ARCHAEOLOGY AND THE CITIES OF ASIA MINOR IN LATE ANTIQUITY

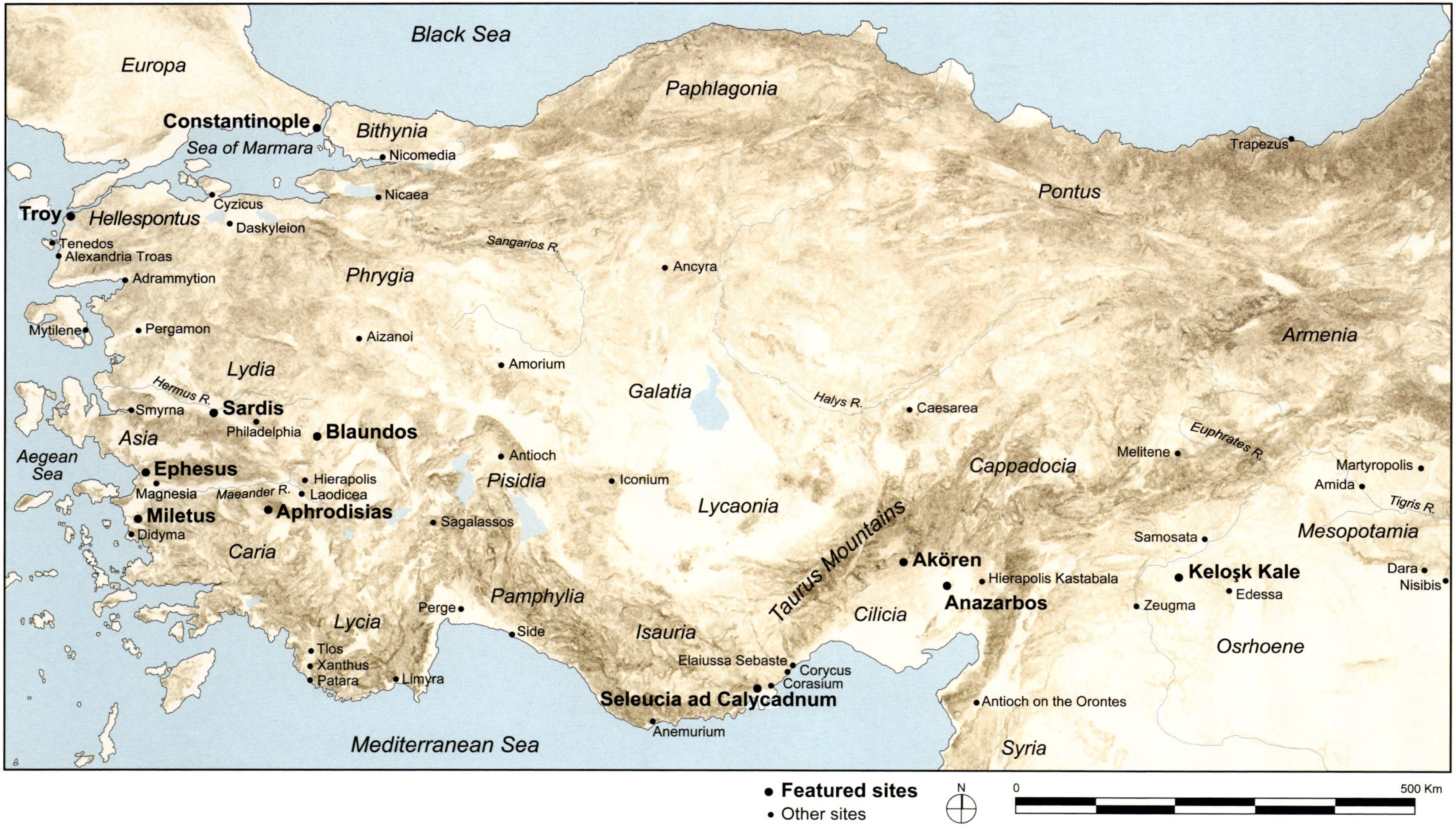
Black Sea
Europa
Paphlagonia
Constantinople
Bithynia
Sea of Marmara
Nicomedia
Trapezus
Nicaea
Pontus
Cyzicus
Troy
Hellespontus
Daskyleion
Tenedos
Alexandria Troas
Sangarios R.
Ancyra
Adrammytion
Phrygia
Mytilene
Pergamon
Aizanoi
Armenia
Amorium
Lydia
Hermus R.
Galatia
Halys R.
Caesarea
Smyrna
Sardis
Philadelphia
Blaundos
Asia
Euphrates R.
Aegean Sea
Antioch
Melitene
Ephesus
Cappadocia
Martyropolis
Hierapolis
Iconium
Pisidia
Amida
Magnesia
Maeander R.
Laodicea
Tigris R.
Lycaonia
Miletus
Aphrodisias
Sagalassos
Mesopotamia
Didyma
Samosata
Taurus Mountains
Caria
Akören
Keloşk Kale
Dara
Hierapolis Kastabala
Nisibis
Edessa
Anazarbos
Perge
Pamphylia
Zeugma
Lycia
Cilicia
Side
Isauria
Osrhoene
Tlos
Xanthus
Elaiussa Sebaste
Corycus
Patara
Limyra
Corasium
Seleucia ad Calycadnum
Antioch on the Orontes
Anemurium
Mediterranean Sea
Syria
Featured sites
Other sites
N
0
500 Km

Archaeology and the Cities of Asia Minor in Late Antiquity

Edited by Ortwin Dally and Christopher Ratté

Kelsey Museum Publication 6

Ann Arbor, Michigan 2011

Published by
Kelsey Museum of Archaeology
The University of Michigan
434 South State Street
Ann Arbor, MI 48109-1390
USA

ISBN 978-0-9741873-5-8

This book is available direct from
The David Brown Book Company
PO Box 511, Oakville, CT 06779, USA
(Telephone 860-945-9329; Fax 860-945-9468)

and

Park End Place, Oxford OX1 1HN, United Kingdom
(Telephone 01865-241249; Fax 01865-794449)
www.oxbowbooks.com

Contents

Preface and Acknowledgments
Ortwin Dally and Christopher Ratté vii

1 Sardis in Late Antiquity
Marcus Rautman 1

2 Sculpture and the Rhetorical Imagination in Late Antique Constantinople
Sarah Bassett 27

3 The Remains of the Centuries. Sculptures and Statue Bases in Late Antique Ephesus: The Evidence of the Upper Agora
Maria Aurenhammer and Alexander Sokolicek 43

4 The Sculptural Decoration of Ephesian Bath Buildings in Late Antiquity
Johanna Auinger 67

5 The Town Center of Miletus from Roman Imperial Times to Late Antiquity
Ortwin Dally, Martin Maischberger, Peter I. Schneider, and Andreas Scholl 81

6 The Riddle of the Market Gate: Miletus and the Character and Date of Earlier Byzantine Fortifications in Anatolia
Philipp Niewöhner 103

7 Survey Evidence for Late Antique Settlement in the Region around Aphrodisias
Christopher Ratté and Peter D. De Staebler 123

8 Buildings and Citizens: Observations from Late Antique and Byzantine Blaundos in Phrygia
Axel Filges 137

9 Troy and the Granicus River Valley in Late Antiquity
Charles Brian Rose 151

10 Trades, Crafts, and Agricultural Production in Town and Countryside in Southeastern Isauria
Günder Varinlioğlu 173

11 Akören: Two Late Antique Villages in Cilicia
Ulrike Wulf-Rheidt 189

12 Anazarbos in Late Antiquity
Richard Posamentir 205

13 Some Aspects of the Development of Osrhoene in Late Antiquity
Peter Baumeister 225

14 Cities in the Eastern Roman Empire from Constantine to Heraclius
David Potter 247

Bibliography 261

Index 289

Preface and Acknowledgments

Ortwin Dally and Christopher Ratté

The city was the fundamental social institution of Greek and Roman culture from the emergence of the Greek polis in the eighth century B.C. to the collapse of the Roman empire fifteen hundred years later. This volume examines the archaeological evidence for the last phase in the life of the cities of Asia Minor, from the early fourth to the early seventh centuries A.D. It also highlights the different kinds of contributions being made by two very different forms of archaeological research: on the one hand, re-examination of the urban sites that have been the focus of long-running excavations, the so-called big digs at places such as Sardis, Miletus, Ephesus, and Aphrodisias; on the other hand, archaeological survey projects both in the hinterlands of cities such as Troy in northwestern western Asia Minor, and in more remote regions such as Cilicia and Osrhoene in southeastern Asia Minor and North Syria. Among the main concerns of the big dig projects is the visual culture of the Graeco-Roman city, and a major contribution of new research both in the capital at Constantinople and in provincial towns has been to highlight the resilience of established traditions of Graeco-Roman civic life, such as the role of private philanthropy or euergetism in the maintenance and beautification of the built environment. Survey archaeology, by contrast, tends to focus on the interaction between town and countryside and in particular on economic issues; as such, it promises to continue to illuminate the widespread if not universal collapse of town life in Asia Minor that marks the transition from antiquity to the Middle Ages.

Asia Minor lay at the center of the late antique world, thanks to the founding of Constantinople in A.D. 330, the many prosperous and well-established cities of its Aegean and Mediterranean coasts, and the emergence of a rich and complex frontier culture to the east. Indeed much of Asia Minor was more heavily urbanized in Roman times than it was until the modern era, and for this reason the archaeological remains of the region's ancient cities are unusually well-preserved. The cities of Asia Minor thus provide a uniquely rich body of evidence for archaeological study of a period of great historical change, characterized by many concerns of real contemporary relevance, such as conflicts over religious identity; urban decay and renewal; and the functioning of empire.

The rise of Christianity, famously identified by Gibbon as a principal cause of the decline and fall of the Roman empire, has always been a major theme of historical study. Archaeology plays a prominent role in debates over subjects such as the degree of conflict and accommodation between different religious communities in late antiquity, and Asia Minor is an area of particular interest. Although it was one of the most thoroughly Christianized regions of the Roman empire, in part because of the attraction of its many Hellenistic Jewish communities to early Christian proselytizers including Paul of Tarsus, some prominent cities such as Aphrodisias still remained centers of pagan learning as late as the fifth century A.D., and new studies of epigraphic and archaeological evidence for the Jewish synagogues at both Aphrodisias and Sardis have shown that they remained vibrant and prosperous public institutions long after the "triumph" of Christianity.[1]

In addition to religious change, a major focus of recent historical and archaeological scholarship on late antiquity has been the "de-urbanization" of the Roman countryside. While Constantinople remained the capital of the eastern Roman empire until A.D. 1453, it is now generally agreed that the provincial cities of Asia Minor—the last holdouts of ancient Mediterranean city life outside the capitals—were substantially abandoned in or before the early seventh century. But the character, causes, and consequences of this change remain controversial subjects. Were the cities depopulated suddenly or over a period of several generations? Were they overwhelmed by disasters, such as earthquakes, the famous "Justinianic plague" of the mid-sixth century, or foreign invasions? Or were cities in rural regions abandoned because of a larger systemic change—because for external reasons including the military threat to both its eastern and its northern frontiers, the Roman empire could no longer afford to maintain the roads and bridges and aqueducts on which city life in rural areas depended? What were the consequences of the loss of cities for the local economies of the surrounding regions? What was its effect on the villages and rural estates in which the vast and largely silent majority of the inhabitants of the Roman empire lived? These are questions central to the study of the end of antiquity which archaeology is uniquely qualified to address.[2]

Indeed, archaeology has played a central role in the investigation of the late antique cities of Asia Minor, especially over the generation following the publication of Clive Foss's "Archaeology and the 'Twenty Cities' of Byzantine Asia,"[3] which drew on contemporary archaeological evidence in arguing for a dramatic break in traditions of civic life in the early seventh century—a major crisis hardly mentioned by medieval Byzantine historians, intent on emphasizing the continuity between the Roman empire and their own day. This same period has witnessed a significant expansion of "survey archaeology" in Asia Minor, focusing on interdisciplinary investigation of the ancient countryside, as opposed to excavation at town sites—and this provides us with our best hope of collecting new evidence to test the hypotheses of Foss and others about the end of the late antique city.[4]

In addition to these kinds of historical and economic questions, classical and late antique archaeology have also traditionally embraced the study of ancient art and architecture, raising questions of interpretation similar to those addressed by students of ancient literature. How did changing habits of patronage affect the production of buildings and statues? How were traditional distinctions of genre, between portrait and "ideal" sculpture, for example, adapted to new circumstances? How were ancient monuments reimagined in the articulation of the relationship between present and past, and in the realization of new ways of envisioning both the private and the public realms?[5]

[1] The 1990s and the first decade of the 21st century witnessed a flowering of studies on late antiquity, marked by a number of major international congresses, of which a sample are cited in this and subsequent footnotes. For a conspectus of recent research on Christianization and the city, see G. Brands and H.-G. Severin (eds.), *Die spätantike Stadt und ihre Christianisierung* (Wiesbaden 2003).

[2] The bibliography is considerable. Recent collections of studies include: N. Christie and S.T. Loseby (eds.), *Towns in Transition. Urban Evolution in Late Antiquity and the Early Middle Ages* (Aldershot 1996); L. Lavan (ed.), *Recent Research in Late-Antique Urbanism, JRA* Suppl. 42 (Portsmouth, RI 2001).

[3] *AJA* 81 (1987) 469–86.

[4] For studies exemplifying the role played by survey archaeology in the study of late antiquity, see T.S. Burns and J.W. Eadie (eds.), *Urban Centers and Rural Contexts in Late Antiquity* (East Lansing 2001); W. Bowden, L. Lavan, and C. Machado (eds.), *Recent Research on the Late Antique Countryside, Late Antique Archaeology* 2 (Leiden 2003); N. Christie (ed.), *Landscapes of Change. Rural Evolutions in Late Antiquity and the Early Middle Ages* (Aldershot 2004).

[5] On sculpture in particular, see F.A. Bauer and C. Witschel (eds.), *Statuen in der Spätantike* (Wiesbaden 2007).

While new monuments were rarer than before, recent research has drawn attention to the continuity of practices such as the erection of honorific statues and civic patronage of baths and other traditional cultural institutions through the fifth century A.D., alongside the "adaptive reuse" of earlier monuments, from the re-carving of sculptures to the conversion of old buildings to new functions. Changes in visual culture were also connected with the political and cultural developments discussed above, beginning with the rise of bishops and imperial officials such as provincial governors as artistic and architectural patrons. Of particular interest are phenomena such as the mutilation of the genitalia of statues still very much on public display (although often with new identities and in new locations) and the adornment of new buildings such as churches and fortification walls with spolia taken from a wide range of earlier structures, from monumental arches to tombs. Current research emphasizes the interpretation of these practices not as signs of decadence, but as evidence for new ways of viewing and for changing habits of representation.

The practice of archaeology in Asia Minor has always been international in character, and this volume, which grows out of a conference co-sponsored by the University of Michigan and the German Archaeological Institute in 2008, features two intellectual traditions that have enjoyed the privilege of conducting archaeological research in Turkey for well over a century: the German-speaking traditions of Germany and Austria, and the Anglophone traditions of Britain and North America. One of the major goals of the original conference was to promote intellectual exchange and cooperation between these two communities, especially between the mid-career and younger scholars who will help to set the agenda for future archaeological research. The language of the conference was English, and it is hoped that the publication of the proceedings will have the added benefit of making research previously published only in German more accessible to an English readership. In addition to its European and North American participants, the conference also featured two young Turkish scholars, both of whom were graduate students at American universities.[6] The final paper in this volume was written especially for this purpose by University of Michigan historian David Potter.

THE CIVIC CULTURE of Asia Minor in late antiquity is one of the most exciting fields in contemporary Old World Archaeology, and one that bridges the gaps between Classicists and Medievalists, and between archaeologists, art-historians, and historians. Archaeology was responsible for a major revision in our understanding of this subject a generation ago, and recent developments in archaeological science, especially in survey archaeology, promise to shed new light on old questions, such as the causes and consequences of the rapid depopulation of the provincial cities of the region in the early seventh century A.D. At the same time, new research on late antique art and architecture offers fresh insights into an era of profound religious and institutional change. It is hoped that this volume will make a useful contribution to the large and growing body of recent scholarship on late antiquity by providing short reports on new research—and new research methods—on a broad range of subjects at a wide variety of different but related archaeological sites.

LIKE ALL FOREIGN RESEARCHERS working in Turkey, the editors would like first of all to acknowledge our debt to the General Directorate of Cultural Resources and Museums of the Ministry of Culture and Tourism of the Republic of Turkey, and to all our Turkish colleagues and friends, for their unstinting hospitality and support. We are also very grateful to the sponsors of the conference that gave rise to

[6] See G. Varinlioğlu's contribution to this volume. The other paper, by Ö. Dalgıç, has already been published: in J.D. Alchemies, H.C. Evans, and T.K. Thomas (eds.), *Anathemata Eortika: Studies in Honor of Thomas F. Mathews* (Mainz 2009).

this volume, including the German Archaeological Institute (collaborating for the first time, but we hope not the last, in the co-sponsorship of an academic symposium at an American university), the American Friends of the German Archaeological Institute, and the following units of the University of Michigan: the Department of Classical Studies; the Kelsey Museum of Archaeology; the College of Literature, Science, and the Arts; the Rackham Graduate School; the International Institute; and the Interdepartmental Program in Classical Art and Archaeology. This volume appears in the series, Kelsey Museum Publications, and we would like to thank the Director of the Museum, Professor Sharon Herbert, and the Director of the Museum's Publications Program, Professor Terry Wilfong, for their interest and advice. We are also pleased to thank Angela Commito, Lydia Herring-Harrington, Jared Secord, and Stephanie Ulmer for their careful and enthusiastic editorial and administrative assistance. Last but not least, for layout and design, we are grateful for the patience and the talents of Margaret Lourie.

1 Sardis in Late Antiquity

Marcus Rautman

Asia Minor has always been central to the study of classical urban culture, particularly during its long late antique twilight.[1] Understanding this transitional phase of ancient settled life has come a long way since the 19th century, when western travelers to Turkey began systematically recording inscriptions and standing walls. By the 1920s there existed enough of a documentary record for Victor Schultze to survey the historical topography of major Anatolian poleis in the first centuries A.D.[2] It was against this limited archaeological background that fifty years ago Ernst Kirsten summarized what then was known of the late classical city's institutional structure, reframing the study of Mediterranean urbanism during the eastern Middle Ages and stimulating a wave of fresh inquiry.[3]

By coincidence, 1958 was the same year that George M.A. Hanfmann began excavating at Sardis. Hanfmann's interest in the site grew out of his work with early Iron Age pottery from Tarsus, and with related material recovered at Sardis by Howard Crosby Butler in 1910–1914, mainly at the famous Artemis Temple and the nearby necropolis.[4] Informed by this experience, Hanfmann targeted the early Lydian capital of Croesus and his predecessors as a primary objective. At the same time he recognized that Sardis was an important place throughout antiquity, with visible remains inescapably calling attention to its classical past. Exploring the city "through all phases of history" was from the beginning one of the expedition's stated aims.[5]

[1] The Michigan-D.A.I. symposium took place during the Sardis Expedition's 50th anniversary year, which prompted this review of the site's contribution to the field. I am grateful to the symposium organizers, Ortwin Dally and Christopher Ratté, for providing the occasion to discuss current work and learn from other participants in Ann Arbor. My thinking about Sardis in all its phases has benefited from years of collaboration with Crawford H. Greenewalt, Jr., and Nicholas D. Cahill, past and present field directors of the Archaeological Exploration of Sardis.

Preliminary expedition reports have appeared in *AASOR*, *AJA*, *BASOR*, and *Kazı Sonuçları Toplantısı*. Abbreviations are used for several fundamental works:

Buckler and Robinson, *Inscriptions* = W.H. Buckler and D.M. Robinson, *Sardis* VII. *Greek and Latin Inscriptions* (Leiden 1932).

Butler, *Sardis* = H.C. Butler, *Sardis* I. *The Excavations, Part 1. 1910–1914* (Leiden 1922).

Foss, *Sardis* = C. Foss, *Byzantine and Turkish Sardis, Sardis* M4 (Cambridge, MA 1976).

Hanfmann, *Sardis* = G.M.A. Hanfmann, *Sardis from Prehistoric to Roman Times. Results of the Archaeological Exploration of Sardis, 1958–1975* (Cambridge, MA 1983).

Hanfmann and Waldbaum, *Survey* = G.M.A. Hanfmann and J.C. Waldbaum, *A Survey of Sardis and the Major Monuments outside the Walls, Sardis* R1 (Cambridge, MA 1975).

Love for Lydia = N.D. Cahill (ed.), *Love for Lydia: A Sardis Anniversary Volume presented to Crawford H. Greenewalt, Jr., Sardis* R4 (Cambridge, MA 2008).

[2] V. Schultze, *Altchristliche Städte und Landschaften* 2. *Kleinasien* (Gütersloh 1922–1926).

[3] E. Kirsten, "Die byzantinische Stadt," in *Berichte zum XI. Internationalen Byzantinisten-Kongress* III (Munich 1958) 1–48; G. Ostrogorsky, "Byzantine cities in the early Middle Ages," *DOP* 13 (1959) 47–66; D. Claude, *Die byzantinische Stadt im 6. Jahrhundert* (Munich 1969).

[4] Butler, *Sardis*. For the site before Butler, see Schultze, *Altchristliche Städte* (supra n. 2), 145–52; Hanfmann and Waldbaum, *Survey*, 1–2.

[5] *BASOR* 154 (1959) 13; Hanfmann, *Sardis*, 139, relying mainly on the epigraphic record compiled by Buckler and Robinson, *Inscriptions*.

The informal dispatches and letters that Hanfmann wrote from the field still make good reading.[6] They anticipate in many ways the lively, often conjectural tone of online excavation blogs posted by field directors; as such they preserve a vivid narrative of discoveries made at Sardis from the archaic through medieval periods, but particularly, as it turned out, during Roman times—and this during the very years that late antiquity was gaining acceptance as a disciplinary field. The appearance of specialist reports over the following generation ensured that Sardis would occupy a prominent place in modern understanding of the period. The opening chapter of Clive Foss's 1976 book, *Byzantine and Turkish Sardis,* gives a sweeping overview of the site from the third through sixth centuries that stands as a landmark synthesis of historical and material evidence in writing urban history. Drawing upon the results of nearly 20 years of excavation, his account remains one of the best-known studies of a late classical city in the eastern Mediterranean. This paper builds on these foundations by reviewing 30 years of further investigation and asking what they add to the story the site can tell.

Sardis's contribution to the archaeology of late antiquity rests mainly on excavations carried out in the northwest part of the urban site. The most significant achievements to date include the following: clearing and reconstructing part of the great Bath-Gymnasium Complex, and so tangibly illustrating the scale of Roman urbanism; identifying and displaying the synagogue, the largest such building known from antiquity; excavating a row of street-side residences or shops and inventorying their considerable contents; and publishing monographic studies of coins, glass, metals, and sculpture. Together with volumes on earlier occupation phases, these publications have made Sardis a key reference point in classical studies.[7] Since 1976, work directed by Crawford H. Greenewalt, Jr., has brought attention to other parts of the site and its environs. This second phase of exploration has produced major discoveries about life in the archaic settlement, of Sardis during the Hellenistic period, and about the Roman city's extent and organization between the first and seventh centuries.[8] Unsurprisingly, traces of late antiquity have been found to be nearly ubiquitous, appearing in abundance from the edge of the Hermus plain to the northern slopes of the acropolis, and along the rising valley of the Pactolus river as well (fig. 1). At the same time, it has been shown that natural landscape changes have left most early habitation levels deeply buried, beyond the reach of casual sampling and remote sensing, but preserved for future excavation.[9]

Sardis occupies a strategic location in the central valley of the Hermus river, the second longest watercourse draining the western Anatolian plateau to the Aegean sea.[10] The situation must not have

[6] G.M.A. Hanfmann, *Letters from Sardis* (Cambridge, MA 1972), covering the first 14 campaigns.

[7] Final expedition reports dealing with Roman and later antiquity include G.E. Bates, *Byzantine Coins*, *Sardis* M1 (Cambridge, MA 1971); Hanfmann and Waldbaum, *Survey*; G.M.A. Hanfmann and N.H. Ramage, *Sculpture from Sardis: The Finds through 1975*, *Sardis* R2 (Cambridge, MA 1978); A. von Saldern, *Ancient and Byzantine Glass from Sardis*, *Sardis* M6 (Cambridge, MA 1980); T.V. Buttrey, A. Johnston, K.M. MacKenzie, and M.L. Bates, *Greek, Roman, and Islamic Coins from Sardis*, *Sardis* M7 (Cambridge, MA 1981); J.C. Waldbaum, *Metalwork from Sardis: The Finds through 1974*, *Sardis* M8 (Cambridge, MA 1983); F.K. Yegül, *The Bath-Gymnasium Complex at Sardis*, *Sardis* R3 (Cambridge, MA 1986); J.S. Crawford, *The Byzantine Shops at Sardis*, *Sardis* M9 (Cambridge, MA 1990).

[8] An illustrated overview of the site and its monuments is assembled by C.H. Greenewalt, Jr., N.D. Cahill, P.T. Stinson, and F.K. Yegül, *The City of Sardis: Approaches in Graphic Recording* (Cambridge, MA 2003). For a summary of research focusing on the pre-Roman period, see C.H. Greenewalt, Jr., "Sardis," in W. Radt (ed.), *Stadtgrabungen und Stadtforschung im westlichen Kleinasien–Geplantes und Erreichtes*, *Byzas* 3 (Istanbul 2006) 359–72.

[9] W. Warfield, "Report on the geology of Sardis," in Butler, *Sardis*, 175–80; Hanfmann and Waldbaum, *Survey*, 54–55; G.W. Olson, "Landslides at Sardis in western Turkey," *Geological Society of America, Reviews in Engineering Geology* 3 (1977) 255–72; *BASOR* 245 (1982) 7–15. For remote sensing, see *BASOR* Suppl. 25 (1988) 55–92, at 62; *AJA* 102 (1998) 500–2; *AJA* 104 (2000) 679–80.

[10] For the wider geographic setting, see C.H. Roosevelt, *The Archaeology of Lydia, from Gyges to Alexander* (Cambridge 2009) 33–58.

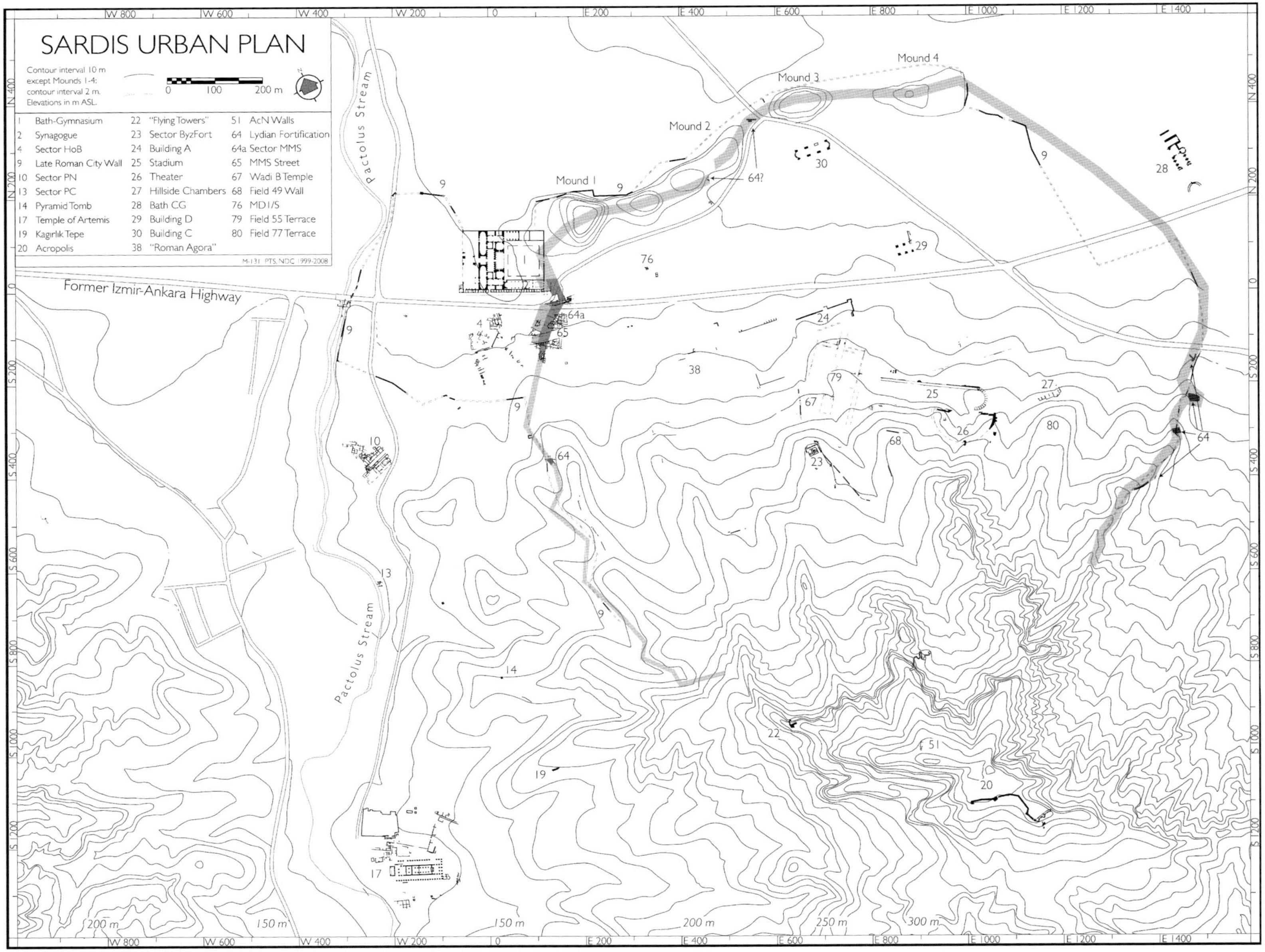

Fig. 1. Sardis, urban plan in late antiquity, with reconstructed circuit of Lydian fortification.

Fig. 2. Sardis, acropolis with theater, from the north.

been particularly convenient from the standpoint of Rome. Travel along the highway from Ephesus, Smyrna, or Pergamon could take up to three days to reach the center of inland Lydia, a geographically diverse territory stretching from the Ionian coast to the highlands of Phrygia. Much of the road ran through the broad, fertile plain of the Hermus valley, which was surrounded by mountains and dotted with the famous tumuli described by Herodotus. Tombs and mausolea of Hellenistic and Roman date appeared along the highway as the Roman traveler neared the city. Crossing the small but fabled Pactolus river, one arrived at Sardis itself (fig. 2).

This was one of the earliest, and surely among the best-known, urban centers of western Asia Minor, with nearly a millennium of occupation preceding late antiquity.[11] Traces of early settlement remain in shadow, but by the seventh to sixth centuries B.C. pockets of habitation had been established on the lower north-facing slopes of the acropolis and along the banks of the Pactolus. The most spectacular discovery of recent years has been the monumental fortification that surrounded the Lydian capital in the mid-sixth century B.C.: a massive structure of stone and mudbrick, some 20 m across at its base and rising more than 10 m high, that descended from the steep acropolis and pushed onto the plain. While most of archaic and Persian Sardis lies beneath deep layers of alluvium and landslide, it has become clear that terraces and buildings set up around this time shaped the terrain for generations to come. The framework of Hellenistic Sardis, either before or after Antiochus intervened in its affairs in 213 B.C., is less evident on the ground.[12] Of known urban monuments, only

[11] For the literary background, see J.G. Pedley, *Ancient Literary Sources*, *Sardis* M2 (Cambridge, MA 1972).

[12] C.H. Greenewalt, Jr., "Sardis in the time of Xenophon," in P. Briant (ed.), *Dans les pas des Dix-Mille*, *Pallas* 43 (Aix 1995) 125–45; C. Ratté, "Reflections on the urban development of Hellenistic Sardis," in *Love for Lydia*, 125–33.

the theater in its earliest phase may plausibly date to this period. The sanctuary of Artemis, situated well apart from the city about 1 km up the Pactolus valley, was clearly an important place even if its appearance is unclear. Much that is known about Hellenistic Sardis takes the form of architectural or sculptural remains that were incorporated into later buildings, or pottery recovered from isolated houses and secondary fills laid down after the site's devastation by earthquake in A.D. 17.[13]

At this point the classical city begins to come into focus. A well-known passage in Tacitus (*Annals* 2.47) records the nocturnal earthquake that rocked western Asia and left Sardis critically damaged. Reconstruction is said to have begun immediately with the support of the imperial treasury under the supervision of a senate-appointed commissioner. Like massive relief operations of recent times, urban recovery must have progressed slowly and was never completed as planned.[14] Clearing debris and restoring essential public services no doubt claimed the highest priority. A series of public commemorations attests imperial interest in the city and other parts of the province. A large statue base found in the western city honors the deified Tiberius as "founder of the city," and a municipal temple dedicated to him is known. Germanicus is similarly honored as "kaisara theon sebaston" in an enormous inscription set up by Caligula.[15] An inscription of A.D. 53/54 commemorates the completion under Claudius of an aqueduct; the presence of standing piers, mortar-lined channels, and terracotta pipes in the surrounding hills and valleys makes clear that multiple sources were eventually needed to supply the city.[16] Excavation regularly encounters thick layers of occupation debris of late Hellenistic and Augustan date, which were leveled to form broad shelves, sometimes 2–3 m deep, on the lower hillslopes and plain.[17]

Recent work has confirmed several key components of Sardis's first-century A.D. reconstruction near the center of the urban site. The combined efforts of topographic study, remote sensing, and selective excavation have sketched the outlines of three great public buildings on the north side of the acropolis: the theater, the stadium, and a temple that faced onto a vast terrace. The theater is the most easterly known monument of the upper city and likely stood atop the remains of a Hellenistic predecessor. The hillside preserves the unmistakable shape of the cavea, which may have accommodated 12,000–15,000 spectators, and both parados walls have long been visible to travelers through the area.[18] Recent excavation on the theater's western slope has identified substantial parts of the eroded structure, including mortared foundations for seats and an intact section of the marble-paved diazoma. The lower cavea and orchestra are still filled by as much as 7 m of tumbled architectural debris, which includes fragments of the building's decoration and seats, some inscribed. Further

[13] For recent assessment of excavated contexts, see S.I. Rotroff, *Hellenistic Pottery from Sardis*, *Sardis* M13 (Cambridge, MA 2003) 11–15.

[14] The slow pace of reconstruction may have been one reason why nine years later Sardis lost to Smyrna in competing to host the provincial temple honoring Tiberius (Tacitus, *Annals* 4.55–56).

[15] For the Tiberius inscription, set up under Claudius and found at Sector MMS/N, see *BASOR* 29 (1983) 13, fig. 15; C. Foss, "Appendix: Inscriptions related to the complex," in Yegül, *Bath-Gymnasium Complex* (supra n. 7), 169 no. 1, fig. 32. Comparable language appears in an inscription seen at Turgutlu, about 30 km west of Sardis, and published in Buckler and Robinson, *Inscriptions*, 57 no. 39. For the 2 m-long block honoring Germanicus, see *BASOR* 203 (1971) 14. All three documents are discussed by P. Herrmann, "Sardeis zur Zeit der iulisch-claudischen Kaiser," in E. Schwertheim (ed.), *Forschungen in Lydien*, *Asia Minor Studien* 17 (Bonn 1995) 21–36, at 31–36. I have benefited from consulting Professor Herrmann's unfinished manuscript on the Sardis inscriptions.

[16] Buckler and Robinson, *Inscriptions*, 29 no. 10; E. Winter, *Staatliche Baupolitik und Baufürsorge in den römischen Provinzen des kaiserzeitlichen Kleinasien*, *Asia Minor Studien* 20 (Bonn 1996) 180; Herrmann, "Sardeis" (supra n. 15), 31–35. Parts of the aqueduct were traced by Butler (*Sardis*, 35–36, map 1), and are still visible.

[17] Hanfmann, *Sardis*, 141; *Kazı Sonuçları Toplantısı* 22.1 (2000) 416–17.

[18] Butler, *Sardis*, 31; R.L. Vann, *The Unexcavated Buildings of Sardis*, *BAR-IS* 538 (Oxford 1989) 47–58.

Fig. 3. Sardis, theater, east parados wall and excavation of stage building area.

Fig. 4. Sardis, reconstructed plan of Roman temple complex, stadium, and theater.

work to the north of the orchestra indicates that many pieces of the freestanding stage building, two or three stories in height and richly decorated in an Asiatic Ionic or related style, lie close to where they originally stood (fig. 3).[19]

Planning and construction of the theater were closely coordinated with the adjacent stadium. The vaulted semicircular *sphendone* lies immediately to the north of the stage building. Long rows of seats were supported by the hillside and vaulted substructures, which stretched westward over a length of some 200 m. The stadium ends below a projecting acropolis spur known as Field 55. Excavation of several sondages on this flat area has established the outlines of a large artificial terrace with deep foundations. At the center of the north side, a 14 m-wide staircase supported by a quadrant vault rose 5 m to the level of an expansive platform, some 100 m wide and 2 ha in area, which apparently was bounded by a portico on columns. Situated on axis to the south, today in a ravine known as Wadi B, was a large Ionic or Corinthian temple, octastyle and pseudoperipteral in plan, with a 22 m-wide façade that would have dominated the precinct (fig. 4).[20] The massive amount of architectural debris that has been found along the terrace's eastern edge likely comes from the superstructure of temple and portico: large column bases, fluted shafts, historiated capitals, and finely finished blocks, many inscribed with personal names and formulaic texts honoring as "twice *neokoros*" this metropolis of Asia and all Lydia.[21] The stratigraphy of terrace and temple foundations suggests that the precinct's development was a sustained effort that began around the middle of the first century A.D. and continued into the second century, a span that broadly applies to the stadium and theater as well. The planning, scale, and execution of all three structures indicate that this was a major initiative, comparable in many ways to the Tiberian-Claudian effort of an earlier generation. Throughout its prolonged construction, this civic showcase would have been a conspicuous feature of the city.[22]

Most of Roman Sardis lay below the level of this vast complex, on the lower hillside and along the edge of the Hermus plain. Inscriptions mention the typical landmarks of urban life during the high empire: streets with public squares and fountains; an agora, archive, basilica, and odeum; multiple baths, confraternities, and temples.[23] None of these features can be securely located, but topography clearly favored the lower and more accessible parts of the site. The direction of projected growth can be inferred from a pair of large public baths: the western Bath-Gymnasium Complex and the eastern Bath CG. These roughly contemporary buildings stood 1400 m apart, along the main highway as it approached the city from both sides. Their peripheral siting suggests that city planners anticipated development far to the northwest and northeast, onto land that may still have

[19] For excavation carried out since 2006, see *Kazı Sonuçları Toplantısı* 29.3 (2007) 372–74, figs. 4–8; *Kazı Sonuçları Toplantısı* 30.4 (2008) 194, fig. 11.

[20] The temple's northeast corner was identified in 1981–1982; see C. Ratté, T.N. Howe, and C. Foss, "An early imperial pseudodipteral temple at Sardis," *AJA* 90 (1986) 45–68. Excavation in 2004–2005 established its breadth and northerly orientation; see *Kazı Sonuçları Toplantısı* 27.2 (2005) 176, fig. 9. The possibility of *neokoros* status for the temple is considered by B. Burrell, *Neokoroi. Greek Cities and Roman Emperors* (Leiden 2004) 100–3; and R.S. Ascough, "Greco-Roman religions in Sardis and Smyrna," in R.S. Ascough (ed.), *Religious Rivalries and the Struggle for Success in Sardis and Smyrna, Studies in Christianity and Judaism* 14 (Waterloo, ON 2005) 40–52, at 44.

[21] Sardis received its second *neokoros* under the Antonines; see Burrell, *Neokoroi* (supra n. 20), 103. The inscriptions from Field 55 are unpublished but employ similar language to Buckler and Robinson, *Inscriptions*, 74–78 nos. 63–70. They may be later than the temple and not directly reflect its status, but certainly predate the area's destruction.

[22] *Kazı Sonuçları Toplantısı* 28.2 (2006) 743–45, fig. 1; N.D. Cahill, "Mapping Sardis," in *Love for Lydia*, 111–24. Some work on the Wadi B temple may still have been underway when it was destroyed by an earthquake, apparently in the late second or early third century.

[23] Buckler and Robinson, *Inscriptions*, particularly the late second-century list of fountains, 37–40 no. 17. Vitruvius (2.8.9–10) and Pliny (*Natural History* 35.172) record that the *gerousia* still met in the remodeled mudbrick palace of Croesus, a dubious tradition that nevertheless suggests a prominent hillside location, similar to Pergamon.

been used for burials.[24] Excavation has established that these quintessential Roman buildings may have been begun in the second half of the first century A.D., but were still under construction in the early 200s.[25] As elsewhere, these massive vaulted structures were among the most essential of urban amenities and would have been among the first buildings seen by travelers coming from west and east.

The lower city occupies the plain between the two baths, its deeply buried remains imperfectly glimpsed by remote sensing.[26] Excavated structures and other visible features nevertheless attest the presence of a coherent urban grid that presumably was laid out around the mid-first century A.D. and developed over the following generations. One or two major thoroughfares spanning the lower site seem to have established the orientation of important cross streets and buildings.[27] The fact that second- and third-century levels have not often been found by excavation elsewhere suggests that most people lived in this little-explored central region. The historical record makes clear the city's status at the time. By the Antonine period, civic concerns reached up the Pactolus valley to the suburban Artemis Temple, whose Hellenistic cella was remodeled to serve as a center of the imperial cult. The Marble Court's dedication to the Severan family in A.D. 211 and the award of a third neokorate under Elagabalus document Sardis's growing urban distinction.[28]

Many of these buildings of the high empire, powerfully built and of imposing scale, would stand for centuries to come, even as the city around them changed during late antiquity. An event of central importance was Diocletian's raising of Sardis to the rank of provincial capital, a decision that suggests the earthquakes and Gothic invasions of the later third century had not seriously affected the area.[29] The city's new status may have had little immediate impact on the lives of local inhabitants, but it ensured that Sardis would be among the places that benefited from the government's move to Constantinople and its growing interest in the Asian heartland. The newly organized province of Lydia included more than 20 cities scattered across the Hermus valley and its surrounding hill country.[30] Administering this expanse would have been the responsibility of a centrally appointed governor who occupied an official *praetorium*; the location of this ceremonial residence and political center is unknown, but its urban prominence is clear from other cities. Within a few years the state had also established a major factory for the production of armaments and shields, named in the *Register of Dignitaries* but unidentified on the ground, to supply troops throughout the diocese of Asia.[31]

[24] Late Hellenistic and Roman burials have been identified at the western Sector HoB and beyond the eastern city walls near Çaltılı; see Buckler and Robinson, *Inscriptions*, 125 no. 146; Hanfmann, *Sardis*, 123–24; *BASOR* 26 (1990) 161–64.

[25] J.C. Waldbaum and G.M.A. Hanfmann, "The Roman Bath CG: Site, plan, and description," in Hanfmann and Waldbaum, *Survey*, 129–50; Yegül, *Bath-Gymnasium Complex* (supra n. 7), 9–16.

[26] For geophysical survey of the area, see *AJA* 102 (1998) 500–2; *AJA* 104 (2000) 679–80.

[27] Suggested by Hanfmann and Waldbaum, *Survey*, 30, fig. 10; and much refined by Cahill, "Mapping Sardis" (supra n. 22).

[28] Buckler and Robinson, *Inscriptions*; for a descriptive overview, see Hanfmann, *Sardis*, 144–48. For the Artemis Temple's status as the city's second *neokoros* foundation, see Burrell, *Neokoroi* (supra n. 20), 103–10; for the third, 110–11.

[29] The localized effects of earthquakes and Goths are clear at Ephesus, but less evident at Aphrodisias; see S. Ladstätter and A. Pülz, "Ephesus in the late Roman and early Byzantine period: Changes in its urban character from the third to the seventh century A.D.," in A.G. Poulter (ed.), *The Transition to Late Antiquity on the Danube and Beyond*, *ProcBritAc* 141 (London 2007) 391–433; compare C. Ratté, "New research on the urban development of Aphrodisias in late antiquity," in D. Parrish (ed.), *Urbanism in Western Asia Minor*, *JRA* Suppl. 45 (Portsmouth, RI 2001) 117–47, at 140–44.

[30] P. Herrmann, *Tituli Lydiae*, *TAM* 5 (Vienna 1981–1989); for the setting, see S. Mitchell, *Anatolia. Land, Men, and Gods in Asia Minor*, vol. 1 (Oxford 1993) 180–83; on the scarcity of sources, idem, "The cities of Asia Minor in the Age of Constantine," in S.N.C. Lieu and D. Montserrat (eds.), *Constantine. History, Historiography, and Legend* (London 1998) 52–73.

[31] For *praetoria* and their functions, see L. Lavan, "The residences of late antique governors: A gazetteer," *Antiquité tardive* 7 (1999) 135–64, concerning Sardis, 147–48; idem, "The *praetoria* of civil governors in late antiquity," in L. Lavan (ed.), *Recent Research in Late-Antique Urbanism*, *JRA*

Fig. 5. Sardis, view of western quarters with city wall and Bath-Gymnasium Complex, looking north.

Safeguarding while at the same time advertising these strategic assets necessitated the building of fortifications, and most of the city wall appears to date around this time. While much of the wall has eroded or been quarried away, surviving sections indicate an open circuit of about 4 km that capitalized on the site's topography. Originating on the westernmost spur of the acropolis, the wall projected 400–600 m onto the plain, proceeded along a series of low mounds eastward about 1 km, and returned along the most easterly ridge, just beyond the theater. One of the most informative discoveries of recent years has been to see how closely late Roman builders followed the course of the archaic mudbrick fortification, whose monumental remains have been documented in several locations (fig. 1).[32] In some places mortared rubble foundations were built immediately next to the archaic structure, which would have been at least 800 years old by this time; elsewhere the two walls may have functioned together, with the later construction closing gaps in the eroding yet still imposing mudbrick defenses. The main departure from precedent is the late Roman wall's 400 m westward extension toward the Pactolus river. On the south side the wall was built atop a sloping mound of residential debris, substantially deposited in the aftermath of the Tiberian earthquake. To the north the builders went out of their way, perhaps scaling back earlier plans, to include the north flank of the western Bath-Gymnasium Complex in the circuit (fig. 5). Protecting this huge structure

---

Suppl. 42 (Portsmouth, RI 2001) 39–56. For arms production, see Foss, *Sardis*, 14–15; S. James, "The *fabricae*: State arms factories of the later Roman empire," in J.C. Coulston (ed.), *Military Equipment and the Identity of Roman Soldiers. Proceedings of the Fourth Roman Military Equipment Conference*, *BAR-IS* 394 (Oxford 1988) 257–331.

[32] *AJA* 104 (2000) 656–68; *Kazı Sonuçları Toplantısı* 22.1 (2000) 416–17. Compare supra n. 23 for the Roman view of archaic mudbrick architecture at Sardis; and for the larger context, see F.K. Yegül, "Memory, metaphor, and meaning in the cities of Asia Minor," in E. Fentress (ed.), *Romanization and the City. Creation, Transformations, and Failures*, *JRA* Suppl. 38 (Portsmouth, RI 2000) 133–53; and F. Rojas, *Empire of Memories: Anatolian Material Culture and the Imagined Past in Hellenistic and Roman Lydia* (Ph.D. dissertation, University of California-Berkeley 2010).

must have been among the builders' primary objectives since a great deal of the enclosed terrain was undeveloped. Altogether the annexation increased the total area of the fortified archaic site by about 20 ha, or nearly 18 per cent.[33]

Fig. 6. Sardis, section of western city wall, looking north.

Most of the wall takes the form of short sections of mortared rubble masonry, deeply founded and nearly 2 m thick, which stand as high as 6–8 m (fig. 6).[34] Design, materials, and construction methods vary considerably along its length. Sections covering level terrain generally are 5–10 m long and join at sharp angles. The fabric consists mainly of fieldstones set in mortar along with very little brick. Reused architectural blocks appear in foundations and lower courses in several places, particularly on the west side of the city. Four towers of rectangular and rounded plan are known, with variations in design and construction probably reflecting different dates. Nothing remains of the main portals that greeted travelers along the valley highway, although these likely resembled the gates once seen at Philadelphia (Alaşehir), 60 km to the east.[35] The smaller road from Hypaepa may have arrived at a narrow opening known as the Southwest Gate, or more plausibly entered the city through a larger portal nearby.

The late Roman city wall marks a turning point in the history of Sardis, yet its date has remained unsettled. From the later third century municipal authorities across the empire were encouraged by the state to build their own fortifications, a move that fundamentally changed the appearance and routines of many classical poleis.[36] Moments of military threat in western Asia Minor could favor a date for the Sardis wall in either the mid-third or late fourth century; building the imperial arms factory here more specifically implies that the location was considered secure by the time of Constantine.[37] It may be equally reasonable to view the wall in more than strategic terms, however, as part of

[33] The area south of the Bath-Gymnasium was used for burials through at least the second century; Hanfmann, *Sardis*, 123–24; *BASOR* 249 (1983) 15–20; *BASOR* Suppl. 26 (1990) 161–64. For estimates of area, see Greenewalt, "Sardis" (supra n. 8), 364 n. 18.

[34] Standing remains are described in D. van Zanten, R.S. Thomas, and G.M.A. Hanfmann, "The city wall," in Hanfmann and Waldbaum, *Survey*, 35-52; see also C. Foss and D. Winfield, *Byzantine Fortifications: An Introduction* (Pretoria 1986) 127–28.

[35] A. Pralong, "Les remparts de Philadelphie," in H. Ahrweiler (ed.), *Philadelphie et autres études, Byzantina Sorbonensia* 4 (Paris 1984) 101–26.

[36] For similar considerations at mid-fourth-century Aphrodisias, see P.D. De Staebler, "The city wall and the making of a late-antique provincial capital," in C. Ratté and R.R.R. Smith (eds.), *Aphrodisias Papers 4. New Research on the City and its Monuments, JRA* Suppl. 70 (Portsmouth, RI 2008) 284–319.

[37] Foss, *Sardis*, 3, 7; James, "*Fabricae*" (supra n. 31), 267; compare Hanfmann, *Sardis*, 143–44; also Mitchell, *Anatolia*, vol. 1 (supra n. 30), 234–36; J. Crow, "Fortifications and urbanism in late antiquity: Thessaloniki and other eastern cities," in Lavan (ed.), *Recent Research* (supra n. 31), 89–105. This also suggests the fortifications encompassed enough open terrain to accommodate a major industrial facility.

an ongoing effort to project a new urban identity throughout antiquity. Construction of a number of vaulted *hypogaea* outside the western wall in the mid- to late fourth century reflects the interest of urban elites in burial close to town.[38] The wall's westward extension clearly encouraged the systematic development of the enclosed area in the early fifth century.[39] The few stratified deposits that can be associated with the Sardis city wall include finds dating through at least the third century, yet other sections received attention in the fourth century and later. In some places the late Roman wall seems to have replaced parts of the archaic fortification that had remained standing until then.[40] Certainly no surviving section of the city wall resembles the neatly banded brick and limestone masonry seen on the acropolis in the western portal known as the Flying Towers, nor the massive spoils-work of the fortified summit. The very different fabric, design, and objective of these high walls suggest the work of military engineers who were detailed to the site in later times, perhaps in the late seventh or eighth century, rather than an initiative of local authorities.[41]

Altogether the late Roman fortification encloses an area of nearly 130 ha, whose 50,000–100,000 inhabitants would have filled a substantial city by contemporary standards. Changing urban priorities appear clearly in the wall's relation to existing features, particularly the decision to incorporate the western Bath-Gymnasium Complex and its southern environs while excluding the eastern Bath CG. Parts of Bath CG were renovated in late antiquity, with some spaces partitioned and decorated with marble incrustation–style paintings, but how late public bathing continued here is unclear. By the fifth century the location had become remote; there are few signs of nearby habitation, and supplying water to the area would have been increasingly burdensome.[42] By contrast, much of the Bath-Gymnasium Complex was conscientiously maintained by local patrons and government officials through the fifth and sixth centuries. Continuing public interest in the facility—its ostentatious Marble Court, the colonnaded palaestra onto which it faced, and the gatherings that took place here—coincides with the local quarter's development in the 400s.[43] Fifty years of excavation have documented how this activity extended to the construction of new streets, imposing public buildings, and elegant private houses. Equally important is the realization that not all parts of the city shared in this expansion.

The scale of development appears clearly in street building. The main thoroughfare of western Sardis was the so-called Marble Road, a broad colonnaded passage that stretched along the south side of the Bath-Gymnasium Complex. In its early form the Marble Road had no clear urban importance, but its reconstruction ca. A.D. 400, presumably as far as a major gate in the new city wall, would have created a grand concourse for travelers coming from the west. Excavation has documented a 20 m-wide paved

[38] For the painted tomb of Flavios Chrysanthios (Tomb 76.1), a high-ranking official in the arms factory, see *BASOR* 229 (1978) 61–64; *BASOR* 233 (1979) 4–8. Several other vaulted tombs have been found nearby, two relatively close to the city wall; see infra n. 87.

[39] The discovery of a late fourth-century burial in a painted *hypogaeum* (Tomb 79.1) east of the Pactolus might be taken to support a later date for the fortifications, but probably shows that the city wall's construction did not end traditional burial practices in this intra-mural yet still undeveloped area; see *BASOR* 239 (1983) 22–25. Another nearby *hypogaeum* (Tomb 07.1), also located within the walls, continued to be visited as late as the seventh century; see *Kazı Sonuçları Toplantısı* 30.4 (2008) 193–94.

[40] For recent exploration of the upper western wall (Sector CW32), see *Kazı Sonuçları Toplantısı* 22.1 (2000) 416, figs. 5–6; for the eastern wall (Sector CW6), *Kazı Sonuçları Toplantısı* 23.2 (2001) 228, figs. 3–4. Compare the multiple phases of Pergamon's fortifications, as documented by M. Klinkott, *Altertümer von Pergamon* XVI. *Die Stadtmauern.* Teil 1. *Die byzantinischen Befestigungsanlagen von Pergamon* (Berlin 2001) 8–33.

[41] *BASOR* 203 (1971) 12, fig. 8; Foss, *Sardis,* 57–61; Hanfmann and Waldbaum, *Survey*, fig. 24.

[42] Waldbaum and Hanfmann, "Bath CG" (supra n. 25), 139, 163–65. At some point, perhaps still in late antiquity, the area was flooded and buried by alluvium.

[43] Yegül, *Bath-Gymnasium Complex* (supra n. 7), 49–51, fig. 124 for late graffiti suggesting the *boule* and *gerousia* met in the Marble Court.

Fig. 7. Sardis, Marble Road, north colonnade, and Byzantine Shops, looking east.

surface flanked by porticoes and a row of modest structures known as the Byzantine Shops (fig. 7). To the east the Marble Road met a broad paved plaza or square at Sector MMS/N, which was redeveloped about the same time. The south portico's oblique orientation here continues the northeasterly alignment of streets in central Sardis. Other passages from the north and south converged on this public expanse, which linked the Bath-Gymnasium Complex with the rest of the city. The renovation of both Marble Road and plaza underscores their increasing ceremonial and commercial roles in the life of the city.[44]

Two roads to the south appear to be new creations of the period. One is an 18 m-wide colonnaded street running diagonally across the House of Bronzes sector (HoB) toward the Southwest Gate. A multi-pier structure built of marble spolia with a brick-arched superstructure marks its intersection with a second street in Sector MMS. This equally broad, sloping thoroughfare had a 10 m roadway flanked by porticoes supported by large piers and semi-finished columns. Construction of the MMS street was an ambitious project that entailed cutting a trough, 20 m wide and 3–4 m deep, through the area. Doing so required late Roman excavators to remove parts of existing houses as well as the buried remains of the archaic fortification, which they selectively incorporated into the new street wall (fig. 8). None of this new street seems to have been paved, however. Limited excavation of the roadway and both porticos has revealed only packed earth surfaces that rose gradually, from the time of construction ca. A.D. 400 through the sixth century. The apparent goal was to extend the line of

[44] Ibid., 17–24; Crawford, *Byzantine Shops* (supra n. 7), 3–11. For the MMS/N plaza, see *AASOR* 53 (1995) 4–6. The Marble Road offered only incidental access to the Bath-Gymnasium, whose main entrance was directly from the plaza or a short colonnaded street leading from it. For monumental urban corridors, see G. Bejor, *Vie colonnate. Paesaggi urbani del mondo antico, RdA* Suppl. 22 (Rome 1999); D. Parrish, "The urban plan and its constituent elements," in Parrish (ed.), *Urbanism* (supra n. 29), 9–41; and P. Ballet, N. Dieudonné-Glad, and C. Saliou (eds.), *La rue dans l'antiquité. Définition, aménagement, devenir* (Renes 2008); compare L. Lavan, "The political topography of the late antique city: Activity spaces in practice," in L. Lavan and W. Bowden (eds.), *Theory and Practice in Late Antique Archaeology, Late Antique Archaeology* 1 (Leiden 2003) 314–37, at 327–31.

Fig. 8. Sardis, MMS street, north colonnade, and remains of Lydian fortification, looking east.

a principal thoroughfare from central Sardis into the new western quarter. An inscription found at the intersection of the two streets identifies one of them as an *embolos* that ran from an unidentified tetrapylon to the *embolos* of Hypaepa, presumably meaning the colonnaded street that led in the direction of the Southwest Gate. An associated text preserves the language of civic euergetism by announcing that this considerable undertaking was carried out without public expense.[45]

Official support is attested elsewhere at Sardis. The emperor Valens is said to have stayed at the site while on campaign ca. A.D. 365, and Arcadius is named by a monumental inscription datable to A.D. 398.[46] Several civic and provincial officials were involved with work at the Bath-Gymnasium Complex. Basiliskos, a governor of Lydia, relocated a gilded bronze sculpture of entwined snakes from a public fountain to a pool inside the bath. Severos Simplikios, vicar of the diocese of Asia, is credited on the architrave of the Marble Court with restoring the *aleipterion*, apparently meaning the entire complex.[47] The nearby MMS/N plaza was decorated by Flavios Archelaos, another *vicarius Asiae*, whose name and title were set in mosaic to greet visitors entering the quarter from the east.[48] A lengthy epigram on the Marble Court podium recalls the restoration of this imposing space by Memnonios, *pater poleos*.[49] All this activity is difficult to date closely but shows that a continuing engagement with civic patronage ran through the fifth and sixth centuries.[50]

[45] *BASOR* 177 (1965) 14–17; *BASOR* 199 (1970) 28–29. *BASOR* Suppl. 25 (1988) 18–20 clarifies the urban context for the inscriptions published by Foss, *Sardis*, 115 nos. 18–19. The project's expressly ambiguous sponsorship may reflect the incomplete state in which it was left.

[46] Zosimus 4.4–8; Ammianus Marcellinus 26.5.8–10.6; Foss, *Sardis*, 7–8. For the unpublished Arcadius inscription, see *Kazı Sonuçları Toplantısı* 23.2 (2001) 229.

[47] Foss, *Sardis*, 113–15 nos. 15, 17; Yegül, *Bath-Gymnasium Complex* (supra n. 7), 12–14, 171 nos. 6–7. For the title ("lamprotatou kometos protou bathmou") and other office holders, see D. Feissel, "Vicaires et proconsuls d'Asie du IVᵉ au VIᵉ siècle," *Antiquité tardive* 6 (1998) 91–104, at 96–97.

[48] *AASOR* 52 (1994) 6–7, fig. 6; V. Scheibelreiter, *Stifterinschriften auf Mosaiken Westkleinasiens*, *Tyche* Suppl. 5 (Vienna 2006) 33–35. For the local context of the name, see G. Petzl, *Tituli Lydiae. Philadelpheia et Ager Philadelphenus*, *TAM* 5.3 (Vienna 2007) 50.

[49] Foss, *Sardis*, 114 no. 16; Yegül, *Bath-Gymnasium Complex* (supra n. 7), 34, 171–72 no. 7. It has been suggested that the text was composed ca. A.D. 570 by the poet and historian Agathias in honor of his father; R. Merkelbach and J. Stauber, *Steinepigramme aus dem griechischen Osten* 1. *Die Westküste Kleinasiens von Knidos bis Ilion* (Stuttgart and Leipzig 1998) 402 no. 04/03/04. However, the name is also known locally from a prominent donor of the synagogue; see J.H. Kroll, "The Greek inscriptions of the Sardis synagogue," *HTR* 94 (2001) 5–127, at 40–41 no. 63.

[50] Coins and pottery date the Flavios Archelaos mosaic to the mid-fifth century. It is tempting to see an earlier drain complex excavated here, out of use by A.D. 400, as the source of Basiliskos's serpent fountain, or at least broadly related to renewal of the city's water supply at the time.

Some degree of official authorization is implicit in the closing of temples and the dismantling of abandoned public structures.[51] The sanctuary of Artemis south of the city seems to have become a minor habitation center around this time. By the late fourth or early fifth century the temple no longer functioned, its cult having been abandoned or suppressed and its fabric neutralized by multiple incised crosses and other Christian graffiti.[52] A small chapel known as Church M was built immediately next to the great structure ca. A.D. 400.[53] The temple at Wadi B had apparently collapsed by the early third century, leaving its superstructure and foundations to be thoroughly quarried and burnt for lime during late antiquity.[54] By the early fifth century parts of the Field 55 terrace were occupied by shops and houses, at least one with attractively painted walls.[55] Official concern would certainly have extended to the nearby stadium and theater, and these buildings may have continued in use a little longer. The considerable architectural debris encountered in the theater obscures the latest activity levels in the lower cavea and orchestra, but at the same time demonstrates that the structure was not entirely robbed for other purposes.[56]

The construction of new temples in the form of churches is poorly attested at Sardis, and it remains uncertain whether deliberate steps were taken to Christianize its urban topography.[57] One would expect Sardis, an ancient see whose metropolitan status was recognized by the Council of Nicaea, to have had an episcopal basilica by the fourth century. Apart from the small Church M at the Artemis Temple, however, the only securely identified example is Church EA. This building was found along the road to Hypaepa, about 120 m outside the southwestern city wall in Sector PN. The peripheral location, on a low bluff overlooking the Pactolus river, apparently relates to earlier burials in the area, which the building may have served as either a martyrium or cemetery church. The 30 m-long plan includes a basilica with three aisles preceded by an atrium and eventually flanked by several chapels. The proposed foundation date in the later fourth century would make this one of the earliest known churches in Asia.[58] The nearby construction of a small bath and residence, beautifully furnished with mosaic floors, reflects the growth of this suburban quarter in the fifth century.[59]

By contrast, urban churches at Sardis are nearly invisible, and this at a time when small towns and even villages across the empire were building multiple basilicas.[60] The most likely candidate for a church within the city is the unexcavated Building D, a large structure located near the center of the lower city (fig. 9). The unexcavated building is known almost entirely by its five massive piers,

[51] J. Alchermes, "Spolia in Roman cities of the late empire: Legislative rationales and architectural reuse," *DOP* 48 (1994) 167–78; H.G. Saradi, *The Byzantine City in the Sixth Century. Literary Images and Historical Reality* (Athens 2006) 355–56.

[52] For varied disposition of the cult images, see Hanfmann, *Sardis*, 193; *AJA* 104 (2000) 675–76. For Christian graffiti, see W.H. Buckler and D.M. Robinson, "Greek inscriptions from Sardes IV," *AJA* 18 (1914) 35–74, at 44 no. 12, fig. 5; idem, *Inscriptions*, 145–46 no. 184; compare mandates to purify pagan monuments by incising crosses on them (*Theodosian Code* 16.10, 25).

[53] For the date, Butler, *Sardis*, 113; Hanfmann, *Sardis*, 195.

[54] Ratté et al., "Temple" (supra n. 20), 67. Lime burning also took place on the terrace above the Wadi B temple, at Sector ByzFort, in the later sixth century; see *BASOR* Suppl. 25 (1988) 35–36.

[55] *Kazı Sonuçları Toplantısı* 28.2 (2006) 745, fig. 7; M. Rautman, "The aura of affluence: Domestic scenery in late Roman Sardis," in *Love for Lydia*, 147–58, at 155, pl. 19.

[56] Much of the theater's quarrying is understood to have occurred in the early 20th century.

[57] See recently G. Brands and H.-G. Severin (eds.), *Die spätantike Stadt und ihre Christianisierung* (Wiesbaden 2003); Saradi, *Byzantine City* (supra n. 51), 385–439.

[58] For Church EA, see H. Buchwald, "Early Christian Basilica EA and Church E," in Hanfmann, *Sardis*, 196–204, and his forthcoming final report on these buildings.

[59] For the bath and residence at Sector PN, see *BASOR* 162 (1961) 24–29; *BASOR* 166 (1962) 15–19; *BASOR* 170 (1963) 18–23; *BASOR* 174 (1964) 20–24.

[60] A fragmentary cornice or lintel invoking the *episkopou theos* was recorded in the late 19th century; Buckler and Robinson, *Inscriptions*, 149 no. 190. The block's large size (at least 0.90 by 0.405 m) and lettering suggest it came from the cathedral, *episkopeion*, or other substantial building of the fifth or sixth century.

Fig. 9. Sardis, Building D, northwest pier, looking north.

which stand to a height of about 10 m. Two elliptical domes or domical vaults are thought to have spanned the 14 m interval between piers. A sixth-century construction date has been proposed on the basis of scale, vaulting forms, and the many architectural spoils built into its piers. An inscription naming the emperor Arcadius was found near one pier, which suggests that by this time at least one major foundation of the late fourth century had become available for reuse. Several of the pier blocks resemble Severan-period ornament seen in the Bath-Gymnasium Complex, whose Marble Court and palaestra were partially restored in the fifth century. The uneven assembly of large blocks contrasts with the careful selection and close fitting of spolia in other buildings, however, and makes possible a slightly later date as well.[61]

Viewed against this background, it is all the more striking that the most impressive known religious foundation of late Roman Sardis is a synagogue. This imposing structure consists of an 80 m-long hall with forecourt that was built into the south palaestra wing of the Bath-Gymnasium Complex (fig. 10). For a diaspora synagogue the scale is without parallel and the orientation to the west is unusual. These features, like the resemblance to Christian basilicas, reflect the special circumstances of the site and the progressive adaptation of standing remains to new purposes. In its main phase the synagogue consisted of a hall over 18 m wide. At the west end was a broad apse with three-tiered semicircular *synthronon*. Three doorways joined the main hall with a peristyle court to the east. Six pairs of piers, carefully built of reused marble blocks, supported a pitched roof spanning the 12 m-wide nave, a clear span greater than some nearby streets.[62] Liturgical furnishings included a monumental table assembled of sculptural spolia and two aedicular shrines, presumably for storing the Torah. Several carved and inscribed menorahs found nearby clearly establish its intended use.[63]

Both the main hall and forecourt of the synagogue were paved with mosaics. The hall features 21 mosaic panels consisting mainly of geometric ornament, with the image of a kantharos amid

[61] Compare the masonry piers of the second- to third-century Building C, discussed in Vann, *Unexcavated Buildings* (supra n. 18), 23–39. For Building D, see Hanfmann, *Sardis*, 196; H. Buchwald, "Western Asia Minor as a generator of architectural forms: Provincial back-wash or dynamic center of production?" *JÖB* 34 (1984) 199–234, at 209–12. For a recent structural assessment, see N.D. Karydis, *Early Byzantine Vaulted Construction in Churches of the Western Coastal Plains and River Valleys of Asia Minor* (Ph.D. thesis, University of Bath 2010).

[62] The form and chronology of the synagogue are laid out by A.R. Seager, "The building history of the Sardis synagogue," *AJA* 76 (1972) 425–35; idem, "The building," in Hanfmann, *Sardis*, 168–78. For a recent reconstruction, see Greenewalt et al., *City of Sardis* (supra n. 8), figs. 114–15 no. 40.

[63] Seager, "Building" (supra n. 62), 175–76; D.G. Mitten and A.F. Scorziello, "Reappropriating antiquity: Some spolia from the synagogue at Sardis," in *Love for Lydia*, 135–46; M. Rautman, "Two menorahs from the synagogue at Sardis," *Qadmoniyot* 43 (2010) 44–48 (in Hebrew).

Fig. 10. Sardis, synagogue, looking southeast.

graceful vines covering the floor of the apse. Other panels included the names of individual donors, of which 11 have been reconstructed from the surviving fragments. The lower walls of the hall were decorated with a particularly elaborate program of polychrome opus sectile (*skoutlosis*), and apparently mosaics as well. A similar combination of floor mosaics and wall revetment appeared in the forecourt. Inscribed revetment plaques found throughout the building record at least 70 additional donations that were made over the course of several generations.[64]

The synagogue must have been one of the most imposing monuments of Sardis and it is unsurprising that its history is complex. For much of late antiquity it would have been a scene of constant construction, with multiple phases attested epigraphically and archaeologically. The building that stands today may have been begun in the later fourth century, although how much of it was completed then is unclear. It seems reasonable that piecemeal decoration of the substantial hall alone, with an interior area of about 1,000 m^2, would have extended into the fifth century, and alterations and repairs continued into the 500s. The floor and roof of such a large timber-covered structure would have required regular maintenance. The need for repairs would have been acute in the forecourt, which saw heavy traffic around its central fountain.[65]

The recent proposal to date the synagogue to the sixth century emphasizes these later interventions apart from their larger setting.[66] The numismatic argument for a later date rests on the

[64] L. Robert, "Inscriptions de la synagogue," in idem, *Nouvelles inscriptions de Sardes* 1 (Paris 1964) 37–57; Kroll, "Greek inscriptions" (supra n. 49); Scheibelreiter, *Stifterinschriften* (supra n. 48), 38–52. For the context of collective donations, see J.-P. Caillet, "Les dédicaces privées de pavements de mosaïques à la fin de l'antiquité. Occident européen et monde grec: données socio-économiques," in X. Barral i Altet (ed.), *Artistes, artisans et production artistique au Moyen Age* 2. *Commande et travail* (Paris 1987) 15–36.

[65] For a recent assessment of the forecourt, see M. Rautman, "Daniel at Sardis," *BASOR* 358 (2010) 29–42.

[66] J. Magness, "The date of the Sardis synagogue in light of the numismatic evidence," *AJA* 109 (2005) 443–75.

discovery of several post-A.D. 400 coins in the eastern part of the main hall and forecourt, but in contexts more plausibly associated with alterations and repairs than with initial construction. The absence of fifth- and sixth-century coins from the building's foundations cannot be attributed to a subsequent withdrawal of currency, since coins of this date are commonly found at Sardis. The bedding of the south portico mosaics at the MMS/N plaza, only a few meters to the southeast, included an uninterrupted series of fourth- to sixth-century coins. A deposit of nearly 700 nummi found in the MMS street portico is only the largest of several excavated hoards of fifth century date.[67] Pottery and lamps recovered from below the floor of the main hall appear consistently early, in contrast to the distinctive fifth- and sixth-century forms found above the floor and elsewhere.[68] Floor mosaics with related decorative patterns and borders turn up in public and domestic contexts across the site, and attest the continuity of local traditions over the span of centuries. As an integral part of the city's architectural and social fabric, the synagogue shared the fortunes of the urban quarter of which it formed an important part.

The synagogue forecourt had two principal entrances: one opening off a colonnade that continued north to the main palaestra gate, and a smaller one from the Marble Road to the south. These and other thoroughfares from east and south met in the MMS/N plaza. This marble-paved expanse clearly played a prominent role in the life of the city. A double portico on large columns dominated the south side. The inner walkway was covered by a brick vault and paved by successive mosaic floors, one installed by Flavios Archelaos in the mid-fifth century and the second by another patron in the later sixth century. Here also rectangular panels of varying sizes suggest the contributions of multiple sponsors. The involvement of the diocesan *vicarius* attests the importance of the plaza, and of the residential quarter that lay behind it.[69]

Excavation at Sectors MMS and MMS/S has traced the long-term development of this neighborhood. For centuries the area was dominated by the elongated mound of the archaic fortification wall, whose buried remains extended the western ridge of the acropolis. Domestic remains of late Hellenistic and early Roman date have been located along the mound's top and east side, while the flat terrain farther west preserves scattered burials of about the same time. Construction of the new city wall made the area ripe for development, and this began ca. A.D. 400 by cutting the MMS street through the area. Municipal approval surely would have been needed for expropriation and development. At a time when urban patronage was increasingly dominated by government officials, the possibility that work was privately funded makes the undertaking all the more impressive.

Once street lines had been established, existing foundations and standing walls offered local property owners a starting point for developing new residences (fig. 11). The process of building and remodeling went on for more than a century. No less than the early houses described by Vitruvius, these late Roman structures expressed the social standing and interests of their occupants. Common concerns included providing courts or open spaces for light and air, maintaining a reliable water supply for personal use and public display, arranging adequate drainage for rain and wastewater, and shaping special rooms for reception and dining. Whatever their specific identify, the owners clearly aspired to the upper levels of local society.

[67] B. Burrell, "A hoard of minimi from Sardis and the currency of the fifth century C.E.," *RN* 163 (2007) 235–82; for the context, ead., "Small bronze hoards at late fifth century C.E. Sardis," in *Love for Lydia*, 159–69. For a hoard of 71 bronze coins, mostly of the late fifth century and concluding with nine issues of Zeno (A.D. 476–491), see *AASOR* 52 (1994) 24, fig. 26.

[68] M.L. Rautman, "Two late Roman wells at Sardis," *AASOR* 53 (1995) 37–84.

[69] *AASOR* 52 (1994) 3–7; Feissel, "Vicaires et proconsuls" (supra n. 47), 97; Scheibelreiter, *Stifterinschriften* (supra n. 48), 33–35 no. 5.

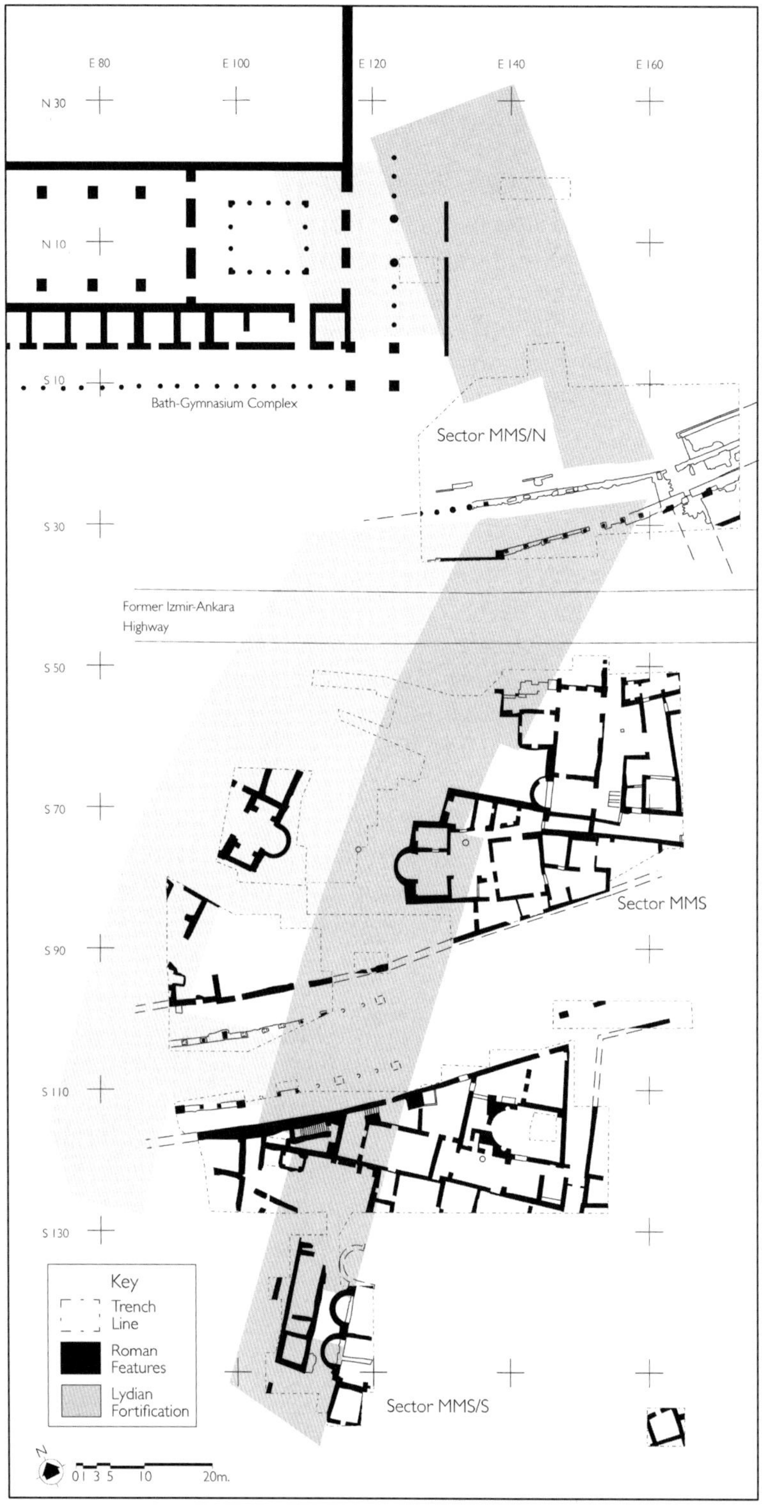

Fig. 11. Sardis, plan of Lydian fortification and late Roman features at Sectors MMS/N, MMS, and MMS/S.

Fig. 12. Sardis, west part of late Roman house at Sector MMS/S, looking north.

The area between the MMS/N plaza and MMS street was filled with interconnected rooms of different sizes. The irregular plans seen at Sector MMS result from the step-by-step combination of at least four living units into a single sprawling residence by around A.D. 500.[70] The more southerly part clearly preserves the lines of a fourth-century predecessor, which arranged small rooms around three or four sides of a peristyle court. After the street was laid out, this house was expanded by adding an apse to one of these rooms, presumably for dining, and building another reception space nearby. By contrast, the more northerly rooms looked toward the nearby plaza and welcomed visitors with greater ceremony. About 10 m behind the plaza's south portico a marble-paved corridor led to a small reception space resembling a daytime office. From here a short corridor reached an apsidal room that could have served equally for reception and dining. The room's well-preserved walls carried a complex program of painted architecture and *skoutlosis*, which reflects the widespread taste for marble decoration and brings the language of public assembly into the heart of the domus.[71] At its greatest extent the complex comprised more than 30 separate spaces, including at least three open courts, six water basins or tanks, and two or more latrines.

A similar picture appears across the street to the south. An earlier peristyle house at Sector MMS/S was partially razed by street construction, but then reorganized as a grand fifth-century residence with more than a dozen rooms on three levels (fig. 12). The main entrances lay behind the street's south portico. One of these led to a broad vestibule that preceded an elaborately decorated apsidal hall. The room originally was paved in marble and had painted walls that included the implicitly Christian invocation, "hagios o theos."[72] The floor of the apse was slightly raised and surfaced with

[70] For an overview, see M.L. Rautman, "A late Roman townhouse at Sardis," in Schwertheim (ed.), *Forschungen in Lydien* (supra n. 15), 49–66.

[71] Rautman, "Aura" (supra n. 55), 147–53, pls. 15–17; compare L. Özgenel, "Public use and privacy in late antique houses in Asia Minor: The architecture of spatial control," in L. Lavan, L. Özgenel, and A. Sarantis (eds.), *Housing in Late Antiquity. From Palaces to Shops, Late Antique Archaeology* 3.2 (Leiden 2007) 239–81.

[72] *AJA* 104 (2000) 650, fig. 6. For similar formulae in

mosaic. Most strikingly, the apse wall and semidome were covered with painted stucco with incised geometric patterns.[73] Such measures effectively underscored the status of the owner, who could enter the apse from a back room when appearing before assembled guests. The discovery here of 21 stamped glass weights suggests that this was the home of a well-to-do businessman, or perhaps a municipal official of the early seventh century. Farther west, another entrance from the street opened onto the surviving part of the earlier peristyle court. The raised east and south porticos were supported by columns and piers, and a large water basin stood in the northwest corner. Surviving wall paintings include the figure of a waiting servant, which echoes the theme of expectant reception. Opening off the court was a long room with marble-paved floor, a raised platform paved in opus sectile and tiles, and painted incrustation-style walls. A marble sigma table, broken in places but complete, makes clear that the room was used for dining as late as the early seventh century. Smaller service spaces were independently accessible from street and alley.[74]

These several houses, and others less extensively excavated, formed part of a relatively homogeneous and certainly prosperous quarter whose development reflects fundamental changes in the late antique city. All were reorganized or built anew in the first half of the fifth century along the lines of domestic fashion seen elsewhere in the Roman east. Open courts, colonnades, and water basins were key themes of household display. Rooms for reception, especially the newly popular apsidal halls, were emphasized by marble or mosaic floors and walls covered with ornate decoration, both real and illusory. Maintaining these scenes of daily elegance required constant renovation and updating, which can be traced in changing floor levels, circulation patterns, and decorative programs. Associated finds reflect the rising level of domestic consumption and specialized use of individual rooms. Several of these houses expanded over time as their owners annexed adjacent properties, and reached their greatest extent in the early sixth century.

The level of residential comfort noted at Sectors MMS and MMS/S may so far be exceptional for Sardis, but similar features appear elsewhere at the site. The so-called House of Bronzes in Sector HoB, discovered during the first season of excavation, occupies a flat, largely undeveloped area south of the Bath-Gymnasium Complex, about 100 m to the west. Contending with earlier burials and other features, the owner nevertheless was able to create two large rooms for reception or other special purposes in the fourth to sixth centuries.[75] Comparable if less well understood houses have been found on the higher parts of the site as well. Several unexplored multilevel units occupy the artificial terrace that overlooks the HoB area.[76] A fifth-century house found at Sector ByzFort had multiple rooms featuring mosaics, marble revetment, wall paintings, and a fine view of the Hermus valley.[77] At a slightly lower level, several houses were established in the fourth to fifth centuries on the Field 55 terrace, within sight of the Wadi B temple foundations. At least one of these buildings included a large rectangular room, carefully paved with tiles and decorated with incrustation-style paintings similar those at Sector MMS.[78]

---

domestic contexts, see C. Roueché, *Aphrodisias in Late Antiquity: The Late Roman and Byzantine Inscriptions*, revised second online edition (2004) <http://insaph.kcl.ac.uk/ala2004>, ISBN 1 897747 17 9, VI.52, no. 134.

[73] Rautman, "Aura" (supra n. 55), 156, fig. 8.

[74] *AJA* 104 (2000) 645–55. The weights are discussed by M.M. Fulghum and F. Heintz, "A hoard of early Byzantine glass weights from Sardis," *AJN* 2nd Ser. 10 (1998) 105–20.

[75] *BASOR* 154 (1959) 22–27; *BASOR* 157 (1960) 22–28; *BASOR* 170 (1963) 13; *BASOR* 249 (1983) 18, fig. 20. For the social standing of its occupants, see S. Ellis, "Middle class houses in late antiquity," in W. Bowden, A. Gutteridge, and C. Machado (eds.), *Social and Political Life in Late Antiquity*, *Late Antique Archaeology* 3.1 (Leiden 2006) 413–37, at 422.

[76] *BASOR* 177 (1965) 14–17.

[77] *BASOR* Suppl. 25 (1988) 36, fig. 22.

[78] *Kazı Sonuçları Toplantısı* 28.2 (2006) 745, fig. 7; Rautman, "Aura" (supra n. 55), 155, pl. 19.

Fig. 13. Sardis, late Roman street and flanking buildings at Sector MD1/N, looking southeast.

Less ambitious residential units found across the site may better reflect how most people lived. Traces of hillside habitation on the east side of Sector ByzFort, overlooking Field 55, include small buildings flanking a 5 m-wide contour road. These structures were solidly built on multiple levels, variously paved, modestly furnished, and occupied mainly in the fifth century. One space was equipped with two large water tanks that seem better suited to light industry than routine household needs.[79] Similar structures have been found on the lower plain. A partially excavated building at Sector MD2 includes at least four rooms, one furnished with a large cement-lined vat, which were occupied in the fifth and sixth centuries. The nearby Sector MD1/N includes a long rectangular structure with a cellar-like space appropriate for commercial storage. Common to both buildings is the combination of small, usually tiled rooms and more utilitarian spaces, together with signs of household production or commerce.[80] This broad sampling of the urban site says little about the overall density of habitation, however. Some sectors are filled with small structures crowded along narrow alleys or roads (fig. 13). Other areas, particularly near lower sections of the city wall, served mainly as neighborhood dumps. Modest, multifunctional structures of the fifth and sixth centuries have been found outside the city as well, along the banks of the Pactolus, around the Artemis Temple, and underneath the present excavation compound.[81]

The so-called Byzantine Shops preserve the most distinctly urban residential experience known so far at Sardis.[82] This long row of unremarkable spaces lies along the south side of the Bath-Gymnasium Complex and synagogue, behind the Marble Road's north portico (see fig. 7). Whatever its earlier history, the area took its present form ca. A.D. 400. The prominent street-side location and uniform construction suggest that portico and shops were built as a coordinated undertaking, perhaps initiated by municipal authorities but modified by individual leaseholders or owners to suit specific needs.[83]

[79] *AASOR* 52 (1994) 23–24.

[80] *AJA* 104 (2000) 669–71.

[81] Hanfmann and Waldbaum, *Survey*, 57–62; *BASOR* 249 (1983) 25–26.

[82] Crawford, *Byzantine Shops* (supra n. 7). The organization of units has been discussed recently by A. Harris, "Shops, retailing and the local economy in the early Byzantine world: The example of Sardis," in K. Dark (ed.), *Secular Buildings and the Archaeology of Everyday Life in the Byzantine Empire* (Oxford 2004) 82–122; K.E. Hammer and M. Murray, "Acquaintances, supporters, and competitors. Evidence of inter-connectedness and rivalry among the religious groups in Sardis," in Ascough (ed.), *Religious Rivalries* (supra n. 20), 175–94; see also Ellis, "Middle class houses" (supra n. 75), 422–23.

[83] For contemporary building legislation see Brands and Severin (eds.), *Spätantike Stadt* (supra n. 57); Saradi, *Byzantine City* (supra n. 51).

The design lent itself to easy alteration: a massive shared back wall with drain and a series of sturdy weight-bearing piers, 5 m to the south, between which slender partitions could be added to shape multiple rooms with doors, windows, and niches. The colonnade's 3 m height allowed space for an upper loft that could be used for sleeping quarters or storage, while street-side rooms were well suited for retail and household industry.

The arrangements of private entrepreneurs must have been in constant, asynchronous flux, which makes it difficult to track changes over time. In its excavated state, the quarter essentially preserves a moment in the early seventh century when fire swept through the crowded, if only partially occupied buildings. At this time there were about 20 independent units, each comprising one to three rooms at street level and perhaps as much floor space above. The presence of service counters, benches, kitchen wares, and amphorae indicates that three of these units likely served for food preparation or service. Two or three others may have been used for dyeing cloth or assembling scraps of glass, metal, and other materials for reuse.[84] Apart from these specialized assemblages, most artifacts recovered from the sector resemble the coins, household wares, tools, and personal effects found in other domestic contexts. Stone mortars, shallow basins, storage vessels, makeshift latrines, hearths, and ovens are equally present in the nearby HoB and MMS houses. These similarities point to a broad convergence of habitation and production at the household level in the late sixth and early seventh centuries.

Such glimpses of Sardis, assembled over the course of 50 years of excavation and study, make clear that the city's appearance changed in important ways during late antiquity. Some of its most prominent early monuments, like the Wadi B temple, stadium, and theater, stood on the terraced slopes of the acropolis. Whether these buildings were ever completed and how long they were maintained are open questions, but before the end of the fourth century the temple was gone and its abandoned precinct had been given over to housing. The stadium and theater, like places of mass entertainment elsewhere, were expensive to maintain and may not have functioned much later. Ideological motives may have contributed to the area's shift from civic showcase to private habitation, but if so, only indirectly. The landmark temple in Wadi B had apparently been destroyed much earlier by earthquake, possibly while the local bishop Melito was still alive. Other centers of traditional cult seem to have been similarly afflicted by natural catastrophe or passive neglect, prompting futile efforts at restoration in the mid-fourth century.[85] There is little sign of violent religious strife at Sardis in the days of the sophist Chrysanthios, teacher of the emperor Julian and high priest of Lydia, and his pupil Eunapios.[86] The traditional flowers, garlands, and peacocks found in painted *hypogaea* of the later fourth century appear equally in Christian and nonspecific tombs of the period

[84] For metals recycling and manufacture, see E. Giannichedda, "Metal production in late antiquity: From continuity of knowledge to changes in consumption," in L. Lavan, E. Zanini, and A. Sarantis (eds.), *Technology in Transition: A.D. 300–650, Late Antique Archaeology* 4 (Leiden 2006) 187–209, at 196.

[85] Traditional religion apparently fared better in rural Lydia; see Foss, *Sardis*, 28–29, 155 n. 73; Mitchell, *Anatolia*, vol. 2 (supra n. 30), 118–19; G. Petzl, "Ländliche Religiosität in Lydien," in Schwertheim (ed.), *Forschungen in Lydien* (supra n. 15), 37–48, at 46–48; M. Ricl, "Society and economy of rural sanctuaries in Roman Lydia and Phrygia," *EpigAnat* 35 (2003) 7–101.

[86] The historical background is summarized by Foss, *Sardis*, 22–34.

[87] For the Christian "Painted Tomb," see Butler, *Sardis*, 174, 181–83, pls. IV–V. The tomb of Flavios Chrysanthios (Tomb 76.1) includes the common Christian formula "kyrie boethei"; *BASOR* 229 (1978) 61–64; *BASOR* 233 (1979) 4–8. For two nearby *hypogaea* (Tombs 79.2, 79.3) without Christian texts, see *BASOR* 249 (1983) 22–25. Two more vaulted tombs (Tombs 07.2, 07.3) with similar paintings have recently been identified closer to the city wall; see *Kazı Sonuçları Toplantısı* 30.4 (2008) 192–93, figs. 3–5. For a comprehensive survey of the painted tombs, see now V. Rousseau, *Late Roman Wall Painting at Sardis* (Ph.D. dissertation, University of Wisconsin-Madison 2010).

Fig. 14. Sardis, wall painting in Tomb 07.3.

(fig. 14).[87] Epigraphic and archaeological evidence for the local Jewish community, together with the monumental synagogue, attests the city's religious pluralism. More pragmatic reasons for relocating public life onto the urban plain were the area's seismic instability, the fortification of the lower city, and the changing priorities of civic leaders.[88]

Monumentalized urban passages, refurbished public buildings, and expanded houses of local residents are unmistakable signs that Sardis saw some of its most prosperous years in late antiquity. The grandiose scale of official and private patronage appears in the elaboration of colonnaded streets and plazas, which were gaining importance as scenes of commercial as well as ceremonial life. The costly but selective maintenance of public buildings could be justified by assigning them new political roles, as may have been the case with the *boule* and *gerousia* meeting in the Marble Court of the Bath-Gymnasium.[89] The bustle of construction echoed in prolonged work at the synagogue and constant remodeling of the MMS houses and the Byzantine Shops. Inescapable in western Sardis but apparent across the site, this restless activity provides vivid background for the well-known builders' inscription that was set up in A.D. 459 to ensure the timely completion of contracted projects.[90]

[88] Olson, "Landslides" (supra n. 9); for the "early Byzantine tectonic paroxysm," see S. Stiros, "The AD 365 Crete earthquake and possible seismic clustering during the fourth and sixth centuries A.D. in the eastern Mediterranean: A review of historical and archaeological data," *Journal of Structural Geology* 23 (2001) 545–602. Compare the effects of third- and fourth-century earthquakes in the region noted by Ladstätter and Pülz, "Ephesus" (supra n. 29). For urban priorities in late antiquity, see J.H.W.G. Liebeschuetz, *The Decline and Fall of the Roman City* (Oxford 2001); J.-M. Spieser, *Urban and Religious Spaces in Late Antiquity and Early Byzantium* (Aldershot 2001); Saradi, *Byzantine City* (supra n. 51).

[89] For sixth-century graffiti from the Marble Court, see Yegül, *Bath-Gymnasium Complex* (supra n. 7), 49, fig. 124. The palaestra of the theater gymnasium at Ephesus may also have seen political activities about this time; see P. Scherrer and E. Trinkle, *Die Tetragonos Agora in Ephesos. Grabungsergebnisse von archaischer bis in byzantinische Zeit—Ein Überblick. Befunde und Funde klassischer Zeit, Forschungen in Ephesos* XIII 2 (Vienna 2006) 11.

[90] For the text, see Buckler and Robinson, *Inscriptions*, 40–43 no. 18; M. Di Branco, "Lavoro e conflittualità in una città tardoantica. Una rilettura dell'epigrafe di Sardi *CIG* 3467," *Antiquité tardive* 8 (2000) 181–208. The text nostal-

Imperial interest tangibly benefited the city as an official base for administration and armsmaking, but more importantly by stimulating traffic to and from this sub-regional economic hub.[91] Like other nearby cities, Sardis was celebrated by contemporary writers for its fine textiles, and perhaps less credibly for its wines. Local workshops have been proposed for the manufacture of bronze vessels, iron tools, glass wares and windowpanes, polychrome jewelry, and carved bone implements.[92] A long ceramic tradition continued in the massive output of bricks, roof tiles, and vessels for table use, transport, and storage. At the same time, the local ceramic environment illustrates the site's distance from the late empire's economic mainstream. The limited nature of interregional exchange appears in the scarcity of imported amphorae compared with local vessels, mainly single-handled transport jars, which are locally ubiquitous but infrequently found elsewhere. On the level of fine wares, the most widely distributed varieties of African Red Slip and Phocean Red Slip pottery appear in fifth- to sixth-century levels, along with imitations made of local clays. Specialized imported objects like lamps, *ampullae*, and *unguentaria* may also have inspired local versions that in some cases outlived their sources of inspiration.[93]

The prosperity Sardis enjoyed in the later fourth to sixth centuries may be the result of local circumstances, but the far-reaching changes it saw around the turn of the seventh century are those seen among its neighbors as well. Many public spaces were poorly maintained if not abandoned altogether; houses were subdivided and put to new purposes; imported pottery decreased in variety and quantity; and the supply of currency dwindled.[94] These phenomena are plainly evident in western Sardis, where coins and pottery preserve a continuous occupation sequence down to the early 600s. The demise of the Byzantine Shops is especially stark: all inhabited units were hastily evacuated before fire swept through the quarter, an event that preserved their diverse contents along with a numismatic break at A.D. 616. Small clusters of coins of Constans II (A.D. 641–655) have been found in the area, mainly in the southern rooms of the Bath-Gymnasium Complex and scattered about the nearby Marble Road, but their scarcity elsewhere speaks to wider dislocations in local routines.[95] Clearly by the mid-seventh century Sardis had become a very different place.

Coming to terms with such signs of urban transformation is one of the central challenges posed by late antiquity.[96] At Sardis, as at many Mediterranean sites, the decision of early excavators to focus on

---

gically invokes the memory of the "most illustrious twice *neokoros* metropolis of the Sardians"; see Burrell, *Neokoroi* (supra n. 20), 113.

[91] For highways and milestones attesting late third- and fourth-century repairs, see Buckler and Robinson, *Inscriptions*, 90 no. 84; Foss, *Sardis*, 6–7, 150–51 nn. 13, 18; D.H. French, *Roman Roads and Milestones of Asia Minor*, Fasc. 2, *An Interim Catalogue of Milestones*, Par. 1, *British Institute of Archaeology at Ankara Monograph* 9 (Oxford 1988) 250–59; Petzl, *Tituli Lydiae* (supra n. 48), 111–13 nos. 1536–37.

[92] For evidence of glassmaking, see von Saldern, *Ancient and Byzantine Glass* (supra n. 7), 1–2; for metalworking, M. Goodway and P. Vandiver, in Crawford, *Byzantine Shops* (supra n. 7), 129–34; Waldbaum, *Metalwork* (supra n. 7), 6–9; for gem-cutting, *BASOR* 249 (1983) 28–29. The remains of bone-cutting on a large scale were found in fifth-century levels near the Wadi B temple.

[93] Rautman, "Two late Roman wells" (supra n. 68), 79–81; idem, "From mainstream to margin among the late Roman amphorae of Sardis," in P. Monsieur and J. Poblome (eds.), *From Amphorae to Modelling the Late Roman Economy* (forthcoming).

[94] The evidence is highly varied with pockets of private stability appearing amid larger areas of public neglect. For ambiguities in perceiving the advent of regional "decline," see M. Whittow, "Recent research on the late-antique city in Asia Minor: The second half of the 6th century revisited," in Lavan (ed.), *Recent Research* (supra n. 31), 137–53, at 140–49.

[95] Bates, *Byzantine Coins* (supra n. 7), 1–3; Crawford, *Byzantine Shops* (supra n. 7), 2–3.

[96] For a recent review of perspectives on change, see J.H.W.G. Liebeschuetz, "Transformation and decline: Are the two really incompatible?" in J.-U. Krause and C. Witschel (eds.), *Die Stadt in der Spätantike–Niedergang oder Wandel?*, *Historia Einzelschriften* 190 (Stuttgart 2006) 463–83.

Fig. 15. Sardis, Sector MMS, apsidal structure with secondary installations, looking east.

two or three major buildings emphasized those aspects of Roman settled life that were highly visible, but at the same time socially complex and politically precarious. The state of pottery studies in the 1960s, when large-scale excavation was underway, provided little framework for addressing questions of production, development, exchange, and use; as a result, coins had to serve as the main chronological guideposts, despite uncertainties about their minting and distribution. For these reasons, the destruction and abandonment of the Byzantine Shops ca. A.D. 616 suggested an irresistible link with the great historical narrative of that decade: the Sassanian incursions in Asia Minor and the heroic resistance of Heraclius. The appealing clarity of this story, with wealthy Sardis falling to an otherwise forgotten attack that year, is apparent from its widespread acceptance.[97]

Recent work validates the broad outlines of this view while introducing some refinements. The city's increasing isolation during a tumultuous period is confirmed by the scarcity of imported pottery and seventh-century coins, and issues of Heraclius's later reign continue to be rare. Maintenance of public spaces and monuments appears inconsistent, with some street-side porticoes resurfaced with mosaics while others were partitioned for commercial use.[98] Private houses underwent complex changes that saw individual spaces selectively maintained, subdivided, stripped, and put to new purposes. Hearths, ovens, vats, drains, and latrines were cut through or set atop marble or mosaic floors, sometimes in grand apsidal rooms (fig. 15).[99] Spaces once intended for ceremony and display were adapted as practical units for generating wealth, primarily at the level of households and other small

[97] C. Foss, "The Persians in Asia Minor and the end of antiquity," *EHR* 90 (1975) 721–43; idem, *Sardis*, 53–55. For reservations, see J. Russell, "The Persian invasions of Syria/Palestine and Asia Minor in the reign of Heraclius: Archaeological, numismatic and epigraphic evidence," in E. Kountoura-Galake (ed.), *The Dark Centuries of Byzantium (7th–9th c.)* (Athens 2001) 47–71. In the same sense that "late antiquity" came of age amid Cold War cultural studies, many of its precepts invite revaluation through the multipolar lens of a globalized 21st century; compare B. Ward-Perkins, *The Fall of Rome and the End of Civilization* (Oxford 2005) 176–83.

[98] The upper portico mosaic of the MMS/N plaza dates to the mid- or late sixth century; *AASOR* 53 (1995) 5–6; Scheibelreiter, *Stifterinschriften* (supra n. 48), 35–36 no. 6. Portico encroachment is known at the MMS street, the Marble Road, and most clearly the colonnade in front of the synagogue; see *BASOR* 174 (1964) 46–47; Crawford, *Byzantine Shops* (supra n. 7), 7, figs. 126, 129; *BASOR* Suppl. 25 (1988) 20.

[99] *BASOR* Suppl. 25 (1988) 58–61; *AASOR* 51 (1993) 11; *AASOR* 53 (1995) 8–10; *AJA* 102 (1998) 481; *AJA* 104 (2000) 653–54. Such phenomena broadly correspond with the demise of the curial class, which saw urban elites move to rural estates, if not the imperial capital itself, and leave their townhouses empty or in the hands of urban workers. For a recent review see Saradi, *Byzantine City* (supra n. 51), 151–63.

social units.[100] Significant parts of the site seem to have been unoccupied by the later sixth century, while others were accumulating debris from unidentified sources. Future excavation may locate areas that survived or even flourished through the seventh century, perhaps as clustered dwellings within a substantially ruralized setting. Byzantine Sardis remained an administrative center and metropolitan capital, but by the eighth century these functions may not have extended far beyond the walled acropolis, which had been laboriously fortified with architectural spoils brought from the city below.[101] Ongoing survey of the Sardis environs aims to clarify the process of urban change by identifying patterns of consolidation, continuity, or expansion in rural land use and settlement.[102]

Every archaeological site has a story to tell, a story that is shaped by research design, methods, and happenstance. The last 50 years of exploration at Sardis have sketched the outlines of a great Roman city that was the administrative, economic, and cultural focus of an inland province. Imperial action benefited its development at two critical junctures: in the early first century A.D. when Tiberius acted to rebuild the polis, and in the late third century when Diocletian decided its political rank. The results of this external involvement can be seen everywhere, but it is the archaeological focus, largely fortuitous, on western Sardis that has brought particular attention to late antiquity and the expansion of one part of the city. Recent work suggests that this area may not be representative of the entire site, but benefited from its proximity to the Bath-Gymnasium Complex and the highway leading west. Construction of urban fortifications in the late third and early fourth century presented local elites and government officials with new opportunities for ceremonial, commercial, and residential development, which took the form of public buildings, colonnaded streets, and houses of pretense that reinforced their standing in late classical society. In the sixth century the city's increasing isolation from the political and economic mainstream, brought about by the centralization of government and accelerated by demographic, economic, environmental, and military crises, left residents to reassess traditional life-ways and their own place in a post-Roman world. The fundamental reasons for the demise of the classical city lay beyond the site and even its territory, in its changing relation with imperial power, and with other points in the urban heartland of Asia Minor.

[100] E. Zanini, "Artisans and traders in the early Byzantine city: Exploring the limits of archaeological evidence," in Bowden, Gutteridge, and Machado (eds.), *Social and Political Life* (supra n. 75), 373–411, at 398–403.

[101] For the acropolis, apparently unoccupied through most of late antiquity, see *BASOR* 162 (1961) 33–34; *BASOR* 166 (1962) 37–39; *BASOR* 170 (1963) 32. Inscriptions built into the walls range in date from Claudius to the time of Justinian; see Buckler and Robinson, *Inscriptions*, 29 no. 10, 43 no. 19; Foss, *Sardis*, 57–60. The careful installation of many inscribed blocks suggests a lingering interest in displaying the city's past.

[102] Intensive long-term survey in the vicinity of Sardis and Bin Tepe is now being extended by systematic regional reconnaissance; see C.H. Roosevelt and C. Luke, "Central Lydia Archaeological Survey," *Araştırma Sonuçları Toplantısı* 24.2 (2007) 135–54; *Araştırma Sonuçları Toplantısı* 25.3 (2008) 305–26; *Araştırma Sonuçları Toplantısı* 26.2 (2009) 433–50; Roosevelt, *Archaeology of Lydia* (supra n. 10).

2 Sculpture and the Rhetorical Imagination in Late Antique Constantinople

Sarah Bassett

A visitor to Constantinople in the middle years of the fifth century would have found a city rich in sculpture, ancient and modern. Amassed almost completely in the century since Byzantium's re-foundation as New Rome in A.D. 324, this monumental urban display included antiquities of pre-fourth-century manufacture which had been gathered from the cities and sanctuaries of the Graeco-Roman world first at the behest of Constantine and his cohort and then at the direction of Theodosius I and the members of his dynasty, as well as works of contemporary manufacture: images of emperors, their wives, family members, and high ranking imperial officials. This varied sculptured array presented the fifth-century viewer with a range of images and with them a vast catalogue of subjects and styles; antiquities such as a fourth-century B.C. statue of Herakles by Lysippos shared the same urban stage as late fourth-century A.D. representations of Roman officials, while mythological figures stood cheek by jowl with images of a more historical bent, works of such venerable antiquity as the Serpent Column of the Plataean Tripod, the great obelisk from the temple of Amon at Thebes in Egypt, or more recent fabrications such as the obelisk's own supporting base showing members of the Theodosian house in attendance at the circus.[1]

This great panoply of sculpture was in many respects characteristic of all late Roman cities, centers such as Rome, Ephesus, and Alexandria that had built their sculptured collections up over time.[2] That this variety was replicated in Constantinople, a city brought to life as a new capital of the Roman world merely a century before, suggests, however, that something deliberate was afoot in the creation of an urban aesthetic that was itself part of a larger project of urban and, ultimately, imperial

[1] The following abbreviations of frequently cited sources are used:
Bassett, *Urban Image* = S. Bassett, *The Urban Image of Late Antique Constantinople* (Cambridge 2004).
Bauer, *Stadt, Platz und Denkmal* = F.A. Bauer, *Stadt, Platz und Denkmal in der Spätantike* (Mainz 1996).
Fıratlı, *Sculpture byzantine* = N. Fıratlı, *La sculpture byzantine figurée au Musée archéologique d'Istanbul* (Paris 1990).
Par. = A. Cameron and J. Herrin (eds.), *Constantinople in the Early Eighth Century: The* Parastaseis Syntomoi Chronikai (Leiden 1984).
Rabe = H. Rabe (ed.), *Hermogenes opera edidit, Rhetores Graeci* 6 (Leipzig 1913).
Stichel, *Kaiserstatue* = R.H.W. Stichel, *Die römische Kaiserstatue am Ausgang der Antike* (Rome 1982).
Wooten = C.W. Wooten, *Hermogenes on Types of Style* (Chapel Hill 1967).
Fıratlı, *Sculpture byzantine*, 1–13 documents the surviving examples of Constantinopolitan honorific statuary. See Stichel, *Kaiserstatue*, 76, 84–87, 90, 94–115 for late fourth- and fifth-century examples. For general discussion of Constantinopolitan public spaces and their sculptured displays, see Bauer, *Stadt, Platz und Denkmal*, 143–86. On ancient statuary see Bassett, *Urban Image*.

[2] On sculptured display in general, see G.M.A. Hanfmann, *From Croesus to Constantine. The Cities of Western Asia Minor and their Arts in Greek and Roman Times* (Ann Arbor 1975); C.C. Vermuele III, *Greek Sculpture and Roman Taste* (Ann Arbor 1977) 87–101; and, more recently, the collected essays in F.A. Bauer and C. Witschel (eds.), *Statuen in der Spätantike* (Wiesbaden 2007). On Rome and Ephesus in particular, see Bauer, *Stadt, Platz und Denkmal*, 3–141 (Rome) and 269–305 (Ephesus). For Alexandria see R.S. Bagnall, "Archaeological work on Hellenistic and Roman Egypt, 1995–2000," *AJA* 105 (2001) 227–43, at 229–30; and J.-Y. Empereur, *La gloire d'Alexandrie* (Paris 1998).

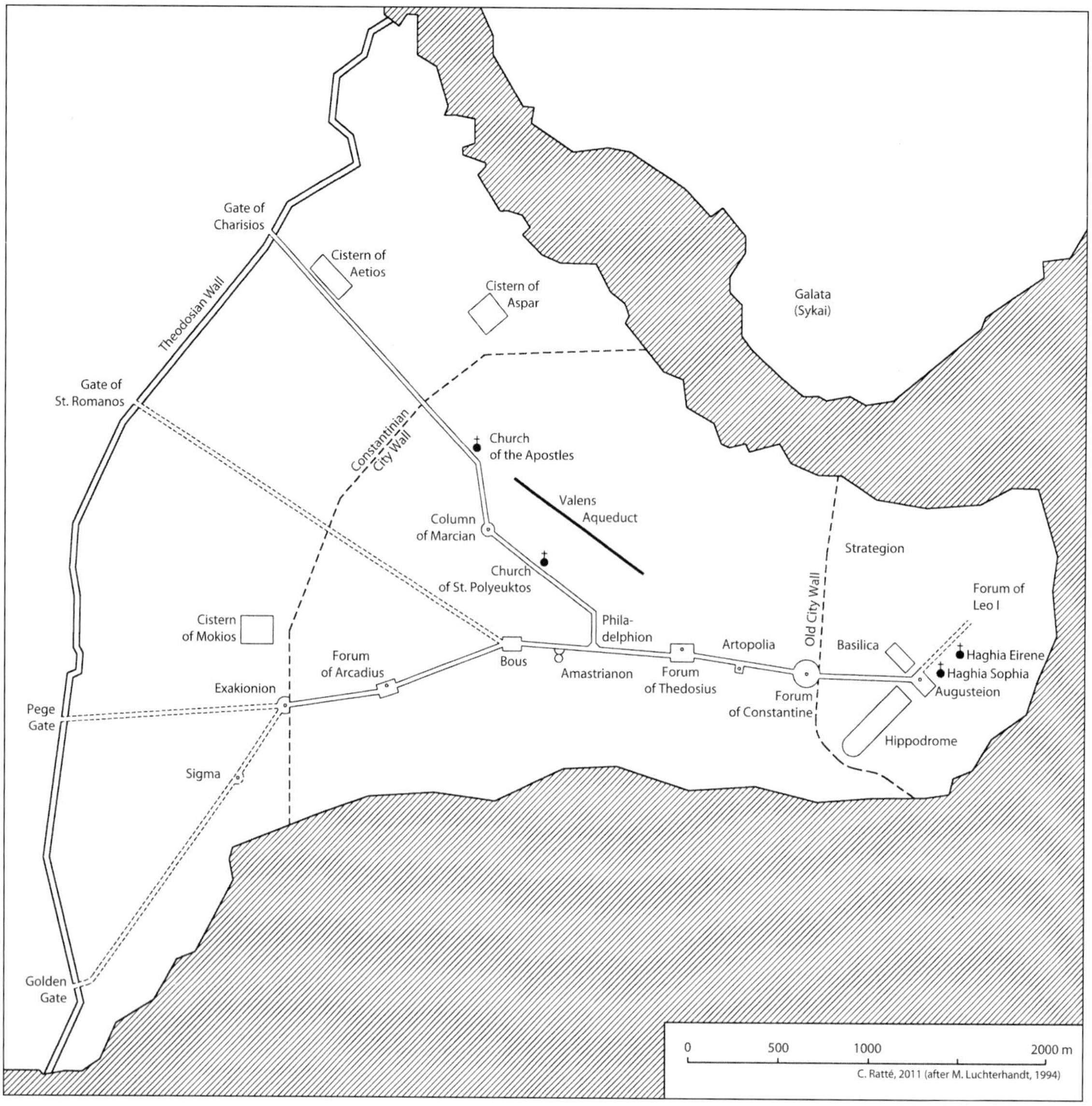

Fig. 1. Plan of Constantinople (Bauer, *Stadt, Plaz und Denkmal in der Spätantike* [Mainz 1996] fig. 47).

glorification. It is this aesthetic that I would like to examine by sketching, first, a picture of the city and its sculptured displays, and offering, second, a proposal for their appreciation derived from an understanding of the late antique "period eye," that package of ideas and assumptions that help determine ways of seeing at an individual point in history, based on late Roman conceptions of rhetorical style.[3]

[3] For the definition of "period eye," see M. Baxandall, *Painting and Experience in Fifteenth-Century Italy, A Primer in the Social History of Pictorial Style* (Oxford 1972). On the relationship between visual and verbal styles in late antiquity, see M. Roberts, *The Jeweled Style. Poetry and Poetics in Late Antiquity* (Ithaca 1989) 66–121; and S. Bassett, "Style and meaning in the imperial panels in San Vitale, Ravenna," *Artibus et Historiae* 57 (2008) 49–57. For consideration of the question in earlier periods of Roman sculpture, see T. Hölscher, *Römische Bildsprache als semantisches System* (Heidelberg 1987); and A. Leibundgut-Maye, "Gleichzeitigkeit des Ungleichzeitigen. Die Stilebenen der trajanischen Kunst und ihre Botschaft," *Antrittsvorlesungen* 5 (Mainz 1989) 15–28. For a different perspective, see F. Fless, *Opferdiener und Kultmusiker auf stadtrömischen historischens Reliefs* (Mainz 1995), who rejects such a formulation. I thank Ortwin Dally for these references.

By the middle of the fifth century Constantinople was replete with venues for the display of public sculpture (fig. 1). The city's monumental core, which had been elaborated according to a Constantinian mandate between A.D. 324 and 330, was built around an armature of streets and public spaces constructed during the reign of Septimius Severus (A.D. 193–211) at the western edge of the old Greek town of Byzantium. At the heart of this armature stood the forum known as the Augusteion, a large, rectangular space of uncertain dimensions. Nearby, the Milion, a quadriform arch marking the confluence of three colonnaded avenues—the major east-west axis of the Mese; its extension, the Regia, which ran along the south flank of the forum; and an avenue that led north to the Golden Horn—offered a second venue. Two further areas—the basilica, a peristyle housing a library and temple; and the military parade ground, or Strategeion—stood northwest of the Augusteion. The hippodrome and the Baths of Zeuxippos rose to the south. To the west, in areas claimed for development under Constantine, three major fora, those of Constantine, Theodosius, and Arcadius, opened out along the Mese. The Mese itself forked halfway between the forum of Theodosius and that of Arcadius. A Capitolium preceded by a space known as the Philadelphion marked this division.[4]

On display in each of these spaces was a range of sculpture, ancient and modern. Archaeological remains together with graphic and literary sources suggest a population somewhere in the area of 250 pieces by the middle of the fifth century.[5] Of the monuments documented approximately two-thirds were ancient imports, the remaining third, contemporary and purpose made. It is this mix of old and new that I wish to consider, examining first the antiquities and then the city's purpose-made sculpture.

Only a handful of the city's antiquities survive. The Serpent Column of the Plataean Tripod from the sanctuary of Apollo at Delphi and an obelisk from the temple of Amon at Thebes in Egypt still stand together on the site of the late antique city's hippodrome, while the column of Constantine, itself of unknown provenance, rises a few blocks away on the site of the emperor's eponymous forum. A statue base dedicated to Theophanes of Mytilene, formerly in the hippodrome, is preserved in the Istanbul Archaeological Museum. Overseas, in Venice, the four bronze horses on the façade of the basilica of St. Mark and the porphyry tetrarchs now built into the southwest corner of the church's exterior

[4] On Constantinopolitan topography, see P. Gilles, *De topographia Constantinopoleos et de illius antiquitatibus libri quattuor* (Lyon 1561); C. Mango, *The Brazen House* (Copenhagen 1954); R. Janin, *Constantinople byzantine* (Paris 1964); R. Guilland, *Études de topographie de Constantinople byzantine* (Berlin and Amsterdam 1969); G. Dagron, *Naissance d'une capitale. Constantinople et ses institutions de 330* (Paris 1974); W. Müller-Wiener, *Bildlexikon zur Topographie Istanbuls* (Tübingen 1977); R. Krautheimer, *Three Christian Capitals* (Berkeley 1983) 41–67; C. Mango, *Le développement urbain de Constantinople (IVe–VIIe siècles)* (Paris 1984); Bauer, *Stadt, Platz und Denkmal*; and, most recently Bassett, *Urban Image*, 17–36.

[5] Literary sources include a range of late Roman and Byzantine texts, the following prime among them: the fifth-century Christodoros of Thebes, *Ekphrasis on the Sculpture in the Baths of Zeuxippos,* translated by W.R. Paton, *The Greek Anthology*, vol. 1, Loeb Classical Library (London and New York 1916) 58–91; the early sixth-century Zosimus, *Historia Nova,* in L. Mendelssohn (ed.), *Zosimi Historia Nova* (Leipzig 1887); the seventh-century *Chronicon Paschale,* in L. Dindorff (ed.), *Chronicon paschale* (Bonn 1832); the eighth-century *Parastaseis syntomoi chronikai* in *Par.* and its 10th-century derivative *Patria Konstantinopoleos* in T. Preger (ed.), *Scriptores originum Constantinopolitanarum* (Leipzig 1903–1907); and Niketas Choniates's 13th-century lament for the fall of Constantinople to the army of the Fourth Crusade, *De Signis Constantinopoleos* in J.L. van Dieten (ed.), *Niketas Choniates Historia* (Berlin 1975) 647–55.

For archaeological documentation see especially S. Casson et al., *Preliminary Report upon the Excavations carried out in and near the Hippodrome of Constantinople in 1927* (London 1928); *Second Report upon the Excavations carried out in and near the Hippodrome of Constantinople in 1928* (London 1929); and "Les fouilles de l'hippodrome de Constantinople," *GBA* 30.1 (1930) 215–42.

Most important among the graphic documentation is the Freshfield Album, a sketchbook made by a German traveler to Constantinople in the 16th century. See E.H. Freshfield, "Notes on a vellum album containing some original sketches of public buildings and monuments drawn by a German artist who visited Constantinople in 1574,"*Archaeologia* 72 (1922) 87–104.

wall stand as testament to the plunder of the city's antiquities in A.D. 1204 by the army of the Fourth Crusade. Finally, at the British Museum, there is a bronze goose from the area of the hippodrome.[6]

Literary sources describe a broader range of figured sculpture than the surviving monuments suggest; images of gods and goddesses, mythic heroes, statesmen, and men-of-letters among them. By the middle of the fifth century these figures, which came from such cities and sanctuaries as Athens, Mytilene, and Rome, probably numbered somewhere between 150 and 200.[7] Preferred display venues included the hippodrome, the Baths of Zeuxippos, and the forum of Constantine.[8] Although there is no overt visual commentary on or criticism of these statues in any of the sources, descriptive details indicate monumental scale, media of bronze, porphyry, and marble, and a preference for works of art from the periods that modern art historians would identify as late classical and Hellenistic. Thus, for example, Christodoros of Thebes's descriptions of a series of statues of the goddess Aphrodite in the Baths of Zeuxippos indicate not only that the goddess was depicted in marble, but also that she was half-draped, an iconography that indicates post-fourth-century B.C. manufacture.[9]

Sculpture of contemporary manufacture also contributed to the luster of the Constantinopolitan environment; however, as with the antiquities, physical evidence is limited. Remains of two statues, the fragments of a marble cuirass figure and a porphyry toga statue, provide evidence for the fourth century A.D.[10] Given the lack of early fourth-century monuments, Theodosian sculptured documentation from the later fourth and the fifth centuries seems rich by comparison. The obelisk base in the hippodrome and fragments from the column of Theodosius are the most well-known examples.[11] Less familiar is the evidence for the city's free-standing honorific sculpture. In Istanbul itself, there are at least eleven statue fragments of emperors or high magistrates from Constantinopolitan venues in the Istanbul Archaeological Museum, prime among them the Beyazit Head identified both as Arcadius (reigned A.D. 395–408) and Theodosius II (reigned A.D. 405–450) (fig. 2).[12] The remaining fragments

[6] For documentation see Bassett, *Urban Image*, 192–204 (Column of Constantine), 216 (Goose), 219–22 (Obelisk), 224–27 (Serpent Column), 222–23 (Horses of San Marco), 232 (Theophanes of Mytilene), 242 (Tetrarchs).

[7] On the provenance of Constantinopolitan antiquities see especially Eusebius of Caesarea, *Vita Constantini* III, 54, who names Delphi, the sanctuary of the Muses at Mt. Helikon, and the temple of Apollo Smintheus at Chryse in the Troad; Jerome, *Chronicon*, 324, who describes a picture of empire-wide origins; and *Patria Konstantinopoleos* (supra n. 5), II, 73, which specifies 22 cities in addition to Rome from which antiquities were brought.

[8] For discussion of these venues and documentation of their contents, see Bassett, *Urban Image*, 50–78; ead., "The antiquities in the hippodrome of Constantinople," *DOP* 45 (1991) 87–96; ead., "*Historiae custos*: Sculpture and tradition in the Baths of Zeuxippos," *AJA* 100 (1996) 491–506.

[9] Christodoros of Thebes, *Ekphrasis* (supra n. 5), 78–81 and 99–101.

[10] For material in the Istanbul Archaeological Museum see Fıratlı, *Sculpture byzantine*, 5 (marble cuirassed figure from Yedikule, inv. no. 1094); 8 (porphyry toga statue from the vicinity of Hagia Sophia, inv. no. 5795).

[11] On the obelisk and its base: G. Bruns, *Die Obelisk und seine Basis auf dem Hippodrom zu Konstantinopel* (Istanbul 1935); B. Kiilerich, *The Obelisk Base in Constantinople: Court Art and Imperial Ideology* (Rome 1998) with extensive bibliography; and, most recently, A. Effenberger, "Nochmals zur Aufstellung des Theodosius—Obelisken in Hippodrome von Konstantinopel," *Gymnasium* 114 (2007) 587–89. On Theodosian sculpture in general: J. Kollwitz, *Oströmische Plastik der theodosianischen Zeit* (Berlin 1941); and B. Kiilerich, *Late Fourth-Century Classicism in the Plastic Arts. Studies in the So-Called Theodosian Renaissance* (Odense 1993) with extensive bibliography. On the columns of Theodosius and Arcadius: Kollwitz, *Oströmische Plastik der theodosianischen Zeit* (supra this note), 3–76; G. Becatti, *La colonna coclide istoriata* (Rome 1960) 83–288; G. Giglioli, *La colonna di Arcadio a Costantinopoli* (Naples 1952); and Kiilerich, *Late Fourth-Century Classicism* (supra this note), 50–55 (Theodosius) and 55–64 (Arcadius) with further recent bibliography.

[12] Fıratlı, *Sculpture byzantine*, 7 (inv. no. 5028) and the majority of scholars identify the portrait as Arcadius. H.-G. Severin, *Zur Porträtplastik des 5 Jahrhunderts n. Chr.* (Munich 1972) 17–20 is less sanguine about specificity, opining that the portrait may represent either Arcadius, Honorius, or Theodosius II. Stichel, *Kaiserstatue*, 51–52 prefers identification with Theodosius II and a date around 414. R. Özgan and D. Stutzinger, "Untersuchungen zu Porträtplastik des 5 Jhs. n. Chr. anhand zweier neugefundener Porträts aus

Fig. 2. Head of an Emperor, Istanbul Archaeological Museum no. 5028 (R. Ousterhout).

Fig. 3. Magistrate, Istanbul Archaeological Museum no. 769 (R. Ousterhout).

include the lone piece of an unidentified imperial bust in porphyry,[13] five draped torsos (fig. 3),[14] a single cuirass statue,[15] and four male heads in various states of preservation.[16] Two further pieces supplement the Constantinopolitan record: a colossal bronze cuirass statue now in Barletta,[17] and a marble head described as that of Theodosius II now in the Louvre.[18]

In addition to the figured remains in the Istanbul Archaeological Museum, statue bases in varying states of preservation document the existence of lost statues, among them representations

---

Stratonikeia," *IstMitt* 35 (1985) 237–74, at 256–61 second identification with Theodosius II, but date the portrait to the second decade of the fifth century.

[13] Inv. no. 73.27: Fıratlı, *Sculpture byzantine*, 8, pl. 4, fig. 8.

[14] Inv. no. 5077: ibid., 8–9, pl. 4, fig. 9a–c; inv. no. 5158A and 5158B: ibid., 9, pl. 5, fig. 10a–b; inv. no. 4417: ibid., 12, pl. 8, fig. 14; inv. no. 769: ibid., 12, pl. 8, fig. 15; inv. no. 4051: ibid., 13, pl. 8, fig. 16a–b.

[15] Inv. no. 5673: ibid, 9–10, pl. 5, fig. 11a–c.

[16] Inv. no. 5278: ibid., 14, pl. 10, fig. 19a–c; inv. no. 6287: ibid., 14, pl. 10, fig. 20a–c; inv. no. 73.26: ibid., 15, pl. 11, fig. 22; inv. no. 4719: ibid., 15, pl. 11, fig. 23.

[17] F.P. Johnson, "The Colossus of Barletta," *AJA* 25 (1929) 20–25; R. Delbreuck, *Spätantike Kaiserporträts* (Berlin 1933) 219–26; Kollwitz, *Oströmische Plastik der Theodosianischen Zeit* (supra n. 11), 109–10; S. Sande, "Zur Porträtplastik des sechsten nachchristlichen Jahrhunderts," *ActaAArtHist* 6 (1975) 65–106, at 75–76; Severin, *Zur Porträtplastik* (supra n. 12), 106–15; J. Breckenridge, in K. Weitzmann (ed.), *Age of Spirituality. Late Antique and Early Christian Art, Third to Seventh Century* (New York 1979) 29–30; Stichel, *Kaiserstatue*, 10, 12, 61–62, pl. 30.

[18] Paris, Musée du Louvre, Départment des Antiquités Grecques et Romaines, MA1036. The head is part of the *ancien fonds* of the Louvre and may have been in the collection from the 17th century. See Weitzmann, *Age of Spirituality* (supra n. 17), 28–29, and Delbrueck, *Spätantike Kaiserporträts* (supra n. 17), 217–19.

of Eudoxia, the wife of Theodosius I, and statues of Theodosius II.[19] In the city itself the base and column of a statue dedicated to Marcian remain, possibly the original support for the colossal figure now in Barletta.[20]

As with the city's antiquities, graphic records and literary sources expand the picture.[21] In addition to the two historiated columns dedicated to Theodosius I and Arcadius, sources report approximately 20 statues of Constantine and other members of his family,[22] a handful of statues representing members of the dynasty of Valentinian I (A.D. 364–375),[23] and around 40 statues of Theodosius the Great (A.D. 379–395) or members of his house.[24] Throughout the city imperial statues predominate; however, there is evidence for other public sculpture, including figures of magistrates and other high-ranking officials, men such as the city prefects, Proclus and Aurelianus, and the senator, Themistius.[25]

Taken together, the physical and literary evidence reveal a combination of historiated columns and honorific statues among the works of contemporary manufacture. With respect to the latter, the medium covers the gamut from marble, alabaster, and porphyry to bronze, silver, and gold.[26] Display venues included the Augusteion, the Milion, the hippodrome, the entrance to the great palace, the Chalke Gate, and the Regia in the city's monumental core. Of these the most popular space for sculptured display was the Augusteion. Approximately 20 statues dedicated to members of each of the city's ruling dynasties, the Constantinian, the Valentinian, and the Theodosian, stood here. The next most populous venue was the Chalke Gate and the Regia leading up to it with approximately eleven statues representing members of the Constantinian and Theodosian houses, followed by the Milion with about six statues, again of members of the Constantinian and Theodosian dynasties.[27] In the western territories the most prominent display areas were the

[19] Stichel, *Kaiserstatue,* 96 no. 91 (Eudoxia), 98–99 nos. 99–100 (Theodosius).

[20] Stichel, *Kaiserstatue,* 100 no. 109; Müller-Wiener, *Bildlexikon zur Topographie Istanbuls* (supra n. 4), 54; Janin, *Constantinople byzantine* (supra n. 4), 84–85; Kollwitz, *Oströmische Plastik der theodosianischen Zeit* (supra n. 11), 69–76.

[21] The literary and graphic sources are essentially the same as those documenting the presence of ancient monuments (supra n. 5).

[22] The numbers are approximate and must remain so given that the overlapping nature of some of the sources precludes an exact count. For Constantinian documentation see John Malalas, *Chronographia*, in L. Dindorff (ed.), *Ioannis Malalae Chronographia* (Bonn 1831) 321; *Chronicon Paschale* (supra n. 5), 528–29; John Lydus, *Liber de mensibus*, in R. Wuensch (ed.), *Liber de mensibus* (Stuttgart 1967) 4.138; George Cedrenus, *Compendium historiarum*, in I. Bekker (ed.), *Georgius Cedrenus [et] Ioannis Scylitzae* (Bonn 1838–39) 1.564; and the various references in *Par.*: 7, 11, 16, 34, 36, 44a, 49, 57, 58, 68. In addition, Mango, *Brazen House* (supra n. 4), 46, 48; Janin, *Constantinople byzantine* (supra n. 4), 59–62, 73, 62–64; and Bauer, *Stadt, Platz und Denkmal*, 148, 162, 166, 173, 227.

[23] *Par.*, 11 reports a statue of Valentinian in the Augusteion without specifying which of the three emperors bearing that name is intended. Likewise, *Par.*, 12 places a statue of an unspecified Valentinian at the modion, or granary. Cameron and Herron in *Par.*, 188, together with Stichel in *Kaiserstatue,* 76 no. 7, suggest identification with Valentinian I, the emperor who established the modion, against Janin in *Constantinople byzantine* (supra n. 4), 66, 69, who favors identification as Valentinian III. *Par.*, 19 documents equestrian statues of Gratian and Valentinian I or II at the *peripatos*, or colonnade, an unidentified location associated either with the hippodrome or the palace. See *Par.*, 194–95, and Stichel, *Kaiserstatue,* 83 no. 47.

[24] Stichel, *Kaiserstatue*, catalogue entries nos. 52, 54–57, 72, 89–91, 95–101, 106–12.

[25] See Bauer, *Stadt, Platz und Denkmal,* 327 on the granting of non-imperial statues and their documentation.

[26] Statue fragments in the Istanbul Archaeological Museum document the range of stone media. See Fıratlı, *Sculpture byzantine*, 8, inv. no. 5797, pl. 4, fig. 7 (porphyry); 8–9, inv. no. 5077, pl. 4, fig. 9a–c (alabaster); 9–10, inv. no. 5673, pl. 5, fig. 11a–c (marble); 12, inv. no. 4417, pl. 8, fig. 14 (marble); 13, inv. no. 4051, pl. 8, fig. 15 (marble). For sculpture in bronze and precious metals, see documentation in Stichel, *Kaiserstatue,* 76 no. 7 (silver); 85 no. 55 (silver), no. 57 (probably bronze); 95 no. 91 (silver); 97 no. 96 (gold). Those statues described as silver or gold are likely to have been silvered or gilded bronze.

[27] For the Augusteion: *Par.*, 11, 31, 68. For the Regia and Chalke Gate: *Par.*, 19, 32, 33, 44a, 77. For the Milion: *Par.*, 34, 35, 35a; *Patria Konstantinopoleos* (supra n. 5), 2.37; Cedrenus (supra n. 22), 1.564; *Suda*, in A. Adler (ed.), *Suidae Lexicon,* pt. 2 (Leipzig 1928–1938) 694–95: s.v. *Theodosios, Basileus Romaion ho micros.*

sequence of imperial spaces along the Mese. Approximately seven statues of Constantine and the members of his family stood at the Capitol-Philadelphion complex and six more in the forum of Constantine. In addition to the historiated columns in the two Theodosian fora, there were at least 12 statues of members of the Theodosian dynasty in the forum of Theodosius and the forum of Arcadius.[28] The peak of this new sculptured production appears to have been in the late fourth and early fifth centuries, during the period of Theodosian rule. At that time the number of imperial figures more than doubled with approximately 43 Theodosian statues described in contrast to the 23 of the Constantinian dynasty.[29]

As in any late Roman city, this sculpture, ancient and modern, was an essential component of the Constantinopolitan civic environment. Its task here as elsewhere was two-fold: to contribute to the overall sense of urban beauty, or *kallos*, and to articulate a distinct vision of history through the selection of individual images and their placement. The sculptured displays of Constantinople achieved these ends in a variety of ways. With respect to the issue of *kallos*, both the presence and the sheer number of monuments on offer contributed overwhelmingly to the sense of urban beauty, a sense enhanced by the rich array of sculptured media and the appreciation of the craftsmanship that went into the creation and display of individual images.[30] Overall, the picture was one of variety, a value particularly appreciated in late antiquity and a point to which I shall return.

Added to this lavish aesthetic appeal was the more sober stuff of history. Over the course of the fourth century this history was created in two overlapping phases using two different kinds of sculpture. The first, based on the gathering and installation of antiquities, aimed to create a mythic-historic past for the city that would legitimate its claims to capital status, and was essentially the work of Constantine. The second, using contemporary sculpture, documented not the past, but the ongoing, living history of Constantinople and was substantially, though not exclusively, the work of the Theodosians.

The importation of some of the ancient world's most evocative monuments to Constantinople was part of a project to create a distinct historical identity for the capital that would support its claims to urban preeminence among the already storied cities of the later Roman world by describing the city not only as the New Rome, the legitimate heir to both the rights and privileges of the old capital on the Tiber and the numinous authority of Rome's own urban precursor, Troy, but also as the steward of the great artistic, literary, and philosophical traditions of the Graeco-Roman world. Thus, the selection of individual antiquities and their organization into discrete gatherings around themes pertinent to the histories of Troy, Rome, and their traditions, in such spaces as the hippodrome, the Baths of Zeuxippos, and the forum of Constantine, described this history by means of subject matter. Displays organized around such stories as the Judgment of Paris in the forum of

[28] Capitol-Philadelphion: *Par.*, 58, 70. Forum of Constantine: *Par.*, 16. Forum of Theodosius: *Par.*, 57, 66; Christodoros of Thebes, *Ekphrasis* (supra n. 5), 16.65; *Chronicon Paschale* (supra n. 5), 565; *Patria Konstantinopoleos* (supra n. 5), 2.47; Constantine the Rhodian, *Ekphrasis*, in E. Legrand, "Description des oeuvres d'art et de l'église des Saints Apotres de Constantinople, poème en vers iambiques par Constantin le Rhodien," *RÉG* 9 (1896) 32–65, at lines 219–40; Cedrenus (supra n. 22), 1.566; Niketas Choniates (supra n. 5), 643, 649. Forum of Arcadius: *Par.*, 71.

[29] Constantinian: *Par.*, 11 (Constantine, Constantios, Constans, Julian, three statues of Helena); 16 (Constantine and Helena, sons of Constantine); 34 (Constantine, Helena); 36 (Constantine); 44a (Julian, Constantine and sons); 46, 49 (Julian); 58 (Constantine, Helena, three sons); 68 (Constantine, his three sons, Julian); 70 (sons of Constantine, Julian, Anastasia, sister of Constantine the Great, here described erroneously as Julian's wife). Theodosian: see documentation in Stichel, *Kaiserstatue*, nos. 47, 52–57, 72, 89–91, 95–101, 106–12.

[30] On the idea of urban *kallos* and its development in the ancient world see H. Saradi, "The *kallos* of the Byzantine city: The development of a rhetorical *topos* and historical reality," *Gesta* 34 (1995) 37–56.

Constantine and the Iliupersis in the Baths of Zeuxippos played up the image of the Trojan link, while images pertinent to the city of Rome and its traditions informed the gathering of monuments in the hippodrome. Elsewhere, in places such as the basilica and the Baths of Zeuxippos, the prominent display of portraits of the great culture heroes of the Graeco-Roman past hammered home the idea of Constantinopolitan cultural primacy.[31]

The physical history of the Constantinopolitan statuary also helped to support these assertions. Not only did the antiquity of the statuary brought to the capital provide the city with a patina of age and respectability that lent credence to the claims mooted in the sculptured displays, it also evoked the concept of spoliation and with it the experience of Rome itself. As spolia, the city's reused monuments stood as tribute from the cities and sanctuaries of the Roman world, at once a physical manifestation of Constantinopolitan hegemony and with it an imitation of Rome, a city rich with its own population of sculptured spoils.[32]

In contrast to the ancient displays, modern sculpture in Constantinople spoke resolutely of contemporary history. The historiated columns dedicated to Theodosius and Arcadius documented the imperial *res gestae*, while portrait images of emperors, members of their families, and the high-ranking imperial officials associated with imperial endeavor honored their subjects by drawing them into the ever-unfolding pageant of Constantinopolitan history.

Comparison of numbers and patterns of distribution between antiquities and contemporary sculpture reveals that Constantine and the members of his house threw their energies into the collection and display of antiquities. Approximately 110 or 115 ancient monuments were brought between A.D. 324 and 360 as opposed to the 21 statues of family members.[33] There was, moreover, widespread distribution of ancient images throughout the city, as opposed to a comparatively limited display of contemporary statues in the Augusteion, the forum, and the Philadelphion. In the later fourth century the numbers reverse themselves. Although the Theodosians revived the reuse of antiquities after a period of hiatus at mid-century, they did so on a much restricted scale, installing only 17 antiquities as opposed to the approximately 43 new portraits.[34] Further, the nature of their ancient installations suggests that many of them represented alterations to or the completion of Constantinian projects. This is the case, for example, with the Theodosian interventions in the hippodrome. Here the erection of the obelisk and with it the nearby Built Obelisk during the reign of Theodosius I brought to fruition projects initiated by Constantine and his planners. Likewise, the addition of a sculpture of Skylla under Arcadius picked up on themes first articulated by the Constantinian installations in the circus.[35] The Theodosian interest instead was in contemporary sculpture. Its widespread distribution throughout the city put a Theodosian stamp on virtually every public space to drive home an idea of continuity with Constantinian rule at the same time that it fostered the developing sense of Constantinople as a predominately Theodosian city.

The shifting balance between ancient and contemporary in fourth- and fifth-century Constantinopolitan sculptured display invites examination not only of the historical and dynastic interests promoted by these two great ruling families by means of subject matter and distribution, but also of the ways in which the various kinds of sculptured displays were seen in terms of style and the extent

[31] Bassett, "Antiquities in the hippodrome" (supra n. 8), 87–96; ead., "*Historiae custos*" (supra n. 8), 491–506. Bassett, *Urban Image*, 50–78.

[32] For a topographical list of Greek statuary and other works of art on display in Rome, see J.J. Pollitt, "The impact of Greek art on Rome," *TAPA* 108 (1978) 170–71; and B.S. Ridgway, *Roman Copies of Greek Originals* (Ann Arbor 1984) 109–11.

[33] Bassett, *Urban Image*, 50–78.

[34] Ibid., 79–97 documents Theodosian use of antiquities.

[35] Ibid., 85–89.

to which an awareness and understanding of such visual form may or may not have contributed to the overall meaning of the assemblage.

Style is a thorny issue, not least because of a lack of a standard definition in archaeological and art historical discussion. For purposes of this essay, I define the term as the manner in which a work of art is executed with respect to such formal elements as line, mass, composition, and color. As such, I see it as distinct from subject matter and technique, although certainly related and in some instances determined by both.[36]

To modern eyes, the Constantinopolitan urban display was stylistically rich and varied. Among the representations of gods, mythological heroes, and historical personages that constituted the bulk of the city's antique holdings there was a marked preference for sculpture that emphasized spatial composition, motion, and the subtle, planar modulation of surfaces, work that would be defined in modern historiography as late classical and Hellenistic. By contrast, the works of fourth- and fifth-century manufacture favored the type of frontal composition, figural stasis, and preference for continuous surfaces with sharp breaks between planes and an interest in surface pattern that modern parlance characterizes as late antique. Coloristic variety, the result of the sculptures' varied media, complemented this stylistic range.

Evidence suggests that late antique viewers were sensitive to such variety and contrast. To begin with, an idea of art and with it style, concepts fundamental to aesthetic categorization and evaluation, certainly existed. Although no specifically late antique treatises on the visual arts survive, a variety of sources make it clear that these basic concepts did. For example, the Theodosian Code (16.10.8) issued at Constantinople in A.D. 382 decrees the preservation of a temple building and its sculpture in the eastern city of Edessa, stating that its images should be "artis pretio quam divinitate metienda iugiter patere" ("measured by the value of their art rather than their divinity").[37] In other words, the Code assumes the existence of art as a category of visual representation into which temple images can be absorbed and by which their numinous powers might be neutralized. Using the more evocative language of poetry, Prudentius expressed a similar point of view in debate with Symmachus:

> deponas iam fest velim puerilia, ritus
> ridiculos tantoque indigna sacraria regno.
> marmora tabenti respergine tincta lavate,
> o procures: liceat statuas consistere puras,

[36] The bibliography on theories of style is enormous and cannot be neatly circumscribed in a single footnote. For an overview of approaches, see J. Elkins, "Style," in J.S. Turner (ed.), *Dictionary of Art*, vol. 29 (New York 1996) 876–83. See also the classic study by M. Schapiro, "On style," in A. Kroeber (ed.), *Anthropology Today: An Encyclopaedic Inventory* (Chicago 1953) 287–312, reprinted in Schapiro's collected essays: *Theory and Philosophy of Art: Style, Artist and Society* (New York 1994) 51–102. For recent considerations of the problem and further bibliography, see B. Lang (ed.), *The Concept of Style* (Philadelphia 1979); W. Sauerlaender, "From stylus to style: Reflections on the fate of a notion," *Art History* 6.3 (1983) 253–70; M.W. Conkey and C.A. Hasdorf (eds.), *The Uses of Style in Archaeology* (Cambridge 1990); C. van Eck, J. McAllister, and R. van de Vall (eds.), *The Question of Style in Philosophy and the Arts* (Cambridge 1995). For theories of style in Roman art, see A. Riegl, *Die Spätrömische Kunstindustrie* (Vienna 1901); O. Brendel, *Prolegomena to the Study of Roman Art* (New Haven 1974); and, most recently, Hölscher, *Römische Bildsprache* (supra n. 3).

[37] For original text: G. Haenel (ed.), *Codex Theodosianus* (Bonn 1837–42) 2, cols. 1614–15. For translation: C. Pharr, *The Theodosian Code and Novels and the Sirmondian Constitutions* (Princeton 1952) 473. On the late imperial attempt to preserve temples and with them the artistic patrimony of the Roman empire, see C. Lepelley, "Le musée des statues divines: la volonté de sauvegarde le patrimoine artistique paeien à l'époque théodosienne," *CahArch* 42 (1994) 5–15. For more general attempts to legislate the preservation of buildings and in so doing maintain urban infrastructure, see J. Alchermes, "Spolia in Roman cities of the late empire: Legislative rationales and architectural reuse," *DOP* 48 (1994) 167–78.

artificium magnorum opera: haec pulcherrima nostrae
ornamenta fuant patriae, nec decolor usus
in vitium versae monumenta coninquinet artis.

You should give up your childish festivals,
your laughable rites, your
shrines unworthy of so great an empire.
Oh noble Romans, wash your marble statues wet
with dripping splatters of gore—
let these statues, the works of great
craftsmen, stand undefiled;
let them become the most beautiful adornments
of our native city—may no
depraved purpose taint the works of art, no
longer in the service of evil.[38]

Further, in Constantinople itself the Lausos collection, a display of Hellenic cult images with dates ranging from the sixth century to the fourth century B.C. amassed by Theodosius II's chamberlain, Lausos, appears to have been organized in such a way as to demonstrate the development and progress of stylistic and technical achievement among the ancients, suggesting a belief in the idea of the perfectibility of art linked to an understanding and appreciation of issues of style.[39]

As these examples suggest, late antique observers not only identified a category of representation as art, but also were attuned in their appreciation of this category to issues of style; however, although the example of the Lausos collection suggests an approach to the understanding of historical styles, it leaves open the question of what fourth- and fifth-century A.D. viewers found aesthetically valuable in contemporary production and display. Analysis of late antique poetry and poetics reveals an appreciation for variety and complexity within the larger structure. Ausonius's hymn to the Moselle provides a good example: using the river as his organizing armature, Ausonius breaks the poem into sections within which he examines the flora and fauna of the river, the inhabitants of its banks, and the activities associated with it in precise and vivid detail. This structure, characterized by Michael Roberts as the "Jeweled Style", is also fundamental to late antique visual composition, as indicated by any one of a number of the period's surviving monuments. In both the fourth-century arch of Constantine and the fifth-century mausoleum of Galla Placidia, for example, the larger composition is composed of a series of smaller, individually framed scenes themselves that together create the whole. Nor is the tactic limited to works of monumental scale. Ivory diptychs, silver plate, and textiles all show the same interest in the division and subdivision of the larger composition into framed elements rich with detail.[40]

What I would like to propose therefore is that the rich sculptured décor of Constantinople, displayed as a series of individual monuments in public gatherings that were themselves set into distinct contexts, spaces such as the Augusteion, the hippodrome, or the forum of Constantine within the larger armature of the city's structure, was itself a manifestation of a "Jeweled Style" aesthetic

[38] *Contra Symmachum* 1, 501–5. H.J. Thomson (ed.), *Prudentius*, vol. 1, Loeb Classical Library (London and Cambridge, MA 1969) 388. Translation from Alchermes, "Spolia" (supra n. 37), 171.

[39] Bassett, *Urban Image*, 98–120.

[40] See Roberts, *Jeweled Style* (supra n. 3), 17–19 for discussion of Ausonius; 66–121 for observations on and illustrations of the visual arts.

that in turn contributed to the sense of urban *kallos*. Throughout the city individual gatherings of statuary organized in discrete spaces articulated themes appropriate to the city's larger image. Thus, the display of antiquities in spaces such as the hippodrome, the Baths of Zeuxippos, and the forum of Constantine detailed aspects of Constantinopolitan history, particularly its roots in the Trojan past and relationship to Rome. In the Augusteion, by contrast, the ranks of imperial portraits of contemporary manufacture legitimated the great Constantinopolitan dynasties and in so doing the ongoing project of imperial rule. Linked within the larger fabric of the city, these varied displays created a picture of the urban whole designed to proclaim Constantinopolitan hegemony among the cities of the later Roman world.

As the range of sculpture within this whole suggests, variety was a key element in the overall composition. How such variety, manifest here both in terms of a range of subject matter and in the combination of works of ancient and contemporary manufacture, might have been understood and appreciated is another question. In the context of Constantinopolitan sculptured display, was variety simply a matter of complexity for complexity's sake, a piling up of forms without rhyme or reason, or did the individual elements accumulated in the service of the larger aesthetic themselves correspond to forms that served some purpose in the overall development of the whole? In the absence of any late antique writings on visual theory and on the basis of the fact that the ancients themselves recognized a link between verbal and visual tradition,[41] rhetorical theory, a literature which not only acknowledged but also elaborated a complex theory of style and from which the aesthetic idea of variety itself derives, offers some insights into the problem.[42]

With respect to style, the most influential of the theoretical treatises for late antiquity, one which had currency into the sixth century and beyond, was a work by the second-century author Hermogenes of Tarsus, *On Style*.[43] As Hermogenes and his readers understood, it was the duty of an orator to consider, first, his subject matter, and second, the most compelling arrangement and presentation of this material. The means to accomplishing this goal was style; that is the way in which the mechanics of language, such elements as sentence structure, word choice, cadence, and rhythm, defined the way of speaking. Style was in large measure determined by subject matter and genre. Thus, not only would a speech crafted for the courtroom have a very different style from one made in honor of a wedding, but among courtroom presentations themselves, accusation was expected to have a different tone from defense.[44] Further, style itself was associated with virtue. Thus, individual styles embodied different virtues and in so doing enhanced the meaning of the oratory.

Hermogenes identified seven basic speaking styles, each with its own subdivisions, in the service of this expression: *Sapheneia* (Clarity), which included *Katharotes* (Purity) and *Eukrineia*

[41] For the link between the verbal and the visual, see not only the famous Horatian dictum, "ut pictura poesis" (*Ars poetica* 361), but also Cicero, *Brutus* (18.70; 73.228; 86.296), and Quintillian, *Institutio oratoria* (12.10), which equate the styles of rhetors to the styles of sculptors. That the equation between verbal and visual form remained viable into late antiquity is evident from Procopius of Gaza, who remarks that painting and poetry have the same agenda: the imitation of gods, men, their passions, and their lives. See *Declamatio* 3 (Venus) in A. Garzya and R.J. Loenertz (eds.), *Procopii Gazaei epistolae et declamationes* (Ettal 1963) 88, lines 1–3.

[42] For a consideration of the relationship between sculptured form and rhetorical tradition in the Roman world, see Hölscher, *Römische Bildsprache* (supra n. 3); Leibundgut-Maye, "Gleichzeitigkeit" (supra n. 3); and R.R.R. Smith, "The public image of Licinius I: Portrait sculpture and imperial ideology in the early fourth century," *JRS* 87 (1997) 170–202.

[43] See Rabe for text. For notes and translation see Wooten. For a discussion of Hermogenes see G. Kennedy, *Greek Rhetoric under Christian Emperors* (Princeton 1983) 96–116. Parts of the following discussion are based on my article "Style and meaning in the imperial panels in San Vitale, Ravenna" (supra n. 3).

[44] For the differences in style between presentations see Rabe, 385, 413, and Wooten, 108–11, 130.

(Distinctness); *Axioma* (Dignity) and *Megethos* (Grandeur), with subsets of *Semnotes* (Solemnity), *Trachytes* (Asperity), *Sphodrotes* (Vehemence), *Lamprotes* (Brilliance), *Akme* (Florescence), and *Peribole* (Abundance) and *Mestotes* (Fullness); *Epimeleia* (carefully wrought style) and *Kallos* (Beauty); *Gorgotes* (Rapidity); *Ethos* (Character), and its subdivisions of *Apheleia* (Simplicity), *Glykytes* (Sweetness), *Dimytes* (Subtlety), and *Epieikeia* (Modesty); and, finally, *Alethinos* (Sincerity) and its subset *Barytes* (Indignation). All of these styles were grouped under the larger designation of *Deinotes* (Force), itself defined as the proper use of style.[45]

In composing and delivering a speech it was understood that no rhetor would adhere solely to one style throughout. Indeed, variation in style from line to line was desirable both as a means to more accurate expression and as a tactic for avoiding the pitfalls of too close an application of a single mode of expression. Given the desirability of varying styles, what determined the ultimate tenor of a speech was the predominance of one mode, for example, *Megethos* (Grandeur), over another.[46]

How might such a scheme, in which specific forms carried specific associations and in so doing constructed specific meanings, have been transported to the streets and squares of late antique Constantinople? Following Hermogenes, subject matter should determine the course of observation. The city's sculptured displays described the mythic origins of the city, its relationship with Rome, and its status as the steward of the larger cultural traditions of the Graeco-Roman world, while simultaneously documenting the imperial dynasties that made this all possible.[47] In this regard, the content of these ensembles conformed to categories of discussion which another great rhetor, Menander of Laodicea (third to fourth century), saw as necessary to the composition of urban encomia.[48] Thus in rhetorical terms the city's sculptured adornment could be seen and understood as a kind of grand urban encomium set in visual terms.

If subject matter determined the rhetorical genre, then genre, as noted, determined style. On the matter of encomium, Hermogenes singled out certain styles as appropriate. Specifically, he claimed that *Semnotes* (Solemnity), *Lamprotes* (Brilliance), and *Peribole* (Abundance), all elements of *Axioma* (Dignity) and *Megethos* (Grandeur), must be present, together with *Glykytes* (Sweetness), an element of *Ethos* (Character). To achieve *Semnotes* (Solemnity) Hermogenes advised the use of direct statement in sentences made of short clauses that read like aphorisms. It is necessary, he opines, to speak dogmatically.[49] Aiding and abetting this cause were words based on broad sounds arranged in rhythms that produce a stately cadence.[50] *Lamprotes* (Brilliance), which, according to Hermogenes, provided an element of luster designed to prevent speech from being overly severe, shares many of the qualities of *Semnotes* (Solemnity), including word choice and rhythm. It, too, is expressed through direct statement, but longer clauses, carefully wrought, soften and dignify the tone.[51] *Peribole* (Abundance) and *Mestotes* (Fullness) may be expressed in a variety of ways. Elaboration of subject matter to include both

[45] *Saphneia* (Clarity): Rabe, 226–42 (Wooten, 8–18); *Axioma* (Dignity) and *Megethos* (Grandeur): Rabe, 242–96 (Wooten, 18–54); *Kallos* (Beauty): Rabe, 296–311 (Wooten, 54–64); *Gorgotes* (Rapidity): Rabe, 312–20 (Wooten, 65–70); *Ethos* (Character): Rabe, 321–52 (Wooten, 70–89); *Alethinos* (Sincerity): Rabe, 321–52 (Wooten, 89–101); *Deinotes* (Force): Rabe, 369–80 (Wooten, 101–8).

[46] On the mixing of styles, see Rabe 221–22, 381 (Wooten 5–6, 108–11) and G. Kennedy, *New History of Classical Rhetoric* (Princeton 1994) 268.

[47] Bassett, *Urban Image*, 50–97.

[48] For Menander see D.A. Russell and N.G. Wilson (eds. and trans.), *Menander Rhetor* (Oxford 1981) 79. On the classification of rhetorical genres, see G.A. Kennedy, "The genres of rhetoric," in S.E. Porter (ed.), *Handbook of Classical Rhetoric in the Hellenistic Period 330 B.C.–A.D. 400* (Leiden 1997) 43–50, and idem., *Greek Rhetoric under Christian Emperors* (supra n. 43), 63.

[49] Rabe, 250 (Wooten, 23).

[50] Ibid., 247 (Wooten, 22). The prescribed rhythms include the dactilic, anapestic, iambic, spondaic, and paeonic. See further ibid., 252–53 (Wooten, 24–25).

[51] Ibid., 264–69 (Wooten, 32–36).

Fig. 4. Colossus, Barletta, Italy (W. Eugene Kleinbauer).

the general and the particular is a clear index of these qualities, as is the use of such devices as the presentation of facts and information in reverse order, parallel construction, repetition and elaboration, and the inclusion of subordinate clauses.[52] Finally, there is *Glykytes* (Sweetness). *Glykytes* (Sweetness) results from the use of short words with few syllables in moderately long phrases of varied rhythm together with an ornamentation of language through the use of such devices as parallelism.[53]

Semnotes (Solemnity) and *Lamprotes* (Brilliance), *Peribole* (Abundance) and *Mestotes* (Fullness), *Glykytes* (Sweetness): how might these forms have been manifest in Constantinopolitan sculpture? If the city's multiple sculptured displays can be understood collectively as an encomium, then I would propose that it is possible to see individual gatherings as well as individual pieces of statuary within those gatherings as embodying elements of these various styles.

Consider, for example, the Barletta Colossus, a bronze cuirass statue of a fifth-century Theodosian emperor (fig. 4).[54] The statue, which washed up on the Adriatic shore in A.D. 1309, is thought to have been plunder from the A.D. 1204 sack of Constantinople by the army of the Fourth Crusade. Although arms below the elbows and the legs are restored, the statue preserves fundamentally its original format. A cuirassed and diademed emperor stands with one foot forward, knees locked and torso stiff. His right arm is raised at a right angle. His left arm, bent at the elbow, extends in front of him and supports a swath of drapery that falls straight.

I would like to suggest that the formal elements of this statue might be understood by analogy to rhetorical categories, and that it therefore is possible to see in it all the necessary elements of *Axioma* (Dignity) and *Megethos* (Grandeur); that is, *Semnotes* (Solemnity) tempered by *Lamprotes* (Brilliance) and *Peribole* (Abundance). For example, monumental scale together with the emphasis on

[52] Ibid., 277–95 (Wooten, 41–54).

[53] Ibid., 330–39 (Wooten, 75–81).

[54] The statue has been identified with various emperors from Valentinian I (A.D. 364–375) to Heraclius (A.D. 610–641). Although the suggested identifications range from the fourth century through the seventh, hairstyle indicates the fifth century. R. Delbrueck, *Spätantike Kaiserporträts* (supra n. 17), 219–26, and Breckenridge (supra n. 17) believed the figure to be that of Marcian (A.D. 450–457) and associated it with the Constantinopolitan column. More recently Stichel, *Kaiserstatue,* 61–62, noting the *pendulae* that hang from the diadem behind the ears, has proposed identification as Honorius (A.D. 395–423), the emperor who first introduced this particular fashion.

frontal composition make the kind of unambiguous direct statement essential to the definition of *Semnotes* (Solemnity). The strong horizontal and vertical arrangement of the limbs around 90 degree angles and the direct fall of the mantle underscore that argument, while an injection of *Lamprotes* (Brilliance) softens this mood. The figure's broken external contour contrasts with the solidity of internal form and the overt statement of the frontal composition as do the linear patterns of the drapery on the torso's surface, adding the sense of complexity so closely associated with *Lamprotes* (Brilliance). *Peribole* (Abundance) too is present. The pose which shows the emperor stepping forward is, paradoxically, without motion, an effect created by the stiff torso and locked knees. Such visual contradictions may be considered analogous to the inversions of word order and the reverse presentation of facts that are among the features of rhetorical *Peribole* (Abundance).

Fig. 5. Hermes fixing his sandal, Ny Carlsberg Glyptothek, Copenhagen no. 2798 (S. Bassett).

What the colossus lacks is *Glykytes* (Sweetness). For that quality it is possible to turn to another Constantinopolitan statue, the Lysippan Sandalbinder from the Baths of Zeuxippos (fig. 5).[55] The statue shows the god Hermes as he bends over his raised right foot while simultaneously turning to look out in the direction of the viewer. The sense of direct statement so vividly imparted by the Barletta statue's pose is here exchanged for a complex composition built around the visual pull of the figure in two directions. This divided movement expressed by the use of diagonals and alternations between mass and space suggests a greater emphasis on *Peribole* (Abundance) and *Mestotes* (Fullness). Likewise, the elaborate tangle of drapery and the sinuous twists and turns of the profile around the hands, some sharp and quick, others long and arching, suggest an analogy to the short words and varied phrasing preferred in the verbal expression of *Glykytes* (Sweetness).

These two statues, the one imperial and contemporary, the other mythic and ancient, suggest the association of certain styles with certain subjects.[56] Specifically, the formal qualities of imperial

[55] Bassett, *Urban Image*, 172–73 no. 63. The statue is dated variously to the fourth, third, and second centuries. B.C.G. Lippold, *Handbüch der Archäologie* (Berlin 1939) 280–81; M. Bieber, *The Sculpture of the Hellenistic Age* (New York 1961) 74; and J. İnan, *Roman Sculpture in Side* (Ankara 1975) 94 consider the work Lysippan on the basis of its proportions and place it in the fourth century B.C. Others, among them F.P. Johnson, *Lysippos* (Durham, NC 1927) 175–77, and J. Dörig, "Lysipps leztes Werke," *JdI* 72 (1957) 19–43 at 55, claim the Hermes for Lysippos's third-century school. B.S. Ridgway, "The date of the so-called Lysippan Jason," *AJA* 68 (1964) 113–28 at 28 suggests that the figure was produced in the eclectic milieu of the second century B.C. Although the range of date and attribution is wide, the statue conforms to the general trend in Constantinopolitan reuse in that it is essentially a product of the late classical age.

[56] Compare Leibundgut-Maye, "Gleichzeitigkeit" (supra n. 3), who observes the use of different visual styles, each

sculpture may be linked to the qualities of *Axioma* (Dignity) and *Megethos* (Grandeur), while those of mythic antiquities are more properly associated with the values of *Glykytes* (Sweetness). In this instance the contrast between the Barletta Colossus and the Lysippan Sandalbinder is one of single statues, but in settings such as the Augusteion or the great Theodosian fora, places given over almost exclusively to dynastic imagery, the preponderance of contemporary imperial portraits sharing visual properties akin to that of the Barletta Colossus would have created an atmosphere portentious with *Axioma* (Dignity) and *Megethos* (Grandeur). Conversely, at the Baths of Zeuxippos, the hippodrome, or the forum of Constantine, venues in which the majority of sculpture was ancient and whose function it was to construct the narratives that created Constantinopolitan history, *Glykytes* (Sweetness) with all its mythic and pleasurable associations held sway.

This visual distinction between the formal qualities of both individual statues and larger groupings of monuments in public spaces suggests further evidence of links to rhetorical thinking, evidence that has bearing on the aesthetic issue of variety. Hermogenes notes that stylistic variety is essential as a means to highlight the most important elements of a composition. In the Hermogenic scheme, each stylistic form has its opposite. Thus, *Katharotes* (Purity) stands in opposition to *Peribole* (Abundance), *Lamprotes* (Brilliance) to *Hyptiotes* (Flatness) and, most importantly for this discussion, *Glykytes* (Sweetness) to *Semnotes* (Solemnity). In rhetorical composition the juxtaposition of such stylistic opposites is desired as a means to underscore and highlight the characteristics of each. Thus, *Glykytes* (Sweetness) at the side of *Semnotes* (Solemnity) sets the charm and grace of the one style against the weighty sobriety of the other. In so doing it not only emphasizes the formal qualities of each style, but with it the virtues associated with them. *Semnotes* (Solemnity) with its glosses of *Lamprotes* (Brilliance) and *Peribole* (Abundance) was the perfect image of imperial grandeur designed to underscore the moral authority of the emperor. By contrast, *Glykytes* (Sweetness), with its intimations of loveliness and pleasure, was construed as the perfect style for the expression of mythic narrative. As Hermogenes himself remarked, it was the purpose of *Glykytes* (Sweetness) to establish the grandeur of *Semnotes* (Solemnity).[57]

If the treatment of visual form can indeed be understood by analogy to the rhetorician's words and phrases, then I would like to conclude with the proposal that the displays of sculpture in Constantinople represent not a direct translation of a set of rules for rhetorical composition into visual language but rather a habit of composition and seeing on the part of artists, planners, and viewers analogous to the habits of writing and listening deployed by rhetors and their audiences, habits that would have been inculcated during the long years of schooling undertaken by the members of the empire's ruling elite.[58] In both the visual and the verbal contexts a shared understanding of subject signaled the genre, in this instance encomium, and within that genre, the structures and their accompanying shades of meaning. Throughout Constantinople these shades were hardly subtle and nothing if not traditional. Here the purpose was to bring the virtues associated with various styles into play to create an environment the grand and varied aesthetic of which stood as an encomium, a *laus Constantinopolitana*, to the empire's premier city.

---

with its own historic and political associations, in the manufacture of busts of Trajan. Leibundgut-Maye draws a direct analogy between these visual traditions and rhetorical styles. Similarly Hölscher, *Römische Bildsprache* (supra n. 3) likens the range of form in Roman sculpture to the range of verbal expression in rhetorical models.

[57] Rabe, 387 (Wooten, 113). In this passage Hermogenes speaks also of *Apheilia* (Simplicity), which shares the same stylistic features of *Glykytes* (Sweetness). See Rabe, 336 (Wooten, 79).

[58] Bassett, *Urban Image,* 98–120, and ead., "'Excellent offerings': The Lausos Collection in Constantinople," *ArtBull* 82 (2000) 6–25.

3 The Remains of the Centuries. Sculptures and Statue Bases in Late Antique Ephesus: The Evidence of the Upper Agora

Maria Aurenhammer and Alexander Sokolicek[1]

Sculptures

The "sculptural landscape" of late antique Ephesus—from the fourth to the sixth century—comprises the accumulated portrait and mythological statuary of several centuries of the Hellenistic and Roman imperial era, continually used or reused, as well as a smaller group of contemporary portrait statues of emperors and governors.[2] Only a few examples attest the existence of contemporary mythological sculpture and ideal portraits, in the public realm mainly in the form of fences adorned by herms, in the private realm documented by portraits of Socrates and Menander and a small-scale female head from Terrace House 1, which was partially reinhabited in late antiquity.[3] The nymphaea

[1] We would like to warmly thank Ortwin Dally and Christopher Ratté, the organizers of the symposium, for the generous invitation. Special thanks to our colleagues J. Auinger, A. Filges, C. Lang-Auinger, S. Karwiese, S. Ladstätter, P. Niewöhner, B. Rose, P. Scherrer, M. Steskal, and H. Thür, and to I. Benda-Weber for the graphics.

In the first part of this preliminary article M. Aurenhammer presents the sculpture found in the area of the Upper Agora. In the second part A. Sokolicek presents the statue bases from this area. Abbreviations for frequently cited sources:

Alzinger, "Regierungsviertel" = W. Alzinger, "Das Regierungsviertel," *ÖJh* 50 (1972–1975) Beiblatt, 230–300.

Auinger and Rathmayr, "Spätantike Statuenausstattung" = J. Auinger and E. Rathmayr, "Zur spätantiken Statuenausstattung der Thermen und Nymphäen in Ephesos," in Bauer and Witschel, *Statuen in der Spätantike*, 237–69.

Aurenhammer, *Idealplastik* = M. Aurenhammer, *Die Skulpturen von Ephesos. Idealplastik* I, *Forschungen in Ephesos* X 1 (Vienna 1990).

Bauer and Witschel, *Statuen in der Spätantike* = F.A. Bauer and C. Witschel (eds.), *Statuen in der Spätantike* (Wiesbaden 2007).

Filges, *Didyma* = A. Filges, *Skulpturen und Statuenbasen von der klassischen Epoche bis in die Kaiserzeit, Didyma* 5 (Mainz 2007).

Højte, *Statue Bases* = J.M. Højte, *Roman Imperial Statue Bases* (Aarhus 2005).

IEph = *Inschriften von Ephesos*, *IK* 17. 1–8 (Bonn 1979–1984).

İnan and Rosenbaum, *Portrait Sculpture* = J. İnan and E. Rosenbaum, *Roman and Early Byzantine Portrait Sculpture in Asia Minor* (London 1966).

İnan and Alföldi-Rosenbaum, *Porträtplastik* = J. İnan and E. Alföldi-Rosenbaum, *Römische und frühbyzantinische Porträtplastik aus der Türkei. Neue Funde* (Mainz 1979).

Ladstätter, *Kuretenstraße* = S. Ladstätter (ed.), *Neue Forschungen zur Kuretenstraße in Ephesos. Akten des Symposiums für H. Thür 2006, DenkschrWien* 382 (2009).

Ladstätter and Pülz, "Ephesus" = S. Ladstätter and A. Pülz, "Ephesus in the late Roman and early Byzantine period: Changes in its urban character from the 3rd to 7th c. A.D.," in A. Poulter (ed.), *The Transition to Late Antiquity on the Danube and Beyond, ProcBritAc* 141 (Oxford 2007) 391–433.

Meyer, *Neue Zeiten* = M. Meyer (ed.), *Neue Zeiten—Neue Sitten. Zu Rezeption und Integration römischen und italischen Kulturguts in Kleinasien, WForsch* 12 (Vienna 2007).

Thür, "Staatsmarkt" = H. Thür, "Wie römisch ist der sog. Staatsmarkt von Ephesos?" in Meyer, *Neue Zeiten*, 77–90.

[2] Recently: Auinger and Rathmayr, "Spätantike Statuenausstattung," passim; J. Auinger and M. Aurenhammer, "Ephesische Skulptur am Ende der Antike," in F. Daim and J. Drauschke (eds.), *Byzanz—Das Römerreich im Mittelalter.* Teil 2.2. *Schauplätze, Monographien des Römisch-Germanischen Zentralmuseums* 84.2.2 (Mainz 2010) 663–96. For the history of Ephesus in late antiquity and in Byzantine times in its various aspects, see numerous articles in the same volume, especially the following ones: S. Ladstätter, "Ephesos in byzantinischer Zeit," 493–519, and A. Pülz, "Das Stadtbild von Ephesos in byzantinischer Zeit," 541–71.

[3] Cf. the herm fence from the Fountain of Trajan: R. Hanslmayr, "Der spätantike Hermenzaun vom Nymphaeum Traiani—eine Planetenbalustrade?" in B. Asamer and W.

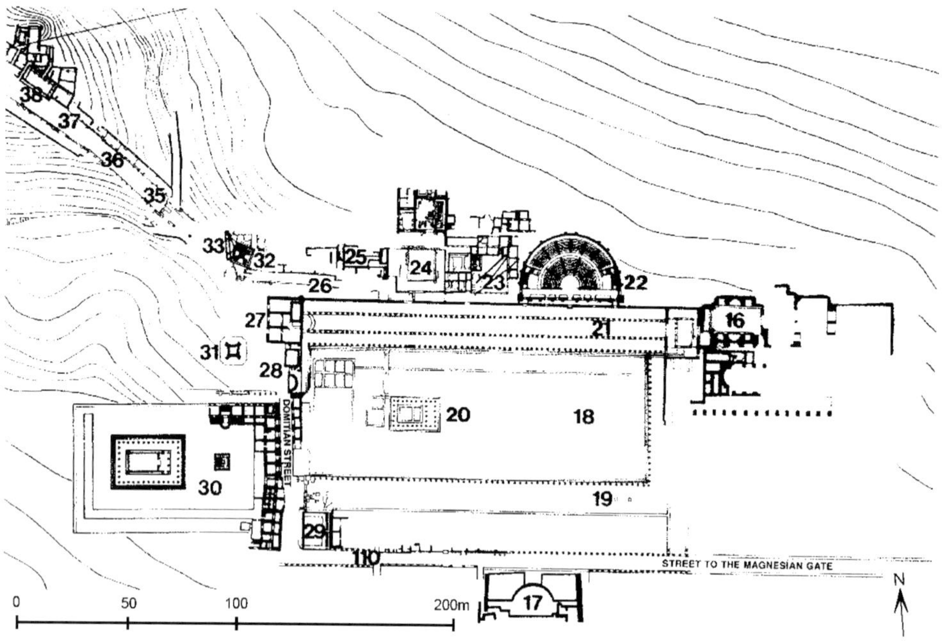

Fig. 1. Ephesus, plan of the Upper Agora (P. Scherrer [ed.], *Ephesus. The New Guide* [Istanbul 2000] 75).

and the baths were maintained at least until the fourth through fifth centuries, and partly renovated. A large amount of their original statuary display was kept through the centuries, with secondary sculptures added during Roman times and in late antiquity, including contemporary statuary of donors. This was shown in a recent study by Johanna Auinger and Elisabeth Rathmayr.[4] A similar case could be made for the theater.[5] From the fourth to the sixth century, the display of contemporary honorific statuary concentrated on the main streets of the city.[6] Recent research on the statuary lining the Embolos or Curetes Street was undertaken by Charlotte Roueché and Auinger.[7]

The first part of this article focuses on the sculptural finds unearthed in several public buildings bordering on the Upper Agora, the plateau stretching between the city's two hills. In the Augustan era, this area was designed as the sacro-political center of the capital of the province (fig. 1).[8] The plateau was framed on three sides by halls, of which the northern stoa—the triple-aisled Basilica-Stoa (fig.

Wohlmayr (eds.), *Akten des 9. Österreichischen Archäologentages am Institut für Klassische Archäologie der Paris Lodron-Universität Salzburg 2001* (Salzburg 2003) 63–68; portrait of Socrates: I. Scheibler, "Rezeptionsphasen des jüngeren Sokratesporträts in der Kaiserzeit," *JdI* 119 (2005) 228–29, 238–39; portrait of Menander: S. Bassett, "The late antique image of Menander," *GRBS* 48 (2008) 205–7, 212, 219, fig. 4; female head from Terrace House 1: M. Aurenhammer, "Skulpturen aus Stein und Bronze," in C. Lang-Auinger (ed.), *Hanghaus 1 in Ephesos. Funde und Ausstattung, Forschungen in Ephesos* VIII 4 (Vienna 2003) 174, 202 no. S 69, pls. 102–3.

[4] Auinger and Rathmayr, "Spätantike Statuenausstattung," passim.

[5] Cf. so far A. Can Özren, "Die Skulpturenausstattung kaiserzeitlicher Theater in der Provinz Asia," *Thetis* 3 (1996) 107–8, 124–27. A comprehensive documentation and interpretation of the sculptural decoration will be published by M. Aurenhammer.

[6] F.A. Bauer, *Stadt, Platz und Denkmal in der Spätantike* (Mainz 1996) 295–97, 299.

[7] J. Auinger, "Zum Umgang mit Statuen hoher Würdenträger in spätantiker und nachantiker Zeit entlang der Kuretenstraße in Ephesos. Fundorte und Fundumstände" and C. Roueché, "The Kuretenstraße: The imperial presence in late antiquity," both in Ladstätter, *Kuretenstraße*, 29–52 and 155–69.

[8] U. Kenzler, "Die augusteische Neugestaltung des Staatsmarkts von Ephesos," *Hephaistos* 24 (2006) 169–81; Thür, "Staatsmarkt," 77–90. Numbers in fig. 1 according to the plan in P. Scherrer (ed.), *Ephesus. The New Guide*, rev. ed. (Istanbul 2000) 75.

1, no. 21)—was the most prominent, dedicated in A.D. 11.[9] The new design incorporated three sacro-political buildings or sacred precincts: the temple in the western part of the plateau (20),[10] a sacred precinct (23, called the Temenos or Rhodian Peristyle in scholarly literature),[11] and the prytaneion (24).[12] The temple and the sacred precinct were dismantled in late antiquity, following the Theodosian edicts; the precinct was heavily built over in Byzantine times.[13] The original functions of both the temple and the precinct as well as the superstructure of the monument enclosed by the precinct have been much discussed. Most recently, Peter Scherrer has argued again for the interpretation of the Temenos as a locale for the cult of Augustus and Artemis,[14] whereas other authors argue for a sanctuary of Divus Iulius and Dea Roma attested by Cassius Dio.[15] The question of the divinity of the temple remains open.[16]

As to the fountain houses at the edges of the plateau, the Flavian building boom led to the erection of the so-called Fontäne (17) and the Fountain of Domitian (28) in A.D. 92/93.[17] According to recent research by Lionel Bier, the bouleuterion (22) was built at the end of the first or the beginning of the second century.[18] The construction date of the baths of the Upper Agora (16) east of the Basilica-Stoa (formerly called "Variusbad"), which were only partially uncovered, is unclear, although a date in the second century is probable.[19]

I will concentrate on the finds from the three sacro-political buildings: the Basilica-Stoa, the bouleuterion, and the prytaneion. The baths on the Upper Agora, the Fontäne, and the Fountain of Domitian will also be mentioned. The Fountain of C. Laecanius Bassus (29)[20] will be excluded here; it is oriented toward the plateau of the temple of the imperial cult (30). According to recent research, this fountain house was in use at least until the fifth century, still displaying its original sculptural decoration of A.D. 78/79.[21] Generally, the status of research differs from monument to monument. Comprehensive studies of the prytaneion, the bouleuterion—and the Fountain of C. Laecanius Bassus—are published, in print or in the final stages of preparation. The basilica has been the focus of many studies dealing with both its architecture and its function. Recently, the small finds discovered

[9] Kenzler, "Staatsmarkt" (supra n. 8), 170–71, 174, 177; Thür, "Staatsmarkt," 82–84; P. Stinson, "Imitation and adaption in architectural design: Two Roman basilical halls at Ephesus and Aphrodisias," in Meyer, *Neue Zeiten*, 91–100.

[10] Kenzler," Staatsmarkt" (supra n. 8), 172–74; Thür, "Staatsmarkt," 78–79, 84–85.

[11] Kenzler, "Staatsmarkt" (supra n. 8), 172–73; Thür, "Staatsmarkt," 81–82.

[12] Kenzler, "Staatsmarkt" (supra n. 8), 172, 175–76; Thür, "Staatsmarkt," 78, 81; M. Steskal, *Das Prytaneion in Ephesos, Forschungen in Ephesos* IX 4 (2010).

[13] Cf. H. Thür, "Das spätantike Ephesos: Aspekte zur Frage der Christianisierung des Stadtbildes," in G. Brands and H.-G. Severin (eds.), *Die spätantike Stadt und ihre Christianisierung* (Wiesbaden 2003) 263–65; Ladstätter and Pülz, "Ephesus," 404, 415. For the prytaneion, see below.

[14] P. Scherrer, "Der *conventus civium Romanorum* und kaiserliche Freigelassene als Bauherrn in Ephesos in augusteischer Zeit," in Meyer, *Neue Zeiten*, 66–70.

[15] Cf. Dio 51.20.7; Kenzler, "Staatsmarkt" (supra n. 8), 172–73, 176.

[16] Kenzler, "Staatsmarkt" (supra n. 8), 173–75.

[17] C. Dorl-Klingenschmid, *Prunkbrunnen in kleinasiatischen Städten, Studien zur antiken Stadt* 7 (Munich 2001) 140–41, 182–84, 189–90 cat. nos. 20 and 27.

[18] L. Bier, *The Bouleuterion at Ephesos, Forschungen in Ephesos* IX 5 (2011). This volume appeared while the current paper was in press. References to it have been added where possible.

[19] *RE* Suppl. XII (1970) s.v. Ephesos (W. Alzinger) 1617–19; H. Vetters, "Ephesos," *ÖJh* 50 (1972–1975) Grabungen 1971/72, 35–39; H. Thür, "Das Gymnasion an der oberen Agora in Ephesos," in E. Christof, G. Koiner, M. Lehner, and E. Pochmarski (eds.), *ΠΟΤΝΙΑ ΘΗΡΩΝ. Festschrift für Gerda Schwarz zum 65. Geburtstag* (Vienna 2007) 406–7; Thür, "Staatsmarkt," 79–80.

[20] Dorl-Klingenschmid, *Prunkbrunnen* (supra n. 17), 186–87 no. 24; K. Jung, "Das Hydrekdocheion des Gaius Laecanius Bassus in Ephesos," in G. Wiplinger (ed.), *Cura Aquarum in Ephesos, BABesch* Suppl. 12 (2006) 79–86. A comprehensive publication by a team of authors is in preparation for *Forschungen in Ephesos* IX 6.

[21] E. Rathmayr, "Die Skulpturenausstattung des C. Laecanius Bassus Nymphaeum in Ephesos," in F. D'Andria and I. Romeo (eds.), *Roman Sculpture in Asia Minor, JRA* Suppl. 80 (Portsmouth, RI 2011), 130–49.

in the excavations of the 1960s and 1970s were published.[22] The excavations of the last century in the baths on the Upper Agora and the Fontäne are not properly published. For all the findspots of the sculptural finds presented here, I rely on the documentation of the excavations in the archives of the Austrian Archaeological Institute in Vienna and on the excavation reports.

The history of the Basilica-Stoa spans six centuries. Replacement bases for the columns in the central aisle and inserted Corinthian capitals of the first two centuries A.D. point to renovations which have been dated to the Theodosian period, after the series of earthquakes of the fourth century.[23] Repair of the floor in the easternmost part of the northern aisle—more about this below—and architectural reuse in the eastern hall of the basilica are documented for the post-Theodosian period. In this eastern hall, architectural members of the upper story of the basilica were reused for the reconstruction of a peristyle court.[24] The excavators assumed that two capitals of the fifth century which were found in this peristyle were also used in this reconstruction,[25] but a proper "Bauaufnahme" (analysis of the architecture) is lacking. In the westernmost part of the middle aisle of the basilica, an eastern apse might point to the erection of a chapel.[26] Small finds and coins attest human activity in the area of the basilica until the early seventh century.[27] The following series of plans with findspots of the sculptural finds and their tentative interpretation can only be preliminary, as the late antique phase of the basilica has not yet been reinvestigated.

The first findspot plan of the basilica (fig. 2) shows a concentration of finds in the eastern part of the building. The over-lifesize group of Augustus and Livia and a portrait of Augustus with the *corona civica* (fig. 2, top row on the left) were found as fill of a floor of tiles near the eastern end of the northern aisle.[28] The floor can be roughly dated by coins, fragments of ceramics, and a male portrait of the second half of the fifth century to the late fifth century (fig. 2, top row on the right).[29] The body parts of the over-lifesize group were smashed to pieces and found scattered over the whole depth of the aisle, just below the level of the stylobate. The late antique portrait was found in the extension of the trench towards the east, at the same level as the Roman portraits. According to the excavation diary, a fragment of a late antique portrait bust (fig. 2, top row on the far right, and fig. 4) was discovered in one of the two late antique walls intersecting the north aisle in this area from north to south.[30] There is no old photograph of the piece, and the fragment shown here has no find number, but it is highly probable that it is in fact the fragment mentioned in the diary. It is part of a portrait bust of the late fifth or early sixth century whose other parts were discovered in a secondary context in the ruins of the baths on the Upper Agora east of the basilica (see fig. 8).[31]

[22] V. Mitsopoulos-Leon and C. Lang-Auinger (eds.), *Die Basilika am Staatsmarkt in Ephesos* 2. Teil: *Funde klassischer bis römischer Zeit*, *Forschungen in Ephesos* IX 2.3 (Vienna 2007).

[23] G. Plattner and A. Schmidt-Colinet, "Beobachtungen zu drei kaiserzeitlichen Bauten in Ephesos," in B. Brandt, V. Gassner, and S. Ladstätter (eds.), *Synergia. Festschrift für F. Krinzinger* (Vienna 2005) 244–45; Ladstätter and Pülz, "Ephesus," 397–98, 404.

[24] Alzinger, "Regierungsviertel," 296–99, fig. 34; E. Fossel, *Die Basilika am Staatsmarkt in Ephesos* (Graz 1982) 33.

[25] The capitals are only mentioned in the file "Marktbasilika. Ruinenbeschreibung" (1971) 4, in the archives of the Austrian Archaeological Institute; they are not published.

[26] F. Miltner, "XXI. Vorläufiger Bericht über die Ausgrabungen in Ephesos," *ÖJh* 43 (1956–1958) Beiblatt, 43–45, fig. 26; Scherrer, "Ephesus" (supra n. 8), 80.

[27] C. Lang-Auinger, in Mitsopoulos-Leon and Lang-Auinger, *Basilika* (supra n. 22), 206.

[28] Alzinger, "Regierungsviertel," 260–65, figs. 16, 18–19. Museum Selçuk inv. nos. 1891 and 1957+1/10/75. İnan and Alföldi-Rosenbaum, *Porträtplastik*, cat. no. 2, 3, 5, pls. 2.4 and 5.1–2.

[29] Lang-Auinger (supra n. 27), 7; coins: 201 nos. 66/031+033 (Anastasios I). Late antique portrait: Alzinger, "Regierungsviertel," 261–63, fig. 17. Museum Selçuk inv. no. 1892. İnan and Alföldi-Rosenbaum, *Porträtplastik*, cat. no. 151, pl. 255.

[30] Excavation diary, 6 June 1970, and "Marktbasilika. Ruinenbeschreibung" (1971) 8, both in the archives of the Austrian Archaeological Institute.

[31] Museum Selçuk inv. no. 2034. İnan and Alföldi-Rosenbaum, *Porträtplastik*, cat. no. 156, pl. 267; F. Krinzinger et al.,

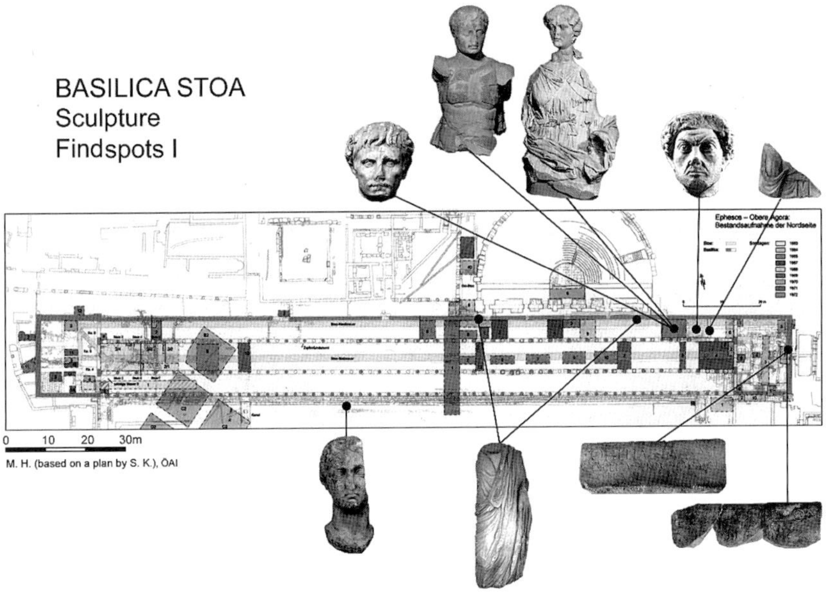

Fig. 2. Basilica-Stoa, plan (S. Karwiese and M. Hofbauer) with findspots (© Österreichisches Archäologisches Institut).

A female Tiberian portrait (fig. 2, bottom row on the left) was discovered on the *krepidoma*.[32] It is tempting to link this portrait with one of the bases of the statues of the basilica's donors—Ofillia Bassa and Sextilius Pollio—which were erected by their son, but as this is the late antique situation we can never be sure. These bases were reused as floor slabs in front of the eastern wall of the east hall of the basilica (fig. 2, bottom row on the far right, and fig. 4).[33] According to the documentation in the photographic archive of the Austrian Archaeological Institute, the torso of a first-century togatus featuring an early form of the toga (fig. 2, bottom row in the middle) was discovered in the hall of the basilica that featured capitals adorned by tauriform protomes ("Stierkopfhalle").[34] It was probably discovered during the excavations of the bouleuterion in 1908, which also included part of the northern aisle of the basilica.[35]

Before proceeding to the findspot plans of the easternmost parts of the basilica, some comments may be offered on the three early imperial portraits found as fill of the fifth-century floor.[36] The three heads were marked with crosses, presumably carved sometime after the Theodosian edicts.[37] The statues of Augustus—as a good emperor—and his wife survived the centuries until they had to give

"Ephesos," *ÖJh* 68 (1999) Jahresbericht 1998, 35–36, fig. 16. For the findspots of the other parts, see below.

[32] Museum Selçuk inv. no. 1894. This portrait is published by M. Aurenhammer, "Late Hellenistic and early Roman imperial portraits from Ephesos," in D'Andria and Romeo, *Roman Sculpture* (supra n. 21), 111–12 fig. 7.12.

[33] Alzinger, "Regierungsviertel," 269–70, fig. 20a–b. *IEph* 407.

[34] Archaeological Museum Izmir inv. no. 33. The torso will be published by J. Auinger.

[35] W. Wilberg, "Stierkopfkapitell aus Ephesos," *ÖJh* 12 (1909) 211–14, figs. 107–9; R. Heberdey, "IX. Vorläufiger Bericht über die Grabungen in Ephesos 1907–1911," *ÖJh* 15 (1912) Beiblatt, 170.

[36] For these and for their setting in the basilica, cf. also Aurenhammer, "Portraits" (supra n. 32).

[37] Cf. recently F.A. Bauer and C. Witschel, "Statuen in der Spätantike," in Bauer and Witschel, *Statuen in der Spätantike*, 6, pl. 3.7; Auinger and Rathmayr, "Spätantike Statuenausstattung," 254–57, pl. 72.10.

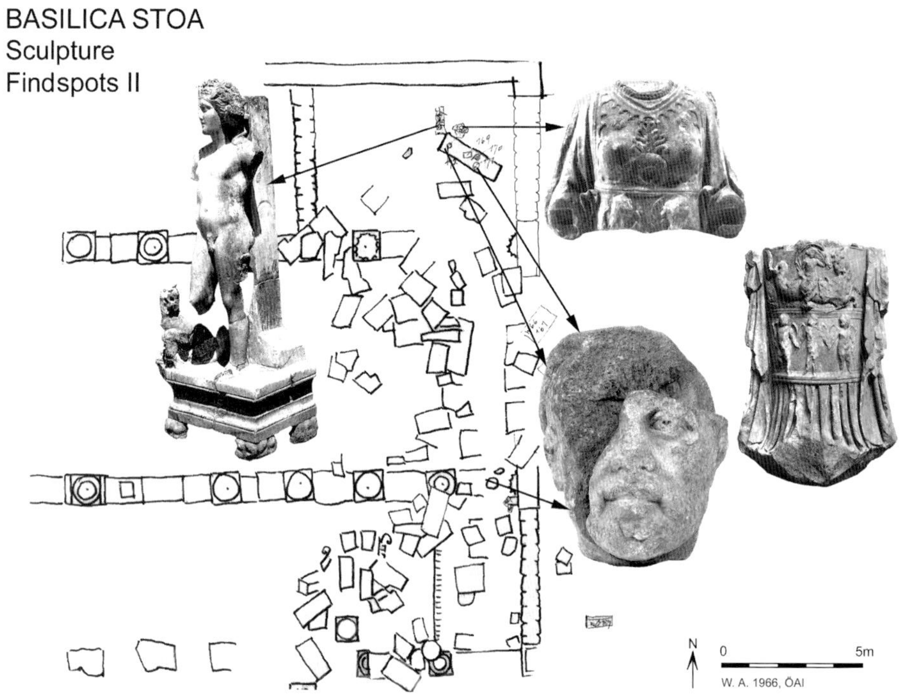

Fig. 3. Eastern end of the Basilica-Stoa, sketch of findspots (W. Alzinger, © Österreichisches Archäologisches Institut. Photograph on the far right: © Kunsthistorisches Museum, Vienna).

way to a refurbishment and adaptation of this part of the building. Whereas Augustus's portrait donning the *corona civica* is contemporary with the erection of the basilica, the over-lifesize group is a later addition of the period of Gaius and Claudius.[38] Generally, enthroned portrait groups of the Julio-Claudian dynasty in divine attire were set up only from the Tiberian period onwards.[39] Their locations range from temples to the locales of augustales (in the west) and to outdoor settings on rostra. The original setting of the Ephesian group in the eastern hall of the basilica has often been assumed, and a cultic function has been ascribed to this hall. P. Scherrer especially has repeatedly argued for the basilica as part of the Ephesian civic Sebasteion and as the setting of an imperial portrait gallery.[40] But there are still many unsolved questions regarding the locales of the early imperial cult at Ephesus and their decoration. An original setting of this cult group in another cult building might also be considered.

Wilhelm Alzinger's sketch of the eastern end of the Basilica-Stoa (fig. 3) shows architectural members of the basilica scattered over the area, and among them three sculptural fragments: a Severan portrait of a priest, which was smashed into three pieces,[41] the upper torso of a first-century copy of the image of Aphrodite of Aphrodisias,[42] and a table leg of a *monopodion* adorned with a figure of

[38] D. Boschung, *Die Bildnisse des Augustus, Das römische Herrscherbild* I 2 (Berlin 1993) 120 cat. no. 26, pls. 24.2–4 and 220.3; 186 cat. no. 186, pls. 175 and 224.3.

[39] C.B. Rose, *Dynastic Commemoration and Imperial Portraiture in the Julio-Claudian Period* (Cambridge 1997) 75, 175 cat. no. 115, 182 cat. no. 125; D. Boschung, *Gens Augusta, Monumenta Artis Romanae* XXXII (Mainz 2002) 97–98; A. Alexandridis, *Die Frauen des römischen Kaiserhauses* (Mainz 2004) 33–34, 93–94.

[40] Most recently Scherrer, "*Conventus*" (supra n. 14), 67. See also (in the same volume) Kenzler, "Staatsmarkt" (supra n. 8), 174 and Thür, "Staatsmarkt," 83–94 and, more cautiously, Stinson, "Imitation" (supra n. 9), 93.

[41] Museum Selçuk inv. no. 11/38/72. İnan and Alföldi-Rosenbaum, *Porträtplastik*, cat. no. 141, pl. 114.3–5.

[42] Museum Selçuk inv. no. 1922. L.R. Brody, *The Aphrodite of Aphrodisias*, *Aphrodisias* III (Mainz 2007) 45–46 cat. no. 20A, pl. 13.

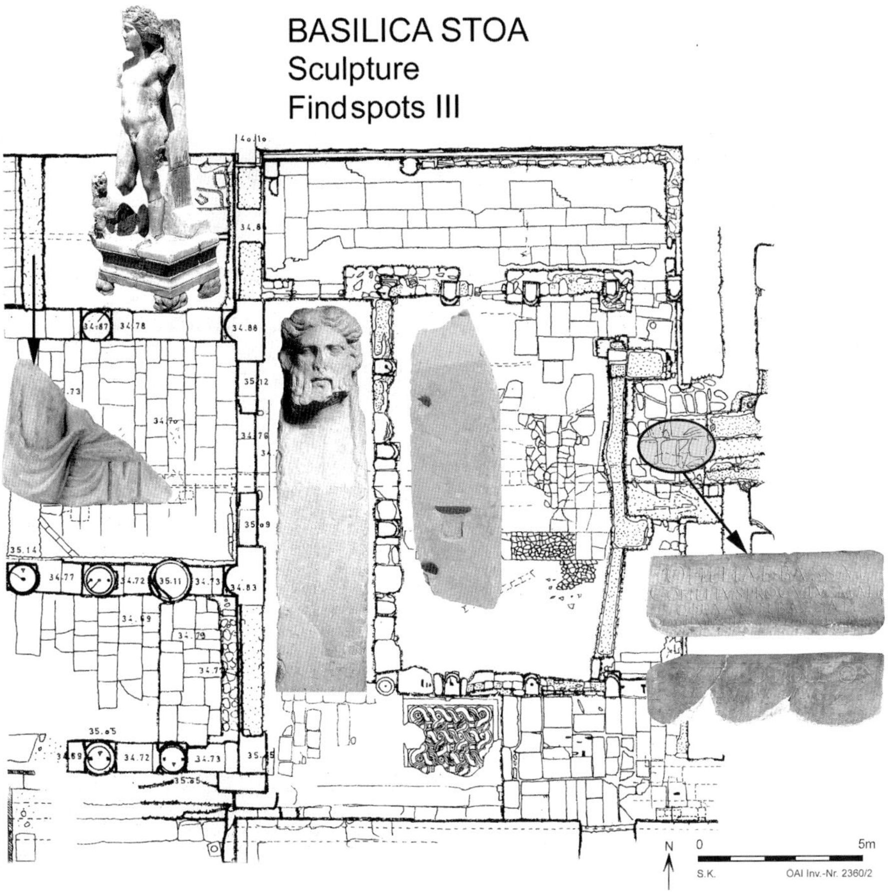

Fig. 4. Eastern end of the Basilica-Stoa including the eastern hall, plan (S. Karwiese) with findspots (© Österreichisches Archäologisches Institut).

Dionysos, of the late Antonine period.[43] The lower part of the image of Aphrodite (fig. 3, on the far right) was discovered in the area of the western gate of the Lower Agora (one decorated tier of the *ependytes* is lacking between the two parts)[44]—so we must be extremely cautious in interpreting this assembly of sculptures. The function of the *monopodion* in this late antique context can probably be linked with two herms found nearby in the peristyle court in the eastern hall of the basilica. This peristyle court (fig. 4) underwent several phases from the fifth to the seventh century, which were tentatively described by the excavators.[45] Alzinger interpreted the peristyle as part of a private dwelling, including two chambers which were created by the insertion of two parallel, north-south running walls intersecting the easternmost part of the northern aisle of the basilica, and by the closure of the

[43] Museum Selçuk inv. no. 1918. F. Eichler, "Die österreichischen Ausgrabungen in Ephesos im Jahre 1966," *AnzWien* 104 (1967) 20–21, pl. 2.4; M. Anabolu, "Efes Müzesinde bulunan masa ayakları," *TürkAD* 29 (1991) 72–73, 79, fig. 9; J. Engemann, "Ein Tischfuß mit Dionysos-Satyr-Darstellung aus Abū Mīnā/Ägypten," *JAC* 41 (1998) 169 n. 1, pl. 3a.

[44] Kunsthistorisches Museum, Vienna inv. no. I 930; Brody, *Aphrodite* (supra n. 42), 45–46 cat. no. 20B, pl. 13.

[45] F. Eichler, "Die österreichischen Ausgrabungen in Ephesos im Jahre 1967," *AnzWien* 105 (1968) 80–82, pl. I 1. More details in the file "Marktbasilika. Ruinenbeschreibung" (1971) in the archives of the Austrian Archaeological Institute.

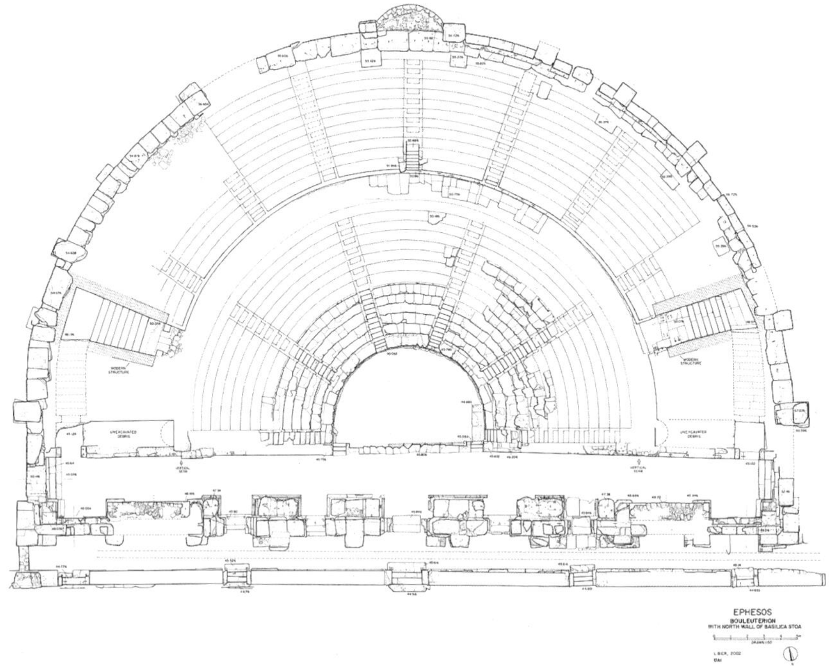

Fig. 5. Bouleuterion, ground plan (L. Bier, © Österreichisches Archäologisches Institut).

intercolumnia in the south.[46] The fragment of the bust of the late fifth or early sixth century was built into the eastern one of these two walls (see fig. 4, on the far left, and fig. 2, top row on the far right). The two double herms of the first or early second century found in the peristyle court—see the fragments in the middle of figure 4—were possibly part of a fence set up between the pillars reused for the peristyle: the depth of the herms matches that of the pillars.[47] These reused pillars were partially re-erected after the excavations.[48] The *monopodion* decorated with the figure of Dionysos probably belonged to the embellishment of this area, too. The irregular, crude spolia wall running more or less parallel to the eastern wall of the east hall obviously marks a last phase (fig. 4, on the far right). It was put up in the course of the enclosure of the enlarged area of a praefurnium of the adjoining baths on the Upper Agora (see fig. 8). At a certain time, the eastern wall of the eastern hall of the basilica was pierced for the erection of this praefurnium (see figs. 4, 8).[49] The bases of the statues of the basilica's donors were reused as floor slabs in the area of the praefurnium; their exact findspots are not documented (figs. 2, 4).

The bouleuterion, located north of the eastern part of the Basilica-Stoa, was erected in the late first or early second century according to recent research by L. Bier (fig. 5).[50] In the mid-second century, an aediculated scaenae frons was dedicated by one of the city's most prominent donors, P. Vedius

[46] Eichler, "Ausgrabungen in Ephesos" (supra n. 45), 82; Alzinger, "Regierungsviertel," 258–59, 299.

[47] Double herm with head: Museum Selçuk inv. no.11/6/77. A. Giumlia, *Die neuattischen Doppelhermen* (Ph.D. dissertation, University of Vienna 1983) 43, 201 cat. no. 2, fig. 1; R. Hanslmayr, *Hermen aus Ephesos* (Ph.D. dissertation, University of Vienna 2006) 18–19, 142–43 cat. no. A5, pl. 6. Fragment: unpublished. For the prestige of herm fences in late antiquity, cf. H. Wrede, "Die spätantike Herme," *JAC* 30 (1987) 129–48.

[48] Alzinger, "Regierungsviertel," 295, fig. 34.

[49] Eichler, "Ausgrabungen in Ephesos" (supra n. 45), 80–82, pl. I 1 (view towards east, peristyle court with ruins of the baths in the background).

[50] Bier, *Bouleuterion* (supra n. 18), 81–85.

Antoninus III, and his wife Flavia Papiane.[51] Late antique and post-antique activity in the bouleuterion is documented by details such as crosses incised above doorways and by an apse constructed at the summa cavea of the auditorium, which must be a very late addition.[52] Two fourth-century Ephesian inscriptions mention the *boule*.[53]

As a full documentation of the evidence and its interpretation has been provided in the comprehensive publication, I will present only a summary here.

Bier's reconstruction of the second-century phase of the stage building is based on the preserved pedestal zone, on the scant remains of the two stories, and on the drawings of inscribed blocks in the archive of the Austrian Archaeological Institute.[54] As to the sculptural finds, only four sculptures are actually extant, whereas the rest of the décor is documented only by drawings of statue bases and by information in the first excavator John Turtle Wood's letters to the British Museum.[55] In the last decade, Klaus Fittschen, Angela Kalinowski, and Hans Taeuber presented the historical and political evidence for the setting of a portrait gallery of the Antonine dynasty in the mid-second century scaenae frons, which underlined P. Vedius Antoninus's ties with the emperor Antoninus Pius.[56] One at least partly preserved statue of this dynastic program is a heroized statue of Lucius Verus in the guise of the Ares Borghese type, set on a low inscribed plinth of oval form.[57] It was found near the central door of the stage building. A profiled base for the statue of Marcus Aurelius is documented in Wood's correspondence, whereas the support for a statue of one of his daughters, a Faustina (Domitia or Annia Galeria Faustina), is preserved in fragments.[58] A finely carved girlish head, which was found near one of the entrances to the stage building, could be a candidate for the portrait of a girl of the early Antonine era.[59] The face is highly idealized and full of sentiment. The hairdo, featuring a tress of hair in the neck, bound by a fillet, is reminiscent of the hairdo of goddesses like Artemis.[60] The loose locks in front of the ears and on the sides of the neck support the interpretation of the head as a portrait. If this head is indeed the portrait of a princess of the Antonine dynasty and can be linked with the base of Faustina, it has implications for the identification of Marcus Aurelius's daughter portrayed in the gallery.[61]

[51] *IEph* 460 (building inscription); *IEph* 1491–93 ("imperial letters"). L. Bier, "The bouleuterion at Ephesos: Some observations for a new survey," in P. Scherrer, H. Taeuber, and H. Thür (eds.), *Steine und Wege. Festschrift für D. Knibbe, Sonderschriften des Österreichischen Archäologischen Institutes* 32 (Vienna 1999) 17; M. Steskal, "Zu den Stiftungen des M. Claudius P. Vedius Antoninus Phaedrus Sabinianus," *Tyche* 16 (2001) 182 –83; A. Kalinowski, "The Vedii Antonini: Aspects of patronage and benefaction in 2nd-c. Ephesos," *Phoenix* 56 (2002) 109–17, 138, 141–44. The inscriptions from the bouleuterion have now been newly discussed by H. Taeuber in Bier, *Bouleuterion* (supra n. 18), 87–98.

[52] Bier, *Bouleuterion* (supra n. 18), 52–53.

[53] *IEph* 43 and 44.

[54] Bier, "Bouleuterion" (supra n. 51), 12, 17; idem, *Bouleuterion* (supra n. 18), 57–64.

[55] K. Fittschen, *Prinzenbildnisse antoninischer Zeit* (1999) 130–31 no. 50; A. Kalinowski and H. Taeuber, "A new Antonine inscription and a new imperial statue-group from the bouleuterion at Ephesos," *JRA* 14 (2001) 351–57; Kalinowski, "Vedii" (supra n. 51), 143–44. The sculptures from the bouleuterion have now been comprehensively presented by M. Aurenhammer and T. Opper in Bier, *Bouleuterion* (supra n. 18), 99–114, which should be consulted in addition to the references cited in following notes.

[56] Supra n. 55.

[57] British Museum inv. no. GR 1865.12-6.1. *IEph* 1505; Fittschen, *Prinzenbildnisse* (supra n. 55), 130–31, pl. 66b–e; Kalinowski and Taeuber, "Inscription" (supra n. 55), 352–57, fig. 1; Kalinowski, "Vedii" (supra n. 51), 143–44, pl. 4.

[58] Marcus Aurelius: Kalinowski and Taeuber, "Inscription" (supra n. 55), 353–57, fig. 2; Kalinowski, "Vedii" (supra n. 51), 143. Faustina: *IEph* 285a; Fittschen, *Prinzenbildnisse* (supra n. 55), 130; Kalinowski and Taeuber, "Inscription" (supra n. 55), 354–57; Kalinowski, "Vedii" (supra n. 51), 143–44.

[59] Istanbul Archaeological Museum inv. no. 53. The height of the head alone is 18 cm. J.T. Wood, *Discoveries at Ephesus* (London 1877) 47; G. Mendel, *Catalogue des sculptures grecques, romaines et byzantines* II (Istanbul 1914) 128 no. 410; Kalinowski and Taeuber, "Inscription" (supra n. 55), 355 n. 23 (an identification with Faustina Minor has clearly to be ruled out).

[60] Cf. portraits of Sabina and Faustina Minor: K. Fittschen and P. Zanker, *Katalog der römischen Porträts in den Capitolinischen Museen und den anderen kommunalen Sammlungen der Stadt Rom* III (Mainz 1983) 12–13 cat. no. 12, pl. 14.

[61] For the identification of M. Aurelius's daughter according

Statues of Antoninus Pius and Faustina the Elder—of which there are no traces—must clearly have supplemented the program.[62] Bier added the fragment of a base for a statue of Demos—discovered in front of the central entrance to the stage—to the sculptural program, which then calls for a statue of Boule.[63] Statues of the donors—of which there are again no traces—were surely also set up;[64] traditional positions would be the terminating blocks of the *analemmata*.

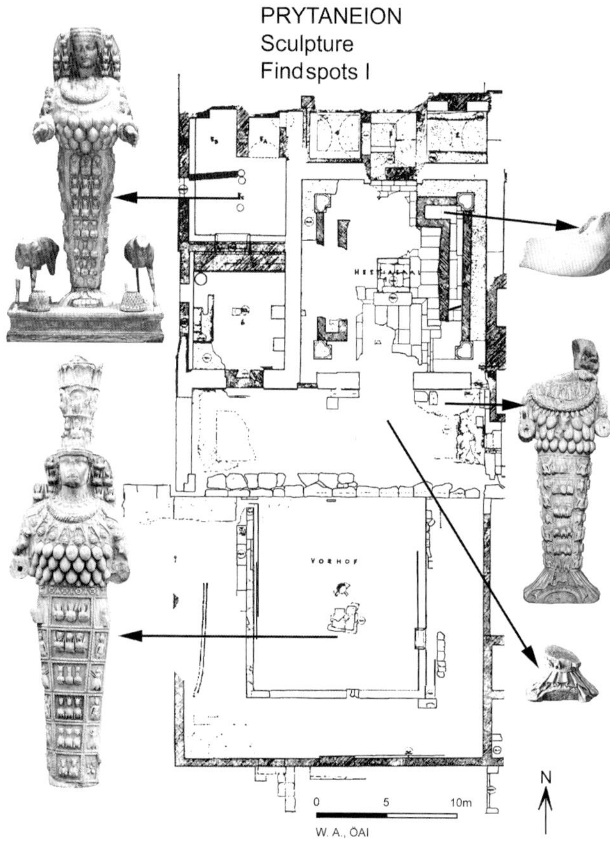

Fig. 6. Prytaneion, plan (W. Alzinger) with findspots (© Österreichisches Archäologisches Institut).

Wood also mentions in his letters to the British Museum torsi of a male portrait statue and of two female statues, one of them seated.[65]

The mythological statuary discovered in front of the stage comprises the torso of an under-lifesize silenus, a supporting figure, which is very similar to the *Silenoi Liknophoroi* from the Canopus in the Villa Adriana, and a statue of the muse Erato.[66] Wood published a drawing of the muse in his book *Discoveries at Ephesus*, complete with a lyre on a base.[67] The statue went down in a shipwreck off the coast of Syros on its way to the British Museum, but was retrieved from the sea in damaged condition. I found it again in the museum of Syros, where it had been displayed unidentified for one and a half centuries. The style of the muse's drapery fits an Antonine or Severan date.[68] According to one of Wood's letters, a fragmentary base of a statue of Melpomene with tragic mask was found during his excavations, too.[69] Statues of muses are of course well suited to the decoration of the multi-functional bouleuteria of the high imperial period, as patrons of orators and musicians.[70]

to the base, cf. Fittschen, *Prinzenbildnisse* (supra n. 55), 130; Kalinowski and Taeuber, "Inscription" (supra n. 55), 354–56; Kalinowski, "Vedii" (supra n. 51), 143–44.

[62] Kalinowski and Taeuber, "Inscription" (supra n. 55), 355–57; Kalinowski, "Vedii" (supra n. 51), 144.

[63] *IEph* 1903 (Demos).

[64] Kalinowski and Taeuber, "Inscription" (supra n. 55), 356–57.

[65] Female statues: Kalinowski and Taeuber, "Inscription" (supra n. 55), 355. Male torso: letter to C.T. Newton (23 March 1866), Archive of the Department of Greek and Roman Antiquities.

[66] Silenus: British Museum inv. no. 1867.11-22.427. Aurenhammer, *Idealplastik*, cat. no. 56, pl. 37. Silenoi in the Villa Adriana: J. Raeder, *Die statuarische Ausstattung der Villa Adriana bei Tivoli, Europäische Hochschulschriften* 38.4 (Frankfurt 1983) 81–82, 85, 230–31, 311–12, pls. 22, 24.

[67] Wood, *Discoveries* (supra n. 59), 50–51. Syros Archaeological Museum inv. no. 682.

[68] Compare the chiton of the statue of Faustina Minor in the Getty Museum in Malibu, C. Schneider, *Die Musengruppe in Milet, Milesische Forschungen* 1 (Mainz 1999) 32–33, pl. 19.

[69] Letter to J.W. Jones (28 November 1866), Archive of the Department of Greek and Roman Antiquities.

[70] Cf. the early Severan statues of muses from the Odeion at Salonica, T. Stephanidou-Tiveriou, "Τὰ ἀγάλματα τῶν

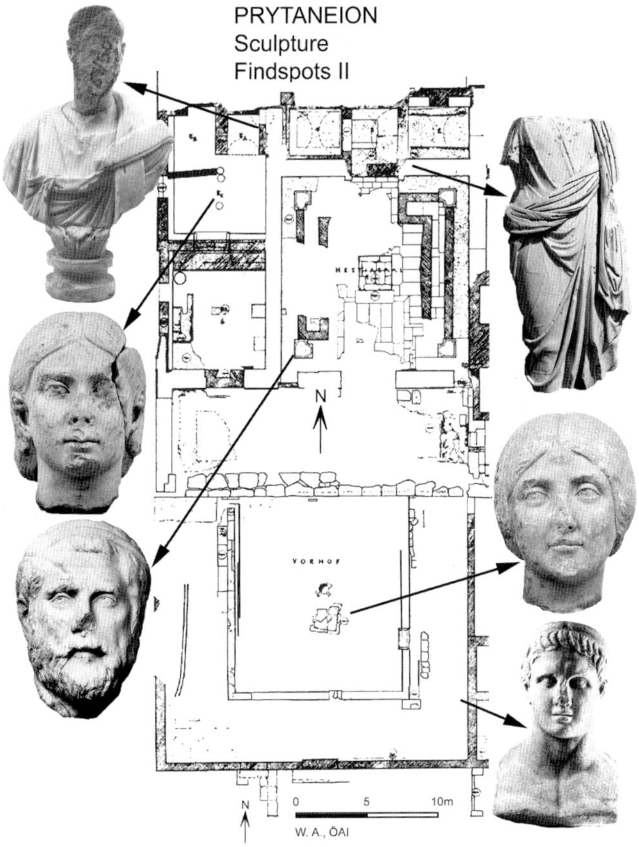

Fig. 7. Prytaneion, plan (W. Alzinger) with findspots (© Österreichisches Archäologisches Institut).

The sculptural decoration of the bouleuterion's stage building obviously comprised a combination of a group of imperial portraits—showing off the donor's standing and his loyalty—with personifications and mythological sculpture suited to the function of the building. The preserved or recorded sculptures of the Antonine portrait gallery allow an initial date in the early Antonine age, which is consistent with the renovation of the stage building, but it is possible that the sculptural program as preserved was assembled over a number of years rather than set up all at once.[71]

The prytaneion is located north of the western part of the basilica, west of the sacred precinct or Temenos (figs. 6–7). Until 2010, our knowledge of the building, its phases, and the hypothetical function of its rooms was based on the documentation of Franz Miltner's excavations of the 1950s, and on studies of its inscriptions and specific phases of its architecture combined with more recent scholarly literature.[72] Recently, Martin Steskal published a comprehensive volume, which should be consulted in connection with the following paragraphs on the prytaneion.[73] An Augustan date for the building is corroborated by epigraphic and architectural evidence and by the small finds from the foundation pits unearthed during Miltner's excavations.[74] A major renovation was undertaken in the second quarter of the third century, using the same ground plan; the brickwork in the walls and the heart-shaped columns of the central room ("Hestiasaal") bear witness to this.[75] In the fourth century, the building was given up and continually used as a quarry. Architectural fragments of the Doric portico were reused in the Baths of Varius (formerly "Baths of Scholasticia") and in the early Justinianic northern hall bordering on the Curetes Street, in the center of the Roman city. According to architectural and archaeological evidence, the erection of this "Curetes Hall" can probably be linked

Μούσων τής Θεσσαλονίκης," *Egnatia* 2 (1990) 73–122; idem, in G. Despinis, T. Stephanidou-Tiveriou, and E. Voutiras, *Κατάλογος γλυπτών τού Αρχαιολογικού Μουσείου Θεσσαλονίκης* (Salonica 1997) cat. no. 93–96. For the function of bouleuteria in the high imperial period, cf. L. Bier, "The Bouleuterion," in C. Ratté and R.R.R. Smith, *Aphrodisias Papers* 4, *JRA* Suppl. 70 (2008) 161–63.

[71] See the discussion by Aurenhammer and Opper in Bier, *Bouleuterion* (supra n. 18), 106.

[72] Cf. H. Thür's summary in Thür, "Staatsmarkt," 81.

[73] Steskal, *Das Prytaneion* (supra n. 12).

[74] Alzinger, "Regierungsviertel," 241–53; W. Alzinger, *Augusteische Architektur in Ephesos*, *Sonderschriften des Österreichischen Archäologischen Institutes* 16 (Vienna 1974) 51–55; D. Knibbe, *Der Staatsmarkt. Die Inschriften des Prytaneions*, *Forschungen in Ephesos* IX 1.1 (Vienna 1981) 75–76.

[75] Alzinger, "Regierungsviertel," 248–49; S.G. Miller, *The Prytaneion* (Berkeley and Los Angeles 1978) 99–102, 106.

with renovations to the Baths of Varius.[76] Byzantine building activity is visible in the prytaneion and in the whole area north and east of the prytaneion, where the Temenos was built over by a maze of walls.[77]

The building comprises the large forecourt ("Vorhof"), the Doric portico ("Vorhalle"), the main hall ("Hestiasaal," the hall designed for the banquets of the *prytaneis*) with supporting walls of the third century for benches, and smaller rooms in the north and west, which were originally not subdivided.[78]

I can offer only a survey of the sculptures found in the prytaneion here, concentrating on the lifesize and over-lifesize monuments. The most spectacular finds are of course the four second-century statues of Artemis Ephesia, discovered in three different spots in the building (fig. 6). The biggest statue was found lying on its front, obviously having fallen or been toppled from the central base in the large peristyle court.[79] The smallest of the three statues was discovered on the floor of the Doric portico.[80] A little farther west, the lowest part of a very similar statuette, obviously of the same workshop, was found.[81] The so-called "Beautiful Artemis" was discovered lying on its back in the northern one of the smaller rooms west of the central hall (5c).[82] According to the studies of the excavations and the documentation of the findspots of the Artemis statues, the evidence does *not* favor the interpretation as a "non-reversible deposition or a ritual burial of pagan statues," as is often stated.[83] Also noteworthy is the fragment of a lower arm of an over-lifesize male statue which was found in the northeastern corner of the "Hestiasaal" (fig. 6, on the upper right).[84]

As for the other sculptural finds, they fall essentially into two parts: two fragments of Hellenistic sculptures, and a group of portraits of the first half of the third century, which might be linked with the contemporary construction phase (fig. 7). The upper part of a late Hellenistic herm of the youthful, athletic Hermes type known from Delos and Rhodes was built into a "late wall" on the eastern side of the peristyle court (fig. 7, on the lower right).[85] The torso of a late Hellenistic portrait statue dressed in a himation was built into the northern wall of the main hall; it is the only extant Hellenistic honorary statue from Ephesus so far (fig. 7, on the upper right).[86] The discovery

[76] Reuse in the Baths of Varius: F. Miltner, "XXII. Vorläufiger Bericht über die Ausgrabungen in Ephesos," *ÖJh* 44 (1959) Beiblatt, 299–305, figs. 145–46; renovation by Scholasticia: statue base *IEph* 453; Curetes Hall: H. Thür, "Die spätantike Bauphase der Kuretenstraße," in R. Pillinger et al. (eds.), *Efeso paleocristiana e bizantina—Frühchristliches und Byzantinisches Ephesos, DenkschrWien* 282 (1999) 112–16; H. Thür and W. Pietsch in S. Karwiese et al., "Ephesos," *ÖJh* 66 (1997) Grabungen 1996, 6–10; Thür, "Spätantike Ephesos" (supra n. 13), 264 with n. 36.

[77] F. Eichler, "Die österreichischen Ausgrabungen in Ephesos im Jahre 1961," *AnzWien* 99 (1962) 39–41, fig. 1; Alzinger, "Regierungsviertel," 243, fig. 5; 247–49; Miller, *Prytaneion* (supra n. 75), 101, 105.

[78] For an interpretation of the halls and rooms, cf. Alzinger, "Regierungsviertel," 244–47; Alzinger, *Architektur* (supra n. 74), 52–54; Thür, "Staatsmarkt," 81.

[79] Museum Selçuk inv. no. 712. Miltner, "Bericht" (supra n. 76), 305–7, figs. 147–48; R. Fleischer, *Artemis von Ephesos und verwandte Kultstatuen aus Anatolien und Syrien, EPRO* 35 (1973) 14 E 45, pls. 12–17.

[80] Museum Selçuk inv. no. 717. Miltner, "Bericht" (supra n. 76), 307, fig. 310; Fleischer, *Artemis* (supra n. 79), 15 E 47, pls. 24–28.

[81] Museum Selçuk (no inventory number). Miltner, "Bericht" (supra n. 76), 308; Fleischer, *Artemis* (supra n. 79), 15 E 48, pl. 29a.

[82] Museum Selçuk inv. no. 78+1637. Miltner, "Bericht" (supra n. 76), 308–9, figs. 150–51; Fleischer, *Artemis* (supra n. 79), 14–15 E 46, pls. 18–23.

[83] Cf. M. Steskal, "Rituelle Bestattungen im Prytaneion von Ephesos? Zu den Fundumständen der Artemis Ephesia—Statuen," *ÖJh* 77 (2008) 363–73, as opposed to, e.g., J. Donderer, "Irreversible Deponierung von Großplastik bei Griechen, Etruskern und Römern," *ÖJh* 61 (1991–1992) Beiblatt, 194, 210, 248–49 cat. no. I 35.

[84] Museum Selçuk. Miltner, "XXI. Vorläufiger Bericht" (supra n. 26), Beiblatt, 34 n. 33.

[85] Museum Selçuk inv. no. 1833. F. Eichler, "Die österreichischen Ausgrabungen in Ephesos im Jahre 1963," *AnzWien* 101 (1964) 40–41, pl. 1; R. Fleischer, in A. Bammer, R. Fleischer, and D. Knibbe, *Führer durch das Archäologische Museum in Selçuk* (Vienna 1974) 16–17, pl. 2; Hanslmayr, *Hermen aus Ephesos* (supra n. 47), 52–55, 154 A 23, pl. 28.

[86] Museum Selçuk inv. no. 776. The torso will be published by J. Auinger.

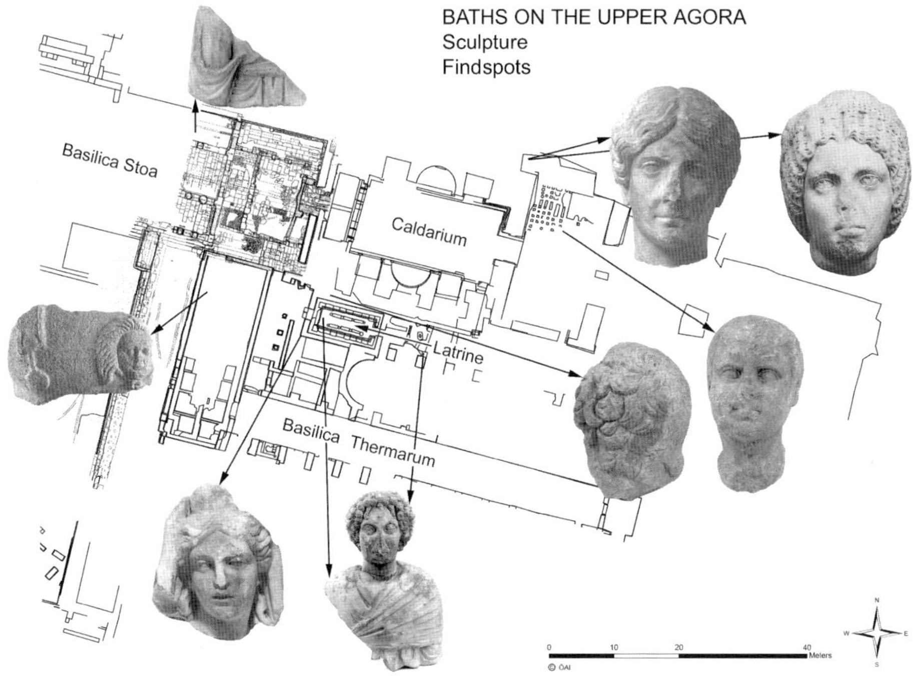

Fig. 8. Eastern end of the Basilica-Stoa and baths on the Upper Agora, detail of the digital plan of Ephesus, with findspots (© Österreichisches Archäologisches Institut).

of several examples of late classical and Hellenistic sculpture in the area of the Upper Agora might be linked with the predecessor of the basilica of the late third century to the first half of the second century B.C. and an epigraphically documented Upper Gymnasium, which was probably located on the plateau of the Upper Agora.[87]

The group of third-century A.D. portraits comprises a Severan head of a priest, which was found in the southwestern corner of the "Hestiasaal," and two Severan female portraits discovered near the base in the middle of the peristyle court and in the room of the "Small Artemis" (5c), respectively.[88] The only unpublished third-century portrait here is a male portrait bust of about A.D. 240 of high quality whose two parts were reused in the eastern wall of room 5c (fig. 7, on the upper left).[89]

Finally, let us examine the finds from the baths on the Upper Agora and the so-called Fontäne. Of the baths on the Upper Agora—which were already mentioned in connection with the basilica—we know unfortunately little. They were only partly uncovered, and the excavations are not properly published.[90] The construction date is unclear, although a date in the second century is probable. The

[87] Cf. also the head of an athlete or Herakles found in the debris of the Byzantine water reservoir north of the prytaneion: Aurenhammer, *Idealplastik*, cat. no. 149, pl. 116. Predecessor of the basilica: Lang-Auinger (supra n. 27), 4–6, 65, 205–6. Gymnasium: H. Thür, "Das Gymnasion" (supra n. 19), 403–14.

[88] Priest: Museum Selçuk inv. no. 643. İnan and Rosenbaum, *Portrait Sculpture*, cat. no. 178, pl. 104.1–2; for its date, cf. K. Fittschen, Review of İnan and Rosenbaum, *Portrait Sculpture*, *GGA* 225 (1973) 52, 62 no. 178. Female portraits: Museum Selçuk inv. no. 705. İnan and Rosenbaum, *Portrait Sculpture*, cat. no. 153, pl. 89.1–2; Museum Selçuk inv. no. 740. İnan and Rosenbaum, *Portrait Sculpture*, cat. no. 172, pl. 100.1–3.

[89] Museum Selçuk inv. nos. 742+2359. The portrait will be published by M. Aurenhammer.

[90] See supra n. 19. The notes and sketches in the excavation diaries, the excavation reports, and F. Miltner's unpublished manuscript on the baths (1952), based on the excavations of 1929, offer additional information.

ground plan (fig. 8) features a row of halls on the north side. A caldarium with seven niches for basins, and two partly heated halls to the east are cut out of the rock in their northern parts. The corridor south of the caldarium led to the main praefurnium on the west side, which was enlarged in late antiquity into the eastern hall of the basilica (see fig. 4). A latrine is located south of the caldarium, which is preserved in its late antique state. The use of the baths in late antiquity is confirmed by a mosaic floor laid in the southern *basilica thermarum* dedicated by Asklepios, a *proconsul Asiae*. The combination of his title ("megaloprepestatos anthypatos") and the decoration of the floor point to a date in the first half of the fifth century.[91]

All the sculptures found in the area were discovered in secondary contexts, including the late antique portraits.[92] Three Roman imperial portraits were dumped into functional parts of the bathing area: the Julio-Claudian head of a boy found in the under-floor heating of the hall east of the caldarium (fig. 8, on the far right), and two female portraits thrown into one of the praefurnia of the same hall—a Tiberian portrait, and the Severan portrait of a priestess of the imperial cult (fig. 8, on the upper right).[93] Two parts of a male portrait bust of the end of the fifth or the beginning of the sixth century were found in the northwestern corner of the latrine and built into a "late wall" in the area east of the latrine, respectively; the already mentioned third fragment was built into a late wall in the northern aisle of the basilica (fig. 8, on the upper left, and figs. 2, 4).[94] According to the inventory of finds, two obviously headless late antique portrait busts were found in the western part of the *basilica thermarum*. Unfortunately, they are not documented by photographs, so we are not able to identify them among the relevant group of busts without find numbers,[95] but they corroborate the evidence of late antique activity in the baths.

Several other fragments of portraits and mythological sculptures were found in the area of the latrine and to the south: a fragment of a head of Hadrianic or Antonine date (fig. 8, right side, bottom row on the left) and two female heads were dumped into channels north and south of the latrine.[96] One of the last mentioned is a fine, small-scale head of Tyche (fig. 8, bottom on the left).[97] The drill-work in the hair on the left side of the head (the principal view) points to a date in the later second century. Among the fragments found lying on the floor of the long, north-south oriented hall south of the eastern hall of the basilica, a fragment of a portrait statue in cuirass is noteworthy (fig. 8, far left).[98]

Our knowledge of the fountain—called "Fontäne" by the excavators—is also incomplete (fig. 9).[99] It borders on the street running south of the Upper Agora, and acted as reservoir and distribution tank for water conduits. Three inscriptions refer to the installation of the Marnas water conduit in A.D. 92/93 (an inscribed part of the architrave and two slabs, obviously parts of the enclosures of water basins).[100] The core of the building is a water-tower, which projects in the form of a semicircle.

[91] V. Scheibelreiter, *Stifterinschriften auf Mosaiken Westkleinasiens*, *Tyche* Suppl. 5 (2006) 36–37 cat.no. 7. Date of the mosaic: V. Scheibelreiter, personal communication.

[92] The following list of sculptures is a selection of the main monuments.

[93] Museum Selçuk inv. nos. 30/46/72–32/46/72. İnan and Alföldi-Rosenbaum, *Porträtplastik*, cat. nos. 124–25 and 137, pls. 102.3–4, 103.1–3, 110.1–4 and 111.1–2.

[94] See supra n. 31.

[95] E.g. H.R. Goette, *Studien zu römischen Togadarstellungen* (Mainz 1990) 147 no. 16, pl. 58.3–4.

[96] Fragment of male portrait (which will be published by J. Auinger): Museum Selçuk inv. no. 1926. Female heads: Museum Selçuk inv. nos. 1952 (Tyche) and 1895 (damaged female head). Both unpublished.

[97] Museum Selçuk inv. no. 1952. Height of the head (without turreted crown) is 14.2 cm.

[98] Museum Selçuk find-no. V 68/6. Unpublished. During the early excavations of the building, fragments of a statue in cuirass were discovered in the caldarium (excavation diary 11 September 1929).

[99] Dorl-Klingenschmid, *Prunkbrunnen* (supra n. 17), 182–83 cat. no. 20, 140–41.

[100] *IEph* 414, 416. P. Scherrer, "Die Fernwasserversorgung

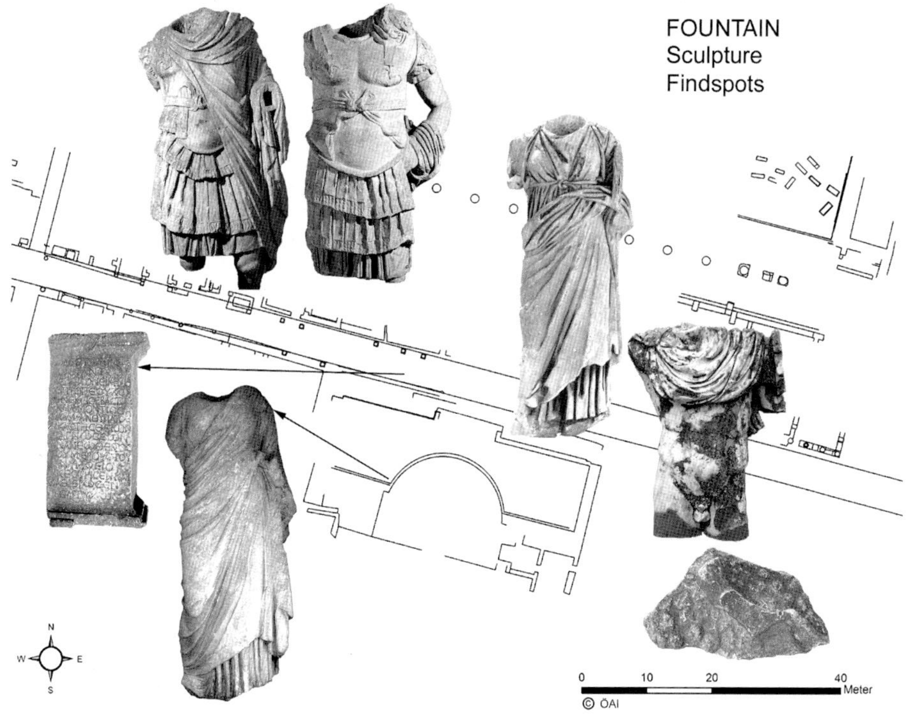

Fig. 9. Fountain, detail of the digital plan of Ephesus, with findspots (© Österreichisches Archäologisches Institut).

It is flanked by lateral wings with columnar façades, fronted by basins. These lateral wings are often described as a second-century phase of the building in scholarly literature, but no study of the architecture has been undertaken.[101] A late antique renovation is documented by a building inscription of the mid-fourth century on the architrave of the "nympheion," which cites the emperors Constantius II and Constans (A.D. 340–350) as well as the proconsul Montius, who also sponsored the *atrium thermarum Constantianarum* in the Harbor Baths.[102] Two bases attest the dedication of statues of the emperors, featuring the same epigraphic formula. One of them was found in front of the fountain (fig. 9, on the far left); it features a drill hole and a pouring channel indicating an adjoining block on top.[103] The other one was reused as a floor-slab in the late antique peristyle court in the eastern hall of the basilica, south of the enlarged praefurnium of the baths.[104]

All the statuary uncovered in the area was found in secondary contexts.[105] The fragment of a reclining river god (fig. 9, on the far right, bottom row) was found in the debris.[106] The position of

von Ephesos in der römischen Kaiserzeit. Synopse der epigraphischen Quellen," in Wiplinger (ed.), *Cura Aquarum* (supra n. 20), 50, 52–53.

[101] This thesis originates from a proposed date of the earlier building inscription (*IEph* 414, dated by Heberdey to the early to mid-second century, cf. Heberdey, "IX. Vorläufiger Bericht" [supra n. 35], Beiblatt, 176–77); and the proposed date of the architecture, cf. F. Eichler, "Die österreichischen Ausgrabungen in Ephesos im Jahre 1962," *AnzWien* 100 (1963) 47 and *RE* Suppl. XII (1970) s.v. Ephesos (W. Alzinger) 1606.

[102] *IEph* 1316–17. Scherrer, "Fernwasserversorgung" (supra n. 100), 51, 53. *Atrium thermarum Constantianarum*: *IEph* 1314–15.

[103] *IEph* 1316.

[104] Roueché, "The Kuretenstraße" (supra n. 7).

[105] For a survey of the sculptures from the fountain, cf. E. Rathmayr, in Auinger and Rathmayr, "Spätantike Statuenausstattung," 253.

[106] Museum Selçuk (no inventory number). I discovered the fragment in one of the depots of the museum. It matches the reference to a rocky plinth with crossed legs of a reclining river god in the excavation diary of 1908 (September 24–26).

its feet and the rocky surface of its plinth are similar to those of the river gods of the Fountain of Domitian (no. 28 on fig. 1), which was also erected in A.D. 92/93 in the northwestern corner of the Upper Agora.[107] Further elements of the primary decoration are preserved in the form of inscribed statue bases (see Alexander Sokolicek's contribution below). All the other preserved sculptures of the fountain can be dated to the second century (or the early third century), but in various decades, and they show different workmanship. A Hadrianic female portrait statue was discovered "in Sturzlage" between two columns, both statue and columns having fallen from the western façade of the fountain (fig. 9, left part, with arrow).[108] It is a headless portrait statue of the Kore type.[109] All the other sculptures—including the fragment of a river god, a second female sculpture, and a female head which I was not able to identify—were discovered in the debris surrounding the building or were built into the walls of the Byzantine structures around the fountain. Chronologically speaking, a male torso of the Dioscuri type (possibly a portrait statue) can be grouped with the female portrait statue according to the style of its drapery (fig. 9, on the far right).[110] The headless statue of a Victory can be dated to the late second or early third century, due to its distinct drill-work (fig. 9, left of the male torso).[111] Two Antonine portrait statues in cuirass feature generalized, in details even crude, workmanship.[112] Matteo Cadario doubted whether they were originally designed as a pair.[113] Considering this assembly of sculptures, we might assume that the river god belonged to the first phase of the building. All the other sculptures, dating to the second century, could have been added in the high imperial period or at the time of the fourth-century renovation. The reuse of the two statues in cuirass for the statues of the fourth-century emperors is often assumed, but the bases seem too small for the heavy, over-lifesize statues, even if they were combined with other blocks.[114]

To sum up, in the area of the Upper Agora, three cult buildings were given up and dismantled in late antiquity: the temple, the prytaneion, and the structures in the Temenos.[115] The basilica and the fountain were renovated in the fourth century, the fountain already before the series of earthquakes in the 350s and 360s.[116] The fifth century is marked by renovations of the baths on the Upper Agora and by the adaptation and refurbishment of the easternmost part of the basilica. We do not yet know how long these buildings were in use. This also applies to the fountain and the bouleuterion. The

[107] Dorl-Klingenschmid, *Prunkbrunnen* (supra n. 17), 189–90 cat. no. 27 ("Brunnenhof auf dem Pollio-Bau"); Plattner and Schmidt-Colinet, "Beobachtungen" (supra n. 23), 246–49; Scherrer, "Fernwasserversorgung" (supra n. 100), 48–49, 52. River gods from this fountain: V.M. Strocka, "Zeus, Marnas und Klaseas. Ephesische Brunnenfiguren von 93 n. Chr.," in N. Başgelen and M. Lugal (eds.), *Festschrift für J. İnan* (Istanbul 1989) 77–85, pls. 39–41; Dorl-Klingenschmid, *Prunkbrunnen* (supra n. 17), 100–1, fig. 60.

[108] As documented in a sketch in the excavation diary of 1908.

[109] Archaeological Museum Izmir inv. no. 27. A. Filges, *Standbilder jugendlicher Göttinnen* (Cologne 1997) 45–48, 255 cat. no. 62.

[110] Aurenhammer, *Idealplastik*, cat. no. 158, pl. 121a.

[111] Archaeological Museum Izmir inv. no. 572. The findspot in the area of the fountain is documented by the excavation diary (10–12 September 1908) and an old photograph. R. Özgan, *Die Skulpturen von Stratonikeia, Asia Minor Studien* 32 (1999) 121–22 K 26, pl. 38c–d wrongly indicates Stratoniceia as the findspot (the inventory number is wrong, too). For the drill-work, compare the statues of barbarians found in and near the propylon of the East Gymnasium, Aurenhammer, *Idealplastik*, cat. nos. 144–45, pl. 99a–b. J. Auinger is preparing a comprehensive publication of the sculptural finds from the East Gymnasium and the Baths of Vedius.

[112] Museum Izmir inv. nos. 6 and 7. M. Cadario, *La corazza di Alessandro. Loricati di tipo ellenistico dal IV secolo a.C. al II d.C., Pubblicazioni della Facoltà di Lettere e Filosofia dell' Università degli Studi di Milano* 218 (2004) 394–95, pl. 52. 1–2.

[113] Ibid., 394.

[114] Bases: height 0.87 m; width 0.53 m; depth 0.39 m. Preserved height of the statues: 1.60 m.

[115] Thür, "Spätantike Ephesos" (supra n. 13), 263–64.

[116] For the earthquakes of the third and fourth centuries affecting Ephesus, cf. recently Ladstätter and Pülz, "Ephesus," 394–98.

Fountain of C. Laecanius Bassus (fig. 1, no. 29) was in use at least until the fifth century. At some time in the fourth century, the fountain (Fontäne) no longer provided water for this structure.[117] After the erection of the so-called Hercules Gate (fig. 1, no. 35) in the later fifth century, which marked the narrow southeastern end of the Embolos, the area of the Upper Agora was transformed into a kind of suburb.[118] Human activity is attested in the area of the Upper Agora until the seventh century and beyond in the form of dwellings, workshops, constructions for water supply, and graves.[119]

As for the sculptures standing in the area in the period between the fourth and sixth centuries, there is continued use of early Roman imperial statuary in the basilica until the end of the fifth century. The reuse of decorative sculpture such as herms and *monopodia* may be assumed for the peristyle court of the basilica in its new function. A part of the original decoration of the stage building of the bouleuterion was obviously on display until late antiquity. The original sculptural decoration of the Fountain of C. Laecanius Bassus was continually used until the fourth century.[120] The main part of the sculptures found in the area of the fountain were probably added to the original decoration of its façade in the high imperial period or even in its fourth-century phase. In the baths on the Upper Agora, sculpture was found exclusively in secondary contexts, including the late antique busts. Generally, six contemporary portraits are preserved or recorded from the area of the Upper Agora, among them three busts. No honorific portrait statue of the fifth century has been found: only the statues of Constantius II and Constans are epigraphically attested at the fountain. No lifesize or small-scale contemporary mythological sculpture was found in the entire area.

It may also be noted that the amount of sculptures found in the other main public square of Ephesus, the Tetragonos Agora,[121] is insignificant when compared to the finds from other areas of the city. Many of the pieces from the Tetragonos Agora were discovered in the vicinity of the gates. A Claudian male portrait was built into a late antique foundation in the southeastern corner of the agora, and two other portraits—one of them a male portrait of the fifth century—were dumped into a drain under the agora, a habit encountered all over the city.[122]

The lack of contemporary portrait statuary of the fifth or sixth century in the form of free-standing statues in both agorai contrasts with the rich evidence of the streets of the late antique city where the display of honorific statuary was concentrated.[123]

[117] This is documented by a change in the course of the water conduits; see K. Jung, "Das Hydrekdocheion" (supra n. 20), 84.

[118] Hercules Gate: A. Bammer, "Ein spätantiker Torbau aus Ephesos," *ÖJh* 51 (1976–1977) 92–126; Bauer, *Stadt* (supra n. 6), 285; Ladstätter and Pülz, "Ephesus," 406.

[119] C. Foss, *Ephesus after Antiquity: A Late Antique, Byzantine and Turkish City* (Cambridge 1979) 82, 134; Bauer, *Stadt* (supra n. 6), 291–92; St. Karwiese, "Die Münzfunde aus dem sog. Sockelbau der Basilica von Ephesos," *NZ* 113/114 (2005) 181–202; Ladstätter and Pülz, "Ephesus," 406, 408.

[120] E. Rathmayr, in Auinger and Rathmayr, "Spätantike Statuenausstattung," 252–53; idem, "Die Skulpturenausstattung" (supra n. 21), 130–49.

[121] See recently P. Scherrer and E. Trinkl, *Die Tetragonos Agora von Ephesos, Forschungen in Ephesos* XIII 2 (Vienna 2006).

[122] M. Aurenhammer, "Drei neue römische Porträtköpfe von der Tetragonos Agora in Ephesos," *ÖJh* 69 (2000) 17–33.

[123] Bauer, *Stadt* (supra n. 6), 271–75, 278–79, 283–90, 295–97; Auinger, "Zum Umgang" (supra n. 7); and Roueché, "The Kuretenstraße" (supra n. 7).

Statue Bases[124]

Sculptural decoration in public space has more than aesthetic value: the display of emperors, officials, and mythological figures in Roman imperial statuary ensembles mirrors the self-representation of urban elites and, more generally, urban identity.[125] Despite the longevity of statuary ensembles, the Roman imperial statue habit ceased to operate as it had toward the end of the third century A.D.[126] In this paper, changes in the adornment of public squares in Ephesus are studied through analysis of the contexts and numbers of known statue bases.[127] The focus is on the bases from the Upper Agora (fig. 1), set against the evidence from the Tetragonos Agora. The overall sum of bases found in Ephesus totals about 1,000 pieces, 33 of which were found in the Upper Agora and 178 in the Tetragonos Agora.

Generally speaking, the reconstruction of the sculptural decoration of public squares is often a matter of reconstructing the after-use of statuary ensembles, and that is itself often a matter of tracing the devices to which statues were originally attached. Statues were never placed on the ground; they were always fixed on bases or on large blocks and were in many cases named by inscriptions placed on the stones on which the statues were set up.[128] Together, a statue and a base form a statuary unit.

Statue bases are valuable objects of study. They are often the only remains of a statue monument, and in many cases they were found near where they originally stood. This is due to the fact that when statuary units were detached and no longer "in use," the forms of statue bases rendered them suitable as building materials, and they were therefore kept in buildings or walls, whereas statues were reused or further "processed" in many different ways.[129] Aside from convenience, this happened because bases do not appear as obviously pagan as statues of gods and goddesses, or of non-Christian emperors. Bases were more neutral in their appearance than individualized sculptures. When the concept of the "ancient city" was challenged by the social and religious transformations of late antiquity,[130] pagan images dominating the cityscape would likely have been removed, whereas statue bases would have remained in place, bearing newly incised signs and words of Christian triumph. The best example of

[124] The dating of the bases is due to the formula of the inscriptions, or, if missing, roughly based on the style of lettering. The author is responsible for the dating if not indicated otherwise. If not stated otherwise, the inscriptions on the bases are Greek.

[125] S. Bassett, "Ancient statuary in fourth-century Constantinople: Subject, style and functions," in Bauer and Witschel, *Statuen in der Spätantike*, 192. More generally see e.g. C.C. Vermeule III, *Greek Sculpture and Roman Taste. The Purpose and Setting of Graeco-Roman Art in Italy and the Greek Imperial East* (Ann Arbor 1977).

[126] B.E. Borg, "Bilder für die Ewigkeit der glanzvoller Auftritt? Zum Repräsentationsverhalten der stadtrömischen Eliten im dritten Jahrhundert n.Chr.," in Bauer and Witschel, *Statuen in der Spätantike*, 43–78; R. Coates-Stephens, "The reuse of ancient statuary in late antique Rome and the end of the statue habit," in Bauer and Witschel, *Statuen in der Spätantike*, 171–87. This becomes especially evident when looking at the preceding periods, especially the second century and Second Sophistic; see the acts of a congress published by B. Borg (ed.), *Paideia. The World of the Second Sophistic* (Berlin 2004) and D. Boschung, "Die Präsentation von Geschichte im Stadtbild der Kaiserzeit," in O.D. Cordovana and M. Galli (eds.), *Arte e memoria culturale nell'età della Seconda Sofistica* (Catania 2007) 103–7.

[127] The changes that affected Ephesus in late antiquity and in early Byzantine times have been presented recently by Ladstätter and Pülz, "Ephesus," 391–433.

[128] Statues could be mounted in different ways: marble statues with plinths were fixed by dowels or clamps; bronze statues do not have plinths and were therefore fixed by lead dowels, having sockets for the feet of the statue on the surface of the bases. See Højte, *Statue Bases*, 150–52; Filges, *Didyma*, 105–6.

[129] Reconstructing the original setting and placing of statue bases can never be totally convincing; the method of reconstructing the original places is discussed below. For the reuse of statues in late antiquity see recently the contributions of a conference on statues in late antiquity, Bauer and Witschel, *Statuen in der Spätantike*, with bibliography.

[130] See W. Liebeschuetz, "The end of the ancient city," in J. Rich (ed.), *The City in Late Antiquity* (London and NewYork 1992) 149; B. Ward-Perkins, "Urban continuity?" in N. Christie and S.T. Loseby (eds.), *Towns in Transition. Urban Evolution in Late Antiquity and the Early Middle Ages* (Aldershot 1996) 4–12, at 4–5 on the definition of a city in late antiquity; G.

these processes in Ephesus is the reworked base of a statue of Artemis, which was demolished and replaced by a cross by a Christian called Demeas in the renewed inscription on the base.[131] More generally and in the context of the changing cityscape in late antiquity, statue bases do not only indicate the original statuary of earlier, Roman imperial times ("portrait"/"statue habit"),[132] they also convey valuable information about the processes of transformation of public squares in the late antique city. Bases tell us about the duration of public monuments, about the re-erection of statues, and about the different roles urban decoration played in different periods.

Whatever their subjects, the majority of the statues in Ephesus—roughly 70 per cent—were made of bronze.[133] This number is reconstructed not by the archaeological record of the statuary but from the bases made for different kinds of statues. According to the form of the fixing holes on their upper surfaces, bases for bronze statues can be clearly distinguished from bases for marble statues.[134] The high proportion of Ephesian bronze sculptures accords with the overall estimation of Roman imperial statues given by Jakob Munk Højte[135] and the numbers from Didyma by Axel Filges,[136] and has to be considered as typical for Roman statuary.[137] Although these figures are taken from different places and contexts, they show that the prevalence of bronze statues in Ephesus is anything but unusual. Bronze statues, however, are rare, "because their value as commemorative monuments soon fell below the relatively high scrap value of bronze,"[138] and consequently, the majority of statues found during excavations are made of marble.[139]

Numbers, Types, Dates, and Findspots of Bases from the Upper Agora

During the excavations in the Upper Agora, 33 bases were found in the central open area and in the surrounding buildings facing the square.[140] Bases from buildings at the west side of the Upper Agora are excluded from this study, because their façades are not turned towards the square and therefore have no significance for its visual composition.[141] Places mentioned here include: 1) the central area, 2) the street to the Magnesian Gate, 3) the baths on the Upper Agora, 4) the fountain at the south side of the agora, 5) the prytaneion, and 6) the bouleuterion (see fig. 1).

Brands, "Die spätantike Stadt und ihre Christianisierung," in Brands and Severin, *Die spätantike Stadt* (supra n. 13), 1–26. For late antique cities in transition see G.P. Brogiolo and B. Ward-Perkins (eds.), *The Idea and Ideal of the Town between Late Antiquity and the Early Middle Ages, The Transformation of the Roman World* 4 (Leiden 1999).

[131] *IEph* 1351. See R. Schwindt, *Das Weltbild des Epheserbriefes* (Tübingen 2002) 81–82.

[132] The study of the statue habits in Ephesus is supervised by M. Aurenhammer.

[133] The percentage of bronze statues is estimated by the numbers of statue bases from Ephesus in Roman imperial times.

[134] The statue bases of Ephesus are currently being studied by the author; for the distinction between bases for marble and bronze statues, see supra n. 5.

[135] Højte, *Statue Bases*, 13–14.

[136] Filges, *Didyma*, 93. According to his studies, only a low percentage (ca. 9 per cent) of the sculptures of the sanctuary in Didyma were made of marble. Considering the different context, this number from Didyma's sanctuary cannot be directly compared with the numbers from the urban area of Ephesus, but it is interesting that in both places the majority of statues are made of metal.

[137] G. Lahusen and E. Formigli, *Römische Bildnisse aus Bronze. Kunst und Technik* (Munich 2001).

[138] Højte, *Statue Bases*, 13.

[139] See Lahusen and Formigli, *Römische Bildnisse aus Bronze* (supra n. 137); E. Formigli, G. Lahusen, and R. Pecchioli, "Grossbronzen der Antike und Renaissance. Ein technisch-formaler Vergleich," in A. Dostert and F. Lang (eds.), *Mittel und Wege. Zur Bedeutung von Material und Technik in der Archäologie* (Möhnesee 2006) 125–37.

[140] About the history of excavation of the Upper Agora, see Mitsopoulos-Leon and Lang-Auinger, *Basilika* (supra n. 22); Thür, "Staatsmarkt"; H. Thür, "Das Gymnasion" (supra n. 19), 403–14.

[141] For that reason, bases from the nymphaeum of C. Laecanius Bassus and the Pollio Nymphaeum are not represented here. The nymphaeum of C. Laecanius Bassus is currently being studied by a team supervised by M. Aurenhammer. See supra, contribution by M. Aurenhammer.

From the central area, we know of nine bases in total. Interestingly, the oldest one is a Hellenistic base found close to the fountain building in the south part of the area. The original context of this base is unknown. It represents a dedication to Hermes and was dedicated by the *gymnasiarch* Hekatokles.[142] The rest of the bases are all of Roman imperial date, and there is not a single late antique piece. Most of the bases are in a fragmentary state of preservation, and the forms of the letters give the only hints for dating. The content of the inscriptions includes private dedications or honorific texts. The majority date to the first and second centuries.[143]

The so-called street of the Magnesian Gate close to the central area yielded only a few pieces, but they are unusually interesting. In total, only four bases were found, two honoring emperors, the other two donated by private persons.[144] Of the imperial bases, one honors the third-century emperor Maximinus; the other bears a Latin inscription,[145] but cannot be ascribed to a specific emperor or dated precisely on other grounds. The base proper is very fragmentary but can be reconstructed as very large and flat; it could have been part of a larger ensemble. The other two bases are dated to the second century. Both were donated by private persons,[146] and they are unusual in comparison with other bases found in the Upper Agora. Both are fragmentary, but it is clear that they are separately worked upper moldings. Only two other separate upper moldings were found nearby in the Upper Agora, both in the prytaneion.[147]

From the buildings bordering on the Upper Agora, there were only two pieces found in the baths, one honoring a victorious athlete probably of the first century,[148] the other a base set up for the emperor Constans by Caelius Montius, proconsul in the years between A.D. 337 and 350.[149]

Inside and in front of the so-called Fontäne, located on the south side of the agora, five bases were found; one additional base unearthed on the north side of the agora close to the baths was probably taken from the fountain.[150] The oldest base dates to the reign of Domitian and is

[142] *IEph* 1102.

[143] Central area: *IEph* 611 (honoring Manius Acilius Glabrio, *legatus Asiae*; upper side simple profile, partially reworked; used as spolium in a late house; date: A.D. 152–170); *IEph* 683C (honoring an unknown person; date: ca. first century according to letter forms); *IEph* 736 (honoring L. Vibius Lentulus; date: first half of the first century according to letter forms); *IEph* 740 (honoring Ulpius Apollonius Plautus, *asiarch*; Ephesus is called *tris neokoros;* found east of the bouleuterion; date: A.D. 212–218); *IEph* 891 (honoring Claudia Basilo, *theoros* at the Olympic games of Ephesus; date: A.D. 161–169); *IEph* 904 (list of names; date: A.D. 120); *IEph* 1076 (fragment of a base; date: ca. second century); *IEph* 1083a (very fragmentary base, mentioning agones; date: first century according to letter forms).

[144] Street to the Magnesian Gate: *IEph* 301 (honoring Maximinus Thrax; date: A.D. 235–238); *IEph* 329,1 (honoring an unknown emperor; fragment of large base; Latin; date: second to third century); *IEph* 475 (donation of Tib. Iulius Celsus; two fragments of upper molding; date: A.D. 105–120); *IEph* 710D (honoring M. Pontius M. f. [Laelianus]; Latin; date: ca. A.D. 161–180). The Latin inscription *IEph* 710D is fragmented and mentions a "M. Pontius M. fil. [". By analogy with *IEph* 1880, a Latin inscription mentioning [M. Pontius] Laelianus on a large slab found on Panayirdağ next to the so-called Hellenistic circular building and dating to the year A.D. 163, our Marcus Pontius [in *IEph* 710D has to be identified with M. Pontius Laelianus. This man was a veteran of L. Verus's Parthian campaign and lived from the beginning of the second century to about the death of the emperor M. Aurelius; see J. Rüpke, "Kaiserliche Religionspolitik und priesterliche Rekrutierungsmechanismen," in H. Cancik and K. Hitzl (eds.), *Die Praxis der Herrscherverehrung in Rom und seinen Provinzen* (Tübingen 2003) 135; A.R. Birley, "From Hadrian to the Antonines," in A.K. Bowman, P. Garnsey, and D. Rathbone (eds.), *The Cambridge Ancient History.* XI. *The High Empire. AD 70–192* (Cambridge 2000) 132–94, about M. Pontius Laelianus at 161–62, 168, 207.

[145] *IEph* 329.1.

[146] *IEph* 475 and *IEph* 710D, see supra n. 21.

[147] *IEph* 613A (date: A.D. 180–192) and *IEph* 985 (date: A.D. 128–250). For more information on the bases, see infra (text).

[148] *IEph* 1118 (date according to letter forms).

[149] Base without number; see C. Roueché, "The Kuretenstraße" (supra n. 7). For the statues, see supra, contribution by M. Aurenhammer and supra n. 103.

[150] *IEph* 236 (base of the demos of Philadelphia honoring the demos of Ephesus; date: Domitian's reign, A.D. 81–96; simple shaft without moldings, probably for a marble statue); *IEph* 1845 (honorific base, mentioning a certain Gerillanus; small fragment of left corner; date: Roman imperial).

Double inscriptions: *IEph* 855 and 855a (two bases honoring

a monument set up by the demos of Philadelphia honoring the demos of Ephesus. Two identical inscriptions honoring T. Fl. Pergamus, both in Latin, were found in the basin of the fountain and were certainly part of the embellishment of the building. Similarly, the latest base, dated to the second quarter of the fourth century and set up by Caelius Montius in honor of the emperor Constans after Montius had re-erected the fountain, bears the same text as the aforementioned base found close to the baths. The analogy of the bases of T. Fl. Pergamus of the late first or early second century would suggest that these bases were part of the embellishment of the building in the fourth century.

From the prytaneion, there are seven bases known, all of Roman imperial date.[151] Among these, there are two upper moldings made for bronze statues.[152] The bouleuterion was embellished with at least six bases, dating to the second and third centuries.[153]

Pattern of Distribution of Bases from the Upper Agora and the Tetragonos Agora

Summing up the situation revealed by the statue bases from the Upper Agora, we can state the following four conclusions:

1) Compared to the number of bases found in Ephesus the amount in the Upper Agora is minimal; in total, there are about 1,000 different bases in Ephesus, and only 33 were found in the Upper Agora, i.e., only 3.3 per cent.
2) Only four out of 33 bases bear Latin inscriptions, i.e., 12 per cent. Excluding the Hellenistic and late antique bases, among the remaining 30 bases of Roman imperial date 13.7 per cent bear Latin inscriptions.
3) Only two bases date to the late antique period, and both bear identical texts honoring Caelius Montius for (re-)building the fountain. Among the others, the latest bases date to the middle of the third century, which is about a century earlier.
4) There are only a few imperial inscriptions on bases and of these, none is earlier than the second century.

T. Fl. Pergamus, *Augustus libertus* and *procurator provinciae Asiae*, *IEph* 855 set up by tabellarii, *IEph* 855a fragmentary; both Latin; date: A.D. 79 to 120); *IEph* 1316 (dedication of the fountain by Caelius Montius, date: between A.D. 337 and 350), probably set up with an identical base transported to the north side of the agora, see supra n. 149. For the statues, see supra, contribution by M. Aurenhammer.

[151] From the Hestia room: *IEph* 1076 (date: middle Roman imperial according to letter forms; base consists of four fragments reconstructed by D. Knibbe as part of one base. The two main pieces were found in the prytaneion, one was found on the way between the prytaneion to the bouleuterion and the other one found in Terrace House 1); *IEph* 609 (fragment of a poem to a woman prytanis; date: unknown); *IEph* 613A (upper molding of a base honoring Alexandros, the son of a certain Dies; date: A.D. 180–192).

Other findspots: *IEph* 715A (honoring the deceased Terentia Tertulla, date: Roman imperial; found in the late houses of the area of the prytaneion); *IEph* 985 (upper molding for Larcia Theogenis Iuliane, prytanis and priestess of Artemis; date: A.D. 128–250; found in the foreroom to the Hestia room); *IEph* 1058 (fragmentary base of the prytanis A(u) runceius, dedicating his words and base to Hestia but also to Demeter and Kore; date: Roman imperial); *IEph* 1926.3 (fragment of an upper molding, no name preserved; date: Roman imperial). For the prytaneion, see supra n. 12.

[152] *IEph* 613A and *IEph* 1926.3, see supra n. 150. For the statues, see supra, contribution by M. Aurenhammer.

[153] *IEph* 285A (honoring Annia Aurelia Galeria Faustina; date: A.D. 161–181; see supra, contribution by M. Aurenhammer); *IEph* 633 (honoring P. Carsidius Pamphilio, prytanis, by the demos; date: A.D. 98–131); *IEph* 1505 (found in the middle entrance to the bouleuterion; base of statue of L. Verus, erected by Vedius Antoninus III in the time of Antoninus Pius); *IEph* 1562 (found south of the bouleuterion by J. Turtle Wood; base honoring Flavius Zoticus, who donated a statue for Claudia, daughter of Tib. Cl. Hermeios; date: A.D. 240–260); *IEph* 1905, 4 (fragmentary upper molding of a statue base with decorated corners, no name preserved; date: Roman imperial); *IEph* 1903 (found in front of the central entrance; base for Demos; date: second century). For the bouleuterion in general and the bases, see supra, contribution by M. Aurenhammer.

These numbers from the Upper Agora, however, reveal the situation of the square only in its "petrified" state, as covered by earth and debris after the area was abandoned.[154] How relevant, then, are these data for reconstructing the situation of statuary ensembles in Roman imperial times and in late antiquity, and what does this situation tell us about use of space in late antiquity?

A comparison of the statue bases from the Upper Agora with the bases from the Tetragonos Agora will bring more light to this problem. In contrast to the small number of 33 bases from the Upper Agora, there are far more statue bases known from the Tetragonos Agora, about 178 in total. This amount is approximately 18 per cent of all bases known from Ephesus, and about five times greater than the number of bases from the Upper Agora. The relatively high number of bases from the Tetragonos Agora is also astonishing when set in comparison to all inscriptions from the Tetragonos Agora, which total 616 examples of all different kinds. From all inscribed stones, nearly a third are statue bases (29 per cent), and this percentage is more than double the corresponding figure of 13 per cent of the 260 inscriptions known from the Upper Agora. Aside from the fact that the two agorai cover areas of comparable size—Upper Agora: ca. 16,500 m^2; Tetragonos Agora: ca. 12,000 m^2—their functions differed in Roman imperial times, with the Tetragonos Agora serving mostly as the place of commerce, and the Upper Agora housing the most important public buildings.[155]

These differences in numbers and functions contrast, however, with certain similarities in percentage apparent on closer examination of the statue bases from both agorai. It is especially interesting that the percentage of bases in Latin from the Tetragonos Agora (ca. 12 per cent or 22 out of 178 bases) equals the percentage of Latin inscriptions of the Upper Agora (ca. 12 per cent or four out of 33 bases).[156] Is this benchmark of 12 per cent for Latin inscriptions among the bases from both agorai only a mere coincidence, or does this situation mirror an overall tendency?

Of the total of 616 inscriptions from the Tetragonos Agora, we know of six bilingual inscriptions (1 per cent), 525 Greek inscriptions (85 per cent), and 66 Latin inscriptions (12 per cent). The language of 19 fragmentary inscriptions (3 per cent) cannot be identified. These are comparable with the numbers of 1 per cent for bilingual and 12 per cent for Latin inscriptions in the total record of inscriptions from the Upper Agora.

Results and Conclusions

Statue bases from large public places in Ephesus are distributed unequally. Whereas 178 bases are known from the Tetragonos Agora, only 33 examples have been found in the Upper Agora. Taking into account that the Tetragonos Agora does not host individual buildings and is some 4,500 m^2 smaller than the Upper Agora, these figures show us that the Upper Agora featured relatively few statue bases. The reason for this phenomenon—the inequality in the representation of individuals by means of statues—is difficult to come by. But despite the differences, the numerical ratios of Greek and Latin inscriptions within the group of statue bases and within all inscriptions found on the agorai do not vary. These disproportionate numbers, to be precise, show equal distribution of Latin-inscribed bases of ca. 12 per cent. This particular number of 12 per cent for bases does not seem to be coincidental in

[154] The phenomenon of "petrified" public places has been described recently by C. Witschel, "Statuen auf spätantiken Platzanlangen in Italien und Africa," in Bauer and Witschel, *Statuen in der Spätantike*, 120–25 with bibliography and discussion.

[155] For functions of the Tetragonos Agora, see P. Scherrer and E. Trinkl, *Die Tetragonos Agora in Ephesos, Forschungen in Ephesos* XIII 2 (Vienna 2006); for the Upper Agora, see Mitsopoulos-Leon and Lang-Auinger, *Basilika* (supra n. 22).

[156] Only one base bears a bilingual inscription: *IEph* 3027 (honoring L. Nonius Calpurnius Torquatus Asprenas; date: A.D. 107).

light of the overall distribution of 11–12 per cent for Latin inscriptions among all inscriptions studied from both Ephesian agorai.

In comparison with other large cities in Asia Minor,[157] Latinity is represented in Ephesus on a much larger scale, and is concentrated in public places.[158] Possibly there was a certain, more or less stable proportion of Latin-speaking citizens, which might be traced back to the descendants of Italian merchants and officials accompanying high Roman magistrates when they visited the Roman province of Asia.[159]

The numbers of Latin inscriptions in public places in Ephesus could be taken to imply a corresponding number of ca. 12 per cent Latin speakers representing themselves in public, because the majority of the inscriptions are not of official but of non-official or "representative" character and thus can be seen as indicative of the linguistic habits of the inhabitants; only two Latin inscriptions from the Tetragonos Agora (one Tetrarchic imperial letter, *IEph* 940, and one imperial decree from the sixth century, *IEph* 39), and none from the Upper Agora are of official character. Apart from their implications for the demography of the Roman imperial town, these figures show that bases in Ephesian public places remained more or less in place, because the stability of the percentages over different genera can hardly be explained as accidental. In other words, the same group of people was presenting itself and its achievements in the same ways and with the same frequency in both places. This assumption of spatial continuity is supported by the location of "twin bases," i.e. bases bearing identical inscriptions, in the fountain located on the Upper Agora.[160] All but one of the bases were found nearby the building; only one base had been carried across the square of the Upper Agora to the north side. Hence, the symmetrical layout of the fountain makes a reconstruction of identical bases on either wing of the building very probable.

In terms of chronology, we should note that there are no late antique bases in either agora, besides the aforementioned bases for L. Montius on the Upper Agora.

In terms of context, we see that neither at the Upper Agora nor at the Tetragonos Agora were bases discovered in their original positions, although they had not moved very far. They were most commonly reused in later buildings, or, as in the Tetragonos Agora, kept in storerooms, presumably for eventual reuse as building materials. This situation contrasts with the contexts of bases on major streets at Ephesus, where both late antique bases and Roman imperial bases reused in late antique contexts either stood upright in their original positions or had fallen onto the pavements of the streets.[161]

[157] R. Kearsley, *Greeks and Romans in Imperial Asia. Mixed Language Inscriptions and Linguistic Evidence for Cultural Interaction until the End of AD III, Inschriften griechischer Städte aus Kleinasien* 59 (Bonn 2001) 1–10, 147–56; P. Herrmann, "Italiker und Römer in Sardeis. Überlegungen zu zwei inschriftlichen Zeugnissen," in J. Spielvogel (ed.), *Res publica reperta. Zur Verfassung und Gesellschaft der römischen Republik und des frühen Prinzipats. Festschrift für Jochen Bleicken zum 75. Geburtstag* (Stuttgart 2002) 36–44; K. Shiuchi, "Bilingual inscriptions in Asia Minor. A preliminary survey," *Kodai* 13/14 (2003–2004) 103–9. More generally: N. Adams, M. Janse, and S. Swain, *Bilingualism in Ancient Society. Language Contact and the Written Text* (Oxford 2002).

[158] See E. Weber, "Zu den lateinischen Inschriften von Ephesos," in F. Krinzinger and H. Friesinger (eds.), *100 Jahre österreichische Forschungen in Ephesos* (Vienna 1999) 139–46, at 139: the percentage of all Latin inscriptions from Ephesus is estimated by Weber to be under 10 per cent. Overall numbers do not necessarily represent social or ethnic realities in ancient cities because excavations reveal only parts of cities; see the problems discussed by Kearsley, *Greeks and Romans* (supra n. 157).

[159] F. Kirbihler, "Die Italiker in Kleinasien, mit besonderer Berücksichtigung von Ephesos (133 v. Chr.–1. Jh. n. Chr.)," in Meyer, *Neue Zeiten*, 19–35.

[160] Pergamus: *IEph* 855 and 855a; Montius: *IEph* 1316 and C. Roueché, "The Kuretenstraße" (supra n. 7).

[161] Bases were unearthed in situ or in fallen positions at the Curetes Street, at the so-called Theater Street between the theater and the stadium, and at the Marble Street between the Embolos and theater. For late antiquity on the Curetes Street see C. Roueché, "Provincial governors and their titulature in the sixth century," *Antiquité tardive* 6 (1998) 83–89 and Ladstätter, *Kuretenstraße*, passim.

Considering contexts and dates, the diversity of the use and reuse of bases in public places (agorai and streets) becomes clear. The transition from a focus on the statuary adornment of public squares to a focus on the statuary adornment of major streets took place in the period between the mid- to late third century (the time of the last bases set up on the agorai) and the fifth and sixth centuries (the time when the bases at the Curetes Street were still standing). This process is very similar to what happened to large public squares in other Roman cities in the Mediterranean. In a recently published study on the situation of fora in late antique Africa and Italy, Christian Witschel argues that there occurred a general decline and removal of statuary representation in the third and fourth centuries and the actual cessation of the erection or re-erection of statues in the beginning of the fifth century,[162] when statuary ensembles shifted to other places of interest.[163] More generally, but tending in the same direction, the overall dislocation of urban centers took place at the time of the transition from the Roman imperial to the late antique city; however, early Christian architecture obviously did not take possession of central public places before the fifth and sixth centuries.[164]

The situation in Ephesus is analogous. The cessation of the setting up of bases in public squares in the third century shows that fora and agorai no longer maintained their role as foci of public interest and active representation; in this respect, the former function of the agora shifted to other public areas such as major streets. The study of the sculpture in the area of both Ephesian agorai leads to the same conclusion: no portrait statues beyond the fourth century were found in these areas, but instead the display of honorific statuary was concentrated on the streets of the late antique city, especially the Embolos. At the same time, contemporary donors to the refurbishment of the buildings on the Upper Agora seem to have preferred the form of the portrait bust for conveying their public image, at least according to the evidence of the baths on the Upper Agora.[165]

[162] Witschel, "Statuen auf Platzanlangen in Italien und Africa" (supra n. 154), 113–69.

[163] Bauer and Witschel, "Statuen in der Spätantike" (supra n. 37), 1–24.

[164] The earliest churches in late antique cities appear in the late fourth century, in most cases located in the outskirts. H.R. Meier, "Zentrumsverlagerung oder Deurbanisierung? Eine Frage zur 'Christianisierung' der spätantiken Stadt," in Brands and Severin, *Die spätantike Stadt* (supra n. 13), 165–77, esp. 176–77; see also W. Hoepfner, "Das Ende der Agora," in ibid., 145–50; but at 149 citing Pergamon as an example of early Christian activity on the agora as an assembly place for the Christian *ekklesia*. C. Witschel, "Betrachtungen zum römischen Städtewesen in der Spätantike," in A. Lampen and A. Ozwar (eds.), *Schrumpfende Städte. Ein Phänomen zwischen Antike und Moderne* (Cologne-Weimar-Vienna 2008) 17–78, esp. 68–9 mentions the dynamics of church constructions in late antique cities where the appropriation of the public space fully developed in the fifth and sixth centuries.

[165] For the evidence of the busts and the chronology of the sculpture, see supra, contribution by M. Aurenhammer.

4 The Sculptural Decoration of Ephesian Bath Buildings in Late Antiquity

Johanna Auinger

Reconstructing the sculptural decoration of Ephesian bath buildings in late antiquity poses significant challenges.[1] The main problem is the incompleteness of the old excavation records. All the major Ephesian bath complexes were excavated between the end of the 19th and the middle of the 20th centuries. The main concerns of the excavators were to clear these large buildings as quickly as possible in order to generate ground plans and to uncover works of decorative architecture and sculpture. As a result, stratigraphic records and other types of archaeological documentation are often missing. At this juncture, it is possible to give only a general overview of the ways in which these buildings and their decoration changed in late antiquity.

In the Hellenistic and Roman city of Ephesus, five large bath-gymnasium complexes[2] and one smaller public bath building[3] are known (fig. 1). While the precise dates of these structures are

[1] I thank Christopher Ratté of the University of Michigan in Ann Arbor and Ortwin Dally of the German Archaeological Institute in Berlin for their invitation to contribute to this volume. This paper represents some of the results of the project "The Sculptural Decoration of the Baths of Vedius and the East Gymnasium in Ephesus" directed by Maria Aurenhammer and funded by the Austrian Research Fund (project no. P 18605) and by the Austrian Archaeological Institute. Furthermore, I also thank Andrew Leung for his architectural documentation and interpretation of the architecture of the East Gymnasium complex.

Abbreviations for frequently cited sources:

Alzinger, "Ephesos" = *RE* Suppl. 12 (1970) 1588–1704, s.v. "Ephesos" (W. Alzinger).

Atalay, *Gewandstatuen* = E. Atalay, *Weibliche Gewandstatuen des 2. Jahrhunderts n. Chr. aus ephesischen Werkstätten* (Vienna 1989).

Auinger, *Skulpturenausstattung* = J. Auinger, *Die Skulpturenausstattung des Vedius- und Ostgymnasiums in Ephesos. Die Funde bis 1931* (Ph.D. dissertation, University of Vienna 2005).

Auinger and Rathmayr, "Spätantike Statuenausstattung" = J. Auinger and E. Rathmayr, "Zur spätantiken Statuenausstattung der Thermen und Nymphäen in Ephesos," in F.A. Bauer and C. Witschel (eds.), *Statuen in der Spätantike* (Wiesbaden 2007) 237–69.

Aurenhammer, *Idealplastik* = M. Aurenhammer, *Die Skulpturen von Ephesos. Idealplastik* I, *Forschungen in Ephesos* X 1 (Vienna 1990).

IEph = *Die Inschriften von Ephesos*, *IK* 17.1–8 (Bonn 1979–1984).

Keil, "XIII. Bericht" = J. Keil, "XIII. Vorläufiger Bericht über die Ausgrabungen in Ephesos," *ÖJh* 24 (1929) Beiblatt, 5–68.

Keil, "XIV. Bericht" = J. Keil, "XIV. Vorläufiger Bericht über die Ausgrabungen in Ephesos," *ÖJh* 25 (1929) Beiblatt, 5–52.

Keil, "XVI. Bericht" = J. Keil, "XVI. Vorläufiger Bericht über die Ausgrabungen in Ephesos," *ÖJh* 27 (1932) Beiblatt, 5–72.

Manderscheid, *Skulpturenausstattung* = H. Manderscheid, *Die Skulpturenausstattung kaiserzeitlicher Thermenanlagen* (Berlin 1981).

Scherrer, *Ephesus* = P. Scherrer (ed.), *Ephesus. The New Guide*, rev. ed. (Istanbul 2000).

Steskal and Ladstätter, "Baugeschichte" = M. Steskal and S. Ladstätter, "Vorbericht zur Baugeschichte des Vediusgymnasiums in Ephesos," *ÖJh* 73 (2004) 237–49.

Steskal and La Torre, *Vediusgymnasium* = M. Steskal and M. La Torre, *Das Vediusgymnasium in Ephesos. Archäologie und Baubefund, Forschungen in Ephesos* XIV 1 (Vienna 2008).

Yegül, *Baths and Bathing* = F.K. Yegül, *Baths and Bathing in Classical Antiquity* (New York 1992).

[2] For a general overview for all Ephesian baths buildings, see esp. Alzinger, "Ephesos," 1608–25 (with older sources) and Yegül, *Baths and Bathing*, 250–313.

[3] The so-called Baths of Scholasticia on the Curetes Street are much smaller than the others and are not a

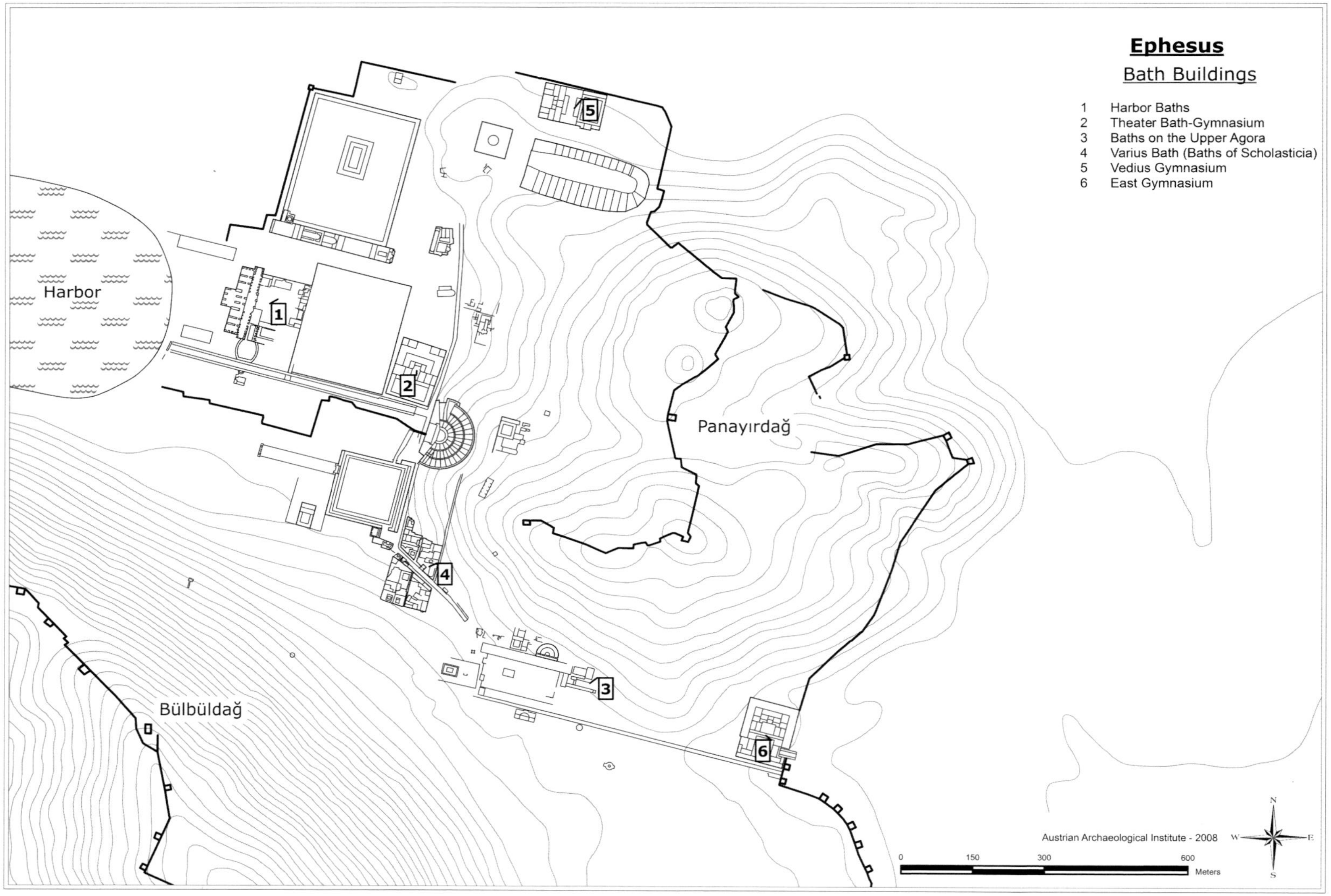

Fig. 1. Map of Ephesus (C. Kurtze, Österreichisches Archäologisches Institut).

unclear,[4] all of them were probably erected in the period between the first century and the end of the second century, and they all remained in use until late antiquity.[5]

The Harbor Baths, the Theater Bath-Gymnasium, the Baths at the Northeast Corner of the Upper Agora, and the Varius Baths

The oldest large bath complex in Ephesus is situated near the harbor area and is therefore called the Harbor Baths (fig. 1, no. 1).[6] Epigraphic references prove that parts of the building were used at least until the mid-fourth century. Lucius Caelius Montius, the proconsul of Asia under the reign of Constantius II and Constans, is recorded in an honorific inscription as the patron of the renovation of the entrance to the Harbor Baths, known as the *atrium thermarum Constantianarum*.[7] The renovation was perhaps made necessary by the partial destruction of the building in the third century.[8] Most of the sculptures found in the Harbor Baths[9] were discovered in the propylon, the Marble Hall, and the frigidarium, with the latest pieces dated to the end of the second century.[10]

Next to the Harbor Baths lies another large bath building, known as the Theater Bath-Gymnasium (fig. 1, no. 2).[11] This complex was probably erected in the Hadrianic period.[12] Surprisingly, no sculpture was found during the excavation. In light of the location of the building in the heart of the late antique city and its proximity to the theater, it would be surprising if it were not still in use in late antiquity, but its later building history remains poorly understood.

We also know very little about the baths situated at the northeast corner of the Upper Agora (fig. 1, no. 3).[13] The layout and dating of this structure are still uncertain. Nevertheless, an inscription

---

bath-gymnasium complex. This paper does not include the smaller baths in private contexts, for example the Sarhoş Hamam (see L. Lavan, "Late antique governors' palaces: A gazetteer," *Antiquité tardive* 7 [1999] 148–49, fig. 11; Scherrer, *Ephesus*, 186 no. 81; S. Ladstätter and A. Pülz, "Ephesus in the late Roman and early Byzantine period: Changes in its urban character from the third to seventh century AD," in A. Poulter [ed.], *The Transition to Late Antiquity on the Danube and Beyond, ProcBritAc 141* [Oxford 2007] 405, figs. 7–8) and the bath in Terrace House 2 in Dwelling Unit 6. For a preliminary report see *ÖJh* 75 (2006) 326–27 (Jahresbericht 2005, 1.1.1, Die Wohneinheit 6 des C. Flavius Furius Aptus).

[4] The Vedius Gymnasium is the only bath building in Ephesus for which the dates are precisely known (infra n. 26).

[5] For a preliminary overview, see Auinger and Rathmayr, "Spätantike Statuenausstattung," 237–69.

[6] See Scherrer, *Ephesus*, 174–77 nos. 91–94; Alzinger, "Ephesos," 1608–11; Yegül, *Baths and Bathing*, 272–73, figs. 335–37.

[7] *IEph* 1314.

[8] Rudolf Heberdey, the excavator at the beginning of the 20th century, suggested that only the palaestra and the adjacent rooms were destroyed in the middle of the third century during the Gothic invasion in A.D. 263. See Auinger and Rathmayr, "Spätantike Statuenausstattung," 238 n. 12.

In the northern part of the palaestra, residential houses of much later date were found; see R. Heberdey, "Vorläufiger Bericht über die Grabungen in Ephesus 1902/3," *ÖJh* 7 (1904) Beiblatt, 39, 43. In 2006, Andreas Pülz of the Austrian Academy of Science began to investigate this area of the palaestra in order to learn more about these structures with respect to the late antique city. See Ladstätter and Pülz, "Ephesus" (supra n. 3), 421 n. 10.

[9] For more information on these sculptures, see Manderscheid, *Skulpturenausstattung*, 86–88 cat. nos. 155–72, pls. 25–26; Aurenhammer, *Idealplastik*, 30 cat. no. 7, pls. 6–7; 59 cat. no. 36, pl. 26b–c; 70 cat. no. 50; 149–52 cat. no. 132, pl. 91a–c; 178–81 cat. no. 148, pls. 110–15. For the sculptural decoration of the Harbor Baths in late antiquity, see Auinger and Rathmayr, "Spätantike Statuenausstattung," 238–40.

[10] The sculptural decoration of the Harbor Baths has not been studied. Without further excavation, it is not possible to draw any additional conclusions about the history of this building.

[11] For the Theater Gymnasium, see Scherrer, *Ephesus*, 162 no. 79; Alzinger, "Ephesos," 1611–13; Yegül, *Baths and Bathing*, 279–82, fig. 353. Concerning the function of the palaestra in late antiquity as the *Forum Theodosianum*, see P. Scherrer and E. Trinkl, *Die Tetragonos Agora in Ephesos. Grabungsergebnisse von archaischer bis in byzantinische Zeit—ein Überblick. Befunde und Funde Klassischer Zeit, Forschungen in Ephesos* XIII 2 (Vienna 2006) 11, 49.

[12] Generally see M. Steskal, "Bemerkungen zur Funktion der Palästren in den ephesischen Bad-Gymnasium-Komplexen," *ÖJh* 72 (2003) 237–39, esp. 231–32 nn. 21–22.

[13] See Scherrer, *Ephesus*, 74 no. 16; J. Keil, "XV. Vorläufiger Bericht über die Ausgrabungen in Ephesos," *ÖJh* 26 (1930) Beiblatt, 5–66, 29–31; Alzinger, "Ephesos," 1617–19; Auinger

informs us that Asklepios, the proconsul of Asia, commissioned a mosaic floor in the southern part of the building at the beginning of the fifth century.[14] In the course of excavation, 20 pieces of sculpture were recovered from the debris and walls (where they had been used as spolia).[15] Among these pieces is a late antique bust datable to the fifth or early sixth century.[16] While the body of the bust was found inside a latrine, the head was discovered in an adjacent room.[17] Another fragment belonging to the same bust was reused in a late antique wall in the Basilica-Stoa on the Upper Agora.[18] The presence of this bust would suggest that this complex was still in use until the beginning or middle of the sixth century.

The Varius Baths on the Curetes Street are smaller in scale than the other bath complexes (fig. 1, no. 4).[19] The first building phase dates to imperial times, and the building remained in use at least until the end of the fourth century. This date is established by an inscription that documents the renovation of the complex by Scholasticia, an affluent female citizen of Ephesus.[20] In the building a seated Antonine female statue was found, refashioned as an image of Scholasticia.[21]

Recent research on the sculptural decoration of the baths in Ephesus has greatly enhanced our knowledge of these structures.[22] The next two bath complexes to be discussed, the Vedius and the East Gymnasia (fig. 1, nos. 5–6), were both originally excavated in the late 1920s, and they have yielded the richest sculptural artifacts. The sculptural decor of the Vedius Gymnasium is especially striking.[23]

and Rathmayr, "Spätantike Statuenausstattung," 240 n. 29. About a predecessor: H. Thür, "Das Gymnasion an der oberen Agora in Ephesos," in E. Christof, G. Koiner, M. Lehner, and E. Pochmarski (eds.), *ΠΟΤΝΙΑ ΘΗΡΩΝ. Festschrift für Gerda Schwarz zum 65. Geburtstag* (Vienna 2007) 406–7; ead., "Wie römisch ist der sog. Staatsmarkt in Ephesos?" in M. Meyer (ed.), *Neue Zeiten—Neue Sitten. Zu Rezeption und Integration römischen und italischen Kulturguts in Kleinasien, Wiener Forschungen zur Archäologie* 12 (Vienna 2007) 79–81.

[14] V. Scheibelreiter, *Stifterinschriften auf Mosaiken Westkleinasien, Tyche* Suppl. 5 (Vienna 2006) 36–37 cat. no. 7.

[15] I thank Maria Aurenhammer for information on the excavations of this bath. For the male mythological sculpture, see Aurenhammer, *Idealplastik*, 132–33 cat. no. 109, pl. 76b–c, and for the portrait sculptures, see Aurenhammer's article in this volume.

[16] For the late antique bust (Selçuk, Efes Müzesi inv. no. 2034) see H. Vetters, "Ephesos," *ÖJh* 49 (1968–1971) Grabungen 1969, 9, fig. 2; J. İnan and E. Alföldi-Rosenbaum, *Römische und frühbyzantinische Porträtplastik aus der Türkei. Neue Funde* (Mainz 1979) 189–90 cat. no. 156, pl. 267; H.R. Goette, *Studien zu römischen Togadarstellungen* (Mainz 1990) 70, 147 cat. no. E 16, 156 cat. no. L 79; *ÖJh* 68 (1999) 35–36, fig. 16 (Jahresbericht 1998, 3, Skulpturen von Ephesos).

[17] Auinger and Rathmayr, "Spätantike Statuenausstattung," 240 n. 32.

[18] Concerning the circumstances of the findspot, see Aurenhammer's article in this volume.

[19] The Varius Baths are also known as the Baths of Scholasticia. See Scherrer, *Ephesus*, 120 no. 41; Alzinger, "Ephesos," 1619–20; Yegül, *Baths and Bathing*, 288–91, figs. 371–72; recently: Auinger and Rathmayr, "Spätantike Statuenausstattung," 241–42.

[20] *IEph* 453; F. Miltner, "XXI. Vorläufiger Bericht über die Ausgrabungen in Ephesos," *ÖJh* 43 (1956–1958) Beiblatt, 23–24.

[21] V.M. Strocka, "Zuviel Ehre für Scholastikia," in M. Kandler, S. Karwiese, and R. Pillinger (eds.), *Lebendige Altertumswissenschaft. Festgabe zur Vollendung des 70. Lebensjahres von Hermann Vetters* (Vienna 1985) 229–32.

[22] For the sculptural decoration, see Manderscheid, *Skulpturenausstattung*, 88–91 cat. nos. 173–91, pls. 26–28; J. Auinger, "Ein Büstenkronenfragment aus Ephesos," in B. Asamer and W. Wohlmayr (eds.), *Akten des 9. Österreichischen Archäologentages am Institut für Klassische Archäologie der Paris-Lodron-Universität Salzburg 2001* (Vienna 2003) 15–19; ead., "Zu dem Neufund eines spätantiken Porträtfragments aus Ephesos. Ein Nachtrag," *ÖJh* 73 (2004) 11–14; Auinger, *Skulpturenausstattung*; F. Slavazzi, "Il ciclo di rilievi nella 'Kaisersaal' del Ginnasio di Vedio a Efeso," in I. Colpo, I. Favaretto, and F. Chedini (eds.), *Iconografia 2005. Immagini e immaginari dell'antichità classica al mondo moderno* (Rome 2006) 235–43; P. Barresi, "Il sofista Flavio Damiano di Efeso e la costruzione di terme-ginnasi nell'Asia Minore romana di età imperiale," in O.D. Cordovana and M. Galli (eds.), *Arte e memoria culturale nell'età della Seconda Sofistica* (Cantania 2007) 137–51; F. Slavazzi, "Uso dei modelli e recupero del passato nei programmi scultorei ufficiali di età antonina in Asia Minore," in Cordovana and Galli (eds.), *Arte e memoria* (supra this note), 123–36; Auinger and Rathmayr, "Spätantike Statuenausstattung."

[23] For more information on the building, see Scherrer, *Ephesus*, 168–70 no. 106; Alzinger, "Ephesos," 1615–17; Yegül, *Baths and Bathing*, 282–84, fig. 359; Steskal and La Torre, *Vediusgymnasium*.

Fig. 2. Vedius Gymnasium, after the excavation of the "Kaisersaal" in 1927 (Österreichisches Archäologisches Institut).

Evidence obtained from the new excavations and from documentation in the archive has allowed us to reconstruct the statuary of this complex from the second to the fifth century.[24]

The Vedius Gymnasium

Situated in the northern part of the city (fig. 1, no. 5), the Vedius Gymnasium owes its name to the building inscription that cites M. Claudius P. Vedius Antoninus Phaedrus Sabinianus and his wife Flavia Papiana as the donors of the complex.[25] They dedicated the building with all its decoration to Artemis, Antoninus Pius, and the people of Ephesus. The building was completed in the middle of the second century.[26] In the Vedius Gymnasium, an exedra, the so-called Kaisersaal, which opens onto the palaestra, was lavishly decorated with statuary and reliefs.

This building was first excavated by Josef Keil from 1927 to 1929. He concentrated on the documentation of the ground plan and the identification of the function of the building.[27] The excavations started in the area of the "Kaisersaal," where most of the sculptural decoration was found (fig. 2).[28] Additional sculptures were discovered in the propylon, in the area south of the palaestra, and in the interior of the bath complex proper. Altogether, more than 60 statues and fragments of statues were

[24] Concerning the excavations and the dating, see Steskal and Ladstätter, "Baugeschichte"; Steskal and La Torre, *Vediusgymnasium*, 92–96.

[25] *IEph* 431; *IEph* 438.

[26] For a summary of the dating differences, see M. Steskal, "Zu den Stiftungen des M. Claudius P. Vedius Antoninus Phaedrus Sabinianus und ihrem Echo in Ephesos," *Tyche* 16 (2001) 182 n. 34 (with older literature) and Steskal and Ladstätter, "Baugeschichte," 241 n. 7.

[27] Keil, "XIII. Bericht," 20–45, figs. 11–31; Keil, "XIV. Bericht," 21–33, figs. 11–19; Keil, "XV. Bericht" (supra n. 13), Beiblatt, 17–20.

[28] For details of the excavation and sculpture of the "Kaisersaal," see Auinger and Rathmayr, "Spätantike Statuenausstattung," 243–44.

found in various places inside the building.[29] The well-preserved statues and reliefs were published in preliminary reports.[30]

From 2001 to 2006, the Vedius Gymnasium was again the focus of fieldwork in Ephesus. Analysis of the ceramics by Sabine Ladstätter has now established a secure chronology for the building.[31] Of particular interest is the evidence for a second phase of architectural decoration, dated to the beginning of the fifth century. This second phase saw the installation of a new opus sectile floor in the "Kaisersaal" as well as mosaics in certain rooms around the palaestra and inside the bath. At the end of the fifth century, the building ceased to be used and the decoration was partly robbed out. In the first half of the sixth century, the Vedius Gymnasium was damaged by fire, and the roof of the structure apparently collapsed in the second half of the sixth century.[32]

Fig. 3. Vedius Gymnasium, lifting of the river god from the north side of the natatio in 1928 (Österreichisches Archäologisches Institut).

In the case of the Vedius Gymnasium, the findspots of the statues supply us with valuable information on the transformation of the sculptural decoration of this building in late antiquity. Some of the statues were found in their original locations. For example, the two river gods, which fell from their bases in the north and south parts of the natatio, had remained undisturbed (fig. 3).[33] Inside the "Kaisersaal" many statues were found lying on the floor, very close to their original positions in the interior aedicular façade.[34] The remaining sculptural pieces from the Vedius Gymnasium were either reused as spolia, or found within the debris of the building. A good example of the former is a small, recently discovered torso of an Aphrodite of the Mazarin type.[35] The lower part of the body was reused in the fabric of a wall

[29] For discoveries before 1931, see Auinger, *Skulpturenausstattung.*

[30] Keil, "XIII. Bericht," 38–44, figs. 19–31; Keil, "XIV. Bericht," 21–25, figs. 13–15, 17–18.

[31] M. Steskal and M. La Torre, "Das Vediusgymnasium in Ephesos. Die Geschichte der archäologischen Erforschung des Vediusgymnasiums und seines Umfeldes," *ÖJh* 70 (2001) 221–44; Steskal and Ladstätter, "Baugeschichte"; S. Ladstätter, "Römische, spätantike und byzantinische Keramik," in Steskal and La Torre, *Vediusgymnasium*, 97–189.

[32] See Steskal and Ladstätter, "Baugeschichte"; Steskal and La Torre, *Vediusgymnasium*, 92–96.

[33] For the two statues mentioned below, only a selection of sources will be cited. For the river god from the north side (İstanbul, Arkeoloji Müzesi inv. no. 4281), see Keil, "XIV. Bericht," 29, fig. 18; Manderscheid, *Skulpturenausstattung*, 88 cat. no. 174, pl. 26; Aurenhammer, *Idealplastik*, 106–7 cat. no. 87, pl. 62a; Auinger, *Skulpturenausstattung*, 169–71 cat. no. V.I.4.1. For the river god from the south side (İzmir, Arkeoloji Müzesi 78), see Keil, "XIV. Bericht," 29, fig. 17; M. Bergmann, *Marc Aurel* (Frankfurt am Main 1978) 17–18, fig. 18; Manderscheid, *Skulpturenausstattung*, 88 cat. no. 173, pl. 26; Aurenhammer, *Idealplastik*, 105–6 cat. no. 86, pl. 61a–b; Auinger, *Skulpturenausstattung*, 171–73 cat. no. V.I.4.2.

[34] For more information on the statues from the "Kaisersaal," see Auinger and Rathmayr, "Spätantike Statuenausstattung," 243–44.

[35] The under-lifesize torso of the Aphrodite (Selçuk, Efes Müzesi inv. no. EVG 5/23/02) is mentioned in Auinger and Rathmayr, "Spätantike Statuenausstattung," 246 n. 80.

Fig. 4. Vedius Gymnasium, statue of Athena of the Giustiniani type (N. Gail, Österreichisches Archäologisches Institut).

in the northern part of the palaestra. The upper portion of the statue has not yet been found. Sculptures discovered in the debris include two slightly over-lifesize herms of Heracles and Hermes and a bath towel of a Cnidian Aphrodite, all found in the propylon.[36] In this same room, the excavators also unearthed the statue of an Athena of the Giustiniani type (fig. 4).[37] Her head, however, was found in a different part of the complex.[38] The findings in the propylon suggest that this was the area where dismantled objects from the gymnasium were stored, such as the statue of Athena or the towel of Aphrodite. This part of the building was poorly preserved, however, and almost nothing of the architecture has survived.

The majority of the sculptures found inside the bath building survive in fragments. Only a few statues are preserved nearly intact. Likewise, the architectural decoration is incomplete, and has obviously been redeployed in various ways, as suggested by a piece of column from the "Kaisersaal" which has been sawed down the middle.[39] The fragmentary nature of the sculptural finds as well as the missing architectural blocks in the

[36] For the Heracles herm (Selçuk, Efes Müzesi, no inventory number), see Keil, "XIV. Bericht," 21; Manderscheid, *Skulpturenausstattung*, 44, 89 cat. no. 179; Auinger, *Skulpturenausstattung*, 158–59 cat. no. V.I.2.1; Auinger and Rathmayr, "Spätantike Statuenausstattung," 246–47 nn. 82–83. For the Hermes herm (Selçuk, Efes Müzesi inv. no. 408), see Keil, "XIV. Bericht," 21; Manderscheid, *Skulpturenausstattung*, 90 cat. no. 188; Auinger, *Skulpturenausstattung*, 160–61 cat. no. V.I.2.2. For the bath towel of a Cnidian Aphrodite (İzmir, Arkeoloji Müzesi inv. no. 239), see Keil, "XIV. Bericht," 21; Manderscheid, *Skulpturenausstattung*, 89 cat. no. 177; Auinger, *Skulpturenausstattung*, 164–66 cat. no. V.I.2.5; Auinger and Rathmayr, "Spätantike Statuenausstattung," 246 n. 79.

[37] For the Athena Giustiniani (İzmir, Arkeoloji Müzesi inv. no. 11), see Keil, "XIV. Bericht," 22, figs. 13–14; Manderscheid, *Skulpturenausstattung*, 89 cat. no. 181, pl. 27; Atalay, *Gewandstatuen*, 18–19, 65–68 cat. no. 5, figs. 5–6; Auinger, *Skulpturenausstattung*, 163–64 cat. no. V.I.2.4; Auinger and Rathmayr, "Spätantike Statuenausstattung," 246 n. 78.

[38] The head was found in room VIII; see Steskal and La Torre, "Vediusgymnasium" (supra n. 31), 224, fig. 4.

[39] Steskal and La Torre, "Vediusgymnasium" (supra n. 31), 236 n. 64.

Vedius Gymnasium suggest that these pieces were taken away, either for reuse as spolia or for other unknown purposes. This is the case, for example, with the fragmentary remains of a Myronian Diskobolos from the "Kaisersaal," a copy of the so-called Aspasia, and an incomplete statue of Hestia.[40]

Fig. 5. Vedius Gymnasium, male head, reworked in the Tetrarchic period (N. Gail, Österreichisches Archäologisches Institut).

But when did the destruction of the sculptural decoration take place? From the investigations of Keil in the 1920s, we know that the building remained in use at least until the time of the Tetrarchy. A male head, produced in imperial times and reworked in this period, was found in the southern part of the ambulatio (fig. 5).[41] This head, probably of Antonine date, originally depicted a bearded man with long hair covering the upper part of the ears. During the reworking of the head, the beard was removed. Another late Roman statue is an unpublished male figure wearing a himation, found in one of the palaestra halls.[42] The head, shoulders, and parts of the arms and hands are missing. This statue dates to ca. A.D. 300, suggesting that the building was still in use at that time.

Excavations in the "Kaisersaal" in 2003 and 2004 were of great importance for research on the sculpture.[43] During routine cleaning, a fragment of a face came to light, which led to further

[40] For the Myronian Diskobolos (İzmir, Arkeoloji Müzesi inv. no. 473), see Keil, "XIII. Bericht," 40 no. 7, fig. 26; Manderscheid, *Skulpturenausstattung*, 45, 90 cat. no. 189, pl. 28; Aurenhammer, *Idealplastik*, 156 cat. no. 138, pl. 95; Auinger, *Skulpturenausstattung*, 148–49 cat. no. V.I.1.1.; Auinger and Rathmayr, "Spätantike Statuenausstattung," 244 n. 63.

For the head of the so-called Aspasia (İzmir, Arkeoloji Müzesi inv. no. 535), see Keil, "XIII. Bericht," 40 no. 6, fig. 25; Manderscheid, *Skulpturenausstattung*, 90–91 cat. no. 183, pl. 27; Atalay, *Gewandstatuen*, 17–18, 61–65 cat. no. 4, fig. 4; Auinger, *Skulpturenausstattung*, 153–54 cat. no. V.I.1.5.

For the statue of Hestia Giustiniani (İzmir, Arkeoloji Müzesi inv. no. 41), see Keil, "XIII. Bericht," 40 no. 5, fig. 23; Manderscheid, *Skulpturenausstattung*, 89–90 cat. no. 182, pl. 27; R. Tölle-Kastenbein, *Frühklassische Peplosfiguren. Typen und Repliken, Antike Plastik* 20 (Berlin 1986) 13, 33–41 no. 51b, pls. 39–41, figs. 31–34; Atalay, *Gewandstatuen*, 16–17, 59–61 cat. no. 3, fig. 3; Auinger, *Skulpturenausstattung*, 155–57 cat. no. V.I.1.6.; Auinger and Rathmayr, "Spätantike Statuenausstattung," 243 n. 58.

[41] For the male portrait head reworked in the age of the Tetrarchy (İzmir, Arkeoloji Müzesi inv. no. 556), see Keil, "XIV. Bericht," 25, 29, fig. 15; J. İnan and E. Rosenbaum, *Roman and Early Byzantine Portrait Sculpture in Asia Minor* (London 1966) 144 cat. no. 182, pl. 106.3–4; Manderscheid, *Skulpturenausstattung*, 12–13, 90 cat. no. 184, pl. 27; Auinger, *Neufund* (supra n. 22), 12 n. 6; Auinger, *Skulpturenausstattung*, 135–38 cat. no. V.P.3.1.

[42] For the torso of the *himation* statue (İzmir, Arkeoloji Müzesi inv. no. 75), see K. Polaschek, *Untersuchungen zu griechischen Mantelstatuen. Der Himationtypus mit Armschlinge* (Berlin 1969) 137, 163–64, pl. 65; Auinger, "Neufund" (supra n. 22), 12 n. 6; Auinger, *Skulpturenausstattung*, 146–47 cat. no. V.P.11.1.

[43] Steskal and Ladstätter, "Baugeschichte," 242–43; Auinger and Rathmayr, "Spätantike Statuenausstattung," 245–46; F. Krinzinger, "Ephesos," in W. Radt (ed.), *Stadtgrabungen und Stadtforschung im westlichen Kleinasien—Geplantes und Erreichtes*, *Byzas* 3 (2006) 97, fig. 12; Steskal and La Torre, *Vediusgymnasium*, 86–87.

archaeological investigations.[44] Study of the stratigraphy yielded more information on the opus sectile floor of the "Kaisersaal." Apparently, it had already been damaged in antiquity and was repaired at the beginning of the fifth century. The repair was undertaken in the following manner: in the area of the sunken parts of the original floor, a leveling stratum was deposited. Included in this stratigraphic unit were numerous small fragments of smashed sculpture consisting of pieces of plinths, limbs, and faces. Fragments of supports, attributes, and reliefs were also used. On top of this layer, the new floor was laid.

The material and workmanship of these fragments are internally consistent with each other. Very likely, they belonged to the original program of the building. Evidence supporting this hypothesis includes fragments of the fringe of the bath towel of the Aphrodite from the propylon.[45]

A minor sensation was the discovery of a miniature torso of a seated sphinx among the hundreds of scattered fragments from the "Kaisersaal." Upon closer examination, this seated sphinx proved in fact to belong to the helmet decoration of the Athena Giustiniani (fig. 4) found in the propylon.[46] This evidence shows that the statue of Athena was no longer part of the sculptural decoration of the building in the fifth century.

What else do these details tell us about the history of sculptural decoration, and what more can we learn from the findspots of these fragments? It is clear from the recent excavations that the findspots of the sculptures discovered in the 1920s cannot necessarily be used to reconstruct the layout of the original sculptural program, but only its last, late antique phase. Reconstruction of the second-century phase of the decoration will be possible only upon completion of a thorough study of the sculptural finds discovered under the late antique floor in the "Kaisersaal" in conjunction with the finds from the original excavations.

Analysis of the roughly 300 fragments found underneath the floor has led to the identification and reconstruction of a number of statues. Among the more important fragments are the plinths of at least 14 statues, most of them with naked feet (fig. 6). Other outstanding pieces include the fragments of a colossal Heracles with a lion skin hanging over his left forearm (fig. 7), and the face of another Heracles of the Landsdowne type.[47] Olympian gods were also present in the assembly, as seen in a small fragment of the head of Dionysus and parts of the neck and the head of a panther, which could also belong to a Dionysian group.[48] In addition to the towel fragments noted above, fragments of the forearms of a female figure probably belong to the copy of the Cnidian Aphrodite whose bath towel was found inside the propylon.[49] Fragments of snakes could have been parts of a statue of Athena, Hygieia, or Asklepios. Surprisingly, no portrait sculpture has been identified.

Above the floor, by contrast, mythological sculptures are mixed with portrait images, raising the question whether the display of sculptures extant at the time of the destruction of the building

[44] A small trench was dug in the northwestern corner of the "Kaisersaal" in which 174 smashed fragments of sculpture were found. In the summer of 2004, the whole room was excavated, yielding an additional 179 fragments of sculpture.

[45] This fringe fragment (Selçuk, Efes Müzesi inv. no. EVG 06/03) is unpublished.

[46] For the sphinx fragment (Selçuk, Efes Müzesi inv. no. EVG 05/03), see Auinger and Rathmayr, "Spätantike Statuenausstattung," 245–46 n. 77, figs. 2–3. For the statue of Athena Giustiniani (İzmir, Arkeoloji Müzesi inv. no. 11), see Keil, "XIV. Bericht," 22, figs. 13–14; Manderscheid, *Skulpturenausstattung*, 89 cat. no. 181. pl. 27; Atalay, *Gewandstatuen*, 18–19, 65–68 cat. no. 5, figs. 5–6; Auinger, *Skulpturenausstattung*, 163–64 cat. no. V.I.2.4.; Auinger and Rathmayr, "Spätantike Statuenausstattung," 246 n. 78.

[47] For the colossal Heracles, see J. Auinger, "Kaisersaal versus 'Kaisersaal.' Zur Funktion der 'Kaisersäle' in ephesischen Thermen," *JRA* (forthcoming), figs. 1–6. The Landsdowne-type Heracles (Selçuk, Efes Müzesi inv. no. EVG 56/03) is unpublished.

[48] The fragment of a head of Dionysus (Selçuk, Efes Müzesi inv. no. EVG 49/03) and the fragment of the neck of a panther (Selçuk, Efes Müzesi inv. no. EVG 30/03) are unpublished.

[49] The forearms of an Aphrodite (Selçuk, Efes Müzesi inv. no. EVG 41/03, 143/03 and EVG 140/03, 02/04) are unpublished.

Fig. 6. Vedius Gymnasium, fragment of a plinth with part of naked toes (N. Gail, Österreichisches Archäologisches Institut).

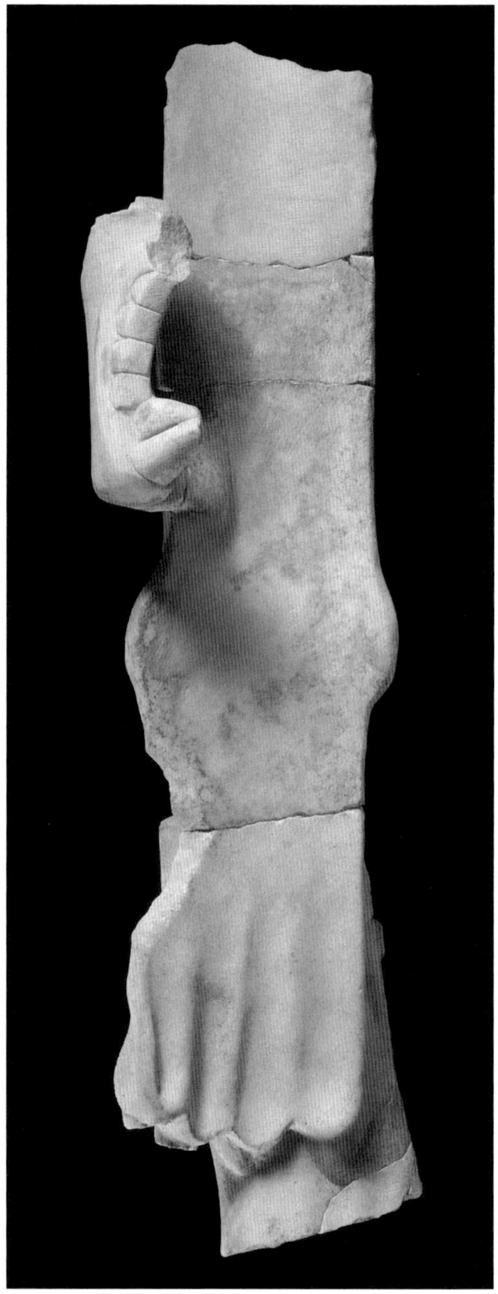

Fig. 7. Vedius Gymnasium, fragment of a lion skin (N. Gail, Österreichisches Archäologisches Institut).

followed a specific program, or was just a more or less arbitrary assemblage of earlier figures. While it is not possible on present evidence to provide definitive explanations for why the fragments of some statues were buried underneath the floor and others remained in use, some possibilities can be suggested.

One possible scenario is that an earthquake caused the demolition of the decoration.[50] This would explain the destruction of the statues buried beneath the pavement, but there are no traces of damage or repair to the sculptures that apparently remained on display. Another possibility could be related to the phenomenon that affected not only Ephesus but many parts of the Roman empire during the rise of Christianity. It was a common practice for nude statues to be destroyed.[51] No Aphrodite in the whole building survived in the fifth century, and the pubic areas of male statues were destroyed. It is also conceivable that gods with pagan attributes had to be removed.

The East Gymnasium

The situation of the East Gymnasium in the southeastern part of the city (fig. 1, no. 6) is closely comparable with that of the Vedius Gymnasium.[52] Located near

[50] For the earthquake theory, see Steskal and Ladstätter, "Baugeschichte," 243.

[51] For the removal of the pubic hair and the complete destruction of the genitalia of statues in Ephesus belonging to bath buildings or nymphaea, see Auinger and Rathmayr, "Spätantike Statuenausstattung," esp. 255 n. 153.

[52] For the building itself, see Scherrer, *Ephesus*, 70–71 no. 12; Alzinger, "Ephesos," 1613–15; Yegül, *Baths and Bathing*, 279–82, figs. 351–52.

Fig. 8. East Gymnasium, after the excavation of the "Kaisersaal" in 1930 (Österreichisches Archäologisches Institut).

the Magnesian Gate, the East Gymnasium is a bath-gymnasium complex very similar in layout to the Vedius Gymnasium. The building was excavated in 1930 and 1931 by J. Keil and Franz Miltner (fig. 8), and has only been cursorily published.[53] The bath complex proper probably dates to the Hadrianic era.[54] The palaestra with adjoining rooms is a later addition, probably commissioned by the same Vedius Antoninus who was the donor of the Vedius Gymnasium. This addition included another lavishly decorated "Kaisersaal," which opens onto the palaestra. Its design closely follows its counterpart in the Vedius Gymnasium.

The sculptural decoration of the "Kaisersaal" of the East Gymnasium is well preserved.[55] So far, however, sculptural finds have been discovered only in the "Kaisersaal" and the propylon; no sculpture has yet been found in the bath complex proper. Very little is known about the chronology of this complex, but it is clear that it was still in use in late antiquity, although its function had changed significantly.

Around the fifth century, a church was built inside the East Gymnasium southeast of the palaestra.[56] Another late Roman modification is a mosaic floor covering the propylon, datable by its decorative scheme to the fourth and fifth centuries.[57] In addition, pillars were erected in the ambulatio to buttress

[53] For sculpture from the East Gymnasium, see Keil, "XVI. Bericht," 25–51, figs. 16–35; J. Keil, "XVII. Vorläufiger Bericht über die Ausgrabungen in Ephesos," *ÖJh* 28 (1933) 11 with fig. 4; Manderscheid, *Skulpturenausstattung*, 91–93 cat. nos. 192–206, pls. 28–30.

[54] Alzinger, "Ephesos," 1615 (middle of the second century A.D.); Steskal, "Bemerkungen" (supra n. 12), 237–39.

[55] Since 2006, the architecture of the "Kaisersaal" and propylon have been studied by A. Leung.

[56] Auinger and Rathmayr, "Spätantike Statuenausstattung," 242 n. 50 (with older literature).

[57] Franz Miltner and Josef Keil found some parts of it, but the greater part remained unearthed. During cleaning while lifting the columns, a mosaic floor came to light. For the preliminary dating of the mosaic floor I offer thanks to Veronika Scheibelreiter at the Austrian Academy of Science.

the outer walls of the bath. Although it is not entirely clear when these pillars were constructed, the masonry suggests a late antique date.

The latest piece of sculpture from the building is datable to the beginning of the third century. The mid-imperial decoration of the "Kaisersaal" includes portrait sculptures and images of goddesses such as Aphrodite, Demeter, and Tyche.[58] Portraits of the donors of the building were found in front of the north and south sides of the "Kaisersaal."[59] In front of the middle niche, a male head, probably depicting Asklepios, was recovered.[60] His body as well as the heads of the goddesses are missing. In addition, a good number of the architectural blocks have been removed. Nevertheless, it seems that many of the fallen statues in the "Kaisersaal" were found not far from their original positions.[61] Unlike the more secure chronology of the Vedius Gymnasium, it is not known how long the "Kaisersaal" in the East Gymnasium was in use. The only good clue is a partly preserved opus sectile floor, which exhibits a technique and design similar to that of the fifth-century floor in the Vedius Gymnasium.[62]

The statues found in the propylon are programmatically different from those in the "Kaisersaal." Inside the propylon, the following statues were discovered: a torso of an Aphrodite, two under-lifesize heads of Pan and Dionysos, and, in or very near the propylon, the fragmentary remains of two barbarians.[63] Barbarians are not typical subjects for the decoration of gymnasia in general, and they do

[58] For the statue of Aphrodite (İzmir, Arkeoloji Müzesi inv. no. 646), see Keil, "XVI. Bericht," 49–50 no. 14, figs. 34–35; Manderscheid, *Skulpturenausstattung*, 91 cat. no. 196, pl. 29; Atalay, *Gewandstatuen*, 29–30, 84–86, cat. no. 20, figs. 47–49; Auinger, *Skulpturenausstattung*, 220–22 cat. no. O.I.1.4. For the statue of Demeter (İzmir, Arkeoloji Müzesi inv. no. 645), see Keil, "XVI. Bericht," 46–47 no. 10, fig. 29; Manderscheid, *Skulpturenausstattung*, 92 cat. no. 199, pl. 29; Atalay, *Gewandstatuen*, 33–34, 89–91 cat. no. 24, fig. 59; Auinger, *Skulpturenausstattung*, 218–20 cat. no. O.I.1.3. For the statue of Tyche (İzmir, Arkeoloji Müzesi inv. no. 647), see Keil, "XVI. Bericht," 48–49 no. 13, fig. 31; Manderscheid, *Skulpturenausstattung*, 92 cat. no. 198, pl. 29; Atalay, *Gewandstatuen*, 32–33, 56–57, cat. no. 23, fig. 58; A. Filges, *Standbilder jugendlicher Göttinnen. Klassische und frühhellenistische Gewandstatuen mit Brustwulst und ihre kaiserzeitliche Rezeption* (Cologne 1997) 123–26, 205, 227, 283 cat. no. 191; Auinger, *Skulpturenausstattung*, 222–23 cat. no. O.I.1.5.

[59] In the north side, a male portrait statue of the so-called Flavius Damianus was found (İzmir, Arkeoloji Müzesi inv. no. 648). See Keil, "XVI. Bericht," 40–41 no. 6, figs. 23, 25; İnan and Alföldi-Rosenbaum, *Porträtplastik* (supra n. 16), 128 cat. no. 151, pls. 83.4, 87.1–2; Manderscheid, *Skulpturenausstattung*, 26–27, 34–35, 37, 92 cat. no. 200, pl. 29; S. Dillon, "The portraits of a civic benefactor of 2nd century Ephesos," *JRA* 9 (1996) 261–74; K. Fittschen, *Prinzenbildnisse antoninischer Zeit* (Mainz 1999) 105–6; J. Rumscheid, *Kranz und Krone. Zu Insignien, Siegespreisen und Ehrenzeichen der römischen Kaiserzeit* (Tübingen 2000) 7 n. 50, 8 n. 52, 34–36, 41 with n. 23, 44, 48–49, 123–24, 143–44 cat. no. 19, pls. 5.2, 9–10; Auinger, *Skulpturenausstattung*, 200–3 cat. no. O.P.1.1.

On the opposite side, a female seated portrait statue was found (Selçuk, Efes Müzesi inv. no. 98); see Keil, "XVI. Bericht," 41–43 no. 7, fig. 2; Manderscheid, *Skulpturenausstattung*, 92 cat. no. 201, pl. 29; Atalay, *Gewandstatuen*, 54–55, 111–12 cat. no. 53, figs. 103, 105; L. Koch, *Weibliche Sitzstatuen der Klassik und des Hellenismus und ihre kaiserzeitliche Rezeption. Die bekleideten Figuren* (Münster 1994) 166–70, 238 cat. no. 147, fig. 8; Auinger, *Skulpturenausstattung*, 203–6 cat. no. O.P.1.2.

[60] For the fragment of the head of a father god (Selçuk, Efes Müzesi inv. no. 2276), see Keil, "XVI. Bericht," 43–44 no. 8, fig. 26; Manderscheid, *Skulpturenausstattung*, 52 n. 125, 93 cat. no. 206, pl. 30; Aurenhammer, *Idealplastik*, 137–38 cat. no. 115, pls. 81a–b, 82a–b; Auinger, *Skulpturenausstattung*, 214–16 cat. no. O.I.1.1.

[61] Therefore it is a relatively straightforward task to reconstruct the decoration. Much information is known from the diaries, unpublished manuscripts, and letters.

[62] For the opus sectile floor of the Vedius Gymnasium, see V. Scheibelreiter, "Mosaik- und *opus-sectile*-Pavimente," in Steskal and La Torre, *Vediusgymnasium*, 259–75, at 263–68.

[63] For the torso of Aphrodite from the propylon (Selçuk, Efes Müzesi inv. no. 86), see Keil, "XVI. Bericht," 34–35 no. 1, figs. 16–17; Manderscheid, *Skulpturenausstattung*, 91 cat. no. 195, pl. 28; Auinger, *Skulpturenausstattung*, 230–31 cat. no. O.I.2.3. For the head of Pan (İzmir, Arkeoloji Müzesi inv. no. 673), see Keil, "XVI. Bericht," 30, 35–36 no. 2, figs. 18, 20; Manderscheid, *Skulpturenausstattung*, 91 cat. no. 194, pl. 28; Aurenhammer, *Idealplastik*, 81–82 cat. no. 60, pl. 42a–c; N. Marquardt, *Pan in der hellenistischen und kaiserzeitlichen Plastik* (Bonn 1995) 185 no. 8; Auinger, *Skulpturenausstattung*, 229–30 cat. no. O.I.2.2.

The findspot of one of them is unknown, except that it was in the immediate surroundings of the propylon. The other was found in front of the propylon. For the first barbarian (İzmir, Arkeoloji Müzesi inv. no. 5), see M. Falkener, *Ephesus, and the Temple of Diana* (London 1862) 87–88; Keil, "XVI.

not fit the specific contexts of either the propylon or the "Kaisersaal." Although both sculptures are of Severan date and are made of the same type of marble, they do not seem to have been originally produced as a pair or part of a group, for they differ greatly in style. It is possible that they were taken from another place and reassembled in the propylon in late antiquity.[64]

Conclusion

The statuary ensembles of the various Ephesian bath-gymnasia raise a variety of chronological and programmatic issues. A combination of epigraphic, stratigraphic, and architectural and sculptural evidence suggests that all the baths in Ephesus were still in use in late antiquity. With the exception of the Theater Gymnasium, large amounts of sculpture were recovered from every complex. In those bath buildings that featured a "Kaisersaal," sculptures were often concentrated in this room as well as in the propyla. This is not surprising in the case of the "Kaisersäle," which also had the richest architectural decoration in Roman imperial times. It is still unclear, on the other hand, whether or not the propyla were similarly decorated. It is possible that these were the places where sculptures were stored and subsequently transferred out of the buildings in late antiquity. One commonality among these complexes is the lack of sculpture in the actual bathing areas. The only exceptions are the two river gods mentioned above from the natatio of the Vedius Gymnasium.

When confronting these problems, it is important to emphasize that the state of research varies greatly among these buildings. For this reason, questions concerning the transformation of their sculptural decoration in late antiquity cannot be answered in the same way in every building. Furthermore, these complexes are located in different parts of the city, and they were not necessarily all abandoned or demolished at the same time.

Like the buildings, the decoration also underwent changes. In late antiquity, very few new sculptures were added to the original decoration; exceptions are the Tetrarchic sculptures from the Vedius Gymnasium.[65] Because of the large number of statues of the latest sculptural assemblages of the East and Vedius Gymnasia, it is very probable that they are more or less complete. The sculptural fragments used in the foundations of the late antique floor in the "Kaisersaal" of the same building also provide valuable evidence for the reconstruction of at least part of the original decorative program.

Bericht," 30, 37–38 no. 4, fig. 22; Aurenhammer, *Idealplastik*, 162 cat. no. 144, pls. 99a, 127a, 127c, 128a–b; Auinger, *Skulpturenausstattung*, 239–40 cat. no. O.I.6.1. For the second (Selçuk, Efes Müzesi inv. no. 372), see Keil, "XVI. Bericht," 30, 38–40 no. 5, fig. 21; Manderscheid, *Skulpturenausstattung*, 93 no. 205, pl. 30; Aurenhammer, *Idealplastik*, 163–64 no. 145, pls. 99b, 127b, 128c–d; Auinger, *Skulpturenausstattung*, 237–38 cat. no. O.I.5.1.

[64] The dispersion of sculpture in Ephesus can also be seen in a late antique statue whose parts were unearthed in the periphery of the East Gymnasium. In 1958, a plinth of a togatus appeared, which eventually turned out to belong to a torso which Rudolf Heberdey discovered on the Marble Street in 1908. For the togatus, see J. Kollwitz, *Oströmische Plastik der theodosianischen Zeit* (Berlin 1941) 86–87, 105–6 no. 7, pls. 24–25; Goette, *Togadarstellungen* (supra n. 16), 147 cat. no. E 11.

[65] This can also been observed at the public fountains in Ephesus; see Auinger and Rathmayr, "Spätantike Statuenausstattung."

5 The Town Center of Miletus from Roman Imperial Times to Late Antiquity

Ortwin Dally, Martin Maischberger, Peter I. Schneider, and Andreas Scholl

Miletus was one of the most important cities in Asia Minor.[1] Already inhabited in the Bronze Age, it became one of the largest cities of the Greek world in the archaic period, and although destroyed by the Persians in the early fifth century B.C., it regained an economic wealth and splendor that lasted until early Byzantine times (fig. 1). In the Hellenistic and Roman periods, benefactors and donors adorned Miletus, like other cities in Asia Minor, with many beautiful buildings and monuments.

Historical Overview

The following overview of the literary and epigraphic evidence for the history of Miletus in later imperial times and in late antiquity until the Byzantine period may give a useful framework for the understanding of the monuments discussed below:

Second century	An earthquake in Miletus is attested in an inscription (*Milet* VI 1, no. 195). Five fragments of a single document found in 1902–1912 and in 1997 in the North Market, to the west of the Delphinion, in the "Justinianic Wall" near the northwest corner of the South Market, on the South Market itself, and in the Selçuk *tekke* refer to: [*Mil*]*esior/um quae* (…) [*terrae m*]*otu deciderunt* (…). ("Of the Milesians who … died in the earthquake …") This may be the same as the major earthquake that occurred during the reign of Antoninus Pius (A.D. 138–161) in Lycia, Caria, and on the islands of the Dodecanese (Pausanias 8.43.4).

[1] The following abbreviations are used in this article:
Dally et al., *ZeitRäume* = O. Dally et al. (eds.), *ZeitRäume. Milet in Kaiserzeit und Spätantike*, Catalogue of the exhibition in Berlin 2009–2010 (Regensburg 2009).
Milet I 5 = J. Hülsen, *Milet* I 5. *Das Nymphäum* (Berlin 1919).
Milet I 7 = H. Knackfuß, *Milet* I 7. *Der Südmarkt und die benachbarten Bauanlagen* (Berlin 1924) 69–151.
Milet I 9 = A. von Gerkan and F. Krischen, *Milet* I 9. *Thermen und Palaestren* (Berlin 1928).
Milet II 1 = A. von Gerkan, *Milet* II 1. *Das Stadion* (Berlin 1921).
Milet V 2 = R. Bol et al., *Milet* V 2. *Marmorskulpturen der römischen Kaiserzeit aus Milet—Aufstellungskontext und programmatische Aussage* (Berlin and New York 2011).
Milet VI 1 = A. Rehm, H. Dessau, and P. Herrmann, *Milet* VI. *Inschriften von Milet.* Teil 1. *A. Inschriften n. 187–406. B. Nachträge und Übersetzungen zu den Inschriften n. 1–406* (Berlin and New York 1997).
Milet VI 2 = P. Herrmann, *Milet* VI. *Inschriften von Milet.* Teil 2. *Inschriften n. 407–1019* (Berlin and New York 1998).
Milet VI 3 = P. Herrmann, W. Günther, and N. Ehrhardt, *Milet* VI. *Inschriften von Milet.* Teil 3. *Inschriften n. 1020–1580* (Berlin and New York 2006).
Pfanner et al., "Forschungen im Sumpf" = M. Pfanner et al., "Forschungen im Sumpf. Neue Untersuchungen zum Markttor und zur Agora in Milet," *Antike Welt* 36.2 (2005) 81–85.
Schneider, *Musengruppe* = C. Schneider, *Die Musengruppe von Milet. Milesische Forschungen* 1 (Mainz 1999).
Weber, "Stadtplan" = B.F. Weber, "Der Stadtplan des kaiserzeitlichen Milet," in L. Schwandner and K. Rheidt (eds.), *Macht der Architektur—Architektur der Macht, Diskussionen zur Archäologischen Bauforschung* 8 (Mainz 2004) 231–40.

Fig. 1. Plan of Miletus in late antiquity and the early Byzantine period (after Dally et al., *ZeitRäume*, inside front cover [J. Denkinger / C. von Bargen / M. Maischberger / I. Blum on the basis of B.F. Weber 2007]).

241–244 An inscription of Gordian III and his wife Tranquillina mentions work on the nymphaeum (*Milet* I 5, no. 2). This inscription has sometimes been interpreted as referring to the complete addition of the third story of the nymphaeum, but more likely concerns limited additions to the sculptural decoration in the basin.

262/263 During the reign of Gallienus (A.D. 253–268) the Goths invaded Asia Minor (Orosius 2.22.7; *Historia Augusta*, *Vita Gallieni* 6.2), leading to the destruction of the temple of Artemis at Ephesus.

	Didyma resists a siege (Festus-epigram n. 159 III [= *SEG* 4.467]: Σκυθικὸς πόλεμος). In Miletus, the Hellenistic city wall was strengthened with spolia ("Gothic Wall"), and probably at the same time, repairs on the Baths of Faustina were carried out by Makarios (*Milet* VI 1, no. 339).
305–363	Repairs or additions to the Sacred Way from Miletus to Didyma are attested by a milestone with inscriptions of the Tetrarchs, of Constantine I and his sons, and of Julian the Apostate (*Milet* VI 3, no. 1387 a–d).
ca. 343	A *vicarius Asiae* Skylakios provides for the building of embankments and channels in order to protect Miletus against flooding, as well as to improve the Milesian harbors in danger of silting up (25th Panegyric of Himerios to Skylakios).
361–363	An honorary inscription for Julian the Apostate is dedicated by the town of Miletus, the "*trophos* of Apollo Didymaios" (*Milet* VI 3, no. 1112).
362	Julian the Apostate orders the destruction of Christian chapels in Didyma, after the destruction by fire of the temple of Apollo at Daphne near Antioch, which occurred on 22 October 362 and was attributed to Christians (Sozomenos, *Historia ecclesiastica* 5.20.7).
ca. 362	Julian the Apostate makes reference to an oracular prophecy of Apollo Didymaios in a letter addressed to the ἡγεμὼν Καρίας (Iulianus, *Epistolae* 88, in B.K. Weis [ed.], *Julian: Briefe* [Munich 1973] 44).
360–378	Antonios Tatianos is *praeses Cariae* = ἡγεμὼν Καρίας under Julian the Apostate and Valens (C. Roueché, *Aphrodisias in Late Antiquity* [London 1989] 39–42 nos. 20–21). Probably he is identical with a Tatianos responsible for the renovation of the Baths of Faustina (*Milet* VI 1, no. 339: δικασπόλος and *Milet* VI 1, no. 340: ἰθυντήρ).
fourth century	The church of St. Michael is built above the former temple of Dionysus.
fourth/fifth century (?)	Hesychios, son of Hesychios, "friend of the powerful king," "orator of the prefects," renovates the Baths of Faustina after 100 years (*Milet* VI 1, nos. 341–343).
late fifth century	Vitianus, *clarissimus consularis Cariae* = λαμπρότατος ὑπατικὸς Καρίας (governor), provides for the building of dikes and embankments near the city "for the wanderers against the floods during winter" (*Milet* VI 3, no. 1129).
533	Flavius Marianus Michaelius Gabrielius Ioannes Eutropius is governor of Caria (*praeses Cariae* = ἡγεμὼν Καρίας).
533–565	Justinian issues a rescript after a dispute between inhabitants of Miletus and members of the provincial administration (*Milet* VI 3, no. 1575 a+b).
538	Justinian orders the construction of a gate in his 12th year, when Nonnos was governor (ὑπατικός) of Caria and Hyakinthos archbishop of Miletus (*Milet* VI 1, no. 206, from the Market Gate).
ca. 539–542	Justinian issues a rescript concerning the right of the church of St. Gabriel (the location of the church is unknown) to provide asylum. At this time, Hyakinthos was bishop of Miletus and Flavius Marianus Patricius was probably governor of Caria (*Milet* VI 3, no. 1576).
early 14th century	Miletus / τα Παλάτια is incorporated into the Selçuk Emirate of Aydın, later into the Menteşe of Milas.
1399	Miletus loses its episcopal see, which is transferred to Aphrodisias.

As in many other cities of Asia Minor, the number of public inscriptions decreases considerably after the third century. In addition, many of the late antique and early Christian inscriptions from Miletus are not well preserved and are known only in fragments.[2] Most earlier public building complexes must have remained in use in late antiquity, but in some cases with very different functions. For example, the Theater, built in the Hellenistic period and reworked during the imperial era, was converted into a castle in early or middle Byzantine times. An inscription on the west side of the northwest pillar of the cavea can be connected with this period. It is apparently an invocation of the archangels.[3]

Numerous statues must have been on display in the South Market until the third century. An official letter of the Roman emperor Macrinus is one of the latest documents preserved in this location.[4] A statue of Tyche was erected in the late fourth century or even later;[5] another inscription refers to the construction of a building in the fourth or fifth century.[6] One of the most important documents is a victory inscription: Nike tells Apollo that the Milesians were successful in defending their city. The inscription can be dated to the third century or later. It is presumably related to the attack of the Goths in A.D. 262/63, but it is not yet clear whether this inscription, which belonged to an unknown building, is a contemporary document of that period, or whether it was carved later, possibly in the fourth century. In the latter case, the inscription could be a replacement for an older inscription, possibly because the building to which it belonged had been restored.[7]

The history of the city after the fourth century is obscure, but we do know that the city must have had some importance at least until the sixth century. The church of St. Michael was built between A.D. 595 and A.D. 606, according to epigraphic sources,[8] and the cathedral and surrounding buildings were rebuilt at the same time. There is some evidence, although recently subject to scholarly debate, that during the rule of the emperor Justinian, the so-called Justinianic Wall was erected.[9] Only one quarter of the city was protected by this wall. The most important document referring to its construction is an inscription preserved in the Pergamon Museum in Berlin.[10]

As in other cities of Asia Minor, we find manifold traces of urban life in Miletus between the fourth and sixth centuries. A beautiful appearance for their city was obviously important to the inhabitants. In the following pages, we would like to demonstrate this by case studies of two buildings: first, the Market Gate, and second, the so-called Baths of Faustina. In the beginning of the 20th century, archaeologists and architects from Berlin excavated these buildings in the city center in the context of the excavations directed by Theodor Wiegand. New excavations took place between 2004 and 2006 in the Market Gate, and from 2006 onward in the Baths of Faustina. The latter project is directed by the Head Office of the German Archaeological Institute and by the Antikensammlung (Collection of Classical Antiquities) in Berlin. The current state of research and of our knowledge in general has recently been presented to the public in an exhibition in the Pergamon Museum entitled "ZeitRäume—Milet in Kaiserzeit und Spätantike" (6 May 2009–21 March 2010), with a homonymous catalogue.[11]

[2] Among the 1,180 inscriptions published in the last two volumes of the inscriptions of Miletus, *Milet* VI 2 and *Milet* VI 3, only 65 are classified as Christian and/or Byzantine. On the number and fragmentary preservation, see P. Herrmann in *Milet* VI 2, 137.

[3] *Milet* VI 2, no. 943, pls. 47.287, 50.304.

[4] *Milet* VI 1, no. 274, pl. 23.1.

[5] *Milet* VI 3, no. 1402, pl. 39.

[6] Ibid., no. 1403.

[7] Ibid., no. 1401, pl. 39.

[8] *Milet* VI 2, no. 1007, pl. 56.343.

[9] See recently P. Niewöhner, in Dally et al., *ZeitRäume*, 60–67; V. Kästner, in Dally et al., *ZeitRäume*, 204–11; and the contribution of P. Niewöhner in this volume.

[10] *Milet* VI 1, no. 206, pl. 16.1; S. Agelidis, in Dally et al., *ZeitRäume*, 186–87, cat. no. 14.

[11] Dally et al., *ZeitRäume*.

Fig. 2. Market Gate of Miletus, reconstruction in the Pergamon Museum in Berlin after completion of the first phase of the recent restoration and installation of the two colossal statues, April 2010 (J. Laurentius, Antikensammlung SMB, 2010).

The Market Gate and the City Center

The Market Gate in the city center was excavated between 1903 and 1905 by Wiegand and Hubert Knackfuß and is world famous for its 1:1 scale reconstruction in the Pergamon Museum in Berlin (fig. 2). An estimated 60 per cent of the building material included in this reconstruction is original (consisting of marble blocks from the quarries near Herakleia under Latmos); the remaining parts are restored in modern marble from Portugal (Estremoz), concrete, plaster, and bricks.[12] Three campaigns focusing on the foundation, "socle," and urban context of the gate were carried out at the initiative of the University of Leipzig (Michael Pfanner and Hans-Ulrich Cain) in 2004, 2005, and 2006; they were financed by the Fritz-Thyssen-Stiftung, and the results will be published in the near future.[13]

The city center is characterized by large public squares: the so-called North Market immediately adjacent to the Lion Harbor, the much larger South Market to the south of the Hellenistic Bouleuterion, and finally a space between the North Market, the Delphinion, the Baths of Capito, and the South Market, which has no archaeological nickname. The North Market and South Market were laid out in the Hellenistic period and were embellished in Roman imperial times by the addition

[12] For the modern history from excavation to reconstruction, see M. Maischberger, "Zwischen Sachzwang und Utopie. Zur Technik von Architekturrekonstruktionen im Museum: Das Markttor von Milet im Berliner Pergamonmuseum," in A. Dostert and F. Lang (eds.), *Mittel und Wege. Zur Bedeutung von Material und Technik in der Archäologie* (Möhnesee 2006) 275–96. For the recent restoration, see M. Maischberger, "Die Restaurierung des Markttors von Milet," in U. Peltz and O. Zorn (eds.), *kulturGUTerhalten. Restaurierung archäologischer Schätze an den Staatlichen Museen zu Berlin*. Catalogue of the exhibition in Berlin 2009 (Mainz 2009) 57–62; M. Maischberger and A. Hoffschildt, "Das Markttor von Milet im Pergamonmuseum. Zur Restaurierung einer musealen Architekturrekonstruktion," in U. Peltz and O. Zorn (eds.), *kulturGUTerhalten. Standards in der Restaurierungswissenschaft und Denkmalpflege*. Proceedings of a conference held in Berlin 2009 (Mainz 2009) 153–62.

[13] For preliminary reports, see Pfanner et al., "Forschungen im Sumpf"; H.-U. Cain and M. Pfanner, in Dally et al., *ZeitRäume*, 82–95.

Fig. 3. Marble statue of a cuirassed emperor with kneeling barbarian to his left (J. Laurentius, Antikensammlung SMB, 2009). Most probably, the statue stood in the tabernacle to the east (left) of the central gateway.

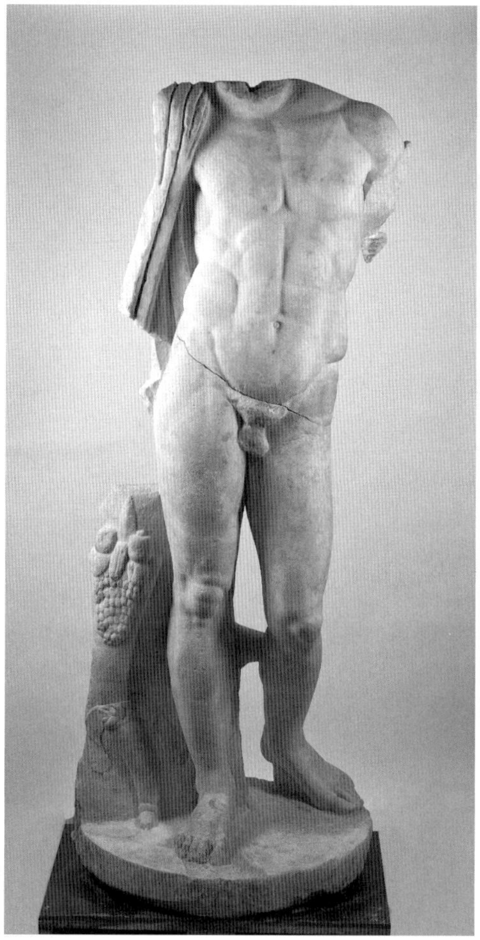

Fig. 4. Marble statue of a naked hero with cornucopia (J. Laurentius, Antikensammlung SMB, 2009). Most probably, the statue stood in the tabernacle to the west (right) of the central gateway.

of new colonnades, porticoes, and entrance buildings. There are reasonable grounds for supposing that the "anonymous" space between the two markets was the oldest agora of Miletus and also the agora proper in later times. Until late antiquity, the city paid a great deal of attention to monuments and altars related to its mythical and historical founders and other important personalities in this area. The southern boundary of the area is bordered by the propylon of the already mentioned bouleuterion, by the famous Market Gate, by the propylon of the late antique basilica, and by the monumental nymphaeum.

The goals of the field project dedicated to the Market Gate were:

1) To verify the reliability of the reconstruction in Berlin, by investigating the "socle," which has remained in situ, in connection with some peculiarities encountered in Berlin.
2) To examine the architectural evidence in situ closely, including searching for further architectural elements left on the site, and determining precisely what materials were used.
3) To investigate the urban context, which had never previously attracted sustained attention.

Fig. 5. The town center of Miletus as shown in the model in the Pergamon Museum in Berlin (1930/1968), with the nymphaeum, the Market Gate, and the bouleuterion in the center, view from the northwest (J. Laurentius, Antikensammlung SMB, 2009).

The building type displays the common features of Roman imperial monumental façades, which can be seen in many theater scaenae, nymphaea, gates, and other public buildings, particularly in Asia Minor: a two-storied structure with three passages in the lower story and corresponding niches in the upper parts, different orders (composite in the lower, Corinthian in the upper story), a richly decorated tabernacle architecture with triangular pediments (the central one being broken), and a garland frieze with *boukephalia*. Most probably, the monument was decorated with statues, two of which were found together with the architectural elements in the excavation debris and were acquired by the Berlin museum. It has recently been proposed that these statues were not placed in the upper story, as earlier research had assumed, but in the lower story, to the left and right of the central gateway.[14] The statues have now been placed in these positions for the first time in the monument's modern history. After many decades in the museum's storerooms, these two larger-than-life marble sculptures, representing a cuirassed emperor with kneeling female barbarian, and a naked hero (figs. 3–4), have been carefully restored and were permanently installed in the tabernacles in November 2009.

The gate served as a monumental entrance to the South Market, although it was placed well off its central axis, and although steps hindered the passage of vehicles. Together with the propylon of the Hellenistic bouleuterion (second century B.C.), the monumental Flavian nymphaeum, which was far more richly decorated with sculptures, and the early third-century propylon, which later served as the entrance to the great Christian basilica, it constituted a magnificent architectural prospect at the south end of the agora (fig. 5). Whether or not the annual ritual procession from the

[14] For consideration of a position on the upper story as an alternative, see V.M. Strocka, *Das Markttor von Milet. 128. Berliner Winckelmann-Programm* (Berlin 1981) 14; for the position on the lower story, see R. Bol in *Milet* V 2, 71; M. Maischberger, in Dally et al., *ZeitRäume*, 111–13; idem, "Zwei marmorne Kolosse. Zur Neuaufstellung der Skulpturen im Markttor von Milet," *Antike Welt* 41.3 (2010) 34–35.

sanctuary of Apollo Delphinios to the extra-urban sanctuary of Apollo Didymaios passed through the gate—the mere evidence of the steps and the narrowness of the openings seems to contradict this hypothesis—the building, together with the other monuments flanking the agora, constituted a splendid setting for this kind of solemn event.[15]

No building inscription or other epigraphic evidence on the monument gives any direct indication of either the building patron or the date of construction. An undated Roman imperial statue base, most probably of the second century, found in the South Market names a private citizen of Miletus who sponsored, among other things, the building of a tripylon (*Milet* VI 1, no. 261). If, as has been reasonably argued, this was the building under consideration, then it was apparently not an imperial commission. The common dating of the gate to the reign of Hadrian was proposed by Volker Michael Strocka on the basis of comparison with the architectural decoration of other monuments in Asia Minor.[16] New research conducted both in the context of the field activities in 2004–2006 as well as on the occasion of the Berlin 2009 exhibition has called this dating into question. The re-examination of the architectural decoration and of technical details, on the one hand, and more general reflections on the urban context and on the historical circumstances, on the other, suggest an earlier dating, ranging from Domitian[17] to Trajan.[18] Moreover, in our view, Strocka seems to be far too confident that the building was completed within a short span of time. There are many indications that the building process lasted much longer or, to be more accurate, that the building was never even fully completed. In the first place, the close examination of the architectural and sculptural decoration which was possible during the recent restoration (the whole gate was covered by scaffolding for many months, thus permitting investigations which had not been possible for decades) revealed a marked heterogeneity in the execution of details, such as the *boukephalia* of the upper frieze.[19] In the second place, a detailed analysis of the monument's "socle," which was left in situ by the excavators, shows clear traces of unfinished elements, for instance on the eastern steps and orthostats.[20] Finally, several architectural elements which were already known to Knackfuß prove that the gate underwent at least one or more restorations in imperial times and in late antiquity. Pillars with unusually shaped capitals were erected to support the lower story, most probably already in the late second or early third century.[21] Knackfuß had thought they dated to the late third or early fourth century, basing this hypothesis on comparison with the ornament of Milesian buildings then dated to the Tetrarchic period. However, all of the buildings mentioned by Knackfuß—the second Roman theater scaenae frons, the east propylon of the stadium, and the propylon between the nymphaeum and Market Gate—can now be dated to the Severan period, which appears to be one of the latest phases of prosperity and of important urban development in Miletus. To the buildings already mentioned, one may also add the palaestra of the Baths of Faustina, the Serapeion, and the so-called Heroon III.[22] Interestingly, the two colossal statues of the Market Gate were apparently left in their original positions and did not suffer any alteration, as happened in many other Roman buildings of

[15] Cain and Pfanner, in Dally et al., *ZeitRäume,* 84–92; Maischberger, in Dally et al., *ZeitRäume,* 109–11, 114.

[16] Strocka, *Markttor* (supra n. 14), 19–32. This dating was also accepted by R. Köster, *Milet* VII. *Die Bauornamentik von Milet.* Teil 1. *Die Bauornamentik der frühen und mittleren Kaiserzeit* (Berlin 2004).

[17] Cain and Pfanner, in Dally et al., *ZeitRäume,* 92–93.

[18] Maischberger, in Dally et al., *ZeitRäume,* 115–17.

[19] M. Pfanner et al., "Das Markttor von Milet. Die Sanierung der römischen Prachtfassade im Pergamonmuseum," *Jahrbuch der Stiftung Preußischer Kulturbesitz* 40 (2003) 183–96, esp. 190–93 with fig. 6.

[20] Pfanner et al., "Forschungen im Sumpf," 82–83 with figs. 3–4.

[21] *Milet* I 7, 151–54 with figs. 167–69; Strocka, *Markttor* (supra n. 14), 22, 45 with fig. 61; Maischberger, in Dally et al., *ZeitRäume,* 117 with figs. 17–18.

[22] Weber, "Stadtplan," 231–240; I. Blum and E. Altenhöfer, in Dally et al., *ZeitRäume,* 42–59.

Miletus such as the nymphaeum, the theater, and the Baths of Faustina. At least, the genitals of the naked hero seem not to have been completely chiseled off (see fig. 4).[23]

The insertion of the supporting pillars in the lower story could have been a response to an earthquake in the second half of the second century. Another possible explanation could be the fact that the surrounding soils were unstable, and therefore the monument was in danger of settling. In fact, measurements taken during the 2004 and 2005 campaigns showed that the Market Gate and the surrounding walls of the north portico of the South Market sank down considerably from west to east. Although it is not clear when exactly this settling occurred,[24] this evidence could explain another peculiarity of the monument that was perceived on the occasion of the restoration in Berlin. The sides of some of the blocks of the central pediment were cut back in modern times, presumably when the reconstruction in the museum was approaching completion in the month of April 1929, and the uppermost blocks proved to be too large to be inserted in the pediment. Apparently, the situation of the reconstructed monument in the museum, on level ground, differed from the situation in situ in Miletus, where the foundations were uneven. Possibly the settling of the foundations had already occurred by the time the builders were ready to put the pediment in place, and so the dimensions of the blocks were adapted to this irregularity.

Another very intriguing question concerns the urban context, both at the time the gate was built and in later periods. Fieldwork in 2005 revealed a clear axial connection with a small structure north of the gate. Small finds unearthed in a trench at the southwest corner of this structure suggest that it was an altar, dating at the latest to the Hellenistic period. Both the nature of the finds and the position of the structure support the idea that this was an important, if not the most important, cult place in the agora, which was preserved until the early sixth century, when its architectural elements were reused for paving the courtyard of the great Christian basilica in the corner between the nymphaeum and Market Gate.[25] The altar and its central position on the agora might explain more plausibly than any other theory proposed to date why the gate was not erected in the middle of the north portico of the South Market.

Finally, there are two particular features of the gate in its late antique phase that deserve mention. First is the part of the back wall of the north portico of the South Market immediately east of the Market Gate, the so-called Antiochos Wall. The survey and documentation of this wall undertaken during the campaigns of 2004 and 2005 clearly showed that it must have been completely rebuilt with reused blocks at some yet undetermined time. This may have happened in connection with the building of the basilica in the sixth century, suggesting a deliberate effort to imitate an older wall.[26] The second feature is the famous block with the inscription mentioning the emperor Justinian dated to the year A.D. 538 (*Milet* VI 1, no. 206), found behind the middle passage of the Market Gate. This inscription and its relation to the Market Gate has been and still is the subject of intense debate on the gate's transformation in later times, on the supposed defense walls, and on Miletus in the sixth century as a whole. The different views on the question are presented together in the "ZeitRäume" catalogue, where Volker Kästner supports the traditional view that the inscribed block belonged to

[23] A. Scholl, in Dally et al., *ZeitRäume,* 148–49; Agelidis, in Dally et al., *ZeitRäume,* 184–85 cat. no. 13; for a different view, see R. Bol in *Milet* V 2, 11.

[24] Pfanner et al., "Forschungen im Sumpf," 84–85 with fig. 8, suggest a slow process from the years 100 to 1000, while Gerhard Tuttahs thinks of an immediate effect during the building of the gate (information kindly given by telephone in 2008).

[25] Cain and Pfanner, in Dally et al., *ZeitRäume,* 84–95 with figs. 4.6.8–12. Philipp Niewöhner is currently working on this problem and will propose a different interpretation of it in the near future.

[26] Pfanner et al., "Forschungen im Sumpf," 84 with fig. 6; Cain and Pfanner, in Dally et al., *ZeitRäume,* 90–91.

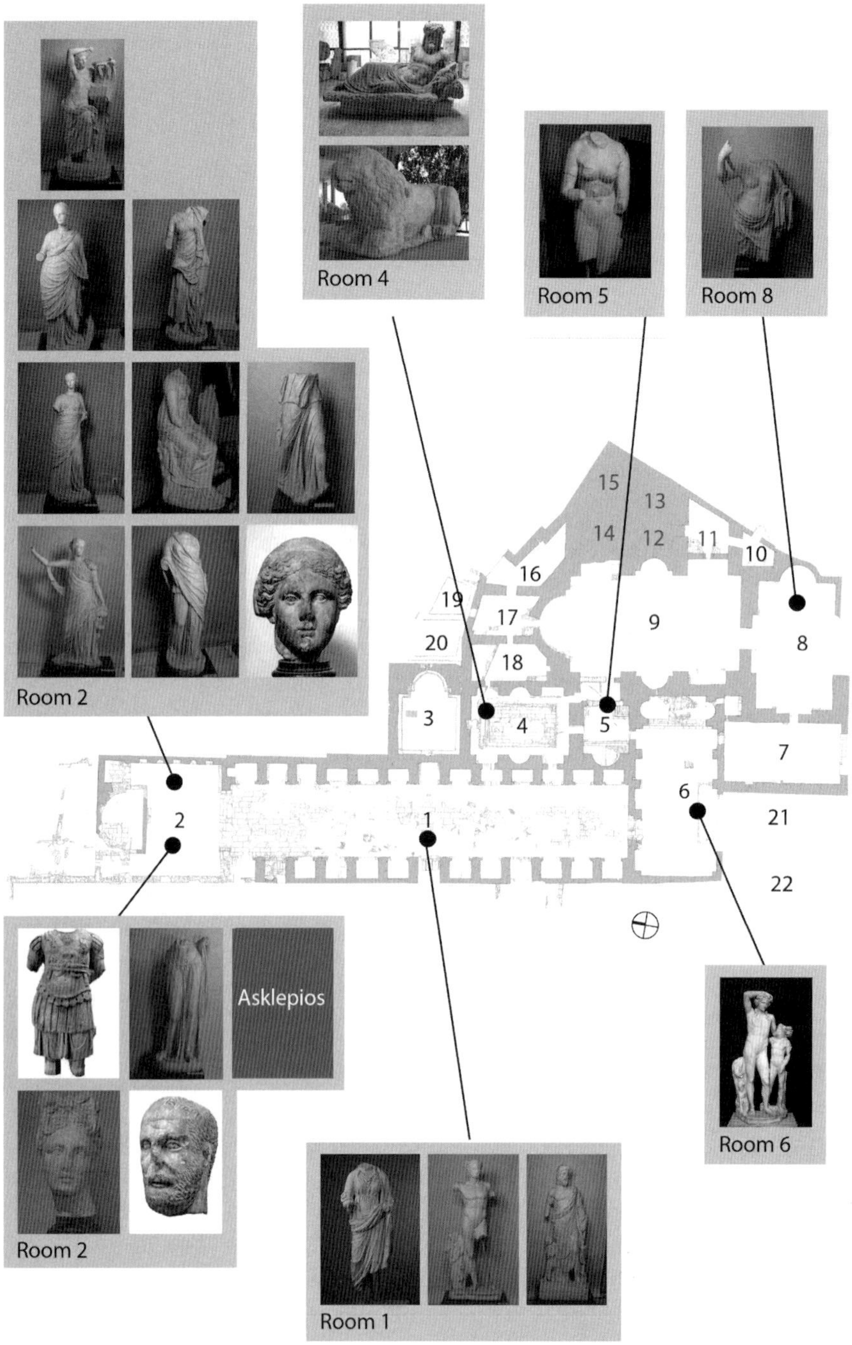

Fig. 6. Plan of the Baths of Faustina complex including the findspots of the sculptures. P. Schneider on the basis of the architectural survey of 2006–2007 and with photographs from the following sources: J. Laurentius 2008, Antikensammlung SMB (Dionysus and Satyr); Arbeitsstelle für Digitale Archäologie–Cologne Digital Archaeology Laboratory (formerly Forschungsarchiv für Antike Plastik [FA Köln]), Archäologisches Institut der Universität zu Köln, FA-SPerg002614-01 (torso of cuirassed emperor); FA Köln Foto Nr. FA-SPerg000095-03 (portrait head); Istanbul, Archaeological Mus. inv. no. 2328 (head of goddess). All other photographs by I. Geske (2006 and 2008).

the gate in the defense wall, thus dated to the time of Justinian, and Philipp Niewöhner argues for a more indirect relation between inscription and gate and therefore for a later dating of the walls.[27]

The Baths of Faustina

The Baths of Faustina complex was excavated in the years 1905–1910 under the direction of Wiegand and published in 1928 by Fritz Krischen.[28] The concept of the combined bath and gymnasium typical of the big thermae of Asia Minor is evident here; its basic components are a marble hall, a palaestra, an ambulacrum, and the massive bathing block (fig. 6). The complex of the Baths of Faustina is located along the strip of empty spaces, public squares, and buildings that connects the southern and northern quarters of Miletus (see fig. 1). In addition, the building is not aligned with the street grid but is instead oriented north-south.[29] Since 2006 the Baths of Faustina complex has been the object of new research on the transformation of Miletus in late antiquity. As noted above, the fieldwork begun in 2006 and still ongoing is part of a joint project of the Head Office of the German Archaeological Institute and the Antikensammlung in Berlin.[30] It started with the "Musensaal" (Hall of the Muses, Room 2) which had been partially studied a decade earlier by C. Schneider, whose research focused mainly on the room's sculptural furnishings.[31] As of the summer of 2008, cleaning and excavation had been restricted mainly to the western rooms of the complex. The heated rooms (Rooms 7–9) and the surrounding subsidiary spaces await archaeological re-evaluation in forthcoming campaigns.

The Baths of Faustina are believed to have been erected when Faustina Minor, the wife of the emperor Marcus Aurelius, visited Ephesus and Asia Minor in the 160s. An inscription consisting of four epigrams carved on the marble slabs of the doorframe between the Hall of the Muses and the ambulacrum[32] names the building "loutron Faustines" ("Bath of Faustina") (fig. 7). The inscription itself was carved much later than the time of Faustina. Makarios, an honorable Milesian who fought against the Goths and restored the Baths of Faustina, together with his wife Eucharia, must have commissioned at least three of the four epigrams. One of the epigrams names a Tatianos, whom A. Rehm identified with the *asiarch* Tatianos recorded for the fourth century. Another inscription on a column in the ambulacrum gives the name of the same Tatianos.[33] If an early dating of the three Makarios epigrams is assumed, then Tatianos must have added his epigram afterwards. The inscription thus gives evidence for three phases of construction or restoration. A fourth phase is then documented by the two inscriptions of Hesychios on the framing of the southern opening of the ambulacrum toward Room 6.[34] According to P. Hermann, Hesychios can be identified with

[27] Compare Kästner, in Dally et al., *ZeitRäume,* 204–11, and Niewöhner, in Dally et al., *ZeitRäume,* 60–67; also see the contribution of Niewöhner in this volume.

[28] *Milet* I 9, 50–93.

[29] According to one explanation, the building was shifted in orientation in order to maximize heat gain. According to another hypothesis, the departure from the grid was a consequence of the terrain on the southeast edge of the Theater Harbor. Respect for structures already extant in the vicinity of the building site might provide a third explanation. Georadar surveying beneath the marble floor of the ambulacrum (Room 1) revealed rectangular structures that follow the same orientation and probably antedate the erection of the complex. The true reason for the unique orientation within the imperial town remains an open question for further research.

[30] Funds were provided by the Gerda Henkel Stiftung and the Deutsche Forschungsgemeinschaft. For preliminary reports, see M. Maischberger, "Ad fontes! Die Berliner Antikensammlung und das Deutsche Archäologische Institut forschen wieder gemeinsam in Milet," *Antike Welt* 38.6 (2007) 33–35; idem, "Milet im Museum und Milet im Felde: Neues von der Restaurierung des Markttors und von den Grabungen in den Faustinathermen," *Jahrbuch der Stiftung Preußischer Kulturbesitz* 44 (2007) 237–51, at 246–51; for a more detailed account, see P. Schneider, in Dally et al., *ZeitRäume,* 120–41.

[31] Schneider, *Musengruppe;* compare also K.A. Neugebauer and T. Wiegand, in *Milet* I 9, 104–18 nos. 8–14 pls. 28–34.

[32] *Milet* VI 1, no. 339.

[33] Ibid., no. 340.

[34] *Milet* VI 3, nos. 341–42.

Fig. 7. Inscription of Makarios and Tatianos mentioning Faustina (I. Geske 2006).

an orator of the fourth/fifth century.[35] His inscriptions then mark a late restoration of the Baths of Faustina.

According to Krischen's description and interpretation of the building's history, the restorations that followed the initial construction did not alter the building significantly, but whatever changes did occur were for the worse! His attractive drawings purport to represent the original architectural concept, by omitting every chronological consideration, as the following observations show.

The first field campaigns demonstrated that the baths were used possibly until the seventh century. A significant number of sculptures were found by the early excavators in several rooms of the building. Most of them came to light in the so-called Hall of the Muses. The statues of Apollo and the Muses after which the hall is named did not necessarily belong to its first phase, although that is the view argued by Renate Bol.[36] Some of the sculptures exhibit traces of restorations. Most of the bases have been cut down, showing that at some point they were rearranged and adjusted for new and smaller positions. The architectural investigation of the building is still ongoing, and so we cannot yet deliver a detailed dating of the different building phases of the baths, but there is some evidence that the new arrangement should be dated not earlier than the second half of the fourth century.

Although statues are not mentioned explicitly in any of the inscriptions, they could have been transferred to the baths in the fourth century. Schneider argued that Tatianos had ordered their transport from an unknown location, because in the building inscription referring to Tatianos, nymphs are mentioned, which are possibly to be identified with the Muses.[37] A related monument is

[35] Ibid., nos. 340–43.

[36] *Milet* V 2, 81–83.

[37] Schneider, *Musengruppe*, 52.

Fig. 8. Gallery/ambulacrum in its actual state looking north toward the theater (P. Schneider 2008).

an inscription on a mosaic of the second or third century that features the heads of the Muses, which mentions a collegium of the *strategoi* and the financial support of the *bouleutai*.[38] It is interesting that the Muses were an important element in the decoration not only of the Baths of Faustina but also of another important private or public building.

There is also further new evidence for the understanding of the sculptures found in the bath building: the sculpture of a lion found in the large frigidarium (Room 4) bears a cross carved on his back. This is not an isolated case of sculptures altered by Christians at Miletus. Also noteworthy are the sculptures of the huge nymphaeum on the agora, which was constructed in A.D. 79/80.[39] The aediculae of the nymphaeum were adorned with numerous statues; fragments of some 30 are known. The old photographs taken by the German excavators show that the genitals of the male statues were very carefully removed with a fine chisel. Especially remarkable is the statue of a young satyr. In addition to genital mutilation, a cross is carved on the right side of his chest. This might indicate that the Christians were also responsible for the removal of the genitals. It is interesting to see that the agora and the Baths of Faustina remained important public building complexes, but that only a restricted number of statues were kept on display.

Ambulacrum (Room 1)

At the center of the complex is the broad gallery regarded as an ambulacrum by F. Yegül[40] and Schneider.[41] The long central hall is flanked by 13 small chambers at either side (fig. 8). The chambers, open

[38] *Milet* VI 3, no. 1400, pl. 38.

[39] *Milet* VI 1, 3–4; *Milet* I 5, 196; Maischberger, in Dally et al., *ZeitRäume*, 96–107.

[40] F. Yegül, *Baths and Bathing in Classical Antiquity* (New York 1992) 414–16.

[41] Schneider, *Musengruppe*, 57.

to the central hall and at a slightly higher floor level, may have been reserved for private entertainment.[42] Krischen reconstructed the hall as covered by a barrel vault with a gold mosaic, supported by plastered and painted walls.[43] The ends of the smaller walls delimiting the chambers featured pilasters with marble revetment and separately worked marble bases and capitals.[44] Only parts of the marble floor and scant traces of the marble revetment have been preserved. In contrast to the lavish original fittings, the plain walls, bare of any covering today, reveal the heterogeneous combination of spolia used in the original construction.

The room must also have been decorated with sculptures on pedestals, as is indicated, for example, by the discovery of a well-preserved statue of Asklepios (Istanbul, Archaeological Mus. inv. no. 1995 T).[45] This very interesting sculpture shows many traces of substantial reworking. Most of these traces were not noticed by earlier scholars, who were mainly interested, as was typical of the early 20th century, in identifying the Greek prototype behind this Roman invention. Many details, of which only some can be mentioned here, show that the original appearance of the statue was very different: 1) the mass of the hair behind the row of locks framing the face has been cut back and is worked in a very superficial manner; 2) the face is extremely flat, lacking any sculptural depth; 3) the upper edge of the chest was clearly recut in order to fit a head reduced in size by remodeling; 4) recutting of the right arm has made it smaller than the left arm; 5) the most remarkable intervention is the transformation of the original marble support on the right side of the sculpture, which was reworked into a figure of Telesphoros (it is clear that the upper part of the original statue support was removed directly beneath the arm); and 6) the slim wooden staff on the left side with the snake curling around it was most likely created out of a massive fold of the himation. No other known sculpture from the Baths of Faustina has been reinterpreted in such dramatic fashion as this figure of Asklepios.

The access to the gallery as the main connection between the palaestra, the outside, and the bathing block underwent considerable change. As there is no other main entrance known so far, the door leading from the stoa west of Rooms 1 and 6, hypothesized by Krischen,[46] to Chamber 4 (west) remains the only major entrance to the complex from the outside. Two other doors in Chambers 7 (west) and 12 (west) provided access from the palaestra, which had an entrance in its southeast corner. The door in Chamber 12 (west) was later closed; a dedicatory inscription to Apollo Didymaios was built into the blocking wall. In Chamber 4 (west) the floor was elevated, and the door opening was narrowed, as was shown by a sounding carried out in 2008. Only the opening of Chamber 7 (west) seems to have remained without any alteration, serving as the only entrance at a later date.

Hall of the Muses (Room 2) and Palaestra

At the north end of the ambulacrum, a broad arch opens onto another hall with an almost square plan. It ends in an apse on the same axis as the gallery (fig. 9). A trench dug in 2006 at the junction

[42] The reconstruction drawing of F. Krischen (*Milet* I 9, pl. 16) shows the floor of the chambers on the same level as the bases of the pilasters. Upon surveying Chamber 4 (east) in 2008, it became evident that the high level of the chambers does not represent the original concept of the ambulacrum but is the result of secondary modification. As F. Yegül (*Baths* [supra n. 40], 414–16) has demonstrated earlier, the hall with the chambers cannot be regarded as the changing room of the baths, but as an ambulacrum, a prominent place of social interaction.

[43] In fact only the rear walls of the chambers are covered by painted plaster. The exception is Chamber 3 (east) which was totally revetted in marble.

[44] Remains of iron and bronze clamps within the joints of the fabric of the pillars imply marble revetment for the main walls of the large hall.

[45] K.A. Neugebauer and T. Wiegand, in *Milet* I 9, 97–98 no. 1 pl. 25.

[46] A sounding (Sounding 1) dug in 2008 did not succeed in verifying the existence of this stoa. The sounding was situated at the connecting point of the stoa with the northwest edge of Room 22.

Fig. 9. The Hall of the Muses in its actual state, view from the southeast (P. Schneider 2008).

of the Hall of the Muses and the gallery proved that both were built at the same stage of the building process.[47] The east wall is articulated by a series of five niches. On the west side, where the corresponding wall is preserved only in the lower layers, the same disposition can be supposed. Four other niches are to be found in the apse, where a stage was inserted at a later date. The access to the stage was via a door that was broken into the outer two niches of the apse. This door led to the two small chambers that flank the apse on the east and west.

As mentioned above, the Hall of the Muses acquired its name from a series of female sculptures that were identified as the Muses, because they were found together with a statue of Apollo. The well-known and well-published group of Apollo and the Muses shows various remarkable traces of recarving, belonging to at least two phases of reuse.[48] The most obvious is again the careful removal of the genitalia in the case of the otherwise very well-preserved figure of Apollo. The intentionally damaged breasts of some of the Muses correspond with this intervention. That the Muses, as mentioned above, were relocated at least once is made clear by the fact that in several instances the plinths and some folds of the garments were recut to adjust them to new positions. The reattached arms of some Muses indicate that they also underwent substantial repair. At some point in time, three or four of the Muses had their heads deliberately knocked off, while other sculptures of the group survived untouched.

The podium in the apse was enlarged at a second stage, as shown by a sounding dug by Schneider in the late 1990s.[49] In the first phase, there was a connection between the Hall of the Muses and the palaestra via a door in the western side chamber. The opening was later filled with marble spolia. The

[47] Schneider, *Musengruppe*, 49, n. 179 suggests a successive construction.

[48] Ibid.; O. Dally and A. Scholl, in Dally et al., *ZeitRäume*.

[49] Schneider, *Musengruppe*, 47–50.

Fig. 10. Room 6, the supposed apodyterium, in its actual state, view from the southwest (P. Schneider 2008).

Fig. 11. Room 6, statue base of the group of Dionysus and a satyr. A water conduit is visible running under the floor to the rear of the statue base (P. Schneider 2008).

use of two seat-blocks from the stadium indicates that the blocking of the door was fairly late. According to A. von Gerkan, the stadium was robbed out when the Byzantine city wall was built.[50] Seat-blocks from the stadium are also found in the ambulacrum (eastern Chambers 1–7), in the frigidaria (Rooms 4, 5, and 5a), and in the niches on the north side of Room 6. Others are lying in the palaestra west of the Hall of the Muses. Furthermore, stadium seat-blocks were reused in the church of St. Michael, in the Great Church, in the baths south of the Ilyas Bey Mosque recently excavated by Niewöhner, and elsewhere. The seat-blocks may well represent the latest additions to the rooms.[51]

The northeast corner of the palaestra, west of the ambulacrum and the Hall of the Muses, had been excavated by Wiegand's team, while excavation in the southeast was limited to a sondage dug to establish the position of the corner. The southwest corner was documented in the context of the excavation of the stadium west of the Baths of Faustina. In the northeast corner, sufficient remains were found of the order and the cornice to enable Krischen to give a complete reconstruction.[52] Re-examination of the decoration suggests a date for the execution of the palaestra in the Severan period.[53]

Tepidarium/Apodyterium (Room 6)

On the south side of the gallery, a smaller archway (as compared to the northern one) led to an oblong rectangular hall. The long walls were articulated by niches defined by buttresses (fig. 10). Krischen identified this room hypothetically as the tepidarium. The room was not heated, however, as there are neither hypocausts under the floor nor tubuli on the walls. Schneider suggested convincingly that this unheated room with separate niches for benches may have served as the apodyterium, and thus as the starting point for the bather's circular tour of the bath complex.[54] From Room 6 the bathing tour may have followed the sequence of Rooms 6–7–8–9–5a–4–5–6 or, alternatively, 6–5–5a–9 (–8–7–8–9)–5a–4–5–6.

The arch of the opening that connects the ambulacrum with Room 6 was constructed of limestone blocks abutting on the neighboring masonry. The sidewalls that carried the vault consisted of two large blocks in the corners and three blocks in the middle. The inscriptions of Hesychios mentioned above are incised on the upper part of the blocks. On one side, the central block was decorated with a roughly incised drawing of a hunter.

On the east end the excavators found a pool flanked by semicircular niches. As Krischen reports, the masonry of these niches was built into the space between the two eastern buttresses of the north and the south sides. The pool was installed later, as indicated by the marble revetment of the niches, which was covered by the border of the basin. In this pool, the excavators found a statuary group of Dionysus and a satyr, which had fallen from its base in the middle of the back wall. The late construction of the pool might indicate that the statuary was also placed there at a later stage. An additional argument for this can be seen in the evidence of the water conduit running under the floor to the rear of the base of the statue, where it must have been used as a fountain (fig. 11). After the cleaning

[50] *Milet* II 1, 41.

[51] The date of the spoliation of the stadium of Miletus needs reconsideration. There are examples of partial modifications in stadia in other cities of the Roman empire already during the third century. Rather than complete demolitions and reusing of the building material for fortification purposes, these acts were due to changes in the spectacles and games given in those buildings. We thank Johannes Lipps and Manuel Flecker for a fruitful discussion on this matter.

[52] *Milet* I 9, fig. 67.

[53] A construction date later than the rest of the Baths of Faustina is also indicated by the joint in the east wall as it springs off north from the Hall of the Muses. A sounding conducted in 2006 at this spot on the outside of the Hall of the Muses revealed a re-enforcement of the wall's lower parts with spoil columns laid down here side by side. Surprisingly, no hints of floors constructed at the level of the stylobate or lower could be identified.

[54] Schneider, *Musengruppe*, 59.

of the floor of Room 6 in 2008, a channel was found underneath on both sides running in front of the buttresses and joining the water conduit of the pool on the north side.

The fine sculptural group of Dionysus and a satyr (Berlin, Antikensammlung Inv. Sk 1797)[55] reflects late Hellenistic prototypes. The head of Dionysus as displayed is a cast of a closely related group in the Vatican Museums; it was added to the statue after its arrival in Berlin at the beginning of the 20th century. The genitalia of both sculptures were very carefully removed—presumably in late antiquity—in a manner identical with that of other nude statues found in the Baths of Faustina (e.g., the Apollo from the group of the Muses). These clear and deliberate manipulations were most likely undertaken to adapt these costly sculptures to the changes in taste that accompanied the emergence of Christianity in Asia Minor. Obvious traces of weathering around the plinth and thick incrustations on the back of the sculpture of Dionysus suggest that the group in its reworked form was part of the thermal display until the very last phases of its use.

Fig. 12. Sounding 2 showing the southwest edge of Room 21 (P. Schneider 2009).

Rooms at the Southwest Corner, Soundings 1–3

Krischen reconstructed the plan of the building south of Room 6 and west of Room 7 on the evidence of the wall remains still visible above ground in the unexcavated parts of the baths, and on the evidence of doors in the west wall of Room 7 and the south wall of Room 6. He hypothesized a room west of Room 7 identical in plan (Room 21 according to our numeration), and another room square in outline and with thick walls farther west (Room 22 according to our numeration). As indicated by the visible wall remains, Room 22 probably projected over the west border of Room 6. A sounding (Sounding 2) was begun in 2008 along the wall between Rooms 21 and 22. It revealed a conspicuous joint between the south walls of Rooms 21 and 22 (fig. 12). Thus the south and west walls of Room 21 seem to form the outer edge of the Baths of Faustina. The south wall of Room 22 was in fact thicker in construction and built up against the outside of Room 21. As the excavation in this area and the study of the ceramics found there are still going on, it is not yet possible to date this annex, but it is very likely that it was added when, according to von Gerkan, the Baths of Faustina were turned into a central castle within the late antique fortification system.[56]

Bathing Block

East of the gallery, the bathing block proper is attached. The frigidaria lie in between the unheated ambulacrum on the west side and the heated spaces (Rooms 7–9) on the east and the south sides.

[55] K.A. Neugebauer and T. Wiegand, in *Milet* I 9, 118–21, no. 15, pl. 35.

[56] *Milet* II 1, 41.

Fig. 13. Large frigidarium (Room 4), actual state, view from the south (P. Schneider 2008).

Large Frigidarium (Room 4)

The ambulacrum and the bathing block are directly connected via the doors in Chambers 3 and 5 (east) of the ambulacrum, giving access to the large frigidarium (Room 4) with a rectangular natatio in its center (fig. 13). Room 3—a non-heated room north of Room 4—provided another means of access via Chamber 7 (east) of the ambulacrum and the door in the separating wall between Rooms 3 and 4. This circulation was cut by turning Room 3 into a water basin. There was a water channel or pipe running from the basin to Room 4 through the pedestal of Maeander, the sculpture of a reclining river god, which was set up directly in front of the blocked door and served as a water spout. Remains of marble slabs in front of the door filling show that the revetment of the wall was installed at the same time as the placement of the Maeander. Another waterspout was the lion sculpture set in the middle of the east edge of the natatio. The water supply for the lion came from the water basin in the subsidiary chamber behind (Room 18). The lion itself was an archaic sculpture modified for Roman tastes by the alteration of its face and mane.[57] A channel was carved from its side to the mouth in order to adjust it to its new function. Possibly at the same time, the lion was "Christianized" by the carving of a cross on its back.

Room 5

Similar changes can be observed in Room 5, a small frigidarium, which lies between the large frigidarium (Room 4) and the presumed apodyterium (Room 6) (fig. 14). It has a central apse on the

[57] V.M. Strocka, "Neue archaische Löwen in Anatolien," *AA* (1977) 481–512, at 495–98, no. 7, figs. 17–20.

Fig. 14. Room 5, panoramic view of the actual state from the south (P. Schneider 2008).

west side with a deepened water basin in front. An opening on the east side gives access to Room 5a, intermediary to the grand caldarium (Room 9). It is obvious at first sight that Room 5 underwent various phases of modification. The first modification was the filling of the two semicircular niches in the north wall with brick, and the covering of the walls with marble revetment. The slabs were attached to the walls at the same time as the installation of the extant floor pavement. The floor with its inserted panels of opus sectile is documented in a better state of preservation by Krischen. It was laid down at a fairly late date, as can be seen in its outer frame, which was composed of a band of plain slabs. The materials used for this purpose were reused screen slabs from a Christian context, either from churches or from private houses, which left the imprints of crosses on the mortar bedding of the floor (see fig. 14). The slabs cannot themselves be dated earlier than the fourth or fifth century; thus their reuse in the baths must be still later. A Christian sign (a cross) is also present on the steps of the marble basin set on top of the opus sectile floor in the southeast corner of the same room (fig. 15). After the marble floor was inserted, a water line was cut into it, feeding the pool in front of the west apse. Here, a remarkable torso of a statue of Aphrodite was found in 1906 (Istanbul, Archaeological Mus. Inv. 1997 T),[58] which shows signs of deliberate manipulation and—perhaps in a later phase—destruction. Clearly both of the arms of the statue were cut off intentionally. Both breasts and the mons veneris have been treated with a pointed chisel, reminiscent of the way in which

[58] K.A. Neugebauer and T. Wiegand, in *Milet* I 9, 122 f., no. 17, pl. 36 right.

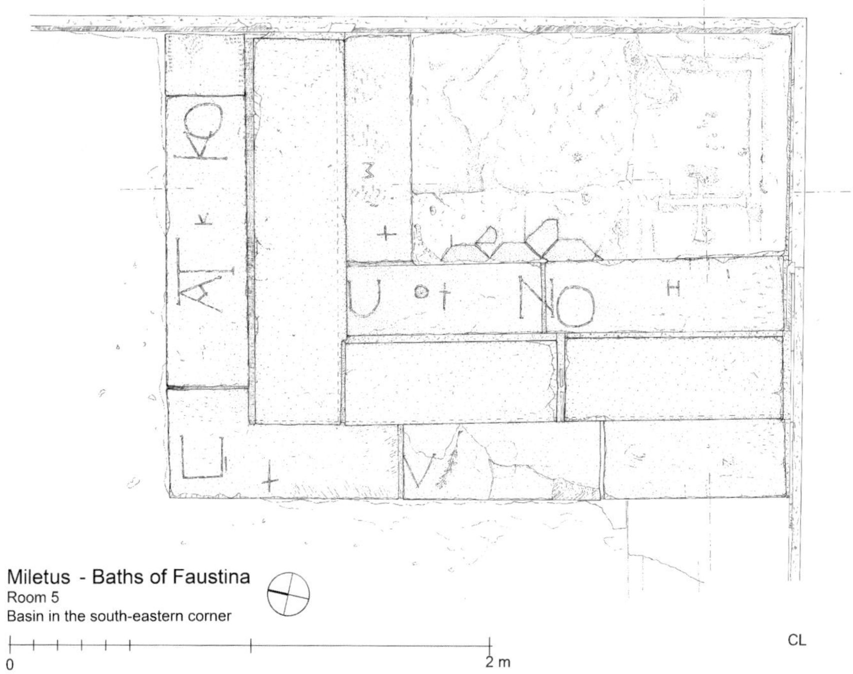

Fig. 15. Room 5, plan of the basin in the southeast corner (C. Lauth 2008).

the male genitalia of the Apollo and the Dionysus were removed without destroying the sculptures as works of art. Like the lion, the Maeander, and the group of Dionysus and a satyr, this sculpture of Aphrodite functioned as secondary fountain decoration as is indicated by the slot running vertically in the middle of the back wall of the apse.

Conclusion and Future Perspectives

The detailed observations made during fieldwork over the last three years permit a fuller understanding of the later phases of the use and appointment of the rooms of the Baths of Faustina, which is more precise than the valuable but in this respect limited presentation of Krischen. Although not all rooms have been investigated in the same way yet, it is now clear that the statuary program as found in the 1905–1910 excavation is a rather late addition. As in Rooms 5 and 6, it seems as if the installation of the statues corresponds to the latest phases of alteration. The precise dating of these alterations remains a major challenge for further investigation. Additionally, more information on the other rooms of the Baths of Faustina, including their functions and changes in use, are expected from future campaigns.

6 The Riddle of the Market Gate: Miletus and the Character and Date of Earlier Byzantine Fortifications in Anatolia

Philipp Niewöhner

The riddle of the Market Gate in Miletus is as old as the archaeology of Byzantine Anatolia. This makes it a useful point of reference for the progress of Byzantine settlement history as well as a stimulant for further research. This essay starts with an exposition of the riddle as it was perceived by Clive Foss in the 1970s. At that time there was as yet little direct archaeological evidence for the settlement history of Byzantine Anatolia, and Foss's hypothesis was based mainly on historical deduction.

The state of research has since changed, and new archaeological evidence from Miletus will be presented. This may not solve the riddle, but it will help to accentuate the problem further. In the search for an answer, recent field work at Aphrodisias, Hierapolis, and elsewhere in Anatolia will be considered. The evidence sheds new light on the date and character of the Byzantine walls of Miletus. These considerations will finally lead to a tentative solution, which—alas—will sound disappointingly familiar and will return to the starting point of historical speculation rather than end with archaeological certainty.

The Riddle of the Market Gate

The riddle of the Market Gate concerns the Byzantine walls that were built up against the back of the Roman Market Gate (fig. 1).[1] The Roman gate faces north and served as a monumental entrance to the South Market. Figure 2 shows a view toward the Theater Hill in the northwest at the time of excavation over a century ago. The four pylons of the Roman gate formed the north face of the Byzantine walls (fig. 3). The south face was added on, and the intervening gap originally filled with mortar and stones. The excavators had the filling taken out in order to search for ancient inscriptions.[2]

The Byzantine walls blocked the two lateral passages of the Roman gate. The western passage now opens into a tower, the remains of which can be seen in figure 2. The tower served to protect a Byzantine gate in the same place as the central passage of the Roman monument.

[1] T. Wiegand, "Fünfter vorläufiger Bericht über die von den Königlichen Museen in Milet unternommenen Ausgrabungen," in *Sitzungsberichte der Königlich Preussischen Akademie der Wissenschaften: Philosophisch-historische Klasse* 1906 VIII (Berlin 1906) 249–65, at 257; H. Knackfuß, *Milet* I 7. *Der Südmarkt und die benachbarten Bauanlagen* (Berlin 1924) 154–55; A. von Gerkan, *Milet* II 3. *Die Stadtmauern* (Berlin 1935) 114–17; P. Niewöhner, "Sind die Mauern die Stadt? Vorbericht über die siedlungsgeschichtlichen Ergebnisse neuer Grabungen im spätantiken und byzantinischen Milet," *AA* (2008/1) 181–201; idem, "Milet in frühbyzantinischer Zeit," in O. Dally et al. (eds.), *ZeitRäume. Milet in Kaiserzeit und Spätantike*, Catalogue of the exhibition in Berlin 2009–2010 (Regensburg 2009) 60–67 (please note corrigendum: p. 65, right column; the second paragraph on alleged fourth-century housing was not written by the author and must be deleted).

[2] T. Wiegand, "Vierter vorläufiger Bericht über die Ausgrabungen der Königlichen Museen zu Milet," in *Sitzungsberichte der Königlich Preussischen Akademie der Wissenschaften: Philosophisch-historische Klasse* 1905 XXV (Berlin 1905) 533–48, at 533–35.

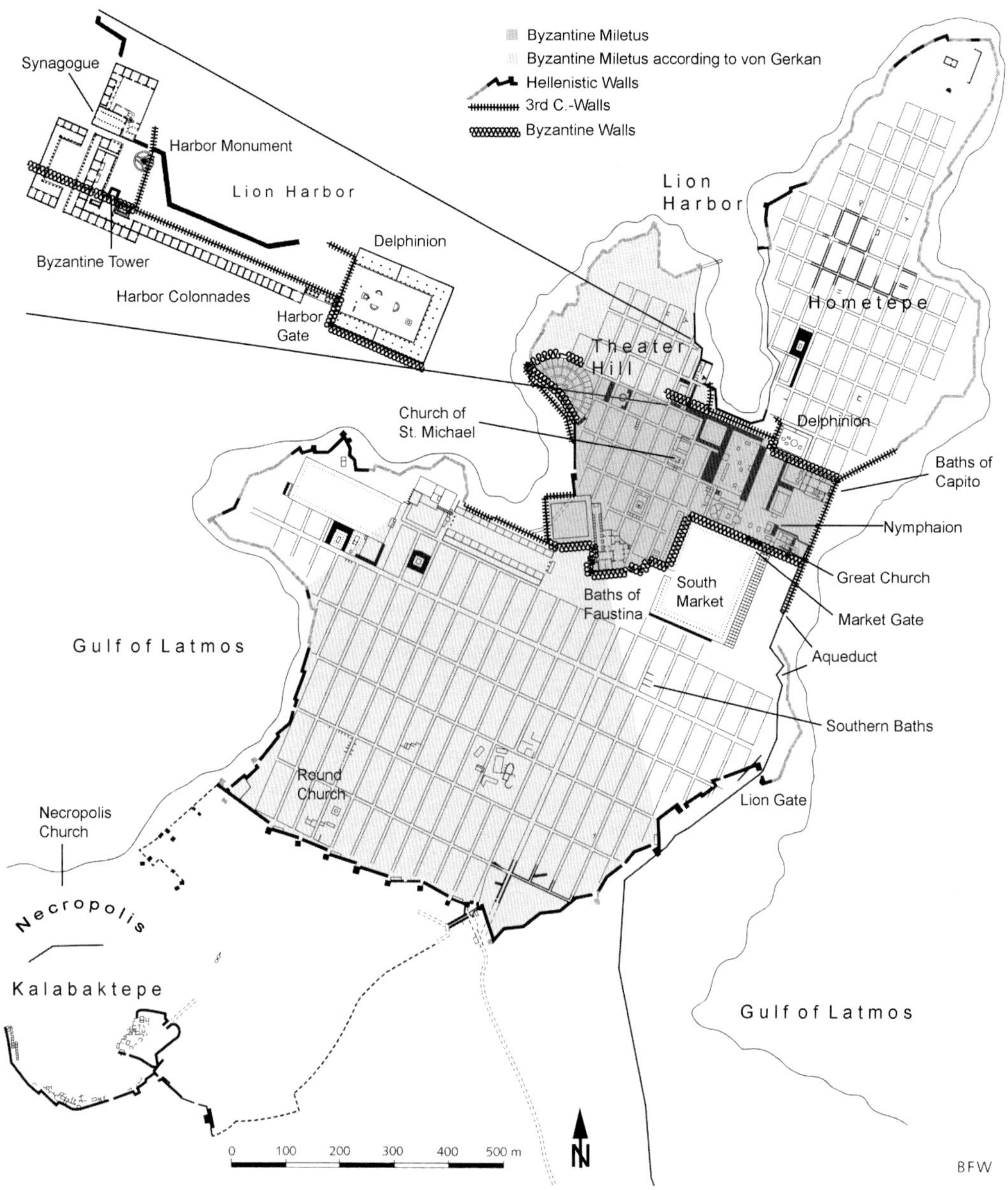

Fig. 1. Byzantine Miletus (P. Niewöhner).

A suggestive inscription was found in front of the gate (fig. 4). This document refers to a gate having been built during the reign of Justinian and can be dated to the year A.D. 538.[3] Armin von Gerkan understood this to date the walls and concluded that Miletus had shrunk to about half its earlier size by the age of Justinian.[4] Nobody objected until Foss pointed out that the inscription is

[3] Wiegand, "Fünfter Bericht" (supra n. 1), 257; Knackfuß, *Milet* I 7 (supra n. 1), 154–55 fig. 170, 303–4, no. 206; A. Rehm, H. Dessau, and P. Herrmann, *Milet* VI. *Inschriften von Milet*. Teil 1 (Berlin and New York 1997) 35–36, 201, no. 206; V. Kästner, "Die Spolie mit der Justiniansinschrift vom milesischen Markttor," in O. Dally et al. (eds.), *ZeitRäume. Milet in Kaiserzeit und Spätantike*, Catalogue of the exhibition in Berlin 2009–2010 (Regensburg 2009) 204–11.

[4] Von Gerkan, *Milet* II 3 (supra n. 1), 127.

Fig. 2. Miletus, Market Gate (foreground) and Theater Hill (background) from the south, around 1905 (Berlin, Antikensammlung, Mil 352).

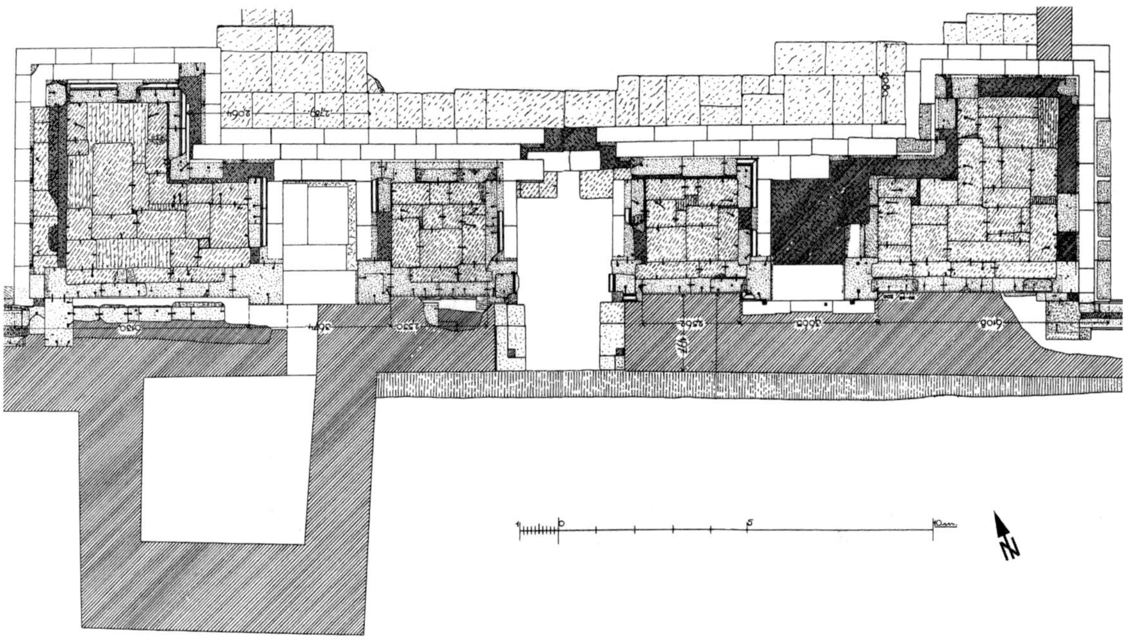

Fig. 3. Miletus, Market Gate, foundations in situ (Knackfuß, *Milet* I 7 [supra n. 1], pl. 2 fig. 3).

Fig. 4. Miletus, Market Gate, Justinianic inscription, now in Berlin, Pergamon Museum (P. Niewöhner).

Fig. 6. Side (Pamphylia), southeast gate from the east (Mansel, *Side* [supra n. 6], 56 fig. 53).

Fig. 5. Miletus, Market Gate, Justinianic inscription (cf. fig. 4), broken right side (P. Niewöhner).

unlike any other inscription from a fortification and does not refer to any walls having been built in addition to the gate.[5] Foss therefore assumed that the inscription refers to some other building activity and does not date the walls.

Closer inspection of the block of marble that carries the inscription is not conclusive. The block is ancient and originally served as a doorpost; it has two ancient inscriptions on the front. The Justinianic inscription is carved on the back. There is no doorstop and no way of telling how many times the block was reused. One end is broken, but the remains of a clamp hole and a dowel hole show that the block was never much longer (fig. 5). The block is too short to bridge the gate properly. This does not, however, preclude its use as a lintel. The gate could have been constructed in the same way as the southeast gate of Side in Pamphylia (fig. 6).[6] In Side the doorframe steps in at the top to accommodate a lintel that would otherwise have been too short.

One could speculate much more about the feasible uses of the block and possible origin of the Justinianic inscription, but probably to no avail. We simply do not know whether the inscription dates the walls.

[5] C. Foss, *Byzantine Cities of Western Asia Minor* (Ph.D. dissertation, Harvard University 1972) 481 no. 45; idem, "Archaeology and the 'Twenty Cities' of Byzantine Asia Minor," *AJA* 81 (1977) 469–86, at 478 no. 49; reprint in: idem, *History and Archaeology of Byzantine Asia Minor* (Aldershot 1990) II.

[6] A.M. Mansel, *Side: 1947–1966 Yılları Kazıları ve Araştırmalarının Sonuçları, Türk Tarih Kurumu Yayınları* ser. 5 v. 33 = *Antalya Bölgesinde Araştırmalar* 10 (Ankara 1978) 56 fig. 53; U. Peschlow, "Mauerbau in krisenloser Zeit? Zur spätantiken Stadtbefestigungen im südlichen Kleinasien. Der Fall Side," in D. Kreikenbom, K.-U. Mahler, and T.M. Weber (eds.), *Krise und Kult. Vorderer Orient und Nordafrika von Aurelian bis Iustinian, Millennium Studies 28* (Wiesbaden 2010) 61–108, at 81–85, 104–7 figs. 30–37.

Foss, however, was sure that this is not the case, because he believed on other grounds that Miletus had not shrunken to half its size by A.D. 538. Foss was convinced that the age of Justinian was still prosperous, and no decline had yet set in.[7] The issue had already troubled von Gerkan (see below) and is further aggravated by new discoveries to be discussed in the following paragraphs.

The Byzantine Walls

Von Gerkan reconstructed the Byzantine walls in the shape of a figure-eight with a north and a south loop (see fig. 1).[8] The north loop has been excavated and includes the Market Gate. The south loop was supposed to turn off at the Baths of Faustina and cut back to the stadium, but there is no archaeological evidence for this.[9] A geomagnetic survey has revealed no traces of the south loop either, although other less massive structures show up clearly, for example a hitherto unknown Roman market basilica to the east of the South Market.[10] This shows beyond a reasonable doubt that the Byzantine walls never included a south loop.

Von Gerkan assumed the existence of a south loop simply because he was convinced that "the area [included in the north loop] is surely too small for [early] Byzantine Miletus."[11] It never occurred to von Gerkan that he might turn this argument around and question the Justinianic date for the Byzantine walls. I shall return to this point, but first there is a second reduction of the Byzantine circuit to be registered.

Figure 1 shows an updated reconstruction of the area included in the Byzantine walls. The tip of the northwestern peninsula that von Gerkan includes in his reconstruction has been cut off as well. The new reconstruction, with a shortcut running in a straight line from the Lion Harbor toward the theater, rests on the alignment of a tower[12] at the eastern end of this line, where it takes off from the harbor (fig. 1, detail). The tower is oriented toward the north and implies that the walls did not turn in the same direction to surround the northern tip of the peninsula.[13] If the walls had turned toward the north, the tower would have been superfluous.

Figure 7 reproduces a photograph of the tower that was taken more than a century ago at the time of excavation. It shows that the tower was built with a variety of spolia. At the time of excavation the chronology of the different fortifications was not yet understood,[14] and later on the tower seems to have been forgotten. Von Gerkan did not mention it in the volume on the walls of Miletus that he published 30 years after the excavation.

[7] C. Foss, "The Persians in Asia Minor and the end of antiquity," *EHR* 90 (1975) 721–43; reprint in: idem, *History and Archaeology of Byzantine Asia Minor* (Aldershot 1990) I; idem, "Archaeology" (supra n. 5); idem, "The Lycian coast in the Byzantine age," *DOP* 48 (1994) 1–52; reprint in: idem, *Cities, Fortresses and Villages of Byzantine Asia Minor* (Aldershot 1996) II. Cf. E. Kirsten, "Die byzantinische Stadt," *Berichte zum XI. Internationalen Byzantinisten-Kongress* III (Munich 1958) 16; W. Müller-Wiener, "Von der Polis zum Kastron: Wandlung der Städte im ägäischen Raum von der Antike zum Mittelalter," *Gymnasium* 93 (1986) 435–75, at 440–51; M. Whittow, "Ruling the late Roman and early Byzantine city: A continuous history," *PastPres* 129 (1990) 3–29; idem, "Recent research on the late-antique city in Asia Minor: The second half of the 6th c. revisited," in L. Lavan (ed.), *Recent Research in Late-Antique Urbanism, JRA* Suppl. 42 (Portsmouth, RI 2001) 137–53; C. Wickham, *Framing the Early Middle Ages: Europe and the Mediterranean 400–800* (Oxford 2005) 626–27.

[8] A. von Gerkan, *Milet* I 6. *Der Nordmarkt und der Hafen an der Löwenbucht* (Berlin 1922) 85; idem, *Stadtmauern* (supra n. 1) 86, 116–17 pl. 1.

[9] Niewöhner, "Mauern" (supra n. 1).

[10] H. Stümpel, "Geophysikalische Prospektion in Milet: Arbeiten in den Kampagnen 2000–2002," *AA* (2005) 183–94, at 186–89.

[11] Von Gerkan, *Milet* II 3 (supra n. 1), 86, 116.

[12] Von Gerkan, *Milet* I 6 (supra n. 8), 17 pls. 8, 11.

[13] W. Müller-Wiener, "Untersuchungen auf dem Theater-Hügel [von Milet]," *IstMitt* 32 (1981) 15–17, at 16; Niewöhner, "Mauern" (supra n. 1). Cf. G. Kleiner, *Die Ruinen von Milet* (Berlin 1968) 59.

[14] Wiegand, "Fünfter Bericht" (supra n. 1), 257; von Gerkan, *Milet* II 3 (supra n. 1), 127.

Fig. 7. Miletus, Lion Harbor, Byzantine Tower from the south, around 1904 (Berlin, Antikensammlung, Mil 293).

The Third-Century Walls

More recently another hitherto unknown stretch of walls has been excavated to the northeast of the Baths of Capito (see fig. 1). The walls fortified the northeastern peninsula, now called Hometepe, and can be identified with a third-century renovation of the ancient circuit.[15] This renovation has been noticed elsewhere along the ancient circuit,[16] but until now not on the northeastern peninsula. It was therefore assumed that Hometepe had not been refortified in the third century and that Miletus had already lost part of its ancient population.[17] Now we know that this was not the case. The newly discovered stretch of walls proves that the entire ancient city was refortified in the third century.

It follows that a Justinianic date for the Byzantine walls does indeed imply a fundamental change in the urban layout within the early Byzantine period. Von Gerkan and Foss were surely right to worry about this, and there are yet more new discoveries to be reported that add to the problem.

The Southern Baths

Outside the Byzantine walls a previously unknown bath building was accidentally discovered in 2008 during cleaning operations connected with the restoration of the Ilyas Bey Mosque. The Selçuk mosque is situated to the south of the South Market, and the baths lie behind the mosque, occupying the southern half of the same insula (see fig. 1). In 2009 stratigraphic excavations were undertaken inside the bath building, which turned out to date originally from the Roman imperial period. A second building phase constituted a renovation and took place after the fifth century, most likely during the reign of Justinian. The renovation included the opening of new passageways and the closing of old ones, probably in connection with the abandonment of the frigidarium. A new hypocaust system was also installed, as well as new marble floors and wall revetment.

In comparison with the other known thermae of Roman Miletus, the southern baths appear small, simple, and utilitarian. They will have served the daily needs of their neighborhood that probably consisted of living quarters. The renovation after the fifth century indicates that the neighborhood was still thriving and poses the question why it should have been excluded from the contemporary fortifications.

[15] Niewöhner, "Mauern" (supra n. 1).

[16] Von Gerkan, *Milet* II 3 (supra n. 1), 81–84, 126–27; I. Blum, "Die Stadtmauern von Alt-Milet: Ergebnisse des Surveys 1996 und 1997," *AA* (1999) 53–76, at 62–63 fig. 12.

[17] Von Gerkan, *Milet* II 3 (supra n. 1), 127; C. Foss and D. Winfield, *Byzantine Fortifications: An Introduction* (Pretoria 1986) 284 fig. 2.

The Necropolis Church

Von Gerkan's reconstruction of a south loop of the Byzantine walls had been partly inspired by a centrally planned building near the outskirts of the Roman city that was turned into a church in the fifth or sixth century (see fig. 1, "Round Church").[18]

Recently yet another, larger church was found to have been built ex novo in the extra-urban necropolis north of Kalabaktepe (see fig. 1).[19] Kalabaktepe is the name of a hill southwest of Miletus. The Necropolis Church was discovered by geomagnetic survey: the two empty stripes on the chart in figure 8 correspond with the ditches on both sides of the field in figure 9. The church extends on both sides beyond the field and has the form of a basilica with atrium. To the south there is a large open square.

Excavation has revealed that the church was built after the fifth century, most probably during the reign of Justinian. The basilica is three-aisled and has a transept. The aisles are paved with mosaics, the transept with marble. The atrium to the west incorporates two earlier graves on its south side. One of them was the object of much attention and seems to have been venerated. This may have been the martyrium of an unidentified saint that is mentioned in a Byzantine inscription from Miletus.[20] The lavish size and monumentality of the Necropolis Church does not accord with the economy and restriction of the Byzantine walls.

The Territory

Further outside town a survey of the territory of Miletus has revealed that the countryside witnessed an unprecedented boom in the fifth and sixth centuries. Rural settlements grew both in number and size beyond any earlier level. The population must have done so, too, and rural churches greatly outnumbered urban ones.[21] The evidence consists mostly of pottery sherds, but churches and stonemasonry were found as well.[22] None of the rural settlements was fortified. This lack of walls was obviously no obstacle to prosperity, so why fortify the town?

The Character and Date of Earlier Byzantine Fortifications of Anatolia

Foss's answer to all this was, of course, that Miletus had not been fortified in A.D. 538 but only later, when from the seventh century onward Anatolia was overrun first by the Persians and then by the Arabs.[23] Carl Humann suggested the same more than a century ago, when he tried to make sense of

[18] T. Wiegand, "Dritter vorläufiger Bericht über die von den Königlichen Museen begonnen Ausgrabungen in Milet," in *Sitzungsberichte der Königlich Preussischen Akademie der Wissenschaften: Philosophisch-historische Klasse* 1904 III (Berlin 1904) 72–91, at 86–89; W. Müller-Wiener, "Rundkirche bei der Süd-Mauer [von Milet]," *IstMitt* 31 (1981) 96–99; O. Feld, "Eine Kirche für Maria in Miletos," in C. Striker (ed.), *Architectural Studies in Memory of Richard Krautheimer* (Mainz 1996) 67–70; O. Feld, "Miletos e Kos: le isole microasiatiche e la terra ferma," in *Corso di cultura sull'arte ravennate e bizantina* 44 (Ravenna 1998) 123–42, at 138–42.

[19] P. Niewöhner, "Die große Friedhofskirche von Milet: Vorbericht über die Ausgrabung einer neuentdeckten Transeptbasilika," *Mitteilungen zur Christlichen Archäologie* 13 (2007) 71–90.

[20] J. Spon, *Voyage d'Italie, de Dalmatie, de Grèce et du Levant, fait aux années 1675 et 1676*, vol. 3.1 (La Haye 1678) 161; P. Herrmann, W. Günther, and N. Ehrhardt, *Milet* VI. *Inschriften von Milet.* Teil 3 (Berlin 2006) 295–96 no. 1578.

[21] H. Lohmann, "Survey in der Chora von Milet: Vorbericht über die Kampagnen der Jahre 1990, 1992 und 1993," *AA* (1995) 293–328, at 323–28; idem, "Survey in der Chora von Milet: Vorbericht über die Kampagnen der Jahre 1996 und 1997," *AA* (1999) 439–73, at 465; M. Berndt, *Funde aus dem Survey auf der Halbinsel von Milet (1992–1999), Internationale Archäologie* 79 (Rahden 2003) 114; H. Lohmann, "Milet und die Milesia: Eine antike Großstadt und ihr Umland im Wandel der Zeit," in F. Kolb (ed.), *Chora und Polis, Schriften des historischen Kollegs: Kolloquien* 54 (Munich 2004) 325–60, at 352.

[22] P. Niewöhner, "Byzantinische Steinmetzarbeiten aus dem Umland von Milet," *Anadolu ve Çevresinde Ortaçağ* 1 (2007) 1–28.

[23] For Foss, see supra n. 5. For the Arab incursions, see H. Ahrweiler, "L'Asie Mineure et les invasions arabes (7e–9e siècles)," *RHist* 227 (1962) 1–32, at 10–12; W. Brandes, *Die Städte Kleinasiens im 7. und 8. Jahrhundert* (Amsterdam 1989) 51–80.

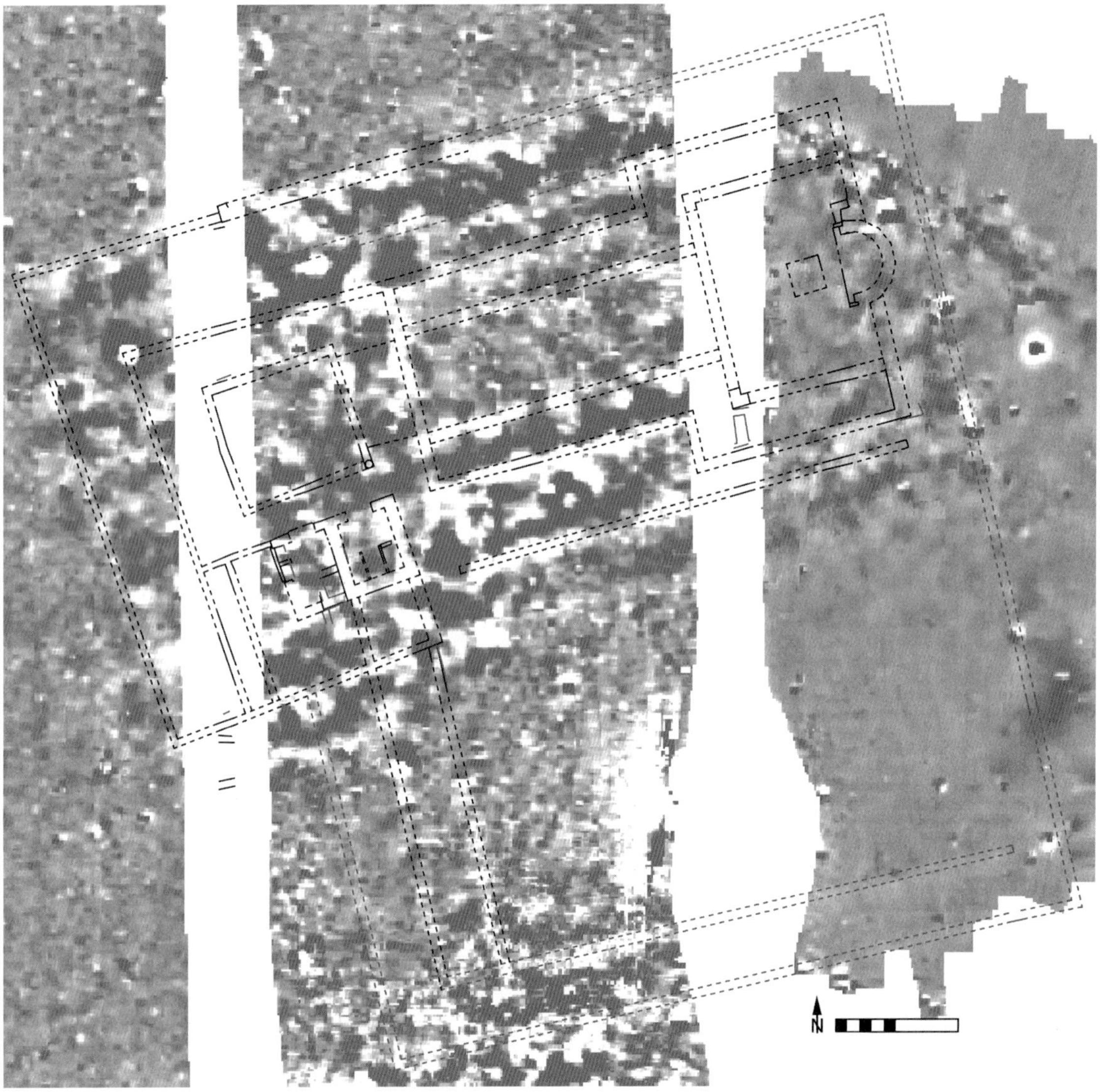

Fig. 8. Miletus, Necropolis Church, geomagnetic chart (H. Stümple) and plan (P. Niewöhner).

Fig. 9. Miletus, Necropolis Church, view from Kalabaktepe looking north (P. Niewöhner).

the Byzantine walls of Magnesia on the Maeander. The fortified area is as small in comparison with the extent of that ancient city as at Miletus.[24]

Elsewhere the situation is similar, but the interpretation veers towards a Justinianic date. The so-called Justinianic walls at Patara offer one example, Ephesus and Side others.[25] This cannot be ignored, because if those towns were constricted by tightening circuits during the sixth century, why not Miletus, too?

Foss simply dates every set of walls to the seventh century or later.[26] At the time of his writing in the 1970s it seemed as if hardly any town in western Anatolia had been fortified during the early Byzantine period. Foss assumes that after some activity in the third century, wall-building died down during the early Byzantine period and was not resumed before the seventh century.[27]

More recently, though, the walls of about a dozen Anatolian towns have been dated to the early Byzantine period. The list includes Aphrodisias, Sardis, Anemurium, Smyrna/Izmir, Sagalassos, Hierapolis in Phrygia, Laodicea on the Lycus, Tlos, Blaundos, Limyra, and Amorium.[28] The dating is

[24] C. Humann, J. Kohte, and C. Watzinger, *Magnesia am Maeander* (Berlin 1904) 33 pls. 2–3; O. Bingöl, *Menderes Magnesiası* (Ankara 1998) 57–58; idem, *Magnesia ad Maeandrum: The City of Artemis with "White Eyebrows"* (Istanbul 2007) 130–32. An early Byzantine date has been proposed by M. Kiel, "Magnesia on the Maeander as Byzantine fortress and Turkish market place: Remarks on the mosque of Aydınoğlu Mehmed şah Çelebi b. Musa Bey," in *Uluslararası Sanat Tarihi Sempozyumu: Prof. Dr. Gönül Öney'e Armağan* (Izmir 2002) 375–85, at 376.

[25] Patara: F. Işık, *Patara. The History and Ruins of the Capital City of Lycian League* (Antalya 2000) 105–6, 172–73; H. Hellenkemper and F. Hild, *Lykien und Pamphylien, Tabula Imperii Byzantini* 8 = *DenkschrWien* 320 (Vienna 2004) II 784–85; U. Peschlow, "Befestigungen lykischer Städte in spätantiker und frühbyzantinischer Zeit," in K. Dörtlük et al., *The 3rd International Symposium on Lycia*, vol. 2 (Antalya 2006) 601–24, at 604; V. Ruggieri, "Patara. Due casi di architettura bizantina e la continuità urbana," *Orientalia Christiana Periodica* 75 (2009) 319–41, at 322–23; S.-G. Bruer and M. Kunze, *Der Stadtplan von Patara und Beobachtungen zu den Stadtmauern, Patara* 1.1 (Istanbul 2010).

Ephesus: H. Thür, "Das spätantike Ephesos: Aspekte zur Frage der Christianisierung des Stadtbilds," in G. Brands and H.-G. Severin (eds.), *Die spätantike Stadt und ihre Christianisierung* (Wiesbaden 2003) 259–73, at 268–69 (note that the early Byzantine acclamations may have been carved before the doorframe was reused at a city gate); A. Pülz, "Das Stadtbild von Ephesos in byzantinischer Zeit," in F. Daim and J. Drauschke (eds.), *Byzanz—Das Römerreich im Mittelalter.* Teil 2.2. *Schauplätze, Monographien des Römisch-Germanischen Zentralmuseums* 84.2.2 (Mainz 2010) 541–71, at 558–60.

Side: A.M. Mansel, *Die Ruinen von Side* (Berlin 1963) 40; F. Hild, review of C. Foss, *History and Archaeology of Byzantine Asia Minor* (Aldershot 1990), *JÖBG* 45 (1995) 385–87, at 386; Hellenkemper and Hild, *Lykien* (supra this note) I 388–389; II 784–785; Peschlow, "Mauerbau" (supra n. 6).

[26] Patara: Foss, "Lycian coast" (supra n. 7), 15.

Ephesus: C. Foss, *Ephesus After Antiquity: A Late Antique, Byzantine and Turkish City* (Cambridge 1979) 106–7; Foss and Winfield, *Fortifications* (supra n. 17), 132–33.

Side: C. Foss, "The cities of Pamphylia in the Byzantine age," in idem, *Cities, Fortresses and Villages of Byzantine Asia Minor*, vol. 3 (Aldershot 1996) 43–44. Cf. Peschlow, "Befestigungen" (supra n. 25), 608–9. An even later, middle Byzantine date has been proposed by C. Gliwitzky, "Die Kirche im sog. Bischofspalast zu Side," *IstMitt* 55 (2005) 337–408, at 376–78.

[27] Foss and Winfield, *Fortifications* (supra n. 17), 129–30. Cf. T. Ulbert, "Stadttore in byzantinischer Zeit," in T.G. Schattner and F. Valdés Fernándes (eds.), *Stadttore: Bautyp und Kunstform, Iberia Archaeologica* 8 (Mainz 2006) 275–90, at 278.

[28] Aphrodisias, second half of the fourth century: C. Roueché, *Aphrodisias in Late Antiquity, JRS Monograph* 5 (London 1989) 42–45 no. 22; C. Ratté, "New Research on the urban development of Aphrodisias in late antiquity," in D. Parrish (ed.), *Urbanism in Western Asia Minor, JRA* Suppl. 45 (Portsmouth, RI 2001) 116–47, at 125–26; C. Ratté and R.R.R. Smith, "Archaeological research at Aphrodisias in Caria, 2002–2005," *AJA* 112 (2008) 713–51, at 734 n. 50; P.D. De Staebler, "The city wall and the making of a late-antique provincial capital," in C. Ratté and R.R.R. Smith (eds.), *Aphrodisias Papers* 4. *New Research on the City and its Monuments, JRA* Suppl. 70 (Portsmouth, RI 2008) 284–318, at 308–11.

Sardis, second half of the fourth century: G.M.A. Hanfmann, R.S. Thomas, and D. Van Zanten, "The city walls," in G.M.A. Hanfmann and J.C. Waldbaum (eds.), *A Survey of Sardis and the Major Monuments Outside the Walls, Archaeological Exploration of Sardis* R1 (Cambridge 1975) 35–52, at 45; G.M.A. Hanfmann, *Sardis from Prehistoric to Roman Times: Results of the Archaeological Exploration of Sardis* 1958–1975 (Cambridge 1983) 143–44; C.H. Greenewalt, "Sardis: Archaeological research and conservation projects in 2000," *Kazı Sonuçları Toplantısı* 23.2 (2001) 227–34, at 228.

Anemurium, around A.D. 382: J. Russell, "The military garrison of Anemurium during the reign of Arcadius," in *Atti*

not always precise, but there can be no doubt that walls continued to be built and rebuilt during the early Byzantine period. It would therefore seem that a Justinianic date for the Byzantine fortification of Miletus cannot be ruled out.

Around A.D. 400

The matter is more complicated, though, as will become apparent on closer examination of the date and character of the various early Byzantine wall circuits. It turns out that most of the securely dated walls were built around A.D. 400,[29] possibly in reaction to the Gothic invasion of the Balkans during the last quarter of the fourth century.[30] This pattern is significant, because it tallies with other building activity. Around A.D. 400 much urban building went on in Anatolia: colonnaded streets and squares were built or rebuilt, for example in Aizanoi, Aphrodisias, Ephesus, Limyra, Nicomedia, Sagalassos, Sardis, Side, and Xanthus.[31]

In Aizanoi the colonnade was constructed solely with reused parts, and the columns lack bases (fig. 10).[32] Nevertheless, the building suffices to suggest an atmosphere of elevated urban lifestyle in the

del XI Congresso Internazionale di Epigrafia Greca e Latina, vol. 1 (Rome 1999) 721–28.

Smyrna/Izmir, reign of emperor Arcadius (395–408): W. Müller-Wiener, "Die Stadtbefestigungen von Izmir, Sığacık und Çandarlı," *IstMitt* 12 (1962) 59–114, at 62–63.

Sagalassos, around A.D. 400: L. Loots, M. Waelkens, and F. Depuydt, "The city fortifications of Sagalassos from the Hellenistic to the Late Roman period," in M. Waelkens and L. Loots (eds.), *Sagalassos* V: *Report on the Survey and Excavation Campaigns 1996 and 1997, ActaArchLov Monographiae* 11 a–b (Leuven 2000) 595–634, at 616–18.

Hierapolis, around A.D. 400: *Reallexikon zur byzantinischen Kunst* II (Stuttgart 1971) 1223 s. v. "Hierapolis" (P. Verzone); F. D'Andria, *Hierapolis in Phrygien, Alte anatolische Städte* 5 (Istanbul 2003) 115.

Laodicea, around A.D. 400: C. Şimşek, *Laodikeia* (Istanbul 2007) 111–14.

Tlos, around A.D. 400 (?): Hellenkemper and Hild, *Lykien* (supra n. 25), II 887.

Blaundos, around A.D. 400 (?): A. Filges, "Stadtentwicklung im Gebiet des oberen Mäander: Die lydisch-phrygische Grenzregion am Beispiel von Blaundos," in E. Schwertheim and E. Winter (eds.), *Stadt und Stadtentwicklung in Kleinasien, Asia Minor Studien* 50 (Bonn 2003) 35–50, at 47; J. Giese, "Baugeschichtliche Einordnung," in A. Filges (ed.), *Blaundos. Berichte zur Erforschung einer Kleinstadt im lydisch-pamphylischen Grenzgebiet, IstForsch* 48 (Tübingen 2006) 114–24, at 116–22.

Limyra, fifth century: J. Borchhardt et al., "Bericht der Grabungskampagne in Limyra 2001," *Kazı Sonuçları Toplantısı* 24.2 (2002) 303–14, at 305, 307 (terminus post quem in the fifth century: ceramics of the fourth and fifth century in the foundation of the gate to the north of the Ptolemaion; terminus ante quem in the sixth century: the addition of the church to the southeast of the Ptolemaion); T. Marksteiner, "Die spätantiken und byzantinischen Befestigungen von Limyra im Bereich des Ptolemaions," in M. Seyer (ed.), *Studien in Lykien, ÖJh Ergh.* 8 (Vienna 2007) 29–45, at 43.

Amorium, probably reign of emperor Zeno (474–491): terminus post quem around the middle of the fifth century: ceramics and the typology of a triangular tower; the roof beams of the tower were cut after A.D. 487: R.M. Harrison, "Amorium excavations 1990: The third preliminary report," *AnatSt* 41 (1991) 215–29, at 225–26 (ceramics); J. Crow, "Fortifications and urbanism in late antiquity: Thessaloniki and other cities," in L. Lavan (ed.), *Recent Research in Late-Antique Urbanism, JRA* Suppl. 42 (Portsmouth, RI 2001) 89–105, at 102 (typology); C. and M. Lightfoot, *Amorium: A Byzantine City in Anatolia* (Istanbul 2007) 108 (dendrochronology). Byzantine sources ascribe the walls to emperor Zeno, Arab sources to his successor Anastasius (491–519): K. Belke, *Galatien und Lykaonien, Tabula Imperii Byzantini* 4 = *DenkschrWien* 172 (Vienna 1984) 123.

29 Supra n. 28.

30 P. Heather, *Goths and Romans 332–489* (Oxford 1991); H. Wolfram, *Die Goten und ihre Geschichte* (Munich 2001); P. Heather, *The Fall of the Roman Empire* (London 2005) 145–90.

31 L. Lavan, "Fora and agorai in Mediterranean cities during the 4th and 5th c. A.D.," in W. Bowden, A. Gutteridge, and C. Machado (eds.), *Social and Political Life in Late Antiquity, Late Antique Archaeology* 3.1 (Leiden 2006) 195–249, at 196–204; P. Niewöhner, *Aizanoi, Dokimion und Anatolien: Stadt und Land, Siedlungs- und Steinmetzwesen vom späteren 4. bis ins 6. Jh. n. Chr., AF* 23 (Wiesbaden 2007) 87–88; F. Martens, "Urban traffic in the hills of the eastern Mediterranean. The development, maintenance, and usage of the street system at Sagalassos in south-western Turkey," in P. Ballet, N. Dieudonné-Glad, and C. Saliou (eds.), *La rue dans l'antiquité. Définition, aménagement et devenir de l'Orient méditerranéen à la Gaule* (Rennes 2008) 191–200, at 196 f.

32 K. Rheidt, "Aizanoi: Bericht über die Ausgrabungen und Untersuchungen 1992 und 1993," *AA* (1995) 693–718, at

Fig. 10. Aizanoi (Phrygia), colonnaded street built around A.D. 400 (K. Rheidt, D-DAI-IST-Ai.95/300).

ancient tradition. The same holds true for thermae that were restored in Aphrodisias, Ephesus, Miletus, Sagalassos, Sardis, and Seleucia on the Calycadnus.[33] More luxury was displayed in large mansions that were built or refurbished in Aphrodisias, Arykanda, Elaiussa Sebaste, Ephesus, Erythrae, Halicarnassus, Hierapolis in Phrygia, Ilion/Troy, Pergamon, Perge, Pessinus, Sagalassos, Sardis, and Xanthos.[34]

699–712; idem, "Archäologie und Spätantike in Anatolien: Methoden, Ergebnisse und Probleme der Ausgrabungen in Aizanoi," in G. Brands and H.-G. Severin (eds.), *Die spätantike Stadt und ihre Christianisierung* (Wiesbaden 2003) 239–47, at 240–41.

[33] Niewöhner, *Aizanoi* (supra n. 31), 89; H. Vanhaverbeke, F. Martens, and M. Waelkens, "Another view on late antiquity. Sagalassos (SW Anatolia), its suburbium and its countryside in late antiquity," in A.G. Poulter (ed.), *The Transition to Late Antiquity on the Danube and Beyond, ProBritAc* 141 (Oxford 2007) 611–48; M. Steskal and M. La Torre, *Das Vediusgymnasium in Ephesos, Forschungen in Ephesos* XIV 1 (Vienna 2008) 310–12.

[34] Niewöhner, *Aizanoi* (supra n. 31), 90–91. Cf. P. Arthur, *Byzantine and Turkish Hierapolis (Pamukkale): An Archaeological Guide* (Istanbul 2006) 105, 148–50; A.-M. Manière-Lévêque, "Habitat proto-byzantin à Xanthos: les espaces de réception de la grande résidence nord-est de l'acropole lycienne," in *The 3rd International Symposium on Lycia* 1 (Antalya 2006) 425–40; S. Ellis, "Late antique housing and the uses of residential buildings. An overview," in L. Lavan, L. Özgenel, and A. Sarantis (eds.), *Housing in Late Antiquity. From Palaces to Shops, Late Antique Archaeology* 3.2 (Leiden 2007) 1–22, at 11 f.; M. Waelkens et al., "Two late antique residential complexes at Sagalassos," in L. Lavan, L. Özgenel, and A. Sarantis (eds.), *Housing in Late Antiquity. From Palaces to Shops, Late Antique Archaeology* 3.2 (Leiden 2007) 495–513; A. Zaccaria Ruggiu, "Regio VIII, insula 104. Le strutture abitative. Fasi e trasformazioni," in F. D'Andria and M. Piera Caggia (eds.), *Hierapolis di Frigia I. Le attività delle campagne di scavo e restauro 2000–2003* (Istanbul 2007) 211–56; M. Rautman, "The aura of affluence: Domestic scenery in Late Roman Sardis," in N.D. Cahill (ed.), *Love for Lydia: A Sardis Anniversary Volume Presented to Crawford H. Greenewalt, Jr., Sardis* R4 (Cambridge, MA 2008) 147–58; E. Equini Schneider, "Elaiussa Sebaste—The 2007 excavation and conservation season," *Kazı Sonuçları Toplantısı* 30.4 (2008) 177–90, at 177 f.; M.L. Berenfeld, "The Triconch House and the predecessors of the Bishop's Palace at Aphrodisias," *AJA* 113 (2009) 203–29; Pülz, "Stadtbild" (supra n. 25), at 552–57.

Fig. 11. Aphrodisias, walls, historic photograph of the exterior façade next to southeast gate (D-DAI-IST-R35.383 Repro).

All this building activity contributed to the embellishment of various townscapes around A.D. 400, and the contemporary wall-building seems to have been part of that effort: for one thing, those earlier circuits were more extensive than the Byzantine walls of Miletus. The earlier walls enclosed all or at least the greater part of the ancient cities.[35] Secondly, the emphasis was on appearance rather than on fortification. I offer a few examples in the following section.

Masonry and Architectural Sculpture

The first example is from Aphrodisias. Figure 11 reproduces an old photograph from the archive of the German Archaeological Institute in Istanbul. This stretch of walls is situated next to the southeast gate, where it would have been noticed by everyone who entered the town. All the building material is reused, but the courses are exceptionally regular and contain a choice selection of ancient reliefs. A cornice runs along the upper part of the walls as had already been the case with the third-century walls at Miletus.[36]

At Aphrodisias the cornice reappears in other sections of the same walls, but the courses are less regular, and there are no reliefs,[37] probably because there is no gate nearby and therefore less attention to be attracted. A similar concentration of unusually careful construction and liberal

[35] Niewöhner, *Aizanoi* (supra n. 31), 93; P. Niewöhner, "Byzantinische Stadtmauern in Anatolien: Vom Statussymbol zum Bollwerk gegen die Araber," in J. Lorentzen et al. (eds.), *Aktuelle Forschungen zur Konstruktion, Funktion und Semantik antiker Stadtbefestigungen, Byzas* 10 (2010) 239–60, at 249–51.

[36] Von Gerkan, *Milet* II 3 (supra n. 1), 81–84 fig. 52; Niewöhner, "Mauern" (supra n. 1).

[37] K.T. Erim, *Aphrodisias: City of Venus and Aphrodite* (London 1986) 53; idem, *Aphrodisias: Ein Führer durch die antike Stadt und das Museum* (Istanbul 1989) 18 fig. 14–15; De Staebler, "City wall" (supra n. 28), 300–1 figs. 18–19.

Fig. 12. Constantinople, Golden Gate, reconstructed exterior façade (F. Krischen, *Die Landmauer von Konstantinopel.* Teil 1. *Denkmäler antiker Architektur* 6 [Berlin 1938] pl. 19).

reuse of architectural sculpture can be observed at the gates of Blaundos, Hierapolis in Phrygia, Limyra, Sagalassos, and Tlos,[38] as opposed to other less carefully built and decorated stretches of the same walls.[39]

Apotropaic Figures. The ancient reliefs next to the southeast gate of Aphrodisias are probably to be understood as apotropes (see fig. 11). In neighboring Hierapolis heads of wild beasts and gorgons were found in the debris of the north gate and must have been affixed to it.[40] Gorgons count among the most common apotropaic figures of antiquity and remained in use in the Byzantine period.[41]

[38] Blaundos: J. Giese, "Das Nordtor," in A. Filges (ed.), *Blaundos: Berichte zur Erforschung einer Kleinstadt im lydisch-pamphylischen Grenzgebiet, IstForsch* 48 (Tübingen 2006) 79–114, at 113–14.

Hierapolis: for the north gate, see *Hierapolis di Frigia 1957–1987* (Milano 1987) 32–33; D'Andria, *Hierapolis* (supra n. 28), 112–14 figs. 92–94 (figural reliefs); Giese, "Nordtor" (supra this note), 123; Arthur, *Hierapolis* (supra n. 34), 129–30 fig. 63; for other gates, see *Hierapolis di Frigia 1957–1987* (Milano 1987) 30 (south gate), 37 (east gate); H. Yıldız, "La porta sud bizantina di Hierapolis (Pamukkale, Denizli)," in F. D'Andria and F. Silvestrelli (eds.), *Ricerche archeologiche turche nella valle del Lykos, Università di Lecce: Scuola di specializzazione in archeologia classica e medievale: Archeologia e storia* 6 (Galatina 2000) 193–207; D'Andria, *Hierapolis* (supra n. 28), 115 fig. 95 (east gate), 202 fig. 177 (south gate); for a city plan, see D. de Bernardi Ferrero (ed.), *Saggi in onore di Paolo Verzone, Hierapolis: Scavi e ricerche* 4 = *Archaeologica* 137 (Rome 2002) foldout.

Limyra: A. Krickel and G. Schartner, "Das Osttor der spätantiken Oststadt von Limyra," *ÖJh* 66 (1997) Beiblatt, 367–74, at 369–72 fig. 20; Peschlow, "Befestigungen" (supra n. 25), 620 fig. 20.

Sagalassos: Loots, Waelkens, and Depuydt, "City fortifications" (supra n. 28), 605, 620.

Tlos: Hellenkemper and Hild, *Lykien* (supra n. 25), II 887 fig. 403.

[39] Blaundos: A. Filges, "Die Stadtmauer: Mauerring und Türme," in idem (ed.), *Blaundos: Berichte zur Erforschung einer Kleinstadt im lydisch-pamphylischen Grenzgebiet, IstForsch* 48 (Tübingen 2006) 67–78, at 77. Hierapolis: *Hierapolis di Frigia 1957–1987* (Milano 1987) 33, 35; D'Andria, *Hierapolis* (supra n. 28), 107 fig. 89.

[40] D'Andria, *Hierapolis* (supra n. 28), 114 fig. 94.

[41] *DACL* 11, 1 (1933) 195–99 s. v. "Méduse" (H. Leclercq); J. Engemann, "Zur Verbreitung magischer Übelabwehr in der nichtchristlichen und christlichen Spätantike," *JAC* 18 (1975) 22–48, at 35–36; *LIMC* 4.1 (Basel 1988) 285–330 s. v. "Gorgo, Gorgones" (I. Krauskopf); *LIMC* 4.1 (Basel 1988) 345–362 s. v. "Gorgones Romanae" (O. Paoletti).

Eagles. The Golden Gate in the Theodosian walls of Constantinople is the most monumental of all Byzantine gates and was built with considerable extra effort in order to effect a grand display (fig. 12). It is the only gate with a triple passage, and the only one with a facing of marble. Its towers are larger and therefore more impressive than normal, and the main doors were sheeted with gold and topped by a statue of the emperor. The gate served as stage for the *adventus*, the ceremonial return to the city after a successful campaign.[42]

The Golden Gate is decorated with a pair of eagles, each sitting on one of the flanking towers and grasping a wreath with fillets hanging down (fig. 13). Other examples of flanking eagles can for instance be found at the entrance to the fifth-century church of St. John Studios at Constantinople and at several Roman gates and arches from the imperial period.[43]

Fig. 13. Constantinople, Golden Gate (cf. fig. 12), southwest corner of north tower (D-DAI-IST-Inst. Neg. 5541).

A gate of the early Byzantine walls at Sagalassos reused a keystone with the relief of an eagle grasping a snake.[44] A similar keystone was newly carved for an early Byzantine aqueduct near Constantinople.[45] The motif was traditionally used on pagan graves and may have been considered apotropaic.[46] During the Christian era it could alternatively have been interpreted as an allegory of Christ fighting Satan.[47]

Nikes. The southern passage of the northwest gate of Aphrodisias used to be decorated with an ancient archivolt, a common feature in early Byzantine fortifications.[48] The archivolt in Aphrodisias has since fallen off. The photograph in figure 14, again from the German Archaeological Institute in Istanbul, must have been taken about a hundred years ago. The lintel carries a building inscription and is flanked on the right side by a relief of Nike.[49] The relief is badly damaged, but one can still make out the spread wings and a body that is turned toward the gate. Although the relief is certainly

[42] B. Meyer-Plath and A.M. Schneider, *Die Landmauer von Konstantinopel.* Teil 2. *Aufnahme, Beschreibung und Geschichte, Denkmäler antiker Architektur* 8 (Berlin 1943) 39–60 pl. 28 I (eagle); J. Kramer, *Skulpturen mit Adlerfiguren an Bauten des 5. Jahrhunderts n. Chr. in Konstantinopel* (Munich 1968) 7–35; J. Bardill, "The Golden Gate of Constantinople. A triumphal arch of Theodosius I," *AJA* 103 (1999) 671–96; N. Asutay-Effenberger, *Die Landmauer von Konstantinopel-Istanbul: Historisch-topographische und baugeschichtliche Untersuchungen, Millennium-Studien* 18 (Wiesbaden 2007) 54–61.

[43] Kramer, *Skulpturen* (supra n. 42), 11.

[44] Northwest gate: Loots, Waelkens, and Depuydt, "City fortifications" (supra n. 28), 620.

[45] At Gümüşpınar to the west of the Long Walls: F. Dirimtekin, "Adduction de l'eau a Byzance dans la région dite 'Bulgarie'," *CahArch* 10 (1959) 217–43, fig. 32.6. I would like to thank James Crow for this reference.

[46] F. Işık, *Girlanden-Sarkophage aus Aphrodisias, Sarkophag-Studien* 5 (Mainz 2007) 85–86.

[47] R. Wittkower, "Eagle and serpent," *JWarb* 2 (1938/39) 293–325; J. Trilling, "The soul of the empire: Style and meaning in the mosaic pavement of the Byzantine imperial palace in Constantinople," *DOP* 43 (1989) 27–72, at 59.

[48] Cf. reused archivolts and architraves above early Byzantine gates at Blaundos: Giese, "Nordtor" (supra n. 38), 81 fig. 73, 83, 85 fig. 77. Limyra: Peschlow, "Befestigungen" (supra n. 25), 620 fig. 20. Sagalassos: Loots, Waelkens, and Depuydt, "City fortifications" (supra n. 28), 620. Tlos: Hellenkemper and Hild, *Lykien* (supra n. 25), II 887 fig. 403.

[49] Cf. L. Robert, *Hellenica* 13 (Paris 1965) pl. 27; Ratté and Smith, "Research" (supra n. 28), 734 fig. 19; De Staebler, "City wall" (supra n. 28), 297–300.

Fig. 14. Aphrodisias, south passage of northwest gate, historic photograph of the exterior façade (D-DAI-IST-R35.362. Repro).

reused, its placement next to the gate is hardly accidental. The Golden Gate as well as a secondary gate of Constantinople were also flanked by Nikes.[50]

Figure 15 shows the northern passage of the northwest gate at Aphrodisias. The passage and the arch on top are both flanked by winged beings. Both reliefs are older, reused blocks, as is the case with all the other building material as well. The winged being at the bottom is part of a longer frieze. The one at the top is badly damaged. The upper body and the head are missing. Still, enough is left to compare with the north façade of the arch of Constantine in Rome. That arch is likewise flanked by two winged beings, a personification of winter at the bottom and one of Nike at the top.[51] The comparison is vague,

[50] The Nike of the Golden Gate was a statue: see supra n. 42. The other Nike—a relief—used to be on display next to a gate at the Golden Horn. Note that it may have been put there later during the Byzantine period and was possibly understood to represent an angel rather than Nike. The relief is now in the Istanbul Archaeological Museum, inv. no. 948: A. Van Millingen, *Byzantine Constantinople: The Walls of the City and Adjoining Historical Sites* (London 1899) 198–205; G. Mendel, *Catalogue des sculptures grecques, romaines et byzantines* (Istanbul 1912–1914) 449–53 cat. no. 667; A.M. Schneider, "Die Blachernen," *Oriens* 4 (1951) 82–120, 90; N. Fıratlı, *La sculpture byzantine figurée au Musée archéologique d'Istanbul, Bibliothèque de l'Institut français d'études anatoliennes d'Istanbul* 30 (Paris 1990) 37–38 cat. no. 68 pl. 26. C.G. Curtis reports that he saw yet another Nike relief with a monogram of Heraclius on a tower at the tip of the historical peninsula of Istanbul during the 19th century: Mendel, *Catalogue* (supra this note), 452.

[51] H.P. L'Orange and A. von Gerkan, *Der spätantike Bildschmuck des Konstantinsbogens, Studien zur spätantiken Kunstgeschichte* 10 (Berlin 1939) 150–55.

but it must be taken into account that the choice of spolia available at Aphrodisias will have been limited. Their use was probably meant to evoke the tradition of Roman triumphal arches.

Fig. 15. Aphrodisias, north passage of northwest gate, historic photograph of the interior façade (E. Steiner, D-DAI-IST-Pe76/153–11 1976).

A Pair of Flanking Towers

Another ancient tradition is yet more common among early Byzantine fortifications: that of the gate with a pair of flanking towers. The most prominent example, the Golden Gate in the Theodosian walls of Constantinople (see fig. 12), has already been mentioned. This sophisticated fortification with an outer wall and ditch is commonly linked to Philo of Byzantium and his manual on the building of Hellenistic defenses.[52] Other early Byzantine walls in provincial Anatolia were less intricate and show that a pair of flanking towers was often built for its own sake without the other features of a textbook fortification.

Hierapolis in Phrygia, the next example to be considered, boasts a dazzling circuit of walls with a number of gates. Some of them are fairly simple, but the north and south gates are more sophisticated.[53] They are situated opposite each other at the ends of the main street or decumanus and form the chief entrances to the town. The north gate has already been mentioned for its wild beasts and gorgons.

The north and south gates are each flanked by a pair of towers. The workmanship is again much better than elsewhere in the circuit. There as everywhere else, besides the two main gates, towers are widely spaced, and an aggressor could have forced his way in relatively easily. The towers flanking the gates overstate the defensive qualities of the fortification as a whole and are of little practical value. Their main purpose was clearly for display. They evoke the tradition of Hellenistic fortifications, easily the most imposing feature of Anatolian urbanism.

Many a Hellenistic fortification was pulled down during the Roman imperial period, but the main gates of Perge and Side were preserved as urban monuments, and each became the focal point of a new square. The flanking towers of the gate in Side came to represent the city on coins.[54] In the late antique and early Byzantine periods, when those towns were refortified, everyone had to pass the paired towers once again.[55] Similarly, the main gates of the late antique or early Byzantine walls

[52] Meyer-Plath and Schneider, *Landmauer* (supra n. 42), 16–22; Foss and Winfield, *Fortifications* (supra n. 17), 44, 180 n. 10; Asutay-Effenberger, *Landmauer* (supra n. 42), 2.

[53] See the literature cited supra n. 38.

[54] Perge: A.M. Mansel, "Bericht über Ausgrabungen und Untersuchungen in Pamphylien in den Jahren 1957–1972," *AA* (1975) 49–96, at 60–75; P. Scherrer, "Hellenistische und römische Stadttore in Kleinasien unter besonderer Berücksichtigung von Ephesos," in T.G. Schattner and F. Valdés Fernándes (eds.), *Stadttore: Bautyp und Kunstform, Iberia Archaeologica* 8 (Mainz 2006) 63–78, at 77.

Side: A.M. Mansel, "Bericht über Ausgrabungen und Untersuchungen in Pamphylien in den Jahren 1946–1955," *AA* (1956) 34–120, at 72–73; Mansel, *Ruinen* (supra n. 25), 36–37 fig. 23.

[55] In Perge an additional outer gate was built in front of the Hellenistic one: Mansel, "Bericht 1957–1972" (supra n. 54), 60–63; Hellenkemper and Hild, *Lykien* (supra n. 25), I 369; U. Peschlow, "Das Südtor von Perge," in I. Delemen et al. (eds.), *Euergetes. Festschrift für Dr. Haluk Abbasoğlu zum 65. Geburtstag* (Antalya 2008) 971–87.

Side: Mansel, *Ruinen* (supra n. 25), 39; A.M. Mansel,

of Ephesus and Sagalassos are Hellenistic in origin and flanked by towers.[56] This motif was passed down through history and became a hallmark of late antique and early Byzantine urbanism, too. One of the finest provincial examples was erected in Blaundos, together with others in Aphrodisias, Laodicea on the Lycus, and Limyra.[57] There, too, other gates have no towers and are less defensive in outward appearance.[58]

The Fifth and Sixth Centuries

In the course of the fifth century wall-building died down in western Anatolia and nothing is reported from the sixth.[59] The same holds true for the other kinds of secular urban building that had flourished around A.D. 400: not only did new building come to a standstill, but the old colonnaded squares and streets fell prey to squatting and lost their formal civic character; ever more thermae ceased to function; and formerly sumptuous urban mansions were downgraded, subdivided, or simply left to decay.[60]

Some walls shared this fate. In Amorium a part of the walls was pulled down to make room for a fifth-century church.[61] The circuit of Sagalassos had been given up by the early sixth century,

---

"Osttor und Waffenreliefs von Side (Pamphylien)," *AA* (1968) 239–79, at 242, 258; Hellenkemper and Hild, *Lykien* (supra n. 25), I 381–82.

[56] Ephesus: Scherrer, "Stadttore" (supra n. 54), 68. Sagalassos, northeast gate: Loots, Waelkens, and Depuydt, "City fortifications" (supra n. 28), 625.

[57] Blaundos: Giese, "Nordtor" (supra n. 38).

Aphrodisias, west gate: C. Ratté and R.R.R. Smith, "Archaeological research at Aphrodisias in Caria, 1997 and 1998," *AJA* 104 (2000) 221–53, at 238–39 (description); Ratté, "Urban development" (supra n. 28), 118 fig. 5-2 (city plan), 125–26 fig. 5-5 (inscription and figural relief); Ratté and Smith, "Research" (supra n. 28), 733–35 (excavation); De Staebler, "City wall" (supra n. 28), 297–300.

Laodicea, eastern Byzantine gate: Şimşek, *Laodikeia* (supra n. 28), 103–11.

Limyra, east gate; the second tower is an addition: Krickel and Schartner, "Osttor" (supra n. 38). Cf. a gate with a pair of flanking towers, but with no certain date, at Philadelphia: E. Curtius, "Philadelphia: Nachtrag zu den Beiträgen zur Geschichte und Topographie Kleinasiens," in *AbhBerl* (Berlin 1872) 93–95, at 94 pl. 8; Hanfmann, Thomas, and Van Zanten, "City walls" (supra n. 28), 41–43; A. Pralong, "Les remparts de Philadelphie," in H. Ahrweiler (ed.), *Philadelphie et autres études, Byzantina Sorbonensia* 4 (Paris 1984) 101–26; R. Meriç, "1985 Yılı Alaşehir Kazı Çalışmaları," *Kazı Sonuçları Toplantısı* 8.2 (1986) 259–71, at 263 map 1; R. Meriç, "1987 Yılı Alaşehir Kazısı," *Kazı Sonuçları Toplantısı* 10.1 (1988) 157–70, at 159, 167–68 figs. 10–11 map 3.

Cf. a gate at Amorium, where one flanking tower has been excavated: "The existence of another matching tower must be postulated to the other side of the gate. Since traces of few other towers are visible in the lower circuit at Amorium it is impossible to say whether the presence of a triangular tower (or pair of towers) is unusual"; Lightfoot, *Amorium* (supra n. 28), 105–6.

[58] Aphrodisias, several gates: Ratté, "Urban development" (supra n. 28), 118 fig. 5-2; De Staebler, "City wall" (supra n. 28), 296–97 fig. 11. Blaundos, south gate: Filges, "Stadtmauer" (supra n. 39), 73–75. Limyra, south gate: H. Alanyalı, A. Pülz, and P. Ruggendorfer, "Urbanistische Forschungen in der Oststadt von Limyra," *ÖJh* 66 (1997) Beiblatt, 374–83, at 375–76 fig. 21. Sagalassos, northwest gate: Loots, Waelkens, and Depuydt, "City fortifications" (supra n. 28), 620.

[59] With the exception of the eastern borderlands toward Armenia and Persia, where Justinian had a number of places fortified, including Caesarea in the Cappadocian hinterland of that border. For the border toward Armenia and Persia, see F. Hild and M. Restle, *Kappadokien, Tabula Imperii Byzantini* 2 = *DenkschrWien* 149 (Vienna 1981) 128–29; F.R. Trombley, "The decline of the seventh-century town: The exception of Euchaita," in S. Vryonis (ed.), *Byzantine Studies in Honor of M.V. Anastos, Byzantina kai Metabyzantina* 4 (Malibu 1985) 65–90, at 77. For the strategic criteria behind the imperial urban and wall building program of the sixth century, see E. Zanini, "The urban ideal and urban planning in Byzantine new cities of the sixth century AD," in W. Bowden and L. Lavan (eds.), *Theory and Practice in Late Antique Archaeology, Late Antique Archaeology* 1 (Leiden 2003) 196–223. The fortification of Caesarea is reported by Procopius, *De aedificiis* 5.4. Cf. Hild and Restle, *Kappadokien* (supra this note), 130–31, 195.

[60] Niewöhner, *Aizanoi* (supra n. 31), 87–88 (squares and streets), 89 (baths), 90–91 (houses); H.G. Saradi, *The Byzantine City in the Sixth Century. Literary Images and Historical Reality* (Athens 2006) 209–352; F. Martens, "Late antique urban streets at Sagalassos," in L. Lavan, A. Sarantis, and E. Zanini (eds.), *Technology in Transition A.D. 300–650, Late Antique Archaeology* 4 (Leiden 2007) 321–65; A. Zaccaria Ruggiu, "Regio VIII" (supra n. 4); M. Waelkens et al., "Complexes" (supra n. 34).

[61] F. Hild and H. Hellenkemper, *Kilikien und Isaurien, Tabula Imperii Byzantini* 5 = *DenkschrWien* 215 (Vienna 1990) I 190; S. Hill, *The Early Byzantine Churches of Cilicia and*

when, after an earthquake, it was used as a dumping ground for debris.[62] At Hierapolis in Phrygia a small bath was built up against the outer façade of the walls during the fifth or sixth century.[63] At Limyra the same happened with a church in the sixth century. This latter example is most instructive, because the church was leveled again some time later, possibly in conjunction with a restoration of the walls,[64] and probably because the structure was hampering defense.

I will come back to this later period at the end of this paper, but first I would like to conclude the discussion of early Byzantine walls in western Anatolia. Their utter neglect in the sixth century confirms that their building around A.D. 400 had more to do with urban embellishment than with a pressing need for fortification.

Urban embellishment came off the agenda in the fifth and sixth centuries as towns lost their key position in the administration and social life of the empire. This development has been studied by Wolf Liebeschuetz and is often referred to as the "flight of the curiales."[65] Afterwards, what remained to be built were churches.[66] As in Limyra they were often placed outside the walls. Other extramural churches may be found in Hierapolis in Phrygia, Sagalassos, and Tlos.[67] In comparison to this later development, the early Byzantine walls look like the fanciful caprices of a wave of overcharged urban building campaigns around A.D. 400.

The Countryside

This image is confirmed by the situation in the countryside. As in the territory of Miletus, recent surveys have shown that all over Anatolia the countryside witnessed an unprecedented boom in the fifth and sixth centuries.[68] In the territory of Aizanoi in Phrygia ancient settlements were confined to

---

Isauria, Birmingham Byzantine and Ottoman Monographs 1 (Aldershot 1996) 92. Cf. Ephesus, where a stretch of wall had to give way to a church during the fifth/sixth century, although the neighboring gate to Magnesia had been renovated only recently: Scherrer, "Stadttore" (supra n. 54), 68.

[62] Loots, Waelkens, and Depuydt, "City fortifications" (supra n. 28), 616–18.

[63] D. de Bernardi Ferrero, "Excavations and restorations during 1994 in Hierapolis of Phrygia," *Kazı Sonuçları Toplantısı* 17.2 (1995) 95–105, at 96–97; F. D'Andria, "Hierapolis of Phrygia: Its evolution in Hellenistic and Roman times," in D. Parrish (ed.), *Urbanism in Western Asia Minor, JRA* Suppl. 45 (Portsmouth, RI 2001) 94–115, at 113; Arthur, *Hierapolis* (supra n. 34), 145.

[64] Borchhardt, "Bericht" (supra n. 28), 305–6; Marksteiner, "Befestigungen" (supra n. 28), 43.

[65] W. Liebeschuetz, "The finances of Antioch in the fourth century AD," *ByzZeit* 52 (1959) 344–56. Reprint in: idem, *From Diocletian to the Arab Conquest: Change in the Late Roman Empire* (Aldershot 1990) XII; A.H.M. Jones, *The Later Roman Empire, 284–602: A Social, Economic and Administrative Survey*, vol. 2 (Oxford 1964) 737–57; J.H.W.G. Liebeschuetz, *The Decline and Fall of the Roman City* (Oxford 2001); A. Laniado, *Recherches sur les notables municipaux dans l'empire protobyzantin, TravMém Monographies* 13 (Paris 2002) 1–129; Saradi, *City* (supra n. 60), 148–85.

[66] J.H.W.G. Liebeschuetz, "Administration and politics in the city of the 5th and 6th centuries with special reference to the circus factions," in C. Lepelley (ed.), *La fin de la cité antique et le début de la cité médiévale: De la fin du 3e siècle a l'avènement de Charlemagne, Studi storici sulla tarda antichità* 8 (Bari 1996) 161–82, at 167–68; Niewöhner, *Aizanoi* (supra n. 31), 105; Saradi, *City* (supra n. 60), 385–440.

[67] Hierapolis, church built into the baths to the north of the Roman agora: *Reallexikon zur byzantinischen Kunst* II (Stuttgart 1971) 1212–15 s. v. "Hierapolis" (P. Verzone); D'Andria, *Hierapolis* (supra n. 28), 62.

Sagalassos: P. Talloen and L. Vercauteren, "The fate of temples in Late Antique Anatolia," in L. Lavan and M. Mulryan (eds.), *The Archaeology of Late Antique "Paganism," Late Antique Archaeology* 7 (Leiden 2011) 347–87, at 352–69.

Tlos, transept basilica: W.W. Wurster, "Antike Siedlungen in Lykien," *AA* (1976) 23–49, at 37 fig. 4; Hellenkemper and Hild, *Lykien* (supra n. 25), II 886–87.

[68] J.M. Cook, *The Troad. An Archaeological and Topographical Study* (Oxford 1973) 369–73; F. Vermeulen, M. de Dapper, and T. Wiedemann, "Vers un approche géo-archéologique intégrée: le territoire antique de Pessinonte (Turquie)," in M. Clavel-Lévêque and A. Vignot (eds.), *Cité et territoire* 2 (Paris 1998) 123–39, at 132 fig. 10; J. Devreker and F. Vermeulen, "Fouilles et prospections à Pessinonte: campagne de 1996," *Anatolia Antiqua* 6 (1998) 249–58, at 257; D. Baird, "Settlement expansion on the Konya Plain, Anatolia: 5th–7th centuries A.D.," in W. Bowden, L. Lavan,

the plain. During the early Byzantine period this changed, and the mountainous regions were settled in addition to the plain. New settlements were built, each with its own church. The driving force behind this extension will have been a growing population that could no longer be accommodated and fed in the plain alone.[69] Neither Aizanoi nor the rural settlements were fortified. There was clearly no need for this in western Anatolia during the early Byzantine period.

Walls Built after Around A.D. 400

There is one more point to be made against an early Byzantine date for walls such as those in Miletus, Magnesia, Patara, Ephesus, and Side: they are stronger but less beautiful than the earlier Byzantine walls of Anatolia. Their strength derives from the greater thickness of the walls as well as from a more careful and regular arrangement of courses.[70] The careful workmanship was not restricted to the gates, as was so often the case with the early Byzantine walls that were built around A.D. 400.

In Side new walls were built across the peninsula. The towers can only be entered on the level of the walkways and have massive bases for additional strength.[71] Other massive towers or bastions occur in Miletus and Patara[72]—about Ephesus and Magnesia I do not know—but not in any earlier Byzantine walls.[73]

---

and C. Machado (eds.), *Recent Research on the Late Antique Countryside, Late Antique Archaeology* 2 (Leiden 2004) 219–46; R.E. Blanton, *Hellenistic, Roman and Byzantine Settlement Patterns of the Coastal Lands of Western Rough Cilicia, BAR-IS* 879 (Oxford 2000) 60.

[69] P. Niewöhner, "Aizanoi and Anatolia. Town and countryside in late late antiquity," *Millennium* 3 (2006) 239–53, at 242–43; Niewöhner, *Aizanoi* (supra n. 31), 76–81.

[70] Ephesus: 3.3–3.4 m: W. Müller-Wiener, "Mittelalterliche Befestigungen im südlichen Jonien," *IstMitt* 11 (1961) 5–122, at 88.

Magnesia: 2.5–3 m: Humann, Kohte, and Watzinger, *Magnesia* (supra n. 24), 33.

Miletus: 1.80–2.60: Knackfuß, *Milet* I 7 (supra n. 1), 154 pls. 2, 25.

Patara: 1.70–2.50 m: M. Kunze, "Bericht über die Arbeiten im archäologischen Gebiet von Patara während der Grabungskampagnen 1993–1996," *Kazı Sonuçları Toplantısı* 19.2 (1998) 61–79, at 63; Bruer and Kunze, *Stadtplan* (supra n. 25).

Side: 2.15–2.40 m: Hellenkemper and Hild, *Lykien* (supra n. 25), I 386; Peschlow, "Mauerbau" (supra n. 6), 73–74, 91–102 figs. 5–6, 9, 12, 26. Cf. M. Klinkott, *Altertümer von Pergamon* XVI. Die *Stadtmauern*. Teil 1. *Die byzantinischen Befestigungsanlagen von Pergamon* (Berlin 2001) 19 f. 97, who dates some walls to the Dark Ages, because they are thicker, have a stronger masonry, and contain more spolia.

Compare the earlier Byzantine walls:

Blaundos: 1.30–1.90 m (first phase; later repairs are up to 2.10 m thick): Filges, "Stadtmauer" (supra n. 39), 70, 72–74, 76.

Hierapolis in Phrygia: 2.5 m: D'Andria, *Hierapolis* (supra n. 28), 115.

Limyra: 1.60–1.75 m: Peschlow, "Befestigungen" (supra n. 25), 604 no. 25; Marksteiner, "Befestigungen" (supra n. 28), 43.

Sagalassos: 2 m: Loots, Waelkens, and Depuydt, "City fortifications" (supra n. 28), 619.

Sardis: 1.25–2.10 m: Hanfmann, Thomas, and Van Zanten, "City walls" (supra n. 28), 39; "on the average somewhat less than two metres": Foss and Winfield, *Fortifications* (supra n. 17), 127.

Tlos: "ca. 1.85–2.00 m": Peschlow, "Befestigungen" (supra n. 25), 608 no. 53.

[71] Hellenkemper and Hild, *Lykien* (supra n. 25), I 387; Peschlow, "Befestigungen" (supra n. 25), 609; Peschlow, "Mauerbau" (supra n. 6), 72–74 .

[72] Miletus: the tower-like corner bastion between the temple of Serapis and the Baths of Faustina. Other towers could be entered: B. Walter, *Milet* II 4. *Topographische Karte von Milet* (Berlin 1968). Patara: Hellenkemper and Hild, *Lykien* (supra n. 25), II 784; Bruer and Kunze, *Stadtplan* (supra n. 25).

[73] The earlier towers included an accessible ground floor:

Anemurium: Russell, "Garrison" (supra n. 28).

Amorium: Harrison, "Amorium excavations 1990" (supra n. 28), 223 fig. 4; N. Christie and R.M. Harrison, "Excavations at Amorium: 1992 interim report," *AnatSt* 43 (1993) 147–62, at 151.

Aphrodisias: Giese, "Baugeschichtliche Einordnung" (supra n. 28), 123; De Staebler, "City wall" (supra n. 28), 296–304.

Blaundos: Giese, "Nordtor" (supra n. 38), 86–101.

Constantinople: Meyer-Plath and Schneider, *Landmauer* (supra n. 42), 71–81.

Hierapolis in Phrygia: Giese, "Baugeschichtliche Einordnung" (supra n. 28), 123.

Laodicea on the Lycus: Şimşek, *Laodikeia* (supra n. 28), 103–11.

Limyra: Krickel and Schartner, "Osttor" (supra n. 38), 368–71.

As for beautification, the builders of the later walls had no qualms about mixing any kind of building material (see figs. 2, 7). The round sections of column drums are exposed everywhere, at the base as well as further up in the wall.[74] The careful workmanship was not extended to the visual aspect, and gates are no longer exceptional. Some gates are flanked by a single tower as in Miletus (see figs. 2–3), but they make no claim to monumentality, let alone the Hellenistic tradition.

To sum up, the later walls are fundamentally different from those built around A.D. 400. It follows that the earlier wall-building does not make a sixth-century date for the later walls of Miletus any more likely. On the contrary, the sixth-century disregard for the earlier fortifications weighs heavily against a contemporary date for the new wall-building program. We may therefore return to the assumption that the later walls were not built before the seventh century.

Conclusions

The Market Gate at Miletus was probably fortified during the Dark Ages, when the permanent Arab threat necessitated a short circuit that could be manned at all times. The Arabs ruled the sea and could attack instantly.[75] Such *razzias* will have left coastal cities such as Miletus, Ephesus, Magnesia, Patara, and Side no time to assemble the troops necessary to defend the extended fortifications of late antiquity and the early Byzantine period; hence the shorter circuits that could be held by a small local garrison.[76] Their simplicity—few towers, no sophisticated gates—is well suited to the ephemeral character of the Arab *razzias*. The Arabs counted on taking the Byzantines by surprise and would not normally bother with the kind of siege that only more sophisticated fortifications could resist.

With this functional explanation for the character and date of the earlier Byzantine fortifications of Anatolia we may return to the beginning of this paper and ask: does it solve the riddle of the Market Gate? It seems advisable to postpone a final verdict until solid evidence has been unearthed by stratigraphic excavation. This kind of evidence is unlikely to turn up in Miletus, however; most of the circuit was already excavated over a century ago, when stratigraphy was less carefully recorded than today, and in any case the stratigraphy is complicated by the fact that the Byzantine walls are founded directly on much earlier walls.[77] It is to be hoped that some other short Byzantine circuit at Ephesus, Magnesia, Patara, Side, or elsewhere will eventually be excavated and dated.

Sagalassos: Loots, Waelkens, and Depuydt, "City fortifications" (supra n. 28), 619–20.

Sardis: Hanfmann, Thomas, and Van Zanten, "City walls" (supra n. 28), 43 fig. 12.

[74] Patara: Işık, *Patara* (supra n. 25), 104 fig. 83, 128 fig. 96; Peschlow, "Befestigungen" (supra n. 25), 612–13 figs. 2–3; Bruer and Kunze, *Stadtplan* (supra n. 25).

Side: Hellenkemper and Hild, *Lykien* (supra n. 25), III figs. 336–39; Peschlow, "Mauerbau" (supra n. 6), 74, 91–102 figs. 5–6, 9, 25–26.

[75] Supra n. 23; V. Christides, "Arab-Byzantine struggle in the sea. Naval tactics (7th–11th centuries A.D.)," in Y.Y. al-Hijji and V. Christides (eds.), *Aspects of Arab Seafaring. An Attempt to Fill in the Gaps of Maritime History* (Athens 2002) 87–106.

[76] P. Niewöhner, "Archäologie und die 'Dunklen Jahrhunderte' im byzantinischen Anatolien," in J. Henning (ed.), *Post-Roman Towns, Trade and Settlement in Europe and Byzantium. Vol. 2, Byzantium, Pliska, and the Balkans, Millennium Studies* 5 (Wiesbaden 2007) 119–58.

[77] Niewöhner, "Mauern" (supra n. 1).

7 Survey Evidence for Late Antique Settlement in the Region around Aphrodisias

Christopher Ratté and Peter D. De Staebler

The city was the fundamental social institution of Greek and Roman culture. More than the sack of Rome, the transformation of provincial towns throughout the Mediterranean world in late antiquity marks the beginning of the Middle Ages. The cities of western and southern Asia Minor were among the last holdouts of traditional Mediterranean urban life outside the capitals, but it is now generally agreed that they were all in large part abandoned in or before the first half of the seventh century. Much else remains hotly debated—why this transformation took place; whether it unfolded suddenly, or gradually, over generations or even centuries; and how to characterize the communities that remained in places such as those examined in this volume. In short, to borrow from the title of a recent German conference, is it better to speak of "Niedergang," or of "Wandel?"[1] The goal of this paper is to investigate the case of Aphrodisias, and in particular, to suggest how regional survey can contribute to the study of "de-urbanization" here and throughout Asia Minor.

First a few words on what has been learned from excavation at the city site of Aphrodisias, and from study of the sculpture and inscriptions. As Charlotte Roueché and R.R.R. Smith have shown, the culture of monuments—the commemoration of civic good deeds by long and fulsome inscriptions, the erection of honorific statues—remained strong at Aphrodisias into the sixth century.[2] Re-examination of the excavated monuments has shown that the same is true of the maintenance of public buildings.[3] Particularly notable was the conversion of the Temple of Aphrodite into a Christian church in ca. A.D. 500. A century to a century and a half later, by contrast, circumstances had changed dramatically. The latest coins in the debris levels found in most areas of the site all date to the reign of Heraclius. Habitation continued only in the area of the theater, converted into a fortified citadel, and in the environs of the temple/church, also partly or wholly surrounded by a post-antique enclosure wall, although the date of that wall is uncertain.

What happened between the end of the fifth century and the beginning of the seventh? The carving of statues and inscriptions came to a virtual halt in the early sixth century, and with it any documentary evidence for the erection or maintenance of public buildings. Does this mean that Aphrodisias had already begun to cease functioning as a city by this time? Should we imagine that urban markets and workshops, educational and recreational institutions, the roads, the water supply, and the drainage system, all started to break down at this time as well? Or was the disappearance

[1] J.-U. Krause and C. Witschel (eds.), *Die Stadt in der Spätantike—Niedergang oder Wandel? Historia Einzelschriften* 190 (Stuttgart 2006).

[2] C. Roueché, *Aphrodisias in Late Antiquity, JRS Monograph* 5 (London 1989) and revised second edition online (2004) <http://insaph.kcl.ac.uk/ala2004> ISBN 1897747 17 9. R.R.R. Smith, "Statue life in the Hadrianic Baths at Aphrodisias, AD 100–600: Local context and historical meaning," in F.A. Bauer and C. Witschel (eds.), *Statuen in der Spätantike, Spätantike, frühes Christentum, Byzanz. Reihe B, Studien und Perspektiven*, Band 23 (Wiesbaden 2007) 203–35, with references to earlier studies.

[3] C. Ratté, "New research on the urban development of Aphrodisias in late antiquity," in D. Parrish (ed.), *Urbanism in Western Asia Minor, JRA* Suppl. 45 (Portsmouth, RI 2001) 117–47.

of the "culture of monuments" a more isolated phenomenon? There had been very little new public building at Aphrodisias for centuries, and it is possible that some late Roman building repairs not epigraphically dated to the fifth century or earlier actually took place in the sixth century. Here it is worth emphasizing that there is stratified archaeological evidence for continued commercial activity on one of the streets south of the agora, and for continued habitation in the area between the Temple of Aphrodite and the stadium, down into the seventh century.[4] This is one good reason for thinking that substantial parts of the city remained vital until just before its partial abandonment.

When we begin to consider developments in the early seventh century, it is no longer possible to keep talking about time without also talking about space. For the abandonment of the city implies that something happened to its inhabitants. The two obvious possibilities are that they died off in significant numbers, or that they moved away. Only by looking outside the city walls, and by looking at the space around Aphrodisias over time, can we hope to determine which of these alternatives is closer to the truth. How does the abandonment of the city appear in a regional perspective? How does it relate to regional settlement patterns? How are population figures for the surrounding area affected? Is there a decline in population in the countryside comparable with that in the city, or is rather the inverse the case—did the population of the hinterland increase as the population of the city declined? Economic questions inevitably arise. Was there more or less farmland under cultivation? How was exploitation of other natural resources affected? Were trade connections with the outside world maintained or cut off? If we enlarge both our temporal and our spatial frames of reference looking not at generations or centuries but at millennia, and not just at Asia Minor but at the entire Mediterranean world, what represents the greater anomaly: the establishment and prosperity of urban ways of life in areas such as northeastern Caria, or a much more diffuse and less dense pattern of settlement in a largely self-sufficient agricultural region?

The present paper cannot of course answer such a wide-ranging set of questions. But it is worth asking them at the outset simply to reinforce an obvious but important point; since the pattern of events seen at Aphrodisias was by no means unique, but rather typical of the contemporary experience of comparable cities throughout Asia Minor (and of the earlier experience of cities across the Latin west), purely local factors, such as earthquakes, cannot provide an adequate account of this change. More systemic explanations are required. The growth of towns in places like Aphrodisias was not the inevitable result of organic developments. These towns had to have reasons for existence. Most were founded at specific points in time and under specific ideological, military, and economic circumstances, which naturally changed over time. The network of towns spread over Asia Minor (and over similar regions around the Mediterranean) had proved remarkably robust for centuries, but history showed that it was still capable of unraveling quickly. Towns everywhere put a strain on local resources, such as arable land and timber supplies; thus they inevitably relied on commercial connections with other towns, especially if they had developed specialized import- or export-based economies; in addition, all these towns also depended to a greater or lesser degree on centralized administration, for example, for the maintenance of roads and aqueducts. Strain on this complex system could have come from many different directions, including natural disaster, war, disease, administrative breakdown, and ideological changes in the general perception of the necessity or desirability of the urban habit as a way of life.

How, then, can regional survey at one site such as Aphrodisias help us to understand this complex phenomenon? The two approaches to addressing this question that we would like to examine

[4] Ratté, "New Research" (supra n. 3), 145–46.

in this paper concern, in the first place, the transformation of a sacred landscape, and in the second place, the evolution of rural settlement in the environs of a major city. We begin with a few words on the scope and methods of the Aphrodisias Regional Survey project, which was begun in 2005 and completed in 2009 with the aim of investigating the interaction between human habitation and the natural environment in an 800 km^2 region around Aphrodisias—the upper valley of the Morsynus river and a plateau and part of an adjacent river valley to the southwest and south—from prehistory to the present day.[5] Research consisted of an architectural survey of the immediate environs of the city as defined by the area between a circle of 1 km radius centered on the city and the city walls—essentially a ring about 500 m wide; intensive survey of a series of 50 m by 5 km transects radiating out from the center of the city; and extensive survey based largely on local information of the entire survey region. Procedures employed for the classification of sites and the collection of surface materials are discussed in greater detail below.

The area around Aphrodisias was investigated field by field in the first part of our survey (fig. 1). The principal aim of this undertaking was to record extra-urban architectural monuments outside Aphrodisias, in particular tombs. In this way, we hoped to gain a better understanding of the suburban cemeteries, and by extension, of the roads leading into and out of town. We examined each field with a team of five, walking up and down the field at 10 m intervals, but we did not rigorously collect or record surface finds. In the intensive transect survey, by contrast, which covered parts of the same area, we counted and collected surface finds in a systematic fashion.

In addition to improving our knowledge of the suburban cemeteries, for instance, of the distribution of sarcophagi of different types in different areas, which provided valuable evidence for the "social history" of the cemeteries,[6] the most important result of this survey was the discovery of at least three and possibly four late antique churches just outside the walls of Aphrodisias. These include a church of essentially basilical plan (but with a central dome) just southwest of the West Gate; a small basilical church (with the nave separated from the side aisles by arcades) in the modern cemetery northeast of Aphrodisias;[7] a large mound, clearly the remains of a monumental east-west oriented apsidal building with several monolithic columns and two composite capitals of which one bears a cross, ca. 200 m southwest of the Southwest Gate; and a doorjamb and two standing columns (one double half-column, one spirally fluted column), just outside the East Gate, possibly also in light of their location and preservation, parts of a church (standing columns or doorjambs at Aphrodisias often represent monuments such as churches still maintained in the middle Byzantine period).[8]

These discoveries represent a major step forward in our understanding of the urban and suburban topography of Aphrodisias in the late Roman and Byzantine periods, illustrating one important aspect of late antique "Wandel." Before the beginning of the survey project, the only late Roman church known at Aphrodisias was the remodeled former poliadic Temple of Aphrodite, and the lack of evidence for other churches in this provincial metropolis was a mystery to us. Aphrodisias is now seen to

[5] The major results of the survey will be published as C. Ratté and P.D. De Staebler (eds.), *Aphrodisias* V. *The Aphrodisias Regional Survey* (Mainz forthcoming). Preliminary reports on the evidence for earlier periods of occupation include C. Ratté, "New research on the region around Aphrodisias," in R. Van Bremen and M. Carbon (eds.), *Hellenistic Karia, Ausonius Éditions, Études* 28 (Bordeaux 2010) 253–67; idem, "The Carians and the Lydians," in F. Rumscheid (ed.), *Die Karer und die Anderen* (Bonn 2009) 135–47.

[6] H. Turnbow, "Roman sarcophagi," forthcoming in Ratté and De Staebler, *Aphrodisias* V (supra n. 5).

[7] This church is also located near an ancient cemetery, including among other monuments a tomb identified by an inscription on its lintel as that of a bishop named Theopropios; see Roueché, *Aphrodisias in Late Antiquity* (supra n. 2), 211–12, nos. 165–66.

[8] Ö. Dalgıç, "Early Christian and Byzantine churches," forthcoming in Ratté and De Staebler, *Aphrodisias* V (supra n. 5).

Fig. 1. Satellite image of Aphrodisias, showing area of suburban survey (scale 1:15,000).

conform to a pattern familiar from numerous other early Christian cities, with a large congregational cathedral situated in the heart of town, and several smaller funerary churches and chapels located just outside the walls. These churches had the effect of sanctifying existing cemeteries, and they may have been situated near martyrs' tombs. They also took possession, as it were, of the major entrances into the city, serving as clear markers of Christian identity, and perhaps also as monumental talismans protecting the community. The centrifugal placement of extramural churches at Aphrodisias and similar towns may be seen as a first step in the de-emphasis of centrally located urban sanctuaries and the growing significance of larger numbers of smaller religious sites more liberally sprinkled across the countryside—in the unraveling, that is, of the traditional fabric of a Roman town. Here it is worth noting that we have quite a bit more evidence for rural churches in the area around Aphrodisias in the late Roman and Byzantine periods than we do for extramural pagan sanctuaries in earlier centuries. One may also see a parallel development in another major transformation of Aphrodisias and other late Roman towns, namely the increased construction of monumental private houses on the edges of the city centers—signifying a departure from traditional public space, and from traditional civic life, and a step toward a new system of social organization.[9]

Let us now turn to the less intensive survey of the surrounding countryside. First a brief look at the distribution of rural churches, shown in figure 2. The principal evidence for these consists of architectural blocks, often bearing carved decoration, and sometimes found in association with in-situ archaeological remains. The churches include four late antique sites on the floor of the Morsynus river valley; a possible late antique monastery low in the hills to the south; a late antique church apparently built on the site of a major pagan sanctuary attached to the city of Attouda, just over the hills to the north of Aphrodisias; two middle Byzantine churches in the hills north and south of the city; and two late antique and three middle Byzantine churches on the southwest plateau.

The main emphasis of this paper lies, however, on the evidence for rural settlement. To begin by stepping back for a moment in time, the earliest substantial settlement in our survey region lies not at Aphrodisias but at Bingeç, apparently ancient Plarasa, on the plateau to the south.[10] This site has never been excavated, and no in situ buildings are known, but it has produced numerous inscriptions, and it has a large Hellenistic tumulus cemetery attached to it—containing at least 28 individual tombs. Aside from Bingeç and Aphrodisias, our main evidence for ancient settlement in the survey region consists of two different kinds of sites, which we have called farmsteads and settlements. Farmsteads are places where we observed unusual concentrations of pottery and roof tiles on the surface, but no extensive in-situ architectural remains. Settlements are places with characteristics similar to farmsteads, but more extensive in-situ architectural remains—a typical example illustrated in figure 3 extends over an area of at least 75 by 25 m. The archaeological distinctions between what we call farmsteads and what we call settlements are real, but as we shall see they may have more to do with changing historical circumstances than with original size and function.

The locations of the 23 ancient settlements identified on the survey are shown in figure 4; 20 of these were identified through the extensive survey, three through the intensive survey. They are concentrated on the hillslopes overlooking the Morsynus river valley and on the plateau to the south, with only three settlements lying below 600 m in elevation. All settlements were mapped and targeted for

[9] On the late Roman houses at Aphrodisias, see M.L. Berenfeld, "The Triconch House and the predecessors of the Bishop's Palace at Aphrodisias," *AJA* 113 (2009) 203–29; I.M. Lockey, *The Atrium House at Aphrodisias* (Ph.D. dissertation, New York University 2010).

[10] On the early history of Aphrodisias and related communities, see C. Ratté, "The Founding of Aphrodisias," in C. Ratté and R.R.R. Smith (eds.), *Aphrodisias Papers 4. New Research on the City and its Monuments*, *JRA* Suppl. 70 (Portsmouth, RI 2008) 7–36, at 10–11, with references.

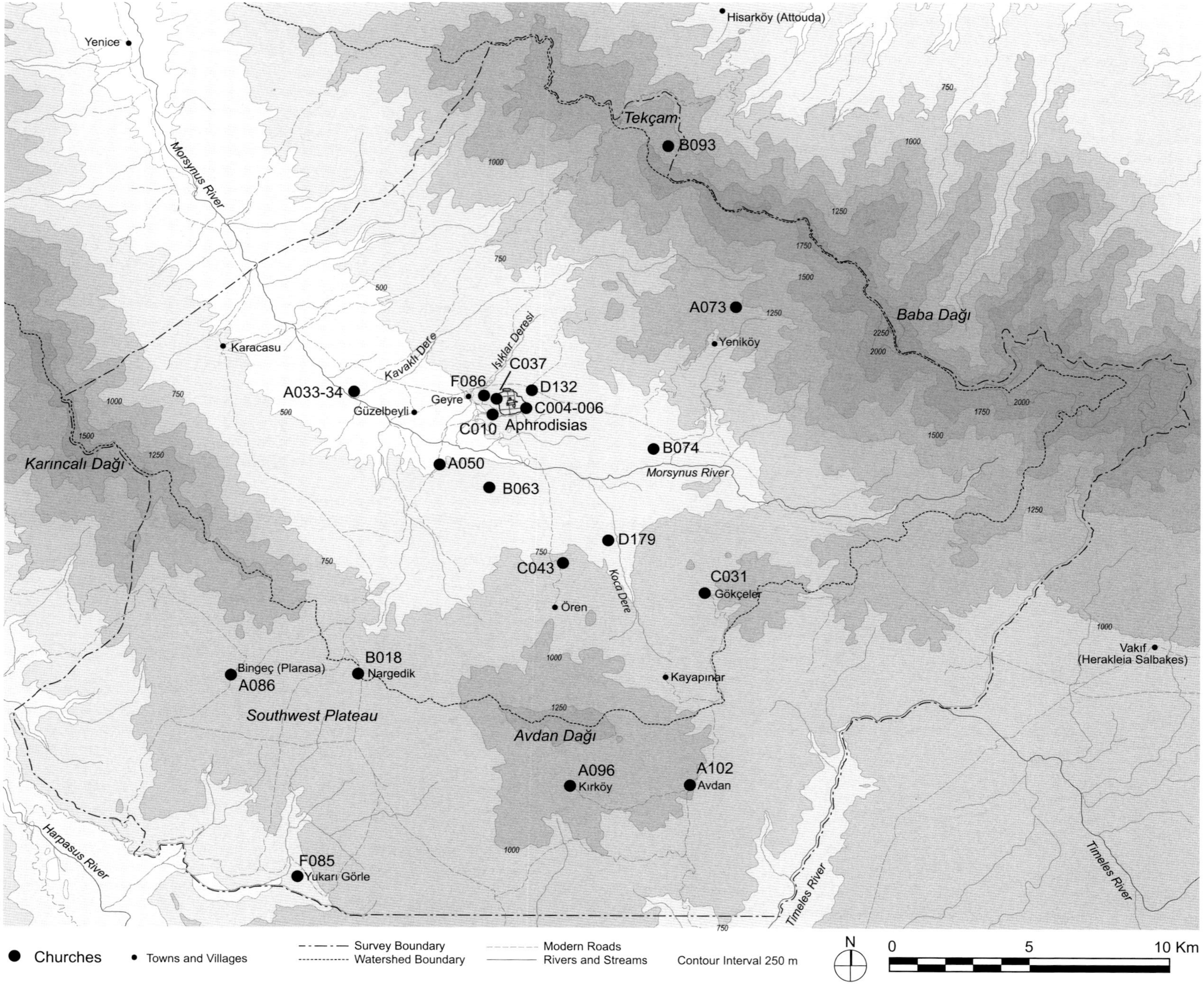

Fig. 2. Map of Aphrodisias survey region, showing locations of churches (scale 1:200,000).

Fig. 3. Map of Settlement A016, showing surface collection transects.

the systematic collection of surface finds, which proceeded as follows (see fig. 3). At each settlement, we laid out an intensive transect consisting of a row of 10 by 10 m squares running through the middle of the site for its whole length, and a series of less intensive transects 10 m wide and equal in length to the intensive transect but without internal subdivisions. The intensive transects were sampled first by a group of four or five persons, walking 2 m apart, collecting all diagnostic materials, and discussing the finds for each separately recorded square. The less intensive transects were then surveyed by pairs walking 5 m apart. We feel that this method of collecting gave us a representative sample of sherds for dating purposes, but we were not collecting intensively enough to detect patterns of use in different areas of the sites. Dating of the pottery depended on comparison with pottery from stratified deposits of Aphrodisias, and on imported pottery or local imitations of datable "international" forms.[11] An

[11] P.D. De Staebler, "Roman pottery," forthcoming in Ratté and De Staebler, *Aphrodisias* V (supra n. 5).

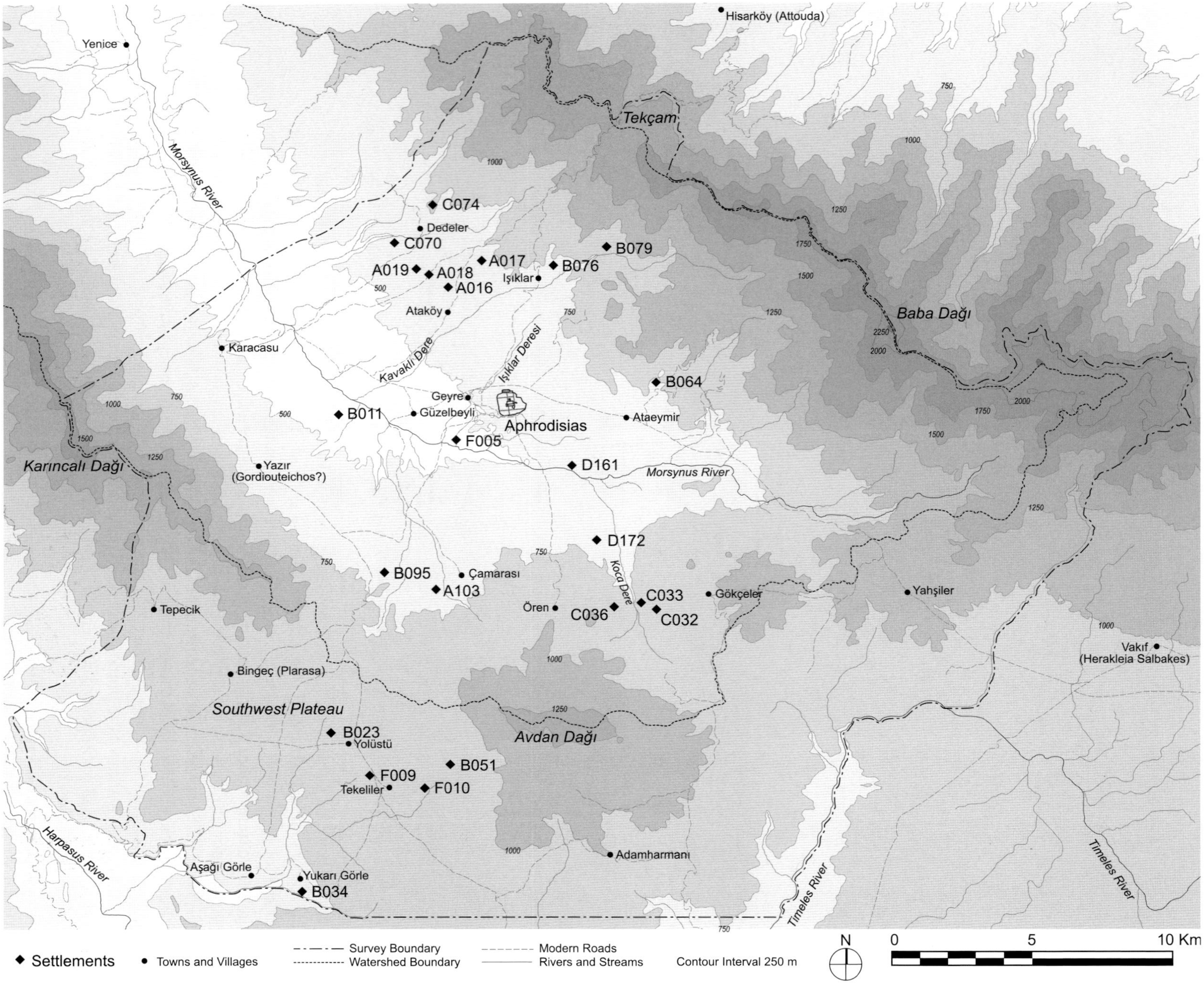

Fig. 4. Map of Aphrodisias survey region, showing locations of settlements (scale 1:200,000).

Table 1. Settlements with datable pottery of the Greek and Roman periods.

Settlements	*Pre-Hell.*	*Hell./ Aug.*	*Early Imp.*	*High Imp.*	*Late Roman*	*Middle Byz.*	*Islamic*	*Mod.*
Hills to North								
Ataköy 1 (A016)	-	++	+	+	-	-	+	+
K. Yaykın (A018)	-	+	+	+	+	+	-	+
Kale Mev. (B064)	+	+	++	+	+	-	+	+
Işıklar (B076)	-	-	++	+	+	-	-	-
Çatak Tep. (B079)	-	++	+	+	-	-	+	+
Pazar Gedii (C070)	-	-	+	+	?	-	+	+
Valley Floor								
Kadıkerim (B011)	-	+	+	+	+	+	+	+
SE 50 (D161)	-	?	+	+	+	-	+	+
SW Trans (F005)	-	-	+	+	?	-	-	+
Hills to South								
Dal Tepesi (A103)	+	+	?	+	-	-	-	-
Yeşilyurt (B095)	-	?	++	+	-	-	-	+
Karakuz Kayası (C032)	-	+	+	?	+	-	-	-
Yıkıntı (C036)	-	++	-	-	-	-	+	+
SE Trans (D172)	+	++	+	-	-	+	+	-
Koca Der. Church (D179)	-	-	-	?	++	+	-	-
Southwest Plateau								
Yolüstü (B023)	-	?	?	?	-	-	-	+
Kara Dere (B051)	-	?	?	?	?	-	-	-
Tekeliler (F009)	-	-	?	?	?	-	-	-
Koca Ören (F010)	-	+	+	+	++	-	+	+

Key: ++ = strong preponderance; + = present; ? = not securely dated; - = absent

obvious problem is our limited knowledge of local pottery from before and after the main periods of occupation, but we were able to associate one unfamiliar fabric with pre-Roman (late classical or Hellenistic) habitation, and another unfamiliar fabric with post-antique (Dark Age) habitation, and we feel comfortable in assigning date ranges to most sites. The dates assigned to the sites are shown in table 1, in which the sites are organized according to geographical location.

The locations of the 32 farmsteads identified on the survey are shown in figure 5. We carried out systematic collection of pottery at 18 or 56 per cent of these: at all those farmsteads where agricultural processing blocks were found (12), at three additional farmsteads found in the course of the intensive survey, and at an additional three farmsteads of special interest. The dates assigned to these sites, again organized by geographical location, are summarized in table 2.

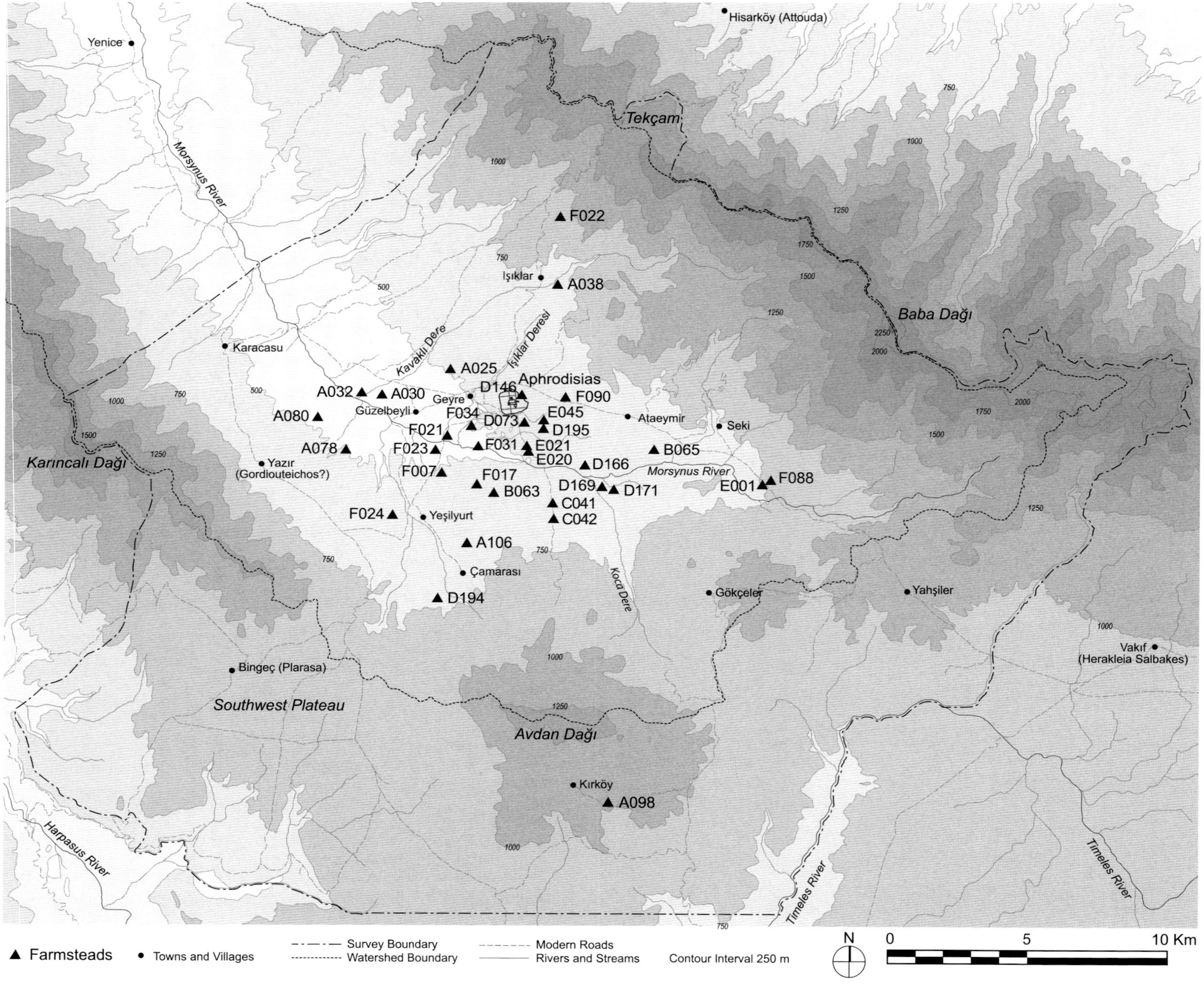

Fig. 5. Map of Aphrodisias survey region, showing locations of farmsteads (scale 1:200,000).

Table 2. Farmsteads where surface finds were collected systematically (18 out of 32 or 56 per cent). Also shown in grey type are five additional sites where some pottery was collected, but not systematically.

Farmsteads	*Pre-Hell.*	*Hell./ Aug.*	*Early Imp.*	*High Imp.*	*Late Roman*	*Middle Byz.*	*Islamic*	*Mod.*
Hills to N								
Işıklar (F022)	-	+	++	+	+	-	+	+
Valley Floor								
Karabuçuk (A030)	-	?	+	+	?	-	-	+
Kavaklı (A032)	-	-	?	+	-	-	-	-
Farm (B063)	-	?	+	?	+	-	+	-
Narlıyer (B065)	-	-	+	?	?	-	-	-
Akdam Der. (C041)	-	-	+	?	+	-	-	+
Villa (D073)	-	-	?	+	?	-		+
SW Trans (D166)	-	-	+	+	+	+	-	-
Farm (D169)	-	-	?	?	-	-	-	-
Farm (D171)	-	-	+	+	?	?	+	+
Farm (D195)	-	-	+	+	?	-	+	-
Farm (E021)	-	+	+	?	+	-	-	-
SW Trans (F007)	-	-	?	?	+	-	-	+
Farm (F017)	-	-	+	?	+	-	+	+
Kaklık Der. (F021)	-	++	+	+	+	-	+	+
Geyre (F023)	-	+	+	+	+	-	-	+
Valga Mev. (F024)	-	-	+	?	+	-	-	+
Farm (F031)	+	+	+	+	-	-	-	+
Farm (F088)	-	-	+	?	?	-	-	+
Farm (F090)	-	+	+	+	?	-	+	+
Hills to S								
Dam Yıkığı (A080)	-	++	+	+	+	-	+	+
Farm (A106)	-	++	+	+	-	-	-	+
Farm (C042)	-	-	-	+	+	-	-	+

Key: ++ = strong preponderance; + = present
? = not securely dated; - = absent

The only other category of site where we carried out systematic collection of surface finds comprised a variety of fortified sites, ranging from isolated watchtowers, to fortified citadels, to a small walled town. The locations of the six sites of this type recorded on the survey are shown in figure 6; the dating evidence is summarized in table 3. Five of these were pre-Roman sites, largely abandoned in the imperial period. One exceptional site is a medieval fortress, probably the site of ancient Tantalus.[12]

[12] On ancient Tantalus, see Roueché, *Aphrodisias in Late Antiquity* (supra n. 2), 167, and ala2004 VII.27. The medieval fortress was first identified in 2005.

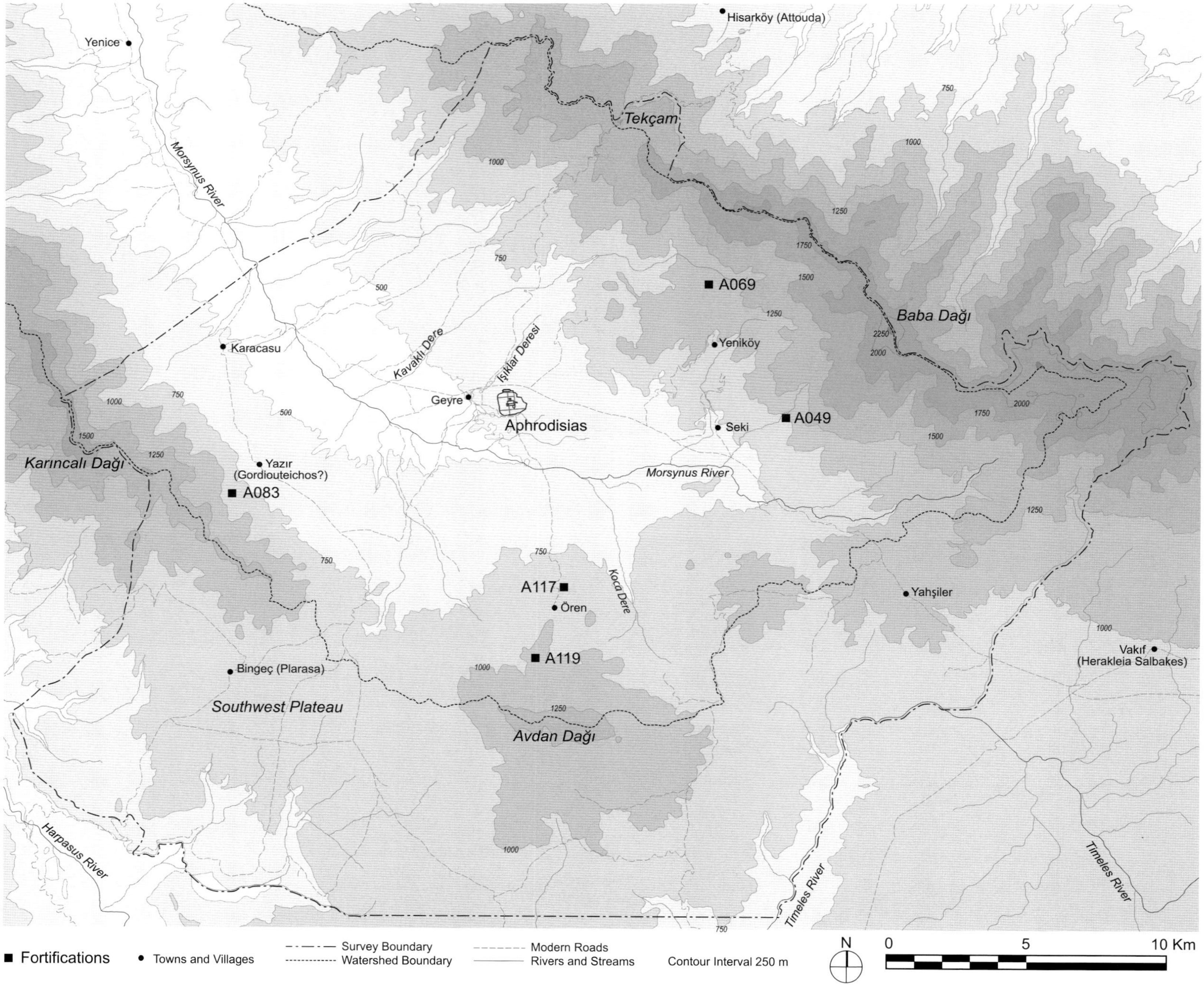

Fig. 6. Map of Aphrodisias survey region, showing locations of territorial fortifications (scale 1:200,000).

Table 3. Fortified sites with datable pottery of the Greek and Roman periods.

Fortified Sites	*Pre-Hell.*	*Hell./ Aug.*	*Early Imp.*	*High Imp.*	*Late Roman*	*Middle Byz.*	*Islamic*	*Mod.*
Seki (A049)	++	+	-	-	-	-	-	-
Yazır (A083)	+	++	+	+	-	-	-	+
Ören (A117)	+	?	?	-	-	-	-	-
Yeniköy (A069)	-	++	+	+	-	-	+	+
Ataeymir (A060)	-	+	+	+	-	-	-	+
Tantalus (A040)	-	-	-	-	-	++	+	-

Key: ++ = strong preponderance; + = present; ? = not securely dated; - = absent

This group of settlements, farmsteads, and citadels comprises all the sites identified on the Aphrodisias Regional Survey where systematic collection of surface finds provides ceramic evidence for dating. What does this evidence tell us about of the history of human habitation in the region? If we focus on the 42 datable settlements and farmsteads, we see that most of the sites in the hills to the north and south of Aphrodisias (16 out of 42) were occupied in the first century B.C. or earlier (11 out of 16 hillside sites, or 69 per cent), and that in almost all of these (nine out of 11), the preponderance of the pottery dates to or before the early imperial period. Occupation on the valley floor tends to start later than occupation in the hills; only six out of 22 valley-sites or 27 per cent were definitely occupied before the early imperial period. On the other hand, most of these sites were occupied at least as late as the third or fourth centuries A.D., and a number were occupied through the late Roman period. We have also seen that the majority of late antique as opposed to middle Byzantine churches lie on the valley floor.

For the Hellenistic and early Roman periods, then, regional settlement at Aphrodisias seems to conform to an understandable pattern. Concentrated in earlier periods on the more remote areas in the hills surrounding the valley and the plateau to the southwest (see below), it moved down to the floor of the valley in Roman times, just as low-lying Aphrodisias came to overshadow highland Plarasa, originally the more important of the two communities. The farmsteads on the floor of the valley may have directly replaced the settlements in the surrounding hills, the archaeological differences between them having less to do with size or original function than with the fact that the sites in the floor of the valley have been subject to constant ploughing, and so appear more as debris scatters than as in-situ architectural remains.

It would not have been surprising to find that the late Hellenistic and early imperial pattern reasserted itself in late antiquity. But that does not seem to have been the case. The sites abandoned in the imperial period do not seem to have been reoccupied (with the exception of the late antique monastery, D179, which is located near settlement D172), and a number of sites occupied into the fourth or fifth century were abandoned at that time. We found very little evidence for habitation after the seventh century.

The significance of this is hard to gauge, for our sample is very small, and heavily biased (toward sites near roads and modern villages, for example). There were surely many more rural settlements in the valley than our extensive survey has found, and modern conditions are not uniform. One category of places we have not been able to survey are the sites of modern villages, and these may be the sites of modern villages precisely because they were ancient villages which were either never abandoned, such as Geyre, the successor of Aphrodisias, or which were in fact reoccupied or settled for the first time in late antiquity. Nevertheless, it remains the case that we have not found evidence for an increase in rural population corresponding to the decrease in urban population in late late antiquity. On this evidence, the large-scale abandonment of Aphrodisias in the early seventh century does not seem to represent simply a dramatic change in settlement pattern, in which a constant regional population redistributed itself differently across the landscape. Rather, it seems to mark a real and significant reduction in population. This could be the result of a variety of factors, including increased mortality, or migration. It could be the result of a declining birth rate and lower life expectancy that had been building up for generations. But it is worth remarking that of the classic explanations for the collapse of the populations of towns like Aphrodisias the only one that would have produced a sudden and significant increase in mortality, especially in urban populations, is the plague.[13]

The plateau southwest of Aphrodisias exhibits a different pattern. At Bingeç, occupation seems to have been constant from the Hellenistic period to late antiquity, as at Aphrodisias. At the nearby village of Görle, also the site of a Hellenistic and Roman town, there are numerous architectural blocks inscribed with Christian symbols, and a large rock-cut tomb cemetery, including one Hellenistic tomb which preserves later painted fresco decoration, tentatively dated to the ninth century[14]—to date, this is the only painted Byzantine tomb known in the region around Aphrodisias. The evidence for middle Byzantine churches at the sites of three modern villages comes from middle Byzantine architectural blocks built into modern houses, a practice not attested at any of the present-day villages in the valley to the north.[15] In addition, we have identified at least two settlements that seem to have been occupied throughout the Roman period (B051 and F009), and one large olive oil factory (F010), which was developed in the late Roman period, and may have been associated with rural production of olive oil for the capital in Constantinople.[16]

If habitation in the region substantially retreated in the late Roman and Byzantine periods to the plateau south of the Morsynus river valley, that, like the increased density of settlement in the floor of the valley in the imperial period, would conform to an understandable pattern. This area could never have sustained the Roman-era population of the region, but perhaps it was adequate to the needs of the greater part of the region's much smaller population in the Dark and Middle Ages—to whom it offered the advantages of a more remote and protected location, the same advantages that explain why it was the principal focus of Hellenistic settlement. At and around Aphrodisias, then, just as at thousands of rural communities throughout the Roman empire, the situation in post-Roman times may have borne interesting similarities to that of the pre-Roman era.

The sketch provided here is only that—a reconstruction that is historically plausible, and that is consistent with the available evidence. Dissatisfying as this may seem in some respects, it remains the case that the kinds of questions raised at the beginning of this paper can only be addressed by the investigation of much larger areas, approximately 800 km^2 in the case of Aphrodisias, than are practical for doctrinaire intensive survey. For this reason, any attempt to answer these questions will have to rely on extrapolation from a relatively small data set. But if comparable results are obtained by surveys at a number of sites, we will be in a better position to draw more robust conclusions from those results.

[13] On the effects of the plague at Aphrodisias, see Roueché, *Aphrodisias in Late Antiquity* (supra n. 2), 140. For possible archaeological evidence in the form of a cluster of infant burials in the substructures of the bouleuterion, see N. Hudson, "Three centuries of Late Roman pottery," in Ratté and Smith, *Aphrodisias Papers* 4 (supra n. 10), 319–45, at 322–24.

[14] Dalgıç, "Early Christian churches" (supra n. 8).

[15] An exception is a middle Byzantine lintel block built into a house at the village of Gökçeler in the southeast corner of the Morsynus river valley, but according to the local inhabitants, the block was actually transported to Gökçeler from Aphrodisias!

[16] I. Lockey, "Olive oil production and rural settlement," forthcoming in Ratté and De Staebler, *Aphrodisias* V (supra n. 5).

8 Buildings and Citizens: Observations from Late Antique and Byzantine Blaundos in Phrygia

Axel Filges

In this paper, I will discuss fieldwork and the attempt to reconstruct urban history from ruins remaining above ground.[1] Buildings or their remains as documented and interpreted during every urban survey offer valuable information as witnesses to historical processes. In addition to simple description, documentation of these buildings often provides absolute or at least relative dating evidence in the form of stylistic or construction details. The "sum total" of the different monuments of a city reveals information about changes in the structure of the city over the course of centuries. Such studies become even more important when they are seen not as an end product but as the starting point to yet other investigations.[2] One point of special interest in the present paper is the question of how well the life of an isolated small village, situated in an impoverished region, fits with or diverges from current views about the late antique cities of Asia Minor in general.[3] Before presenting some aspects of the archaeology of late antique Blaundos, it is first essential to explain the situation of the city in earlier periods.

Blaundos in the Hellenistic and Roman Imperial Eras

The investigated ruins are situated in the Turkish province of Uşak, approximately 40 km south of the provincial capital of the same name and 200 km east of Izmir.[4] The city was first settled in the Hellenistic period and continued to exist as a community at least until A.D. 900, probably even until A.D. 1200.

Blaundos is located on a high plateau surrounded on three sides by steep bluffs (fig. 1). The area occupied by the ruins of the city, both on the plateau and on the slopes below, spread over 820 by 520 m at its greatest extent. The city was situated several kilometers away from the nearest major trade route. Thus it can be assumed that it was not a regular station for traveling traders. The hinterland today is not very productive and was probably comparable during the Roman imperial

[1] Most of this text is identical with the paper given in Ann Arbor on 9 January 2008, but footnotes and some remarks have been added. A German version is published in N. Burkhardt and R. Stichel (eds.), *Die antike Stadt im Umbruch*, Kolloquium Darmstadt Mai 2006 (Wiesbaden 2010) 154–64. I would like to express my thanks to the organizers and editors both for the invitation to the congress in Ann Arbor as well as for the revision of my English version of this paper.

Abbreviations for frequently cited sources:

Blaundos, Berichte = A. Filges (ed.), *Blaundos. Berichte zur Erforschung einer Kleinstadt im lydisch-phrygischen Grenzgebiet, IstForsch* 48 (Tübingen 2006).

[2] For prescriptions on the reconstruction of political and social landscapes from the results of topographical surveys see L. Lavan, "Late Antique urban topography. From architecture to human space," in L. Lavan and W. Bowden (eds.), *Theory and Practice in Late Antique Archaeology, Late Antique Archaeology* 1 (Leiden and Boston 2003) 171–95, at 176–81.

[3] M. Waelkens, "The late antique to early Byzantine city in southwest Anatolia. Sagalassos and its territory: A case study," in J.-U. Krause and C. Witschel (eds.), *Die Stadt in der Spätantike—Niedergang oder Wandel? Historia Einzelschriften* 190 (Stuttgart 2006) 208.

[4] For the geographical setting, see the maps by D. Roos in *Blaundos, Berichte*, figs. 1, 13.

Fig. 1. Overall view from the south, showing the steep slope and the habitation area on the plateau (A. Filges).

period. Nevertheless, there is no explanation I can offer for the high quality marble buildings (fig. 2) other than that farming, animal husbandry, and probably vine cultivation were sources of a certain considerable prosperity.

The Hellenistic settlement is known only from pottery and coins. Not a single surviving building or architectural fragment can be considered to belong to this period. However, this early settlement, which carried the native Luvian name Mlaundos, is known from Roman imperial inscriptions, where it is mentioned as a Macedonian military outpost. Such outposts were numerous in western Asia Minor.[5] The natural protection afforded by the steep slopes of the canyons on three sides made this a suitable site for such an installation.

The settlement made a tremendous—and archaeologically well-attested—advance in its development during the last third of the first century A.D., especially in the Flavian era. Within this period most of the public buildings were erected, out of, as it seems, a kind of urban nothingness, which may have been the result of damage caused by an earthquake known to have occurred in the A.D. 60s.[6]

One characteristic of Blaundos during the first two centuries A.D. attested in the inscriptions from the site is the large proportion of persons of Italic origin. Roman influence can also be seen in other details: of the 55 fragments of inscriptions from Blaundos, at least seven display a Latin text, including two bilingual temple building inscriptions.[7] The construction of two temples with their very tall relief friezes follows the style of the capital of the Roman empire more closely than local traditions.[8] In addition, the oblong forum with the basilica on one of its narrow sides also points to the Italic west.[9]

[5] A. Filges, "Stadtentwicklung im Gebiet des oberen Mäander. Die lydisch-phrygische Grenzregion am Beispiel von Blaundos," in E. Schwertheim and E. Winter (eds.), *Stadt und Stadtentwicklung in Kleinasien, Asia Minor Studien* 50 (Bonn 2003) 37–43; idem, "Von Mlaundos zu Blaundos. Literarische Quellen und Überlegungen zur frühen Geschichte bis zur Integration in das pergamenische Reich," in *Blaundos, Berichte*, 17–21; idem, "Die Fundkeramik," in *Blaundos, Berichte*, 304–10.

[6] A. Filges, "Blaundos im Laufe der Zeiten," in *Blaundos, Berichte*, 312–15.

[7] F. von Saldern, "Die Inschriften des Ceres-Tempels," in *Blaundos, Berichte*, 189–97, 321–50.

[8] A. Filges, "Der Tempel 1 (Ceres-Tempel)," in *Blaundos, Berichte*, 175–76.

[9] D. Roos, "Das Steinfachwerk-Gebäude," in *Blaundos, Berichte*, 212–15.

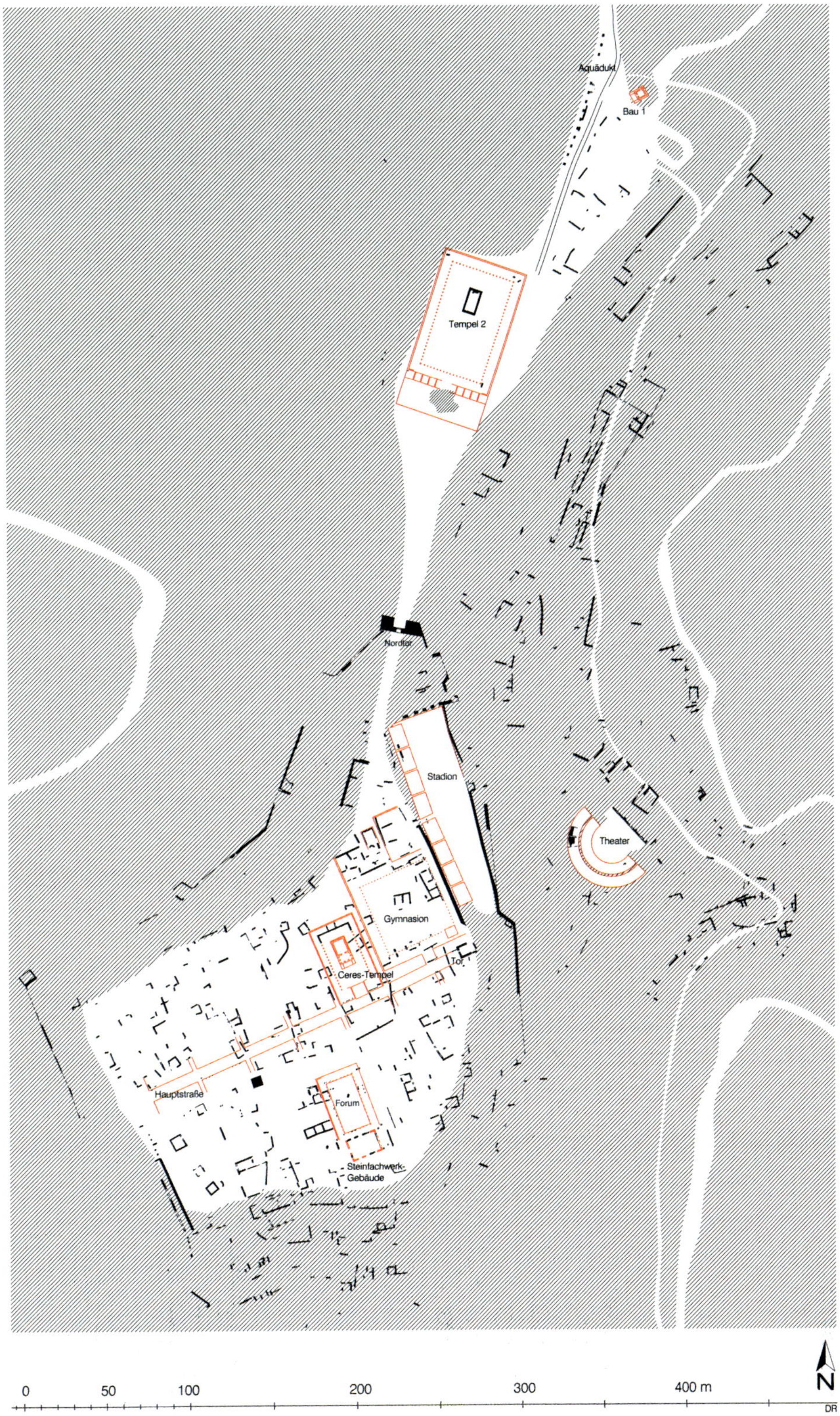

Fig. 2. City map with public areas in red (D. Roos).

Fig. 3. Center of Blaundos from the northeast with the northern gate in the foreground and the so-called Doric Portico in the middle (A. Filges).

Apart from this Italic influence, however, inspiration from the cities of the Maeander valley can be seen clearly in the halls, built of yellow marl, on both sides of the main street (fig. 3).[10] Identical framings of the main streets, consisting of colonnades with halls and shops, built from the same materials and with the same structures, were erected during the last decade of the first century in Hierapolis, Laodikeia, and Tripolis, cities which all lie in the Maeander valley, approximately 50 km to the south.[11] In spite of its geographical location, therefore, it is clear that this small town was by no means culturally isolated.

Three centuries later, this textbook metropolis "en miniature" experienced a second important impulse for development. With this, we reach the principal topic of this paper, the small town of Blaundos during the late antique period.

Blaundos in Late Antiquity

Written sources including Stephanos of Byzantium, council or synod files, and ecclesiastical registers (the *Notitiae Episcopatuum*), repeatedly mention certain variations of the village's name, as well as single persons who are connected with Blaundos.[12] These are of little help, however, in the attempt to recreate the life of the town in late antiquity.

Analysis of ceramic finds (identifiably late Roman/late antique sherds make up at most 10 per cent of the total of the pottery from the site, and consist mainly of large dishes) reveals that they were produced in Phocaea (Phocaean Red Slip), the most important regional center of production, supplying most of western Asia Minor. This fact shows that a regular connection to long distance trade was maintained into late Roman times.[13] Inscriptions from the late antique and Byzantine periods are rare in Blaundos and are mainly found in connection with graves.[14] Surprisingly, only one inscription is identifiably Christian.

[10] Filges, "Stadtentwicklung" (supra n. 5), 44–45; idem, "Zeiten" (supra n. 6), 318–20.

[11] D. Roos and A. Filges, "Die 'Dorische Portikus' und die Hauptstraße von Blaundos," in *Blaundos, Berichte*, 198–204.

[12] In the council files, three bishops are mentioned for the fifth century A.D. and one for both the eighth and the ninth centuries: A. Filges, "Das byzantinische Blaundos in Schriftquellen und Karten," in *Blaundos, Berichte*, 26–27.

[13] Filges, "Fundkeramik" (supra n. 5), 309.

[14] F. von Saldern, "Katalog der Inschriften," in *Blaundos, Berichte*, 344 nos. 37–39.

Now I would like to direct attention to two groups of monuments dated to the late antique or early Byzantine period, which survive in the form of different kinds of walls: these are the fortifications of the town, with its city wall and gate, and the structures in the town center, which belong mostly to dwellings.

The City Wall

I turn first to the best-preserved building, the northern gate, which was the main gate to the town.[15] Situated on the narrowest part of the plateau (only 10 m wide), the gate is positioned optimally from a strategic point of view. The plateau's width of approximately 22 m, and the local topography with its steep slopes, make it nearly impossible to circumvent the gate structure with its two differently sized projecting towers (fig. 4). On the exterior, the space between the two towers forms a small courtyard in front of the actual entranceway, which consists of a rectangular doorframe leading to a barrel-vaulted passage. On the interior, the back walls of the towers are flush with the connecting wall, so that the gate presents a continuous façade.

All the blocks of the gate are marl spolia; only three blocks of marble are visible. The secondary character of the materials is shown by the integration of ornamented and misappropriated elements as well as the numerous lewis holes on the exposed surfaces.[16]

The exterior doorway to the 2.5 m-wide passage is spanned by a horizontal arch. The east tower exhibits a large opening towards the town, made of reused archivolts. A reconstruction of the history of the gate by Jürgen Giese interprets the structure as a well-fortified autonomous complex within the town's defensive system.[17] Each tower originally consisted of several stories, accessible only by ladders. There were embrasures on the third floor, and platforms on the fourth floor (the top floor) for the operation of larger defensive artillery. Above the gate passage, the top floors of the towers were connected by a battlement parapet.

I close this section with a few notes on the city's circuit wall, which is 1250 m long. In the east and west, it follows the edge of the plateau. In some parts, just above the bluffs, the wall is founded directly on the bedrock. For this reason, it is not surprising that large parts of the wall are missing, as they were washed into the canyons over the course of the centuries. Only in the south were attempts undertaken to build a wall that climbs up and down the hill in order to include as much of the hillslope as possible.

The City and City Wall

The next question to be addressed is how the fortification relates to the rest of the town. The map shows that the wall divides the imperial city into two parts (fig. 5). The gate is located at a strategic point of the plateau, with the wall enclosing the bowl of a spoon, as it were, but not its handle. Large parts of the earlier town, including the presumptive main sanctuary of Apollo and the theater, were excluded (fig. 6). There is reason to believe that the ashlar stones reused in the gate came from the quadriporticus of the temenos of the sanctuary of Apollo.

Another public structure whose function is usually significant, the aqueduct, was obviously no longer in use when the fortification walls were built.[18] Indeed, the archivolts of the north tower display exactly the same dimensions as the only preserved arch of the aqueduct, and it can be assumed that they come from this monument.

Thus it is clear that buildings with a variety of different functions, such as the theater, sanctuaries, and other official structures, were deliberately quarried for building materials for the fortification

[15] See the detailed analysis by J. Giese, "Das Nordtor," in *Blaundos, Berichte*, 79–110.

[16] Ibid., 110–12.

[17] Ibid., 109, fig. 100.

[18] P. Baumeister, "Die Wasserversorgung," in *Blaundos, Berichte*, 261, 267.

a

b

Fig. 4a–b. Northern gate, external (a) and internal (b) views (A. Filges).

of the town. It is possible that these structures were exploited because they were no longer required, or because they were already out of use. Especially for the aqueduct, the latter seems to be the case, as it seems unlikely that the means for supplying fresh water to the town was dismantled solely so that its materials could be used in the construction of the fortifications.

Initially, only materials from buildings excluded from the newly fortified city were used in the construction of the walls. Only with later modifications to the wall did people begin to use material from within the town itself. For example, the seat-blocks from the stadium were reused for a secondary reconstruction of a part of the wall originally situated slightly further down-slope.[19] The town

[19] A section of 125 m of the city wall in the northeastern area was cut; in the second phase, the wall runs farther to the west at a higher level up the slope (A. Filges, "Die Stadtmauer: Mauerring und Türme," in *Blaundos, Berichte*, 69–70, figs. 54–56).

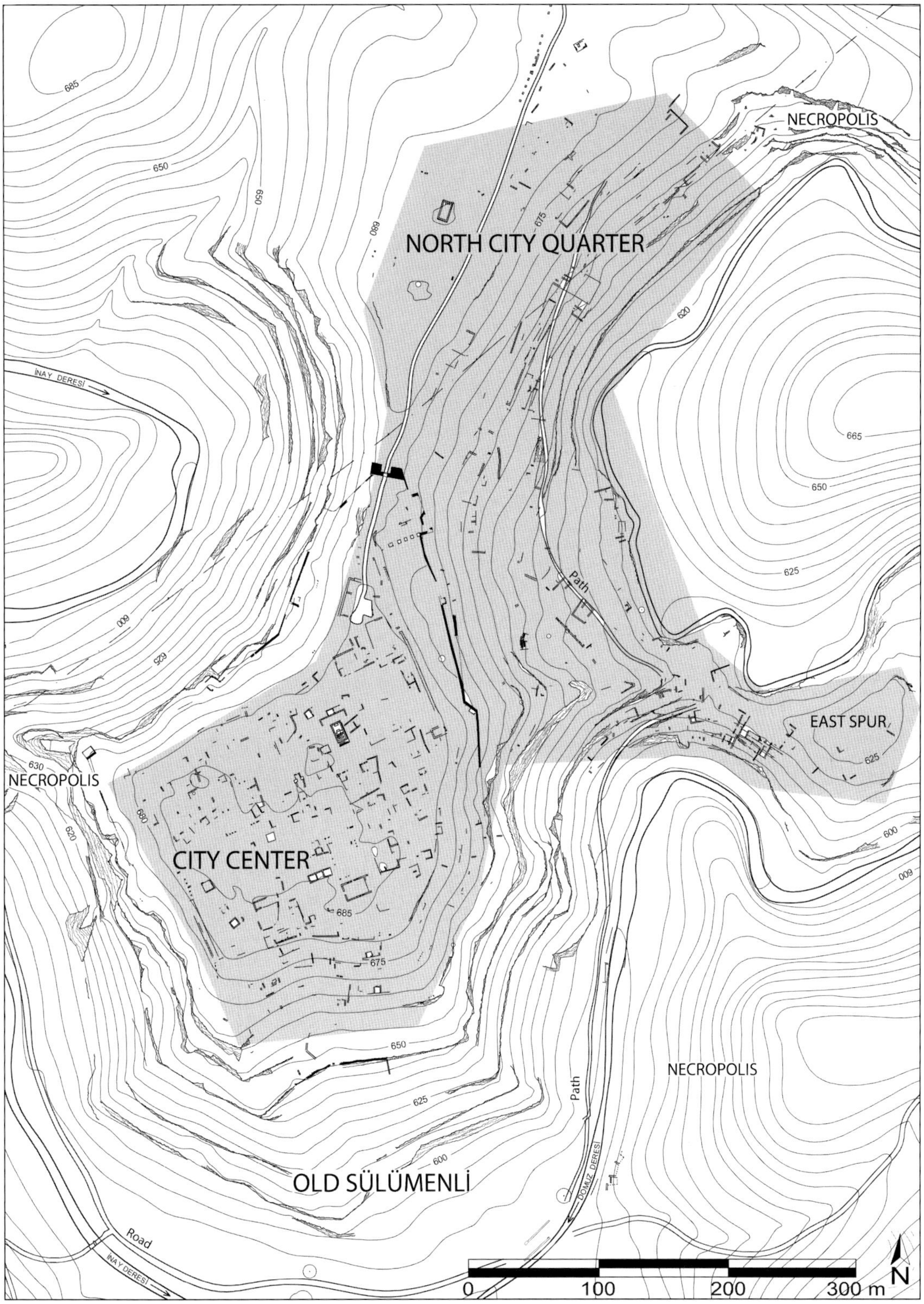

Fig. 5. Habitation area in the first and second centuries A.D. (modified plan: J. Giese).

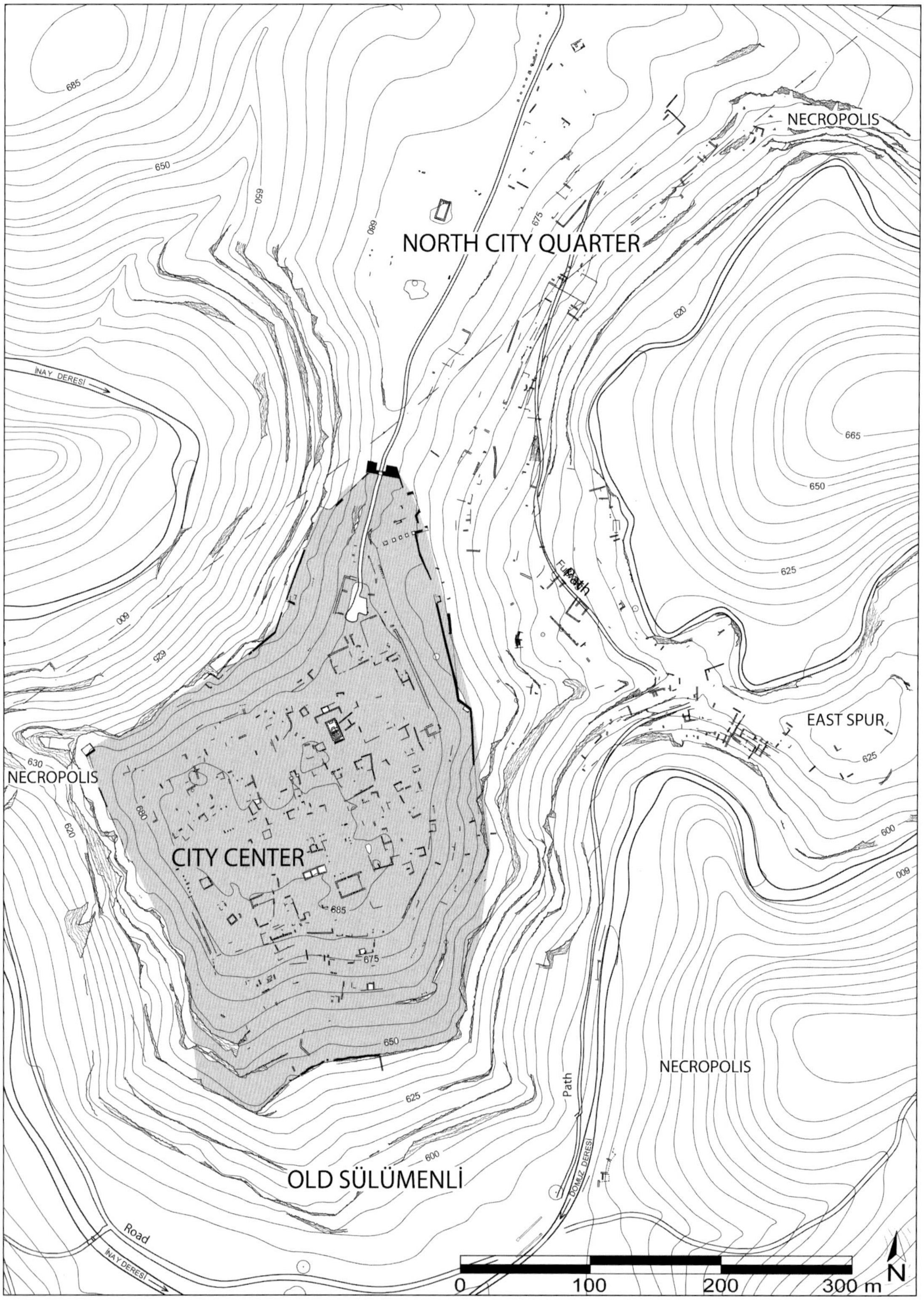

Fig. 6. Habitation area in the sixth century A.D. (modified plan: J. Giese).

used up the available building materials first from the outside, then from the inside, thus slowly but gradually consuming itself.

Trying to Date the City Wall

Now I shall attempt to date the construction of the wall more precisely. It is a well-known phenomenon, both in western Asia Minor and in other parts of the empire, that most towns that originally did not have city walls—such as Blaundos—eventually began to invest the necessary money and labor required for the building of such fortifications. It seems plausible that fortifications became necessary only when the *pax Romana* drew towards a close, and armed invaders made the defense of life and possessions mandatory. The earliest such invaders were apparently the Goths, whose raids led them as far as Ionia during the second half of the third century. After A.D. 396, a law of Arcadius regulated the response to external threats, and the erection of city walls became obligatory. Funds for these buildings were to come from well-situated local landowners.[20]

It is hard to judge today, whether in less important and more isolated regions, migrating groups such as the Goths were regarded as concrete threats or rather as symbols of a more general latent peril. However, towns were secured, and Blaundos did not stand alone. Hierapolis, Tripolis, Laodikeia, and Philadelphia also display very similar fortifications. Traditionally, scholars have dated all these wall projects to around A.D. 400, on the basis of the date assigned to the walls of Hierapolis—a date that was itself based on the aforementioned law and did not consider internal factors.[21]

The chronology of the fortifications of Blaundos should be reconsidered in light of the now relatively well-dated wall of Aphrodisias.[22] During the third quarter of the fourth century, not only was the construction of the city wall taking place, but also new buildings were being built within the town. For Aphrodisias, it seems that after the crisis of the third century, an economic boom began. In my opinion, this allows for the general hypothesis that many city fortifications in Asia Minor were not built during times of threat, but during times of prosperity, initiated by imperial investments, as is witnessed for Aphrodisias.[23] Another example for dating fortifications as early as the fourth century is the wall of Sagalassos, which has been dated to the final quarter of the fourth century on the evidence of stratified coin finds.[24] Unlike Aphrodisias, the urban area was reduced, as was also the case in Blaundos. On this point, different towns used different strategies. Some were enclosed completely, some only partially.[25] But the reduction of the urban area itself seemed to be the most practical solution in the long run, as was the case in Asia Minor regularly from the sixth to the eighth centuries.[26]

For Blaundos itself, it is assumed by analogy with the aforementioned cities that its walls were erected during the second half of the fourth century.[27] For this small town, the erection of the city wall certainly meant a large effort with a high cost. Unfortunately, we do not know whether the money came from the people of the town itself or whether it was granted from outside.

[20] A. Demandt, *Die Spätantike, Handbuch der Altertumswissenschaften* III 6 (Munich 1989) 402.

[21] See Giese, "Nordtor" (supra n. 15), 119–20.

[22] P.D. De Staebler, "The city wall and the making of a late-antique provincial capital," in C. Ratté and R.R.R. Smith (eds.), *Aphrodisias Papers 4. New Research on the City and its Monuments*, *JRA* Suppl. 70 (Portsmouth, RI 2008) 284–318.

[23] C. Ratté, "New research on the urban development of Aphrodisias in late antiquity," in D. Parrish (ed.), *Urbanism in Western Asia Minor*, *JRA* Suppl. 45 (Portsmouth, RI 2001) 125–30.

[24] L. Loots, M. Waelkens, and F. Depuydt, "The city fortifications of Sagalassos from the Hellenistic to the Late Roman period," in M. Waelkens and M. Loots (eds.), *Sagalassos* V (Leuven 2000) 614–19.

[25] This phenomenon was already observed in the 1980s: W. Müller-Wiener, "Von der Polis zum Kastron," *Gymnasium* 93 (1986) 453–57, fig. 7; W. Brandes, *Die Städte Kleinasiens im 7. und 8. Jahrhundert* (Amsterdam 1982) 82–111.

[26] See also the remarks by P. Niewöhner in this volume.

[27] This is the result of Giese's detailed analysis ("Nordtor" [supra n. 15], 122), with which I totally agree.

Citizens and Fortifications

What does the city wall tell us more generally about the town and its citizens in the second half of the fourth century? In the first place, the course chosen for the line of the wall prompts speculation about the status and influence of certain citizens. Given that the northern part of the town was still inhabited when the wall was built, the conscious abandonment of at least some immobile goods in case of attack is implied. The terrain next to the sanctuary of Apollo is uneven and slopes down both eastwards and westwards. It was still possible to erect houses in this location, but conditions were not ideal, and I would suggest therefore that the citizens who lived here belonged to the less rather than the more privileged sectors of the population. This assumption is supported by an analysis of the course of the wall, which does not follow the edges of the center of town (the most sensible course for the purposes of fortification),[28] but instead appears to cover as much of the southern plateau as possible (fig. 7). This was only possible by building the wall across a number of precipices, a very laborious process.

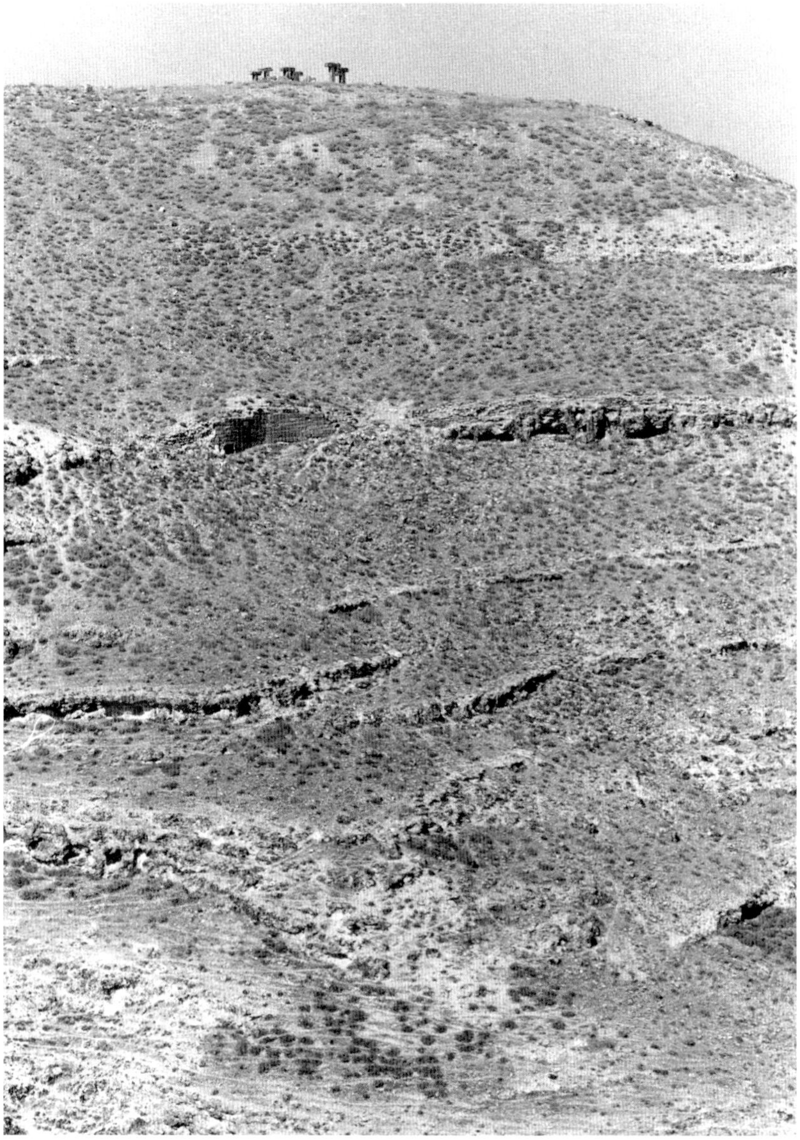

Fig. 7. Detail of the south slope with the city wall below the plateau (A. Filges).

By way of explaining the preference given to the southern plateau, I would like to offer a suggestion that complements the suggestions made above in discussion of the northern area. In general, in Greek and Roman antiquity, a southward orientation for private houses was preferred. For Blaundos and other cities, this means that those premises that allowed for a southward orientation of a house were the most valuable. The gently sloping hillside just beneath the southern edge of the plateau of

[28] Giese, "Nordtor" (supra n. 15), 115.

Blaundos with its attractive view toward the canyon and the adjacent valley can be considered the best "address" for private houses. Thus it is likely that the most important families lived here. That this area was not abandoned despite its defensive weakness reveals, in my opinion, the influence that the urban elite had on the course of the wall. The hypothesis seems to be permitted that citizens of this social class also financed its construction.

The layout of city walls thus helps illuminate the social topography of the city. What if anything does it tell us about demographic change? Several explanations can be given for the exclusion of a large part of the built-up area:

1) The population had diminished in the fourth century from its level in the imperial period. This diminution could be attributed to a lower birth rate or to higher mortality.[29] The space inside the wall was sufficient for the remaining people.
2) The rural population had emigrated to the provincial metropolis before the late antique period, as has recently been postulated for the sixth century by Mark Whittow.[30] Thus, the space within the city walls would also have been sufficient.
3) The urban citizens of all classes had left for good or for the time being for the chora.[31] An edict by Constantine from A.D. 321, which prohibited the removal of columns and marble building elements from the towns into the country,[32] could be regarded as an official response to, and therefore as evidence for, this tendency. Blaundos would then have been merely a place to retreat to, in case of attack.[33]
4) However, it also seems possible that little had changed concerning the number of people who lived in the town and the location of the houses. The population of the northern outskirts would have lived a carefree and content life, and only when attacked would they have been forced to retreat behind the city walls and leave their belongings and houses unprotected.

Which one of these scenarios—or what combination of several—might have happened, we cannot yet decide. However, I think it is important to list and postulate the possibilities. This gives us a basis upon which we can discuss and modify our ideas and models of urban history.

Blaundos in the Late Antique and Early Byzantine Periods

Dwellings

Let us now turn to the buildings that occupy the center of town.[34] On the whole plateau only a few remains of walls are preserved above ground. In the frame of our urban survey, these remains were studied by Ute Schwertheim, and I would like to present a summary of her results.

As building material for the residential houses, spolia as well as undressed blocks of marl were used. The construction of walls is uniform. They are usually ca. 70 cm wide. Their interior and exterior

[29] In Aphrodisias there is no longer any reason to postulate a shrinking number of citizens: Ratté, "Research" (supra n. 23), 138.

[30] M. Whittow, "Recent research on the late-antique city in Asia Minor: The second half of the 6th c. revisited," in L. Lavan (ed.), *Recent Research in Late-Antique Urbanism*, *JRA* Suppl. 42 (Portsmouth, RI 2001) 151.

[31] F.R. Trombley, "Town and territorium in Late Roman Anatolia (late 5th to early 7th c.)," in L. Lavan (ed.), *Recent Research in Late-Antique Urbanism*, *JRA* Suppl. 42 (Portsmouth, RI 2001) 230. For Aphrodisias, see Ratté, "Research" (supra n. 23), 147; this interpretation was reconsidered in C. Ratté, "Aphrodisias," in W. Radt (ed.), *Stadtgrabungen und Stadtforschung im westlichen Kleinasien. Geplantes und Erreichtes*, International Symposion Bergama, 6–7 August 2004, *Byzas* 3 (Istanbul 2006) 48.

[32] Demandt, *Spätantike* (supra n. 20), 285.

[33] From the start the Blaundos survey project intentionally concentrated on the city center, although this meant neglecting the environs: A. Filges, "Blaundos," in W. Radt (ed.), *Stadtgrabungen und Stadtforschung im westlichen Kleinasien. Geplantes und Erreichtes*, International Symposion Bergama, 6–7 August 2004, *Byzas* 3 (Istanbul 2006) 58–59.

[34] See the detailed analysis by U. Schwertheim, "Die spätantik-byzantinische Bebauung," in *Blaundos, Berichte*, 216–22.

faces are not tied together; that is, there are no headers extending through the full thickness of the walls. Only rarely are in-fills of mortar and gravel found. Spolia were used at the corners and doorways. Unfortunately, without excavation, we cannot determine the heights of the walls with respect to the original ground surface, but it is assumed that they represent the lower parts of the buildings.

In total, around 100 rooms of residential buildings can be reconstructed (fig. 8). Two-thirds display a square outline, though they lack properly right-angled corners. The floor spaces of the rooms measure between 4 and 64 m^2. The remains allow for the reconstruction of different types of houses: most common were one-room houses, followed by two-room houses. The latter type shows several variations in how the two rooms were combined, meaning that in some cases rooms are situated at catercorners to each other. Interesting is the type where three rooms are set in a row, where we assume that the middle one was probably an unroofed courtyard. We can also reconstruct some special types of houses, including two houses which are trapezoidal in outline, and some buildings with more than three rooms.

It is difficult to date the buildings that were constructed after the imperial era. The fact that in Blaundos bricks are rarely found in wall construction may be significant. In Pergamon, this is a characteristic feature of early Byzantine walls. However, it is not clear that the same held true for Blaundos. Most likely, the available building material will have had a certain influence on the construction of the walls. Nevertheless, the obvious absence of pottery from Byzantine times compared to the abundance of ceramics of the fourth to sixth centuries seems to be significant.[35] This could imply a decreasing importance and population from the sixth century onward.

Structural Changes in the Layout of the City

More informative for the topic of this colloquium is the overall character of late antique development of the town center. The open spaces of the sanctuaries, the main street and its colonnades, and the other streets were all filled in with new buildings.

The structure of the town thus changed fundamentally. The formerly planned and grid-patterned town with its strong composition of public and open spaces and private buildings (see fig. 2) was transformed into a town with a much more loosely-patterned arrangement of buildings, nearly like a dispersed settlement (see fig. 8). This late transformation, which I date to the period following the erection of the city walls, seems to have abjured large buildings as well as large open spaces, except for the forum.[36] Whether the population no longer attached any great value to "representative" buildings is as yet unclear.

Conclusions

What kinds of answers can a small town such as Blaundos provide to general questions about the transition from the Roman imperial to the late antique and Byzantine city in Asia Minor? This short section may function as something of a summary, albeit one that concentrates on specific questions.

Continuity of Types of Construction and Abandonment of Older Buildings

The one element of the city that continued unchanged into Byzantine times was the central square formed by the relatively small forum of Blaundos. It was probably never overbuilt, though its function during late antique and Byzantine times is uncertain. Otherwise, it seems to have been easy to put older building components to new uses. Many older structures were apparently abandoned, a supposition that is corroborated by the incorporation of building elements of public structures into

[35] Filges, "Fundkeramik" (supra n. 5), 310.

[36] Roos, "Steinfachwerk-Gebäude" (supra n. 9), 204–15.

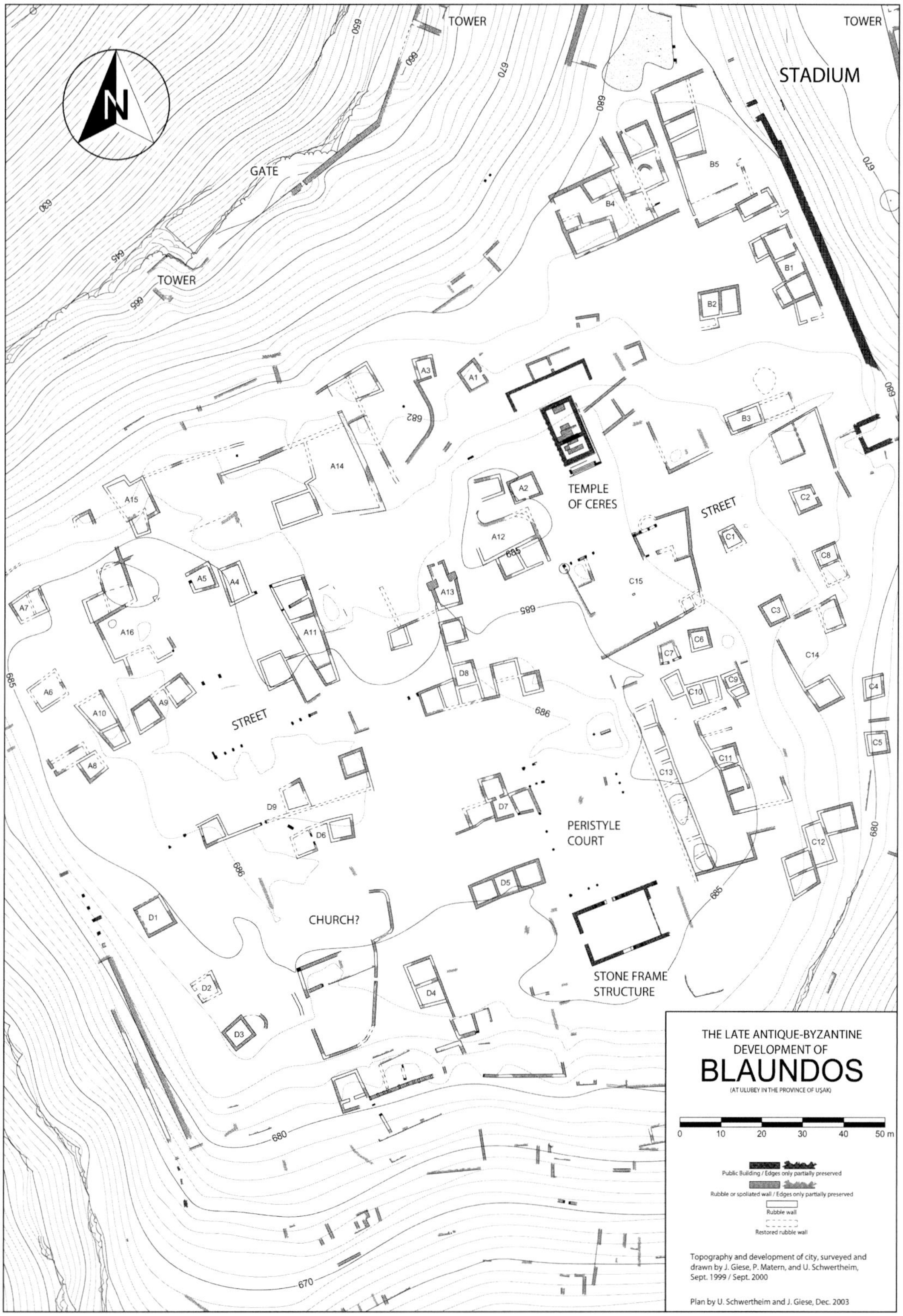

Fig. 8. Plan of dwellings, probably early Byzantine (U. Schwertheim and J. Giese).

the fortification walls. Whether these monuments were out of use before being dismantled for building material is not known.

Processes of Rearrangement

The rearrangement of living space and reorganization of the town structure seems to have been accomplished in several steps: the erection of the city walls emphasized one part of the city at the expense of the other, and led to a significant reduction in size. What might have happened to the contemporary residential buildings, we do not know. Instead, we know only the remains of the last period of the town's occupation, which may be dated to late antique or early Byzantine times. This phase is characterized by a conscious defiance of former structural principals. Most of the open squares and streets were built over. The settlement on the plateau thus took on an unstructured but relatively homogenous appearance.

New Types of Buildings

New types of buildings were developed in the fourth century, of which the most striking example is the city wall with its grand northern gate. In addition, later residential buildings do not seem to follow the rules of their unknown predecessors, since room numbers and arrangements are characteristic for Byzantine, but not for Roman imperial settlements.

Conflicts and Breaks

Since the pagan temples were excluded from the city and so presumably no longer in use when the city walls were built in the second half of the fourth century, a break in religious tradition is implied. Interestingly, however, there is almost no contemporary or later archaeological evidence for Christianity at Blaundos, although some bishops of Blaundos are mentioned in the literary sources. While the city wall as a whole can be taken as a witness to the existence of an impending external threat, the shift of the town's center towards the south implies a latent conflict between different status groups within the population of the town. The enlargement of the southern plateau to protect the richer citizens required extreme efforts, while other parts of the city were left unprotected from potential threats.

Summing Up: The Value of Ruins

To use architectural remains as the sole source of evidence for the reconstruction of the history of a city, as has been done in this paper, poses obvious dangers of misinterpretation. However, these are the only sources of information currently available for Blaundos, as well as for many other late antique and Byzantine settlements.

In cases such as these, surface investigation can provide a reasonably complete picture of a city at the time it was abandoned. For more detailed and more precise diachronic as well as synchronic reconstructions of cities and their citizens' social lives, however, surface investigation must be supplemented by the excavation of subsurface remains.

9 Troy and the Granicus River Valley in Late Antiquity

Charles Brian Rose

I have had the good fortune of conducting fieldwork in two unusually historic areas during the last two decades: Troy and the Granicus river valley, neither of which has traditionally been noted for its late Roman settlements.[1] What I have found, in the course of two decades of excavation, is that the evidence from the two areas is complementary; placing them side by side, as I will do here, yields a relatively clear diachronic overview of settlement patterns in the Troad from the third to the seventh century. I begin with an outline of our excavations at Troy and then conclude with recent discoveries between the Granicus and Aesepus rivers.

Ilion's prominence during the Hellenistic and Roman periods was tied to its identification as the site where the Trojan War had taken place (figs. 1–3).[2] The date at which this identification first occurred is unclear, but it was in place by the early archaic period, and the late Bronze Age fortification walls, which were always partly visible, constantly reminded visitors of the site's Homeric heritage.[3] That heritage was responsible for a series of high profile visits over the next millennium, as well as a wealth of benefactions. Xerxes stopped here in 480 B.C. on his way to sack Greece, as did Alexander on his way to conquer the Persians.[4] Specific areas of the site were subsequently tied to key episodes in Trojan mythology; Caesar, for example, was shown the spot from which Zeus carried off Ganymede, the place where Anchises and Aphrodite made love, and the site of the Judgment of Paris.[5] Meanwhile, the tumuli lining the Dardanelles came to be associated with the burial mounds of the Homeric heroes, who included Ajax, Patroclus, and Achilles, among others.[6]

Both Augustus and Hadrian visited the site, and their statues have been found during excavations in the agora at Ilion.[7] Augustus assisted in the restoration of the acropolis following the devastation

[1] I would like to thank Christopher Ratté and Ortwin Dally for organizing this conference; Robert Ousterhout, Lee Striker, and Ray Van Dam for advice on various points raised in this article; and Gabriel Pizzorno for having prepared the map.

[2] For an overview of the post-Bronze Age excavations at Ilion, see C.B. Rose, "The Granicus River Valley Archaeological Survey Project, 2004–2005," *Studia Troica* 17 (2007) 65–150. For the Granicus river valley, see C.B. Rose and R. Körpe, "The Granicus River Valley Survey Project, 2006," *Araştırma Sonuçları Toplantısı* 25.2 (2007) 103–16.

[3] M. Basedow, "What the blind man saw: New information from the Iron Age at Troy," in C. Mattusch, A. Brauer, and A.A. Donohue (eds.), *Common Ground: Archaeology, Art, Science, and Humanities. Proceedings of the XVIth International Congress of Classical Archaeology, Boston, August 23–26, 2003* (Oxford 2006) 88–92; C.B. Rose, "Separating fact from fiction in the Aeolian migration," *Hesperia* 77.3 (2008) 399–430.

[4] Xerxes: Herodotus 7.43; Alexander: Arrian, *Anabasis* 1.11.7–8; Diodorus 17.17.6–7, 17.18.1; Strabo 13.1.26; Plutarch, *Alexander* 15.7.

[5] Lucan, *Civil War* 9.970–73.

[6] J.M. Cook, *The Troad* (Oxford 1973) 159–65; C.B. Rose, "The 1998 post-Bronze Age excavations at Troy," *Studia Troica* 9 (1999) 35–71, at 61–63; idem, "Greek, Roman, and Byzantine research at Troy, 1999," *Studia Troica* 10 (2000) 53–72, at 55–56.

[7] Augustus: H. Halfmann, *Itinera Principum. Geschichte und Typologie der Kaiserreisen im Römischen Reich* (Stuttgart 1986) 158; *IGR* 4.203; Hadrian: Philostratus, *Heroicus* 137; D. Magie, *Roman Rule in Asia Minor* (Princeton 1950) 613, 1470 n. 6; Halfmann, *Itinera* (supra this note), 43, 191.

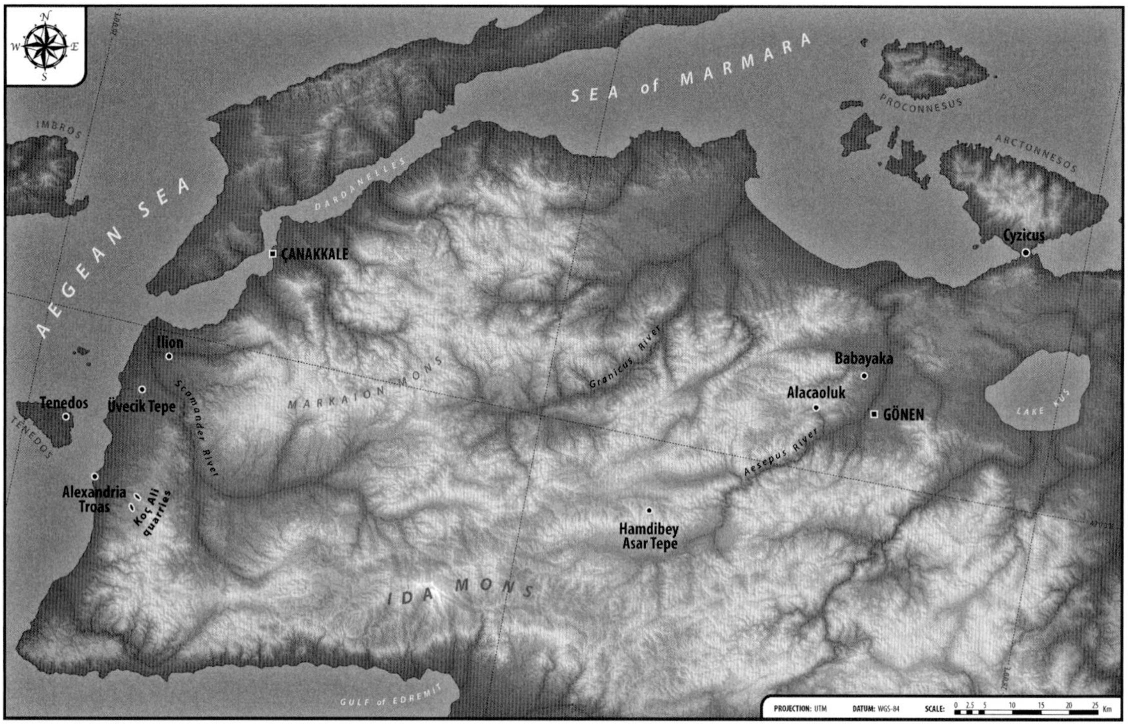

Fig. 1. Map of the Troad (G. Pizzorno).

of the Mithridatic Wars, and Hadrian restored the tomb of Ajax; both reaffirmed Ilion's status as a free and federate city, as did most other members of the imperial family who traveled there.[8] As the mother city of the Romans, it had a privileged status similar to that of Aphrodisias.

At some point toward the end of the second century A.D. there was a major catastrophe at Ilion, possibly caused by a earthquake, although that is merely a guess.[9] The destruction hit both the public and private areas of the city, and there are enormous pits that represent massive cleanup operations in the early third century.[10] Assistance may have been provided by the emperors Caracalla and Macrinus. During Caracalla's visit to Ilion he reportedly honored Achilles with sacrifices and races in armor around the latter's alleged tomb, as Alexander had done 550 years earlier, and set up a bronze statue of Achilles. He also constructed an enormous tumulus for his recently deceased freedman named Festus, now known as Uveciktepe (fig. 4).[11] This is the largest of the Troad tumuli,

[8] C.B. Rose, "Ilion in the early empire," in C. Berns (ed.), *Patris und Imperium. Kulturelle und politische Identität in den Städten der römischen Provinzen Kleinasiens in der frühen Kaiserzeit* (Leuven 2002) 33–47, at 44–45; W. Aylward, "The portico and propylaia of the sanctuary of Athena at Ilion," *Studia Troica* 15 (2005) 160–61. Hadrian was referred to as "restitutor coloniae suae" at Alexandria Troas: A. Ricl, *The Inscriptions of Alexandria Troas* (Bonn 1997) 229, T124; *CIL* 3.7282.

[9] B. Tekkök, S. Wallrodt, C. Günden, and C.B. Rose, "Two Roman wells in the Lower City of Ilion. Quadrats C29 and w28," *Studia Troica* 11 (2001) 343–82, at 344.

[10] C.B. Rose, "The 1996 post-Bronze Age excavations at Troy," *Studia Troica* 7 (1997) 73–110, at 102; idem, "The 1997 post-Bronze Age excavations at Troy," *Studia Troica* 8 (1998) 71–113, at 102; idem, "1998 excavations at Troy" (supra n. 6), 35–71, at 52.

[11] Caracalla: Dio 78.16.10; Herodian 4.8.4–5; Cook, *Troad* (supra n. 6), 172–73; Halfmann, *Itinera* (supra n. 7), 224; Rose, "1996 excavations at Troy" (supra n. 10), 101–2; idem, "1997 excavations at Troy" (supra n. 10), 96–97; S. Alcock, "Material witness: An archaeological context for the *Heroikos*," in E. Bradshaw Aitken and J.K. Berenson Maclean (eds.), *Philostratus'* Heroikos. *Religion and Cultural Identity in the Third Century C.E.* (Leiden 2005) 159–68, at 161–62.

Fig. 2. Aerial view of Troy (Troy Excavation Project).

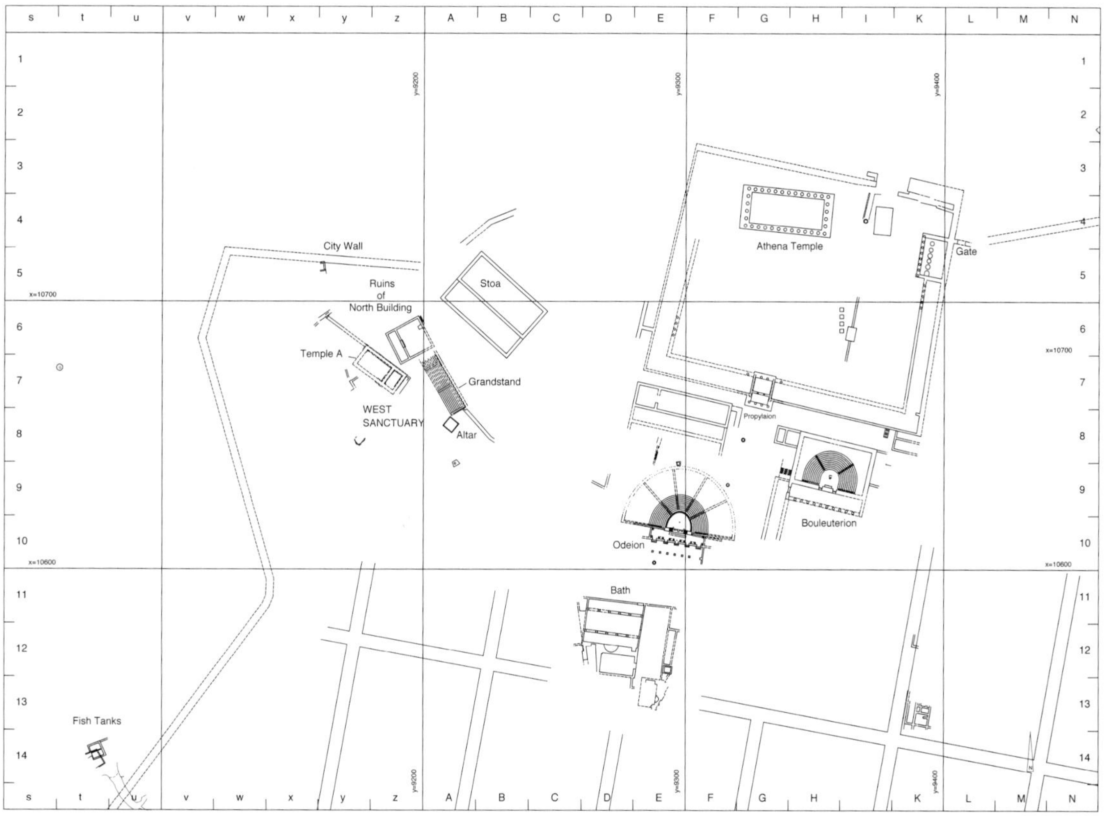

Fig. 3. Plan of Troy IX (Troy Excavation Project).

Fig. 4. Uveciktepe, the tumulus of Festus (courtesy Rüstem Aslan).

nearly 25 m high, and it represents yet another attempt on Caracalla's part to link himself to the Homeric tradition by echoing the mourning of Achilles for Patroclus.

An inscription recently discovered in the earthquake collapse of the Odeion also indicates the involvement of Macrinus, the praetorian prefect who had Caracalla murdered in A.D. 217 (fig. 5):[12]

Αὐτοκρά[τωρ Καῖσαρ]
Μᾶρκος Ὀ[πέλλιος]
Σεουῆρο[ς Μακρεῖνος]
Εὐσεβὴς [- - - - - - - -]
[- - - - -]ọṣạ[- - - - - -]
- -

Fig. 5. Inscription of Macrinus (Troy Excavation Project).

Macrinus occupied the throne for only 14 months and suffered a senatorial *damnatio memoriae* after his assassination, so few dedications to him have been recovered.[13] The most interesting feature of the Troy inscription is that Macrinus's name appears in the nominative case, which indicates a dedication on his part. The nature of the dedication would have been described in the now missing lower section of the inscription, but there is enough evidence to suggest that the benefaction in question may relate to the Odeion. Beneath the marble paving at the west end of the stage were enough coins and pottery to indicate that the stage received its final form during the reign of Caracalla, or

[12] Rose, "1997 excavations at Troy" (supra n. 10), 96–97; *SEG* 48 (1998) no. 1478.

[13] Dio 79.2.5–6; P. Cavuoto, *Macrino* (Naples 1983) 42–48, 61.

shortly thereafter, as did the portico that separated the Odeion from the agora. Given the findspot of Macrinus's inscription, it is possible that the city recognized him for assistance that was actually offered by Caracalla.[14]

During the Severan period there was also a substantial reconstruction of two buildings that lined the agora. In the Antonine baths, on the southern side of the agora, a new apsed hall nearly 16 m wide was divided by two parallel colonnades and paved in marble, thereby replacing an earlier building decorated with mosaics of boxers, bath attendants, and pygmies, among others.[15] It would have been fed by water from an imposing aqueduct bridge with a span of 16 m, still standing in the village of Kemerdere, which formed part of a water system 20–30 km in length that channeled water from the Ida mountains.[16]

Our best evidence for reconstruction during the first half of the third century appears in the residential area of the Lower City, south of the citadel. Magnetic prospection, conducted over the course of 15 years, has revealed the entire plan of the Roman residential district (fig. 6).[17] A network of insulae covered nearly the entire area within the confines of the city wall. The insula system measures 900 m east-west and slightly over 700 m north-south, encompassing as many as 72 insulae of different sizes across a total area of about 45 ha. Although housing in this area began in the third century B.C., shortly after the city wall was built, the most active period of construction was the second quarter of the third century A.D. It was only at this time that occupation in the Lower City became dense, with the walls of one building abutting another. A network of new stone-paved streets, nearly 5 m wide, was also laid at this time.[18] The density of new housing at Ilion points to a significant influx of people into Ilion during the second quarter of the third century, and the ceramic record suggests a simultaneous rise in the local economy.

Also constructed at or near this time were a series of fish tanks in front of the Spring Cave on the southwestern side of the Lower City, 180 m from the citadel (figs. 3, 7). The walls of these basins feature terracotta tubes blocked at one end, which indicates their function as fresh water fish farms, wherein the tubes would have provided shade for the fish. Similar basins have been excavated in Crete, Egypt, and Italy, among others, but the Trojan examples seem to be the only ones found thus far in Asia Minor.[19]

The cave is one large aquifer, with water seeping from its walls and roof, and tool marks visible throughout the interior reflect an attempt to increase the amount of water it discharged. The entrance corridor branches off into three passages, each with smaller dependent corridors, and the central one extends for a length of over 100 m. Cut into the roof of the central passage at staggered intervals are four funnel-shaped shafts intended to channel groundwater into the cave's main corridor, and

[14] W. Aylward, *The Roman Agora at Ilion and its Predecessors* (Ph.D. dissertation, University of Cincinnati 2000) 140.

[15] C.W. Blegen, "Excavations at Troy 1932," *AJA* 36 (1932) 445–46; idem, "Excavations at Troy 1933," *AJA* 38 (1934) 223–48, at 244–46; C.W. Blegen, J. Caskey, M. Rawson, and J. Sperling, *Troy I. The First and Second Settlements* (Princeton 1950) figs. 117–19; Aylward, *Ilion* (supra n. 14), 154–63.

[16] Aqueduct: W. Aylward, G. Bieg, and R. Aslan, "The aqueduct of Roman Ilion and the bridge across the Kemerdere valley in the Troad," *Studia Troica* 12 (2002) 397–427.

[17] P. Jablonka, "Ausgrabungen südlich der Unterstadt von Troia im Bereich des Troia VI—Verteidigungsgrabens. Grabungsbericht 1994," *Studia Troica* 5 (1995) 39–79, at 49; C.-S. Giese Huebner, "Geomagnetische Prospektion 2002 bis 2005 in der Unterstadt von Troia," *Studia Troica* 16 (2006) 125–29; H.G. Jansen, "Das unsichtbare Troia sichtbar gemacht—Chancen und Ergebnisse der Anwendung neuer Prospektionsmethoden," in M.O. Korfmann (ed.), *Troia. Archaeologie eines Siedlungshuegels und seiner Landschaft* (Mainz 2006) 309–16.

[18] Rose, "1998 excavations at Troy" (supra n. 6), 52–54.

[19] Ibid., 55–61. For the type, see J. Higginbotham, *Piscinae: Artificial Fishponds in Roman Italy* (Chapel Hill 1997) passim.

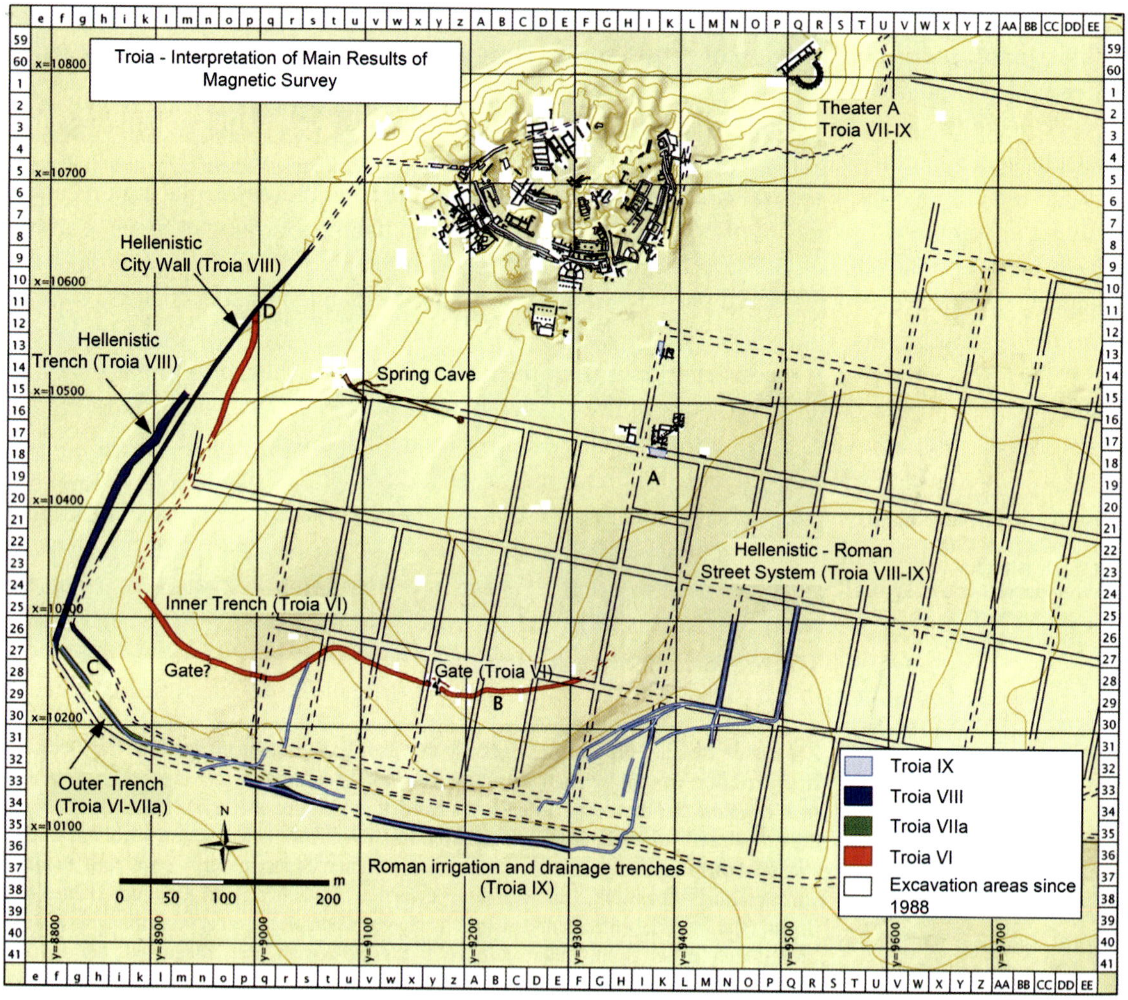

Fig. 6. Plan of the Lower City of Ilion (Troy Excavation Project).

at least two of the shafts end in basins in the floor of the cave.[20] This is a qanat system, well known in the Near East, but the Ilion example is the first to have been discovered in western Asia Minor.[21]

Especially striking is the extent to which the building sequence in the Lower City parallels the history of the "Hanghäuser" at Ephesus.[22] Those houses had been damaged at more or less the same

[20] C. Wolkersdorfer and J. Göbel, "Hydrogeologie der Troianischen Landschaft—eine Bestandsaufnahme," *Studia Troica* 14 (2004) 157–67; M. Korfmann, N. Frank, and A. Mangini, "Eingang in die Unterwelt—die Hoehle von Troia und ihre Datierung," in Korfmann, *Troia* (supra n. 17), 337–42.

[21] For the qanat system, see R.J. Forbes, *Studies in Ancient Technology* I (Leiden 1964) 156–63; R. Tölle-Kastenbein, *Antike Wasserkultur* (Munich 1990) 39–42; D. Crouch, *Water Management in Ancient Greek Cities* (New York 1993) 117; P. Briant, *Irrigation et drainage dans l'antiquité, qanats et canalisations souterraines en Iran, en Égypte, et en Grèce* (Paris 2001).

[22] S. Ladstätter, "Die Chronologie des Hanghauses 2," in F. Krinzinger (ed.), *Das Hanghaus 2 von Ephesos. Studien zu Baugeschichte und Chronologie* (Vienna 2002) 9–40, at 11, 19, 38; H. Thür, "Die Bauphasen der Wohneinheit 4 (und 6)," in Krinzinger, *Hanghaus 2* (supra this note), 41–66, at 57; N. Zimmermann, "Ausstattungen von Haupt- und Nebenräumen. Zur Datierung der Wandmalerein des Hanghauses 2 in Ephesos," in Krinzinger, *Hanghaus 2* (supra this note), 101–17, at 111. "Im Hanghaus 2 kommt es im 2. Viertel des 3.

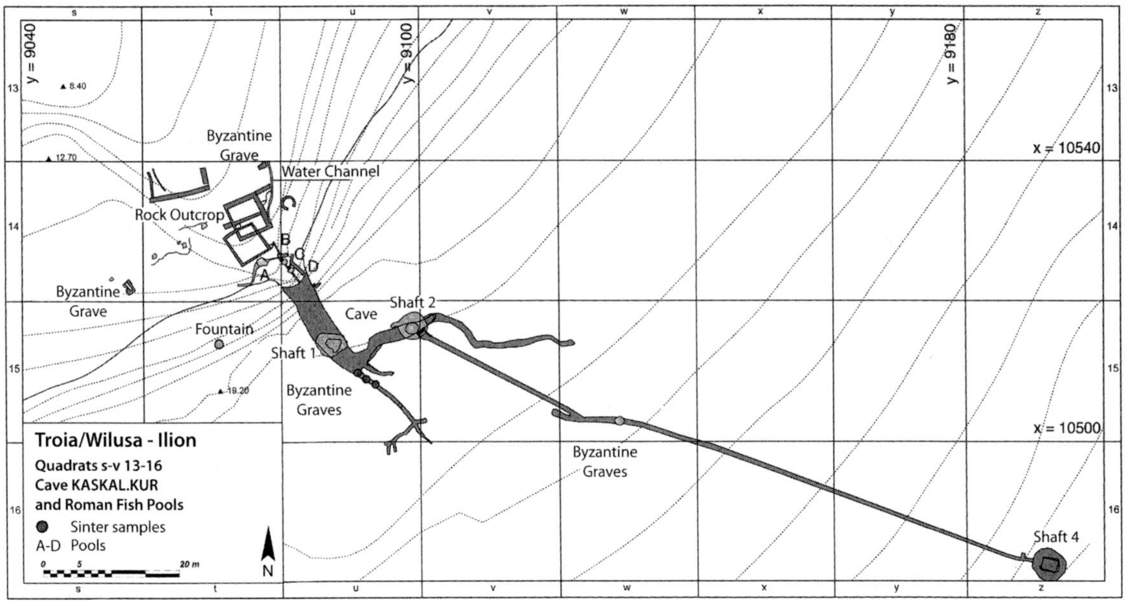

Fig. 7. Plan of the Spring Cave at Troy (Troy Excavation Project).

time as the structures at Ilion, after which there was a similarly dramatic rise in reconstruction. The majority of the mosaics and wall paintings from the Ephesian houses, formerly dated to the fourth and fifth centuries, have now been redated to the second quarter of the third century.[23] Other cities in western Asia Minor, especially in Ionia, benefited as well, and inscriptions refer to new construction, civic improvements, and elaborate spectacles.[24]

Meanwhile, in the area of Alexandria Troas, 25 km away, an extraordinary series of granite quarries (now in the village of Koç Ali) were in operation (figs. 1, 8). Large-scale quarrying appears to have begun here in the early second century, especially for columns, with the products shipped from the harbor at Alexandria Troas.[25] Koç Ali granite columns enjoyed great popularity throughout the Mediterranean, especially between the second and fourth centuries; examples have been found as far east as Palmyra and Nazareth, as far south as Lepcis Magna, and as far west as Arles and Tarraco.[26] The 20 columns still lying in the quarries demonstrate the scale of operations: each has a diameter of ca. 1.65 m and a length of nearly 40 Roman feet—only a few centimeters shorter than those used in the porch of the Pantheon.[27]

There was extensive destruction again ca. A.D. 260–270, which was caused by an attack of the Herulians, although it looks as if an earthquake a few years earlier also weakened the city. One of

Jhs., wohl als folge eines Erdbebens, zu einer umfassenden Bauphase mit teilweiser Neuorganisation der Nutzung und fast durchgängiger Neuasstattung der Räume."

[23] Zimmermann, "Hanghauses" (supra n. 22), superseding M.V. Strocka, *Die Wandmalerei der Hanghäuser in Ephesos, Forschungen in Ephesos* VIII 1 (Vienna 1977).

[24] Magie, *Roman Rule* (supra n. 7), 692–93, 1559 n. 9. This rise in the economy is not visible in the material record of Pergamon: U. Wulf, *Altertümer von Pergamon* XV. *Die Stadtgrabung.* Teil 3. *Die hellenistischen und römischen Wohnhäuser von Pergamon* (Berlin 1999) 209–11.

[25] G. Ponti, "Marmor Troadense: Granite quarries in the Troad. A preliminary survey," *Studia Troica* 5 (1995) 291–320. The discovery of one of the Koç Ali granite columns in the Alexandria Troad harbor makes this certain.

[26] L. Lazzarini, "I graniti dei monumenti italiani ed i loro problemi di deterioramento," *BdA* Suppl. 41 (1987) 157–72, at 163, fig. 24.

[27] Ponti, "Marmor Troadense" (supra n. 25), 319 n. 40. The earliest appearance of Koç Ali granite columns in central Italy is Hadrianic: the Piazza d'Oro in the villa at Tivoli, and the Hadrianic building in the forum at Ostia.

Fig. 8. The quarry at Koç Ali, near Alexandria Troas (C.B. Rose).

Fig. 9. Reconstruction of the temple of Athena (courtesy Elizabeth Riorden).

the residents in the Lower City, who had a prized marble statuette of Cybele, apparently feared the impending devastation of the attackers, and lowered the statuette into a well in an attempt to hide it.[28] There was limited reconstruction following the disaster, and we have found several of the trash pits from the cleanup activities, one of which contained the portrait of Augustus.

[28] Tekkök et al., "Roman wells," (supra n. 9), 371–72.

Fig. 10. The inscribed architrave from the temple of Athena (F. Goethert and H. Schleif, *Der Athenatempel von Ilion, Denkmäler antiker Architektur* 10 [Berlin 1962] fig. 25b).

After A.D. 270, it looks as if the residents once again abandoned much of the Lower City, at least temporarily, and sought shelter closer to the acropolis, as they had done in the late second century B.C. during the Mithridatic Wars.[29] In general, Ilion seems to have entered a period of economic decline after this attack. Inscriptions refer to a Tetrarchic dedication of silver statues of Zeus and Asklepios to Athena Ilias, but the gift appears to have been accompanied by no economic assistance.[30]

Nevertheless, at least some imperial visits continued to occur. Constantine reportedly came in the early fourth century and considered moving the capital either here or to Alexandria Troas.[31] The future emperor Julian actually wrote a letter describing his arrival at Ilion in A.D. 354, wherein we learn that the heroon of Hector was still in existence, as was a bronze statue of Achilles in an open air precinct, presumably the one set up by Caracalla.[32] At some point in the late Roman period a series of Greek epigrams were inscribed on statues of Homeric heroes (Priam, Hector, and Ajax) that probably stood in the Athenaion or the agora.[33] The temple to Athena was still functioning, and there is no evidence that it was subsequently transformed into a church, or that any churches were erected on the acropolis (fig. 9).

Julian was honored with a statue by the residents of Ilion, and it is conceivable that his name was actually featured on the temple.[34] One block of the temple's inscribed epistyle survives, with an incised inscription over which the bronze letters of a second inscription were subsequently placed (fig. 10):[35]

Inscribed: Αὐτοκράτ[ωρ Καῖσαρ Θεοῦ] υἱος Σεβα[στὸς . . .]
Bronze:]οῦ Ἰουλ[

The bronze letters would have been at least 0.20 m in height judging by the position of the holes. Other than Ilion, there are no examples in which building inscriptions, once incised, were replaced by identical inscriptions in bronze, and one can easily understand why. The surfaces that received these inscriptions were exposed to the elements year round, and any plaster meant to cover an incised inscription would have quickly washed away, thereby leaving an ugly shadow under the gilded bronze letters.

[29] A.M. Berlin, "Studies in Hellenistic Ilion: The Lower City. Stratified assemblages and chronology," *Studia Troica* 9 (1999) 73–157, at 147–51.

[30] P. Frisch, *Die Inschriften von Ilion* (Bonn 1975) nos. 96, 97, 103.

[31] Zosimus 2.30; W. Dörpfeld, *Troia und Ilion. Ergebnisse der Ausgrabungen in den vorhistorischen und historischen Schichten von Ilion 1870–1894* (Athens 1902) 592.

[32] Julian, *Letters* 19; M. Sage, "Roman visitors to Ilium in the Roman imperial and late antique period: The symbolic functions of a landscape," *Studia Troica* 10 (2000) 211–31, at 215. He also visited Alexandria Troas: Ricl, *Inscriptions* (supra n. 8), 182, T19.

[33] Frisch, *Inschriften* (supra n. 30), nos. 141, 142, 145.

[34] For the statue, see ibid., no. 100.

[35] Dörpfeld, *Troia* (supra n. 31), 223–25; F. Goethert and H. Schleif, *Der Athenatempel von Ilion, Denkmäler antiker Architektur* 10 (Berlin 1962) 37; Frisch, *Inschriften* (supra n. 30), no. 84; C.B. Rose, "The temple of Athena at Ilion," *Studia Troica* 13 (2003) 27–88, at 65–66; D. Hertel, "Zum Heiligtum der Athena Ilias von Troia IX und zur frühhellenistischen Stadtanlage von Ilion," *AA* (2004) 177–205. The incised letters are certainly Augustan in date, and can be paralleled on other Augustan inscriptions from Ilion: Frisch, *Inschriften* (supra n. 30), nos. 81–83, 85. They feature barely perceptible seriphs, and the crossbars of the "A"s are formed by intersecting diagonal strokes rather than a single horizontal. The inscribed block has now disappeared.

The authors of the first monograph on the Athena temple assumed that both the incised and bronze inscriptions referred to Augustus, with one replacing the other within a very short period of time. The bronze section was consequently restored as: Θε]οῦ'Ιουλ[ίου υἱός].

Such a restoration is certainly incorrect, in that Caesar was never called *theos Ioulios* in the inscriptions of Ilion; Augustan inscriptions in the east refer to Caesar merely as *theos*.[36] There is consequently no reason to associate the bronze letters with Augustus, and the fact that the bronze inscription obscures but does not completely erase the first one argues strongly against it. I suspect that the bronze inscription of the Ilion Athenaion concerned a different emperor, and was inset at a much later time. No words in the second inscription repeat those in the first, and only two fragmentary words survive from the bronze version:]οῦ'Ιουλ[.

The only certainty here is that 1) one of the words begins with'Ιουλ; 2) the name of an emperor was probably featured; and 3) the inscription was set in at a time when it would not have been considered anathema to deface or replace the name of Augustus. All of this evidence points toward a late antique date, and almost certainly to the emperor Julian. The preserved section of the inscription can easily be restored as [Φλαβίου Κλαυδί]ου'Ιουλ[ιανοῦ], which is the usual formula for Julian's name.[37] Julian's statue would have been erected at Ilion at the same time, and his name was probably added to the propylon architrave of the Aphrodisias Sebasteion as well, although it was later defaced.[38]

Shortly after this visit, and for the remainder of the fourth century, the Lower City of Ilion witnessed more building activity than in any of the preceding centuries. Throughout the center of the Lower City there is evidence for reconstruction: this included a monumental portico flanking one of the major streets, and a large glass-working center in the middle of the Lower City, where we found abundant quantities of glass wasters, ingots, and slag, as well as a crucible and new water channels.[39] The manufacture of glass requires large quantities of silicate sand and an abundant supply of fuel, both of which were readily available due to the proximity of the Scamander river and the forests in the foothills of Mt. Ida.

Two opulent houses were built with elaborate polychromatic stone mosaics featuring geometric schemes, datable to the late fourth century, as well as a painted plaster ceiling with floral designs (fig. 11).[40] The entire ceiling was framed by a plaster bead and reel molding with a course of sea shells at the edges, and our best comparanda come from the "Hanghäuser" at Ephesus, where there are two that feature similar designs, although ours is considerably later.[41] It is noteworthy that in none of these houses is there evidence for private baths or opus sectile floors such as one finds at Ephesus and Pergamon.

[36] C. Damon, *Res Gestae divi Augusti* (Bryn Mawr 1995) 60 no. 2.

[37] For the dedication to Julian at Ilion, see Frisch, *Inschriften* (supra n. 30), no. 100. For the inscriptions of Julian in general, see J. Arce, *Estudios sobre el Emperador Fl. Cl. Juliano: fuentes literarias, epigrafía, numismatics* (Madrid 1984) 93–176, op. cit. 109–12, 154–66. To his list add *SEG* 37 (1987) no. 863 (Iasos); *SEG* 41 (1991) nos. 1544 (Askalon), 1614 (Prokynema, Egypt); *SEG* 45 (1995) no. 1682 (Yirce, Mysia); *SEG* 47 (1997) no. 2066 (Jerash); *SEG* 48 (1998) nos. 1912, 1913 (Jerash).

[38] For the Aphrodisias propylon dedication, see K. Erim, *Aphrodisias: City of Venus Aphrodite* (London 1986) 112 (the two lower fasciae of the architrave, later erased). Two other inscriptions to Julian at Aphrodisias were also erased: C. Roueché, *Aphrodisias in Late Antiquity, JRS Monograph* 5 (London 1989) 35–42 nos. 19, 20. The dedication to Julian at Ilion is in Latin, which is interesting in itself. Altogether, five Latin inscriptions can be confidently attributed to Ilion, four of which concern late Roman emperors (Alexander Severus, Diocletian, Constantine II, and Julian: Frisch, *Inschriften* [supra n. 30], nos. 95, 98–100). None of the inscriptions associated with Athena or the koinon were in Latin. On the use of Greek vs. Latin in Asia Minor during the fourth century, see R. Van Dam, *The Roman Revolution of Constantine* (Cambridge 2007) 184–216.

[39] C.B. Rose, "The 1991 post-Bronze Age excavations at Troy," *Studia Troica* 2 (1992) 43–60, at 55–56; idem, "1996 excavations at Troy" (supra n. 10), 102–3; idem, "1997 excavations at Troy" (supra n. 10), 101–2; idem, "1998 excavations at Troy" (supra n. 6), 52–54.

[40] C.B. Rose, "The 1993 post-Bronze Age excavations at Troy," *Studia Troica* 4 (1994) 75–104, at 93–94.

[41] Strocka, *Hanghäuser* (supra n. 23), 58, fig. 91; 91, fig. 349. Another preserved ceiling (ibid., 36, fig. 27) contains inter-

Fig. 11. The mosaic floor of a late Roman house in the Lower City (Troy Excavation Project).

Fig. 12. The mosaic floor of the early Christian church at Ilion (C.W. Blegen et al., *Troy I. The First and Second Settlements* [Princeton 1950] fig. 120).

Some of the new construction gradually encroached upon the paved streets, thereby decreasing their width by several meters and spurring the spoliation of their stone pavers. This is part of a larger late antique trend in the eastern Mediterranean wherein commerce shifted from the agorai and fora to more residential areas along major roads, with the shops often set up behind new porticoes.[42] In spite of the fact that some of these structures were commercial as well as residential, there was no evidence of window grills to discourage theft, although the presence of keys indicates that the doors were locked.

Although Ilion was reportedly the seat of a bishopric until at least the ninth century, only one church has been excavated at the site—on the eastern side of the Lower City. The entire floor of the narthex was paved with mosaics that feature medallions, some of which were filled by images of animals and birds (fig. 12). The total dimensions of the building were quite sizable—approximately

locking squares with floral elements. For the new chronology, see P. Scherrer, "The historical topography of Ephesus," in D. Parrish (ed.), *Urbanism in Western Asia Minor, JRA* Suppl. 45 (Portsmouth, RI 2001) 57–96, at 77–79.

[42] C. Foss, *Byzantine and Turkish Sardis* (Cambridge 1976) 16, 42–43; idem, *Ephesus after Antiquity: A Late Antique, Byzantine, and Turkish City* (Cambridge 1979) 54–67; M.L. Rautman, "A late Roman townhouse in Sardis," in E. Schwertheim (ed.), *Forschungen in Lydien, Asia Minor Studien* 17 (Bonn 1995) 49–66, at 52; C. Lang-Auinger, "Hanghaus 1," in ead. (ed.), *Hanghaus 1 in Ephesos. Funde und Ausstattung, Forschungen in Ephesos* VIII 4 (Vienna 2003) 333.

30 by 18 m, and it may have been the principal church of Ilion during late antiquity. The church was probably constructed during the period of prosperity that occurred at Ilion on either side of A.D. 400, and it was clearly built here because of a pre-existing cemetery in the area.[43]

The quarries at Koç Ali were still in operation during this period: newly quarried columns were shipped to Lepcis Magna in A.D. 313 for use in the restored Forum Vetus basilica, and both the *Theodosian Code* and the *Ecclesiastical History* of Socrates demonstrate continued activity in the first quarter of the fifth century.[44] By the middle of the fifth century, however, the economic picture appears to have become considerably bleaker. The agora at Ilion gradually lost its commercial function due to the steady movement of shops to the Lower City, and it was being used as a cemetery by the middle of the fifth century.[45] A crippling blow occurred around A.D. 500, when two sizable earthquakes struck the western Troad within a relatively short period of time. The coins and pottery associated with the earthquake collapse include an extensive amount of LRC Hayes Form 3, and allow us to date the catastrophe to A.D. 500 or shortly thereafter.[46] Even before the earthquake struck, the city appears to have been largely abandoned: few small finds were discovered in the houses under the earthquake collapse, leading one to posit that the houses had been emptied of their contents prior to A.D. 500.

As in the late Bronze Age, the remaining residents once again took shelter on the acropolis. The northeast gate of the city was completely blocked by a wall composed of fallen architectural elements, and on the southern side of the acropolis, the survivors constructed another defensive wall composed of spolitated architectural elements set in a hard mortar (fig. 13). Both of these seem to have formed part of a new security system, and only one entrance to the acropolis may have remained open.[47]

How long habitation continued here is unclear. But on the southern side of the acropolis Carl Blegen found three coins from the second half of the sixth century: Justin I and Sophia (A.D. 565–568), Tiberius II (A.D. 578–579), and Maurice Tiberius (A.D. 587–588), while a coin of Heraclius (A.D. 610–641) was unearthed in Quadrat D6, to the northwest. These are the latest early Byzantine coins that have been found at the site, and it seems likely that the acropolis was the last locus of activity in post-earthquake Ilion.[48] The date of these coins is particularly important, however, because it means that at least a few of the residents survived the plague that swept through Asia Minor during the reign of Justinian.[49]

The last residents appear to have abandoned the site, including the acropolis, by the early seventh century. Late Byzantine coins and pottery on the south and west sides of the acropolis indicate some renewed activity in the 11th and 13th centuries, but this may have been related only to spoliation of stones.[50] When a settlement was established again in the late 12th century, the water-bearing cave

[43] C.W. Blegen, "Excavations at Troy, 1935," *AJA* 39 (1935) 550–87, at 582–83; Blegen et al., *Troy* (supra n. 15), 13; Frisch, *Inschriften* (supra n. 30), 242–43 no. 156 (inscription); Sage, "Roman visitors" (supra n. 32), 219; C.B. Rose, "Von Konstantin bis Mehmet II," in *Troia. Traum und Wirklichkeit* (Stuttgart 2001) 280–81, at 280.

[44] J.M. Reynolds and J.B. Ward-Perkins, *The Inscriptions of Roman Tripolitania* (Rome 1952) 132 no. 467; Ricl, *Inscriptions* (supra n. 8), 236, T139 (*Theodosian Code*); 234–35, T134 (Socrates, *Ecclesiastical History* 7.37). There is no evidence that the quarries continued operations after ca. A.D. 420.

[45] C.B. Rose, "The 1992 post-Bronze Age excavations at Troy," *Studia Troica* 3 (1993) 97–116, at 110.

[46] Rose, "1996 excavations at Troy" (supra n. 10), 96–101. Featured in the assemblage is Hayes Form 87b: Behälter P18.0093:1.

[47] Rose, "1996 excavations at Troy" (supra n. 10), 99; idem, "Temple" (supra n. 35), 64.

[48] Two coins of Justinian (A.D. 518–565) were found in Quadrat H17, in the center of the Lower City (C55, 58), and a nummus, apparently of Justinian (C143), was found under one of the blocks of the bouleuterion (Rose, "1991 excavations at Troy" [supra n. 39], 53). The coins of Maurice Tiberius, Tiberius II, Justin, and Heraclius were not catalogued by Bellinger in his monograph on the coins of Troy, but they appear in the C.W. Blegen inventory of coins on pages 12 no. 144 (Justin), no. 146 (Maurice Tiberius), no. 152 (Tiberius II); 18 no. 224 (Heraclius). See also Rose, "Temple" (supra n. 35), 65.

[49] For the plague see L. Little (ed.), *Plague and the End of Antiquity: The Pandemic of 541–750* (Cambridge 2007).

[50] These were found in Quadrats F8/9 and D3/4/5. F8/9: Inventory of coins notebook, 11 no. 131 (ca. A.D. 1050), no. 132

Fig. 13. The blocked entrance to the acropolis near Ilion's Northeast Bastion (Troy Excavation Project).

in Quadrat t14 emerged as its nucleus, and the stones of the Athenaion gradually began to travel to the surrounding villages.[51]

There was still a considerable amount of activity in this area of the Troad during the sixth century: Justinian built an enormous granary on the island of Tenedus so that grain ships from Egypt had a place to unload their cargo if the winds and currents of the Dardanelles hindered sailing, and an inscription from Abydus, probably dating to the reign of Anastasius I, records the tarifs imposed on ships crossing the Dardanelles.[52] But this would have had little effect on Ilion or the coastal cities of the Troad, whose public buildings now lay in ruins.

Some of the gaps in the archaeological record of Ilion can be filled by the Granicus River Valley Survey Project, where I have conducted four seasons of work.[53] Our goal in this project is to survey and map all of the settlements and tumuli that lie on or between the Granicus and Aesepus rivers (see fig. 1). This area encompasses a significant portion of the satrapy of Hellespontine Phyrgia, and although tumuli dating to the period of Persian control constitute the most dominant feature of the landscape, there is an abundance of evidence for habitation of late Roman date.[54]

(ca. A.D. 1050); 12 no. 147 (A.D. 1204–1255). D3: ibid., 16 no. 199 (A.D. 1081–1095). D4: ibid., 18 no. 220 (A.D. 1259–1261), no. 221 (A.D. 1260–1261). D5: ibid., 22 no. 280 (12th century).

[51] Rose, "1997 excavations at Troy" (supra n. 10), 102–3; idem, "1998 excavations at Troy" (supra n. 6), 35–71, at 55–61; idem, "Research at Troy, 1999" (supra n. 6), 53–72, at 61–65.

[52] Procopius, *On Buildings* 5.1 (ca. A.D. 560); J. Durliat and A. Guillou, "Le tarif d'Abydos (vers 492)," *BCH* 108 (1984) 581–98. For Byzantine settlements in the vicinity of Ilion, see G. Bieg, K. Belke, and B. Tekkök, "Die Mittel- bis Spätbyzantinische Besiedlung innerhalb des Nationalparks 'Troia und die Troas,'" *Studia Troica* 18 (2008) 163–97.

[53] The first two seasons of work have been presented in Rose et al., "Granicus 2006" (supra n. 2). For a recent survey of the western Troad, see G. Bieg, B. Tekkök, and R. Aslan, "Die Spätrömische Besiedlung der Troas—ein Überblick," *Studia Troica* 16 (2006) 147–70.

[54] For a historical overview of habitation in the area, see N. Sekunda, "Persian settlement in Hellespontine Phrygia," in A. Kuhrt and H. Sancisi-Weerdenburg (eds.), *Achaemenid History* III: *Method and Theory* (Leiden 1988) 175–96; B. Tenger, "Troas zwischen Königsfrieden und Ankunft Alexanders," in E. Schwertheim and H. Wiegartz (eds.), *Die Troas. Neue Forschungen zu Neandria und Alexandria Troas*

The ceramic record points to an unusual sequence of habitation in this area. Less than 1 per cent of the ceramics are Bronze Age (and all second millennium B.C.); 41 per cent are archaic or classical (with the vast majority dating from the late sixth through the early fourth century B.C.); 5 per cent Hellenistic (the majority is early Hellenistic); just over 1 per cent are early to mid-Roman (primarily third century A.D.); nearly 29 per cent are late Roman; 14 per cent Byzantine (with the majority being late 12th or early 13th century), and nearly 10 per cent Ottoman (with the majority dating to the 19th century). In other words, the primary settlements date to the period of Persian occupation, and to the late Roman period. Nearly 60 per cent of the 86 sites that we have identified in the Granicus and Aesepus river valleys have a late Roman phase of occupation.[55]

The significant increase in population here during late antiquity can be explained in part by the rise in seismic activity throughout the Troad, which brought down most of the buildings in the coastal settlements.[56] Disrupted waterways turned to swamps and ultimately prompted a rise in malaria, followed by plague. The abandonment of those sites spurred a return to the agricultural areas that had remained largely uncultivated since the end of Persian control. Indeed, at many sites in our survey area there were virtually no sherds that dated between the late classical and late Roman periods.

Fig. 14. Milestone of Gordian III, from Gümüşçay (Granicus River Valley Archaeological Project).

There is a considerable amount of information relating to the ancient road system that crossed the region. In Gümüşçay we discovered a milestone that bears five inscriptions—Gordian III, Valerian and Gallienus, Licinius, Constantine I with his sons, and Valentinian I (fig. 14). This is an especially important discovery in that no other milestones from this area have been discovered, even though they have appeared on the west coast of the Troad and in the region around Cyzicus. We know from the ancient sources that there was a road that crossed the Granicus in the vicinity of Didymateiche (Gümüşçay), not far from the bridge that would have been used by the Persian army during the Battle of the Granicus. Our new milestone probably belonged to this road.[57]

Altogether, five milestones linked to the Cyzicus-Daskyleion road have been identified. Although their dates range from the Antonine period to Theodosius I, the majority of the inscriptions date to the fourth century, and three of them include dedications to Constantine I and Valentinian I,

---

II, *Asia Minor Studien* 22 (Bonn 1996) 125–47; idem, "Zur Geographie und Geschichte der Troas," in E. Schwertheim (ed.), *Die Troas. Neue Forschungen* III, *Asia Minor Studien* 33 (Bonn 1999) 103–80, at 131–33.

[55] Rose et al., "Granicus 2006" (supra n. 2), 104–5.

[56] E. Guidoboni, *Catalogue of Ancient Earthquakes in the Mediterranean Area up to the 10th Century* (Rome 1994) 302–5 no. 189.

[57] Rose et al., "Granicus 2006" (supra n. 2), 110–13.

Fig. 15. The remains of the ecclesiastical complex at Babayaka (Granicus River Valley Archaeological Project).

like the Gümüşçay milestone.[58] All of these improvements are undoubtedly by-products of Diocletian's establishment of Cyzicus as the capital of Troas and Lesser Phrygia.[59]

Approximately 10 km southeast of Biga, near Taşoluk, we actually discovered part of an ancient road with wheelruts. The remains measure nearly 100 m in length, with a width of 2 m, and they appear never to have been mapped before. The road has been cut between the natural rocks on the high crest of a hill, from which one can see Priapus and the sea of Marmara. The road may originally have been created during the period of Persian domination, but in its current form, it most closely resembles roads of Roman date.[60]

Within this area, we found abundant evidence for settlements, religious complexes, and fortified citadels. Our most important discovery was at Babayaka, which looks out on the Aesepus river and lies about 5 km southeast of Gönen. Here we found a well-preserved building constructed of brick and stone, measuring 20 by 15 m. Most of the first floor is still standing, and it appears never to have been recorded or published (fig. 15). The plan of the building features a triconch or three-apsed room, with each of the apses flanked by semicircular niches, while the outer vestibule is in the form of a double-apsed narthex. This is probably the mausoleum of an important member of the community. Judging by the plan of the building, and the pottery found around it, a date of construction in the fifth or sixth century seems likely.[61]

[58] D.H. French, *Roman Roads and Milestones of Asia Minor*. Fasc. 2, *An Interim Catalogue of Milestones, BAR-IS* 392, *British Institute of Archaeology at Ankara Monograph* 9 (Oxford 1988) nos. 213 (Septimius Severus/Constantine I), 214 (Constantine I, Valentinian I, Theodosius I), 216 (M. Aurelius/Julian), 218 (Constantine I/Valentinian I), 221 (Diocletian).

[59] For Diocletian's reorganization of the province see Tenger, "Geographie" (supra n. 54), 171.

[60] Rose et al., "Granicus 2006" (supra n. 2), 103–16, at 108.

[61] Ibid., 106.

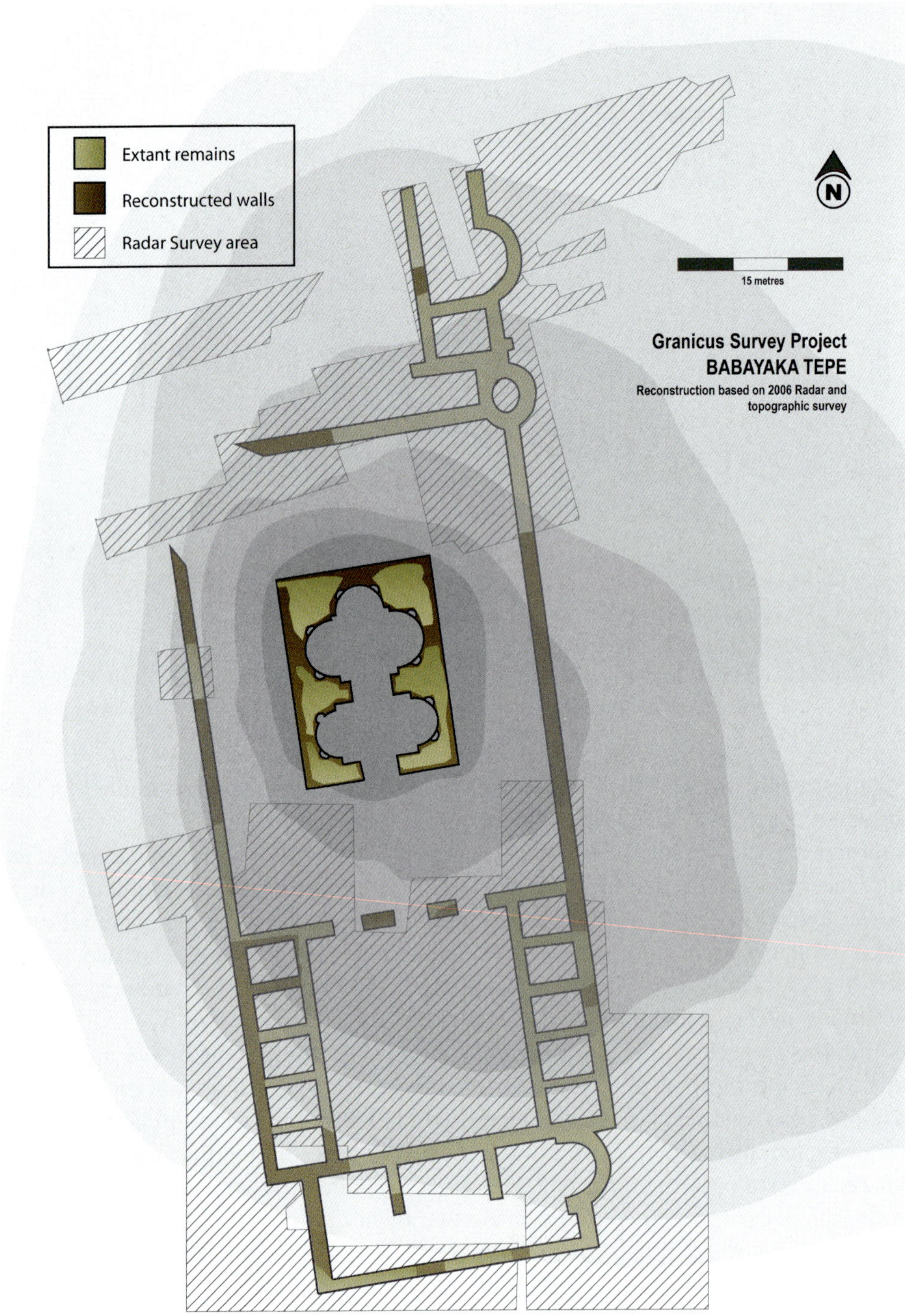

Fig. 16. Restored plan of the ecclesiastical complex at Babayaka (Granicus River Valley Archaeological Project).

We used remote sensing, primarily radar, in the area to the north and south of the building; the results, which were unusually clear, revealed the entire plan (fig. 16). The complex featured a large structure with an apse at the east, probably a church, which is linked to a courtyard, each side of which contained five rooms of equal dimensions. Further to the north is another structure with an apse at the east and an additional set of rooms. This is one of the largest early Byzantine ecclesiastical complexes in the Troad, and it is especially remarkable in that there is no major ancient settlement in the vicinity, as far as we know.[62]

The roads that crossed through the Aesepus, Empelus, and Macestus river valleys in the eastern Troad/Mysia were guarded by citadels situated on high hills that, in some cases, provided views as far as the sea of Marmara.[63] Most of these roads were in operation for long periods of time, as were several of the citadels—from the Achaemenid period through the late Byzantine/early Ottoman periods. There were at least four of them along the Aesepus river, which marked the main road from Cyzicus to Adramyttion and Pergamon, and the distance between them ranged from 6 to 25 km.[64]

Two of these, Alacaoluk and Asartepe, occupy very defensible terrain in the Aesepus river valley, and feature walls of mortared rubble faced in ashlar masonry with neat headers and stretchers, especially on towers and around gates (see fig. 1). The existence of both had been noted by 19th-century topographers who dated them generally to the Byzantine period, but a sketch existed only for Alacaoluk, which was done quickly.[65] Conducting a careful examination of the two citadels, which are unusually well preserved, was one of the principal goals of the Granicus River Valley Survey Project, as was the preparation of new measured plans.

Alacaoluk is located on a high outcropping of bedrock that rises from the floor of a deep gorge about 15 km southwest of Gönen (figs. 17–18).[66] The fortress has an oval shape, about 175 by 105 m in size, and the main citadel wall was fortified by an outer wall on the north and east sides. There are 11 towers overall, the largest of which is approximately 15 m in height. Two gates are preserved, each of which had a barrel-vaulted tunnel about 7 m long made of mortared rubble. Built against the inside of one of the walls were three brick-lined, barrel-vaulted cisterns. Marble spolia appear regularly on the facing, especially near gates and on towers. The walls appear to have been built in three phases that took place over a relatively short period of time, perhaps within the same generation of builders.

Asartepe is located 35 km southwest of Alacaoluk (fig. 19).[67] The elevation of the citadel is extraordinarily high, with views of both the Aesepus and Granicus river valleys, and on clear days, one can see the sea of Marmara from here. The fortress is long and narrow, 325 m long and between 45 and 75 m wide. These walls are not as well preserved as those of Alacaoluk (the highest preserved tower is only about 7 m tall), but aspects of the design and construction indicate that the two fortresses were contemporary. The fortress had 10 towers (excluding bastions that flanked the gates) and three cisterns. Many millstones were found here, which suggests a grain storage and processing facility—

[62] There is nothing comparable in A. Grabar, *Martyrium: recherches sur le culte des reliques et l'art chrétien* (Paris 1943–46), or in M.-F. Auzépy, "Survey of the Byzantine monasteries of the south coast of the sea of Marmara 2004," *Araştırma Sonuçları Toplantısı* 23.2 (2005) 23–34.

[63] T. Wiegand, "Reisen in Mysien," *AM* 29 (1904) 254–339, at 335–39.

[64] See the plan at the back of F.W. Hasluck, *Cyzicus* (Cambridge 1910). A few of these can be dated by literary sources, such as Achyraus, near Hadrianutherae (Balıkesir), which was built by John Comnenus to guard the southern roads (Niketas Choniates, *Annals* 44B).

[65] For the dating, see Wiegand, "Reisen in Mysien" (supra n. 63), 274, 337–38.

[66] Ibid., 335–39, with fig. 47; Hasluck, *Cyzicus* (supra n. 64), 104, fig. 11.

[67] Ibid., 110–11 (identified as Palaeoscepsis); Wiegand, "Reisen in Mysien" (supra n. 63), 274; A.D. Mordtmann, "Ruines de Scepsis en Troade," *RA* 11 (1855) 767–70.

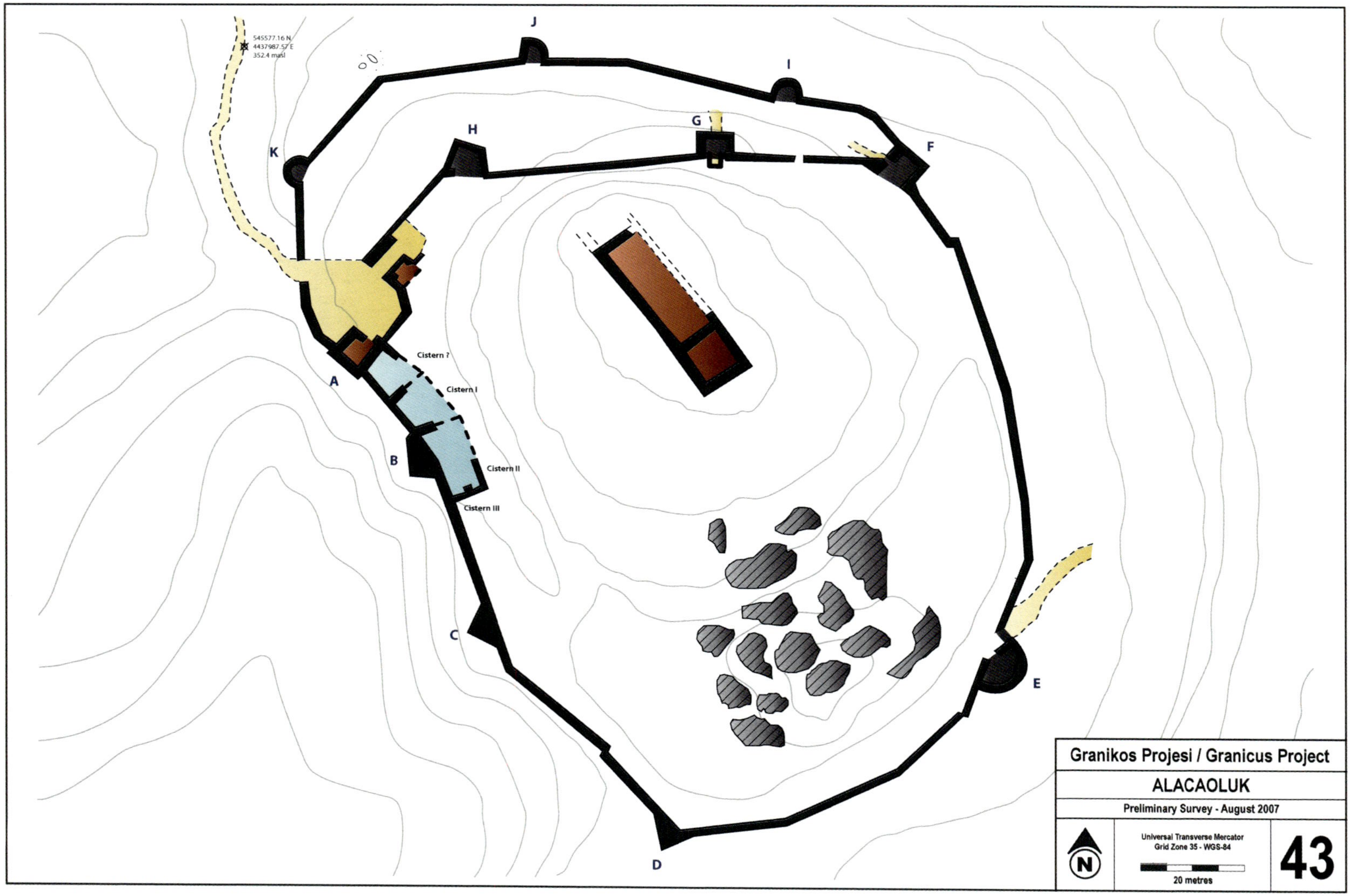

Fig. 17. The late Roman citadel at Alacaoluk (prepared by G. Pizzorno, Granicus River Valley Archaeological Project).

Fig. 18. Remains of the late Roman citadel at Alacaoluk (Granicus River Valley Archaeological Project).

something that would have been important for a garrison. Also like Alacaoluk, marble spolia, including a Doric frieze and window mullions, appear regularly on the facing, with higher frequency at gates and towers.

Dating the citadels of Asartepe and Alacaoluk is difficult, although the style and technique of the walls suggest a date between ca. A.D. 400 and 600. Without excavation, the date can be narrowed only by focusing on the history of the area, and examining when such constructions would have been most plausible. Within the fifth century, one likely period is the reign of Theodosius II (A.D. 401–450), when the combined threat of the Goths and Huns made it clear that the defenses of Constantinople, and of the empire in general, needed to be strengthened. In A.D. 413–414 Theodosius II built the triple fortifications around the city of Constantinople, 18 m in height. This could conceivably have prompted a "ripple effect" wherein other regions in the empire also strengthened their fortifications and began to establish points of protection along the roads to protect commercial routes.[68]

A second possible phase of construction, and the more likely one, would be the reign of the emperor Anastasius I (A.D. 498–518). Anastasius constructed fortification walls across Thrace ca. A.D. 500, probably to counter military threats from the Bulgars, and similar walls were built across the Gallipoli peninsula.[69] These were enormous fortification projects, built as new lines of defense to supplement the existing walls in the face of increasing security problems, and the citadels at Asartepe and Alacaoluk may have been by-products of the building program. With the rise in population in the interior during the early sixth century, and a subsequent increase in commercial traffic, the construction of such citadels along major roads is to be expected.[70]

Structural changes in the regional administration occurred under Heraclius, with the establishment of new geographic units or themes.[71] The Hellespont region was now joined to Bithynia with a new capital at Nicaea, which lay over 300 km east of Ilion and Alexandria Troas. Although

[68] F. Krischen, *Die Landmauer von Konstantinopel* (Berlin 1938); R.M. Errington, *Roman Imperial Policy from Julian to Theodosius* (Chapel Hill 2006) 142–70.

[69] J. Crow, "The long walls of Thrace," in C. Mango and G. Dagron (eds.), *Constantinople and its Hinterland* (Aldershot 1995) 109–24; G. Greatrex, "Procopius and Agathias on the defenses of the Thracian Chersonese," in Mango and Dagron, *Constantinople* (supra this note), 125–30; J. Crow and A. Ricci, "Investigating the hinterland of Constantinople. Interim report on the Anastasian long walls," *JRA* 10 (1997) 235–62; J. Crow, "The infrastructure of a great city: Earth, walls and water in late antique Constantinople," in L. Lavan, E. Zanini, and A. Sarantis (eds.), *Technology in Transition: A.D. 300–650, Late Antique Archaeology* 4.1 (Leiden 2007) 251–85.

[70] The use of window mullion fragments as spolia also points to the later date.

[71] Hasluck, *Cyzicus* (supra n. 64), 193–94; J.F. Haldon, *Byzantium in the Seventh Century. The Transformation of a Culture* (Cambridge 1997).

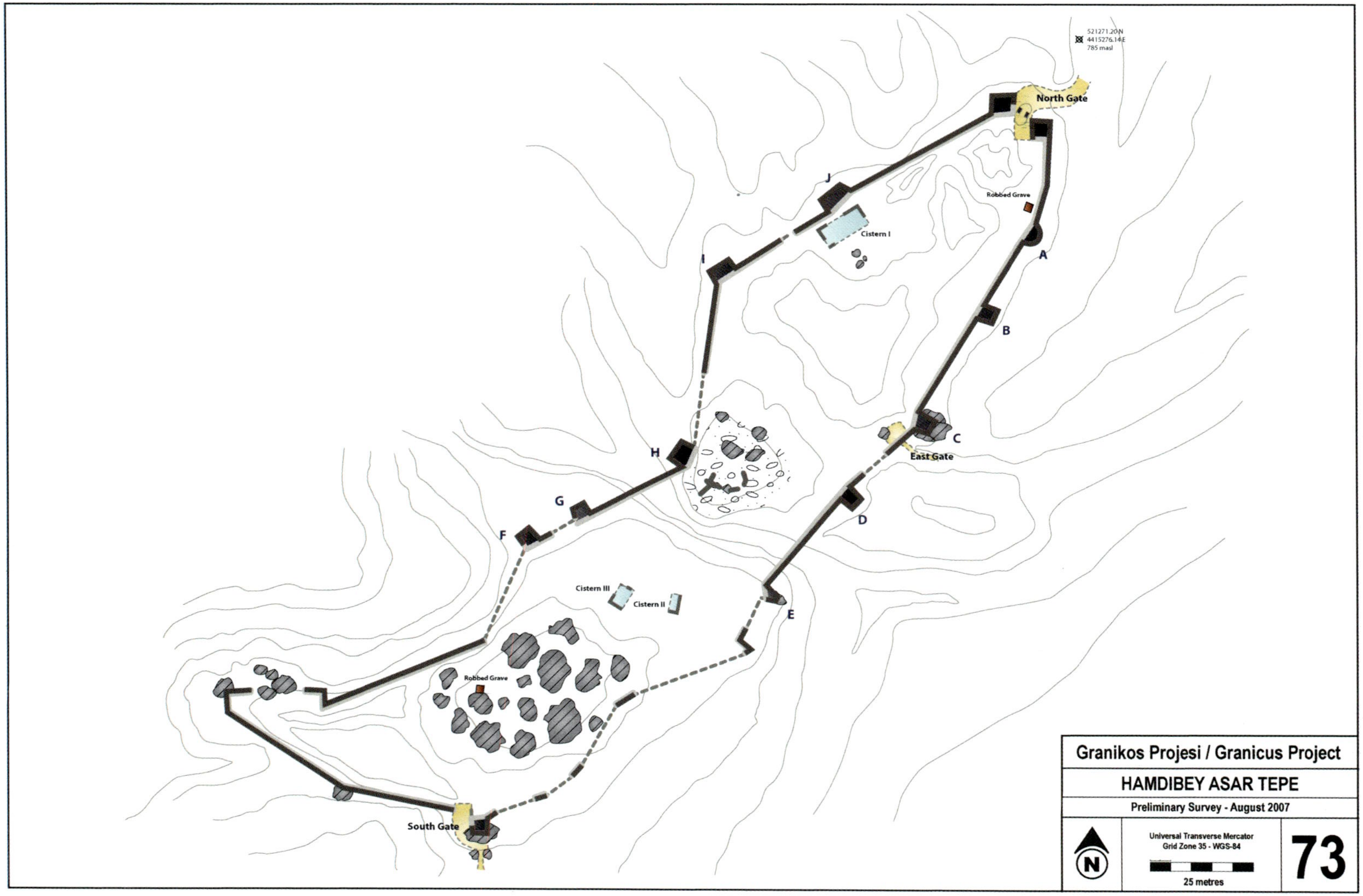

Fig. 19. The late Roman citadel at Asartepe (prepared by G. Pizzorno, Granicus River Valley Archaeological Project).

the Heraclian hoard of silver ecclesiastical spoons found at Lampsacus in 1847 attests the wealth of the local churches in the Troad, the new administrative changes clearly had a negative effect on the area's commerce.[72] Subsequent raids by both Sassanians and Arabs further decimated the population, and there would be no recovery until the empire of Nicaea in the 13th century, and even then, it would be short-lived.[73]

Conclusion

Research in Ilion and the Granicus river valley, city and country, has provided a significant body of evidence regarding late antique occupation in the Troad. The evidence from Ilion demonstrates the rise in the city's fortunes between A.D. 230 and 250, as well as during the second half of the fourth century. The Granicus survey, in particular, has clarified the shift in population from coastal cities to the interior after the earthquakes of ca. A.D. 500, and has elucidated the new fortification systems. Binding both areas, of course, was the Homeric tradition. The Granicus valley, like Troy, came equipped with its share of legendary landmarks, including the tombs of Memnon, Paris, and Oenone, and Ganymede's point of abduction by Zeus.[74] Although those legends would cease to be an economic engine for the Troad following the advent of Christianity, the region would continue to attract a distinguished group of visitors eager to co-opt the Homeric landscapes for their own purposes.

This was particularly apparent in the nationalist movements of medieval Europe when so many groups laid claim to Trojan ancestry, including the Franks, the Normans, and the Danes, among others.[75] Those reassessments of ethnic identity were accompanied by public speeches, some of which have survived in one form or another, and they highlight the applicability of Troy to a variety of new historical circumstances. Both Pierre of Bracheux, the French Crusader of the early 13th century, and Mehmet II, the Ottoman Sultan in the mid-15th century, reportedly delivered similarly structured speeches after their respective conquests of Byzantine Constantinople, wherein they argued that they had finally avenged the attacks on their kinsmen, the Trojans, by sacking the Greeks in Constantinople.[76] Even though Pierre and Mehmet represented very different constituencies that were often at war with each other, both claimed kinship with the Trojans, and therefore, by extension, with each other. Such striking reconfigurations of the past succinctly illustrate the power and versatility of the Trojan tradition, as well as the distinctive blend of east and west that separated the Troad from other areas with a Homeric pedigree.

[72] S. Hauser, *Spätantike und frühbyzantinische Silberlöffel* (Münster 1992) 31–42.

[73] Rose, "1997 excavations at Troy" (supra n. 10), 102–3; Rose, "Research at Troy, 1999" (supra n. 6), 55–61; H. Kiesewetter, "Spätbyzantinische Gräber bei der Quellhöhle in der Unterstadt von Troia/Ilion," *Studia Troica* 9 (1999) 411–35. A much larger citadel was constructed at Priapus/Pegae (modern Karabiga) during the middle and late Byzantine periods: W. Aylward, "The Byzantine fortifications at Pegae (Priapus) on the sea of Marmara," *Studia Troica* 16 (2006) 179–203.

[74] Strabo 13.1.11 (Ganymede/Memnon), 13.1.33 (Paris, Oenone).

[75] S.J. Harris, *Race and Ethnicity in Anglo-Saxon Literature* (New York 2003).

[76] D. Jacoby, "Knightly values and class consciousness in the Crusader states of the eastern Mediterranean," *Mediterranean Historical Review* 1 (1986) 170–73; Sage, "Roman visitors" (supra n. 32).

10 Trades, Crafts, and Agricultural Production in Town and Countryside in Southeastern Isauria

Günder Varinlioğlu

Strabo describes Rough Cilicia as an agriculturally poor region whose natural resources were limited to ship-building, timber, and saffron: "its coast is narrow and has no level ground, or scarcely any; and besides that, it lies at the foot of the Taurus, which affords a poor livelihood."[1] The archaeological and epigraphic evidence of the late antique period, especially of the fifth and sixth centuries, paints a different picture for the eastern section of Rough Cilicia. A wide range of crafts, professions, and products recorded in funerary inscriptions testifies to commercial ties within the region and across the Mediterranean. Rural settlements built entirely of labor-intensive and costly masonry indicate the availability of a considerable economic surplus in the countryside. Mills, presses, and threshing floors ubiquitous in the limestone hills of southeastern Isauria were the main facilities used in agro-pastoral production.

The rural landscapes studied in this article lie in the hinterland of Seleucia ad Calycadnum, the capital of the late antique province of Isauria, corresponding to Roman Rough Cilicia (fig. 1). The countryside had an outlet to the Mediterranean primarily through the harbor-village of Corasium. The city of Corycus, located 7 km east of Corasium, was the main harbor and commercial center along this coast. Rural settlements in the hinterlands of Seleucia ad Calycadnum, Corycus, and Elaiussa-Sebaste occupy the limestone hills that rise above a narrow strip of coastal plains. This geography is characterized by a lack of water sources and scarcity of fields suitable for agriculture. Villages, hamlets, farmsteads, and isolated buildings are widely dispersed in the territory, in such a way to be close to agriculturally and pastorally exploitable lands. Surface pottery indicates intensive activity between the fourth and seventh centuries, while the fifth and sixth centuries in particular are marked by the growth of settlements and the construction of basilicas.[2] The creation of an economic surplus was possible through the intensive exploitation of natural resources in marginal areas, parallel to the development of similar landscapes all over the Mediterranean, such as at Tripolitania, North Syria, and Palestine.[3]

Epigraphic Evidence for Urban Trades and Crafts

The epigraphic records of Corycus, Corasium, Diocaesarea, Olba, Seleucia ad Calycadnum, and St. Thecla are exceptional sources that shed light on the commercial ties between the countryside and coastal towns. This evidence, quantitatively large enough for a statistical study, provides valuable

[1] Strabo 14.5.1.

[2] G. Varinlioğlu, *Rural Landscape and Built Environment at the End of Antiquity: Limestone Villages of Southeastern Isauria* (Ph.D. dissertation, University of Pennsylvania 2008) and ead., "Living in a marginal environment: Rural habitat and landscape in southeastern Isauria," *DOP* 61 (2008) 287–317.

[3] G. Barker, *Farming the Desert: The UNESCO Libyan Valleys Archaeological Survey* (Paris 1996); G. Tate, *Les campagnes de la Syrie du Nord du IIe au VIIe siècle: un exemple d'expansion démographique et économique dans les campagnes à la fin de l'antiquité*, *Bibliothèque archéologique et historique* 133 (Paris 1992); and J. Lefort, C. Morrisson, and J.-P. Sodini, *Les villages dans l'empire byzantin: IVe–XVe siècle* (Paris 2005).

Fig. 1. Map of southeastern Isauria (drawn by K. Rasmussen from Archaeographics; G. Varinlioğlu, "Living in a marginal environment: Rural habitat and landscape in southeastern Isauria," *DOP* 61 [2008] 291, fig. 1).

information about trades and crafts prominent in the region. The exceptionally large and diverse corpus of funerary inscriptions from Corycus is especially well known.[4] My study incorporates the evidence from Corasium, Diocaesarea, Olba (referred to as the survey area), Seleucia ad Calycadnum, and St. Thecla, examining it in comparison to the epigraphic evidence for trades and crafts throughout western Cilicia.[5] I contextualize these results using the archaeological remains of presses, mills, and threshing floors studied and recorded during my survey in the hinterland of Seleucia ad Calycadnum (in 2003–2007).

Trade and craft names appear 568 times in the epigraphic corpus of Corasium, Corycus, Diocaesarea, Olba, Seleucia ad Calycadnum, and St. Thecla.[6] Out of these, 451 (79 per cent) were found in Corycus, followed by a total of 57 in Seleucia and St. Thecla, 32 in Corasium, and 28 in Diocaesarea and Olba, while 93 were recorded elsewhere in western Cilicia. The statistical distribution of professions in the survey area is comparable with that of western Cilicia (table 1 and graph 1). Sixty-four per cent of the corpus of inscriptions from the survey area (versus 61 per cent in western Cilicia) is formed by three major groups of professions: manufacture, ecclesiastical posts, and food-related trades. Twenty-two per cent (versus 25 per cent in western Cilicia) belongs to public officials, retail, construction, and the service sector. The remaining 14 per cent (same percentage in western Cilicia) is divided somewhat equally among the military, finance, maritime, and health-related professions.

In the survey area, the largest trade community consisted of various manufacturing craftsmen (28.2 per cent), using as raw materials predominantly metal, clay, wool and goat hair, leather, and flax/linen. Industries dealing with murex, glass, unguents, gems, papyrus, potash/soap, and wood are represented in small numbers (3.7 per cent). Two leading groups are the manufacturers of metal (7.4 per cent) and animal products such as wool/goat hair and leather (7.5 per cent). Metal manufacturers, such as key- and cleaver-makers, cutlers, tool-grinders, and copper/bronzesmiths, alongside craftsmen using precious metals such as silver and gold, served the needs not only of civilians but also, and perhaps more importantly, of the legions stationed in Seleucia ad Calycadnum. The city's arms factory, already in existence by the seventh century, would have required iron in particularly large quantities. Agricultural production, construction, and seafaring also contributed to the demand for metal implements.

The manufacture of clay products (5.3 per cent) included the production of pottery as well as floor and roof tiles, which are ubiquitous throughout the countryside and were obviously in high demand. As the hinterlands of coastal cities lacked clay and water sources, pottery production must have been carried out along and near river mouths; hence clay products were traded between the coast and the hinterlands. Although several kiln sites were discovered in Flat Cilicia, at Elaiussa-Sebaste, and at Bıçkıcı/Syedra in western Rough Cilicia, none have been located so far between Seleucia and Corycus.[7]

Textile production (e.g., brocade-makers, embroiderers, and weavers) is represented by 4.4 per cent; wool and goat hair by 4.1 per cent; and leather (e.g., shoemakers, tanners, and saddlers) by 3.4

[4] T.R.S. Broughton, "Roman Asia," in T. Frank and A.C. Johnson (eds.), *An Economic Survey of Ancient Rome* (Baltimore 1933) 499–916; F. Hild and H. Hellenkemper, *Kilikien und Isaurien, Tabula Imperii Byzantini* 5 (Vienna 1990) 108-27; E. Patlagean, *Pauvreté économique et pauvreté sociale à Byzance, 4ᵉ–7ᵉ siècles* (Paris 1977) 156–81; and most notably F. Trombley, "Korykos in Cilicia Trachis: The economy of a small coastal city in late antiquity (saec. V–VI)—a précis," *Ancient History Bulletin* 1.1 (1987) 16–23.

[5] I used exclusively the inscriptions brought together by S. Hagel and K. Tomaschitz, *Repertorium der westkilikischen Inschriften: Nach den Scheden der kleinasiatischen Kommission der Österreichischen Akademie der Wissenschaften* (Vienna 1998).

[6] These values correspond to the record of a trade/profession and not strictly to the number of inscriptions. Some inscriptions contain more than one trade name.

[7] E. Equini Schneider, *Elaiussa Sebaste I: Campagne di scavo, 1995–1997* (Rome 1999); N.K. Rauh and K.W. Slane, "Possible amphora kiln sites in W Rough Cilicia," *JRA* 13 (2000) 319–30.

Table 1. Percentages of trade and craft groups in the epigraphic record of Western Cilicia in comparison to the survey area.

Main Category		*Survey Area (Corasium, Corycus, Diocaesarea, Olba, Seleucia ad Calycadnum, St. Thecla) (%)*		*Western Cilicia (including the survey area) (%)*	
Manufacture		28.2		24.4	
Metal			7.4		6.4
Clay			5.3		4.6
Textile			4.4		3.8
Wool/goat hair	*animal products*		4.1		3.5
Leather	*animal products*		3.4		2.9
Other (murex, glass, unguents, gems, papyrus, wood, etc.)			3.7		3.3
Ecclesiastical		20.3		23.2	
Food		15.3 (+ 4.4* = 19.7)		13.3 (+ 3.8* = 17.1)	
Production			8.4		7.4
Distribution			6.9		5.9
Public Official		8.4		11.6	
Retail		7.5		6.5	
Food-wares			4.4		3.8
Textiles			3.1		2.7
Construction		5.9		6.9	
Service		4.4		3.7	
Military		2.4		3.4	
Finance		2.4 (+ 1.5** = 3.9)		2.2 (+ 1.5** = 3.7)	
Maritime		2.3		2.1	
Health		2.3		2.1	
Other		0.5		0.5	

* the percentage of food retail
** the percentage of the manufacturing of precious metals (silver and gold)

per cent. In this category, the linen industry, comprising linen-workers (λινοξός), dealers (λινοπώλης), weavers (λινυφαντάριος, ὑφαντάριος), loom-makers (ἱστοποιός), and perhaps also embroiderers (πλουμάριος), constitute 3 per cent of the assemblage. Although flax grew easily almost everywhere in the Mediterranean, the highest quality linen of the Roman imperial period was produced in Tarsus.[8]

[8] Flax grows well in alluvial and deep loamy soils, while its processing requires large quantities of water. For this reason linen production must have been a coastal industry. For an ethno-archaeological study of linseed oil production in Anatolia, see F. Ertuğ, "Linseed oil and oil mills in central Turkey. Flax/linum and Eruca, important oil plants of Anatolia," *AnatSt* 50 (2000) 171–84. Diocletian's Price Edict lists expensive linen products (e.g., undergarments, mantles, and sheets) of Tarsus and Alexandretta in eastern Cilicia. For a discussion of the linen industry in Tarsus, see E. Ertekin, "İlkçağ'da Tarsus 'ketenciler'i ve ketenleri," *Olba* 11 (2005) 155–75.

Graph 1. Trade categories in the epigraphic record of the survey area.

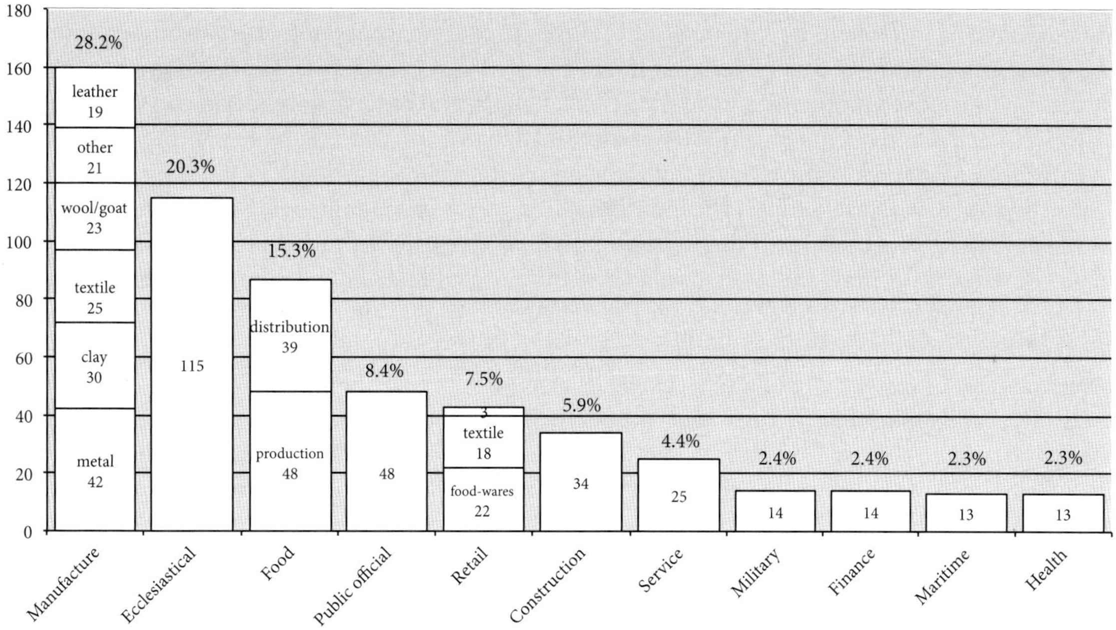

Guilds of linen workers/dealers are documented at Anazarbos and Corycus, where linen-dealers are buried in the same sarcophagus as the members of the customs officials' guild.

The categories discussed above may be regrouped and recalculated on the basis of the raw materials used in manufacture. Crafts processing animal products (leather, wool, and goat hair) form 7.5 per cent, a value that virtually equals that of the metal industry. Likewise, if the category of textiles is expanded in such a way as to include wool and goat hair products, the sum reaches 8.5 per cent, surpassing the manufacture of both metal and animal products. Wool, goat hair, and leather products were demanded in large quantities by the military troops, as well as by ecclesiastical and administrative officials. *Cilicium* articles made of the hair of the long-haired goat took their name from the province of Cilicia.[9] Livestock played an important role in the local economy, especially in the marginal limestone hills where pastoralism was certainly widely practiced, although it is not as archaeologically visible as agricultural exploitation.[10]

The financial and social rise of the church is well attested epigraphically. Ecclesiastical officials (e.g., presbyters, deacons, vicars, and lectors) are the second largest group with 20.3 per cent, while public officials (e.g. notaries, night-watchmen, customs-house officials, and prison guards) occupy only the fourth place (8.4 per cent).

The production and distribution of food constitutes 15.3 per cent of the corpus. Producers, such as fishermen, bakers, gardeners, and makers of cider, sausage, and hot drinks, amount to 8.4 per cent;

[9] *Cilicium* was used for numerous military items, such as garments, tents, shields, horse blankets, sacks, as well as curtains, carpets, boat equipment, and clothes for monks and priests. See Procopius, *History of the Wars* 2.26; Columella, *On Agriculture* 1.26; and Cicero, *Verrine Orations* 2.1.38. Patlagean, *Pauvreté* (supra n. 4), 161; L. Robert, "Noms de métiers dans des documents byzantins," in idem (ed.), *Opera minora selecta, épigraphie et antiquités greques* (Amsterdam 1969) 915–21.

[10] Troughs and tethering holes, common in the North Syrian and Palestinian countryside, are rare in the survey area. But the ground floors and courtyards of houses and structures built with perishable materials or less durable masonry could be used as stables.

while distributors, such as sellers of olive oil, wine, cumin, pistachios, meat, and green grocers make up 6.9 per cent of the assemblage.[11] In the latter category, taverns, inns, restaurants, and pastry shops were in particular demand by ship personnel stopping at the harbors of Corycus and Corasium. In the food business, 56 per cent of merchants dealt in fruits and vegetables. Sellers of grains and producers of flour-based products (e.g., wheat sellers, bakers, and pastry cooks) form 22 per cent, while sellers of meat stand at 10 per cent. The predominance of fruit and vegetable commerce is indicative of the exploitation of the irrigated and fertile coastal plains, particularly the Calycadnus delta, whose products would also supply the limestone hills, where gardening would hardly yield sufficient produce to meet the demands of the rural population. In return, the marginal countryside supplied olive oil, wine, pistachios, and perhaps also cumin. The small percentage of meat dealers in coastal settlements may have a twofold explanation. Villagers brought their animals to the local markets themselves, instead of holding permanent shops in cities. Second, the meat business may not have been lucrative or respected enough to secure its purveyors a place in the necropolis.

The category of retail (7.5 per cent) is equally divided between retailers of textiles and those of foods and wares, followed closely by the building trades (5.9 per cent) and a diverse group of services, including those of the grave-digger, the bath-keeper, the barber, and the professional reciter, which add up to 4.4 per cent. The remaining 9.9 per cent of the epigraphic assemblage is evenly divided among the military, financial (e.g., banker, accountant, and silver-dealer) and maritime occupations (e.g., shipwright, sailor, and sail-maker), and health professionals (e.g., doctor and midwife).

The funerary inscriptions also record individuals who specialized in two compatible or completely unrelated trades.[12] Tavern-keeper/fishmonger, tavern-keeper/pistachio-dealer, gardener/cumin-dealer, builder/tool-grinder, and shipwright/wine-dealer are complementary businesses. However, tavern-keeper/grave-digger, gardener/goldsmith, marble-worker/bread-baker, and potter/sack-maker are more difficult to interpret. It may be argued that one profession was the family business, while the other was a new skill acquired by the individual, as suggested, for example, by a potter/sack-maker, who was the son of a sack-maker. Although the inheritance of trades (e.g., gardener and potter) and family businesses (e.g., potter, shoemaker, and wine-dealer) are attested, in many other cases, the father and son had completely different professions, such as the potter son of a construction worker, the gardener son of a carpenter, the weaver son of a goldsmith, and the baker son of a gardener. Ecclesiastical officials often held an additional trade, such as a presbyter who worked as a perfumer, gem-engraver, potter, banker, goldsmith, or sail-maker. Deacons and archdeacons were relatively "upscale" professionals (e.g., doubling as linen-makers, cider-makers, copper/bronzesmiths, doctors, reciters, treasury-keepers, or accountants).

People holding different trades and having no apparent family ties could be buried in the same sarcophagus (e.g. a clothes-mender with a marble-worker and a baker with a messenger). This might be explained by financial constraints for less lucrative crafts. The cases of a gem-engraver and a perfumer, a doctor and a baker, and a gardener and a shoemaker suggest social and/or family ties between the occupants of the sarcophagus. The partnering of a tavern-keeper and a wine-dealer, and of a confectioner and a tavern-keeper/pistachio-dealer, may indicate commercial relationships. The case of the sarcophagus shared by the guild of customs house officials and the guild of linen-dealers underlines the importance of linen trade in Corycus.

[11] There is no clear-cut distinction between food producers and distributors. Olive oil- and wine-sellers were probably procuring supplies in bulk from villagers. Merchants, such as bakers, cooks, hot drink-makers, and tavern-keepers, would be involved in both the production and the distribution of food.

[12] For a complete list, see Varinlioğlu, *Rural Landscape* (supra n. 2), 193–97.

What does the quantification of the professions in the epigraphic record tell us about the socio-economic structure of Isaurian-Cilician cities and their economic ties with the rural countryside? Funerary inscriptions portray a picture biased towards religious and public officials and wealthy citizens who could afford a sarcophagus in the necropolis. Non-lucrative or non-reputable trades are completely absent from the record. Members of lower classes would be buried either in mass graves or in modest, uninscribed graves.[13] In other words, the percentages of the professions do not directly correlate with their places in the local economy. Moreover, the habit of inscribing tombs is an urban phenomenon; the few examples of inscribed sarcophagi, tombstones, and arcosolia in the countryside rarely include the professions of the deceased or their family.[14]

Nevertheless, the epigraphic evidence underlines the importance of manufacturing crafts using animal products in the economy of coastal settlements. The main suppliers of this industry were the pastoralists of the limestone hills. The countryside was also a main producer of olive oil and wine. The remains of threshing floors, mills, and presses, used mainly for processing grains, olives, and grapes, provide ample material evidence for discussion of the role of grape and olive cultivation in the limestone hills, a region suitable for both crops.

Archaeological Evidence for Rural Agricultural Production

Wines of Isauria and Cilicia are attested both textually and epigraphically.[15] In addition to the local epigraphic record for wine-dealers, a late fifth-century Abydus tariff gives Cilician shipwrights transporting wine special privileges on their way to and from Constantinople.[16] The vine iconography on sarcophagi and the existence of kiln sites for LR 1 amphorae—although they could also contain olive oil—in Cyprus, North Syria, Flat Cilicia, and western Rough Cilicia—might be considered as further evidence for wine production and trade throughout this region. We do not know whether Isaurian/Cilician olive oil was exported, yet the size and number of presses indicate that the hinterlands were well equipped to produce it in large quantities. However, until all presses are documented and their capacities are calculated, it is not possible to speculate about the scale of production.

The press is the ubiquitous material evidence for olive oil and wine production. It is often very difficult or impossible to differentiate olive and wine presses without excavation or the chemical study of organic residue samples. My discussion is based on the limited study of a small number of presses from the survey territory west of the Yenibahçe ravine (see fig. 1) in comparison to the well-known types from Cyprus, Syria, Palestine, and western Asia Minor.[17]

[13] Patlagean, *Pauvreté* (supra n. 4), 158.

[14] The only exception in the survey area is the sarcophagus at Çaltıören of a presbyter, who was also a teacher (διδάσκαλος) and treasurer (νομικός).

[15] Ammianus Marcellinus (14.8.1) writes about Isaurian wine and fruit, and *Expositio Totius Mundi* (39) praises Cilician wines. Pliny (14.11, 19) lists sweet raisin wine and hyssop wine from Cilicia. The wine from Abates in Cilicia was known for its medicinal uses. See M. Decker, "The wine trade of Cilicia in late antiquity," *ARAM* 17 (2005) 52–53.

[16] By A.D. 492, Cilicia I, Cilicia II, and Isauria were distinct provinces; therefore official documents like the Anazarbos inscription and the Abydus tariff (J. Durliat and A. Guillou, "Le tarif d'Abydos [vers 492]," *BCH* 108 [1984] 581–98) must have used the proper nomenclature referring to Cilicians, i.e. from Cilicia I and II. Cilician shipwrights in the Abydus tariff might be carrying mainly the produce of the fertile Cilician plain. But they may have also carried the products of other regions (e.g., Syrian oil and Palestinian wine). Cilician merchants may also have been active in the transportation of the annona to the military in the Danube region. See O. Karagiorgou, "LR2: A container for the military annona on the Danubian border?" in S. Kingsley and M. Decker (eds.), *Economy and Exchange in the East Mediterranean during Late Antiquity* (Oxford 2001) 129–66.

[17] For Cyprus, see S. Hadjisavvas, *Olive Oil Processing in Cyprus: From the Bronze Age to the Byzantine Period* (Nicosia 1992); for Syria, see O. Callot, *Huileries antiques de Syrie du Nord* (Paris 1984); for Palestine, see R. Frankel, S. Avitsur, and E. Ayalon, *History and Technology of Olive Oil in the Holy Land* (Tel Aviv 1994); for western Asia Minor, see A. Diler, "Akdeniz bölgesi antik çağ zeytinyağı

Although the same equipment can be used to extract grape juice and olive oil, the mechanics of the two processes are significantly different.[18] The extraction of the must from the grapes was fairly easy; the expertise came into play during fermentation. On the other hand, the operation of the press for the extraction of olive oil required trained personnel who knew how to operate the heavy and complicated pressing equipment. The grapes were treaded almost always with feet and only rarely using stone rollers (e.g., in Palestine and North Syria). For larger-scale production, treading took place on a rock-cut floor connected to a collecting vat, which could be rock-cut, ceramic, or made of perishable materials. The remaining grape stalks and skins could be pressed using several types of equipment (lever and weights press, lever and screw press, or fixed screw press) often identical to the ones used for extracting olive oil.[19]

Olives were first crushed into pulp with stone rollers on a flat surface, in rotary crushers, or, more rarely, in horizontal mills.[20] The bitter juice (*amurca*) released by crushing was alleviated by the addition of water in equal amounts.[21] The resulting olive pulp was placed in woven baskets or mats and pressed several times on a pressing bed or treading floor. At this stage, hot water was poured over the crushed olives to facilitate the extraction of oil. After the completion of the pressing, the baskets containing olive paste had to be thoroughly cleansed with hot water. Finally, the mixture of lees and oil was left to settle in the collecting vat. The oil, being less dense than the rest, would rise to the surface. To enhance the separation of oil, more water could be added to the vat. In conclusion, for the extraction of olive oil for commercial purposes, there were two major requirements: heavy pressing equipment and large quantities of water.

The most common press types in the Mediterranean are the lever and weights, lever and drum, lever and screw, and fixed screw presses, all known at the latest by the first century B.C.[22] As in North Syria, the great majority of the presses in the survey territory were open air installations, although they might have been covered with tents or temporary structures for protection against the sun during the grape harvesting period and against the rain during the olive harvesting period.

In the survey territory, the lever and weights press is the most common type, followed by a variation of the lever and screw press. A third group is the simple press consisting of small shallow depressions and treading surfaces in the bedrock, found mainly outside settlements throughout the survey territory.[23] Some examples have a shallow, roughly rectangular treading floor connected to a

---

ve şarap işlikleri," *Araştırma Sonuçları Toplantısı* 11 (1993) 505–20; idem, "Akdeniz bölgesi antik çağ zeytin ve üzüm presleri—1993," *Araştırma Sonuçları Toplantısı* 12 (1994) 441–57; idem, "İç Karia yüzey araştırmaları 1994," *Araştırma Sonuçları Toplantısı* 13 (1995) 315–33; and idem, "İç Karia yüzey araştırması 1995," *Araştırma Sonuçları Toplantısı* 14 (1996) 189–206.

[18] In traditional communities, often the same equipment is used for processing textiles, cheese, dates, sesame, nuts, and flax. See J.-P. Brun, "La discrimination entre les installations oléicoles et vinicoles," in M.-C. Amouretti and J.-P. Brun (eds.), *La production du vin et de l'huile en Méditerranée* (Athens 1993) 511–37.

[19] The fermentation, which started already during treading, could take place in the collecting vat, which was covered to avoid exposure to the sun or alternatively in other containers, such as in pithoi and dolia, often buried in the soil and placed in enclosed spaces to avoid heat. See J.-P. Brun, *Le vin et l'huile dans la Méditerranée antique: Viticulture, oléiculture et procédés de transformation* (Paris 2003) 70, 77–79.

[20] For smaller-scale production, olives could be crushed by stamping with wooden utensils, treading with wooden shoes, or by placing heavy stones on the pile of olives.

[21] Callot, *Huileries antiques* (supra n. 17), 20.

[22] Presses described by Cato, Pliny the Elder, Vitruvius, and Hero of Alexandria are studied in A.G. Drachmann, *Ancient Oil Mills and Presses* (Kobenhavn 1932). For the typology of Mediterranean presses, see R. Frankel, *Wine and Oil Production in Antiquity in Israel and Other Mediterranean Countries* (Sheffield 1999) 27, 86–88.

[23] Our documentation of the agricultural installations was based on chance finds, rather than a systematic study. The physical properties of the installations and their relationship to associated fields, structures, and settlements were cursorily investigated. The results of another survey focusing on oileries and wineries between the Calycadnus and Lamus rivers was published in Ü. Aydınoğlu, *Dağlık*

Fig. 2. Simple press at Meydankalesi.

Fig. 3. Lever and weights press at Işıkkale.

shallow vat, without a lateral niche for the insertion of the press beam. In others, the circular pressing surface is connected to one or two small holes, which serve as collecting and settling vats, while the rock-cut surface on one side has a niche for a small portable or disposable beam (fig. 2). The presses without lateral walls were probably more suitable for pressing grapes, fruits, and grains, which did not require much pressure. Similar simple presses are commonly found close to vineyards in the Palestinian countryside.[24]

The lever and weights press, ubiquitous in the survey territory as well as in the hinterlands of Corycus and Elaiussa-Sebaste, is a well-known type in the eastern Mediterranean, often associated with the production of wine. As I argue below, however, this type of press was used for the production of both wine and olive oil. It consists of a rock-cut shallow (25–40 cm) treading floor/pressing platform connected by a channel to a rock-cut single large storage vat (fig. 3).[25] A longitudinal rock-cut or masonry wall on one side of the floor housed a niche (fulcrum) for the insertion of the press beam. In the survey territory, the fulcrum exhibits slight variations in form (rectangular, rectangular with a curved upper edge, T-shaped, or inverse L-shaped), indicating different methods used to stabilize the beam by inserting wooden sticks (fig. 4). The press beam was anchored into this recess; treaded grapes or olive mash were placed under the beam; and force was applied on its other end using stone weights, screw weights, or simply human effort in order to extract the liquid, which was collected in the storage vat located on one—or rarely two—of the short sides of the floor. In the simplest versions, the weights were hung on the beam to increase pressure, while more complicated systems comprised a mechanism of winches, pulleys, and screws to control the movement of the beam, and hence pressure.[26]

Kilikia Bölgesinde Antik Çağda Zeytinyağı ve Şarap Üretimi: Üretimin Arkeolojik Kanıtları (İstanbul 2009). However, this work does not contextualize the presses in the agricultural and settlement landscape.

[24] Frankel, *Wine and Oil* (supra n. 22), 53–54.

[25] In Syria, the floors may be as deep as 75 cm.

[26] Weight stones are rarely found on the surface. Lever weights are recognizable by their mortises, used to hang the weight stone to the beam directly by ropes or a pulley system. The reversed-T mortise typical of the Levant is common in southeastern Isauria in several variations. The perforation of the T receives a wooden rod, tied by a rope to the beam of the lever press. Weights whose upper section has been recarved into regular symmetrical cavities might indicate the modification of lever weights into screw weights.

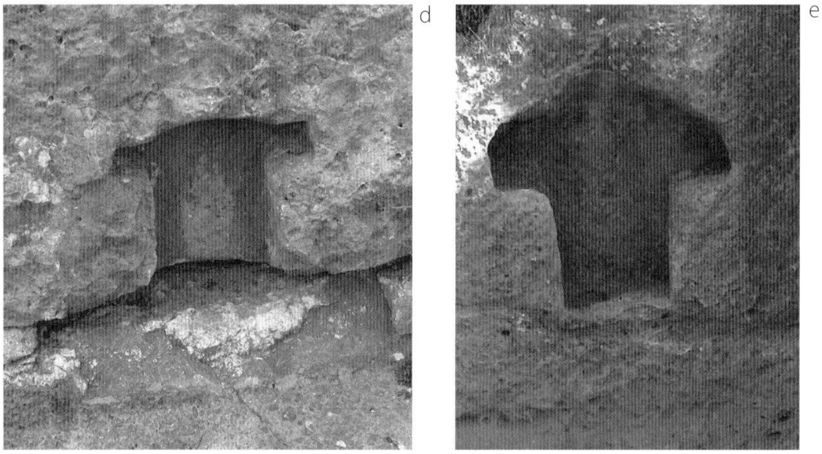

Fig. 4. Types of fulcra at Işıkkale (a, c), Aşağıdünya (b), Gökkale (d), and Hayvalı (e).

Fig. 5. Olive press at Payambelen (a) with perforated fulcrum zone (b).

Fig. 6. Screw weight near Karadedeli.

The lever and screw press, which is much less common in the survey territory, is found inside buildings within settlements. It is characterized by a larger fulcrum in the form of a deep rectangular niche or hole, with projecting perforated stones on either side (fig. 5). These circular perforations must have been used for the insertion of a wooden rod or ropes to anchor the beam securely to the fulcrum. The design of the press at the fulcrum resembles Cypriot perforated monoliths and Palestinian perforated piers.[27] But this particular form is characteristic of the region, perhaps a local innovation for the stabilization of the lever.[28] The fulcrum hole going through the wall would allow the operators to push the beam out without disturbing the setup inside the building. The fulcrum is always located adjacent to a corner of the building, so for this reason it was possible to work on only one side of the lever. The combination of a large fulcrum, perforated piers, and adjacent wall may be interpreted as methods to control the movement of the beam in lever and screw mechanisms that created higher forces, and thus required better operational skills. If the beam got free of the fulcrum in an uncontrolled manner, it would present a great danger both for the equipment and for the workers. The screw weights of the survey area follow a well-known type, which was the dominant form in North Syria, with a central socket connected to two dovetail mortises (fig. 6). It probably originated in the Levant some time during the Hellenistic or Roman period, while all dated Palestinian screw weights are Byzantine.[29] But the introduction of the new and more efficient technology did not displace traditional methods of production. In the survey territory, newly built pressing installations were equipped with lever and screw presses, but the previously existing installations continued to be used, perhaps with minor changes such as the transformation of lever weights into screw weights.

The structures that enclose the lever and screw press type described above were either built or revamped in the early Byzantine period. Building B at the village of Işıkkale is an enclosed pressing facility equipped with a lever and screw press and rotary mills (fig. 7). Its walls are built of mortared ashlar masonry at the lower registers, while the upper parts of the walls, which do not survive, were probably built of mortared squared-stone masonry like the adjacent Building A. This complex of structures corresponds to the expansion of Işıkkale marked by the construction of its basilica in the first half of the sixth century, and thus might be dated tentatively to the late fifth and early sixth centuries. Similarly, the lever and screw press at the village of Akhayat is enclosed in a large rectangular building built with mortared squared-stone masonry, also corresponding to the Byzantine

[27] Frankel, *Wine and Oil* (supra n. 22), 82–83.

[28] In Palestine, perforated piers are also always associated with lever and screw presses used in wine production, while Cypriot perforated monoliths are elements of oileries. See Frankel, Avitsur, and Ayalon, *History and Technology* (supra n. 17), 62, and Hadjisavvas, *Olive Oil* (supra n. 17), 137–49. Frankel (*Wine and Oil* [supra n. 22], 146) describes devices resembling rock-cut tethering rings located below the beam hole and used to operate the beam with the help of ropes. These perforations are located below the beam end in Palestine, and above in southeastern Isauria, where ropes instead of wooden rods may have been used to control the movement of the beam.

[29] The Palestinian type known as "Kasfa Screw Weight" is also the dominant type—in several variations—in North Syria. See Frankel, *Wine and Oil* (supra n. 22), 114–18, 173.

Fig. 7. Aerial view of Buildings A and B at Işıkkale.

Fig. 8. Lever and screw press at Akhayat.

phase of the village (fig. 8). Another press at Demircili is enclosed in a structure using spolia from a Roman-period peristyle house. Structures equipped with lever and screw presses also include crushing basins and large rotary mills, associated with large-scale, commercial production of olive oil. The creation or adoption of this particular lever and screw press seems to be closely linked to an increase in the production of olive oil, which probably occurred some time during the fifth and sixth centuries. This suggests that the export of olive oil played a crucial role in the prosperity and development of the rural countryside. The construction of large and expensive structures to house olive presses indicates the increasing importance and market value of the production of olive oil for this territory during late antiquity.

Rectangular treading floors connected to a collecting vat are often associated with the production of wine.[30] If this type of installation is identified as a wine press, then the Isaurian and Cilician countryside was predominantly a producer of wine, and olive oil production was either non-existent or carried out only at the domestic scale until the introduction of the lever and screw press discussed above. But how can we then explain the reference to olive in the name of the city of Elaiussa-Sebaste? Furthermore, this type of installation was used in North Africa mainly for olive oil production.[31] Frankel argues that the volume of the collecting vats (larger or smaller than 1 m^3) may be a criterion for differentiating wine presses from olive oil presses, because treading grapes produces a large quantity of juice.[32] The amount of oil extracted from a given volume of olives is indeed much less than the amount of juice produced by a similar volume of grapes, but during the pressing of olives, a large quantity of hot water is added to the paste, first to facilitate the extraction, then for the separation of the oil from the residues. Therefore, the extraction of olive oil also necessitates large containers. A more reliable criterion is the presence of crushing devices (e.g., mills and rollers) around presses.[33] But these are much less frequently found in the archaeological record, because they were often carried off for reuse.[34] The existence of crushing equipment is solid proof for the production of olive oil at a commercial scale, but its absence is not enough to justify the identification of a facility as a wine press.

Throughout the survey territory, threshing floors, cisterns, and lever and weights presses are found side by side, suggesting a production workflow that necessitated the use of all three.[35] (Lever and screw presses are never found in association with threshing floors.) The necessity of supplying drinking water to animals and workers does not justify the construction of large cisterns near threshing floors. Pressing grapes used a certain amount of water, but not in large quantities. How can we explain the coexistence of these three elements? I argue that the surface of the threshing floors was used for crushing olives, which would then be pressed in the adjacent press facility. The cistern would supply the large amount of water used at all stages of olive oil production. Crushing the olives on the threshing floor instead of on the treading floor of the press would increase the speed of production. The heavy equipment required to press the olives on the treading surface could be left in place instead of being continually removed before crushing the olives and reinstalled for

30 Decker, "Wine trade" (supra n. 15), 57.

31 Brun, "Discrimination" (supra n. 18), 521–23.

32 In North Africa, Syria, and Palestine, vats of 5 m^3 are quite common, while some reach 10 m^3. See Frankel, *Wine and Oil* (supra n. 22), 57, 157.

33 Callot's survey of presses of North Syria shows that olives were crushed with rollers in the basins where they were subsequently pressed. Only a small number of open air installations had a separate surface for crushing purposes. In enclosed installations, the press is separated from the rotary crusher, as in the lever and screw presses of the survey territory. However, Callot assumes that all the presses in the Syrian countryside are olive presses and does not consider the possibility that some of these installations may have served mainly for wine production. See Callot, *Huileries antiques* (supra n. 17).

34 Brun, "Discrimination" (supra n. 18), 518.

35 For a detailed discussion of the use of threshing floors and their association with cisterns and presses, see Varinlioğlu, "Marginal environment" (supra n. 2), 304–8.

Graph 2. Distribution of pottery types in the survey area and Işıkkale (Ç. Toskay).

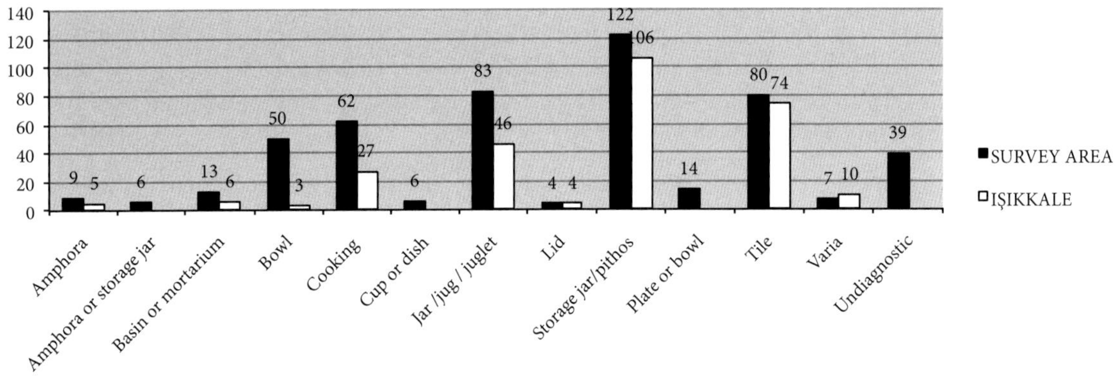

pressing them. In addition, the bitter juice of the olives covering the threshing floor would work as an insecticide. Lever and weight presses could also be used for wine production, which took place during a different season of the year. In Isauria and Cilicia, grape harvesting started in the first half of September, while olives were picked biennially between the end of October and January. By the time olive harvesting started, wine production would be long finished; thus the same presses could be used for both operations. In other words, the lever and weights presses found in the survey area should not be categorized exclusively as wine presses.

The limited and unsystematic pottery collection focusing on diagnostic sherds revealed a striking predominance of storage jars and pithoi, as opposed to the extremely limited number of fineware and amphorae (graph 2).[36] Fineware and products carried in amphorae rarely reached the limestone hills at any period, even when trade was booming in the Mediterranean. Without a systematic and extensive pottery survey, it is not possible to reach conclusions about the intensity, patterns, or chronological changes in the imports. But common imported wares well known in the Mediterranean seem to have penetrated the countryside only in small quantities. Roman Eastern Sigillata A wares, probably produced in Eastern Cilicia, and Cypriot Late Roman Red Slip Wares were imported more than other long-distance trade wares, such as African Red Slip or Phocaean Red Slip. Among the few amphora sherds found, LR 1, which was produced at many sites in the eastern Mediterranean, is the most common. Yet the extreme rarity of amphora sherds suggests that LR 1 was not used to transport the products of the countryside to the coast. Perishable containers, such as skin or goat-hair sacks and wooden containers, are the most plausible carriers. The products of the countryside could then be transferred to amphorae produced and filled at the harbor facilities. The transportation of olive oil in goatskins from the press to the harbor to be transferred into amphorae is attested in North Africa and Baetica, which were major olive oil exporters in the first three centuries of the Common Era.[37]

In the epigraphic record of Corycus, wine-dealers occupy 17.2 per cent of the food business, while olive oil-sellers stand at 11.5 per cent. These numbers by themselves, however, are not sufficient to support the conclusion that wine production was more important than olive oil production. Without a systematic survey focusing on the documentation of all agricultural installations, it is not possible to calculate the scale of production.[38] However, the presence of permanent presses and mills is an

[36] The discussion on pottery presented in this article is based on Çiğdem Toskay's study of this material.

[37] The use of goatskin to transport both wine and olive oil is a practice attested as early as the 15th century B.C. Goatskin bags would be cheaper alternatives to amphorae. See Brun, *Le vin et l'huile* (supra n. 19), 164–66.

[38] Aydınoğlu, *Dağlık Kilikia* (supra n. 23) does not provide data towards the calculation of the scale of production.

indication of surplus production, because such an investment would be superfluous for producing wine and olive oil purely for domestic use. A well-organized collective operation, involving teams trained in handling the presses, was a requirement during the olive harvesting season, so that investment in these presses, mills, and threshing floors paid off. Unlike North African or Syrian oil, Isaurian and Cilician oil may not have traveled very long distances, but the rural hinterlands most certainly supplied the regional demand, which must have been considerable due to the stationing of the army.

The lever and screw press typical of the region, designed specifically for olive oil extraction, was found in early Byzantine structures. Therefore, the expansion of settlements and the rise of prosperity in the countryside from the fifth century onwards may be closely related to the intensification of olive oil production. Despite the importance of olive oil for the marginal hills, however, it was certainly not a monoculture, but rather was practiced together with other agro-pastoral activities, especially viticulture and animal husbandry, as the epigraphic record clearly indicates.[39]

Conclusions

The marginal territory studied in this paper allowed for a combination of economic strategies, including the cultivation of grains, grapes, and olives, as well as gardening, and the herding of sheep and goats, whose hair and skin were processed in Isaurian-Cilician cities and harbor settlements. The metal industry and arms factory in Seleucia required large quantities of wood from the hinterland. The exploitation of other miscellaneous products, such as saffron, plants used in dyeing textiles, game animals, pistachios (a seller of which is known in Corycus), and laurel (whose leaves and fruits were used in cooking, soap-making, and medicine), was part of the rural economy, although these products did not leave material evidence. The place of specialized crafts such as the manufacturing of linen, weaving (wool and goat hair), and architectural trades needs to be further investigated. Our understanding of the relationship between towns and countryside in southeastern Isauria is still in its infancy despite the increasing number of archaeological investigations in the region.

[39] F. Hild and H. Hellenkemper (*Kilikien und Isaurien* [supra n. 4], 109) argue that olive production was a monoculture following Tchalenko's model for the Syrian Massif Calcaire. See G. Tchalenko, *Villages antiques de la Syrie du Nord: le Massif du Bélus à l'époque romaine*, 3 vols., *Bibliothèque archéologie et historique* 50 (Paris 1953–1958); contra Tate, *Campagnes* (supra n. 3); idem, "Un cas de croissance économique en zone marginale: la Syrie du Nord," *Histoire, économie et société* 3 (1997) 353–59.

11 Akören: Two Late Antique Villages in Cilicia

Ulrike Wulf-Rheidt

Cilicia, a flourishing landscape in antiquity, rarely appears in surveys of late antique Asia Minor. This is astonishing, when one considers the many remains of buildings of this period preserved in remarkably good condition.[1] Most previous investigations of late Roman Cilicia have been largely restricted to church buildings.[2] With a few exceptions we know little about the houses or the overall surroundings of the people who went to the Cilician churches.[3] For this reason, the primary concern of the survey of Akören was the investigation of residential architecture and urban organization, in addition to the four well-preserved churches.[4] This article will focus, therefore, not on the churches but rather on the surrounding settlements.[5]

The remains of the two late antique settlements, called Akören I and Akören II, are situated only 1 km apart in the immediate vicinity of the present-day village of Akören (fig. 1).[6] They are located about 100 km north of Adana in the rugged foothills of the Taurus mountains. The smaller

[1] The best compilation to this day is F. Hild and H. Hellenkemper, *Kilikien und Isaurien, Tabula Imperii Byzantini* 5 (Vienna 1990). See also S. Eyice, "Silifke ve dolaylarında yapılan toprakűstü arkeolojik araştırmalar raporu 1979," *Belleten* 44 (1980) 111–24; idem, "Einige byzantinische Kleinstädte im Rauhen Kilikien," in *150 Jahre Deutsches Archäologisches Institut* (Mainz 1981) 204–9.

[2] For example, S. Hill, *The Early Byzantine Churches of Cilicia and Isauria, Birmingham Byzantine and Ottoman Monographs* I (Hampshire 1996); H. Hellenkemper, "Early church architecture in southern Asia Minor," in K. Painter (ed.), *Churches Built in Ancient Times, Recent Studies in Early Christian Archaeology* (London 1994) 213–38.

[3] For example, I. Eichner, *Frühbyzantinische Wohnhäuser in Kilikien. Baugeschichtliche Untersuchung zu den Wohnformen der Region um Seleukeia am Kalykadnos, Istanbuler Forschungen* 52 (Tübingen 2011). See also the preliminary report, I. Eichner, "Frühbyzantinische Wohnhäuser in Kilikien. Arbeitsbericht über die Kampagne 1998," *Araştırma Sonuçları Toplantısı* 17 (2000) 275–82. For the layout of cities in Cilicia, see R. Posamentir's publications on Anazarbos, including the contribution in this volume.

[4] The survey headed by Dr. Gabriele Mietke from the Museum for Late Antiquity and Byzantine Art in Berlin lasted four years (1994–1998) and was funded by the German Research Foundation (DFG). The surveying was undertaken by Dr. Katja Heine and Dr. Ulrich Weferling (Chair of Surveying at the Brandenburg University of Technology Cottbus). The students of architecture came from the chairs of Building History at the Brandenburg University of Technology Cottbus and the University of Applied Sciences Konstanz. The results are so far only published in preliminary reports: G. Mietke, "Survey der römisch-frühbyzantinischen Siedlung bei Akören in Kilikien 1994," *Araştırma Sonuçları Toplantısı* 13.1 (1996) 35–48; ead., "Survey der römisch-frühbyzantinischen Siedlung bei Akören in Kilikien 1995," *Araştırma Sonuçları Toplantısı* 14.1 (1997) 423–34; ead., "Survey der römisch-frühbyzantinischen Siedlung bei Akören in Kilikien 1996 und 1997," *Araştırma Sonuçları Toplantısı* 16.1 (1999) 75–93. See also U. Wulf, "Akören. Zur Stadtplanung und Wohnarchitektur zweier Siedlungen in Kilikien," in G. Brands and H.-G. Severin (eds.), *Die spätantike Stadt und ihre Christianisierung* (Wiesbaden 2003) 299–307, pls. 116–25.

[5] For the churches, see Mietke, "Survey 1994" (supra n. 4), 36–41, figs. 1–5; ead., "Survey 1995" (supra n. 4), 426–27, fig. 7; Hellenkemper, "Early church architecture" (supra n. 2), 226–32, figs. 14–22.

[6] Although the churches and the tombs contain various inscriptions, the antique names of the two settlements are not known. Therefore Hansgerd Hellenkemper and Friedrich Hild, the first to describe the settlements briefly, named the western one Akören I and the eastern one Akören II. Hild and Hellenkemper, *Kilikien und Isaurien* (supra n. 1), 168.

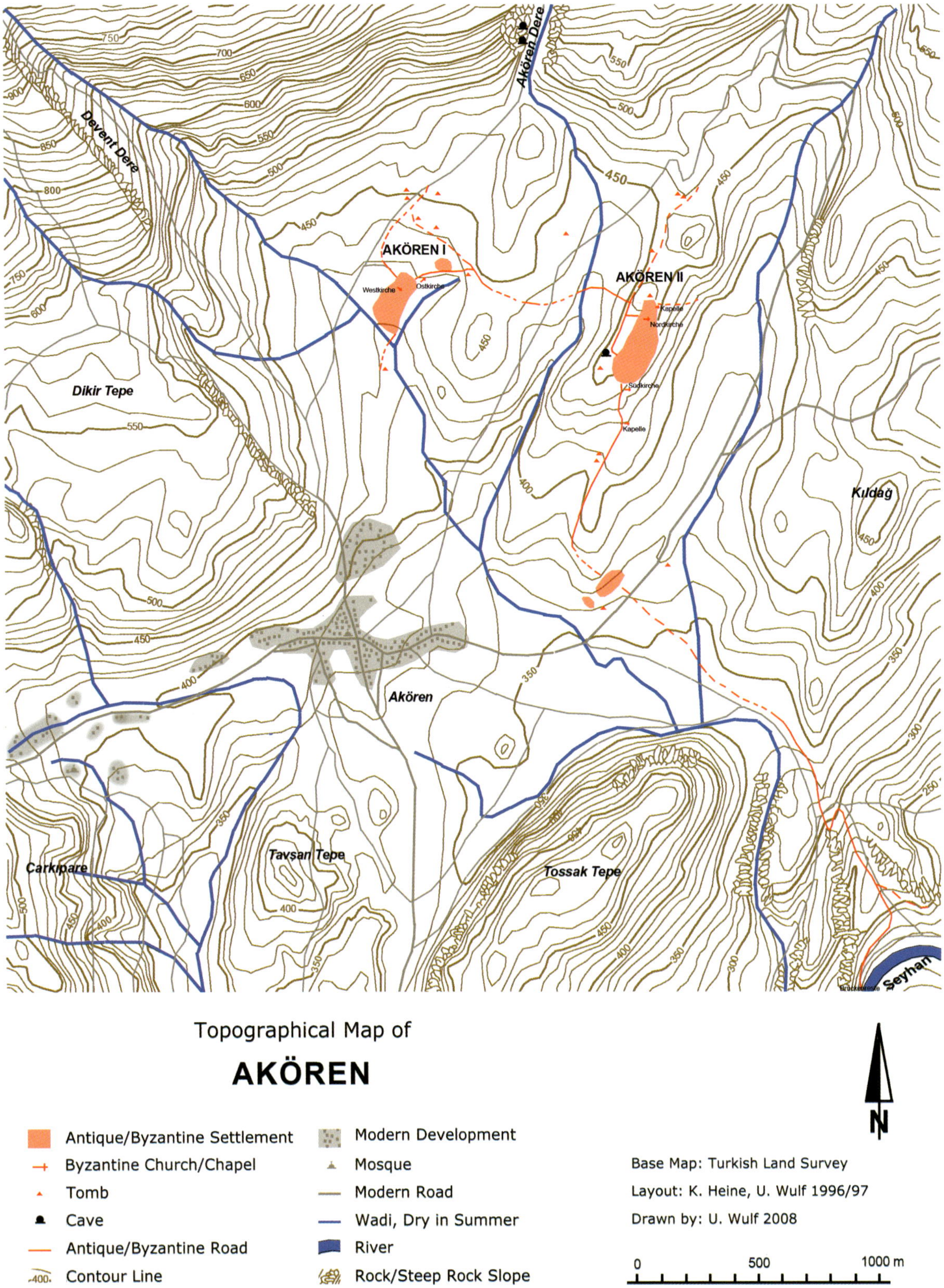

Fig. 1. Akören. Topographical map of Akören I and II with the remains of ancient roads (scale 1:25,000) (U. Wulf-Rheidt).

Fig. 2. Akören II. Model of the topographical situation (U. Wulf-Rheidt).

settlement, Akören I, lies in the valley of an intermittent stream, while Akören II occupies an elevated ridge. Each settlement was dominated by two churches. The residential areas around the churches are in parts well preserved, in other parts densely overgrown with shrubbery. Topographic surveys of both settlements produced detailed maps of each village, showing all the walls, the locations of all door entrances and staircases, all mill and grinding stones, and all watering troughs and signs of cisterns visible on the surface. With these maps, it is possible to recognize the alleys, housing plots, and even ground plans of individual houses. The finished maps also reveal at first glance that both sites were not small villages with a couple of farms but rather densely developed, organized settlements.

Akören II

The better-preserved settlement, Akören II, is built on a ridge, which runs almost exactly north-south (figs. 2–3). Between the so-called South Church at the lowest point and the North Church on the highest hilltop, a densely built settlement extends about 300 m in length and 150 m in width. The spine of the settlement is a street, in some places only 2.5 m wide, which originates at the South Church and follows the topography from south to north. Numerous alleys branch off of this street to the east and west, subdividing the settlement into units, each about 40 to 45 m wide.

The North Church is not integrated into this relatively regular scheme, nor is it located along the main axis; rather it is accessible via the lateral alleys. The narrow and winding alleys to the church as well as its irregular location show that the church was added to an already existing settlement. An imperial inscription on a block near the church, dated to A.D. 82, suggests that it was built on the site of an earlier Roman building. According to Mustafa Sayar, the inscription is in honor of or

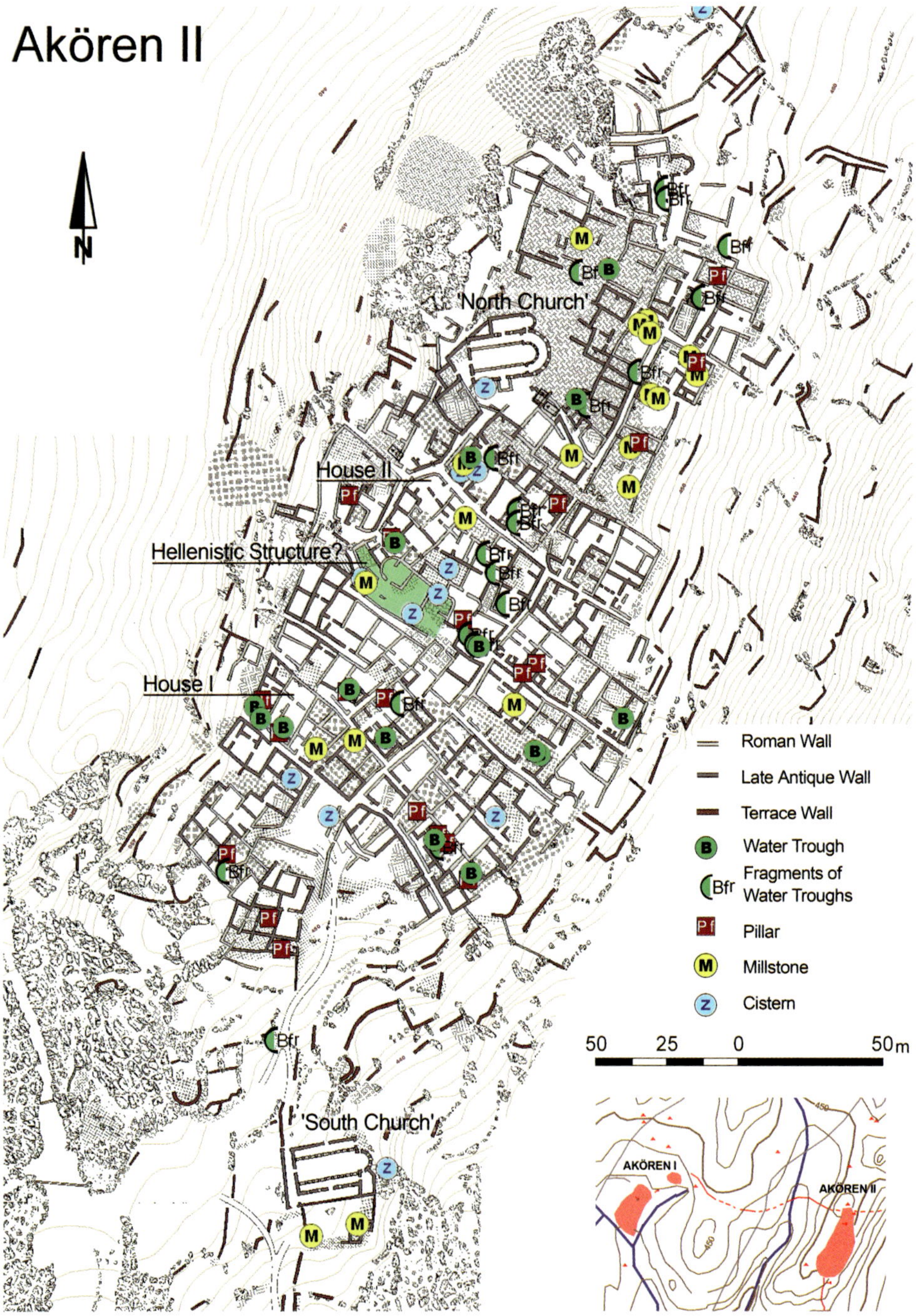

Fig. 3. Akören II. Topographical map. Marked in green is the probably earlier structure of a fortified country-seat, possibly Hellenistic (scale 1:2,500) (U. Wulf-Rheidt).

Fig. 4. The different types of masonry found in Akören I and II. Left: unifacial masonry, probably Roman (first to third century). Right: bifacial masonry, probably late antique (fifth to sixth century) (U. Wulf-Rheidt).

consecrated to an imperial association or society.[7] Thus the church may have been built in the place of the Roman building that once housed this association or society.

That the settlement was not first built in late antiquity is also supported by numerous burial structures, all dating to Roman times. A total of 18 graves in the vicinity of the two settlements were found in good condition (see fig. 1). Some of these can be precisely dated on the evidence of their inscriptions. The graves range from a tumulus, which according to its inscription dates to the first years of the second century, to a mausoleum, the inscription of which names the year A.D. 270.[8] The ancient ceramic finds from the surface indicate the same period, from the first to the third centuries.

The residential architecture from both sites exhibits two distinct masonry techniques (fig. 4), and it seems reasonable to connect these techniques with the two known periods of occupation, that of the tombs, on the one hand, and that of the churches, on the other. The first, "bifacial" masonry type consists of rectangular blocks of stone laid in continuous courses without headers. This kind of masonry compares very well with that of the church buildings. The second, "unifacial" type of masonry consists, by contrast, of walls one block thick built of barely treated blocks of stone of generally polygonal shape. Elsewhere in Cilicia, there is a rough division between unifacial masonry for buildings from the imperial period and bifacial masonry for buildings from late antiquity. For this reason, granted that dating by masonry type is always problematic, we would like to propose tentative dates of the first to third centuries for the unifacial masonry, thus contemporary with the tombs, and the fifth and sixth centuries for the bifacial masonry, that is, the same time as the construction of the large churches.

A chart of the different masonry techniques shows that the parcellation of the plots of land as well as the laying out of the infrastructure of the settlement is associated with the masonry technique dated to the Roman period (see fig. 3). One installation, however, situated roughly in the center of the settlement, stands out. This is a large area with a room that ends in a semicircle, to which additional rooms are attached to the west, one of which protrudes like a tower (see figs. 3, 11, marked in green). The quality of the masonry of the tower is far better than that of the walls of the houses (fig. 5). It could have been an older, fortified country-seat, possibly of Hellenistic origin, something frequently encountered in this region.[9] Many indicators suggest that a Roman settlement developed and remained in use while the large churches were built during the fifth and sixth centuries.

[7] I thank Mustafa Sayar, who dealt with the inscriptions of Akören, for this information. The inscriptions will be included in the final publication.

[8] Mietke, "Survey 1995" (supra n. 4), 426–27, fig. 7.

[9] S. Durugönül, *Türme und Siedlungen im Rauhen Kilikien: Eine Untersuchung zu den archäologischen Hinterlassenschaften im Olbischen Territorium, Asia Minor Studien* 28 (Bonn 1998) 28–33. Comparable to the structure at Akören II is, for example, Catıören.

Fig. 5. Akören II. Additional tower-like room probably of an earlier, Hellenistic structure (U. Wulf-Rheidt).

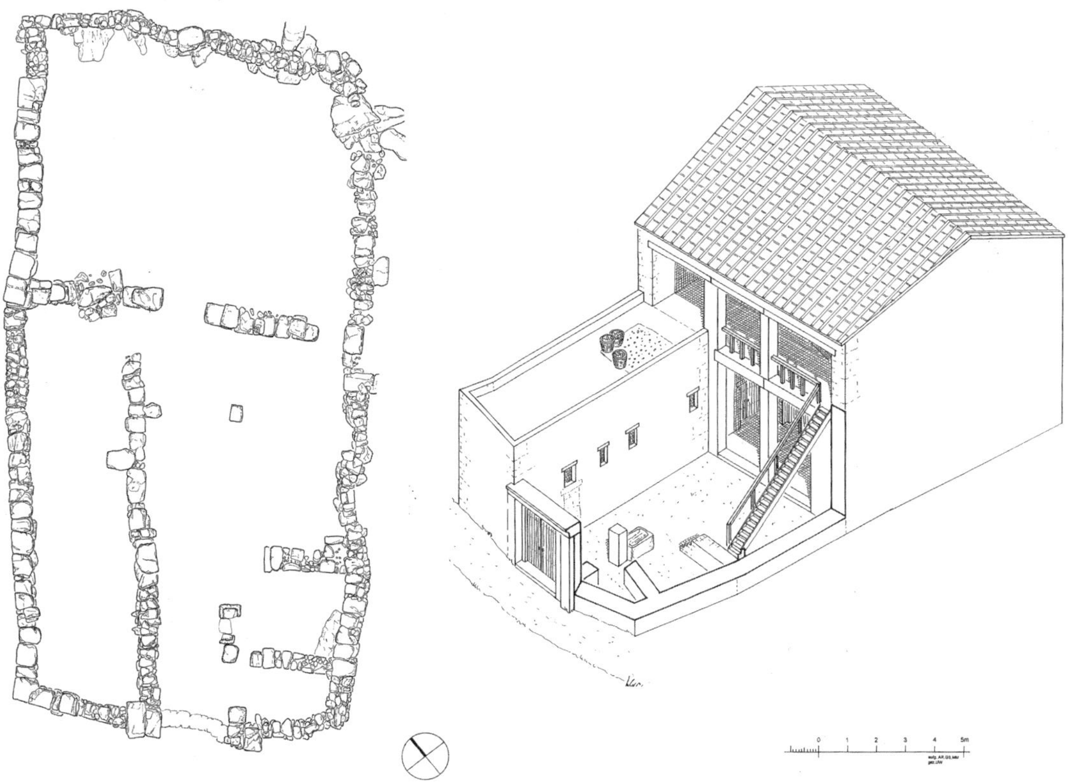

Fig. 6. Akören II. House I. Ground plan (scale 1:250) and reconstruction of the late antique phase (U. Wulf-Rheidt).

Not only the structure of the settlement but also some houses can be reconstructed very well, such as a house in the area of the possible fortified country-seat (see fig. 3, marked "House I"). It exhibits masonry of both types, and was probably originally constructed in Roman times (fig. 6). The nearly 300 m^2 house is oriented north-south. The rooms are grouped in an L-shape around a relatively small yard. In the northeast part of the house is a room about 90 m^2 in area that could be entered through two doors but had no windows. Two pillars indicate that there was a hall about 2.5 m wide in front of this room. The smaller space in the northwest was probably organized into a suite of three smaller rooms. The bifacial masonry shows that in some areas the house was renovated in late antiquity. It was expanded to the north, although the original north boundary of the structure was left in place. The main purpose of the expansion of the ground floor was apparently to support a larger upper floor, the existence of which can be established at least for this phase, because remains of a staircase are still visible today.

This type of elongated house can be detected in Akören in diverse variations, with a yard generally to the south and the main rooms to the north (figs. 7, 9). The long rectangular main part of the house may have had a smaller room attached to the north end. There are even houses that obviously had both an anteroom facing south and an additional small space facing north.

The organization of these houses recalls classical or Hellenistic examples, for instance, the houses of Dystos in Euboea.[10] Because at present no evidence indicates extensive habitation of Akören during the Hellenistic period or earlier,[11] these conspicuous parallels in the layout of ground plans must represent continuity of traditional house-forms until late Roman times in this region. This continuity can also be detected in late antiquity. Although Roman houses were partially renovated or rebuilt, almost all the late antique houses seem to have originated as Roman buildings. New buildings were quite obviously exceptional.

Extensive renovations are also exceptional in late antique Akören. One rare example is a house southwest of the North Church (see fig. 3, marked "House II"). Its interior was fundamentally transformed, but the Roman perimeter walls had already determined its basic character (fig. 8). Departing from the model of an elongated house extending from north to south, the house was converted so as to have a transverse yard area in the northeast, with five rooms attached in the southwest. In the west, there seems to have been a single room accessible only from an alley, because there are no doors leading from it to the other rooms. Thus it could have been a store or workshop, as seen in several other places in Akören. The approximately square room in the east part of the house was probably the main room, to which an additional smaller room was attached to the southwest. No remains of a staircase have been found, but the possibility cannot be excluded that there was a wooden staircase in the yard, and that at least the main room had two stories, as similar houses suggest.

In general the houses follow the typical Roman ground plan. In the architecture of residential dwellings, therefore, we cannot detect a break between Roman and late antique buildings. On the contrary, the ground plans, presumably of Hellenistic origin, speak to an extremely long-term adherence to traditional ways of dwelling. This is also true of the overall settlement pattern. Although individual houses were partially rebuilt, the existing Roman settlement pattern was maintained with only a few exceptions (see fig. 3). This pattern can be reconstructed as a densely developed row house

[10] For the houses of Dystos in Euboea, see W. Hoepfner (ed.), *Geschichte des Wohnens*, Band 1 (Stuttgart 1999) 359–67. Hoepfner dates the first phase of the house to the middle of the fourth century B.C. The houses with the main room and only an additional small space at the rear are reminiscent of the houses of Delos from the archaic period. See also ibid., 510–14, especially Houses IIIA–C and IIIE–F.

[11] The ceramic finds are, according to the investigation of Neşe Atik, not earlier than the first century A.D. Mietke, "Survey 1996 and 1997" (supra n. 4), 81.

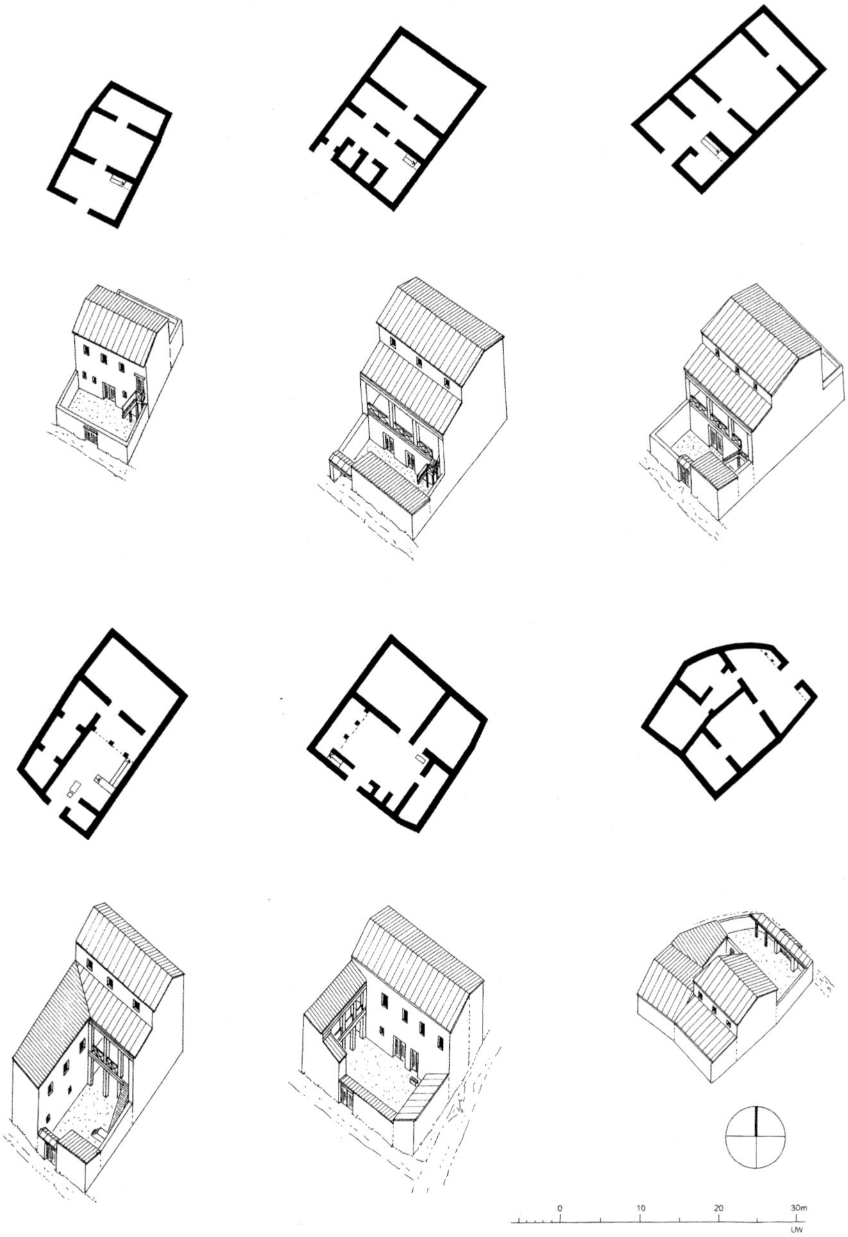

Fig. 7. Akören. Variations of house types in the late antique period (scale 1:1,000) (U. Wulf-Rheidt).

settlement oriented approximately north-south. The insulae bounded by the transverse alleys were rather short, about 18 to 20 m deep, and each comprised four to five units (fig. 9).

In the densely developed settlement hardly any vacant areas can be detected. Only in the southern part of the settlement does there exist a large, apparently vacant square with a cistern, which could have been a marketplace or public area (see figs. 3, 9). In this case, too, it appears that the square goes back to the Roman settlement pattern. On the north side of this area are two structures that do not conform to the usual arrangement of residential dwellings (see figs. 3, 11 [marked in orange]). Moreover, in the area of a freestanding structure subdivided into four rooms of approximately equal

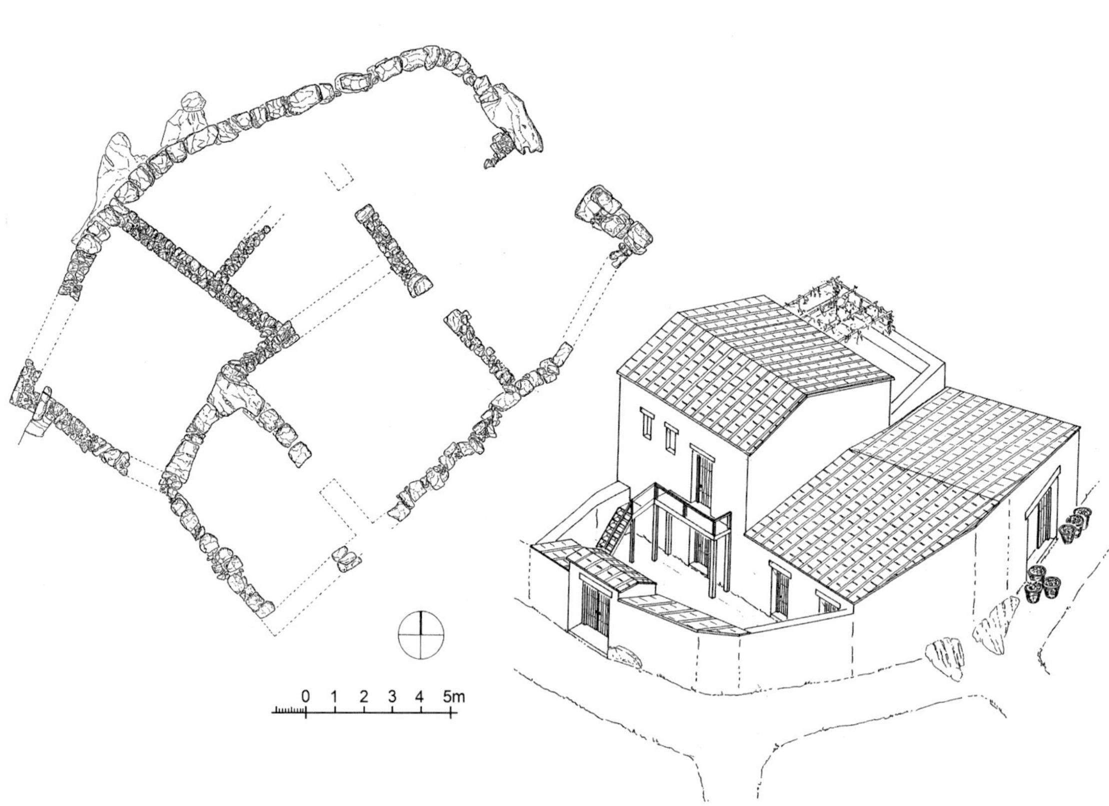

Fig. 8. Akören II. House II. Ground plan (scale 1:250) and reconstruction of the late antique phase (U. Wulf-Rheidt).

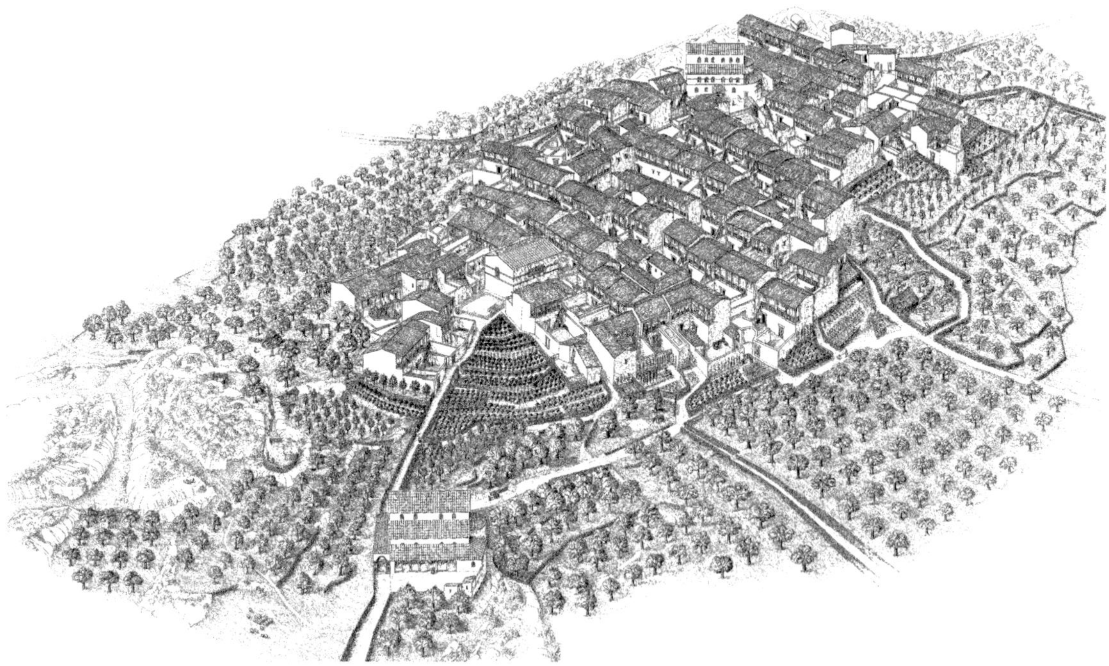

Fig. 9. Akören II. Reconstruction of the village in late antiquity (J. Denkinger, Architekturreferat DAI Berlin).

size and covering about 15 by 18 m, decorated architectural fragments were found that seem too elaborate for a simple dwelling. These fragments include an elaborately profiled cornice and stone mullions indicative of large subdivided windows usually not found in residential architecture (fig. 9). Crosses on the mullions point to an origin in late antiquity. The layout of the structure and the architectural elements indicate a special building, possibly associated with ecclesiastical or civic administration.

For the late antique settlement, about 90 residences can be reconstructed, and we may assume a similar number for the Roman settlement. Therefore the average population at Akören II could be estimated at about 500 to 700 people.[12]

Obviously, the people depended largely on agriculture. Despite the difficult topography, the entire area around the settlement was terraced (see figs. 3, 9). With the exception of the steep, rocky slopes, every centimeter of land was cultivated, beginning with fields immediately adjacent to the settlement. In many yards, a pillar with a hole for tying animals (see fig. 3, marked "Pf") and a water trough (fig. 3, marked "B") in front have been found intact, indicating that the houses also sheltered animals. In addition, fragments of basins were found in most houses (see fig. 3, marked "Bfr") so it can be assumed that almost every house was equipped with such basins and troughs.

We also found numerous grindstones and counterweights that must have come from large olive oil presses (see fig. 3, marked "M").[13] Numerous grindstones for the production of flour were also discovered. We did not detect buildings that were used exclusively as olive oil factories or flour mills, as can be found in the region today, but given the widespread distribution of grindstones and weights, it may be assumed that domestic production of both oil and flour was widespread.

The ground plans of the Roman houses with their small yards were unsuitable for this kind of intensive agricultural use, as is shown by the fact that in many cases they were further developed in late antiquity. A comparison with present-day houses in Akören suggests that the barely lit basement was presumably used exclusively for agricultural purposes, for example, as stables, storage areas, and workshops (fig. 10). In particular, the small rooms facing the yards could not have accommodated the large presses. Thus the presses probably were installed in the larger rooms on the ground floor. Accordingly, the actual living quarters were on the upper floor and in general could be reached through an entrance hall in which, particularly during summer, the main activities of life took place (see figs. 6–8).

Because many fragments of roof tiles remained on the surface, at least the late antique houses apparently had tile roofs, partially sloped (see fig. 7). The set-back, narrow structures attached to the main rooms and possibly the additional installations may have had flat roofs. As is still customary today in this region, the flat roofs were likely used as additional outdoor spaces for work and for spreading and drying fruits and vegetables (fig. 10).

Akören I

Although it is not as well preserved, an absolutely comparable settlement pattern can be reconstructed in Akören I (fig. 11). The pattern also goes back to a previous Roman development. A closed semicircular installation along the southeast wing might even indicate an older core here as a departure

[12] For averages of comparable settlements, see P.J. Watson, *Archaeological Ethnography in Western Iran* (Arizona 1979) 42–44, 153–54, 236–37.

[13] The grindstones and counterweights belonged to olive oil presses comparable to Syrian examples, such as in O. Callot, *Huileries antiques de Syrie du Nord* (Paris 1984); and to examples from Palestine, for which see R. Frankel, "Oil and wine presses in the southern Levant in antiquity," *DOP* 51 (1997) 73–84. For the construction of olive oil presses in Asia Minor, see also the contribution of G. Varinlioğlu in this volume.

Fig. 10. Akören. Two examples of modern village houses showing that to this day the dimly lit rooms of the ground floors are used as stables and storage rooms and the flat roofs for drying fruits and vegetables (U. Wulf-Rheidt).

Fig. 11. Akören I and II. Schematic layout of the two settlements (scale 1:5,000) (U. Wulf-Rheidt).

point for the development of the settlement. The settlement is also made accessible by two roads running north-south, and subdivided by cross streets into individual quarters. Here, too, the houses exhibit a predominantly north-south orientation and the same pattern of ground plans that we have seen already in Akören II. Akören I consists of about 55 houses and therefore must have had about 300 to 450 inhabitants. Thus the settlement is smaller than Akören II by roughly a third.

Fig. 12. The so-called North Church, a three-nave ambulatory basilica built at the end of the fifth century (U. Wulf-Rheidt).

Judging by an accumulation of capitals and fragments of architectural profiles, this settlement, too, appears to have had a lavishly furnished building for special purposes. It was situated at a square with public access to a relatively huge cistern and around it were grouped three other buildings that were probably not used as houses (see fig. 11, marked in orange). There was a row of stores or workshops in the immediate vicinity and another huge, publicly accessible cistern.

The irregular location of the so-called West Church at the core of the settlement also is conspicuous in Akören I (see fig. 11). The church had to fit into an existing scheme, so irregularities were accepted. This may indicate that here, too, an ancient building existed prior to the church, comparable to the North Church in Akören II.

Comparison of Akören I and II

Both settlements appear to have originated from an older core, perhaps a Hellenistic fortified country-seat, and both densely developed late antique settlements have Roman predecessors that shaped the planning of each settlement (see fig. 11).

The almost identically organized settlements Akören I and II are situated in close proximity to each other, barely one km apart as the crow flies (see fig. 1). It is notable that despite the agricultural character of the surrounding area, the dense urban structures of the Roman settlements prevailed until late antiquity. Despite intensive inspection, we were not able to detect any free-standing farmsteads or other agricultural buildings in the areas around the settlements. The entire region, so far as possible, appears to have been terraced or subdivided into fields and thus to have been reserved for agricultural use. Apparently the characteristic settlement pattern in this region was the village community consisting of densely grouped houses of approximately the same size; thus we can perceive no social hierarchy of plantation owners and smaller family yards. This settlement pattern continues seamlessly from Roman times into the sixth century.

Although we can detect hardly any breaks or changes in the residential architecture, the new construction of churches in each case strongly altered the appearance of the settlements and reshaped them. Here, too, we can detect a uniform scheme. In each of the two settlements, one church is located a short distance away from the settlement, while the other quite obviously took the place of a larger previous building, possibly replacing a pagan shrine. Three of the four churches are oriental basilicas, a type of church frequently found throughout Cilicia.

Unusual and rare, by contrast, is the North Church, a three-nave ambulatory basilica with an additional chapel in the north part of Akören II (fig. 12). The chapel added later on can be dated by an inscription to A.D. 504;[14] therefore, the ambulatory church must have been built earlier, possibly at the end of the fifth century. Because an inscription also dates the beginning of the construction of the South Church exactly to the year A.D. 525,[15] we know that the unusual ambulatory basilica is the first large church building in Akören. The construction of large, almost oversized churches amid the densely developed settlement thus began at the end of the fifth century. The model for the first such church building must have been the Church of the Apostles at Anazarbos,[16] a church in the capital of the province of Cilicia II, in which the two settlements in Akören are also located.[17] Because the ambulatory church in Akören quite obviously is a copy of the church in the capital, it appears that there were close ties between the settlement in the province and the capital.

Two additional buildings in Akören II demonstrate a religious character: a small chapel located in the south outside the settlement (fig. 13) and another at the northwestern edge that was built into a Roman installation and must have been a part of this complex (see fig. 11, marked "Chapel").

The Overall Settlement Structure

The relatively rare ambulatory church and the additional religious buildings make it probable that the larger settlement, Akören II, played a more important role within the overall settlement structure (see fig. 1). This is also indicated by the infrastructure that connected the two settlements to the hinterland, which we were able to clarify largely through intensive exploration of the surroundings. To this day, the remains of a bridge across the Şehan river, the ancient Saros, are evident, although its construction techniques suggest that it is post-antique, probably Ottoman, in date (see fig. 15). It is likely, however, that as early as the Roman period, the main road crossed the river at this point before it continued to Akören II. The road then went uphill and after going around a hill gave a view of the small chapel that indicated—visible from afar—the approach to the settlement with the South Church at the edge (see fig. 13). Once this chapel was reached, the lavish arch of the South Church marked the next important point on the way to the settlement (see figs. 3, 14). The construction history of the church leaves no doubt that the arch, which according to an inscription was built in A.D. 546, originally stood alone.[18] Only in the year A.D. 594, when the vestibule was built, was the arch integrated into the church building.

Visible from a distance, the arch frames the main entranceway that leads past the church to the settlement, thus making clear the entry into both the church district and the settlement (see figs. 3, 14). Here an ancient theme lives on; the arch marks the boundary of the city as it does in innumerable Roman examples and as we encounter it in Anazarbos, the provincial capital.[19]

[14] Mietke, "Survey 1994" (supra n. 4), 40.

[15] Ibid., 38.

[16] M. Gough, "Anazarbus," *AnatSt* 2 (1952) 116–18; Hild and Hellenkemper, *Kilikien und Isaurien* (supra n. 1), 116–20, fig. 7; G. Mietke, "Die Apostelkirche von Anazarbos und Syrien," *Olba* 2 (1999) 227–39.

[17] Hild and Hellenkemper, *Kilikien und Isaurien* (supra n. 1), 38–39.

[18] Mietke, "Survey 1994" (supra n. 4), 36–38.

[19] Gough, "Anazarbus" (supra n. 16), figs. 2–3.

Fig. 13. The chapel at the rise to Akören II. On the left side, the arch of the South Church is visible (U. Wulf-Rheidt).

Fig. 14. The so-called South Church with the arch built in A.D. 546, which was integrated into the vestibule of the church building in the year A.D. 594. In front is the ancient road leading through the arch to the settlement (U. Wulf-Rheidt).

Fig. 15. Remains of a bridge across the Şehan river that probably replaced a late antique bridge (U. Wulf-Rheidt).

Conclusions

With the exceptions of the quite significant church buildings and the few special structures adorned with typical late Roman architectural fragments, the architecture of the Akören settlements is largely modeled after that of traditional Graeco-Roman houses, revealing the longstanding continuity of much older traditions in the vernacular architecture of this remote agricultural region. Akören shows how in the residential architecture of the rural settlements of Cilicia, far away from modern centers, elements from earlier periods survived for many centuries despite Christianization. At the same time, ancient symbols of urban prestige such as arches marking the boundaries of settlements were adopted and effectively used in a contemporary language of forms. The history of the two settlements of Akören shows how ancient urban traditions remained astonishingly current well into the sixth century and demonstrates once again that a new religion does not immediately affect material culture in all areas.

12 Anazarbos in Late Antiquity

Richard Posamentir

Without question, the appearance of most ancient cities in Asia Minor underwent significant, even fundamental changes between the fourth and the eighth centuries A.D.[1] The archaeological and architectural traces of these changes are in many cases impressively obvious, even though few written sources shed light on the various and specific processes that accompanied the transition from the antique, through the late antique, to the post-antique era. It is noteworthy that these changes happened in different ways and at different moments, if one considers, for example, the cities of eastern as opposed to western Asia Minor. These variations are due not only to the different urban structures that particular cities had from their very beginnings, but also and even more so to their different historical backgrounds, which were strongly connected to their topographical situations.

A look at the less well-explored cities of the eastern Roman empire reveals that our knowledge of this period of transition is still extremely limited, and that the prerequisites for archaeological investigations in this region are totally different from those in the west. While monumental fortification systems and impressive Christian sanctuaries of the post-antique era survive in rather good condition (though often of uncertain date), remains of earlier periods (especially of Hellenistic and Roman imperial times) have vanished almost entirely. It is no coincidence that only a few publications by classical archaeologists are devoted to the cities in the area east of modern Adana and that

The Anazarbos field survey 2004–2007 was a joint project of Istanbul University (Prof. Dr. M. H. Sayar) and the German Archaeological Institute, Istanbul branch.

[1] The following abbreviations will be used in this paper:
Foss, "Cities" = C. Foss, "The Cities of Pamphylia in the Byzantine age" in idem, *Cities, Fortresses and Villages of Byzantine Asia Minor* (Aldershot 1996) 1–62.
Gough, "Anazarbus" = M. Gough, "Anazarbus," *AnatSt* 2 (1952) 85–150.
Hellenkemper, "Stadtmauern" = H. Hellenkemper, "Die Stadtmauern von Anazarbos / Ayn Zarba," in W. Diem and A. Falaturi (eds.), *XXIV. Deutscher Orientalistentag, Zeitschrift der Deutschen Morgenländischen Gesellschaft* Suppl. 8 (Stuttgart 1990) 71–76.
Hellenkemper = F. Hild, H. Hellenkemper, and G. Hellenkemper-Salies, "Kommagene-Kilikien-Isaurien," *Reallexikon zur Byzantinischen Kunst* IV (1990) 191–356.
Hild and Hellenkemper, *Kilikien und Isaurien* = F. Hild and H. Hellenkemper, *Kilikien und Isaurien, Tabula Imperii Byzantini* 5 (Vienna 1990).
Posamentir, "Säulenstrasse" = R. Posamentir, "Ohne Mass und Ziel?—Anmerkungen zur Säulenstrasse von Anazarbos," in I. Delemen et al. (eds.), *Euergetes. Festschrift für Haluk Abbasoğlu zum 65. Geburtstag* (Istanbul 2008) 1013–33.
Posamentir, "Innovation" = R. Posamentir, "Innovation und Kulturtransfer in Anazarbos, der einstigen Metropole Kilikiens," in F. Pirson and U. Wulf-Rheidt (eds.), *Austausch und Inspiration. Kolloquium anlässlich des 65. Geburtstages von Adolf Hoffmann* (Berlin 2008) 89–106.
Posamentir and Sayar, "Anazarbos" = R. Posamentir and M.H. Sayar, "Anazarbos—ein Zwischenbericht aus der Metropole des Ebenen Kilikien," *IstMitt* 56 (2006) 317–57.
Sayar, *Inschriften* = M.H. Sayar, *Die Inschriften von Anazarbos und Umgebung I, Inschriften griechischer Städte aus Kleinasien* 56 (Bonn 2000).

For changes in cities in Asia Minor between the fourth and eighth centuries A.D., cf. D. Claude, *Die byzantinische Stadt im 6. Jahrhundert* (Munich 1969); A. Cameron, *The Mediterranean World in Late Antiquity AD 395–600* (London and New York 1993); J.H.W.G. Liebeschuetz, *Decline and Fall of the Roman City* (Oxford 2001); B. Brenk, "Zur Christianisierung der spätrömischen Stadt im östlichen Mittelmeerraum," in G. Brands and H.-G. Severin (eds.), *Die spätantike Stadt und ihre Christianisierung* (Wiesbaden 2003) 85–95.

Fig. 1. View of the urban area of Anazarbos and the mountain range with the Armenian castle on top, from the south (R. Posamentir).

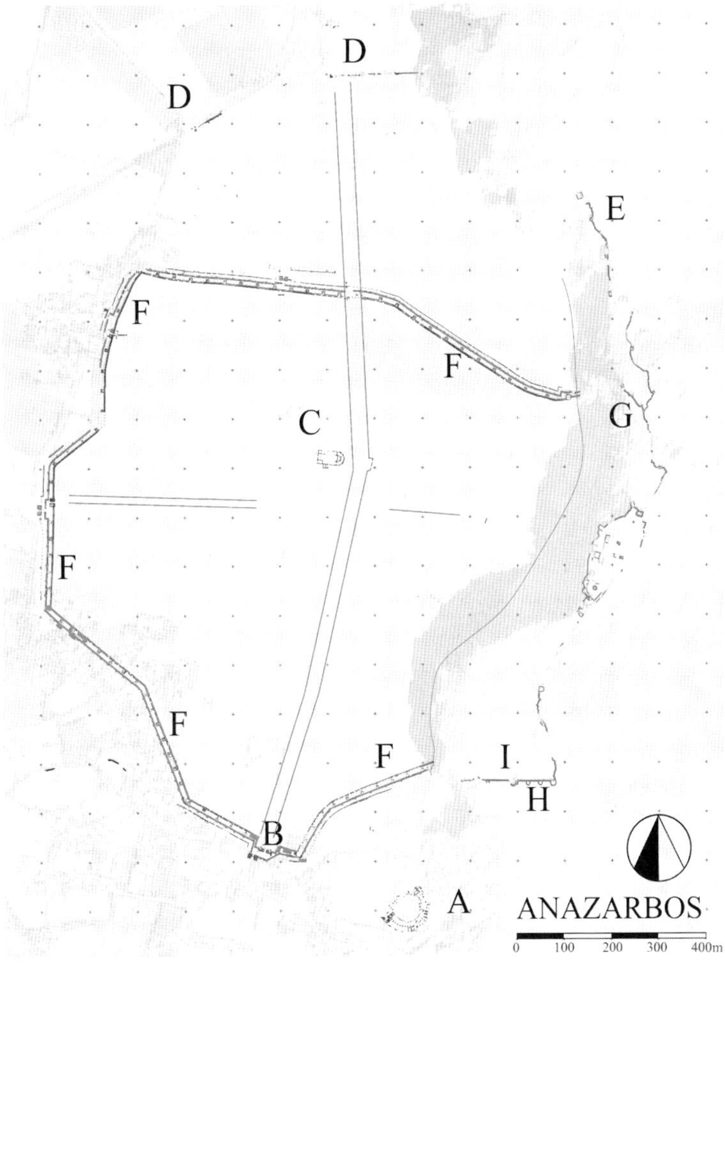

Fig. 2. Schematic overall plan of the urban area of Anazarbos, showing only selected monuments:
A = Theater
B = Monumental arch
C = Church of the Apostles
D = First circuit wall (Theodosian?)
E = Section of the first circuit wall on top of the rock
F = Second circuit wall (Justinian?)
G = Section of the second circuit wall on top of the rock
H = Armenian walls
I = Byzantine gate (Justinian?)
(H. Birk/R. Posamentir)

many sites are dealt with only in rather superficial reports, which—understandably—have had to leave many questions unanswered.

Still, this situation is not only the result of insufficient preservation of monuments of the pre-late antique era; another fact must be held responsible as well. The cities of the east were in danger of being overrun by intruders from the south and east much earlier and for a much longer period than the cities of the west. Therefore, one of the most fascinating problems revolves around the question whether indications of decline in the ancient cities of eastern Asia Minor were solely the result of an inevitable "process of ruralization" or "deurbanization" during Christian late antiquity, or whether they should be seen in direct connection with the Arab threat and later the early Islamic era.[2] This specific question will be addressed in the following pages with the aid of evidence from a place called Anazarbos.

The spectacular site of Anazarbos (fig. 1), a city of the Roman Near East, located some 60 km northeast of modern Adana, carries the name of a large and 4.5 km-long range of hills that rises more than 220 m above the Çukurova plain.[3] At its foot, along the western side and on top of an obviously much smaller Hellenistic predecessor, stretches a Roman city of the same name, covering an area of about 250 acres. The city gained enormous strategic importance during the second half of the second century and the first half of the third century A.D. for Roman troops on their way to the east.[4]

Of the Hellenistic period, only a handful of pottery sherds have been found so far, but more remains of the Roman imperial era survive (fig. 2). In certain areas, at least traces of an orthogonal grid system can be discerned, arranged along a monumental north-south oriented colonnaded street, which was up to 34 m wide and 1.75 km long.[5] This disproportionately wide street terminates at both ends in archways,[6] and has recently been carefully studied.[7] A second main street, likewise accompanied by columns, crosses the city from west to east. The unusual combination of theater, amphitheater, and circus can be observed in the south part of the city, right next to or possibly in the middle of three wide-ranging necropoleis, dated from the first century B.C. to approximately the sixth century A.D.[8] City walls apparently did not exist during the Roman imperial period, while several public buildings, including two baths, a basilica (?), and at least three sanctuaries (located along the main axes) have been partially detected by means of geophysical prospection.[9] Coins from the first century A.D. onward show a massive castle on the rock above the city.[10] However, actual remains from this era are scarce on top of the hills, apart from a huge grave monument,[11] a propylon,[12] and a processional staircase leading directly to a huge foundation of stone and mortar, which most likely

[2] Cf. for example Foss, "Cities," 43–45, 48–50.

[3] Gough, "Anazarbus," 92; Hild and Hellenkemper, *Kilikien und Isaurien,* 179; Sayar, *Inschriften*, 9–10 no. LZ 1–6.

[4] For an overview see Gough, "Anazarbus," 85–150; Hild and Hellenkemper, *Kilikien und Isaurien*, 178–85; and most recently Posamentir and Sayar, "Anazarbos," 317–57.

[5] Posamentir and Sayar, "Anazarbos," 343, fig. 31; Posamentir, "Säulenstrasse," 1025, fig. 2.

[6] For the north arch see Hild and Hellenkemper, *Kilikien und Isaurien*, pl. 67, or recently Posamentir and Sayar, "Anazarbos," 330–31, fig. 14.

[7] Posamentir, "Säulenstrasse,"1013–33.

[8] Posamentir and Sayar, "Anazarbos," 351–54, figs. 41–45; for one especially interesting rock chamber tomb with relief decoration, see recently U. Kelp, "Darüber wachen Verderben und Schrecken und Todeslos: Erinyen als Grabwächter: Zum Eunuchengrab in Anazarbos," in I. Delemen et al. (eds.), *Euergetes. Festschrift für Haluk Abbasoğlu zum 65. Geburtstag* (Istanbul 2008) 675–98.

[9] See Posamentir and Sayar, "Anazarbos," 343–45, figs. 31–33; Posamentir, "Säulenstrasse," 1017, figs. 13–14; 1019–21, fig. 26.

[10] R. Ziegler, *Kaiser, Heer und städtisches Geld. Untersuchungen zur Münzprägung von Anazarbos und anderer ostkilikischer Städte, ETAM* 16 (Vienna 1993) 29 nos. 35–43, pls. 1–2.

[11] Posamentir and Sayar, "Anazarbos," 340–42, figs. 28–29; Posamentir, "Innovation," 102–5, fig. 15.

[12] Posamentir and Sayar, "Anazarbos," 339–40, fig. 27.

once carried the temple of Aphrodite Kasalitis.[13] Almost all other remains on top of the rock belong to several building phases from presumably the sixth to the 14th centuries.

Otherwise, the post-Roman imperial eras are represented by two circuits of fortification walls, the first embracing almost the entire Roman city (cutting off only a short section of the colonnaded street at its north end)[14] and only partially preserved. The second, more impressive and doubtless later in date, is almost fully intact in its lower levels and reduces the inhabited area significantly.[15] Inside and outside of the two fortification rings, at least six huge church complexes can be distinguished,[16] in some places well preserved and in other places recognizable only through remote sensing, while a remarkable number of large but ramshackle peristyle-like structures and smaller brick buildings cover the whole area.[17] It is noteworthy that both of the latter classes of buildings are to a significant degree not aligned with the Roman grid plan, and must therefore be considered post-antique. A third arch with five passages in the south-central part of the city proper corresponds to the colonnaded street with its porticoes and taverns and should also be considered post-antique, in view of its manner of construction, its extensive use of spolia, and its architectural design, including projecting Christian symbols.[18]

Since this contribution is focused on the cities of Asia Minor and their transformation from Roman imperial times to late antiquity, two very specific complexes of problems will be treated here. In the first place, an investigation of this process of transformation in Anazarbos should attempt to respond to questions such as:

1) What exactly happened to the city, and what is actually visible to us from what happened?
2) How and why did the organization and structure of Anazarbos change?
3) Can these visible changes be correlated with specific dates or historical circumstances?

In the second place, and closely connected to these subjects, is the issue of the way in which the inhabitants of the late antique era treated the architectural and structural remains of the preceding period.

Although these are wide-ranging questions that cannot be fully resolved here, I hope nevertheless to be able to show that certain phenomena that occurred in Anazarbos can add valuable information to our understanding of this very interesting time of dynamic change. Naturally, these phenomena can only be mentioned briefly here, but they might be of importance not only for the region, but for other sites as well, namely, sites where:

1) similar phenomena are well known and already well documented,
2) the same phenomena are known but not properly interpreted, or
3) these phenomena have simply been overlooked until now.

Starting with minor details it will soon become clear that all of the following observations are in one way or another connected with each other.

[13] For the inscriptions, see Sayar, *Inschriften*, 40–41 nos. 29–34, pl. 25; for the cult, see M.H. Sayar, "Aphrodite Kasalitis in Anazarbos," in M. Meyer and R. Ziegler (eds.), *Kulturbegegnung in einem Brückenland: Gottheiten und Kulte als Indikatoren von Akkulturationsprozessen im Ebenen Kilikien*, *Asia Minor Studien* 53 (Bonn 2004) 185–89; 239–42 nos. 35–39; and, for the tentative identification of the sanctuary, see Posamentir and Sayar, "Anazarbos," 337–39, figs. 23–26.

[14] Posamentir, "Säulenstrasse," 1021, fig. 26.

[15] Hellenkemper, "Stadtmauern," 71–76; Posamentir, "Innovation," 93–95, fig. 4.

[16] For the three most prominent ones see Hellenkemper, 198–201, figs. 6–7.

[17] Posamentir and Sayar, "Anazarbos," 332–33, figs. 16–17.

[18] C.J. Williams, *The Development of Monumental Street Architecture* (Ph.D. thesis, London 1979) 178–79; Posamentir and Sayar, "Anazarbos," 329–30, figs. 10–13; Posamentir, "Säulenstrasse," 1016–17, figs. 8–13.

Fig. 3. Outer face of the Roman imperial arch at the southernmost end of the colonnaded street, from the south (R. Posamentir).

Fig. 4. Inner face of the Roman imperial arch at the southernmost end of the colonnaded street, from the north (R. Posamentir).

One of the few well-preserved monuments of Roman imperial times is represented by an impressive triumphal arch in the south part of the city of Anazarbos.[19] Although severely damaged by occasional earthquakes, it is still a showpiece of Roman craftsmanship of the late second century A.D. and can be fully reconstructed, because all of its architectural elements are either still in situ or are lying around the structure. However, the arch itself, which forms the beginning of one of the longest and widest colonnaded streets of antiquity, has two very different faces. The side facing the area outside of the city is well preserved, while the inner side is completely blank; almost all of its decorative architectural elements have been removed and are nowhere to be found in the vicinity (figs. 3–4).

The question immediately arises why the outer façade remained so remarkably well preserved—and even why the monument as a whole is still standing—while within the city proper, not much else of the original architectural fabric remains.[20] And furthermore, to where did the architectural elements of the inner side disappear? The first question is relatively easy to answer, since the whole arch with its original three passages was integrated into the second (and perhaps also the first) fortification circuit mentioned above, which partly enclosed the area of the Roman imperial city. Looking at the ground plan of the monumental arch and its immediate vicinity, it is clear that the circuit walls respected the existence of the porticoes that start there and that accompany the colonnaded street (fig. 5). This detail would suggest that the old structures were still

[19] Gough, "Anazarbus," 110–13; P. Verzone, "Città ellenistiche e romane dell'Asia Minore: Anazarbos," *Palladio* N.S. 7 (1957) 9–25, at 13–24; Hild and Hellenkemper, *Kilikien und Isaurien*, 181, fig. 68; Posamentir and Sayar, "Anazarbos," 325–27, fig. 8; 330–31; 334–36, fig. 20; Posamentir, "Säulenstrasse," 1015–16, figs. 2–5.

[20] Cf. Hild and Hellenkemper, *Kilikien und Isaurien*, figs. 71, 77, 79–82; Sayar, *Inschriften*, pls. 1–4; and most recently Posamentir and Sayar, "Anazarbos," 318, fig. 1.

in good shape and in use when the fortifications were built. It would seem likely, therefore, that the arch was meant to serve at the time of the construction of the walls as a city gate, representing the wealth and splendor of the city to visitors from outside. The outer façade, therefore, was left untouched and formed a true "Porta Aurea" of Anazarbos, while the inner side was of minor importance and could be relieved—so to speak—of its decoration. In any case, the contrast between the elaborately ornamented outer façade and the modest, almost shabby inner side is characteristic of city gates of the late antique era, as more prominent examples in other cities of Asia Minor suggest.

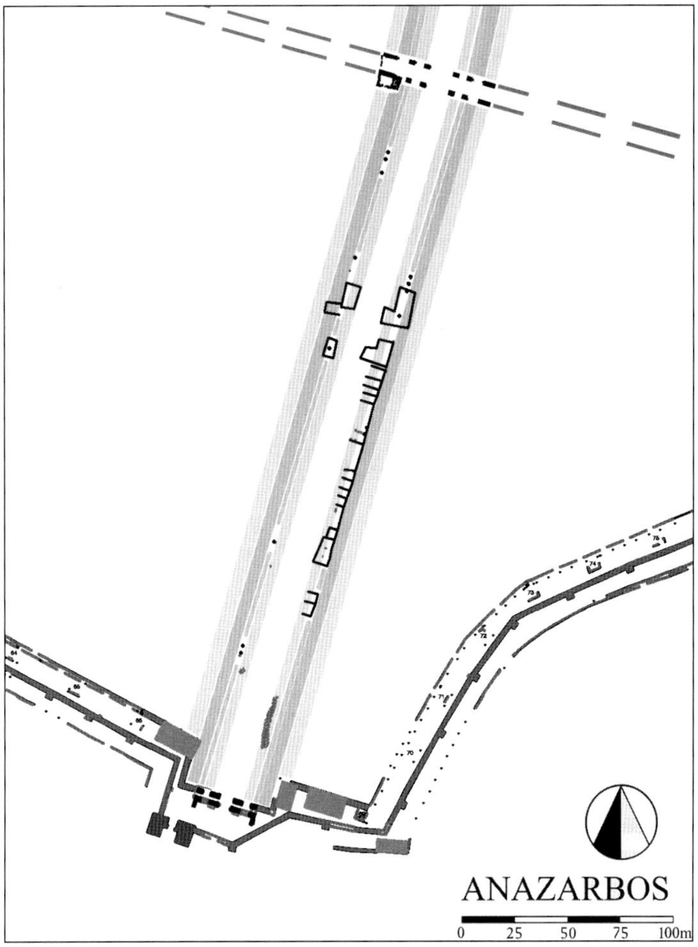

Fig. 5. Schematic plan of the southernmost section of the colonnaded street with late antique additions constraining its original width; the four lines to each side represent the paved pedestrian way, the course of columns, the porticoes, and the taverns (from inside to outside) (H. Birk/R. Posamentir).

The fact remains that the people who erected the walls obviously paid specific attention to the preservation of the monument, even though it might not have been the most practical and valuable part of a strong fortification system.[21] On the other hand, the architectural decoration of the inner side, which was not needed to represent the city's splendor to the outside world, was obviously an attractive source of materials for reuse in other buildings. If one searches for the architectural decoration that once adorned the inner side of the arch, one almost immediately encounters a huge church complex within the city center, the so-called Church of the Apostles.[22] This structure is built almost entirely out of reused stones,[23] and the origin of some of the spolia can be easily determined: the north side incorporates various elements of a huge temple complex that has been detected in the north part of the city (outside the second circuit wall), while the south side consists of architraves, friezes, and *geisa* which are extremely similar to the missing blocks of the triumphal

[21] Cf. the somehow similar situation in Constantinople, which led to the discussion whether the "Porta Aurea" must be dated earlier than the adjacent walls. See B. Meyer-Plath and A.M. Schneider, *Die Landmauer von Konstantinopel.* Teil 2. *Denkmäler antiker Architektur* 8 (Berlin 1943) 42–44.

[22] Gough, "Anazarbus," 116–18, figs. 7–8; Hellenkemper, 198–201, fig. 6; G. Mietke, "Die Apostelkirche von Anazarbos und Syrien," *Olba* 2 (1999) 227–39; Posamentir and Sayar, "Anazarbos," 334–36, figs. 18–20.

[23] Already mentioned by F.W. Deichmann, "Die Spolien in der spätantiken Architektur," *SBMünch* 6 (Munich 1975) 34–36.

Fig. 7. Projection of the polygonal apse of the Church of the Apostles (northern face) with reworked tendriled frieze blocks in the socle zone, from the southeast (R. Posamentir).

Fig. 6. One of the granite columns of the outer face of the Roman imperial arch, now lying in the apse of the Church of the Apostles in the city center (R. Posamentir).

arch.[24] The friezes are too small and too heterogeneous to have been part of the monumental gate, but the *geisa* likely belonged to the arch or at least the adjacent halls (the latter might hold true for some of the frieze blocks and architraves as well). The columns that lie inside the apse of the church, on the other hand, were almost certainly taken from the monumental arch (fig. 6).

Truly remarkable is the care and respect that craftsmen of around A.D. 500—the approximate date of the construction of the church[25]—paid to three- or four-hundred-year-old blocks. The friezes, especially, are not only reused, but even partly "reanimated" by the addition of new bands of ornament or even entire new blocks with decorative elements carved in the style of the second or third centuries. This becomes apparent in certain places, in which spolia of different date, style, and motif are connected with the aid of so-called "architectural ties" in order to effect smooth transitions.[26] Some of these "imitations" are so accurate and well done that one has to look twice to determine what is old and what is new (fig. 7). And it is certainly possible that this practice is also more frequent than has been realized in other places.[27] A comprehensive study of this phenomenon at Anazarbos is in preparation and has already shown, for example, that various types of friezes from at least four different ancient buildings were reused and assembled in the manner described.[28] A similar handling

[24] Posamentir and Sayar, "Anazarbos," 334–35, fig. 19.

[25] Mietke, "Apostelkirche" (supra n. 22), 236–37.

[26] Posamentir, "Innovation," 92–93, figs. 2–3.

[27] Cf. in general H. Brandenburg, "Die Verwendung von Spolien und originalen Werkstücken in der spätantiken Architektur," in J. Poeschke (ed.), *Antike Spolien in der Architektur des Mittelalters und der Renaissance* (Munich 1996) 11–48; idem, "Prachtentfaltung und Monumentalität als Bauaufgaben frühchristlicher Kirchenbaukunst," in J. Gebauer et al. (eds.), *Bildergeschichte. Festschrift für Klaus Stähler* (Möhnesee 2004) 59–76.

For a comparable process in northern Italy, see C. Jäggi, "Spolie oder Neuanfertigung? Überlegungen zur Bauskulptur des Tempietto sul Clitunno," in U. Peschlow and S. Möllers (eds.), *Spätantike und byzantinische Bauskulptur* (Stuttgart 1998) 105–11.

[28] I. Engelmann and P. Niewöhner, "Bauen nach der Krise. Die Spoliengalerie an der Apsis der Apostelkirche

Fig. 8. View of the outer face of the apse of the church next to the colonnaded street in Hierapolis Kastabala with architraves in the socle zone, from the west (R. Posamentir).

Fig. 9. Newly produced architectural element (pipe frieze) from one of the churches in Akören imitating antique models (R. Posamentir).

of comparable spolia can also be seen in old photographs taken by Gertrude Bell in the area of the three other gates in the second circuit wall (see fig. 19).

Interestingly, a similarly respectful handling of spolia can also be detected at sites closely related to Anazarbos (since Anazarbos was their metropolis); this can be seen, for example, in one of the churches in Hierapolis Kastabala,[29] where architraves were reused in a similar position (fig. 8), thoughtfully assembled, although here without imitations. Some antique capitals have also been reused here in a very careful way. In other places, such as Akören, for example,[30] where no original material from Roman imperial times was at hand, craftsmen actually imitated earlier architectural elements, such as pipe friezes (fig. 9). In this case, however, the skills of the craftsmen were simply not adequate to deceive the viewer. It is no coincidence that the capitals from these churches are among the oddest creations in the entire region. In any case, it is clear that the people who erected the Church of the Apostles in Anazarbos and related provincial buildings held great respect for an earlier era of wealth and splendor; the respectful reuse of earlier blocks might even be described as a conscious referential process, establishing a bridge between two epochs.[31] A similarly referential process is apparent in the topographical situation of the Church of the Apostles, as the examination of the building in its larger context shows.

Upon close inspection of the results of the remote sensing that revealed part of the grid plan of the Roman city, a clear structural difference becomes visible between the areas inside and outside the second circuit walls, which were erected at an as yet uncertain date (fig. 10). The orthogonal organization of the city has almost completely dissolved in the city center. When did this happen, and why?

In order to answer these questions, it is necessary first to consider the datable late antique buildings, in order to determine whether or not they respected the urban layout of the Roman city.

von Anazarbos," in D. Kreikenbom (ed.), *Krise und Kult. Vorderer Orient und Nordafrika von Aurelian bis Justinian, Millennium Studies* 28 (Mainz 2010) 109–37.

[29] O. Feld, "Die beiden Kirchen in Hierapolis Kastabala," in idem (ed.), *Studien zur spätantiken und byzantinischen Kunst 1, F. W. Deichmann gewidmet* (Bonn 1986) 77–86.

[30] U. Wulf-Rheidt, "Akören. Zur Stadtplanung und Wohnarchitektur zweier Siedlungen in Kilikien," in G. Brands and H.-G. Severin (eds.), *Die spätantike Stadt und ihre Christianisierung* (Wiesbaden 2003) 299–307.

[31] Cf. for example the church of Julianos in Brād for a similar process; C. Strube, *Die "Toten Städte." Stadt und Land in Nordsyrien während der Spätantike* (Mainz 1996) 36, fig. 64b.

Fig. 5. Akören II. Additional tower-like room probably of an earlier, Hellenistic structure (U. Wulf-Rheidt).

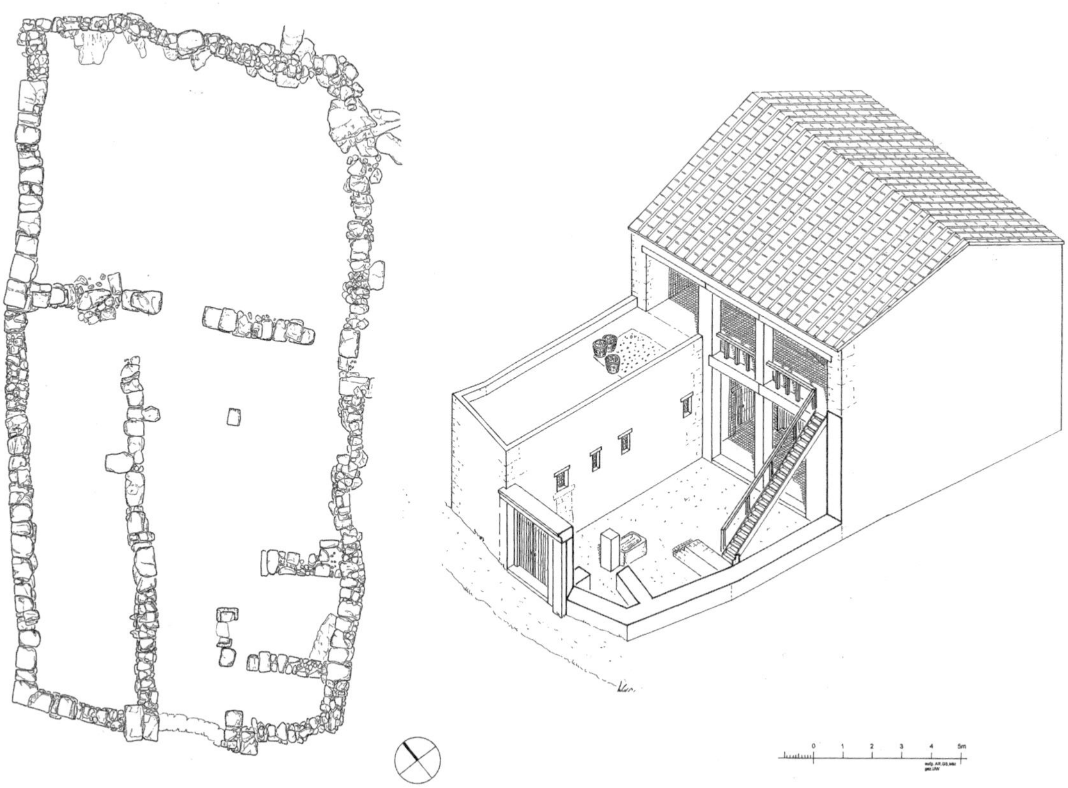

Fig. 6. Akören II. House I. Ground plan (scale 1:250) and reconstruction of the late antique phase (U. Wulf-Rheidt).

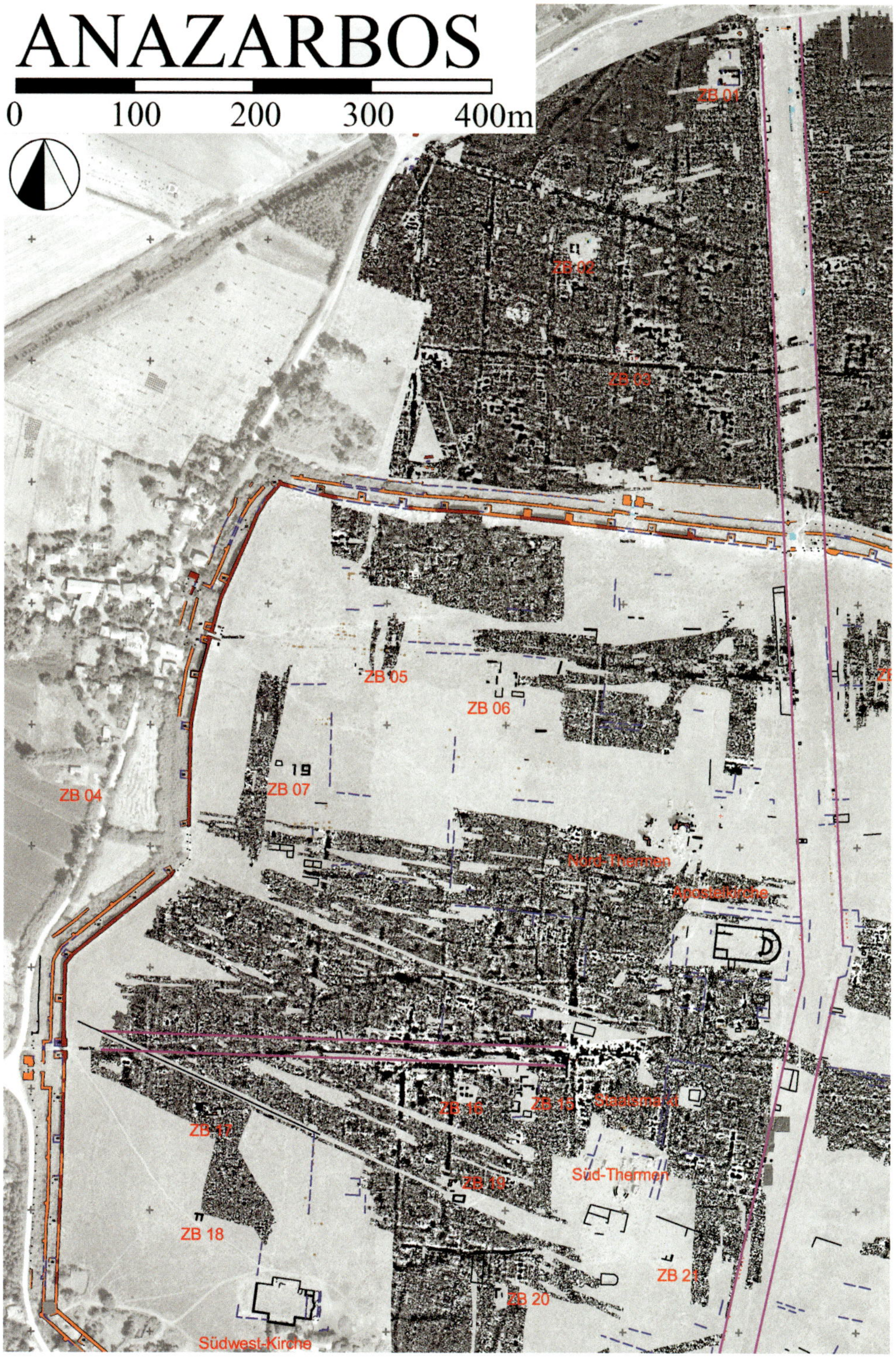

Fig. 10. Differences in urban structure between the areas inside and outside the circuit walls; results of remote sensing work (geomagnetic survey) show the orthogonal grid plan from Roman imperial times outside and the typical phenomenon of "deurbanization" inside (H. Birk/H. Stümpel).

Fig. 11a. Detail of remote sensing work (geomagnetic survey) outside the circuit walls showing the orthogonal grid plan from Roman imperial times and a three- or four-leaved, light anomaly embedded within the antique insula system (H. Stümpel).

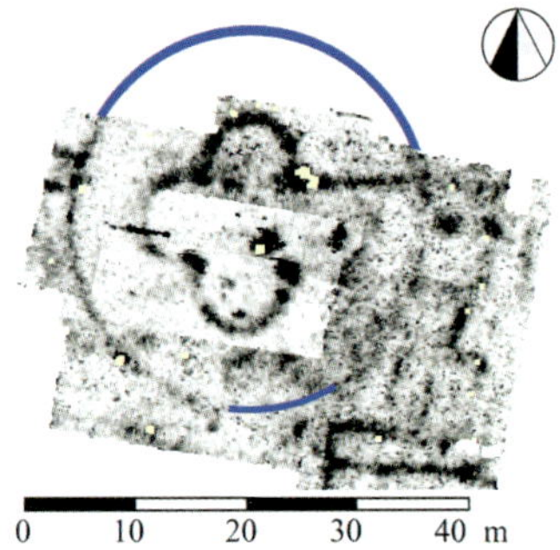

Fig. 11b. Detail of remote sensing work (georadar) outside the circuit walls showing the ground plan of a church surrounded by a circular wall (sanctuary of St. Menas?) (H. Stümpel).

Immediately outside the enclosing walls of the second circuit, and in the middle of the grid-planned part of the city, a tetra- or triconch building is perfectly visible in both the geomagnetic and the georadar images (fig. 11).[32] Surface finds, including glass mosaic tesserae, marble panels of various colors, and diagnostic architectural elements prove that the interpretation of this structure as a Christian sanctuary is correct. Similar structures are well known from the fourth and especially fifth centuries, but most interesting for us at this point is the precision with which the building is integrated into the former insula system. It seems that the church, perhaps a "martyrion," was erected at a time when the urban structures of Roman Anazarbos were still fully functional.

The impression made by looking at the aforementioned Church of the Apostles in the city center is similar: again, both the orientation and the layout seem to respect older structures. Perhaps this orientation was even determined by an earlier, pagan sanctuary upon which the church was built, as one would be tempted to assume in view of its prominent location. Moreover, the entrance to an enclosure-like area around the church, formed by an ornamented door made of spolia,[33] is exactly aligned with the back wall of the tabernae flanking the colonnaded street (fig. 12). The unusual plan of the church with a passage around the apse allows the dating of the structure to around A.D. 500.[34] Indeed, a similar type of church in Akören, a small village dependent on Anazarbos, can be securely dated by an inscription and should be slightly later in time.[35]

A somewhat similar case in Anazarbos that can be dated precisely—according to an inscription—to the year A.D. 516 is the so-called Rock-cut Church.[36] It does not lie within the city proper, but is also equipped with a comparable surrounding enclosure, including a monumental gate and important architectural decoration. As this structure has a very different orientation,[37] it can probably be assumed that the Church of the Apostles followed an older alignment. Another monument that matches these observations is the aforementioned arch (or probably better considered a monumental crossing) in the south-

[32] Posamentir and Sayar, "Anazarbos," 343–44, fig. 31.

[33] Posamentir, "Säulenstrasse," 1019, fig. 19.

[34] Deichmann, "Spolien" (supra n. 23), 34–35; Hellenkemper, 198–201.

[35] Hild and Hellenkemper, *Kilikien und Isaurien*, 169, figs. 45–48; Mietke, "Apostelkirche" (supra n. 22), 237.

[36] Gough, "Anazarbus," 108, 137 no. 14; Hild and Hellenkemper, *Kilikien und Isaurien*, 182; Sayar, *Inschriften*, 53, no. 62, pl. 23.

[37] Posamentir and Sayar, "Anazarbos," 336–37, fig. 21.

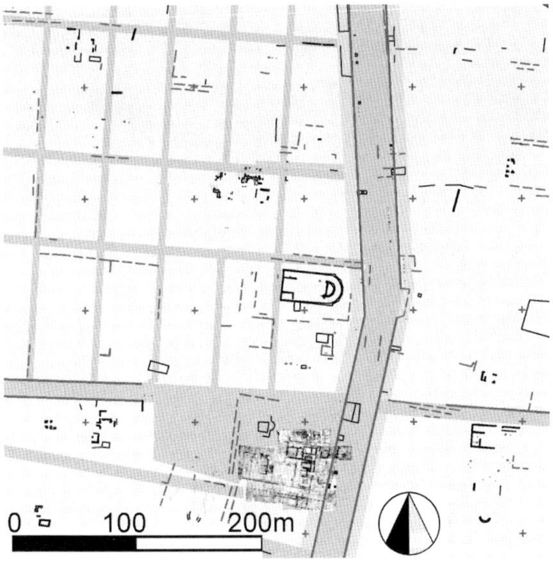

Fig. 12a. Schematic and tentative reconstruction of Roman imperial grid plan within the city center (based on remote sensing and surface survey), showing the correspondence of the Church of the Apostles with the former insula system (R. Posamentir).

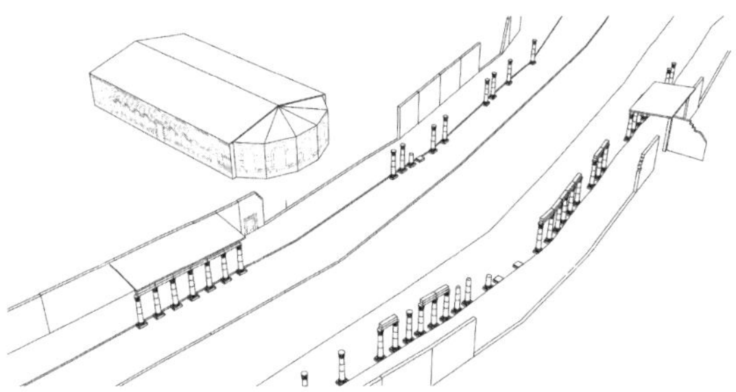

Fig. 12b. Schematic reconstruction showing the spatial relationship between the colonnaded street and the Church of the Apostles (I. Engelmann).

central part of the city. Building techniques, the reuse of certain architectural elements, and the various crosses again suggest a date around A.D. 500. With its five passages, the building clearly responds to the composition of the colonnaded street.[38] At that time and at least in this area, the main axis of the city obviously still existed in its original layout. Not far from this point a well-known phenomenon can be observed, which might in fact be contemporary (or slightly later), namely the inclusion of the other triumphal arch into the large fortification system; since the three entrances of the arch did not exactly conform to the requirements of a functioning and successful defense system, the two side passages were blocked. It is tempting to assume that the reduction of the width of the colonnaded street by the construction of taberna-like installations, right next to the arch and consisting of shabby cross walls, was also undertaken at this time.[39]

Nevertheless, all of these structures seem to indicate that the organization of the city was still very much like that of the Roman imperial period, and that the fundamental urban transformation did not take place before the sixth century. Closely connected with late Roman developments are—as already mentioned and beyond any doubt—the fortification walls, which seemingly have no earlier predecessors.[40] The first circuit ("D" on fig. 2; in the south part underneath "F"), here described briefly, embraced almost the entire Roman city and was almost wholly erased, like so many other buildings of the city. The blocks in the still extant parts originally belonged in all identifiable cases to pagan sanctuaries, some of which can even be identified.[41] A Theodosian dating, already proposed by Friedrich Hild and Hansgerd Hellenkemper,[42] would go well together with the promotion of Anazarbos to the metropolis of the province Cilicia Secunda and, furthermore, would match sources of this time concerning the looting and reuse of pagan sanctuaries perfectly.[43] Since

[38] Williams, "Development" (supra n. 18), 178–79; Posamentir, "Säulenstrasse," 1016–17, figs. 8–13.

[39] Posamentir, "Säulenstrasse," 1015, fig. 3.

[40] Posamentir, "Innovation," 93–94, fig. 4.

[41] Posamentir and Sayar, "Anazarbos," 343–45, figs. 31–33.

[42] Hild and Hellenkemper, *Kilikien und Isaurien*, 181–82, fig. 69.

[43] H.-R. Meier, "Alte Tempel—neue Kulte. Zum Schutz obsoleter Sakralbauten in der Spätantike und zur Adaption alter Bauten an den christlichen Kult," in B. Brenk (ed.), *Inno-*

the remarkable differences between orthogonal grid and chaotic confusion can both be detected within this very circle, the walls of the first fortification ring are obviously not relevant for our question. It is only interesting to point out that certain walls on top of the rock overlooking the city obviously correspond with this ring wall in the plain, as is not surprising ("E" on fig. 2).

The second circuit wall ("F" on fig. 2), on the other hand, merits close examination.[44] This wall consists of three different elements (fig. 13): a fortified ditch, a forewall, and a main wall. The last exhibits in its construction a division between huge limestone blocks in the lower courses, and smaller, softer, and lighter stones in the upper courses; the forewall and ditch wall are built entirely of the aforementioned large and heavy limestone blocks. A brief glance at these blocks reveals that nearly the entire Roman imperial city and its building materials have been pillaged in order to erect the second ring wall. As we have already seen, clear differences between the city structure inside and outside these walls were revealed by remote sensing; this means that the construction of the walls and the transformation of the city can be seen as related, and indeed, as different aspects of a single process.

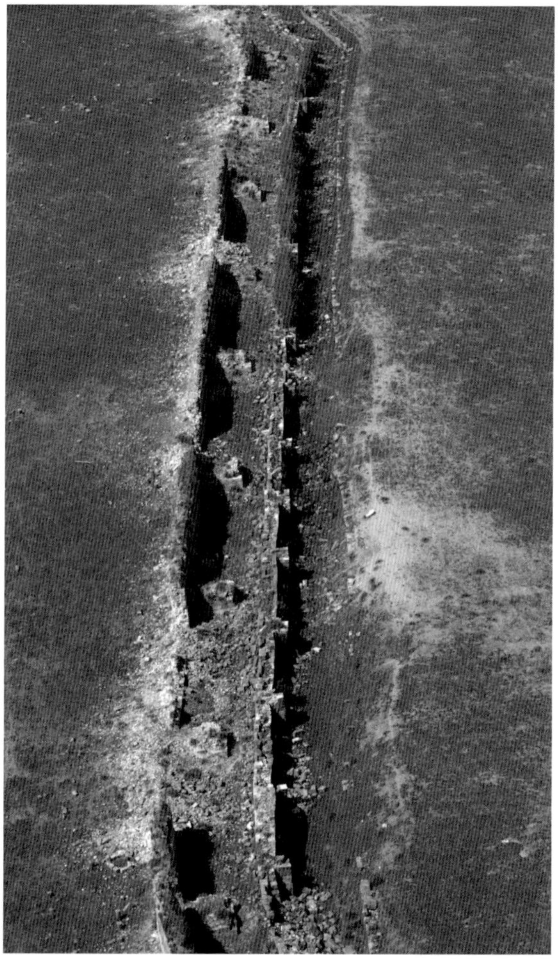

Fig. 13. View from the rock of Anazarbos of the northern section of the tripartite circuit wall with its main wall (with demolished towers), its forewall, and a fortified ditch, from the east (R. Posamentir).

A smooth transition from order to chaos between the sixth and eighth centuries, initiated by the same people who had previously inhabited the city and simply because of altered circumstances, does not seem very likely. Under what circumstances, then, is such a process imaginable? It is possible that the orthogonal street system of the Roman city disappeared so completely in the city center, simply because there were actually no structures left to indicate it. And there were possibly no structures left, because all of the earlier building materials had been used to construct the walls. Moreover, these walls could have been built—and the structures that provided the necessary building materials demolished—without any resistance by the city's inhabitants, because the city had already been severely damaged by a catastrophe—either natural or manmade. Here especially the earthquakes of the sixth century come to mind, as well as the Arab threat and eventual conquest of around A.D. 800.

---

vation in der Spätantike (Wiesbaden 1996) 361–76, esp. 368; K.L. Noethlichs, "Baurecht und Religionspolitik: Vorchristlicher und christlicher Städtebau der römischen Kaiserzeit im Lichte weltlicher und kirchlicher Rechtsvorschriften," in G. Brands and H.-G. Severin (eds.), *Die spätantike Stadt und ihre Christianisierung* (Wiesbaden 2003) 179–97, esp. 191.

[44] Posamentir, "Innovation," 96–103, figs. 6–14d.

Still other explanations are also plausible: the process of "deurbanizing" an existing city could be due to a radical change that was ultimately caused by intruders; in this case it would be the Arabs overrunning Anazarbos in ca. A.D. 800. The process of demolition might be attributed to the need for different structures built according to different settlement traditions. Again, the clue for this problem seems to lie within the walls, in particular whether they were erected by the Byzantines or by the Arabs. In order to find answers to these questions, an extensive survey of these walls was carried out in the season of 2007, with several goals in mind.

First, the stones reused in these walls might not only offer information concerning the date of the fortification systems, but might also enable us to understand more about the development of the city itself. A statistical approach after accurate documentation of all datable stones should tell us about periods of extensive building activity in contrast to times without any or only restricted architectural output. Preliminary results suggest that the latest spolia used for building the walls can be dated to the sixth century.

Second, and equally important, we pursued the question as to which classes of architectural elements had actually been used to erect the walls and whether all types of buildings from both inside and outside the walls had been included, or whether certain building types had been spared. In this connection, the state of preservation of at least two huge church complexes and one Christian gateway within the enclosed area seems significant, especially since no other stone buildings except these three within the city proper seem to have been spared, whereas the material obtained from at least two churches on the outside obviously were used for the walls.

Apart from new evidence gathered from the survey of the walls, it should also be mentioned that two theories concerning the dating and origin of the walls have already been proposed. They will be briefly presented here, in order to provide a background for a better understanding of this process. One theory was presented by Michael Gough, who carried out two field surveys in Anazarbos in the middle of the 20th century. In his reports he expressed the opinion that a first phase (the lower levels of these walls) should be interpreted as Byzantine, while a second phase, represented by the upper section of the main walls, probably should be ascribed to the Armenian occupation, which extended from the 12th to the 14th century.[45] In Gough's view, the similarity between the upper levels of the walls and the stonework of the Armenian fortification systems on top of the overlooking rock would justify such an assumption. Furthermore, the staircases leading up to the wall-walks would also appear to be very similar to those of the upper fortifications.

Arguments against Gough's interpretation can easily be raised. Staircases of this type are similar in construction in all epochs for technical reasons.[46] The walls on top of the rock are in fact completely different in both building material and technique: a different kind of stone was used in a different way by the Armenian architects. Armenian occupation was—as shown by the results of an extensive pottery survey—in any case limited to the settlement on top of the hills during the 12th through 14th centuries.

In a brief paper published in a conference volume in 1988, Hellenkemper (agreeing with Gough on the existence of two phases of construction) proposed that the walls of Anazarbos should be dated to the ninth and 10th centuries respectively, both phases falling in the period of Arab occupation.[47] His main pieces of evidence were two inscriptions (lost today) recording enormous sums of money spent by Mutawakkil and finally Saifaddaula for the renovation, and eventually even the new erection, of the walls

[45] Gough, "Anazarbus," 103–4.

[46] Posamentir, "Innovation," 95–98, fig. 9.

[47] Hellenkemper, "Stadtmauern," 71–76.

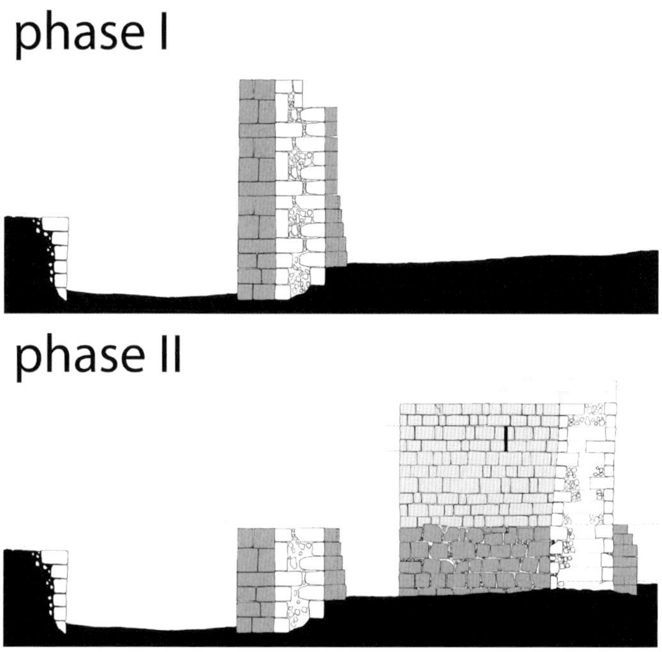

Fig. 14. Reconstructed cross-section of the two (Arab) construction phases of the tripartite circuit wall according to H. Hellenkemper (I. Engelmann).

of Anazarbos.[48] Hellenkemper views as additional proof the horseshoe-like shape of the gates, ornaments such as the twisted fillets (both being decisive for the dating of the upper levels only), and some signs painted on a few blocks, possibly Kufic mason marks.[49] According to Hellenkemper, a first enclosing wall consisting of only a ditch and a rather thin wall with retaining pillars serving as towers was built in the ninth century, while in the 10th century this wall was partly demolished in order to construct the lower levels of the main wall with the stone material previously used for the upper levels of the forewall (fig. 14).

Arguments against Hellenkemper's theory can also easily be found. The gates of the main walls correspond with the old street system, while the slightly displaced gates of the forewall do not, which would mean that architects would have neglected existing traffic ties in the ninth century, but would have returned to them some generations later, which seems unlikely.[50] The displaced gates of the forewall, on the other hand, are more common than one might suppose; they can be seen in late antique fortification systems, for example, such as those in Dara, Martyropolis, and Antiocheia ad Orontes.

In addition, the southern part of the main wall is built almost entirely of stone seats from the nearby theater.[51] If the forewall had been erected first, either the theater seats would have remained unused in the ninth century, and then in the 10th century been transported across the fortification ditch, or, alternatively, they would have first formed the upper part of the forewall, which seems unlikely in view of static considerations.

Several inscriptions mentioning repair and building activities in the sixth century are also at hand, and do not seem to belong to the first circuit wall.[52] Moreover, horseshoe-shaped gates can no longer be viewed only as a characteristic feature of Arab building techniques; they are just as possible in Byzantine times, and the same holds true for the twisted fillets.[53] Last but not least, the retaining pillars seem far too small to have served as towers.

[48] Hild and Hellenkemper, *Kilikien und Isaurien*, 180, 183.

[49] Hellenkemper, "Stadtmauern," 76 pl. 12.

[50] Posamentir, "Innovation," 97–100, fig. 11.

[51] Posamentir and Sayar, "Anazarbos," 346–47, figs. 34–35.

[52] Hild and Hellenkemper, *Kilikien und Isaurien*, 179–83; M.H. Sayar, "Mauererneuerungsinschriften aus Anazarbos," *Epigraphica Anatolica* 29 (1997) 111–15; Sayar, *Inschriften*, 32–34.

[53] Posamentir, "Innovation," 102–3, fig. 14b–d; cf. A. Arbeiter, "Die Anfänge der Quaderarchitektur im westgotenzeitlichen Hispanien," in B. Brenk (ed.), *Innovation in der Spätantike* (Wiesbaden 1996) 11–51, at 34 pls. 5–7; C. Strube, *Baudekoration im nordsyrischen Kalksteinmassiv, Bd. 2: Das 6. und frühe 7. Jahrhundert, Damaszener Forschungen* 11 (Mainz 2002) pl. 79c, for horseshoe-shaped arcs; ibid., pls. 16b, 43c, 45c–d, for the twisted fillets of Byzantine origin.

Fig. 15. Photograph of the northern section of the tripartite circuit wall taken by Gertrude Bell in 1905, from the west (G. Bell, with kind permission of the Gertrude Bell Archives/M.P.C. Jackson, Newcastle upon Tyne).

Since it is obvious that the dating of these walls yields significant information for the development—in this case the shrinking or, more positively judged, the concentration—of the city, some new arguments that seem to favor a Byzantine dating of at least the first phase (which means the lower levels of the main wall, the forewall, and the fortified ditch) should be considered. After all, it should be stated that these walls are unique in many aspects—regardless of whether they belong to the Byzantine, Arab, or Armenian era—and they would be even more outstanding today, if Turkish farmers had not reduced large parts of the upper levels (second phase) within the last 100 years (fig. 15).[54]

First of all, the similarities of the layout to the Theodosian land walls of Constantinople are striking.[55] Both consist of three elements: a main wall, a forewall, and a fortified ditch in rather close proximity to each other, even though we do not know exactly what the first layout of the Theodosian walls with forewall and fortified ditch actually looked like.[56] Both display rectangular towers (this concerns only certain sections of the walls in Constantinople; there are 80 towers in Anazarbos and 96 towers in Constantinople) at remarkably short distances from each other and small rectangular retaining pillars in the walls of the ditch, referring rhythmically to each other. The main difference lies in the fact that in Anazarbos, the forewall also serves as one of the walls of the ditch; in this way

[54] Posamentir, "Innovation," 96–97, figs. 6–7. The photographs of 1905 were taken by Gertrude Bell; the author is extremely thankful to J. Crow and M.P.C. Jackson, Newcastle upon Tyne, for granting access to the Gertrude Bell archive and for permission to publish selected images in this contribution.

[55] Meyer-Plath and Schneider, *Landmauer* (supra n. 21), 21–22, pls. 1–3; W. Müller-Wiener, *Bildlexikon zur Topographie Istanbuls* (Tübingen 1977) 290–91; Posamentir, "Innovation," 98–102, figs. 10–14a.

[56] Meyer-Plath and Schneider, *Landmauer* (supra n. 21), 16–26.

Fig. 16. View of the southernmost section of the fortified area on top of the mountain range with Byzantine (left) and Armenian (right) walls in the foreground and the Armenian Donjon in the background (R. Posamentir).

Fig. 17. View of one of the Armenian half round towers, built over a rectangular Byzantine tower that formed part of a gate, from the east (R. Posamentir).

the whole ensemble gives the impression that it was a compressed variation of its Constantinopolitan forerunner.

The logical continuation of the wall on top of the rock overlooking the city seems at first glance to be completely different (fig. 16; "H" on fig. 2). However, detailed mapping in the 2007 season showed that the typically Armenian semicircular towers are superimposed not only upon a typical Byzantine gate (fig. 17; "I" on fig. 2),[57] but also upon a number of rectangular towers spaced at the usual interval. Used in their lower parts as cisterns, they offer an explanation for the fact that the entrances to the Armenian towers are situated at a surprising height.

[57] Already mentioned by Gough, "Anazarbus," 119.

In addition, as already mentioned, of all the stone structures in the city proper, only the two churches have been spared, as well as the Christian arch. Also, the pottery found in the area outside the walls is not later in date than the sixth century, whereas continuous occupation inside the wall until the 12th century is clearly attested.[58] There are also no architectural elements later than the sixth century reused within the walls.[59]

Procopius criticizes the emperor Justinian for tearing down theaters in order to erect other buildings,[60] and this occurred in Anazarbos and many other cities of Asia Minor.[61] According to literary sources, the city was rebuilt after the earthquakes of the sixth century during Justinian's rule and renamed Justinianupolis.[62]

A block with a projecting cross, which had been part of the wall in a now collapsed section, was found in 2007 (fig. 18).[63] The surfaces of the other faces of the block are smeared with mortar and prove that the cross had once been visible.

Cities such as Antioch (but probably many others in the region as well) seem to tell a very similar story, with a Theodosian (?) wall and a second and stronger wall with forewall and ditch (not in all areas), possibly erected during the reign of Justinian.[64] The latter also reduces the city's area, while, on the other hand, no comparable walls of Arab times are at hand within the whole area.[65] Walls of definite Byzantine origin such as the ones in Martyropolis, Melitene, Dara-Anastasiupolis, Amida, or Side are, moreover, at least similar in their general layout (partly their usage of spolia) and appearance.[66]

[58] According to Prof. Dr. A. DiGiorgi, Case Western Reserve University of Cleveland, Ohio, who has agreed to publish the pottery of the Anazarbos survey. A certain amount of coarseware of a later date seems to indicate a rural utilization of the area.

[59] According to C. Nowak (Rome), who has agreed to publish the architectural elements of Anazarbos.

[60] Procopius, *Anecdota* 26, 5–9. For the integration of antique gateways into Justinian fortification systems cf. for example the case of Palmyra; O. Puchstein, "Grundplan der Stadt Palmyra. Straßen und Plätze, Basilica und Wohnbauten," in T. Wiegand (ed.), *Palmyra. Ergebnisse der Expeditionen von 1902 und 1917* (Berlin 1932) 17–35, at 29–31, figs. 30–31.

[61] Cf. for example the late antique walls of Blaundos in Phrygia: A. Filges, "Die Stadtmauer: Mauerring und Türme," in idem (ed.), *Blaundos. Berichte zur Erforschung einer Kleinstadt im lydisch-phrygischen Grenzgebiet, IstForsch* 48 (Tübingen 2006) 67–78, at 70; 78, fig. 55. This phenomenon is certainly to be found in late antiquity in other parts of the ancient world as well; cf. A. Oepen, "Die Nutzung kaiserzeitlicher Theaterbauten in Hispanien während der Spätantike und der Westgotenzeit," in G. Brands and H.-G. Severin (eds.), *Die spätantike Stadt und ihre Christianisierung* (Wiesbaden 2003) 199–217; P. Pinon, "Approche typologique des modes de réutilisationdes amphithéâtres de la fin de l'Antiquité au XIXe siècle," in C. Domergue, C. Landes, and J.-M. Pailler (eds.), *Spectacula I, Gladiateurs et amphithéâtres* (1990) 103–13.

[62] Hild and Hellenkemper, *Kilikien und Isaurien*, 179; Sayar, *Inschriften*, 12–13. For the role of Justinian in comparable processes, see e.g., Oepen, "Theaterbauten," (supra n. 61), 200.

[63] The block was found by architect C. Brasse on the occasion of a short survey in order to compare the walls of Anazarbos to those of Antioch. C. Brasse is in the process of writing a Ph.D. thesis on the walls of Antioch.

[64] The walls of Antioch are in the process of reinvestigation by architect C. Brasse to whom I owe much valuable information; see C. Brasse, "Von der Stadtmauer zur Stadtgeschichte. Das Befestigungssystem von Antiochia am Orontes," in J. Lorentzen, F. Pirson, P.I. Schneider, and U. Wulf-Rheidt (eds.), *Aktuelle Forschungen zur Konstruktion, Funktion und Semantik antiker Stadtbefestigungen, Byzas* 10 (Istanbul 2010) 261–82. Cf. as well T.A. Sinclair, *Eastern Turkey: An Architectural and Archaeological Survey*, 4 vols. (London 1987–1990) 4.242–48. For Justinian's policy concerning the fortification of the east, see Cameron, *Mediterranean World* (supra n. 1), 104–13, 118–20, and Brenk, "Christianisierung" (supra n. 1), 85–95.

[65] This holds true for sites such as Tarsus and Misis as well, where huge Arab fortification systems have been postulated; see Hellenkemper, 72–73.

[66] Side: Foss, "Cities," 43–45, fig. 6; Melitene: Sinclair, *Eastern Turkey* (supra n. 64), 3.3–4, 8–10; Diyarbakır: ibid., 3.164–76; esp. 170; Martyropolis: ibid., 3.287–89 (with displaced gates of the forewalls!); Dara: ibid., 3.219–21.

Fig. 18. Inner face of the northwestern section of the circuit wall (main wall) with collapsed curtain wall and associated block featuring a projecting cross, from the south (R. Posamentir).

Finally it must be stressed that the framing fillets and profiles of the gates resemble those of the Church of the Apostles[67]—and related to this observation it must be stated that the use of earlier blocks for decorative purposes, as in the Church of the Apostles, can be detected in various places along the walls and especially close to the gates (fig. 19). This also holds true for an inscription that can (most likely) be attributed to the tetra- or triconch building outside the walls.[68] In the inscription, immediately visible to people entering the city (although not vertically arranged), a round building is mentioned, in which Saint Menas was worshipped. According to the remote sensing, the church had a round encircling wall, which means that the actual building was apparently only a few meters away.

Arguments against a Byzantine dating are in fact few and concern almost exclusively the upper levels or a second phase of the walls. A small amount of pottery originating from the late eighth to 10th centuries from a single section of the north part of the wall was found during the 2007 season. However, this phenomenon could be explained as evidence for a partial repair of the walls. Also, some of the strange reliefs once present but now lost in one of the gateways (fig. 20) do not seem

[67] Posamentir, "Innovation," 102–3, fig. 14b–d; the churches of North Syria often show a similar feature; C. Strube, *Baudekoration im nordsyrischen Kalksteinmassiv* I: *Kapitell-, Tür- und Gesimsformen der Kirchen des 4. und 5. Jahrhunderts n. Chr.*, *Damaszener Forschungen* 5 (Mainz 1993) pls. 38a–b, 45a, 116a–d; idem, *Baudekoration* (supra n. 53), pl. 78d.

[68] Sayar, *Inschriften*, 50 no. 58 pl. 24.

Fig. 19. Photograph of a tendriled frieze block reused in one of the towers of the northern gate of the tripartite circuit wall (main wall) taken by Gertrude Bell in 1905, from the west (G. Bell, with kind permission of the Gertrude Bell Archives/M.P.C. Jackson, Newcastle upon Tyne).

Fig. 20. Photograph of a panel of ornamental decoration carved on one of the towers of the southwestern (?) gate of the tripartite circuit wall (main wall) taken by Gertrude Bell in 1905, from the west (G. Bell, with kind permission of the Gertrude Bell Archives/M.P.C. Jackson, Newcastle upon Tyne).

to fit an early date, but they too could have been added later.[69] This does not hold true for several projecting *tabulae ansatae*, but these do not seem to be of Arab craftsmanship and are most likely spolia. Finally, the existence of oriels in at least one place is truly odd, but even such elements do have parallels in at least seventh-century monastery architecture in Syria.

Taking all of this information together, the preponderance of the evidence seems to favor a Byzantine or even a sixth-century date for at least the lower levels of the second circuit wall. If this interpretation is correct, then the organization and appearance of the Roman imperial city may have remained in many respects unchanged until the fifth century before the destructive earthquakes (or the constantly rising Arab threat), which should be held responsible for the reorganization and the dissolution of the once regular urban structure.[70]

At this time, the streets would have been filled with building materials, ready and available for use in the construction of new and massive fortifications (in combination with a concentration of the city proper). Interestingly, there were no efforts made to return to a regular grid system. Therefore, a natural catastrophe might have been the accelerating and decisive turning point in a slow process of decline, which in any case was ongoing and inevitable. Before this turning point, people in the east were obviously still very close to and conscious of their past—probably even more so than in the west.

[69] The author is again extremely thankful to J. Crow and M.P.C. Jackson, Newcastle upon Tyne, for granting access to the Gertrude Bell archive and for permission to publish selected images in this contribution. The originally Byzantine city walls of Martyropolis show a similar phenomenon, but also underwent substantial renovation and repair work in later times; cf. Sinclair, *Eastern Turkey* (supra n. 64), 3.289.

[70] Comparable processes of urban transformation in the sixth or seventh centuries can probably be seen in Anemurium in Asia Minor or in Apamea in Syria; see Foss, "Cities," 45.

However, Anazarbos obviously suffered the same fate as, for instance, Side, and there too no reliable sources are available to date major construction works such as the Byzantine city walls.[71] Especially remarkable are the similarities between the towers of these walls and those of Anazarbos; wall-walks built against the inner face of the wall, inner chambers with arrow slits, and the innumerable quantity of spolia are immediately comparable. The second circuit wall of Side seems also to have been built after a serious disaster that made such a radical change possible or at least much easier.

Clive Foss dated the second circuit walls of Side to the mid-seventh century and also saw a connection between the process of demolishing and transforming the urban organization and the erection of the walls.[72] However, his date is based solely on inference, and one might ask whether it is not more likely that the construction of the walls—and accordingly the reduction of the city—were steps taken in advance, before the Arab threat became more than just a threat. There is an undeniable similarity between the two processes in these two different cities, since in Anazarbos, too, late antiquity was obviously a prosperous time, followed by a "dark age catastrophe and very limited Byzantine recovery."[73] At least all identifiable bodies of evidence, such as architecture, pottery, and sculpture, seem to point in this direction. Nevertheless, one should certainly be cautious when offering a generalizing statement: every city has its own history.

[71] Ibid., 43–45, fig. 6.

[72] Ibid., 43.

[73] Ibid., 50.

13 Some Aspects of the Development of Osrhoene in Late Antiquity

Peter Baumeister

The following contribution turns the spotlight on the eastern part of Asia Minor, especially the northern area of the ancient territory of Osrhoene, in the hope that a view to the east will be helpful in the context of a volume devoted largely to the archaeology and the cities of the west. Since Osrhoene has always been a borderland between the Hellenistic and Roman sphere of influence, on the one hand, and the Persian and Sassanian kingdoms as well as the Arab empires, on the other, its intercultural contacts with its eastern neighbors were much more intensive than in other parts of Asia Minor. The importance of Osrhoene as a borderland was not limited to the sphere of political interaction. In addition, Osrhoene was a contact zone where socioeconomic, religious, and philosophical developments emanating from both east and west were focused, and thus a place from which new trends emerged.

The importance of Osrhoene as a dynamic borderland has not been adequately recognized, however, for a number of reasons, among them the modern political situation, especially in the latter half of the 20th century. This paper attempts to begin to redress this deficit, by giving a short overview of a current research project in the northern part of the region.[1]

The Ancient Landscape of Osrhoene—A Brief Introduction

The ancient landscape of Osrhoene is located between the Euphrates and the Habur rivers, today the borderland between modern Turkey and Syria.[2] The origin of the name of this region is uncertain; its etymological roots have been discussed by several scholars, but no consensus has been reached.[3]

[1] The following abbreviations will be used in this paper:
Baumeister et al., "Keloşk Kale" = P. Baumeister, D. Roos, and T. Saner, "Die Keloşk Kale. Ein spätantiker Gebäudekomplex im türkischen Euphratbogen. Studien zu Osrhoene in der Spätantike I," *IstMitt* 57 (2007) 623–74.
Segal, *Edessa* = J.B. Segal, *Edessa. The Blessed City* (Oxford 1970).

This project is a cooperative undertaking of the German Archaeological Institute Berlin, the Institute for Architectural History, Technical University of Karlsruhe, and the İstanbul Teknik Üniversitesi. The cooperating partners are Dr.-Ing. Dorothea Roos and Prof. Dr. Turgut Saner. The project is supported generously by the Fritz Thyssen Foundation.

[2] For Osrhoene in general, see A. von Gutschmid, *Untersuchungen über die Geschichte des Königreichs Osroëne*, *Mémoires de l'Académie impériale des sciences de St.-Pétersbourg, VIIe Série* 35.1 (1887); O. Krückmann, *RE* XVIII 1 (1942) 1589–90 s. v. Osroene; K. Kessler, *Der Neue Pauly* 9 (2000) 88 s. v. Osroene; see also J. Wagner, "Provincia Osrhoenae. New archaeological finds illustrating the military organization under the Severan Dynasty," in S. Mitchell (ed.), *Armies and Frontiers in Roman and Byzantine Anatolia*, *BAR-IS* 156 (Oxford 1983) 103–29, and cf. M.G. Angeli Bertinelli, "I Romani oltre l'Eufrate nel II secolo d. C. (le province di Assiria, di Mesopotamia e di Osroene)," *ANRW* II 9.1 (1976) 3–45, at 17–22, 39–41.

[3] See in general Krückmann, "Osroene" (supra n. 2); Kessler, "Osroene" (supra n. 2); for "Orhay/Orhai" see also J. Marquart, cited in E. Hertzfeld, "Hatra," *ZDMG* 68 (1914) 665–66; E. Kirsten, "Edessa, eine römische Grenzstadt des 4. bis 6. Jahrhunderts im Orient," *JAC* 6 (1963) 144–72, at 149; Segal, *Edessa*, 2; H.J.W. Drijvers, "Hatra, Palmyra und Edessa. Die Städte der syrisch-mesopotamischen Wüste in politischer, kulturgeschichtlicher und religionsgeschichtlicher Bedeutung," *ANRW* II 8 (1977) 799–906, at 866; A. Harrack, "The ancient name of Edessa," *JNES* 51 (1992)

The major political and economic center of northern Osrhoene was Edessa, modern Şanlıurfa.[4] According to the literary sources, the kingdom of Osrhoene was established in the year 131/130 B.C. after the defeat of Antiochos Sidetes by the Parthian Empire. When Antiochos was forced to pull his troops back behind the Euphrates, a local king named Aryu is said to have formed an independent principality near his capital Edessa.[5] Thanks to numismatic evidence and comparatively rich historical sources, we have a complete list of the kings of Edessa.[6] Among the early members of this dynasty were some who were involved in events of world-historical importance. One such was Abgar II, who was responsible for the disastrous defeat of the Roman general Crassus by the Parthians in which the Roman insignia were lost.[7]

A major development of the second century was the establishment of the *Provincia Mesopotamiae* by the emperor Trajan, but even then the kingdom of Osrhoene was still able to benefit from the ongoing conflicts between the great powers, and to maintain at least a degree of independence between the Roman and the Parthian spheres of influence. Caracalla and especially Gordian III brought this tradition to an end. In A.D. 242 the last king of Edessa was forced to withdraw from the throne.[8]

Turning now to the northern part of Osrhoene, the main focus of this article, the *Chronicles* of Edessa and several other literary sources give us a sense of the historical development of the region over the following centuries, at least in Edessa and its vicinity. More than anything else, repeated conflicts with Rome's eastern neighbors—first the wars against Persia, later the Arab conquest—determined the historical development of Osrhoene, although the regions in the vicinity of the Euphrates lay behind the frontier line, especially in the conflicts with Persia.[9] Nevertheless, before Edessa was finally conquered by the Arabs in A.D. 638, the Persian kings threatened northern Osrhoene more than three times, especially in A.D. 363 after the defeat of Julian, but also in A.D. 544, and particularly in A.D. 609, when Chosraw II managed to conquer Edessa and to keep it for a few years.[10]

The history of northern Osrhoene was also influenced by internal religious conflicts. It is not possible to give a short summary of these events, but it is important to state that these conflicts sometimes nearly reached the status of a civil war, and that the different religious disputes frequently ended in persecutions and martyrdom.

Admittedly, most of our knowledge about early Edessa is derived from the so-called *Chronicles* of Edessa or from the work of Christian historians such as Eusebius.[11] These sources are dated

---

209–14; S.K. Ross, *Roman Edessa. Politics and Culture on the Eastern Fringes of the Roman Empire, 114–242 CE* (London and New York 2001) 5.

[4] For Edessa in general, see Kirsten, "Edessa" (supra n. 3); A.F. Klijn, *Edessa, die Stadt des Apostels Thomas. Das älteste Christentum in Syrien* (Neunkirchen-Vluyn 1965); Segal, *Edessa*; Drijvers, "Hatra, Palmyra und Edessa" (supra n. 3), 863–85; Ross, *Roman Edessa* (supra n. 3); cf. also R. Duval, *Histoire d'Édesse, politique, religieuse et littéraire* (Paris 1892, reprint Amsterdam 1975).

[5] For the early chronology, see in general Gutschmid, "Königreich Osroëne" (supra n. 2); A.R. Bellinger and C.B. Welles, "A third-century contract of sale from Edessa in Osrhoene," *YCS* 5 (1935) 93–154, at 142–54; Drijvers, "Hatra, Palmyra und Edessa" (supra n. 3), 867.

[6] See Gutschmid, "Königreich Osroëne" (supra n. 2); for the later discussions, see the literature cited infra n. 8; cf. also E. Babelon, *Numismatique d'Édesse en Mésopotamie, Mélanges Numismatiques, 2-éme série* (Paris 1893) 209–96; G.F. Hill, *Catalogue of the Greek Coins of Arabia, Mesopotamia and Persia* (London 1922) xciv–cvii, 91–118, pls. III–VIII.

[7] Plutarch, *Crassus* 21–22; Cassius Dio 40.20–23; see also Drijvers, "Hatra, Palmyra und Edessa" (supra n. 3), 871.

[8] See in general Segal, *Edessa*, 14–15; Drijvers, "Hatra, Palmyra und Edessa" (supra n. 3), 878–79; see also M. Gawlikowski, "The last kings of Edessa," in R. Lavenant (ed.), *VII. Symposium Syriacum, Orientalia Christiana Analecta* 256 (Rome 1998) 421–28; S.K. Ross, "The last king of Edessa: New evidence from the Middle Euphrates," *ZPE* 97 (2003) 187–206.

[9] See below, nn. 51–52.

[10] See in general Segal, *Edessa*, 74, 77, 112.

[11] *Chronicon Edessenum*, in I. Guidi (ed.), *Chronica Minora*, vol. 1, *Corpus Scriptorum Christianorum Orientalium* 1, 2 (Paris 1903) 1–13; other important sources are: *Doctrina Addai*, in G. Phillips (ed.), *The Doctrine of Addai, the Apostle*

to the fourth or sixth century, and are of uncertain reliability for events in the first, second, and third centuries. That the religious conversion of this part of northern Mesopotamia happened at an early date[12] is therefore an assumption—still to be proven by modern historical or archaeological research.

Edessa itself claimed to have played an important role in early Christianity. This self-professed reputation is based on legends of the third or fourth century: the correspondence between Abgar II and Jesus Christ, and the conversion of Abgar the Great to Christianity in the second or early third century.[13]

Looking at the archaeological remains and modern research, it must be admitted that the material evidence for the late antique and early Christian periods as currently known does not give the same impression as the literary sources. Especially in Edessa, the former capital of the kingdom of Osrhoene and in late antiquity still a major center in northern Mesopotamia, there are only few traces of early Christian architecture left. We do not have any substantial knowledge of the churches and buildings that we know of from the literary sources and that must have been famous throughout a major part of the Mediterranean in ancient times.[14] From the *Chronicles* of Edessa (for instance) and other sources we learn that a church already existed, probably near the pools in the center of the city, in A.D. 201. And especially in the fourth and sixth centuries the bishops of Edessa erected a great number of churches, martyria, and other public buildings such as infirmaries.

When we shift our focus from the cities to the countryside, it becomes clear that our knowledge of rural Osrhoene in late antiquity is even more deficient. Apart from the reports of 19th- and early 20th-century scholars traveling through this region on their way to Mesopotamia, Osrhoene—especially the northern part—has not been the focus of major archaeological projects.[15] A few single buildings have been the subjects of isolated studies, without regard for their larger contexts. But apart from the major traffic routes between Zeugma, Samosata, and other cities, Osrhoene and other areas have not been investigated consistently. During the preparations for the dam projects of the 1970s, large surveys along the Euphrates and its tributary streams took place, but mainly in the areas to be inundated after the construction of the dams.[16] Despite intensive and careful surveys and investigations, the lack of time did not permit detailed documentation of the sites visited. Due to the mass of material, the publications which resulted give only overviews of the results of fieldwork and catalogue-like presentations of sites. Further detailed research and analysis of recorded data are still lacking.

New Research in the Area of Northern Osrhoene

A new research project can now give some new clues as to the history of the northern part of Osrhoene in late Roman and early Byzantine times. The initial goal of the project to be presented here was

(London 1876); Jacob of Edessa, *Chronicon Iacobi Edesseni*, in E.W. Brooks (ed.), *Chronica Minora*, vol. 3, *Corpus Scriptorum Christianorum Orientalium* 5, 6 (Paris 1905–1907); J.-B. Chabot (ed.), *Chronique de Michel le syrien* (Paris 1899–1905); for the *Chronicle* of Joshua Stylites, see A. Luther, *Die syrische Chronik des Josua Stylites, Untersuchungen zur antiken Literatur und Geschichte* 49 (Berlin and New York 1997); cf. also *Chronicon ad annum Christi 1234 pertinens*, in J.-B. Chabot (ed.), *Corpus Scriptorum Christianorum Orientalium* 81, 82, 109 (Paris 1916–1920); see also Segal, *Edessa*, 20–21.

[12] W. Cureton, *Ancient Syriac Documents Relative to the Earliest Establishment of Christianity in Edessa and the Neighbouring Countries* (London 1864, reprint 1967); L.W. Barnard, "The origins and emergence of the church in Edessa during the first two centuries A.D.," *VigChr* 22 (1968) 161–75.

[13] See in general Klijn, *Edessa* (supra n. 4), 14–20; Segal, *Edessa*, 62–70.

[14] For the archaeological remains in Edessa, see especially Kirsten, "Edessa" (supra n. 3); Segal, *Edessa*.

[15] For the region north of Şanlıurfa, see E. Sachau, *Reise in Syrien und Mesopotamien* (Leipzig 1883) 446–52; the route that Ainsworth took (cf. W.F. Ainsworth, *A Personal Narrative of the Euphrates Expedition* I–II [London 1888]), is recorded in the map of Kiepert (R. Kiepert, *Karte von Kleinasien* [Berlin 1902–1906] CV Malatya).

[16] See infra n. 42.

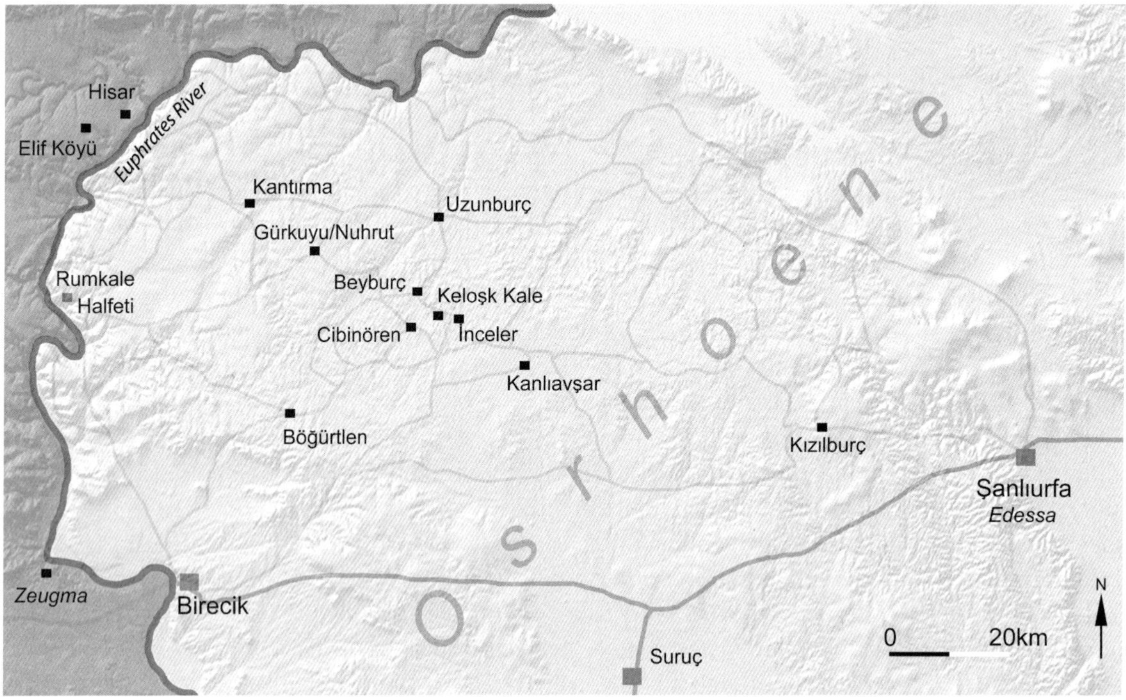

Fig. 1. Map of the northwestern part of Osrhoene.

the archaeological documentation of a single building complex in the area between Şanlıurfa and Birecik, the so-called Keloşk Kale (fig. 1).[17] During the fieldwork for this project we noticed, however, that there were extensive archaeological remains of the late Roman and early Byzantine periods in particular throughout the whole area. The relevant literature showed that none of these remains had previously been noticed or published in any way. This then was the starting point for a more ambitious research program in the northern part of Osrhoene, especially in the area between Şanlıurfa and the Euphrates, north of the modern highway leading eastward from Birecik. The preliminary results of the survey can help to illuminate the development of late antique Osrhoene from a new angle; these results will be presented in the following pages.

The So-Called Keloşk Kale

As mentioned above, a building complex north of the Birecik-Şanlıurfa Highway gave the initial impetus for the new research project. Since the documentation of the so-called Keloşk Kale has recently been published in *Istanbuler Mitteilungen*,[18] only a brief summary of the results will be presented here.

Until recently, this complex was unknown to scholarship, in part because the area is accessible only by rough dirt roads. A team of architects from the İstanbul Teknik Üniversitesi discovered the ruins during a survey of modern Turkish village architecture in this region in 2001. The ruins, situated on a small hilltop, are called "Keloşk Kale" by the local villagers. "Kale" is the Turkish word for "castle" or "fortress"; the word "keloşk" is the Kurdish equivalent. The building complex consists of three units surrounding a small courtyard (fig. 2). Buildings 1 and 2 are in a good condition, but

[17] The final report of the first campaign was published recently; see Baumeister et al., "Keloşk Kale."

[18] For the following summary of the results at Keloşk Kale no specific references will be given here; see instead the detailed discussion in Baumeister et al., "Keloşk Kale"; see also the preliminary report in T. Saner, D. Roos, and P. Baumeister, "Keloşk Kale (Birecik) 2004," *Araştırma Sonuçları Toplantısı* 23.2 (2005) 217–41.

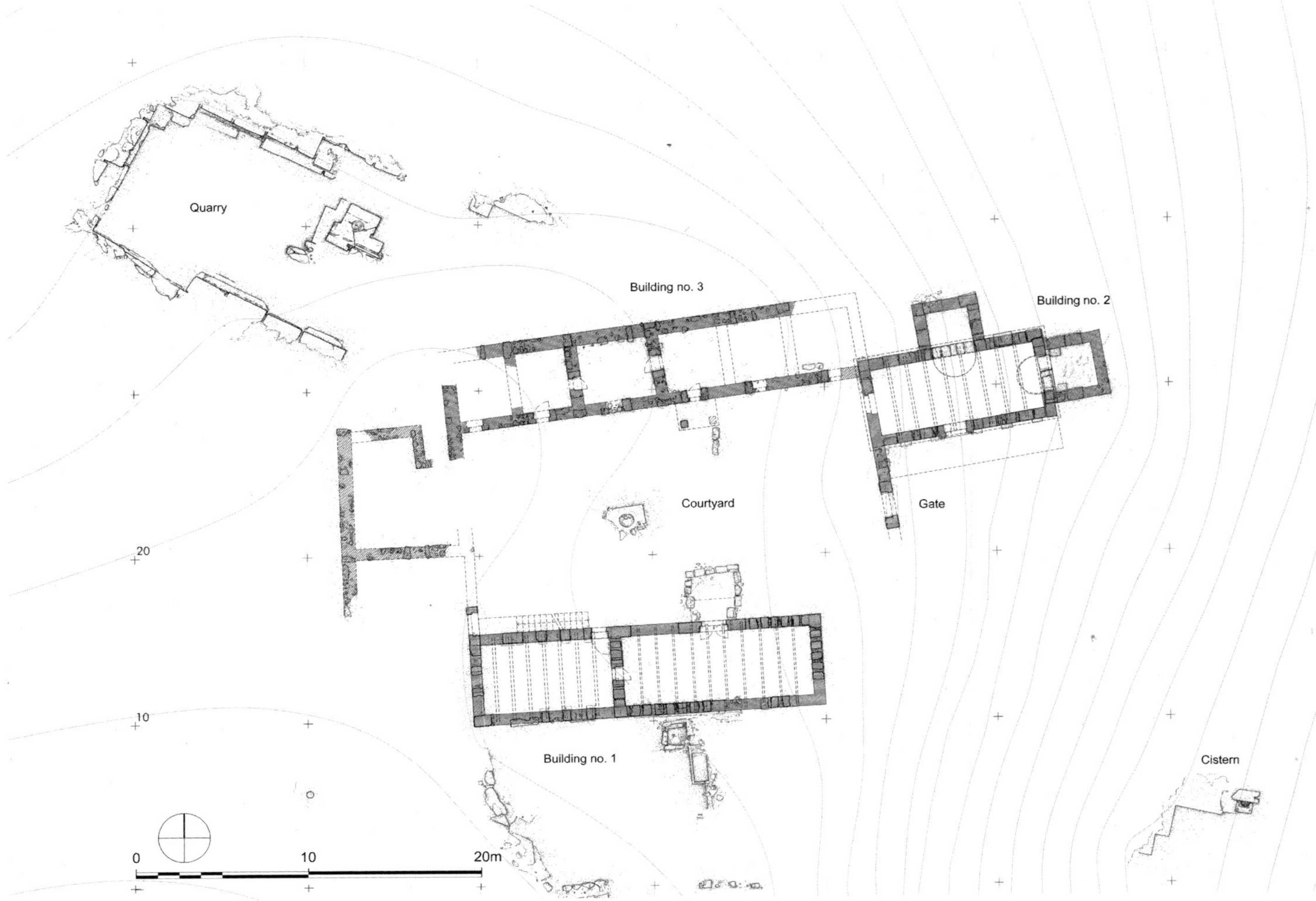

Fig. 2. Ground plan of the so-called Keloşk Kale (scale 1:400).

Fig. 3. Keloşk Kale, Building 1, view from the southwest.

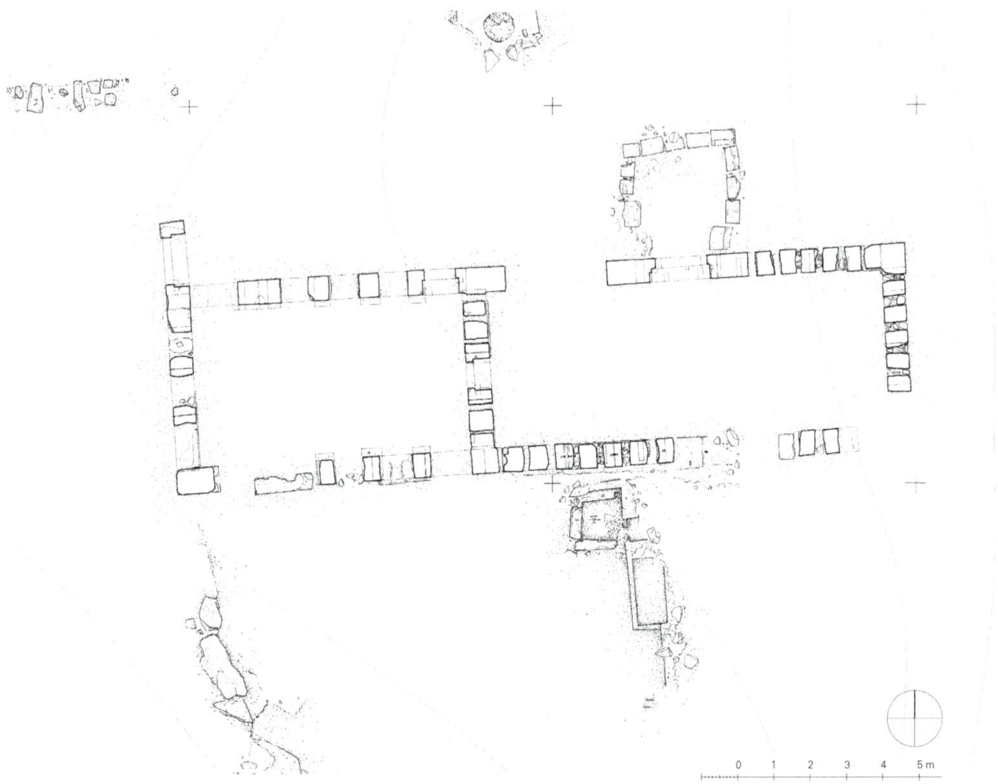

Fig. 4. Keloşk Kale, ground plan of Building 1 (scale 1:200).

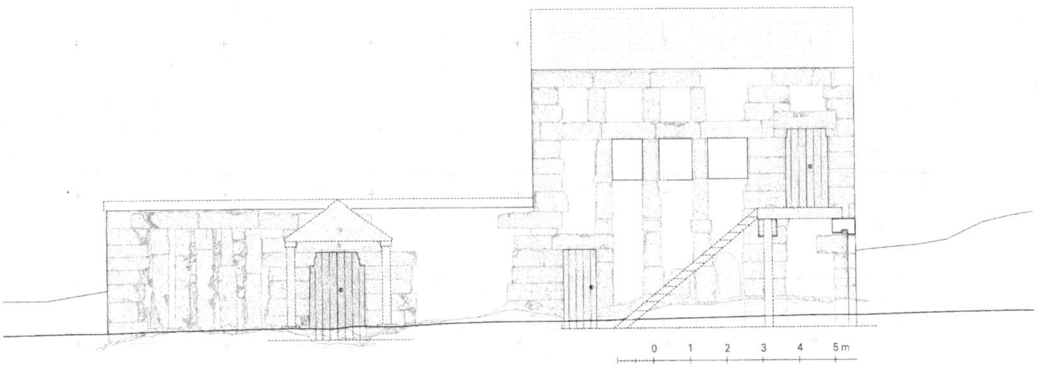

Fig. 5. Keloşk Kale, Building 1 (scale 1:200).

Building 3 has been completely destroyed. The complex was originally enclosed by a circuit wall, portions of which can be seen in the southwest part of the area. There are also two cisterns, a rock-cut tomb, and a gate, which marks the main entrance to the courtyard. In addition, traces are still visible of a road leading to the complex, carved into the surrounding limestone plateau.

Because of its construction technique, Building 1 is the most prominent part of this complex (figs. 3–5). It was built using a stone-beam construction, in which the framing skeleton consists of large stone beams. The panels between the framing elements were probably filled with masonry. The building consists of two parts: a single-story wing to the east, and a two-story wing to the west. As the ground plan shows, the building has three entrances. A double-leafed door provides access to the eastern part; a second entrance is located in the north wall of the west wing, and a small staircase leads to the upper floor.

The construction technique seems very unusual. The east wing consists of closely set vertical stone beams. It is possible but not certain that the small-scale masonry still surviving between the beams is a remnant of the original construction. The horizontal blocks on top of the vertical beams show cuttings for the roof structure.

The western part of the building consists of a framework construction. Almost a dozen windows in the walls of the upper story brought in light and fresh air. The uppermost small rectangular panels once were filled with masonry, but no traces remain.

It is not possible to reconstruct the roof of Building 1 with absolute certainty. One possibility is a reconstruction with a pitched roof over the western part of the building and a flat roof over the eastern one—the latter to provide a place for drying fruits and vegetables, as in modern houses.

Building 2 is not well preserved (figs. 6–8). It consists of a rectangular central room with an additional room to the north and another to the east, both separated from the main room by arches. The ground plan shows two entrances: one from the exterior of the complex, and another from the courtyard. The southern doorframe bears traces of a decorative molding that is important for dating the structure.

In the north and south walls there are traces of windows. In the roof zone of the eastern wall, a single block of the pediment remains. This suggests a pitched roof with at least one window in the center of the pediment. The reconstruction shows that the main room and the additional room to the east had different floor levels.

Fig. 6. Keloşk Kale, Building 2, view from the southwest.

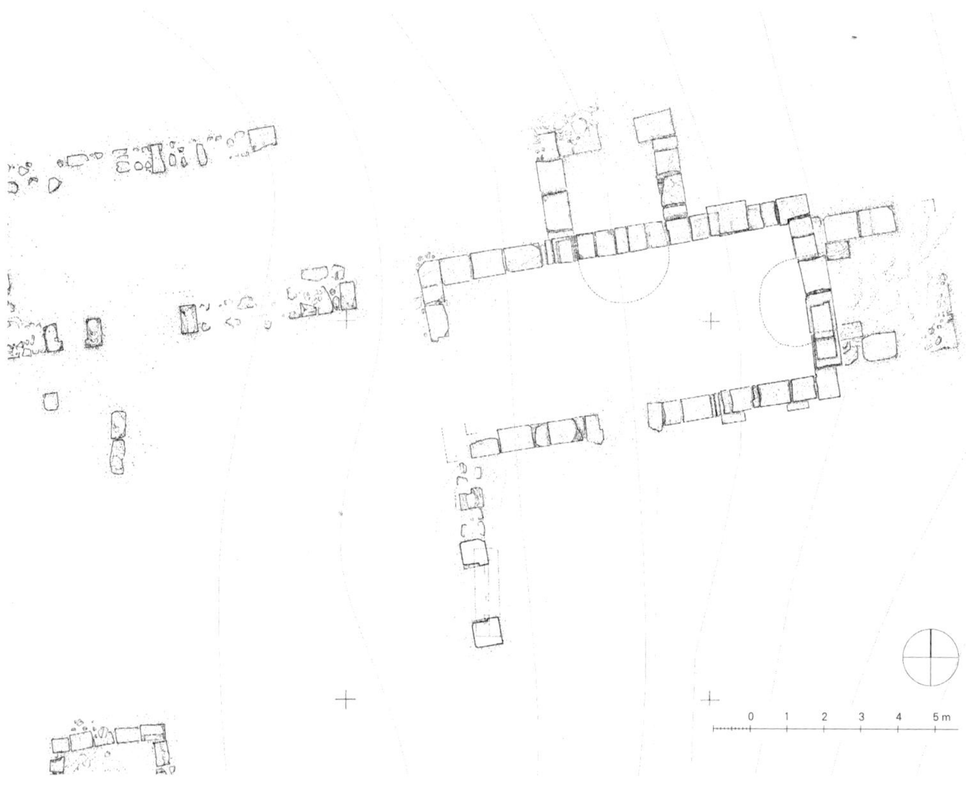

Fig. 7. Keloşk Kale, ground plan of Building 2 (scale 1:200).

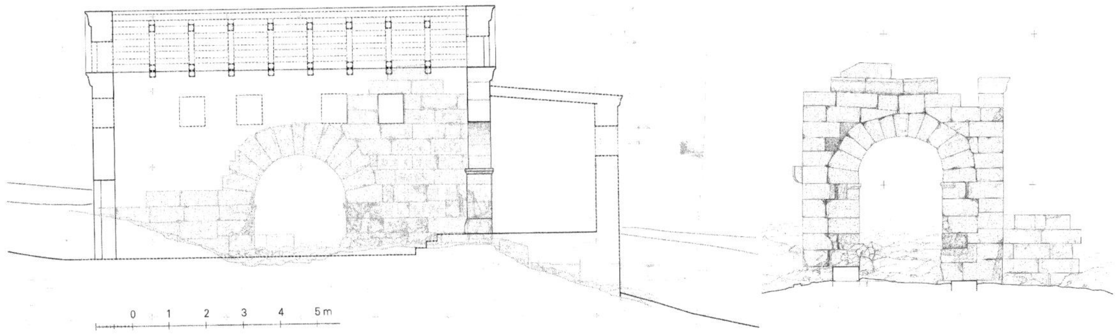

Fig. 8. Keloşk Kale, Building 2 (scale 1:200).

Building 3 requires only brief mention, because it is almost completely destroyed (see fig. 2). The building consisted of five rooms. One feature is remarkable: two fallen blocks of a pillar that carried the roof of a small porch still remain in situ in front of one of the entrances.

What were the date and function of this extraordinary building complex? There is no external evidence for dating, such as inscriptions (except two from a later period), coins, significant ceramic fragments,[19] or ornamental decoration. Comparison with similar buildings in northern Syria, however, especially in the limestone massif and the so-called dead cities, may be helpful. Building 2 in particular has many parallels with Syrian churches with only one nave. Not only their typology, but also their construction techniques are comparable with those of the building at Keloşk Kale.

A sixth-century church in Sitt er-Rum has features very similar to Building 2 at Keloşk Kale (fig. 9). It is east-west oriented and has a similar narrow oblong plan. The small windows and the prominent profiles underneath the roof zone are comparable, as is the shape of the roof pediment. Another similar feature is the doorframe with its narrow moldings, although the corresponding moldings are unfortunately not well preserved at Keloşk Kale.

A remarkable detail is the dressing of the blocks of the arch, in which both some of the voussoirs and some of the surrounding blocks are cut in polygonal shapes so as to tie in with the horizontal masonry. Exactly the same construction technique seems to be used in both places, in Sitt er-Rum and at Keloşk Kale (fig. 10).[20]

The list of similar buildings of the fifth and sixth centuries in northern Syria is very long and cannot be discussed in detail here.[21] Suffice it to say that these examples strongly suggest that Building 2 at Keloşk Kale was also built in the fifth or sixth century. And it is also very probable that it was erected as a church with a small sanctuary to the east, although diagnostic features such as a bema—which an excavation in the main room might well bring to light—are still lacking.

Returning to Building 1, it is almost impossible to find exact parallels for the skeleton-like stone-beam construction.[22] Again, the best comparisons can be found in late antique northern Syria.

[19] Although many ceramic fragments are still to be found within the whole building complex, it was almost impossible to find diagnostic fragments of rims or sherds that bear any kind of decoration. An exception is a fragment with a spiral which is comparable to the decorations of amphorae from northern Syria, especially from the vicinity of Resafa (Baumeister et al., "Keloşk Kale," 667, fig. 50).

[20] See discussion below, 244.

[21] For a more detailed discussion and further comparisons, see Baumeister et al., "Keloşk Kale," 662–68.

[22] Although there are comparable technical solutions in the ancient world, the framework of Building 1 seems to be unique—at least we have not yet found any close parallels. The so-called *opus africanum*, which we know for example

Fig. 9. Church in Sitt er-Rum.

Fig. 10. Building 2 at Keloşk Kale (left) and the church in Sitt er-Rum (right): parallels in construction technique.

The façades of the convent-buildings or guesthouses of the monasteries of the limestone massif in particular exhibit similar methods of construction. Kasr el-Benat, built in the fifth century, is one example. Another striking feature is the corner treatment, where the skeleton-like framework joins masonry laid in horizontal courses.[23] The monastery at Deir Siman and several other examples show that there is much comparable construction in Syria.[24] There are, however, also significant differences. The stone-frame panels of the building in Kasr el-Benat and of other examples in northern Syria were

from nothern Africa, Pompeii, and elsewhere, is different in its static structure, as the examples from Dougga or Selinus show. For a discussion, see Baumeister et al., "Keloşk Kale," 646–47 with nn. 36–38.

[23] H.C. Butler, *Syria. Publications of the Princeton University Archaeological Expeditions to Syria from 1904–5 and 1909*. II, *Architecture*. B, *Northern Syria* (Leiden 1920) 214–22, fig. 220.

[24] C. Mango, *Byzantinische Architektur* (Stuttgart 1975) fig. 89; C. Strube, *Die "Toten Städte." Stadt und Land in Nordsyrien während der Spätantike* (Mainz 1996) fig. 41.

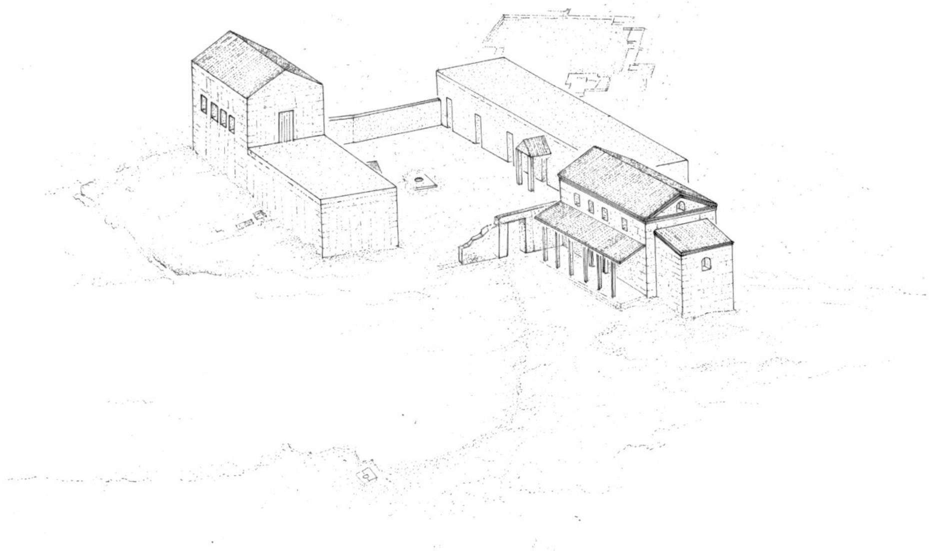

Fig. 11. Keloşk Kale, reconstruction of the building complex.

never filled with masonry, because these skeleton-frames were used in the construction of loggias and not for solid load-bearing walls as seen at Keloşk Kale. But in spite of these differences, it seems clear that the stone-beam construction can also be dated to the fifth or sixth century, although greater chronological precision is beyond reach.

We do not know why this type of construction was chosen at Keloşk Kale. Of course its static quality is outstanding: the best proof is the fact that the building is still standing up to the roof in a region prone to frequent earthquakes. But there may be other reasons why this unusual construction technique was used in this context. Perhaps, in fact, the similarities with the complexes in northern Syria were intentional. Perhaps the owner of the complex wanted to draw an explicit parallel with those northern Syrian buildings, which were very famous in late antiquity. Possibly this was the reason why Building 1 at Keloşk Kale shows this unusual construction technique.

Let us turn now to the function of the complex (fig. 11). Generally speaking, there are two possible interpretations. The first one is that the complex was the center of a farm, in other words, the homestead of a more or less wealthy landowner. We know such *villae rusticae* very well in late antique northern Syria. Even if Building 2 is a church, this explanation would not contradict this interpretation, since we know of a number of chapels built by wealthy private citizens within their homesteads. Another possibility is that Keloşk Kale was a *koinobion*, a kind of monastery or convent.[25] But without epigraphic evidence this interpretation is still hypothetical.

Some Notes on the Area of Keloşk Kale

After finishing our work at Keloşk Kale, we conducted a brief survey of the surrounding area. First, we visited the village of İnceler Köyü. This tiny hamlet consists of only a few houses on top of a hill, several hundred meters away from Keloşk Kale. The hill was also the site of an ancient settlement.

[25] See the discussion in Baumeister et al., "Keloşk Kale," 669–72.

Fig. 12. İnceler Köyu, courtyard with traces of a foundation (?).

Fig. 13. İnceler Köyu, chamber-like structure cut in the bedrock.

Within the courtyard of the modern village, traces of large blocks are still visible (fig. 12). The sizes of the blocks and their alignment suggests that they are the remains of the foundations of a major building, just opposite Keloşk Kale.

On the western slope of the hill, a chamber-like structure is cut into the bedrock (fig. 13). A few surviving blocks show that masonry walls once completed this structure. According to the local

Fig. 14. Pillar capitals from İnceler Köyü (left and center); pillar capital from Sitt er-Rum (right).

villagers, traces of wall paintings, no longer visible, could be seen within the chamber until just a few years ago. Without any other information, the function of this structure is uncertain. Its position on the edge of the hilltop and its partially rock-cut construction technique may indicate that it was a tomb. There are remains of at least two other rock-cut tombs in the hamlet of İnceler Köyü,[26] which may add weight to this interpretation.

Although ancient building materials were clearly reused in the construction of the modern village houses, no diagnostic pieces—for example, blocks with architectural moldings—were identified. However, different architectural elements are scattered throughout the village courtyards, including the capital of a half-column decorated with a molded profile (fig. 14, left) and a block that probably served as a pillar capital, characterized by wedge-like projections at the top (fig. 14, center).

Without detailed examination of the site including excavation, it is not possible to determine its function or to date it precisely, but a few further observations may be made. At the moment, the two capitals provide the only evidence for dating. The preserved decoration of the half-column capital is not chronologically diagnostic. But the pillar capital with its wedge-like projections shows similarities to the late antique architecture of northern Syria. A striking parallel is a pillar capital of a building in Sitt er-Rum, the site mentioned above (fig. 14, right). Although the simple forms of these capitals are not closely datable, this similarity does at least constitute some evidence for a late antique date for our capital, possibly in the fifth or sixth century. Since there is no corresponding structure at Keloşk Kale to which the capital could have belonged, we may exclude the possibility of a post-antique dislocation of the piece. The building to which the capital belonged at İnceler Köyü presumably lies beneath one of the modern houses.

To sum up: in addition to Keloşk Kale, there was a small settlement at İnceler Köyü nearby. As at Keloşk Kale, a close relationship to the late antique settlements in northern Syria is suggested by the type of the pillar capital found at this settlement. Whether the traces of the large building within the modern village courtyard belong to this period is uncertain. In any case, its construction technique does not suggest a military function, which might have indicated a date in the second or third century, following the pattern of the facilities at Eski Hisar or Uzunburç.[27] Although it is tempting to date the settlement at İnceler Köyü to late antiquity, which would fit into a pattern to be discussed later, this identification must remain on present evidence conjectural.

A very similar situation has come to light in Cibinören, a village situated a few kilometers southwest of Keloşk Kale. As at İnceler Köyü, we have identified modern houses clearly built of reused ancient materials, and there are traces of walls and foundations made of similarly-sized stone

[26] There are apparently still more tombs in the vicinity of İnceler Köyü, according to the local villagers.

[27] See infra 242 f.

Fig. 15. Carved joining surfaces of the wall blocks: Building 2 at Keloşk Kale (left); church in Sitt er-Rum (right).

blocks. Of particular note are a great number of rock-cut tombs scattered through the modern village. Not only the number but also the large size of these tombs would seem to indicate a significant degree of prosperity.

Since no traces of architectural ornament, inscriptions, or any other chronologically diagnostic remains were found during our brief visit, any suggestions as to the date are entirely speculative. In light of the establishment of other ancient settlements in this area in late antiquity (as at Keloşk Kale) and of the general prosperity of the region in this period (as attested at Beyburç, discussed below), it would not be surprising if the ancient settlement at Cibinören also experienced a period of growth and prosperity in the fifth or sixth century.

A few kilometers northwest of Keloşk Kale, in a village called Beyburç, the evidence for an extensive late antique settlement is striking. The remains of two ancient buildings within the modern village are still especially prominent.[28] One of these is the almost entirely intact exterior north wall of a major building, preserved along its whole length. Even the profiled blocks of the sima are still in situ. The walls of the other three sides of the building are missing.

The profiled blocks of the sima on top of the wall help to date the building. Their elongated s-shaped curvature is very similar to that of blocks in the same architectural context at Building 2 at Keloşk Kale (see figs. 6–8) and at the comparable buildings in northern Syria discussed above in connection with the dating of Keloşk Kale.[29] Another detail reminiscent of Building 2 at Keloşk Kale is the treatment of the joining surfaces of the blocks, concave in plan and tightly fitted only at the front and back (fig. 15).[30] All these details suggest that the building in Beyburç was also built during the fifth or sixth century, although precise dating is not possible. The function of the building is not clear. A religious function is possible, but since the plan of the complete building is not known, any such proposal is speculative.

The function of the second prominent building in Beyburç, however, seems obvious.[31] The remains of this structure are located in the eastern part of the modern village. The plan of the building is still legible on the ground. It consisted of two rooms: a main room in the west, separated by a still-standing archway decorated with a sequence of moldings from a second room in the east. The floor levels of the two rooms differ, and the steps leading up from the west room to the east room are still preserved. The east-west alignment of the building, the molded arch, and the small room in the east

[28] Thanks to an anonymous inhabitant, the ruins of Beyburç are now well documented in informative photographs on Google Earth.

[29] Baumeister et al., "Keloşk Kale," 662–65.

[30] See infra 245.

[31] See also the photographs on Google Earth (supra n. 28).

with its elevated ground level (which can be interpreted as the remains of an apse or *sanctuarium*), indicate that the building functioned as a small chapel or church.

All these features are also reminiscent of Building 2 at Keloşk Kale (see figs. 6–8), and the molded arch could indicate that this chapel was also built in the fifth or sixth century. As will be seen below during the discussion of the church in Gürkuyu, an especially common architectural feature of this period is the sequence of the various moldings, which follow the shape of the arch and then continue horizontally on either side in the manner of the "Syrian lintel."[32] In sum, the preserved buildings thus suggest that there was a settlement of the fifth or sixth century at Beyburç, as at İnceler Köyü and Keloşk Kale.[33] Like the other settlements, the one at Beyburç seems to have been prosperous, to judge by the extent and quality of its remains.

Thus the late antique building complex at Keloşk Kale is by no means unique. It is evident that there were several settlements in the immediate vicinity, which also experienced a period of prosperity at the same time. This is clear in the cases of İnceler Köyü and Beyburç, and it is likely that the architectural remains in Cibinören, which are not precisely datable, also belong to this period, and that this settlement also reached an urban and cultural climax in the fifth and sixth centuries.

Widening the range of our analysis, we shall see that this pattern of remarkable expansion in fifth- and sixth-century settlements can be observed in a larger area around Keloşk Kale and throughout the region east of the Euphrates in general. One example is the village of Gürkuyu, formerly known as Nuhrut or Monastirli Köy, a few kilometers west of Keloşk Kale. On the outskirts of the modern village, there is a remarkably well-preserved church.[34] In addition to a main nave of three bays, there is a side aisle in the south, separated from the nave by three arches. Only one of the two piers of the nave arcade preserves its capital. The arch that separates the main nave from the apse is decorated with a sequence of plain moldings.

Although R. Kiepert recorded Nuhrut as "Monastirli Köy"—which means that he was aware of Christian ruins—the church was not known to scholarship until 2001. Although it has been published only in a brief article,[35] there is no doubt that the church can be dated to the fifth or sixth century. The church recalls the so-called "Weitarkaden-Basilika" type especially well known from northern Syria. Although the buildings differ in details, such as the construction of the piers, the shape of the windows, and the architectural decoration with various moldings on the eastern arch, it will suffice for present purposes to cite the parallel of the basilica at Qalblozeh, together with further examples such as the churches in Fidreh[36] and in Brad.[37] Lack of time prevented us from examining the rest of the modern village intensively, but it seems very probable that further remains of a late antique village are to be found within the modern settlement.

[32] For an early example, see the arch of the church of A.D. 492 in Kalota: G. Tchalenko, *Villages Antiques de la Syrie du Nord: le massif du Bélus à l'époque romaine*, vol. 2, *Bibliothèque archéologique et historique* 50 (Paris 1953) pls. 39, 113; cf. C. Strube, *Baudekoration im nordsyrischen Kalksteinmassiv I: Kapitell-, Tür-, und Gesimsformen der Kirchen des 4. und 5. Jahrhunderts n. Chr., Damaszener Forschungen* 5 (Mainz 1993) 258–61; Strube, *Tote Städte* (supra n. 24), 210–13. See also the church in Fafertin: Tchalenko (supra this note), pls. 15, 42. Similar moldings also occur above doorways, e.g. in Qalat Siman or Qalblozeh, cf. Strube, *Baudekoration* (supra this note), pl. 111e; Tchalenko (supra this note), pl. 160.1.

[33] Although it is probable that this settlement was also inhabited in earlier periods, we did not find any traces during our short visit. The watchtower, mentioned by J. Wagner ("Provincia Osrhoenae" [supra n. 2], 107, fig. 8.1 [map]; 109), seems to have been removed completely by the local villagers. On the other hand, Wagner does not mention the late antique structures that are described here.

[34] A. Zäh, "Eine spätantike Kirche in Nuhrud (heute Gürkuyu) im nördlichen Mesopotamien," *JÖB* 51 (2001) 365–71, figs. 1–17.

[35] Ibid.

[36] H.C. Butler, *Early Churches in Syria. Fourth to Seventh Centuries* (Princeton 1929) 70–71, fig. 72.

[37] Butler, *Syria* (supra n. 23), 310; Butler, *Early Churches* (supra n. 36), 196, fig. 197b. For an example in southern Syria, cf. the church in Um Idj-Djimal: ibid., 118, fig. 115.

Another example of an outstanding construction of this period is a building in Kantırma, about 5 km west of Nuhrut. Near the main road at the foot of a hillock, three well-preserved arcades survive.[38] Their construction technique suggests that these rows of pier-based arches are most likely the remains of the substructure of a storage building. The arcades—which compensated for the slope of the hill—were useful for the ventilation of the building, so that organic materials such as corn could be stored in the upper story.

This structure has already been mentioned in some articles, but its date deserves further examination. A. Comfort thought of it as a Hellenistic or early Roman building,[39] while S. Gündüz speaks of a medieval han.[40] Although the structure still awaits proper documentation, some details suggest a different date; indeed, comparisons with the buildings at Keloşk Kale, Beyburç, and Gürkuyu indicate that this building also dates to the fifth or sixth century. The most striking criterion is the construction of the arches. The manner in which the voussoirs are cut and prepared in relation to the horizontal masonry is reminiscent of the arch of Building 2 at Keloşk Kale (see fig. 10). This treatment can be seen in Kantırma at the junction between two arches, which is covered with a horizontal slab. As at Keloşk Kale, the outer edges of the arch are cut horizontally and vertically to form a bedding for the upper courses. This feature can also be seen at Gürkuyu. The dressing of the blocks at the base of the arch is also comparable to that of Gürkuyu. The presence and shape of the abutment moldings also seem comparable to those of Gürkuyu and Building 2 at Keloşk Kale. As further discussed below, these features also occur in northern Syria, especially in the fifth and sixth centuries. In conclusion, one may suggest that the storage building also belongs to the fifth or sixth century. This would match very well with the pattern of the cultural development of this area.

Some Preliminary Conclusions

Before attempting to summarize the preliminary results of the new project presented above, it must first be acknowledged that our understanding of the material culture of northern Osrhoene is still not sufficient to justify wide-ranging reconstructions of the cultural development of the region. Nevertheless, it seems worthwhile to attempt to contextualize the results of our fieldwork, even if the following conclusions must be expressed very carefully.

Although the evidence remains scanty, at least the general outlines of the cultural history of the region are beginning to take shape. First of all, it is apparent that the area east of the Euphrates and north of the Birecik-Şanlıurfa Highway experienced considerable prosperity in the fifth and sixth centuries. Although we know from both literary sources and archaeological evidence that the emperors—especially Diocletian and Justinian—made serious efforts to improve the infrastructure of the eastern border region,[41] it is still surprising to find such varied and elaborate remains of urban and religious life outside the main centers. As the churches in Gürkuyu and Beyburç show, this region was not an underdeveloped area in a critical and endangered region. The elaborate construction of both the churches and the storage building in Kantırma, as well as other structures, attest an impressive level of economic and cultural prosperity in the fifth and sixth centuries.

This means that the overall well-being we can observe in major cities such as Edessa was not concentrated exclusively in the well-fortified capitals, but also extended to the hinterland. Considering

[38] Zäh, "Eine spätantike Kirche" (supra n. 34), figs. 18–19; S. Gündüz, "Kalkan Village, Kantarma Field Han," in A. Durukan (ed.), *The Cultural Heritage in the Towns Birecik, Halfeti, Suruç, Bozova and Rumkale* (Ankara 2003) 265–67, pls. 368–73.

[39] A. Comfort, C. Abadie-Reynal, and R. Ergeç, "Crossing the Euphrates in antiquity: Zeugma seen from space," *AnatSt* 50 (2000) 99–126A, at 115.

[40] Gündüz, "Kalkan Village" (supra n. 38), 265–67, pls. 368–73.

[41] See infra nn. 51–53.

the ever-present threat of war in this region—and the geographical and agricultural realities that still exist today—such a florescence seems remarkable. Furthermore, the lack of major fortifications in this region shows that this area seems to have been reasonably safe—or at least that its inhabitants felt it to be safe. Another important point is that religious life seems to have been of great importance—even in small villages. Within a comparatively small radius there are a surprisingly large number of churches, including a possible monastery at Keloşk Kale.

For the development of the Euphrates region, the results of the surveys that were carried out during the preparation of the dam projects in eastern Anatolia are of great importance—although the catalogue-like publication of the sites does not allow for very detailed conclusions.[42] Thanks to the research of G. Algaze, J. Wagner, and especially Comfort, we have a relatively precise idea of the distribution of settlements along the Euphrates valley and also of the road system along the Euphrates, and the connections between Samosata, Seleucia/Zeugma, and Edessa.[43]

It seems clear that the Euphrates region north of Carchemish experienced significant economic prosperity in late Roman and Byzantine times, as suggested by the evidence for increasing population in this period. As Algaze points out, various farmsteads, hamlets, and "villas" were spread around the major centers such as Zeugma, and many new settlements were founded to replace older settlements nearby.[44] He also notes a "substantial peak" of inhabitation in the Birecik-Carchemish area.[45] Although these conclusions seem to corroborate our theory about a prosperous development and a certain cultural florescence in northern Osrhoene at that time, it must be remembered that the material on which they are based is very limited. Algaze's results refer to a period of almost 400 years, that is, from the third to the seventh century, and without more evidence, a more nuanced view will not be possible.[46]

[42] M. Özdoğan, *Lower Euphrates Basin 1977 Survey, Middle East Technical University, Lower Euphrates Project Publications* I 2 (Istanbul 1977); Ü. Serdaroğlu, *Surveys in the Lower Euphrates Basin* (Ankara 1977); G. Algaze, R. Breuninger, and C. Lightfoot, "The Tigris-Euphrates Archaeological Reconnaissance Project: A preliminary report of the 1989–1990 seasons," *Anatolica* 17 (1991) 175–240, at 199–208; G. Algaze, R. Breuninger, and J. Knudstad, "The Tigris-Euphrates Archaeological Reconnaissance Project: Final report of the Birecik and Carchemish Dam survey areas," *Anatolica* 20 (1993) 1–96; see also G. Algaze, "The cultural aspects of the Güneydoğu Anadolu Projesi," *Arkeoloji ve Sanat* 56/57 (1993) 3–15. For other surveys in this area, see also T.B. Mitford, "Survey of the Euphrates limes," *AnatSt* 17 (1967) 13–14; idem, "The Euphrates frontier in Cappadocia," in D. Haupt and H.G. Horn (eds.), *Studien zu den Militärgrenzen Roms* II, *Beih. BJb.* 38 (Cologne 1977) 501–10; J.G. Crow and D.H. French, "New research on the Euphrates frontier in Turkey," in W.S. Hanson and L.J.F. Keppie (eds.), *Roman Frontier Studies* 1979, *BAR-IS* 71 (Oxford 1980) 903–12; T.B. Mitford, "The Roman frontier on the Upper Euphrates," in R. Matthews (ed.), *Ancient Anatolia* (Oxford 1998) 255–72; Comfort et al., "Crossing the Euphrates" (supra n. 39); A. Comfort and R. Ergeç, "Following the Euphrates in antiquity: North-south routes around Zeugma," *AnatSt* 51 (2001) 19–49, and cf. also D.H. French, "New research on the Euphrates frontier: Supplementary notes 1 and 2," in Mitchell, *Armies and Frontiers* (supra n. 2), 71–101; J. Crow, "A review of the physical remains of the frontier of Cappadocia," in P.W.M. Freeman and D. Kennedy (eds.), *Defence of the Roman and Byzantine East, BAR-IS* 297, *British Institute of Archaeology at Ankara Monograph* 8 (Oxford 1986) 77–91.

[43] Algaze et al., "Tigris-Euphrates preliminary report" (supra n. 42), 199–208; Algaze et al., "Tigris-Euphrates final report" (supra n. 42); J. Wagner, "Legio IIII Scythica in Zeugma am Euphrat," in Haupt and Horn, *Studien zu den Militärgrenzen Roms* II (supra n. 42), 517–39; Wagner, "Provincia Osrhoenae" (supra n. 2); J. Wagner, *Die Römer an Euphrat und Tigris, Sondernummer Antike Welt* (Feldmeilen 1985) 52–56; Comfort et al., "Crossing the Euphrates" (supra n. 39); Comfort and Ergeç, "Following the Euphrates" (supra n. 42); also important is H. Hellenkemper, "Der Limes am nordsyrischen Euphrat. Bericht zu einer archäologischen Landesaufnahme," in Haupt and Horn, *Studien zu den Militärgrenzen Roms* II (supra n. 42), 461–71, at 466–71.

[44] Algaze et al., "Tigris-Euphrates final report," (supra n. 42), 21–23, cf. the phase-map 81 (fig. 17b).

[45] Ibid., 22.

[46] The results are based primarily on the study of ceramic evidence. Detailed photographic documentation of architectural remains has not yet been completed. Crossing the Euphrates, the state of current research is comparable to the situation in the Euphrates region. For the results of a survey in the Gaziantep region, see A. Archi, P.E. Pecorella, and

That said, it should be noted that at least some monuments in other parts of northern Osrhoene and adjacent areas illustrate the same fifth- and sixth-century florescence that we have noticed in the area around Keloşk Kale. And this does seem to be a more general regional phenomenon. One example of a building complex built at the same time and with a comparable religious function is Deyr Yakup, located about 8 km south of Şanlıurfa.[47]

Returning to the typological and architectural characteristics of the buildings at and around Keloşk Kale, one can only assume that at least some of the remains in northwestern Osrhoene listed in Algaze's catalogue and elsewhere exhibit similar features, but for certainty on this point, we must await further study and publication.[48]

No other intensive investigations of this part of Osrhoene have been undertaken. Thanks to various surveys, however, we do at least have a more detailed picture of this region in high imperial and late Roman times, which can provide a background for understanding the developments of the following centuries. Until the second century, the culture of the area between the Euphrates and the modern Birecik-Şanlıurfa Highway was dominated by its function as a border region and by the presence of military units. An example of this military presence is the fort at Eski Hisar (fig. 16). This camp was erected in A.D. 197 by the *Legio Scythica IIII* on a hill near Gürkuyu, not far away from Keloşk Kale. Except for impressive quarries located a few hundred meters away in a nearby valley, no trace of the building itself remains.[49] Similar military facilities such as watchtowers were built throughout the whole area; examples include the watchtowers at Uzunburç, Kızılburç, and Beyburç (the latter village is located close to Keloşk Kale, as mentioned above).[50]

The most important reason for the transformation of this region from a frontier zone with a heavy military presence to a landscape exhibiting a widespread florescence of civil and religious life and a highly developed civic infrastructure is of course the expansion of the Roman empire. After the wars of Septimius Severus against the Parthians, and especially after the fortification program of Diocletian, the Euphrates lost its significance as a major borderline, and cities such as Amida, Kiphas, and Dara served as the main line of defense in the frontier area near the Tigris river.[51] In

---

M. Salvini, *Gaziantep e la sua regione. Uno studio storico e topografico degli insediamenti preclassici, Incunabula graeca* 48 (Rome 1971). Archi also gives a description of the sites in a catalogue-like form, and only a small part of the documentation seems to be published. It is immediately clear that more detailed classification of some of the remains would be helpful, as for example in the case of the "Ionic" capital (ibid., pl. 19 fig. 68) or of the "Islamic" building (ibid., pl. 10 figs. 29–30).

[47] F.W. Deichmann and U. Peschlow, *Zwei spätantike Ruinenstätte in Nordmesopotamien, Sitzungsberichte der Bayerischen Akademie der Wissenschaften, philosophisch-historische Klasse* 1977/2 (Munich 1977) 41–63. Another could be the church at Ehneş, on the west bank of the Euphrates—in the case that the problem of its building chronology can be solved. Thanks to the generosity of Doç. Dr. Kutalmış Görkay and the Zeugma Archaeological Project this building was documented in 2009 by D. Roos and P. Baumeister. The questions concerning the chronology will be discussed in a forthcoming article. For the church, see V. Eid, *Im Land des Ararat. Völker und Kulturen im Osten Anatoliens* (Stuttgart 2006) 97; for Ehneş in general, see Hellenkemper, "Limes" (supra n. 43), 467 with n. 28 and cf. Comfort et al., "Crossing the Euphrates" (supra n. 39), 114.

[48] For example, the "ruined church" (Algaze, "Güneydoğu Anadolu" [supra n. 42], 28) or the churches in Savaşan (Comfort et al., "Crossing the Euphrates" [supra n. 39], 115) and in Saylakkaya (Ainsworth, *Euphrates Expedition* [supra n. 15], 193).

[49] For the fort, see S. Guyer, "Eski Hissar, ein römisches Lagerkastell im Gebiet von Edessa," in *Mélanges syriens offerts à R. Dussaud* (Paris 1939) 183–90; Wagner, "Provincia Osrhoenae" (supra n. 2), 107–9.

[50] For the watchtowers in this area, see ibid., 107, fig. 8.1 (map); 109; see also supra n. 33 for Beyburç.

[51] For the general development, see Wagner, *Die Römer* (supra n. 43), 64–69; J. Eadie, "The transformation of the eastern frontier, 260–305," in R.W. Mathisen and H.S. Sivan (eds.), *Shifting Frontiers in Late Antiquity* (Aldershot 1995) 72–82. For the eastern frontier after A.D. 298, see E. Winter, "On the regulations of the eastern frontier of the Roman empire in 298," in D.H. French and C.S. Lightfoot (eds.), *The*

Fig. 16. Roman fort in Eski Hisar (S. Guyer, "Eski Hissar, ein römisches Lagerkastell im Gebiet von Edessa," in *Mélanges syriens offerts à R. Dussaud* [Paris 1939] figs. 2, 4).

spite of periods of disturbance, this Tigris region continued to function as a buffer zone until the Arab invasion in the seventh century.[52] This becomes especially evident during the reign of Justinian, who enlarged the fortifications of Diocletian massively in addition to founding new military facilities. From Procopius's *Buildings of Justinian* we also know that the infrastructure of the region between the Euphrates and Tigris rivers was remarkably improved, especially by the construction of new roads and of cisterns along major traffic routes.[53] Although the prosperity and economic power

---

Eastern Frontier of the Roman Empire, BAR-IS 553 (Oxford 1989) 555–71.

[52] For the character and the development of the eastern border, see N. Hodgson, "The east as part of the wider Roman imperial frontier policy," in French and Lightfoot, *The Eastern Frontier* (supra n. 51), 177–89; B. Isaac, "An open frontier," in P. Brun, S. van der Leeuw, and C.R. Whittaker (eds.), *Fontières d'empire. Nature et signification des frontières romaines* (Nemours 1993) 105–14; W. Liebeschuetz, "The defences of Syria in the sixth century," in Haupt and Horn, *Studien zu den Militärgrenzen Roms* II (supra n. 42), 487–99; W.E. Kaegi, "Reconceptualizing Byzantium's eastern frontiers in the seventh century," in Mathisen and Sivan, *Shifting Frontiers* (supra n. 51), 83–92, cf. also V. Chapot, *La frontière de l'Euphrate de Pompée à la conquête arabe* (Paris 1907); E. Dabrowa (ed.), *The Roman and Byzantine Army in the East, Proceedings of a Colloquium held at the Jagiellonian University, Kraków in September 1992* (Kraków 1994); M.H. Dodgeon and S.N.C. Lieu, *The Roman Eastern Frontier and the Persian Wars: A.D. 226–363* (London and New York 1991); see also the articles in French and Lightfoot, *The Eastern Frontier* (supra n. 51); in Mathisen and Sivan, *Shifting Frontiers* (supra n. 51); and in Mitchell, *Armies and Frontiers* (supra n. 2). For the upper Euphrates, see T.B. Mitford, "The Roman frontier" (supra n. 42).

[53] For a discussion of Procopius's description within the archaeological context in general, see L.M. Whitby, "Procopius and the development of Roman defences in Upper Mesopotamia," in Freeman and Kennedy, *Defence* (supra n. 42), 717–35 and cf. A.M. Cameron, *Procopius and the Sixth Century* (London 1985) 84–112; see also G. Downey, "Justinian as a builder," *ArtB* 22 (1950) 262–66; idem, "The Persian campaign in Syria in A.D. 540," *Speculum* 28.2 (1953) 340–48. For Dara, see L.M. Whitby, "Procopius' description of Dara," in Freeman and Kennedy, *Defence* (supra n. 42), 737–83.

of the major cities of the region, such as Edessa, were based on their locations along the main trading routes to the east, the improvement of the civil and military infrastructure of the area—and the emperor's direct support—was surely of more general benefit for regional development. At Edessa in particular, several literary sources attest the construction of many new churches as well as other official buildings of religious character—all of which reflect the city's economic power.[54]

The settlements in northwestern Osrhoene presented above are important in this context; they suggest that regions in the hinterland far from the major traffic routes exhibit a comparable development. The fact that even rural areas seemed to be prospering in this period may be a sign that this economic growth was followed by some kind of administrative consolidation. This specific area was not disturbed by the warfare that afflicted the general region several times during the fifth and sixth centuries. The seventh century shows how fragile this situation was. After the breakdown of the eastern frontier following the Arab invasion, the entire area around the Euphrates experienced a massive decline of population.[55]

Before drawing final conclusions I would like to focus attention on another point of interest which may be the most important of all. As discussed above, there are many links between the architecture of northwestern Osrhoene and the architecture of northern Syria. The skeleton-like framework of the Building 1 at Keloşk Kale (see figs. 3, 5), the typological features of Building 2 (see figs. 6–8), and several of its architectural details (e.g., the molded blocks in the roof zone and the decorated doorframes) show a very close relationship to the architecture of northern Syria. As we have seen, the pillar capital with wedge-like projections from İnceler Köyü may also serve as an indicator of this link, as a very similar piece from Sitt er-Rum suggests (see fig. 14, right), as well as the molded arch of the chapel in Beyburç and the molded blocks of the wall at the same village.[56] The most striking parallel is the church in Gürkuyu, which in form and decoration follows a common Syrian type.[57]

But the similarities are not only typological. Corresponding similarities in technical details may indicate even closer connections, possibly at the workshop level. This is apparent in the comparison between details of the church at Keloşk Kale and the chapel in Sitt er-Rum. The manner in which the voussoirs of the arch are cut and prepared for integration into the surrounding masonry shows that the same tradition of workmanship is found in both places. In figure 10 these parallels are obvious: the voussoirs differ in size, especially in the lower zone. The upper surfaces are cut horizontally and vertically to form a bedding for the blocks of the horizontal courses of masonry. The wedge-shaped stones, which compensate for the curve of the arch and which also have beddings for the courses above, also show close similarities.

[54] The following list, which is of course not complete, gives only a rough impression of the building activity in Edessa in the fourth and fifth centuries. *Probably A.D. 313*: Bishop Qona started to build a new "cathedral," which was finished by his successor. *A.D. 327–28*: Bishop Aithallaha enlarged this church. *Probably A.D. 345*: Bishop Abraham built a church for the martyrs of Edessa (Shmona, Gurya, and Habbib). *A.D. 369–70*: Bishop Barsai built a "great baptisterium." *A.D. 379*: Bishop Walagash (Eulogios) built a church for Daniel. *A.D. 394*: Bishop Qona transfered the sarcophagus of St. Thomas to Edessa. *A.D. 408*: Bishop Diogenes started to build a church for the martyr Barlaha. *Probably A.D. 435*: Bishop Rabbula converted a synagogue in the center of the city to the church of St. Stephen. *After A.D. 435*: Bishop Hiba built a church of the twelve apostles. *A.D. 437/8*: A silver altar was built in the "old church," i.e. the cathedral. *A.D. 442*: A silver chapel was built for the bones of St. Thomas. *After A.D. 457*: Bishop Nona built a church for John the Baptist. At the end of the fifth century the bones of the evangelist Addai were transfered to this church. *After A.D. 457*: Bishop Nona built a martyrium for Kosmas and Damian. This list is compiled mainly from Kirsten, "Edessa" (supra n. 3), 1963; Segal, *Edessa*; the dates are approximate and will have to be discussed elsewhere. For the sources, see supra n. 11.

[55] See Algaze et al., "Tigris-Euphrates final report," (supra n. 42), 23; cf. also T.J. Wilkinson, *Town and Country in Southeastern Anatolia* I, *Settlement and Land Use in the Lower Karababa Basin* (Chicago 1990) 126–27.

[56] See supra n. 28.

[57] Zäh, "Eine spätantike Kirche" (supra n. 34), figs. 1–17.

Another comparable feature is the type of joints used in the masonry of the walls. As already discussed in connection with Beyburç and Keloşk Kale, the joints are concave as seen in plan, tight at front and back for a clean and neat appearance, and hollowed out to a depth of a few centimeters in the middle, so as to avoid the expense of carving flush joints in places where they are not visible. The similarities between the joints of Keloşk Kale and those of Sitt er-Rum are particularly clear (see fig. 15).

These resemblances lead to the conclusion that the workmen followed exactly the same method of construction. In other words, workmen with the same technical training were employed both in northern Syria and the area which is in the focus of our current research. Although only elaborate ornamental decoration would provide conclusive proof, it is possible that workshops from Syria were also operating in northern Osrhoene and vice versa—an important connection that only the new evidence presented here has brought to light.

As mentioned above, these special technical features can also be observed in other buildings of northern Osrhoene. The arches of the storehouse-like building in Kantırma show the same method of construction as the arches at Keloşk Kale and Sitt er-Rum.[58] And as we have seen, the same type of concave joint is also found in the blocks of the huge wall at Beyburç.

The close relation in typology and construction technique of the northwestern part of Osrhoene with the limestone massif in northern Syria sheds a new and important light on the development of this region in late antiquity.[59] Although this is a subject that needs further intensive investigation, our observations suggest that this relationship represents more than purely temporary or localized influence. Bearing in mind not only historical developments but also geographical and geological realities, it is likely that the entire region was once a cohesive cultural area with a very homogenous development and typical cultural features.

The archaeological work at Keloşk Kale and the preliminary reconnaissance of the surrounding area make it clear that this region has a rich and remarkable historical heritage, which has not yet received adequate scientific attention. A major research project in this part of northern Osrhoene would be very fruitful for the discipline. The work presented here should be understood as a first attempt to shed new light on the development of this fascinating landscape, especially in late Roman and early Byzantine times.

[58] Gündüz, "Kalkan Village" (supra n. 38), 266, pls. 370–71.

[59] Similar relations for typology and workmanship have already been suggested, but only for a much earlier time, especially the second century A.D., cf. S. Guyer, "Zwei spätantike Grabmonumente Nordmesopotamiens und der älteste Märtyrergrab-Typus der christlichen Kunst," in E.F. Weidner (ed.), *Aus fünf Jahrtausenden morgenländischer Kultur. Festschrift Max Freiherr von Oppenheim* (Berlin 1933) 148–56, at 148, 150; Guyer, "Lagerkastell" (supra n. 49), 184, 188.

14 Cities in the Eastern Roman Empire from Constantine to Heraclius

David Potter

The story of the classical city in the eastern portions of the Roman empire in the 350 years after Constantine's death centers on the replacement of traditional and parochial forms of organization with more universal and centralized institutions. The result was a long-term decline in the importance of classical urbanism that may be seen as a transition from the centrality the polis as a socio-economic and political entity, limited to a very few sites by the end of the seventh century, to the *kastron*, a much less ambitious entity whose very name emphasized an essentially military function.[1] One factor in this transformation was the great world crisis of the seventh century resulting in the rise of the Islamic empires, but this is not a sufficient explanation, and the rise of Islam may itself be seen as a partial result of changes that were already underway. The question of just how significant these changes were is the focus of what remains a significant debate. One pole was planted in 1975 when Clive Foss published the first in a pair of stirring articles, arguing that it was the Persian invasion that dealt the final blow to the classical city in Asia Minor.[2] A decade later, Hugh Kennedy showed that, south of the Taurus, urban landscapes were changing well in advance of the Persian invasion or Arab conquest in that public spaces were being put to new, more private uses.[3] From both studies the crucial point that emerged was that in the period leading up to the collapse of Roman authority south of the Taurus, urban history had diverged significantly between the regions where Semitic languages and Coptic predominated amongst the population, and the regions where Greek was the predominant language.[4] More recently, work done on the Balkans has offered fresh insight into the economic collapse of another neighboring region of the Roman empire, suggesting that we need to read the Anatolian evidence not just in light of that from the south but also in light of that from the west.[5]

I am grateful to Professor Ratté for the invitation to contribute this essay; the framework for the discussion of the issues treated at the end of this paper owes much to a conversation in February of 2011 with Professor Stephen Mitchell. I am also extremely grateful to Professor Nate Andrade for his perceptive reading and detailed commentary on an earlier draft of this paper.

[1] W. Brandes, *Die Städte Kleinasiens im 7. und 8. Jahrhundert* (Amsterdam 1989) 28–43.

[2] C. Foss, "The Persians in Asia Minor and the end of antiquity," *EHR* 90 (1975) 721–47; idem, "Archaeology and the 'Twenty Cities' of Byzantine Asia," *AJA* 81 (1977) 469–86, but see also the nuanced treatment in his "The Persians in the Roman Near East (602–630 AD)," *JRAS* Ser. 3 13 (2003) 149–70, showing continuities of administration in the occupied zones of Syria and Egypt.

[3] H. Kennedy, "From polis to madina: Urban change in late antiquity," *Past and Present* 106 (1985) 3–27. The process that he observed is not limited to the Near East, and is a feature of changing government styles more generally; see now the important discussion of the agora at Nicopolis in P. Vladkova, "The late Roman agora and the state of civic organization," in A.G. Poulter (ed.), *The Transition to Late Antiquity on the Danube and Beyond*, *ProcBritAc* 141 (Oxford 2007) 203–17. On the other hand it was not always the case that new construction was haphazard; see A. Walmsley, *Early Islamic Syria: An Archaeological Assessment* (London 2007) 38–39.

[4] See also J. Haldon, "Social transformation in the 6th–9th c. East," in W. Bowden, A. Gutteridge, and C. Machado (eds.), *Social and Political Life in Late Antiquity, Late Antique Archaeology* 3.1 (Leiden 2006) 603–47, on the difficulties inherent in universalizing theories of change in relation to the evidence for this period.

[5] See now the essays collected in Poulter, *Transition to Late Antiquity* (supra n. 3).

Looking specifically at the textual evidence for urban life, major changes in the course of the fourth to sixth centuries began with the replacement of the local councils, which had administered cities by distributing necessary tasks to be performed as "gifts" by their members to the people, by groups of "leaders" who often held imperial rather than local positions. Other changes included the development of regional institutions, linked with the circus factions that dominated the capital, replacing traditional infrastructures for the production of public spectacles, while Christianity replaced local cult, in ways that integrated city politics into the politics of imperial religion.[6] A further point is that the model so far described held good only for the lands of Asia Minor. In the Balkans, urban structures collapsed in the face of Hunnic invasion and Slavic migration from the middle of the fifth to the middle of the sixth century, leaving the imperial administration to govern a few enclaves in this crucial region, while the regions south of the Taurus, extending as far as Egypt, are marked by the rise of economically powerful villages. In some places village societies may have challenged the economic dominance of cities and, in their appeal to extra-urban authority figures—monks of either the Hermetic or coenobic sort—their political dominance. In other places, these villages may have formed part or all of the property of powerful imperial administrative functionaries whose main residence was elsewhere.[7] A important contribution, common to both Foss and Kennedy, was to focus attention on the question of how well the trends evident in the texts could be reconciled with archaeological data, and how that data could be allowed to paint the backdrop for the stage upon which the dramatic events of the late sixth and early seventh centuries played out.

The essays in the current volume contribute to the overall study of late imperial urbanism on a range of significant topics. One is the issue of visual styling—how did people envision an urban landscape? Another is that of impact—how did the building choices made at an imperial capital affect choices made at local levels? A third is whether there was a consistent pattern of urban devolution in Asia Minor, and what "urban devolution" might actually look like. The final question is how Asia Minor compares with the lands beyond the Taurus.

Late Antique Cityscapes

Any study of style needs to begin at the empire's heart. Sarah Bassett's discussion of statuary at Constantinople draws attention to the issue of public art in a late imperial setting, and the importance in late antique city planning of what Helen Saradi has shown to be the interest in civic *kosmos* and *kallos*.[8] There were a lot of statues in Constantinople: examples mentioned in the sources number somewhere in the area of 250 pieces by the middle of the fifth century, roughly two-thirds of which were ancient imports, while a third were created after the decision to relocate the center of power to the city. The primary areas for display were the hippodrome, the Baths of Zeuxippus, and the Forum of Constantine. In each area the display combined pieces of great antiquity such as the Serpent Column, erected at Delphi to commemorate the Battle of Platea in 479 B.C., which was on display in the

[6] The basic treatment of civic government from which this derives is J.H.W.G. Liebeschuetz, *The Decline and Fall of the Roman City* (Oxford 2001) 104–68, 203–20; for the role of the Church see also F. Millar, *A Greek Roman Empire: Power and Belief under Theodosius II (408–450), Sather Classical Lectures* 64 (Berkeley 2006) 130–40 and C. Rapp, "Bishops in late antiquity: A new social and urban elite?" in J. Haldon and L.I. Conrad (eds.), *The Byzantine and Early Islamic Near East* VI. *Elites Old and New, Studies in Late Antiquity and Early Islam* 1 (Princeton 2004) 149–78.

[7] On this point see esp. H. Kennedy, "Syrian elites from Byzantium to Islam: Survival or extinction?" in J. Haldon (ed.), *Money, Power and Politics in Early Islamic Syria: A Review of Current Debates* (Farnham 2010) 181–200, at 181–89.

[8] H. Saradi, "The *kallos* of the Byzantine city: The development of a rhetorical *topos* and historical reality," *Gesta* 34 (1995) 37–56, esp. 40–45; see also the valuable summary in K.G. Holum, "The Classical city in the sixth century: Survival and transformation," in M. Maas (ed.), *The Cambridge Companion to the Age of Justinian* (Cambridge 2005) 87–112, esp. 89–90.

hippodrome by the fifth century together with an Egyptian obelisk and the Column of Theodosius. The Column of Theodosius was typical of modern work in that it was directly related with the emperors who had lived in the city, meaning that by the end of the first quarter of the fifth century, visitors might see the massive new Column of Arcadius, commemorating the defeat of Gainas; 20 statues of Constantine and his family members, a few representing members of the dynasty of Valentinian; and numerous statues of the Theodosian house along with a few important officials, such as the city prefects Proclus and Aurelianus. While on the one hand the result was simply to make the city more decorous, it also served to illuminate the different agendas of the Constantinian and Theodosian houses. The massive importation of old statues under Constantine served to establish the city's claim to be a worthy imperial capital, while the newer works favored by the house of Theodosius tended to stress the family's place in imperial history. While the array of statuary conforms, as Bassett shows, to rhetorical theory about the way that style might create pleasure, it also offers a visual complement to the point made in the second quarter of the fifth century by the compilers of the Theodosian Code that the regime of the Theodosian house built upon that of Constantine.

Although Byzantium was an older city than Ephesus, Ephesus had a much longer history as an important place and is one of four major centers (all provincial capitals) for which recent evidence is reviewed in this volume. The city itself was famously embellished in the fourth and early fifth centuries, in the wake of a series of earthquakes in the second half of the fourth century. The city's recovery began with the improvement of the water system, both through the reconstruction of the infrastructure for bringing water into the city and through rebuilding of the fountains that were crucial to the distribution network.[9] There followed work on prestige projects such as the lavish avenue leading to the harbor from the theater—the Arcadiane—which would be enhanced in Justinian's reign with a four-columned monument advertising the city's attachment to the imperial house, the public baths that were built at the behest of Constantius II, and numerous churches (often constructed on sites of earlier public buildings that had been damaged in earthquakes). The most famous of these, the Church of St. Mary, which would host the great Church Councils of A.D. 431 and 449, was also located near the harbor.[10] It may have stood next to a new palace built for the governor of Asia.[11] This redevelopment of urban elegance was not, however, universal, for the immensely impressive "Terrace Houses," which were ruined in an earthquake around A.D. 300, were not rebuilt; the poorer structures replacing them turned what was once a high rent district into a slum, but that may be seen as the kind of thing that routinely happens in old cities, and the fact that members of the local gentry were living somewhere else does not mean that they were not living in Ephesus.[12]

The "new Ephesus" coexisted with memorials of the city's past just as the "new Constantinople" built upon Byzantium, though in this case it may have had greater indigenous artistic resources, as Maria Aurenhammer shows in her discussion of the use of public art to create an appropriate civic image. Perhaps the most significant point of comparison between the Constantinople and Ephesus

[9] S. Ladstätter and A. Pülz, "Ephesus in the late Roman and early Byzantine period: Changes in its urban character from the third to seventh century AD," in Poulter, *The Transition to Late Antiquity* (supra n. 3), 391–433, at 398–402.

[10] See in general C. Foss, *Ephesus after Antiquity: A Late Antique, Byzantine and Turkish City* (Cambridge 1979) 47–95; on the Justinianic monument previously thought to be of the evangelists, see Ladstätter and Pülz, "Ephesus in the late Roman and early Byzantine period" (supra n. 9), 402, 415–16 (on churches).

[11] Ladstätter and Pulz, "Ephesus in the late Roman and early Byzantine period" (supra n. 9), 405.

[12] For the date and a somewhat different view, see ibid., 395–97; A.G. Poulter, "The transition to late antiquity," in idem, *Transition to Late Antiquity* (supra n. 3), 1–50, at 24.

is, however, in the treatment of mythological statuary. In neither city was there any hesitation about displaying images of the old gods in public contexts, even though, as Aurenhammer shows, Ephesus's cult buildings tended to be dismantled, and as Alexander Sokolicek points out, the study of statue bases does show that despite their role in enhancing a cityscape, statues could be the object of occasional vandalism. A moment of vandalism lasts forever in the archaeological record, and it is unfortunate that although we can identify the vandals in question as local Christians, we cannot now know the date at which, for instance, the Christian Demeas defaced the statue base of Artemis, or the date of the seeming mass castration of statues in the nymphaeum at Miletus and in Miletus's Baths of Faustina (though plainly well into the Christian period), as well as of the mutilation of the statue of Aphrodite from Room 5 in the same facility, a fate also suffered by statues in the bathhouses of Ephesus. Nor sadly can we reconstruct the aesthetic sense that lay behind the desire to gaze upon the genitally mutilated statues that were left in situ, though it does not stretch the bounds of credulity to associate these acts with the growing Christian discomfort with the public nudity that was characteristic of the classical city.[13] In Constantinople, by way of contrast, statues seem to have been a good deal safer, possibly because they did not seem so much to represent a pagan past as they did an imperial present.

What the study of the inscribed bases at Ephesus does show is that there is a significant change in the venue for the erection of statues from those agorai to the street, not obviously because the old venues were filled up. This transition began in the mid- to late third century and continued into the sixth century. It is a process that has been observed in other cities and that would seem to reflect the gradual restructuring of public spaces, possibly as the traditional organs of civic government were undermined by the rise of the supra-regional groups—church and imperial officials—which came to dominate civic life. As this happened, some of the more important traditional spaces, such as Ephesus's Tetragonos Agora, ceased to be used as they had been in the past (though the Ephesian agora appears to have continued in use for commercial purposes), and the living could reflect that the memorials of the dead were being repurposed before their eyes—a fate perhaps less grim than that of the agora of the Upper City at Ilion which, as activity shifted to the Lower City, began to be used as a cemetery.[14] The upper agora remained in use until the middle of the fifth century, when after yet another earthquake it seems to have been given over to private occupancy.[15]

Designer city walls are another feature of the late antique cityscape. In the first several centuries A.D., as Simon Esmonde Cleary has shown, there was a tendency for circuits of walls in the Roman world to be linked with assertions of civic status rather than the necessities of defense. This is especially the case in places where, as at Arles, circuit walls could be breached to add other urban prestige projects—an amphitheater—or where the circuit encompasses significantly more territory than was needed by the population.[16] In the mid-third century it is possible to identify some emergency or reactive fortifications such as the post-Herulian wall at Athens or the nearly contemporary wall built around Verona.[17] Likewise there are some signs of places that were able to revamp existing defensive circuits just in time to avoid catastrophe, as seems to have been the case at Thessalonika, where the Hellenistic

[13] P. Brown, *The Body and Society: Men, Women, and Sexual Renunciation in Early Christianity* (New York 1988) 315–17 (with especial reference to John Chrysostom), 437–38 (more generally).

[14] For the use of the Tetragonos Agora, see Landstätter and Pülz, "Ephesus in the late Roman and early Byzantine period" (supra n. 9), 405.

[15] Ibid., 406.

[16] S. Esmonde Cleary, "Civil defences in the west under the high empire," in P. Wilson (ed.), *The Archaeology of Roman Towns. Studies in Honour of John S. Wacher* (Oxford 2003) 72–85.

[17] On the characteristics of these walls, see H.W. Dey, *The Aurelian Wall and the Refashioning of Imperial Rome, AD 271–855* (Cambridge 2011) 120.

wall was strengthened in time to save the city from sack, as was also the case at Miletus. Other walled cities were not so fortunate, which is perhaps an important reminder that a new circuit was not necessarily a prophylactic panacea: Philippopolis may have been betrayed by its own defenders in A.D. 251, while it is uncertain if the defences of Antioch were betrayed in A.D. 252 or taken with the aid of the massive ram that Ammianus would later see in Dura.[18] A new move towards walls arguably as urban status symbols begins with the Aurelianic wall at Rome in the 270s, and continues with the elaborate fortification of new tetrarchic capitals such as Trier or Milan, which might be seen as the inspiration for new wall building throughout western Europe.[19] Philipp Niewöhner makes an important contribution to our understanding of this phenomenon in Asia Minor, showing that there are in fact two distinctive phases of circuit construction in Asia Minor, the first around A.D. 400 (roughly contemporary with the massive new Theodosian walls at Constantinople), the other after A.D. 600. The fifth-century circuits can be seen in the context of other urban embellishments such as "churches and a palace and stoas and lodgings for the magistrates"—all structures, for instance, that Procopius says Justinian added to Helenopolis in Bithynia.[20] The cities that display tetrarchic and post-tetrarchic circuits include Aphrodisias, Sardis, Anemurium, Smyrna/Izmir, Sagalassos, Hierapolis in Phrygia, Laodicea on the Lycus, Tlos, Blaundos, Limyra, Amorium, and, as Richard Posamentir shows, Anazarbos. These new walls sometimes sought to preserve impressive features of earlier walls as was the case with the gates of Perge and Side. Functional walls, lacking elaborate towers and sophisticated gates, and surrounding far less area than the early circuits, can now more clearly be seen as characteristic of the circumstances of the seventh century A.D., though Procopius observes that Justinian replaced a number of "display walls" in Cappadocia with defensible circuits in the previous century. Caesarea, for instance had been:

> ... surrounded by a wall which, by reason of its immoderate extent, was very easy to attack and altogether impossible to defend. For it embraced a great expanse of land that was not at all necessary to the city, and by reason of its excessive size it was easily assailable by an attacking force. High hills rise there, not standing very close together, but far apart. These the founder of the city was anxious to enclose within the circuit-wall so that they might not be a threat against the city; and in the name of safety he did a thing which was fraught with danger. For he enclosed within the walls many open fields and gardens as well as rocky cliffs and pasture-lands for flocks. However, even at a later time the inhabitants of the place decided not to build anything in this area, but it remained exactly as it had been. Even such houses as did chance to be in this district have continued to be isolated and solitary up to the present day. And neither could the garrison maintain a proper defense in keeping with the extent of the wall, nor was it possible for the inhabitants to keep it in repair, seeing that it was so large. And because they seemed to be unprotected, they were in constant terror. But the Emperor Justinian tore down the unnecessary portions of the circuit-wall and surrounded the city with a wall which was truly safe, and made defenses which would be thoroughly impregnable in case of attack; and then he made the place strong by the addition of a sufficient garrison (Procopius, *De aedificiis* 5.4.7 [Loeb translation, minimally adapted]).

Urban and Rural Economy

The state of the eastern empire's urban economy in the century prior to the seventh century revolves around the dichotomy between evident urban decline of Asia Minor and the seeming prosperity of

[18] D.S. Potter, *The Roman Empire at Bay, AD 180–395*, *Routledge History of the Ancient World* (London 2004) 246, 249.

[19] Dey, *The Aurelian Wall* (supra n. 17), 126–28.

[20] Procopius, *De aedificiis* 5.2.5; the oft-noted inaccuracies of this work are not significant to the present argument, which is concerned with ideology rather than reality; see also the review of the issues in Poulter, "The transition to late antiquity" (supra n. 12), 9–11.

the regions beyond the Anatolian plateau from the fifth to seventh centuries. Georges Tchalenko's justifiably famous publication of his study of the villages on the limestone massif south of Antioch made it impossible to write a unified story of urban collapse across the eastern empire, even with Jean-Pierre Sodoni's and Georges Tate's important observation that the economy of these villages was not based as Tchalenko had suggested on the olive oil export business, raising the question of whether what we are seeing in this area is "aggregate growth" resulting from a shift of population into the area, or "intensive growth" stemming from increased efficiency of production as well as a change in the population.[21] It remains the case that there does seem to be a rise in the importance of this area, and it is possible that the increased prosperity of villages is connected with the fascination with the holy men who often seem to have acted as patrons of these places. At the same time, work on early Byzantine Egypt, perhaps most provocatively by Jairus Banaji, focused attention on the increasing prosperity of village elites in the fifth and sixth centuries, while James Keenan notes that any picture of rural decline in Egypt from the sixth to ninth century remains "ragged."[22] The great unanswered (and sometimes unasked) question is whether it is possible to gauge the surplus created by these places, and whether it is possible to quantify the scale of change. In order to understand what is happening, it is useful to be able gain a view of regional developments in turn (even allowing that there is not absolute coherence in the evidence across the region), in this case beginning with the Anatolian evidence and then turning to the zone across the Taurus. In trying to assess the significance of what has been found, it is also important to be able to look at what we can know about how the institutions of the state were able to function, which is the purpose of the final section of this paper.

This volume contributes three important studies of the situation in Asia Minor for the period in question. In presenting the results of their survey of the region around Aphrodisias, Christopher Ratté and Peter De Staebler show that while the development of the late Hellenistic and Roman city involved a definite shift of population away from upland sites into the valley, there is no comparable shift in late antiquity of the population out of the city into the previously occupied sites of the hinterland. The data suggest that while the development of the city may or may not be connected with significant growth in the population of the area, the deurbanization of Aphrodisias in the early seventh century seems to be connected with a genuine decline. What we do not see here is a phenomenon similar to that postulated in other regions—e.g., Britain—where the end of Roman rule was marked by a return of the population to immediately pre-Roman modes of existence.[23] A further point of interest here is that Aphrodisias was out of the area most affected by the Persian invasion or later Arab raids, which perforce concentrated on urban areas that were along the route to Constantinople, and if—as seems

[21] G. Tchalenko, *Villages antiques de la Syrie du Nord: le massif du Bélus à l'époque romaine*, 3 vols, *Bibliothèque archéologique et historique* 50 (Paris 1953–1958); G. Tate, *Les campagnes de la Syrie du Nord du IIe au VIIe siècle: un exemple d'expansion démographique et économique dans les campagnes à la fin de l'antiquité*, *Bibliothèque archéologique et historique* 133 (Paris 1992); C. Foss, "Syria in transition, A.D. 550–750: An archaeological approach," *DOP* 51 (1997) 189–269, at 197–204; see also C. Wickham, *Framing the Early Middle Ages. Europe and the Mediterranean, 400–800* (Oxford 2005) 442–59, challenging Tate's challenge to Tchalenko, by arguing that inter-regional transport of mass produced goods (e.g., olive oil) enhanced the economy of the region, but the institutions he looks at were not new and evidence from the time of Heraclius suggests that the economic expansion here was the result of aggregate rather than intensive growth. For the distinction between these forms of growth, see now A. Bowman and A. Wilson, "Quantifying the Roman economy: Integration, growth, decline?" in eidem (eds.), *Quantifying the Roman Economy: Methods and Problems*, *Oxford Studies in the Roman Economy* 1 (Oxford 2009) 3–84, at 28.

[22] J. Banaji, *Agrarian Change in Late Antiquity: Gold, Labour, and Aristocratic Dominance* (Oxford 2001); J.G. Keenan, "Byzantine Egyptian villages" in R.S. Bagnall (ed.), *Egypt in the Byzantine World, 300–700* (Cambridge 2007) 226–43, at 240.

[23] S. Esmonde Cleary, *The Ending of Roman Britain* (London 1989) 130–61.

very likely—there had been an inflated mortality rate stemming from the great epidemic of the sixth century, it would have been reasonable to expect that a recovery would have been underway if people were still seeking to live in this area. While warfare and disease may be contributory factors to this tale of urban decline, neither is sufficient to explain the phenomenon.

What is also striking about the Aphrodisias survey is that its results seem quite different from those of the survey carried out in the area of Sagalassos, where the shift in settlement away from the urban center is both earlier and may be more closely connected with rural expansion. At Sagalassos, as at Aphrodisias and elsewhere, urban life appeared to follow a consistent pattern, with the city plan remaining intact into the middle of the fifth century. After that the city appears to have entered into a period of rapid decline, in which stately homes become less elegant (one has a stable built into it), and suburbs lose their residential function and are used for more intensive cultivation, while villages, now located in more remote spots, appear to become more significant. Various explanations have been canvassed for the systemic collapse of the area, including problems with the water supply, security breakdowns, earthquakes, declines in trade, plague, and changes in local government, some of which might reasonably be seen as effects rather than causes, and none of which are necessarily unique (even in combination) to the sixth century.[24] Still, perhaps the salient point that emerges from Hannelore Vanhaverbeke's important survey is that a single model or chronology for the collapse of urban life is not viable, nor, as she indicates in her conclusion, should it be necessarily assumed that an urban economy was the most viable economy for regions such as this one (a point that is reasonably extended to Syria and Osrhoene).

The second Turkish survey reviewed in this volume covers the Granicus region. It remains to be seen whether this will tell the same tale as the Aphrodisias survey or resemble more closely that of the Sagalassos survey. For the sixth to seventh century more work is plainly needed to place the fortifications at Alacaoluk and Asartepe in their proper context. For the earlier period, however, the results are very promising. The fresh analysis of the road system offers important insight into the development of the region, which, with Nicomedia and Constantinople, was the "capital district" of the fourth-century Roman world. Another promising survey, this one of the region around Sardis, is still at too early a stage to enable us to know if the trend in the sixth to seventh century was that of actual population decline or population transfer, as Sardis itself underwent the transition from classical to post-classical city, though it does not seem that there is yet evidence to suggest a repopulation of the countryside on the scale of the Lydian period.[25] That development is traced in Marcus Rautman's important review of work on the late Roman aspects of the site in the last three decades.

One fascinating feature of the urban landscape of early fourth-century Sardis is that the line of the original Lydian wall was still evident, a feature of the cultural archaism of the previous centuries and of the importance that cities could attach to the preservation of genuine antiquities.[26] The continued importance of this relic is reflected by the incorporation of portions of the old wall into the 4 km "designer" circuit that was built in the fourth century, surrounding an area evidently

[24] H. Vanhaverbeke, F. Martens, and M. Waelkens, "Another view on late antiquity: Sagalassos (SW Anatolia), its suburbium and its countryside in late antiquity," in Poulter, *Transition to Late Antiquity* (supra n. 3), 611–48.

[25] C.H. Roosevelt, "Central Lydia Archaeological Survey: 2005 results," *Araştırma Sonuçları Toplantısı* 24.2 (2007) 135–54; C.H. Roosevelt and C. Luke, "Central Lydia Archaeological Survey: 2006 results," *Araştırma Sonuçları Toplantısı* 25.3 (2008) 305–26; eidem, "Central Lydia Archaeological Survey: 2007 results," *Araştırma Sonuçları Toplantısı* 26.2 (2009) 433–50.

[26] D. Potter, "Cultural archaism and community identity: The case of Xanthus and Paphos," *Διαλέξεις, Ομιλίες, Εκδηλώσεις A* (Nicosia 1994) 427–41; F.K. Yegül, "Memory, metaphor, and meaning in the cities of Asia Minor," in E. Fentress (ed.), *Romanization and the City. Creation, Transformations, and Failures*, *JRA* Suppl. 38 (Portsmouth, RI 2000) 133–53.

rather larger than required by the actual population. One curiosity that Rautman notices is that even while there are some characteristic construction projects of this period, such as the reconstruction of the Marble Road, and some new luxury properties for the town's elite (a possible reflection of the increasing economic gap between the new "leading" men and earlier curiales), there does not seem to have been a great deal of money spent on new churches. This is not to say that there were not churches being built, as in the case of Church M near the Temple of Artemis or Building D in the heart of the city, now provisionally identified as a church, but rather to say that the scale of this construction appears to have been less than in other major cities, such as Ephesus. The most significant new religious building that has been identified from the fourth century is in fact the synagogue near the Bath-Gymnasium Complex. The city's well-being into the second half of the sixth century makes the testimony for decline around the year A.D. 600 all the more striking, and there appears to be clear evidence for the damage done to the city in the course of the Persian campaign against Constantinople in the destruction of the "Byzantine Shops" in A.D. 616. Such destruction should not, of course, have had a long-term impact on the economic vitality of the city—and Persian administration in newly occupied lands tended to rely heavily on existing elites—but the failure of the area to recover suggests that the Persian invasion is part of the longer-term process that left the cities of the region in a state of extreme economic fragility.

Troy and Blaundos offer important counter-examples to the relatively consistent stories told by the ruins of provincial capitals. In the case of Troy, as Brian Rose points out, the city, still thriving at the beginning of the fourth century when Constantine allegedly thought of using it as the site of his capital, was in serious decline before A.D. 500 as witnessed by the use of the upper agora as a cemetery in the previous half century. In A.D. 500 a devastating earthquake struck the city. At this time the Lower City was abandoned and the remaining population withdrew to the acropolis, and somewhat later it would seem that the city sank into the shadow of the massive new granary Justinian constructed on Tenedus to facilitate the rapid turnaround by the grain fleet from Alexandria.[27] The last residents left the area in the early seventh century. Whether this can be blamed on their location in the path of Persian and Arab armies is, however, an open question, as any analysis of this situation must also take account of the cities that continued as urban centers after A.D. 600, including Smyrna, Nicaea, Trebizond, and Attaleia.[28] Such analysis needs also to take account of a place like Blaundos, whose decline cannot be self-evidently associated with the wars of the world crisis. It appears that Blaundos was doing well enough to equip itself with a designer wall around A.D. 400, built in the most laborious way possible. A century later, or so it seems, things had changed. As Axel Filges notes, the obvious absence of Byzantine pottery compared to that of the previous two centuries might reasonably imply a decreasing importance and population. At the same time, there was significant change in the town's structure as the previously planned and grid-patterned town with its strong composition of public and open spaces and private buildings changed into a town with a much more loosely patterned arrangement of buildings, avoiding large buildings and large open spaces other than the agora.

The new evidence from the Anatolian surveys sharpens the focus on the seeming disconnect between the development of lands south or east of the Taurus and those to north and west of the mountains. As Posamentir's analysis of Anazarbos in Cilicia reminds us, all generalization is somewhat risky. At Anazarbos, the redating of the second circuit of walls to the second half of the sixth century

[27] Procopius, *De aedificiis* 5.1.8–14.

[28] For these cities see Brandes, *Die Städte Kleinasiens* (supra n. 1), 124–31.

makes clear a sudden decline in the city's fortunes. This is all the more striking as the outlines of the Roman city are clearly respected in the new building (largely, it seems, Christian) that took place in the early sixth century; the fifth-century walls took care to respect the existing city plan; and artisans working on new buildings took care to respect the traditions of the past. Indeed, in the construction of the new Church of the Apostles, the craftsmen "reanimated" the ancient blocks (some 300 or 400 years old) that they incorporated into their building through the addition of new bands of ornament or created new blocks with decorative elements carved in the style of the second or third centuries. Similar respect for the past appears in one of the churches in Hierapolis Kastabala, where architraves were reused in a similar position. There is similar evidence at Akören in the territory of Anazarbos, where the remains of two small villages, one of about 55 houses (Akören I), the other of about 90 (Akören II), are the object of Ulrike Wulf-Rheidt's careful survey. Here, where there was no original material from Roman imperial times, craftsmen imitated earlier architectural elements, and individual house plans in the fifth and sixth centuries seem to echo earlier patterns. In both places, the characteristic settlement pattern consisting of densely grouped, roughly similarly sized houses with no obvious social hierarchy suggests that they were independent peasant communities.[29] The pattern continues seamlessly into the sixth century, and the most obvious breaks in continuity may be associated with the replacement of pagan shrines by the early sixth-century churches that looked to stylistic models from Anazarbos. The sudden decline in the area, which must also now be dated to the second half of the sixth century, was so striking that earlier studies had tended to look for a considerably later date—as late as A.D. 800—than now seems plausible.

Outside of a strictly urban context, a great deal of attention has long been focused on the development of the limestone massif south of Antioch. It is thus of great importance that these studies can now be supplemented by Peter Baumeister's survey of Osrhoene. It should perhaps not be surprising that the limestone massif south of Antioch should provide the most significant comparanda for the material that he and his team have published since, as he notes, it is likely that the entire region was once a cohesive cultural area with a very homogenous development and typical cultural features, and it can now be demonstrated that workmen with the same technical training were employed across the region. Furthermore, as Baumeister points out, Procopius's work on Justinian's building projects reveals the imperial government's devotion of significant resources to this area's development. At Edessa, the chief city of the region, evidence for the construction of many new churches and other official buildings of religious character reflect the city's economic power. In this context, the settlements in northwestern Osrhoene suggest that the hinterland, removed as it was from major traffic routes, showed comparable development. The problem, of course, is how we might gain some insight into the significance of this growth. Does it simply mean that more people were moving into the countryside and existing at a level that might not be far above that of subsistence, or does it mean that there was more extensive growth, producing a significant surplus?

Archaeological and epigraphic studies of local economies are of enormous value in providing an impression of the sorts of industries that might exist and the extent to which the needs of cities shaped the economic activity of the countryside. Thus in the marginal territory of southern Isauria that forms the basis of Günder Varinlioğlu's study, there is evidence for a combination of economic strategies, including the cultivation of grains, grapes, and olives, as well as gardening, and the herding of sheep and goats, whose hair and skin were processed in Isaurian-Cilician cities and harbor

[29] On the significance of this for our understanding of social conditions within the village, see Wickham, *Framing the Early Middle Ages* (supra n. 21), 447.

settlements. The metal industry and arms factory in Seleucia required large quantities of wood, while there is also evidence for miscellaneous products, such as saffron, plants used in dyeing textiles, game animals, pistachios (a seller of which is known in Corycus), and laurel (whose leaves and fruits were used in cooking, soap making, and medicine). This study complements other useful analyses such as those of the municipal tariffs for Anazarbos with its mixture of goods including saffron, garum, heavy cordage, gourds, fennel, garlic, fried foods, wine, salt, plant grafts, common silk, tin, lead, slaves, cattle and carob.[30] The problem with such studies, however, is whether or not they can offer a clear view of the relative importance of the various elements of the local economy. Of the inscriptions with which G. Varinlioğlu has worked, only 13 and 15.3 per cent represent people working in food production, while those recording people engaged in manufacture range, by region, from roughly 24 to roughly 28 per cent, and those related to ecclesiastical employment (a clear indication that the data are unlikely to reflect true proportions) range from roughly 20 to roughly 23 per cent. If we focus specifically on Frank Trombley's examination of occupations on sixth- to eighth-century inscriptions from Corycus, a coastal community in Rough Cilicia, we see that of some 456 inscriptions listing occupations, some 25 per cent were clerical or administrative, while the evidence from other trades suggested that there was a heavy class bias in reportage of other occupations within categories. Hence while five net-makers are attested, there is only one fisherman on record. On the other hand, Trombley's statistics also suggest that within categories of "peer occupations" such as people working in food preparation, the heavier representation of people working with bread products (e.g., running granaries or bakeries) than people running butcher shops might represent the greater importance of bread in the diet (though the relatively small number of people dealing in vegetables might again reflect a class rather than a dietary bias).[31] In sum, these are important studies, but studies that need to be read with considerable care and alongside evidence offered by papyrological data. One (admittedly preliminary) survey of the best-attested occupations for Arsinoe, Hermopolis, and Aphridito offers the following breakdown:[32]

	Arsinoe	Hermopolis	Aphridito
centuries covered	*sixth–eighth*	*fifth–eighth*	*sixth and eighth*
food	36.1%	35.6%	16.5%
textile	18.8%	17.85%	8.35%
construction	17%	17.85%	7.85%
river trades	5.85%	5.9%	19.0%

Other data, also imprecise, suggest that somewhere between 25 and 30 per cent of people in Egypt might engage in an occupation other than farming, but also that there could be substantial variation between metropolitan sites and villages; relatively small numbers of people, for instance, could be engaged in crafts in villages, whereas a higher percentage could be engaged in crafts in larger

[30] G. Dagron and D. Feissel, *Inscriptions de Cilicie, Travaux et mémoires du Centre de recherche d'histoire et civilisation de Byzance* 4 (Paris 1987) n. 128, with discussion of the local aspect in the review by D. Potter, "Recent inscriptions from Flat Cilicia," *JRA* 2 (1989) 305–12, at 311; C. Morrisson and J.-P. Sodini, "The sixth-century economy," in A. Laiou (ed.), *The Economic History of Byzantium from the Seventh through the Fifteenth Century* (Washington 2002) 207.

[31] F.R. Trombley, "Korykos in Cilicia Trachis: The economy of a small coastal city in late antiquity (saec. V–VI)—a précis," *The Ancient History Bulletin* 1.1 (1987) 16–23; he should not be blamed for the discussion of peer occupations in the text above.

[32] P. van Minnen, "The other cities in later Roman Egypt," in Bagnall, *Egypt in the Byzantine World* (supra n. 22), 207–25, at 222.

areas, with some occupations such as wine merchant, linen-weaver, or silversmith being limited to larger places.[33] If the Egyptian and other epigraphic data are allowed as reasonable comparanda for Varinlioğlu's, then it would seem that agricultural labor is likely very much under-represented, but that the proportion of those who might have been engaged in some sort of manufacturing (which would not, presumably, have ruled some household agricultural employment out) was somewhat over-represented; it is also possible that the clothing production in Cilicia was somewhat differently structured than it was in Egypt—but even this conclusion may presume too much on the very impressionistic nature of the evidence.

Economic Decline and the Wars of the Seventh Century

The papers collected in this volume cannot completely explain what happened to the classical city in Asia Minor during the sixth and seventh centuries. What they can (and do) achieve is to place interpretative problems in clearer focus. One of these problems is the impact of the great sixth-century plague. Although it is plausible that the plague did severe harm, that alone is not a sufficient explanation of the picture of diverse declines that are evident in these papers, and neither is the political crisis of the early seventh century.[34] Another problem is the impact of the Persian invasion. Although it can be said with some certainty that some cities of Asia Minor show signs of serious damage at Persian hands, it can also be said with equal certainty that they did not fall into decline simply because Persian armies showed up in the decade after A.D. 614. The military failures in the years after Phocas murdered Maurice may more readily be seen as a result of existing problems than as their cause.

In the reign of Justinian there were already signs that the Roman government lacked the power to restrain a full-scale Persian invasion. While this might have something to do with the plague, the plague actually seems to have exercised some restraint over the Persians who withdrew in the face of the horror. Although Roman armies were spectacularly successful against Persian forces in the reign of Maurice, some allowance needs to be made for highly competent Roman exploitation of disunity and ineptitude on the part of the Persians. In the main, the imperial government relied on a defense in depth to keep the Persians from launching deep raids into their own territory—a strategic concept that should not be seen as a modern construct as it is explicitly attributed to Justinian in the case of the Balkans.[35]

Although the strategy of defense in depth was by and large successful over many centuries, it reflected the fact that the eastern provinces could not support a military establishment capable of launching a sustained offensive into Persian territory.[36] The progressive collapse of imperial control over the Balkans in the half century after Justinian, robbed the imperial regime, already stretched thin by the need to garrison Africa, Italy, and Spain in the post-Justinianic era, of crucial reserves.

[33] R. Alston, *The City in Roman and Byzantine Egypt* (London 2002) 224–337; the figure preferred by Alston is 28 per cent, but he admits that this is speculative.

[34] For a sensible treatment of the problem see W. Brandes, "Byzantine cities in the seventh and eighth centuries—different sources, different histories?" in G.P. Brogiolo and B. Ward-Perkins (eds.), *The Idea and Ideal of the Town between Late Antiquity and the Early Middle Ages* (Leiden 1999) 25–58, at 32–36.

[35] Procopius, *De aedificiis* 4.11.20.

[36] L.M. Whitby, "Recruitment in Roman armies from Justinian to Heraclius (ca. 565–615)," in A. Cameron (ed.), *The Byzantine and Early Islamic Near East* III. *States, Resources and Armies, Studies in Late Antiquity and Early Islam* 1 (Princeton 1995) 61–124 offers a balanced analysis of Byzantine resources, while J. Howard-Johnston, "The two great powers in late antiquity: A comparison," in Cameron, *The Byzantine and Islamic Near East* III (supra this note), 157–226 shows that the Sassanian state was likely more efficient in the extraction of resources from its people and mustered forces that were on a par with Roman armies, though it should be noted that neither study places the stress on the problem of the Balkans that is asserted here.

It perhaps might also be the case that the collapse of urban society in the Balkans had an impact on the cities of Asia Minor, for it is in the context of failure in the Balkans that we begin to see signs of significant economic slowdown in what is now Turkey.[37] This was a gradual process, for "post-curial" government and what might be described as "post-classical" settlements had become commonplace in the course of the fifth century. So it was that, for instance, by A.D. 450 Nicopolis ad Istrum had already declined significantly—and then it was sacked by the Huns. In the reign of Maurice the citizens, garrison, and bishop of Arsemus (60 km northwest of Nicopolis, and a place that had once resisted Attila with success) united in refusing to contribute to a campaign against the Avars; which may be a sign that both places had become centers for local landowners who, lacking the means to flee, were stuck finding a way forward on their own.[38] If that is the case, then Nicopolis and Arsemus may also be seen as exemplifying a particular model of urban devolution unlike those seen so far in Anatolia.

Does the decline of urban life in the Balkans suggest that a viable Aegean economy was necessary to the stability of Asia Minor, and that the loss of trading partners on the far side of the Aegean severely harmed the regional economy? The weakened cities of the Balkans while still under Roman control had begun planting new crops, preferring legumes and millet to winter-sown grains. This meant that they had to import wheat, and that the population, living on a more tenuous diet, was less healthy.[39] Certainly it might suggest that the region was not making much of a net contribution to the economy of the empire as a whole, and if we see the developments of Syria or Oshroene as an imperial ideal, the situation in the Balkans appears to have been the opposite of that in the second half of the fifth century—even imperial victories such as those of Maurice in the 590s could not alter the course of decline.[40] Economic collapse and social transition do not happen overnight, but the process was beyond the capacity of a weakened pre-modern polity to change, and after each challenge the state was less able to withstand another.[41] Certainly the loss of the Balkans was a far more sustained blow to the empire than even the horrendous pestilence of Justinian's time.

It has long been noted that there was a great deal of continuity between the economic regime of Syria and Egypt in the late Roman period and that of the Umayyads. Not only are there no signs of any immediate change in patterns of land exploitation, there is also evidence for continuity within the elite, a concept which is itself problematic as the requirements for admission to such a group varied wildly from place to place. As Dorotheus of Gaza famously put the problem, a man who was great at Gaza would be of the middling sort at Caesarea, a peasant at Antioch, and poor in Constantinople.[42] The middling, or Gaza-esque, elite of Syria and Egypt appears to have suffered little long-term effect

[37] For evidence on the loss of Balkan cities see Brandes, "Byzantine cities" (supra n. 34), 41–43; J.H.W.G. Liebeschuetz, "The lower Danube region under pressure: From Valens to Heraclius," in Poulter, *Transition to Late Antiquity* (supra n. 3), 101–34, at 108; J.-P. Sodini, "The transformation of cities in late antiquity within the provinces of Macedonia and Epirus," in Poulter, *Transition to Late Antiquity* (supra n. 3), 311–36, at 314–15.

[38] Priscus, Fr. 9 (Blockley) with Liebeschuetz, "The lower Danube region under pressure" (supra n. 37), 104–105; Theoph. 7.3.1 for the sixth century, with M. Whittow, "Nicopolis ad Istrum: Backward and Balkan?" in Poulter, *Transition to Late Antiquity* (supra n. 3), 375–89, at 386.

[39] A.G. Poulter, *Nicopolis ad Istrum: A Roman, Late Roman, and Early Byzantine City. Excavations 1985–1992, JRS Monograph* 8 (London 1995) 44.

[40] Liebeschuetz, "The lower Danube region under pressure" (supra n. 37), 128–29.

[41] See also Poulter, "The transition to late antiquity" (supra n. 12), 46.

[42] Dorotheos, *Didaskalia* 2.6, with C. Wickham, "Conclusion," in Haldon and Conrad, *The Byzantine and Early Islamic Near East* VI (supra n. 6), 285–98, at 285; for further discussion of the problem in archaeological terms, see J.-P. Sodini, "Archaeology and late antique social structures," in L. Lavan and W. Bowden (eds.), *Theory and Practice in Late Antique Archaeology, Late Antique Archaeology* 1 (Leiden 2003) 25–56, and several of the contributions in Bowden, Gutteridge, and Machado, *Social and Political Life in Late Antiquity* (supra n. 4).

from the changes in government, if its members survived the immediate shock (most did) of the Persian conquest, which was genuinely vicious in some places—Jerusalem, where seven mass burials have been uncovered, is a prime example—and caused such dread that the population of a place like Abu Mina would flee before the coming of the enemy.[43] Such people were also not in a position to leave, though in the case of those who had achieved a status within the imperial regime it may have been harder to stay put. Although there is some continuity between members of the Roman and Umayyad elite, there is also a fair amount of evidence to suggest that suspected supporters of the old regime were exiled as part of settlements with their cities.[44]

Still, even if continuity is evident, the question remains as to just how much surplus value was being produced in the agricultural lands of Syria and Mesopotamia. The answer may be provided by Tabari's account of the trial of Chosroes II after his deposition in A.D. 628, which, as James Howard-Johnston has convincingly shown, reflects a late Sassanian history, *The Book of Lords*.[45] The Roman victories at the root of the political chaos in Persia were the result of extraordinary miscalculations on the Sassanian side, for their main army had been left in the west and was unable to intervene against Heraclius's forces as they advanced south from Armenia. These same forces withdrew to Armenia after ravaging the area around Ctesiphon before having to confront the main army. At his trial the king (who, unsurprisingly, was executed in the aftermath) was accused of the murder of his predecessor (true), the ill-treatment of his sons, the brutality of his lengthy prison terms, lack of affection towards his harem, treacherous behavior towards Maurice, and:

> [Fifth,] what you have inflicted on your subjects generally in levying the land tax and in treating them with harshness and violence. [Sixth,] your amassing a great amount of wealth, which you exacted from the people with great brutality so that you drove them to consider your rule hateful and thereby brought them into affliction and deprivation. [Seventh,] your stationing the troops for long periods along the frontiers with the Byzantines and on other frontiers, thereby separating them from their families (al-Tabari [Nöldeke p. 1047, tr. Bosworth]).[46]

There is no obvious reason to believe that taxation was not in fact a serious issue, for Chosroes's successor promptly repealed some of the taxes that Chosroes had imposed, and while it is possible that the charge that Chosroes hoarded his wealth may have some validity—in his defense Chosroes does say that only a fool does not realize that a king maintains his authority through wealth and armies—the fact of these charges suggests that, although having taken possession of Syria, Osrhoene, and Egypt, Chosroes was unable to extract sufficient surplus from these lands to fund war and avoid alienating his subjects. In Roman lands it is apparent that he retained the Roman tax system and many of the collectors who had been in post at the time of the conquest. A reasonable conclusion is that the surplus generated by these lands was not sufficiently robust to support the costs of aggressive warfare. This might also suggest that the economic expansion of these regions was not significantly above the subsistence level.

[43] On continuity of the elite, see Foss, "The Persians in the Roman Near East" (supra n. 2), 154; on mass graves at Jerusalem at the time of the Persian sack, see G. Avni, "The Persian conquest of Jerusalem (614 C.E.)—an archaeological assessment," *BASOR* 357 (2010) 35–48, at 36–37, and 44 for the lack of longer-term consequences; for the situation at Abu Mina see N. Litinas, *Greek Ostraca from Abu Mina (O.AbuMina), Archiv für Papyrusforschung und verwandte Gebeite Beiheft* 25 (Berlin 2008) x (the population returned when the Persians left).

[44] Kennedy, "Syrian elites from Byzantium to Islam" (supra n. 7), 189–98.

[45] J. Howard-Johnston, *Witnesses to a World Crisis: Historians and Histories of the Middle East in the Seventh Century* (Oxford 2010) 367–68.

[46] C.E. Bosworth, *The History of al-Tabari*, vol. 5. *The Sasanids, the Byzantines, the Lakhmids, and Yemen* (Albany 1999) 383.

The relative fragility of the imperial tax system had direct consequences for the empire's ability to defend itself. Although the Persians left the infrastructure of taxation intact, there is no reason to think that in the few years that intervened between the end of the Persian war and the Arab invasion of Palestine that the Roman state had become suddenly more powerful. In the wake of Roman defeats in Palestine and Syria, cities saw it better to negotiate with the new arrivals than to resist. The leaders of these cities saw no reason to sacrifice themselves for a regime that had proved ineffective and, with its aggressive stance against the monophysite population of the area, offensive. The extreme monotheists who followed the revelation of Mohammed were not yet obviously followers of a new religion, and it seems that their leaders were happy to leave existing administrative regimes in place. If we knew more about the settlements that were reached in Syria and Palestine we might be better able to interpret the settlement for one-year's joint rule as the Romans evacuated Egypt in A.D. 642, but as it is the recent publication of two Rainier papyri from the year of the Arab conquest have shed important light upon the situation. In one we find reference to a boat "bearing the seal of Amr" amongst a number of others in the harbor at Hermopolis.[47] In the second we read in a letter from the pagarch Athanasius to the notarius Senouthis:

> The letter carrying *moagaritai* having come asking for boats, give them the boats where they want in your district so that in the future they do not come to me if they wish to get on the boats (*P. Rain.* 30 n. 11).

The term *moagaritai* is well known from papyri as a Greek rendition of *muhâjirûn*, indicating "militarily active members of the community of Believers," or, it seems, more simply, Arab soldiers serving in the armies of the Amirs, and it is clear that accommodation was the order of the day.[48] The years of the Arab conquest are the years during which poleis largely disappeared or were replaced in Asia Minor by *castra*. In looking at urban history in these years and in the previous two centuries, we seem often to be finding areas whose economic prosperity was marginal. This though raises the question addressed in both the Sagalassos and Aphrodisias surveys: in looking ahead, are we also not failing to look far enough back to the pre-Roman period in which the city-state was rare? That might in turn raise the question of what form of the Roman imperial system was necessary to support urban culture. That system would seem to be the system of the first three centuries A.D., which could guarantee peace and security, because, even if the state could only hope to raise marginal surpluses from the regions under its control, the accumulation of those surpluses from across the Mediterranean basin enabled Augustus and his immediate successors to achieve overwhelming military power on the frontiers so long as only one frontier was subjected to a serious threat at any one time. It is perhaps worth noting that the great Islamic state that would come into being during the seventh century could not itself achieve the conquest of the vestigial Roman empire.

[47] See in general F. Morelli, *L'Archivio di Senouthios Anystes e testi connessi: lettere e documenti per la costruzione di una capitale, Corpus papyrorum Raineri Archiducis Austriae* 30 (Berlin 2010) 11–14; for the broader circumstances see H. Kennedy, *The Great Arab Conquests: How the Spread of Islam Changed the World We Live In* (London 2007) 152–53.

[48] For the term see *SB* 8.9755 and the discussion in H.I. Bell, *Greek Papyri in the British Museum* IV. *The Aphrodito Papyri* (London 1910) xxxiv, and F. Donner, *Muhammed and the Believers: At the Origins of Islam* (Cambridge, MA 2010) 203–204 on *muhâjirûn* and 98–99 on the proper title for the early leaders of the community being *amir al-mu'minin* rather than Caliph.

Bibliography

N. Adams, M. Janse, and S. Swain, *Bilingualism in Ancient Society. Language Contact and the Written Text* (Oxford 2002).

A. Adler (ed.), *Suidae Lexicon* (Leipzig 1928–1938).

S. Agelidis et al., "Katalog," in O. Dally et al. (eds.), *ZeitRäume. Milet in Kaiserzeit und Spätantike* (Regensburg 2009) 161–203.

H. Ahrweiler, "L'Asie Mineure et les invasions arabes (7ᵉ–9ᵉ siècles)," *RHist* 227 (1962) 1–32.

W.F. Ainsworth, *A Personal Narrative of the Euphrates Expedition*, 2 vols. (London 1888).

H. Alanyalı, A. Pülz, and P. Ruggendorfer, "Urbanistische Forschungen in der Oststadt von Limyra," *ÖJh* 66 (1997) Beiblatt, 374–83.

J. Alchermes, "Spolia in Roman cities of the late empire: Legislative rationales and architectural reuse," *DOP* 48 (1994) 167–78.

S. Alcock, "Material witness: An archaeological context for the *Heroikos*," in E. Bradshaw Aitken and J.K. Berenson Maclean (eds.), *Philostratus'* Heroikos. *Religion and Cultural Identity in the Third Century C.E.* (Leiden 2005) 159–68.

A. Alexandridis, *Die Frauen des römischen Kaiserhauses* (Mainz 2004).

G. Algaze, "The cultural aspects of the Güneydoğu Anadolu Projesi," *Arkeoloji ve Sanat* 56/57 (1993) 3–15.

G. Algaze, R. Breuninger, and J. Knudstad, "The Tigris-Euphrates Archaeological Reconnaissance Project: Final report of the Birecik and Carchemish Dam survey areas," *Anatolica* 20 (1993) 1–96.

G. Algaze, R. Breuninger, and C. Lightfoot, "The Tigris-Euphrates Archaeological Reconnaissance Project: A preliminary report of the 1989–1990 seasons," *Anatolica* 17 (1991) 175–240.

R. Alston, *The City in Roman and Byzantine Egypt* (London 2002).

W. Alzinger, "Ephesos," *RE* Suppl. XII (1970) 1588–1704.

W. Alzinger, *Augusteische Architektur in Ephesos, Sonderschriften des Österreichischen Archäologischen Institutes* 16 (Vienna 1974).

W. Alzinger, "Das Regierungsviertel," *ÖJh* 50 (1972–1975) Beiblatt, 230–300.

M. Anabolu, "Efes Müzesinde bulunan masa ayakları," *TürkAD* 29 (1991) 71–85.

M.G. Angeli Bertinelli, "I Romani oltre l'Eufrate nel II secolo d. C. (le province di Assiria, di Mesopotamia e di Osroene)," *ANRW* II.9.1 (1976) 3–45.

A. Arbeiter, "Die Anfänge der Quaderarchitektur im westgotenzeitlichen Hispanien," in B. Brenk (ed.), *Innovation in der Spätantike* (Wiesbaden 1996) 11–51.

J. Arce, *Estudios sobre el Emperador Fl. Cl. Juliano: fuentes literarias, epigrafia, numismatica* (Madrid 1984).

A. Archi, P.E. Pecorella, and M. Salvini, *Gaziantep e la sua regione. Uno studio storico e topografico degli insediamenti preclassici, Incunabula Graeca* 48 (Rome 1971).

P. Arthur, *Byzantine and Turkish Hierapolis (Pamukkale): An Archaeological Guide* (Istanbul 2006).

R.S. Ascough, "Greco-Roman religions in Sardis and Smyrna," in R.S. Ascough (ed.), *Religious Rivalries and the Struggle for Success in Sardis and Smyrna, Studies in Christianity and Judaism* 14 (Waterloo, ON 2005) 40–52.

N. Asutay-Effenberger, *Die Landmauer von Konstantinopel-Istanbul: Historisch-topographische und baugeschichtliche Untersuchungen, Millennium Studies* 18 (Wiesbaden 2007).

E. Atalay, *Weibliche Gewandstatuen des 2. Jahrhunderts n. Chr. aus ephesischen Werkstätten* (Vienna 1989).

J. Auinger, "Ein Büstenkronenfragment aus Ephesos," in B. Asamer and W. Wohlmayr (eds.), *Akten des 9. Österreichischen Archäologentages am Institut für Klassische Archäologie des Paris-Lodron-Universität Salzburg 2001* (Vienna 2003) 15–19.

J. Auinger, "Zu dem Neufund eines spätantiken Porträtfragments aus Ephesos. Ein Nachtrag," *ÖJh* 73 (2004) 11–14.

J. Auinger, *Die Skulpturenausstattung des Vedius- und Ostgymnasiums in Ephesos. Die Funde bis 1931* (Ph.D. dissertation, University of Vienna 2005).

J. Auinger, "Zum Umgang mit Statuen hoher Würdenträger in spätantiker und nachantiker Zeit entlang der Kuretenstraße in Ephesos. Fundorte und Fundumstände," in S. Ladstätter (ed.), *Neue Forschungen zur Kuretenstraße in Ephesos, DenkschrWien* 382 (2009) 29–52.

J. Auinger, "Kaisersaal versus 'Kaisersaal'. Zur Funktion der 'Kaisersäle' in ephesischen Thermen," *JRA* (forthcoming).

J. Auinger and M. Aurenhammer, "Ephesische Skulptur am Ende der Antike," in F. Daim and J. Drauschke (eds.), *Byzanz—Das Römerreich im Mittelalter.* Teil 2.2. *Schauplätze, Monographien des Römisch-Germanischen Zentralmuseums* 84.2.2 (Mainz 2010) 663–96.

J. Auinger and E. Rathmayr, "Zur spätantiken Statuenausstattung der Thermen und Nymphäen in Ephesos," in F.A. Bauer and C. Witschel (eds.), *Statuen in der Spätantike* (Wiesbaden 2007) 237–69.

M. Aurenhammer, *Die Skulpturen von Ephesos. Idealplastik* I, *Forschungen in Ephesos* X 1 (Vienna 1990).

M. Aurenhammer, "Drei neue römische Porträtköpfe von der Tetragonos Agora in Ephesos," *ÖJh* 69 (2000) 17–33.

M. Aurenhammer, "Skulpturen aus Stein und Bronze," in C. Lang-Auinger (ed.), *Hanghaus 1 in Ephesos. Funde und Ausstattung, Forschungen in Ephesos* VIII 4 (Vienna 2003) 153–208.

M. Aurenhammer, "Late Hellenistic and early Roman imperial portraits from Ephesos," in F. D'Andria and I. Romeo (eds.), *Roman Sculpture in Asia Minor, JRA* Suppl. 80 (Portsmouth, RI 2011) 101–16.

M.-F. Auzépy, "Survey of the Byzantine monasteries of the south coast of the sea of Marmara 2004," *Araştırma Sonuçları Toplantısı* 23.2 (2005) 23–34.

G. Avni, "The Persian conquest of Jerusalem (614 C.E.)—an archaeological assessment," *BASOR* 357 (2010) 35–48.

W. Aylward, *The Roman Agora at Ilion and its Predecessors* (Ph.D. dissertation, University of Cincinnati 2000).

W. Aylward, "The portico and propylaia of the sanctuary of Athena at Ilion," *Studia Troica* 15 (2005) 160–61.

W. Aylward, "The Byzantine fortifications at Pegae (Priapus) on the sea of Marmara," *Studia Troica* 16 (2006) 179–203.

W. Aylward, G. Bieg, and R. Aslan, "The aqueduct of Roman Ilion and the bridge across the Kemerdere valley in the Troad," *Studia Troica* 12 (2002) 397–427.

E. Babelon, *Numismatique d'Édesse en Mésopotamie, Mélanges Numismatiques, 2e série* (Paris 1893).

R.S. Bagnall, "Archaeological work on Hellenistic and Roman Egypt, 1995–2000," *AJA* 105 (2001) 227–43.

D. Baird, "Settlement expansion on the Konya Plain, Anatolia: 5th–7th centuries A.D.," in W. Bowden, L. Lavan, and C. Machado (eds.), *Recent Research on the Late Antique Countryside, Late Antique Archaeology* 2 (Leiden 2004) 219–46.

P. Ballet, N. Dieudonné-Glad, and C. Saliou (eds.), *La rue dans l'antiquité. Définition, aménagement, devenir* (Renes 2008).

A. Bammer, "Ein spätantiker Torbau aus Ephesos," *ÖJh* 51 (1976–1977) Beiblatt, 92–126.

A. Bammer, R. Fleischer, and D. Knibbe, *Führer durch das Archäologische Museum in Selçuk-Ephesos* (Vienna 1974).

J. Banaji, *Agrarian Change in Late Antiquity: Gold, Labour, and Aristocratic Domination* (Oxford 2001).

J. Bardill, "The Golden Gate of Constantinople. A triumphal arch of Theodosius I," *AJA* 103 (1999) 671–96.

G. Barker, *Farming the Desert: The UNESCO Libyan Valleys Archaeological Survey* (Paris 1996).

L.W. Barnard, "The origins and emergence of the church in Edessa during the first two centuries A.D.," *VigChr* 22 (1968) 161–75.

P. Barresi, "Il sofista Flavio Damiano di Efeso e la costruzione di terme-ginnasi nell'Asia Minore romana di età imperiale," in O.D. Cordovana and M. Galli (eds.), *Arte e memoria culturale nell'età della Seconda Sofistica* (Cantania 2007) 137–51.

M. Basedow, "What the blind man saw: New information from the Iron Age at Troy," in C. Mattusch, A. Brauer, and A.A. Donohue (eds.), *Common Ground: Archaeology, Art, Science, and Humanities* (Oxford 2006) 88–92.

S. Bassett, "The antiquities in the hippodrome of Constantinople," *DOP* 45 (1991) 87–96.

S. Bassett, "*Historiae custos*: Sculpture and tradition in the baths of Zeuxippos," *AJA* 100 (1996) 491–506.

S. Bassett, "'Excellent offerings': The Lausos collection in Constantinople," *ArtBull* 82 (2000) 6–25.

S. Bassett, *The Urban Image of Late Antique Constantinople* (Cambridge 2004).

S. Bassett, "Ancient statuary in fourth-century Constantinople: Subject, style and function," in F.A. Bauer and C. Witschel (eds.), *Statuen in der Spätantike* (Wiesbaden 2007) 189–202.

S. Bassett, "The late antique image of Menander," *GRBS* 48 (2008) 201–25.

S. Bassett, "Style and meaning in the imperial panels in San Vitale, Ravenna," *Artibus et Historiae* 57 (2008) 49–57.

G.E. Bates, *Byzantine Coins*, *Sardis* M1 (Cambridge, MA 1971).

F.A. Bauer, *Stadt, Platz und Denkmal in der Spätantike: Untersuchungen zur Ausstattung des öffentlichen Raums in den spätantiken Städten Rom, Konstantinopel und Ephesos* (Mainz 1996).

F.A. Bauer and C. Witschel, "Statuen in der Spätantike," in eidem (eds.), *Statuen in der Spätantike* (Wiesbaden 2007) 1–26.

F.A. Bauer and C. Witschel (eds.), *Statuen in der Spätantike* (Wiesbaden 2007).

P. Baumeister, "Die Wasserversorgung," in A. Filges (ed.), *Blaundos. Berichte zur Erforschung einer Kleinstadt im lydisch-phrygischen Grenzgebiet*, *IstForsch* 48 (Tübingen 2006) 261–68.

P. Baumeister, D. Roos, and T. Saner, "Die Keloşk Kale. Ein spätantiker Gebäudekomplex im türkischen Euphratbogen. Studien zu Osrhoene in der Spätantike I," *IstMitt* 57 (2007) 623–74.

M. Baxandall, *Painting and Experience in Fifteenth-Century Italy, A Primer in the Social History of Pictorial Style* (Oxford 1972).

G. Becatti, *La colonna coclide istoriata* (Rome 1960).

G. Bejor, *Vie colonnate. Paesaggi urbani del mondo antico*, *RdA* Suppl. 22 (Rome 1999).

I. Bekker (ed.), *Georgius Cedrenus [et] Ioannis Scylitzae* (Bonn 1838–1839).

K. Belke, *Galatien und Lykaonien, Tabula Imperii Byzantini* 4 (Vienna 1984).

H.I. Bell, *Greek Papyri in the British Museum* IV. *The Aphrodito Papyri* (London 1910).

A.R. Bellinger and C.B. Welles, "A third-century contract of sale from Edessa in Osrhoene," *YCS* 5 (1935) 93–154.

M.L. Berenfeld, "The Triconch House and the predecessors of the Bishop's Palace at Aphrodisias," *AJA* 113 (2009) 203–29.

M. Bergmann, *Marc Aurel* (Frankfurt 1978).

A.M. Berlin, "Studies in Hellenistic Ilion: The Lower City. Stratified assemblages and chronology," *Studia Troica* 9 (1999) 73–157.

M. Berndt, *Funde aus dem Survey auf der Halbinsel von Milet (1992–1999)*, *Internationale Archäologie* 79 (Rahden 2003).

M. Bieber, *The Sculpture of the Hellenistic Age* (New York 1961).

G. Bieg, K. Belke, and B. Tekkök, "Die mittel-bis spätbyzantinische Besiedlung innerhalb des Nationalparks 'Troia und die Troas'," *Studia Troica* 18 (2008) 163–97.

G. Bieg, B. Tekkök, and R. Aslan, "Die spätrömische Besiedlung der Troas—ein Überblick," *Studia Troica* 16 (2006) 147–70.

L. Bier, "The bouleuterion at Ephesos: Some observations for a new survey," in P. Scherrer, H. Taeuber, and H. Thür (eds.), *Steine und Wege, Festschrift für D. Knibbe, Sonderschriften des Österreichischen Archäologischen Institutes* 32 (Vienna 1999) 7–18.

L. Bier, "The Bouleuterion," in C. Ratté and R.R.R. Smith, *Aphrodisias Papers* 4. *New Research on the City and its Monuments*, *JRA* Suppl. 70 (Portsmouth, RI 2008) 144–68.

L. Bier, *The Bouleuterion at Ephesos, Forschungen in Ephesos* IX 5 (Vienna 2011).

O. Bingöl, *Menderes Magnesiası* (Ankara 1998).

O. Bingöl, *Magnesia ad Maeandrum: The City of Artemis with "White Eyebrows"* (Istanbul 2007).

A.R. Birley, "From Hadrian to the Antonines," in A.K. Bowman, P. Garnsey, and D. Rathbone (eds.), *The Cambridge Ancient History*. XI. *The High Empire. AD 70–192* (Cambridge 2000) 132–94.

R.E. Blanton, *Hellenistic, Roman and Byzantine Settlement Patterns of the Coastal Lands of Western Rough Cilicia, BAR-IS* 879 (Oxford 2000).

C.W. Blegen, "The excavations at Troy, 1932," *AJA* 36 (1932) 445–46.

C.W. Blegen, "Excavations at Troy, 1933," *AJA* 38 (1934) 223–48.

C.W. Blegen, "Excavations at Troy, 1935," *AJA* 39 (1935) 550–87.

C.W. Blegen, J. Caskey, M. Rawson, and J. Sperling, *Troy I. The First and Second Settlements* (Princeton 1950).

I. Blum, "Die Stadtmauern von Alt-Milet: Ergebnisse des Surveys 1996 und 1997," *AA* (1999) 53–76.

I. Blum and E. Altenhöfer, "Milet in der römischen Kaiserzeit," in O. Dally et al. (eds.), *ZeitRäume. Milet in Kaiserzeit und Spätantike* (Regensburg 2009) 43–59.

R. Bol et al., *Milet* V 2. *Marmorskulpturen der römischen Kaiserzeit aus Milet—Aufstellungskontext und programmatische Aussage* (Berlin and New York 2011).

J. Borchhardt et al., "Bericht der Grabungskampagne in Limyra 2001," *Kazı Sonuçları Toplantısı* 24.2 (2002) 303–14.

B. Borg (ed.), *Paideia. The World of the Second Sophistic* (Berlin 2004).

B. Borg, "Bilder für die Ewigkeit der glanzvoller Auftritt? Zum Repräsentationsverhalten der stadtrömischen Eliten im dritten Jahrhundert n.Chr.," in F.A. Bauer and C. Witschel (eds.), *Statuen in der Spätantike* (Wiesbaden 2007) 43–78.

D. Boschung, *Die Bildnisse des Augustus, Das römische Herrscherbild* I 2 (Berlin 1993).

D. Boschung, *Gens Augusta, Monumenta Artis Romanae* XXXII (Mainz 2002).

D. Boschung, "Die Präsentation von Geschichte im Stadtbild der Kaiserzeit," in O.D. Cordovana and M. Galli (eds.), *Arte e memoria culturale nell'età della Seconda Sofistica* (Catania 2007) 103–07.

C.E. Bosworth, *The History of al-Tabari* 5. *The Sasanids, the Byzantines, the Lakhmids, and Yemen* (Albany 1999).

W. Bowden, A. Gutteridge, and C. Machado (eds.), *Social and Political Life in Late Antiquity, Late Antique Archaeology* 3.1 (Leiden 2006).

A. Bowman and A. Wilson, "Quantifying the Roman economy: Integration, growth, decline?" in eidem (eds.), *Quantifying the Roman Economy: Methods and Problems, Oxford Studies in the Roman Economy* 1 (Oxford 2009) 3–84.

H. Brandenburg, "Die Verwendung von Spolien und originalen Werkstücken in der spätantiken Architektur," in J. Poeschke (ed.), *Antike Spolien in der Architektur des Mittelalters und der Renaissance* (Munich 1996) 11–48.

H. Brandenburg, "Prachtentfaltung und Monumentalität als Bauaufgaben frühchristlicher Kirchenbaukunst," in J. Gebauer et al. (eds.), *Bildergeschichte. Festschrift für Klaus Stähler* (Möhnesee 2004) 59–76.

W. Brandes, *Die Städte Kleinasiens im 7. und 8. Jahrhundert* (Amsterdam 1989).

W. Brandes, "Byzantine cities in the seventh and eighth centuries—different sources, different histories?" in G.P. Brogiolo and B. Ward-Perkins (eds.), *The Idea and Ideal of the Town between Late Antiquity and the Early Middle Ages, The Transformation of the Roman World* 4 (Leiden 1999) 25–58.

G. Brands, "Die spätantike Stadt und ihre Christianisierung," in G. Brands and H.-G. Severin (eds.), *Die spätantike Stadt und ihre Christianisierung* (Wiesbaden 2003) 1–26.

G. Brands and H.-G. Severin (eds.), *Die spätantike Stadt und ihre Christianisierung* (Wiesbaden 2003).

C. Brasse, "Von der Stadtmauer zur Stadtgeschichte. Das Befestigungssystem von Antiochia am Orontes," in J. Lorentzen et al. (eds.), *Aktuelle Forschungen zur Konstruktion, Funktion und Semantik antiker Stadtbefestigungen, Byzas* 10 (Istanbul 2010) 261–82.

O. Brendel, *Prolegomena to the Study of Roman Art* (New Haven, CT 1974).

B. Brenk, "Zur Christianisierung der spätrömischen Stadt im östlichen Mittelmeerraum," in G. Brands and H.-G. Severin (eds.), *Die spätantike Stadt und ihre Christianisierung* (Wiesbaden 2003) 85–95.

P. Briant, *Irrigation et drainage dans l'antiquité, qanats et canalisations souterraines en Iran, en Égypte, et en Grèce* (Paris 2001).

L.R. Brody, *The Aphrodite of Aphrodisias, Aphrodisias* III (Mainz 2007).

G.P. Brogiolo and B. Ward-Perkins (eds.), *The Idea and Ideal of the Town between Late Antiquity and the Early Middle Ages, The Transformation of the Roman World* 4 (Leiden 1999).

E.W. Brooks (ed.), *Chronica Minora* 3, *Corpus Scriptorum Christianorum Orientalium* 5, 6 (Paris 1905–1907).
T.R.S. Broughton, "Roman Asia," in T. Frank and A.C. Johnson (eds.), *An Economic Survey of Ancient Rome* (Baltimore 1933) 499–916.
P. Brown, *The Body and Society: Men, Women, and Sexual Renunciation in Early Christianity* (New York 1988).
S.-G. Bruer and M. Kunze, *Der Stadtplan von Patara und Beobachtungen zu den Stadtmauern, Patara* I.1 (Istanbul 2010).
J.-P. Brun, "La discrimination entre les installations oléicoles et vinicoles," in M.-C. Amouretti and J.-P. Brun (eds.), *La production du vin et de l'huile en Méditerranée* (Athens 1993) 511–37.
J.-P. Brun, *Le vin et l'huile dans la Méditerranée antique: Viticulture, oléiculture et procédés de transformation* (Paris 2003).
G. Bruns, *Die Obelisk und seine Basis auf dem Hippodrom zu Konstantinopel* (Istanbul 1935).
H. Buchwald, "Early Christian Basilica EA and Church E," in G.M.A. Hanfmann, *Sardis from Prehistoric to Roman Times. Results of the Archaeological Exploration of Sardis, 1958–1975* (Cambridge, MA 1983) 196–204.
H. Buchwald, "Western Asia Minor as a generator of architectural forms: Provincial back-wash or dynamic center of production?" *JÖB* 34 (1984) 199–234.
W.H. Buckler and D.M. Robinson, "Greek inscriptions from Sardes IV," *AJA* 18 (1914) 35–74.
W.H. Buckler and D.M. Robinson, *Sardis* VII. *Greek and Latin Inscriptions* (Leiden 1932).
B. Burrell, *Neokoroi. Greek Cities and Roman Emperors* (Leiden 2004).
B. Burrell, "A hoard of minimi from Sardis and the currency of the fifth century C.E.," *RN* 163 (2007) 235–82.
B. Burrell, "Small bronze hoards at late fifth century C.E. Sardis," in N.D. Cahill (ed.), *Love for Lydia: A Sardis Anniversary Volume Presented to Crawford H. Greenewalt, Jr., Sardis* R4 (Cambridge, MA 2008) 159–69.
H.C. Butler, *Syria. Publications of the Princeton University Archaeological Expeditions to Syria from 1904–5 and 1909.* II, *Architecture.* B, *Northern Syria* (Leiden 1920).
H.C. Butler, *Sardis* I. *The Excavations.* Pt. 1, *1910–1914* (Leiden 1922).
H.C. Butler, *Early Churches in Syria. Fourth to Seventh Centuries* (Princeton 1929).
T.V. Buttrey, A. Johnston, K.M. MacKenzie, and M.L. Bates, *Greek, Roman, and Islamic Coins from Sardis, Sardis* M7 (Cambridge, MA 1981).
M. Cadario, *La corazza di Alessandro. Loricati di tipo ellenistico dal IV secolo a.C. al II d.C., Pubblicazioni della Facoltà di Lettere e Filosofia dell'Università degli Studi di Milano* 218 (2004).
N.D. Cahill (ed.), *Love for Lydia: A Sardis Anniversary Volume Presented to Crawford H. Greenewalt, Jr., Sardis* R4 (Cambridge, MA 2008).
N.D. Cahill, "Mapping Sardis," in N.D. Cahill (ed.), *Love for Lydia: A Sardis Anniversary Volume Presented to Crawford H. Greenewalt, Jr., Sardis* R4 (Cambridge, MA 2008) 111–24.
J.-P. Caillet, "Les dédicaces privées de pavements de mosaïques à la fin de l'antiquité. Occident européen et monde grec: données socio-économiques," in X. Barral i Altet (ed.), *Artistes, artisans et production artistique au Moyen Age* 2. *Commande et travail* (Paris 1987) 15–36.
H.-U. Cain and M. Pfanner, "Die Agora Milets in der Kaiserzeit und Spätantike," in O. Dally et al. (eds.), *ZeitRäume. Milet in Kaiserzeit und Spätantike* (Regensburg 2009) 83–95.
O. Callot, *Huileries antiques de Syrie du Nord* (Paris 1984).
A. Cameron, *Procopius and the Sixth Century* (London 1985) 84–112.
A. Cameron, *The Mediterranean World in Late Antiquity AD 395–600* (London and New York 1993).
A. Cameron and J. Herrin (eds.), *Constantinople in the Early Eighth Century: The* Parastaseis Syntomoi Chronikai (Leiden 1984).
A. Can Özren, "Die Skulpturenausstattung kaiserzeitlicher Theater in der Provinz Asia," *Thetis* 3 (1996) 99–128.
S. Casson et al., *Preliminary Report upon the Excavations carried out in and near the Hippodrome of Constantinople in 1927* (London 1928).
S. Casson et al., *Second Report upon the Excavations carried out in and near the Hippodrome of Constantinople in 1928* (London 1929).
S. Casson et al., "Les fouilles de l'hippodrome de Constantinople," *GBA* 30.1 (1930) 215–42.
P. Cavuoto, *Macrino* (Naples 1983).

J.-B. Chabot (ed.), *Chronique de Michel le syrien* (Paris 1899–1905).

J.-B. Chabot (ed.), *Chronicon ad annum Christi 1234 pertinens, Corpus Scriptorum Christianorum Orientalium* 81, 82, 109 (Paris 1916–1920).

V. Chapot, *La frontière de l'Euphrate de Pompée à la conquête arabe* (Paris 1907).

V. Christides, "Arab-Byzantine struggle in the sea. Naval tactics (7th–11th centuries A.D.)," in Y.Y. al-Hijji and V. Christides (ed.), *Aspects of Arab Seafaring. An Attempt to Fill in the Gaps of Maritime History* (Athens 2002) 87–106.

N. Christie and R.M. Harrison, "Excavations at Amorium: 1992 interim report," *AnatSt* 43 (1993) 147–62.

D. Claude, *Die byzantinische Stadt im 6. Jahrhundert* (Munich 1969).

R. Coates-Stephens, "The reuse of ancient statuary in late antique Rome and the end of the statue habit," in F.A. Bauer and C. Witschel (eds.), *Statuen in der Spätantike* (Wiesbaden 2007) 171–87.

A. Comfort, C. Abadie-Reynal, and R. Ergeç, "Crossing the Euphrates in antiquity: Zeugma seen from space," *AnatSt* 50 (2000) 99–126A.

A. Comfort and R. Ergeç, "Following the Euphrates in antiquity: North-south routes around Zeugma," *AnatSt* 51 (2001) 19–49.

M.W. Conkey and C.A. Hasdorf (eds.), *The Uses of Style in Archaeology* (Cambridge 1990).

J.M. Cook, *The Troad. An Archaeological and Topographical Study* (Oxford 1973).

J.S. Crawford, *The Byzantine Shops at Sardis, Sardis* M9 (Cambridge, MA 1990).

D. Crouch, *Water Management in Ancient Greek Cities* (New York 1993).

J. Crow, "A review of the physical remains of the frontiers of Cappadocia," in P.W.M. Freeman and D. Kennedy (eds.), *The Defence of the Roman and Byzantine East, BAR-IS* 297, *British Institute of Archaeology at Ankara Monograph* 8 (Oxford 1986) 77–91.

J. Crow, "The long walls of Thrace," in C. Mango and G. Dagron (eds.), *Constantinople and its Hinterland* (Aldershot 1995) 109–24.

J. Crow, "Fortifications and urbanism in late antiquity: Thessaloniki and other eastern cities," in L. Lavan (ed.), *Recent Research in Late-Antique Urbanism, JRA* Suppl. 42 (Portsmouth, RI 2001) 89–105.

J. Crow, "The infrastructure of a great city: Earth, walls and water in late antique Constantinople," in L. Lavan, E. Zanini, and A. Sarantis (eds.), *Technology in Transition: A.D. 300–650, Late Antique Archaeology* 4 (Boston 2007) 251–85.

J. Crow and D.H. French, "New research on the Euphrates frontier in Turkey," in W.S. Hanson and L.J.F. Keppie (eds.), *Roman Frontier Studies, 1979, BAR-IS* 71 (Oxford 1980) 903–12.

J. Crow and A. Ricci, "Investigating the hinterland of Constantinople. Interim report on the Anastasian Long Wall," *JRA* 10 (1997) 235–62.

W. Cureton, *Ancient Syriac Documents Relative to the Earliest Establishment of Christianity in Edessa and the Neighbouring Countries* (London 1864, reprint 1967).

E. Curtius, "Philadelphia: Nachtrag zu den Beiträgen zur Geschichte und Topographie Kleinasiens," *AbhBerl* (1872) 93–95.

E. Dabrowa (ed.), *The Roman and Byzantine Army in the East* (Kraków 1994).

G. Dagron, *Naissance d'une capitale. Constantinople et ses institutions de 330* (Paris 1974).

G. Dagron and D. Feissel, *Inscriptions de Cilicie, Travaux et mémoires du Centre de recherche d'histoire et civilisation de Byzance* 4 (Paris 1987).

Ö. Dalgıç, "Early Christian and Byzantine churches," in C. Ratté and P.D. De Staebler (eds.), *Aphrodisias* V. *The Aphrodisias Regional Survey* (Mainz forthcoming).

O. Dally and A. Scholl, "Skulptur und Raum," in O. Dally et al. (eds.), *ZeitRäume. Milet in Kaiserzeit und Spätantike* (Regensburg 2009) 143–53.

O. Dally et al. (eds.), *ZeitRäume. Milet in Kaiserzeit und Spätantike* (Regensburg 2009).

C. Damon, *Res Gestae divi Augusti* (Bryn Mawr 1995).

F. D'Andria, "Hierapolis of Phrygia: Its evolution in Hellenistic and Roman times," in D. Parrish (ed.), *Urbanism in Western Asia Minor: New Studies on Aphrodisias, Ephesos, Hierapolis, Pergamon, Perge and Xanthos, JRA* Suppl. 45 (Portsmouth, RI 2001) 96–115.

F. D'Andria, *Hierapolis in Phrygien, Alte anatolische Städte* 5 (Istanbul 2003).
D. de Bernardi Ferrero, "Excavations and restorations during 1994 in Hierapolis of Phrygia," *Kazı Sonuçları Toplantısı* 17.2 (1995) 95–105.
D. de Bernardi Ferrero (ed.), *Saggi in onore di Paolo Verzone, Hierapolis: Scavi e ricerche* 4 = *Archaeologica* 137 (Rome 2002).
M. Decker, "The wine trade of Cilicia in late antiquity," *ARAM* 17 (2005) 52–53.
F.W. Deichmann, "Die Spolien in der spätantiken Architektur," *SBMünch* 6 (Munich 1975) 34–36.
F.W. Deichmann and U. Peschlow, *Zwei spätantike Ruinenstätte in Nordmesopotamien, Sitzungsberichte der Bayerischen Akademie der Wissenschaften, philosophisch-historische Klasse* 1977/2 (Munich 1977).
R. Delbreuck, *Spätantike Kaiserporträts* (Berlin 1933).
A. Demandt, *Die Spätantike, Handbuch der Altertumswissenschaften* III 6 (Munich 1989).
G. Despinis, T. Stefanidou-Tiveriou, and E. Voutiras, *Κατάλογος Γλυπτών τού Αρχαιολογικού Μουσείου Θεσσαλονίκης* (Thessaloniki 1997).
P.D. De Staebler, "The city wall and the making of a late-antique provincial capital," in C. Ratté and R.R.R. Smith (eds.), *Aphrodisias Papers* 4. *New Research on the City and its Monuments, JRA* Suppl. 70 (Portsmouth, RI 2008) 284–318.
P.D. De Staebler, "Roman pottery," in C. Ratté and P.D. De Staebler (eds.), *Aphrodisias* V. *The Aphrodisias Regional Survey* (Mainz forthcoming).
W.G. Dever (ed.), *Preliminary Excavation Reports: Sardis, Paphos, Caesarea Maritima, Shiqmim, 'Ain Ghazal, AASOR* 51 (New Haven, CT 1993) 1–126.
W.G. Dever (ed.), *Preliminary Excavation Reports: Sardis, Bir Umm Fawakhir, Tell el-'Umeri, The Combined Caesarea Expeditions, and Tell Dothan, AASOR* 52 (New Haven, CT 1994) 1–190.
W.G. Dever (ed.), *Preliminary Excavation Reports: Sardis, Idalion, and Tell el-Handaquq North, AASOR* 53 (New Haven, CT 1995) 1–154.
J. Devreker and F. Vermeulen, "Fouilles et prospections à Pessinonte: campagne de 1996," *Anatolia Antiqua* 6 (1998) 249–58.
H.W. Dey, *The Aurelian Wall and the Refashioning of Imperial Rome, AD 271–855* (Cambridge 2011).
M. Di Branco, "Lavoro e conflittualità in una città tardoantica. Una rilettura dell'epigrafe di Sardi *CIG* 3467," *Antiquité tardive* 8 (2000) 181–208.
A. Diler, "Akdeniz bölgesi antik çağ zeytinyağı ve şarap işlikleri," *Araştırma Sonuçları Toplantısı* 11 (1993) 505–20.
A. Diler, "Akdeniz bölgesi antik çağ zeytin ve üzüm presleri–1993," *Araştırma Sonuçları Toplantısı* 12 (1994) 441–57.
A. Diler, "İç Karia yüzey araştırmaları 1994," *Araştırma Sonuçları Toplantısı* 13 (1995) 315–33.
A. Diler, "İç Karia yüzey araştırması 1995," *Araştırma Sonuçları Toplantısı* 14 (1996) 189–206.
S. Dillon, "The portraits of a civic benefactor of 2nd century Ephesos," *JRA* 9 (1996) 261–74.
L. Dindorff (ed.), *Ioannis Malalae Chronographia* (Bonn 1831).
L. Dindorff (ed.), *Chronicon paschale* (Bonn 1832).
F. Dirimtekin, "Adduction de l'eau a Byzance dans la région dite 'Bulgarie'," *CahArch* 10 (1959) 217–43.
M.H. Dodgeon and S.N.C. Lieu, *The Roman Eastern Frontier and the Persian Wars. A.D. 226–363* (London and New York 1991).
J. Donderer, "Irreversible Deponierung von Großplastik bei Griechen, Etruskern und Römern," *ÖJh* 61 (1991–1992) Beiblatt, 194–276.
F. Donner, *Muhammed and the Believers: At the Origins of Islam* (Cambridge, MA 2010).
J. Dörig, "Lysipps leztes Werke," *JdI* 72 (1957) 19–43.
C. Dorl-Klingenschmid, *Prunkbrunnen in kleinasiatischen Städten, Studien zur antiken Stadt* 7 (Munich 2001).
W. Dörpfeld, *Troia und Ilion. Ergebnisse der Ausgrabungen in den vorhistorischen und historischen Schichten von Ilion 1870–1894* (Athen 1902).
G. Downey, "Justinian as a builder," *ArtB* 22 (1950) 262–66.
G. Downey, "The Persian campaign in Syria in A.D. 540," *Speculum* 28.2 (1953) 340–48.
A.G. Drachmann, *Ancient Oil Mills and Presses* (Kobenhavn 1932).

H.J.W. Drijvers, "Hatra, Palmyra und Edessa. Die Städte der syrisch-mesopotamischen Wüste in politischer, kulturgeschichtlicher und religionsgeschichtlicher Bedeutung," *ANRW* II 8 (1977) 799–906.

J. Durliat and A. Guillou, "Le tarif d'Abydos (vers 492)," *BCH* 108 (1984) 581–98.

S. Durugönül, *Türme und Siedlungen im Rauhen Kilikien: Eine Untersuchung zu den archäologischen Hinterlassenschaften im Olbischen Territorium, Asia Minor Studien* 28 (Bonn 1998) 28–33.

R. Duval, *Histoire d'Édesse, politique, religieuse et littéraire* (Paris 1892, reprint Amsterdam 1975).

J. Eadie, "The transformation of the eastern frontier, 260–305," in R.W. Mathisen and H.S. Sivan (eds.), *Shifting Frontiers in Late Antiquity* (Aldershot 1996) 72–82.

A. Effenberger, "Nochmals zur Aufstellung des Theodosius - Obelisken in Hippodrome von Konstantinopel," *Gymnasium* 114 (2007) 587–89.

F. Eichler, "Die österreichischen Ausgrabungen in Ephesos im Jahre 1961," *AnzWien* 99 (1962) 39–41.

F. Eichler, "Die österreichischen Ausgrabungen in Ephesos im Jahre 1962," *AnzWien* 100 (1963) 47.

F. Eichler, "Die österreichischen Ausgrabungen in Ephesos im Jahre 1963," *AnzWien* 101 (1964) 40–41.

F. Eichler, "Die österreichischen Ausgrabungen in Ephesos im Jahre 1966," *AnzWien* 104 (1967) 20–21.

F. Eichler, "Die österreichischen Ausgrabungen in Ephesos im Jahre 1967," *AnzWien* 105 (1968) 80–82.

I. Eichner, "Frühbyzantinische Wohnhäuser in Kilikien. Arbeitsbericht über die Kampagne 1998," *Araştırma Sonuçları Toplantısı* 17 (2000) 275–82.

I. Eichner, *Frühbyzantinische Wohnhäuser in Kilikien. Baugeschichtliche Untersuchung zu den Wohnformen der Region um Seleukia am Kalykadnos, IstForsch* 52 (Tübingen 2011).

V. Eid, *Im Land des Ararat. Völker und Kulturen im Osten Anatoliens* (Stuttgart 2006).

J. Elkins, "Style," in J.S. Turner (ed.), *Dictionary of Art*, vol. 29 (New York 1996) 876–83.

S. Ellis, "Middle class houses in late antiquity," in W. Bowden, A. Gutteridge, and C. Machado (eds.), *Social and Political Life in Late Antiquity, Late Antique Archaeology* 3.1 (Leiden 2006) 413–37.

S. Ellis, "Late antique housing and the uses of residential buildings. An overview," in L. Lavan, L. Özgenel, and A. Sarantis (eds.), *Housing in Late Antiquity. From Palaces to Shops, Late Antique Archaeology* 3.2 (Leiden 2007) 1–22.

J.-Y. Empereur, *La gloire d'Alexandrie* (Paris 1998).

I. Engelmann and P. Niewöhner, "Bauen nach der Krise. Die Spoliengalerie an der Apsis der Apostelkirche von Anazarbos," in D. Kreikenbom et al. (eds.), *Krise und Kult. Vorderer Orient und Nordafrika von Aurelian bis Justinian, Millennium Studies* 28 (Mainz 2010) 109–37.

J. Engemann, "Zur Verbreitung magischer Übelabwehr in der nichtchristlichen und christlichen Spätantike," *JAC* 18 (1975) 22–48.

J. Engemann, "Ein Tischfuß mit Dionysos-Satyr-Darstellung aus Abū Mīnā/Ägypten," *JAC* 41 (1998) 169.

E. Equini Schneider, *Elaiussa Sebaste I: Campagne di scavo, 1995–1997* (Rome 1999).

E. Equini Schneider, "Elaiussa Sebaste—The 2007 excavation and conservation season," *Kazı Sonuçları Toplantısı* 30.4 (2008) 177–90.

K. Erim, *Aphrodisias: City of Venus Aphrodite* (London 1986).

K. Erim, *Aphrodisias: Ein Führer durch die antike Stadt und das Museum* (Istanbul 1989).

R.M. Errington, *Roman Imperial Policy from Julian to Theodosius* (Chapel Hill 2006).

E. Ertekin, "İlkçağ'da Tarsus 'ketenciler'i ve ketenleri," *Olba* 11 (2005) 155–75.

F. Ertuğ, "Linseed oil and oil mills in central Turkey. Flax/linum and Eruca, important oil plants of Anatolia," *AnatSt* 50 (2000) 171–84.

S. Esmonde Cleary, *The Ending of Roman Britain* (London 1989).

S. Esmonde Cleary, "Civil defences in the west under the high empire," in P. Wilson (ed.), *The Archaeology of Roman Towns. Studies in Honour of John S. Wacher* (Oxford 2003) 72–85.

S. Eyice, "Silifke ve dolaylarında yapılan toprakiüstü arkeolojik araştırmalar raporu 1979," *Belleten* 44 (1980) 111–24.

S. Eyice, "Einige byzantinische Kleinstädte im Rauhen Kilikien," in *150 Jahre Deutsches Archäologisches Institut* (Mainz 1981) 204–09.

M. Falkener, *Ephesus, and the Temple of Diana* (London 1862).

D. Feissel, "Vicaires et proconsuls d'Asie du IVe au VIe siècle," *Antiquité tardive* 6 (1998) 91–104.

O. Feld, "Die beiden Kirchen in Hierapolis Kastabala," in O. Feld (ed.), *Studien zur spätantiken und byzantinischen Kunst: F.W. Deichmann gewidmet* 1 (Bonn 1986) 77–86.

O. Feld, "Eine Kirche für Maria in Miletos," in C. Striker (ed.), *Architectural Studies in Memory of Richard Krautheimer* (Mainz 1996) 67–70.

O. Feld, "Miletos e Kos: le isole microasiatiche e la terra ferma," *Corso di cultura sull'arte ravennate e bizantina* 44 (1998) 123–42.

A. Filges, *Standbilder jugendlicher Göttinnen. Klassische und frühhellenistische Gewandstatuen mit Brustwulst und ihre kaiserzeitliche Rezeption, Arbeiten zur Archäologie* (Cologne 1997).

A. Filges, "Stadtentwicklung im Gebiet des oberen Mäander. Die lydisch-phrygische Grenzregion am Beispiel von Blaundos," in E. Schwertheim and E. Winter (eds.), *Stadt und Stadtentwicklung in Kleinasien, Asia Minor Studien* 50 (Bonn 2003) 37–42.

A. Filges, "Blaundos," in W. Radt (ed.), *Stadtgrabungen und Stadtforschung im westlichen Kleinasien. Geplantes und Erreichtes, Byzas* 3 (Istanbul 2006) 49–60.

A. Filges (ed.), *Blaundos. Berichte zur Erforschung einer Kleinstadt im lydisch-phrygischen Grenzgebiet, IstForsch* 48 (Tübingen 2006).

A. Filges, "Blaundos im Laufe der Zeiten: Eine Zusammenschau und der Versuch einer Einbindung in die Regionalgeschichte," in A. Filges (ed.), *Blaundos. Berichte zur Erforschung einer Kleinstadt im lydisch-phrygischen Grenzgebiet, IstForsch* 48 (Tübingen 2006) 312–20.

A. Filges, "Das byzantinische Blaundos in Schriftquellen und Karten," in A. Filges (ed.), *Blaundos. Berichte zur Erforschung einer Kleinstadt im lydisch-phrygischen Grenzgebiet, IstForsch* 48 (Tübingen 2006) 26–29.

A. Filges, "Die Fundkeramik," in A. Filges (ed.), *Blaundos. Berichte zur Erforschung einer Kleinstadt im lydisch-phrygischen Grenzgebiet, IstForsch* 48 (Tübingen 2006) 304–11.

A. Filges, "Die Stadtmauer: Mauerring und Türme," in A. Filges (ed.), *Blaundos. Berichte zur Erforschung einer Kleinstadt im lydisch-phrygischen Grenzgebiet, IstForsch* 48 (Tübingen 2006) 67–78.

A. Filges, "Der Tempel 1 (Ceres-Tempel)," in A. Filges (ed.), *Blaundos. Berichte zur Erforschung einer Kleinstadt im lydisch-phrygischen Grenzgebiet, IstForsch* 48 (Tübingen 2006) 175–76.

A. Filges, "Von Mlaundos zu Blaundos. Literarische Quellen und Überlegungen zur frühen Geschichte bis zur Integration in das pergamenische Reich," in A. Filges (ed.), *Blaundos. Berichte zur Erforschung einer Kleinstadt im lydisch-phrygischen Grenzgebiet, IstForsch* 48 (Tübingen 2006) 17–20.

A. Filges, *Skulpturen und Statuenbasen von der klassischen Epoche bis in die Kaiserzeit, Didyma* 5 (Mainz 2007).

N. Fıratlı, *La sculpture byzantine figurée au Musée archéologique d'Istanbul, Bibliothèque de l'Institut français d'études anatoliennes d'Istanbul* 30 (Paris 1990).

K. Fittschen, review of J. İnan and E. Rosenbaum, *Roman and Early Byzantine Portrait Sculpture in Asia Minor* (London 1966), *GGA* 225 (1973) 46–67.

K. Fittschen, *Prinzenbildnisse antoninischer Zeit, Beiträge zur Erschliessung hellenistischer und kaiserzeitlicher Skulptur und Architektur* 18 (Mainz 1999).

K. Fittschen and P. Zanker, *Katalog der römischen Porträts in den Capitolinischen Museen und den anderen kommunalen Sammlungen der Stadt Rom* III (Mainz 1983).

R. Fleischer, *Artemis von Ephesos und verwandte Kultstatuen aus Anatolien und Syrien, EPRO* 35 (Leiden 1973).

F. Fless, *Opferdiener und Kultmusiker auf stadtrömischen historisches Reliefs: Untersuchungen zur Ikonographie, Funktion und Benennung* (Mainz 1995).

R.J. Forbes, *Studies in Ancient Technology* I (Leiden 1964).

E. Formigli, G. Lahusen, and R. Pecchioli, "Grossbronzen der Antike und Renaissance. Ein technisch-formaler Vergleich," in A. Dostert and F. Lang (eds.), *Mittel und Wege. Zur Bedeutung von Material und Technik in der Archäologie* (Möhnesee 2006) 125–37.

C. Foss, *Byzantine Cities of Western Asia Minor* (Ph.D. dissertation, Harvard University 1972).

C. Foss, "The Persians in Asia Minor and the end of antiquity," *EHR* 90 (1975) 721–47.

C. Foss, *Byzantine and Turkish Sardis, Sardis* M4 (Cambridge, MA 1976).

C. Foss, "Archaeology and the 'Twenty Cities' of Byzantine Asia," *AJA* 81 (1977) 469–86.

C. Foss, *Ephesus after Antiquity: A Late Antique, Byzantine and Turkish City* (Cambridge 1979).

C. Foss, "Appendix: Inscriptions related to the complex," in F.K. Yegül, *The Bath-Gymnasium Complex at Sardis*, *Sardis* R3 (Cambridge, MA 1986) 169–72.

C. Foss, "The Lycian coast in the Byzantine age," *DOP* 48 (1994) 1–52.

C. Foss, "The cities of Pamphylia in the Byzantine age," in idem, *Cities, Fortresses and Villages of Byzantine Asia Minor* 3, *Collected Studies, CS 538* (Aldershot 1996) 1–62.

C. Foss, "Syria in transition, AD 550–750: An archaeological approach," *DOP* 51 (1997) 189–269.

C. Foss, "The Persians in the Roman Near East (602–630 AD)," *JRAS* Ser. 3 13 (2003) 149–70.

C. Foss and D. Winfield, *Byzantine Fortifications: An Introduction* (Pretoria 1986).

E. Fossel, *Die Basilika am Staatsmarkt in Ephesos* (Graz 1982).

R. Frankel, "Oil and wine presses in the southern Levant in antiquity," *DOP* 51 (1997) 73–84.

R. Frankel, *Wine and Oil Production in Antiquity in Israel and Other Mediterranean Countries* (Sheffield 1999).

R. Frankel, S. Avitsur, and E. Ayalon, *History and Technology of Olive Oil in the Holy Land* (Tel Aviv 1994).

D.H. French, "New research on the Euphrates frontier: Supplementary notes 1 and 2," in S. Mitchell (ed.), *Armies and Frontiers in Roman and Byzantine Anatolia*, *BAR-IS* 156 (Oxford 1983) 71–101.

D.H. French, *Roman Roads and Milestones of Asia Minor*. Fasc. 2, *An Interim Catalogue of Milestones*, Part 1, *BAR-IS* 392, *British Institute of Archaeology at Ankara Monograph* 9 (Oxford 1988).

E.H. Freshfield, "Notes on a vellum album containing some original sketches of public buildings and monuments drawn by a German artist who visited Constantinople in 1574," *Archaeologia* 72 (1922) 87–104.

P. Frisch, *Die Inschriften von Ilion* (Bonn 1975).

M.M. Fulghum and F. Heintz, "A hoard of early Byzantine glass weights from Sardis," *AJN* second ser. 10 (1998) 105–20.

A. Garzya and R.J. Loenertz (eds.), *Procopii Gazaei epistolae et declamationes* (Ettal 1963).

M. Gawlikowski, "The last kings of Edessa," in R. Lavenant (ed.), *VII. Symposium Syriacum*, *Orientalia Christiana Analecta* 256 (Rome 1998) 421–28.

E. Giannichedda, "Metal production in late antiquity: From continuity of knowledge to changes in consumption," in L. Lavan, E. Zanini, and A. Sarantis (eds.), *Technology in Transition: A.D. 300–650*, *Late Antique Archaeology* 4 (Leiden 2006) 187–209.

J. Giese, "Baugeschichtliche Einordnung," in A. Filges (ed.), *Blaundos. Berichte zur Erforschung einer Kleinstadt im lydisch-pamphylischen Grenzgebiet*, *IstForsch* 48 (Tübingen 2006) 114–23.

J. Giese, "Das Nordtor," in A. Filges (ed.), *Blaundos. Berichte zur Erforschung einer Kleinstadt im lydisch-phrygischen Grenzgebiet*, *IstForsch* 48 (Tübingen 2006) 79–113.

C.-S. Giese Huebner, "Geomagnetische Prospektion 2002 bis 2005 in der Unterstadt von Troia," *Studia Troica* 16 (2006) 125–29.

G. Giglioli, *La colonna di Arcadio a Costantinopoli* (Naples 1952).

P. Gilles, *De topographia Constantinopoleos et de illius antiquitatibus libri quattuor* (Lyon 1561).

A. Giumlia, *Die neuattischen Doppelhermen* (Ph.D. dissertation, University of Vienna 1983).

C. Gliwitzkiy, "Die Kirche im sog. Bischofspalast zu Side," *IstMitt* 55 (2005) 337–408.

F. Goethert and H. Schleif, *Der Athenatempel von Ilion*, *Denkmäler antiker Architektur* 10 (Berlin 1962).

H.R. Goette, *Studien zu römischen Togadarstellungen* (Mainz 1990).

M. Goodway and P. Vandiver, in J.S. Crawford, *The Byzantine Shops at Sardis*, *Sardis* M9 (Cambridge, MA 1990) 129–34.

M. Gough, "Anazarbus," *AnatSt* 2 (1952) 85–150.

A. Grabar, *Martyrium: recherches sur le culte des reliques et l'art chrétien* (Paris 1943–46).

G. Greatrex, "Procopius and Agathias on the defenses of the Thracian Chersonese," in C. Mango and G. Dagron (eds.), *Constantinople and its Hinterland* (Aldershot 1995) 125–30.

C.H. Greenewalt, Jr., "The Sardis campaign of 1976," *BASOR* 229 (1978) 57–73.

C.H. Greenewalt, Jr., "Sardis in the age of Xenophon," in P. Briant (ed.), *Dans les pas des Dix-Mille*, *Pallas* 43 (Aix 1995) 125–45.

C.H. Greenewalt, Jr., "Sardis: Archaeological research and conservation projects in 1999," *Kazı Sonuçları Toplantısı* 22.1 (2000) 415–24.

C.H. Greenewalt, Jr., "Sardis: Archaeological research and conservation projects in 2000," *Kazı Sonuçları Toplantısı* 23.2 (2001) 227–34.
C.H. Greenewalt, Jr., "Sardis: Archaeological research and conservation projects in 2004," *Kazı Sonuçları Toplantısı* 27.2 (2005) 175–86.
C.H. Greenewalt, Jr., "Sardis," in W. Radt (ed.), *Stadtgrabungen und Stadtforschung im westlichen Kleinasien. Geplantes und Erreichtes, Byzas* 3 (Istanbul 2006) 359–72.
C.H. Greenewalt, Jr., "Sardis: Archaeological research and conservation projects in 2005," *Kazı Sonuçları Toplantısı* 28.2 (2006) 743–56.
C.H. Greenewalt, Jr., "Sardis: Archaeological research and conservation projects in 2006," *Kazı Sonuçları Toplantısı* 29.3 (2007) 371–86.
C.H. Greenewalt, Jr., "Sardis: Archaoelogical research and conservation projects in 2007," *Kazı Sonuçları Toplantısı* 30.4 (2008) 191–204.
C.H. Greenewalt, Jr., N.D. Cahill, and M.L. Rautman, "The Sardis campaign of 1984," *BASOR* Suppl. 25 (1988) 13–54.
C.H. Greenewalt, Jr., and E.E. Freedman, "The Sardis campaign of 1977," *BASOR* 233 (1979) 1–32.
C.H. Greenewalt, Jr., and M.L. Rautman, "The Sardis campaigns of 1994 and 1995," *AJA* 102 (1998) 469–505.
C.H. Greenewalt, Jr., and M.L. Rautman, "The Sardis campaigns of 1996, 1997, and 1998," *AJA* 104 (2000) 643–81.
C.H. Greenewalt, Jr., M.L. Rautman, and N.D. Cahill, "The Sardis campaign of 1985," *BASOR* Suppl. 25 (1988) 55–92.
C.H. Greenewalt, Jr., E.L. Sterud, and D.F. Belknap, "The Sardis campaign of 1978," *BASOR* 245 (1982) 1–34.
C.H. Greenewalt, Jr., et al., "The Sardis campaigns of 1979 and 1980," *BASOR* 249 (1983) 1–44.
C.H. Greenewalt, Jr., et al., "The Sardis campaign of 1986," *BASOR* Suppl. 26 (1990) 137–77.
C.H. Greenewalt, Jr., et al., *The City of Sardis: Approaches in Graphic Recording* (Cambridge, MA 2003).
I. Guidi (ed.), *Chronica Minora* 1, *Corpus Scriptorum Christianorum Orientalium* 1, 2 (Paris 1903).
E. Guidoboni, *Catalogue of Ancient Earthquakes in the Mediterranean Area up to the 10th Century* (Rome 1994).
R. Guilland, *Etudes de topographie de Constantinople byzantine* (Berlin and Amsterdam 1969).
S. Gündüz, "Kalkan Village, Kantarma Field Han," in A. Durukan (ed.), *The Cultural Heritage in the Towns of Birecik, Halfeti, Suruç, Bozova and Rumkale* (Ankara 2004) 265–66.
S. Guyer, "Zwei spätantike Grabmonumente Nordmesopotamiens und der älteste Märtyrergrab-Typus der christlichen Kunst," in E.F. Weidner (ed.), *Aus fünf Jahrtausenden morgenländischer Kultur. Festschrift für Max Freiherr von Oppenheim* (Berlin 1933) 148–56.
S. Guyer, "Eski-Hissar, ein römisches Lagerkastell im Gebiet von Edessa," in *Mélanges syriens offerts à R. Dussaud* (Paris 1939) 183–90.
S. Hadjisavvas, *Olive Oil Processing in Cyprus: From the Bronze Age to the Byzantine Period* (Nicosia 1992).
G. Haenel (ed.), *Codex Theodosianus* (Bonn 1837–1842).
S. Hagel and K. Tomaschitz, *Repertorium der westkilikischen Inschriften: Nach den Scheden der kleinasiatischen Kommission der Österreichischen Akademie der Wissenschaften* (Vienna 1998).
J. Haldon, *Byzantium in the Seventh Century. The Transformation of a Culture* (Cambridge 1997).
J. Haldon, "Social transformation in the 6th–9th c. East," in W. Bowden, A. Gutteridge, and C. Machado (eds.), *Social and Political Life in Late Antiquity, Late Antique Archaeology* 3.1 (Leiden 2006) 603–47.
H. Halfmann, *Itinera Principum. Geschichte und Typologie der Kaiserreisen im Römischen Reich* (Stuttgart 1986).
K.E. Hammer and M. Murray, "Acquaintances, supporters, and competitors. Evidence of inter-connectedness and rivalry among the religious groups in Sardis," in R.S. Ascough (ed.), *Religious Rivalries and the Struggle for Success in Sardis and Smyrna, Studies in Christianity and Judaism* 14 (Waterloo, ON 2005) 175–94.
G.M.A. Hanfmann, "Excavations at Sardis, 1958," *BASOR* 154 (1959) 5–35.
G.M.A. Hanfmann, "Excavations at Sardis, 1959," *BASOR* 157 (1960) 8–43.
G.M.A. Hanfmann, "The third campaign at Sardis (1960)," *BASOR* 162 (1961) 8–49.
G.M.A. Hanfmann, "The fourth campaign at Sardis (1961)," *BASOR* 166 (1962) 1–57.
G.M.A. Hanfmann, "The fifth campaign at Sardis (1962)," *BASOR* 170 (1963) 1–65.
G.M.A. Hanfmann, "The sixth campaign at Sardis (1963)," *BASOR* 174 (1964) 3–58.
G.M.A. Hanfmann, "The seventh campaign at Sardis (1964)," *BASOR* 177 (1965) 2–37.

G.M.A. Hanfmann, *Letters from Sardis* (Cambridge, MA 1972).

G.M.A. Hanfmann, *From Croesus to Constantine. The Cities of Western Asia Minor and their Arts in Greek and Roman Times* (Ann Arbor 1975).

G.M.A. Hanfmann, *Sardis from Prehistoric to Roman Times. Results of the Archaeological Exploration of Sardis, 1958–1975* (Cambridge, MA 1983).

G.M.A. Hanfmann and N.H. Ramage, *Sculpture from Sardis: The Finds through 1975*, *Sardis* R2 (Cambridge, MA 1978).

G.M.A. Hanfmann and R.S. Thomas, "The thirteenth campaign at Sardis (1970)," *BASOR* 203 (1971) 5–22.

G.M.A. Hanfmann and J.C. Waldbaum, *A Survey of Sardis and the Major Monuments outside the City Walls*, *Sardis* R1 (Cambridge, MA 1975).

G.M.A. Hanfmann et al., "The eleventh and twelfth campaigns at Sardis (1968, 1969)," *BASOR* 199 (1970) 7–58.

R. Hanslmayr, "Der spätantike Hermenzaun vom Nymphaeum Traiani—eine Planetenbalustrade?" in B. Asamer and W. Wohlmayr (eds.), *Akten des 9. Österreichischen Archäologentages am Institut für Klassische Archäologie der Paris-Lodron-Universität Salzburg 2001* (Salzburg 2003) 63–68.

R. Hanslmayr, *Hermen aus Ephesos* (Ph.D. dissertation, University of Vienna 2006).

A. Harrack, "The ancient name of Edessa," *JNES* 51 (1992) 209–14.

A. Harris, "Shops, retailing and the local economy in the early Byzantine world: The example of Sardis," in K. Dark (ed.), *Secular Buildings and the Archaeology of Everyday Life in the Byzantine Empire* (Oxford 2004) 82–122.

S.J. Harris, *Race and Ethnicity in Anglo-Saxon Literature* (New York 2003).

R.M. Harrison, "Amorium excavations 1990: The third preliminary report," *AnatSt* 41 (1991) 215–29.

F.W. Hasluck, *Cyzicus* (Cambridge 1910).

S. Hauser, *Spätantike und frühbyzantinische Silberlöffel* (Münster 1992).

P. Heather, *Goths and Romans 332–489* (Oxford 1991).

P. Heather, *The Fall of the Roman Empire* (London 2005).

R. Heberdey, "Vorläufiger Bericht über die Grabungen in Ephesus 1902/3," *ÖJh* 7 (1904) Beiblatt, 38–56.

R. Heberdey, "IX. Vorläufiger Bericht über die Grabungen in Ephesos 1907–1911," *ÖJh* 15 (1912) Beiblatt, 157–182.

H. Hellenkemper, "Der Limes am nordsyrischen Euphrat. Bericht zu einer archäologischen Landesaufnahme," in D. Haupt and H.G. Horn (eds.), *Studien zu den Militärgrenzen Roms* II, *Beih. BJb.* 38 (Cologne 1977) 461–71.

H. Hellenkemper, "Die Stadtmauern von Anazarbos / Ayn Zarba," in W. Diem and A. Falaturi (eds.), *XXIV. Deutscher Orientalistentag, Zeitschrift der Deutschen Morgenländischen Gesellschaft* Suppl. 8 (Stuttgart 1990) 71–76.

H. Hellenkemper, "Early church architecture in southern Asia Minor," in K. Painter (ed.), *Churches Built in Ancient Times, Recent Studies in Early Christian Archaeology* (London 1994) 213–38.

H. Hellenkemper and F. Hild, *Lykien und Pamphylien, Tabula Imperii Byzantini* 8 (Vienna 2004).

P. Herrmann, "Sardeis zur Zeit der iulisch-claudischen Kaiser," in E. Schwertheim (ed.), *Forschungen in Lydien, Asia Minor Studien* 17 (Bonn 1995) 21–36.

P. Herrmann, *Milet* VI. *Inschriften von Milet.* Teil 2. *Inschriften n. 407–1019* (Berlin 1998).

P. Herrmann, "Italiker und Römer in Sardeis. Überlegungen zu zwei inschriftlichen Zeugnissen," in J. Spielvogel (ed.), *Res publica reperta. Zur Verfassung und Gesellschaft der römischen Republik und des frühen Prinzipats. Festschrift für Jochen Bleicken zum 75.Geburtstag* (Stuttgart 2002) 36–44.

P. Herrmann, W. Günther, and N. Ehrhardt, *Milet* VI. *Inschriften von Milet.* Teil 3. *Inschriften n. 1020–1580* (Berlin 2006).

P. Herrmann and J. Keil, *Tituli Lydiae*, *TAM* 5 (Vienna 1981–1989).

D. Hertel, "Zum Heiligtum der Athena Ilias von Troia IX und zur frühhellenistischen Stadtanlage von Ilion," *AA* (2004) 177–205.

E. Hertzfeld, "Hatra," *ZDMG* 68 (1914) 665–66.

J. Higginbotham, *Piscinae: Artificial Fishponds in Roman Italy* (Chapel Hill 1997).

F. Hild, review of C. Foss, *History and Archaeology of Byzantine Asia Minor* (Aldershot 1990), *JÖBG* 45 (1995) 385–87.

F. Hild and H. Hellenkemper, *Kilikien und Isaurien, Tabula Imperii Byzantini* 5 (Vienna 1990).

F. Hild, H. Hellenkemper, and G. Hellenkemper-Salies, "Kommagene-Kilikien-Isaurien," *Reallexikon zur Byzantinischen Kunst* IV (Stuttgart 1990) 182–356.

F. Hild and M. Restle, *Kappadokien, Tabula Imperii Byzantini* 2 (Vienna 1981).

G.F. Hill, *Catalogue of the Greek Coins of Arabia, Mesopotamia and Persia* (London 1922).

S. Hill, *The Early Byzantine Churches of Cilicia and Isauria, Birmingham Byzantine and Ottoman Monographs* 1 (Aldershot 1996).

N. Hodgson, "The east as part of the wider Roman imperial frontier policy," in D.H. French and C.S. Lightfoot (eds.), *The Eastern Frontier of the Roman Empire, BAR-IS* 553 (Oxford 1989) 177–89.

W. Hoepfner (ed.), *Geschichte des Wohnens* 1 (Stuttgart 1999).

W. Hoepfner, "Das Ende der Agora," in G. Brands and H.-G. Severin (eds.), *Die spätantike Stadt und ihre Christianisierung* (Wiesbaden 2003) 145–50.

M. Højte, *Roman Imperial Statue Bases* (Aarhus 2005).

T. Hölscher, *Römische Bildsprache als semantisches System* (Heidelberg 1987).

K.G. Holum, "The Classical city in the sixth century: Survival and transformation," in M. Maas (ed.), *The Cambridge Companion to the Age of Justinian* (Cambridge 2005) 87–112.

J. Howard-Johnston, "The two great powers in late antiquity: A comparison," in A. Cameron (ed.), *The Byzantine and Early Islamic Near East* III. *States, Resources and Armies, Studies in Late Antiquity and Early Islam* 1 (Princeton 1995) 157–226.

J. Howard-Johnston, *Witnesses to a World Crisis: Historians and Histories of the Middle East in the Seventh Century* (Oxford 2010).

N. Hudson, "Three centuries of late Roman pottery," in C. Ratté and R.R.R. Smith (eds.), *Aphrodisias Papers* 4. *New Research on the City and its Monuments, JRA* Suppl. 70 (Portsmouth, RI 2008) 319–45.

J. Hülsen, *Milet* I 5. *Das Nymphäum* (Berlin 1919).

C. Humann, J. Kohte, and C. Watzinger, *Magnesia am Maeander* (Berlin 1904).

J. İnan, *Roman Sculpture in Side* (Ankara 1975).

J. İnan and E. Alföldi-Rosenbaum, *Römische und frühbyzantinische Porträtplastik aus der Türkei. Neue Funde* (Mainz 1979).

J. İnan and E. Rosenbaum, *Roman and Early Byzantine Portrait Sculpture in Asia Minor* (London 1966).

B. Isaac, "An open frontier," in P. Brun, S. van der Leeuw, and C.R. Whittaker (eds.), *Fontières d'empire. Nature et signification des frontières romaines* (Nemours 1993) 105–14.

F. Işık, *Patara. The History and Ruins of the Capital City of Lycian League* (Antalya 2000).

F. Işık, *Girlanden-Sarkophage aus Aphrodisias, Sarkophag-Studien* 5 (Mainz 2007).

P. Jablonka, "Ausgrabungen südlich der Unterstadt von Troia im Bereich des Troia VI-Verteidigungsgrabens. Grabungsbericht 1994," *Studia Troica* 5 (1995) 39–79.

D. Jacoby, "Knightly values and class consciousness in the Crusader states of the eastern Mediterranean," *Mediterranean Historical Review* 1 (1986) 170–73.

C. Jäggi, "Spolie oder Neuanfertigung? Überlegungen zur Bauskulptur des Tempietto sul Clitunno," in U. Peschlow and S. Möllers (eds.), *Spätantike und byzantinische Bauskulptur* (Stuttgart 1998) 105–11.

S. James, "The *fabricae*: State arms factories of the later Roman empire," in J.C. Coulston (ed.), *Military Equipment and the Identity of Roman Soldiers, BAR-IS* 394 (Oxford 1988) 257–331.

R. Janin, *Constantinople byzantine* (Paris 1964).

H.G. Jansen, "Das unsichtbare Troia sichtbar gemacht—Chancen und Ergebnisse der Anwendung neuer Prospektionsmethoden," in M.O. Korfmann (ed.), *Troia. Archäologie eines Siedlungshügels und seiner Landschaft* (Mainz 2006) 309–16.

F.P. Johnson, *Lysippos* (Durham, NC 1927).

F.P. Johnson, "The colossus of Barletta," *AJA* 25 (1929) 20–25.

A.H.M. Jones, *The Later Roman Empire, 284–602: A Social, Economic and Administrative Survey*, 2 vols. (Oxford 1964).

K. Jung, "Das Hydrekdocheion des Gaius Laecanius Bassus in Ephesos," in G. Wiplinger (ed.), *Cura Aquarum in Ephesos, BABesch* Suppl. 12 (2006) 79–86.

W.E. Kaegi, "Reconceptualizing Byzantium's eastern frontiers in the seventh century," in R.W. Mathisen and H.S. Sivan (eds.), *Shifting Frontiers in Late Antiquity* (Aldershot 1996) 83–92.

A. Kalinowski, "The Vedii Antonini: Aspects of patronage and benefaction in 2nd c. Ephesos," *Phoenix* 56 (2002) 109–49.

A. Kalinowski and H. Taeuber, "A new Antonine inscription and a new imperial statue-group from the bouleuterion at Ephesos," *JRA* 14 (2001) 351–57.

O. Karagiorgou, "LR2: A container for the military annona on the Danubian border?" in S. Kingsley and M. Decker (eds.), *Economy and Exchange in the East Mediterranean during Late Antiquity* (Oxford 2001) 129–66.

S. Karwiese, *Groß ist die Artemis von Ephesos. Die Geschichte einer der großen Städte der Antike* (Vienna 1995).

S. Karwiese, "Die Münzfunde aus dem sog. Sockelbau der Basilica von Ephesos," *NZ* 113/114 (2005) 181–202.

N.D. Karydis, *Early Byzantine Vaulted Construction in Churches of the Western Coastal Plains and River Valleys of Asia Minor* (Ph.D. thesis, University of Bath 2010).

V. Kästner, "Die Spolie mit der Justiniansinschrift vom milesischen Markttor," in O. Dally et al. (eds.), *ZeitRäume. Milet in Kaiserzeit und Spätantike* (Regensburg 2009) 205–11.

R. Kearsley (ed.), *Greeks and Romans in Imperial Asia. Mixed Language Inscriptions and Linguistic Evidence for Cultural Interaction until the End of AD III, Inschriften griechischer Städte aus Kleinasien* 59 (Bonn 2001).

J.G. Keenan, "Byzantine Egyptian villages," in R.S. Bagnall (ed.), *Egypt in the Byzantine World, 300–700* (Cambridge 2007) 226–43.

J. Keil, "XIII. Vorläufiger Bericht über die Ausgrabungen in Ephesos," *ÖJh* 24 (1929) Beiblatt, 5–68.

J. Keil, "XIV. Vorläufiger Bericht über die Ausgrabungen in Ephesos," *ÖJh* 25 (1929) Beiblatt, 5–52.

J. Keil, "XV. Vorläufiger Bericht über die Ausgrabungen in Ephesos," *ÖJh* 26 (1930) Beiblatt, 5–66.

J. Keil, "XVI. Vorläufiger Bericht über die Ausgrabungen in Ephesos," *ÖJh* 27 (1932) Beiblatt, 5–72.

J. Keil, "XVII. Vorläufiger Bericht über die Ausgrabungen in Ephesos," *ÖJh* 28 (1933) Beiblatt, 5–44.

U. Kelp, "Darüber wachen Verderben und Schrecken und Todeslos. Erinyen als Grabwächter: Zum Eunuchengrab in Anazarbos (Kilikien)," in I. Delemen et al. (eds.), *Euergetes. Festschrift für Prof. Dr. Haluk Abbasoğlu zum 65. Geburtstag* (Istanbul 2008) 675–98.

G.A. Kennedy, *Greek Rhetoric under Christian Emperors* (Princeton 1983).

G.A. Kennedy, *New History of Classical Rhetoric* (Princeton 1994).

G.A. Kennedy, "The genres of rhetoric," in S.E. Porter (ed.), *Handbook of Classical Rhetoric in the Hellenistic Period 330 B.C.–A.D. 400* (Leiden 1997) 43–50.

H. Kennedy, "From polis to madina: Urban change in late antiquity," *Past and Present* 106 (1985) 3–27.

H. Kennedy, *The Great Arab Conquests: How the Spread of Islam Changed the World We Live In* (London 2007).

H. Kennedy, "Syrian elites from Byzantium to Islam: Survival or extinction?" in J. Haldon (ed.), *Money, Power and Politics in Early Islamic Syria: A Review of Current Debates* (Farnham 2010) 181–200.

U. Kenzler, "Die augusteische Neugestaltung des Staatsmarkts von Ephesos," *Hephaistos* 24 (2006) 169–81.

K. Kessler, "Osroene," *Der Neue Pauly* 9 (2000) 88.

M. Kiel, "Magnesia on the Maeander as Byzantine fortress and Turkish market place: Remarks on the mosque of Aydınoğlu Mehmed şah Çelebi b. Musa Bey," in R. Ünal, I. Kuyulu, and Z. Mercangöz (eds.), *Uluslararası Sanat Tarihi Sempozyumu: Prof. Dr. Gönül Öney'e Armağan* (Izmir 2002) 375–85.

R. Kiepert, *Karte von Kleinasien in 24 Blatt. Blatt CV, Malatya* (Berlin 1902).

H. Kiesewetter, "Spätbyzantinische Gräber bei der Quellhöhle in der Unterstadt von Troia/Ilion," *Studia Troica* 9 (1999) 411–35.

B. Kiilerich, *Late Fourth-Century Classicism in the Plastic Arts. Studies in the So-Called Theodosian Renaissance* (Odense 1993).

B. Kiilerich, *The Obelisk Base in Constantinople: Court Art and Imperial Ideology* (Rome 1998).

F. Kirbihler, "Die Italiker in Kleinasien, mit besonderer Berücksichtigung von Ephesos (133 v. Chr.–1. Jh. n. Chr.)," in M. Meyer (ed.), *Neue Zeiten—Neue Sitten. Zu Rezeption und Integration römischen und italischen Kulturguts in Kleinasien, WForsch* 12 (Vienna 2007) 19–35.

E. Kirsten, "Die byzantinische Stadt," in *Berichte zum XI. Internationalen Byzantinisten-Kongress* III (Munich 1958).

E. Kirsten, "Edessa, eine römische Grenzstadt des 4. bis 6. Jahrhunderts im Orient," *JAC* 6 (1963) 144–72.

G. Kleiner, *Die Ruinen von Milet* (Berlin 1968).

A.F. Klijn, *Edessa, die Stadt des Apostels Thomas. Das älteste Christentum in Syrien* (Neunkirchen-Vluyn 1965).

M. Klinkott, *Altertümer von Pergamon* XVI. *Die Stadtmauern.* Teil 1. *Die byzantinischen Befestigungsanlagen von Pergamon mit ihrer Wehr- und Baugeschichte* (Berlin 2001).

H. Knackfuß, *Milet* I 7. *Der Südmarkt und die benachbarten Bauanlagen* (Berlin 1924).

D. Knibbe, *Der Staatsmarkt. Die Inschriften des Prytaneions* 1. Teil: *Die Kureteninschriften und sonstige religiöse Texte, Forschungen in Ephesos* IX 1.1 (Vienna 1981).

L. Koch, *Weibliche Sitzstatuen der Klassik und des Hellenismus und ihre kaiserzeitliche Rezeption. Die bekleideten Figuren* (Münster 1994).

J. Kollwitz, *Oströmische Plastik der theodosianischen Zeit* (Berlin 1941).

M.O. Korfmann, N. Frank, and A. Mangini, "Eingang in die Unterwelt—die Höhle von Troia und ihre Datierung," in M.O. Korfmann (ed.), *Troia. Archäologie eines Siedlungshügels und seiner Landschaft* (Mainz 2006) 337–42.

R. Köster, *Milet* VII. *Die Bauornamentik von Milet.* Teil 1. *Die Bauornamentik der frühen und mittleren Kaiserzeit* (Berlin 2004).

J. Kramer, *Skulpturen mit Adlerfiguren an Bauten des 5. Jahrhunderts n. Chr. in Konstantinopel* (Munich 1968).

J.-U. Krause and C. Witschel (eds.), *Die Stadt in der Spätantike—Niedergang oder Wandel?, Historia Einzelschriften* 190 (Stuttgart 2006).

I. Krauskopf, "Gorgo, Gorgones," *LIMC* 4.1 (Basel 1988) 285–330.

R. Krautheimer, *Three Christian Capitals* (Berkeley 1983).

A. Krickel and G. Schartner, "Das Osttor der spätantiken Oststadt von Limyra," *ÖJh* 66 (1997) Beiblatt, 367–74.

F. Krinzinger, "Ephesos," in W. Radt (ed.), *Stadtgrabungen und Stadtforschung im westlichen Kleinasien. Geplantes und Erreichtes, Byzas* 3 (Istanbul 2006) 81–101.

F. Krinzinger et al., "Ephesos," *ÖJh* 68 (1999) Jahresbericht 1998, 12–46.

F. Krischen, *Die Landmauer von Konstantinopel.* Teil 1. *Denkmäler antiker Architektur* 6 (Berlin 1938).

J.H. Kroll, "The Greek inscriptions of the Sardis synagogue," *HTR* 94 (2001) 5–127.

O. Krückmann, "Osroene," *RE* XVIII.1 (Stuttgart 1942) 1589–1590.

M. Kunze, "Bericht über die Arbeiten im archäologischen Gebiet von Patara während der Grabungskampagnen 1993–1996," *Kazı Sonuçları Toplantısı* 19.2 (1998) 61–79.

S. Ladstätter, "Die Chronologie des Hanghauses 2," in F. Krinzinger (ed.), *Das Hanghaus 2 von Ephesos. Studien zu Baugeschichte und Chronologie* (Vienna 2002) 9–40.

S. Ladstätter, "Römische, spätantike und byzantinische Keramik," in M. Steskal and M. La Torre, *Das Vediusgymnasium in Ephesos. Archäologie und Baubefund, Forschungen in Ephesos* XIV 1 (Vienna 2008) 97–189.

S. Ladstätter (ed.), *Neue Forschungen zur Kuretenstraße in Ephesos, Akten des Symposions für Hilke Thür 2006, DenkschrWien* 382 (2009).

S. Ladstätter, "Ephesos in byzantinischer Zeit: Das letzte Kapitel der Geschichte einer antiken Großstadt," in F. Daim and J. Drauschke (eds.), *Byzanz—Das Römerreich im Mittelalter.* Teil 2.2. *Schauplätze, Monographien des Römisch-Germanischen Zentralmuseums* 84.2.2 (Mainz 2010) 493–519.

S. Ladstätter and A. Pülz, "Ephesus in the late Roman and early Byzantine period: Changes in its urban character from the third to seventh century AD," in A.G. Poulter (ed.), *The Transition to Late Antiquity on the Danube and Beyond, ProcBritAc* 141 (Oxford 2007) 391–433.

G. Lahusen and E. Formigli, *Römische Bildnisse aus Bronze. Kunst und Technik* (Munich 2001).

B. Lang (ed.), *The Concept of Style* (Philadelphia 1979).

C. Lang-Auinger, "Ergebnisse," in ead., *Hanghaus 1 in Ephesos. Funde und Ausstattung, Forschungen in Ephesos* VIII 4 (Vienna 2003) 328–33.

C. Lang-Auinger, "Zusammenfassung," in V. Mitsopoulos-Leon and C. Lang-Auinger (eds.), *Die Basilika am Staatsmarkt in Ephesos* 2.Teil: *Funde klassischer bis römischer Zeit, Forschungen in Ephesos* IX 2.3 (Vienna 2007) 205–6.

A. Laniado, *Recherches sur les notables municipaux dans l'empire protobyzantin, TravMém Monographies* 13 (Paris 2002).

L. Lavan, "The residences of late antique governors: A gazetteer," *Antiquité tardive* 7 (1999) 135–64.

L. Lavan, "The *praetoria* of civil governors in late antiquity," in L. Lavan (ed.), *Recent Research in Late-Antique Urbanism, JRA* Suppl. 42 (Portsmouth, RI 2001) 39–56.

L. Lavan, "Late Antique urban topography: From architecture to human space," in L. Lavan and W. Bowden (eds.), *Theory and Practice in Late Antique Archaeology, Late Antique Archaeology* 1 (Leiden 2003) 171–95.

L. Lavan, "The political topography of the late antique City: Activity spaces in practice," in L. Lavan and W. Bowden (eds.), *Theory and Practice in Late Antique Archaeology, Late Antique Archaeology* 1 (Leiden 2003) 314–37.

L. Lavan, "Fora and agorai in Mediterranean cities during the 4th and 5th c. A.D.," in W. Bowden, A. Gutteridge, and C. Machado (eds.), *Social and Political Life in Late Antiquity, Late Antique Archaeology* 3.1 (Leiden 2006) 195–249.

L. Lazzarini, "I graniti dei monumenti italiani ed i loro problemi di deterioramento," *BdA* Suppl. 41 (1987) 157–72.

H. Leclercq, "Méduse," *DACL* 11.1 (1933) 195–99.

J. Lefort, C. Morrisson, and J.-P. Sodini, *Les villages dans l'empire byzantin: IVe–XVe siècle* (Paris 2005).

E. Legrand, "Description des oeuvres d'art et de l'église des Saints Apotres de Constantinople, poème en vers iambiques par Constantin le Rhodien," *REG* 9 (1896) 32–65.

A. Leibundgut-Maye, "Gleichzeitigkeit des Ungleichzeitigen. Die Stilebenen der trajanischen Kunst und ihre Botschaft," *Antrittsvorlesungen* 5 (Mainz 1989) 15–28.

C. Lepelley, "Le musée des statues divines: la volonté de sauvegarde le patrimoine artistique paeien à l'époque théodosienne," *CahArch* 42 (1994) 5–15.

J.H.W.G. Liebeschuetz, "The finances of Antioch in the fourth century AD," *ByzZeit* 52 (1959) 344–56.

J.H.W.G. Liebeschuetz, "The defences of Syria in the sixth century," in D. Haupt and H.G. Horn (eds.), *Studien zu den Militärgrenzen Roms* II, *Beih. BJb.* 38 (Cologne 1977) 487–99.

J.H.W.G. Liebeschuetz, "The end of the ancient city," in J. Rich (ed.), *The City in Late Antiquity* (London and New York 1992) 1–49.

J.H.W.G. Liebeschuetz, "Administration and politics in the city of the 5th and 6th centuries with special reference to the circus factions," in C. Lepelley (ed.), *La fin de la cité antique et le début de la cité médiévale: de la fin du 3e siècle a l'avènement de Charlemagne, Studi storici sulla tarda antichità* 8 (Bari 1996) 161–82.

J.H.W.G. Liebeschuetz, *The Decline and Fall of the Roman City* (Oxford 2001).

J.H.W.G. Liebeschuetz, "Transformation and decline: Are the two really incompatible?" in J.-U. Krause and C. Witschel (eds.), *Die Stadt in der Spätantike—Niedergang oder Wandel?, Historia Einzelschriften* 190 (Stuttgart 2006) 463–83.

J.H.W.G. Liebeschuetz, "The lower Danube region under pressure: From Valens to Heraclius," in A.G. Poulter (ed.), *The Transition to Late Antiquity on the Danube and Beyond, ProcBritAc* 141 (Oxford 2007) 101–34.

C. and M. Lightfoot, *Amorium: A Byzantine City in Anatolia* (Istanbul 2007).

B.C.G. Lippold, *Handbüch der Archäologie* (Berlin 1939).

N. Litinas, *Greek Ostraca from Abu Mina (O.AbuMina), Archiv für Papyrusforschung und verwandte Gebeite Beiheft* 25 (Berlin 2008).

L. Little (ed.), *Plague and the End of Antiquity: The Pandemic of 541–750* (Cambridge 2007).

I.M. Lockey, *The Atrium House at Aphrodisias* (Ph.D. dissertation, New York University 2010).

H. Lohmann, "Survey in der Chora von Milet: Vorbericht über die Kampagnen der Jahre 1990, 1992 und 1993," *AA* (1995) 293–328.

H. Lohmann, "Survey in der Chora von Milet: Vorbericht über die Kampagnen der Jahre 1996 und 1997," *AA* (1999) 439–73.

H. Lohmann, "Milet und die Milesia: Eine antike Großstadt und ihr Umland im Wandel der Zeit," in F. Kolb (ed.), *Chora und Polis, Schriften des historischen Kollegs: Kolloquien* 54 (Munich 2004) 325–60.

L. Loots, M. Waelkens, and F. Depuydt, "The city fortifications of Sagalassos from the Hellenistic to the late Roman period," in M. Waelkens and L. Loots (eds.), *Sagalassos* V: *Report on the Survey and Excavation Campaigns 1996 and 1997, ActaArchLov Monographiae* 11a–b (Leuven 2000) 595–634.

H.P. L'Orange and A. von Gerkan, *Der spätantike Bildschmuck des Konstantinsbogens, Studien zur spätantiken Kunstgeschichte* 10 (Berlin 1939).

A. Luther, *Die syrische Chronik des Josua Stylites, Untersuchungen zur antiken Literatur und Geschichte* 49 (Berlin 1997).
D. Magie, *Roman Rule in Asia Minor* (Princeton 1950).
J. Magness, "The date of the Sardis synagogue in light of the numismatic evidence," *AJA* 109 (2005) 443–75.
M. Maischberger, "Zwischen Sachzwang und Utopie. Zur Technik von Architekturrekonstruktionen im Museum: Das Markttor von Milet im Berliner Pergamonmuseum," in A. Dostert and F. Lang (eds.), *Mittel und Wege. Zur Bedeutung von Material und Technik in der Archäologie* (Möhnesee 2006) 275–96.
M. Maischberger, "Ad fontes! Die Berliner Antikensammlung und das Deutsche Archäologische Institut forschen wieder gemeinsam in Milet," *Antike Welt* 38.6 (2007) 33–35.
M. Maischberger, "Milet im Museum und Milet im Felde: Neues von der Restaurierung des Markttors und von den Grabungen in den Faustinathermen," *Jahrbuch der Stiftung Preußischer Kulturbesitz* 44 (2007) 237–51.
M. Maischberger, "Das Nordtor des Südmarktes, sog. Markttor," in O. Dally et al. (eds.), *ZeitRäume. Milet in Kaiserzeit und Spätantike* (Regensburg 2009) 109–19.
M. Maischberger, "Die Restaurierung des Markttors von Milet," in U. Peltz and O. Zorn (eds.), *kulturGUTerhalten. Restaurierung archäologischer Schätze an den Staatlichen Museen zu Berlin* (Mainz 2009) 57–62.
M. Maischberger, "Zwei marmorne Kolosse. Zur Neuaufstellung der Skulpturen im Markttor von Milet," *Antike Welt* 41.3 (2010) 34–35.
M. Maischberger and A. Hoffschildt, "Das Markttor von Milet im Pergamonmuseum. Zur Restaurierung einer musealen Architekturrekonstruktion," in U. Peltz and O. Zorn (eds.), *kulturGUTerhalten. Standards in der Restaurierungswissenschaft und Denkmalpflege* (Mainz 2009) 153–62.
H. Manderscheid, *Die Skulpturenausstattung kaiserzeitlicher Thermenanlagen* (Berlin 1981).
C. Mango, *The Brazen House* (Copenhagen 1954).
C. Mango, *Byzantinische Architektur* (Stuttgart 1975).
C. Mango, *Le developpement urbain de Constantinople (IVe–VIIe siècles)* (Paris 1984).
A.-M. Manière-Lévêque, "Habitat proto-byzantin à Xanthos: les espaces de réception de la grande résidence nord-est de l'acropole lycienne," in K. Dörtlük et al. (eds.), *The 3rd International Symposium on Lycia* 1 (Antalya 2006) 425–40.
A.M. Mansel, "Bericht über Ausgrabungen und Untersuchungen in Pamphylien in den Jahren 1946–1955," *AA* (1956) 34–120.
A.M. Mansel, *Die Ruinen von Side* (Berlin 1963).
A.M. Mansel, "Osttor und Waffenreliefs von Side (Pamphylien)," *AA* (1968) 239–79.
A.M. Mansel, "Bericht über Ausgrabungen und Untersuchungen in Pamphylien in den Jahren 1957–1972," *AA* (1975) 49–96.
A.M. Mansel, *Side: 1947–1966 Yılları Kazıları ve Araştırmalarının Sonuçları, Antalya Bölgesinde Araştırmalar* 10 (Ankara 1978).
T. Marksteiner, "Die spätantiken und byzantinischen Befestigungen von Limyra im Bereich des Ptolemaions," in M. Seyer (ed.), *Studien in Lykien, ÖJh Ergh.* 8 (Vienna 2007) 29–45.
N. Marquardt, *Pan in der hellenistischen und kaiserzeitlichen Plastik* (Bonn 1995).
F. Martens, "Late antique urban streets at Sagalassos," in L. Lavan, A. Sarantis, and E. Zanini (eds.), *Technology in Transition: A.D. 300–650, Late Antique Archaeology* 4 (Leiden 2007) 321–65.
F. Martens, "Urban traffic in the hills of the eastern Mediterranean. The development, maintenance, and usage of the street system of Sagalassos in south-western Turkey," in P. Ballet, N. Dieudonné-Glad, and C. Saliou (eds.), *La rue dans l'antiquité. Définition, aménagement et devenir de l'Orient mediterranéen à la Gaule* (Rennes 2008) 191–200.
H.-R. Meier, "Alte Tempel—neue Kulte. Zum Schutz obsoleter Sakralbauten in der Spätantike und zur Adaption alter Bauten an den christlichen Kult," in B. Brenk (ed.), *Innovation in der Spätantike* (Wiesbaden 1996) 361–74.
H.-R. Meier, "Zentrumsverlagerung oder Deurbanisierung? Eine Frage zur 'Christianisierung' der spätantiken Stadt," in G. Brands and H.-G. Severin (eds.), *Die spätantike Stadt und ihre Christianisierung* (Wiesbaden 2003) 165–77.
G. Mendel, *Catalogue des sculptures grecques, romaines et byzantines* (Istanbul 1912–1914).

L. Mendelssohn (ed.), *Zosimi Historia Nova* (Leipzig 1887).

R. Meriç, "1985 Yılı Alaşehir Kazı Çalışmaları," *Kazı Sonuçları Toplantısı* 8.2 (1986) 259–71.

R. Meriç, "1987 Yılı Alaşehir Kazısı," *Kazı Sonuçları Toplantısı* 10.1 (1988) 157–70.

R. Merkelbach and J. Stauber, *Steinepigramme aus dem griechischen Osten* 1. *Die Westküste Kleinasiens von Knidos bis Ilion* (Stuttgart and Leipzig 1998).

M. Meyer (ed.), *Neue Zeiten—Neue Sitten. Zu Rezeption und Integration römischen und italischen Kulturguts in Kleinasien*, *WForsch* 12 (Vienna 2007).

B. Meyer-Plath and A.M. Schneider, *Die Landmauer von Konstantinopel*. Teil 2. *Denkmäler antiker Architektur* 8 (Berlin 1943).

G. Mietke, "Survey der römisch-frühbyzantinischen Siedlung bei Akören in Kilikien 1994," *Araştırma Sonuçları Toplantısı* 13.1 (1996) 35–48.

G. Mietke, "Survey der römisch-frühbyzantinischen Siedlung bei Akören in Kilikien 1995," *Araştırma Sonuçları Toplantısı* 14.1 (1997) 423–34.

G. Mietke, "Die Apostelkirche von Anazarbos und Syrien," *Olba* 2 (1999) 227–39.

G. Mietke, "Survey der römisch-frühbyzantinischen Siedlung bei Akören in Kilikien 1996 und 1997," *Araştırma Sonuçları Toplantısı* 16.1 (1999) 75–93.

F. Millar, *A Greek Roman Empire: Power and Belief under Theodosius II (408–450)*, *Sather Classical Lectures* 64 (Berkeley 2006).

S.G. Miller, *The Prytaneion* (Berkeley and Los Angeles 1978).

F. Miltner, "XXI. Vorläufiger Bericht über die Ausgrabungen in Ephesos," *ÖJh* 43 (1956–1958) Beiblatt, 2–64.

F. Miltner, "XXII. Vorläufiger Bericht über die Ausgrabungen in Ephesos," *ÖJh* 44 (1959) Beiblatt, 244–380.

S. Mitchell, *Anatolia. Land, Men, and Gods in Asia Minor*, 2 vols. (Oxford 1993).

S. Mitchell, "The cities of Asia Minor in the Age of Constantine," in S.N.C. Lieu and D. Montserrat (eds.), *Constantine. History, Historiography, and Legend* (London 1998) 52–73.

T.B. Mitford, "Survey of the Euphrates limes," *AnatSt* 17 (1967) 13–14.

T.B. Mitford, "The Euphrates frontier in Cappadocia," in D. Haupt and H.G. Horn (eds.), *Studien zu den Militärgrenzen Roms* II, *Beih. BJb.* 38 (Cologne 1977) 501–10.

T.B. Mitford, "The Roman frontier on the Upper Euphrates," in R. Matthews (ed.), *Ancient Anatolia* (Oxford 1998) 255–72.

V. Mitsopoulos-Leon and C. Lang-Auinger (eds.), *Die Basilika am Staatsmarkt in Ephesos* 2. Teil: *Funde klassischer bis römischer Zeit*, *Forschungen in Ephesos* IX 2.3 (Vienna 2007).

D.G. Mitten and A.F. Scorziello, "Reappropriating antiquity: Some spolia from the synagogue at Sardis," in N.D. Cahill (ed.), *Love for Lydia: A Sardis Anniversary Volume Presented to Crawford H. Greenewalt, Jr.*, *Sardis* R4 (Cambridge, MA 2008) 135–46.

A.D. Mordtmann, "Ruines de Scepsis en Troade," *RA* 11 (1855) 767–70.

F. Morelli, *L'Archivio di Senouthios Anystes e testi connessi: lettere e documenti per la costruzione di una capitale*, *Corpus papyrorum Raineri Archiducis Austriae* 30 (Berlin 2010).

C. Morrisson and J.-P. Sodini, "The sixth-century economy," in A. Laiou (ed.), *The Economic History of Byzantium from the Seventh through the Fifteenth Century* (Washington 2002).

W. Müller-Wiener, "Mittelalterliche Befestigungen im südlichen Jonien," *IstMitt* 11 (1961) 5–122.

W. Müller-Wiener, "Die Stadtbefestigungen von Izmir, Sığacık und Çandarlı," *IstMitt* 12 (1962) 59–114.

W. Müller-Wiener, *Bildlexikon zur Topographie Istanbuls* (Tübingen 1977).

W. Müller-Wiener, "Rundkirche bei der Süd-Mauer [von Milet]," *IstMitt* 31 (1981) 96–99.

W. Müller-Wiener, "Untersuchungen auf dem Theater-Hügel [von Milet]," *IstMitt* 32 (1981) 15–17.

W. Müller-Wiener, "Von der Polis zum Kastron: Wandlungen der Stadt im ägäischen Raum von der Antike zum Mittelalter," *Gymnasium* 93 (1986) 435–74.

K.A. Neugebauer and T. Wiegand, "Die Faustinathermen. Die Skulpturen," in A. von Gerkan and F. Krischen (eds.), *Milet* I 9. *Thermen und Palaestren* (Berlin 1928) 97–125.

P. Niewöhner, "Aizanoi and Anatolia. Town and countryside in late late antiquity," *Millennium* 3 (2006) 239–53.

P. Niewöhner, *Aizanoi, Dokimion und Anatolien: Stadt und Land, Siedlungs- und Steinmetzwesen vom späteren 4. bis ins 6. Jh. n. Chr., AF* 23 (Wiesbaden 2007).

P. Niewöhner, "Archäologie und die 'Dunklen Jahrhunderte' im byzantinischen Anatolien," in J. Henning (ed.), *Post-Roman Towns, Trade and Settlement in Europe and Byzantium* 2, *Byzantium, Pliska, and the Balkans, Millennium Studies* 5 (Wiesbaden 2007) 119–57.

P. Niewöhner, "Byzantinische Steinmetzarbeiten aus dem Umland von Milet," *Anadolu ve Çevresinde Ortaçağ* 1 (2007) 1–28.

P. Niewöhner, "Die große Friedhofskirche von Milet: Vorbericht über die Ausgrabung einer neuentdeckten Transeptbasilika," *Mitteilungen zur Christlichen Archäologie* 13 (2007) 71–90.

P. Niewöhner, "Sind die Mauern die Stadt? Vorbericht über die siedlungsgeschichtlichen Ergebnisse neuer Grabungen im spätantiken und byzantinischen Milet," *AA* (2008/1) 181–201.

P. Niewöhner, "Milet in frühbyzantinischer Zeit," in O. Dally et al. (eds.), *ZeitRäume. Milet in Kaiserzeit und Spätantike* (Regensburg 2009) 61–67.

P. Niewöhner, "Byzantinische Stadtmauern in Anatolien: Vom Statussymbol zum Bollwerk gegen die Araber," in J. Lorentzen et al. (eds.), *Aktuelle Forschungen zur Konstruktion, Funktion und Semantik antiker Stadtbefestigungen, Byzas* 10 (Istanbul 2010) 239–60.

K.L. Noethlichs, "Baurecht und Religionspolitik: Vorchristlicher und christlicher Städtebau der römischen Kaiserzeit im Lichte weltlicher und kirchlicher Rechtsvorschriften," in G. Brands and H.-G. Severin (eds.), *Die spätantike Stadt und ihre Christianisierung* (Wiesbaden 2003) 179–97.

A. Oepen, "Die Nutzung kaiserzeitlicher Theaterbauten in Hispanien während der Spätantike und der Westgotenzeit," in G. Brands and H.-G. Severin (eds.), *Die spätantike Stadt und ihre Christianisierung* (Wiesbaden 2003) 199–217.

G.W. Olson, "Landslides at Sardis in western Turkey," *Geological Society of America, Reviews in Engineering Geology* 3 (1977) 255–72.

G. Ostrogorsky, "Byzantine cities in the early Middle Ages," *DOP* 13 (1959) 47–66.

M. Özdoğan, *Lower Euphrates Basin 1977 Survey, Middle East Technical University, Lower Euphrates Project Publications* I 2 (Istanbul 1977).

R. Özgan, *Die Skulpturen von Stratonikeia, Asia Minor Studien* 32 (Bonn 1999).

R. Özgan and D. Stutzinger, "Untersuchungen zu Porträtplastik des 5 Jhs. n. Chr. anhand zweier neugefundener Porträts aus Stratonikeia," *IstMitt* 35 (1985) 237–74.

L. Özgenel, "Public use and privacy in late antique houses in Asia Minor: The architecture of spatial control," in L. Lavan, L. Özgenel, and A. Sarantis (eds.), *Housing in Late Antiquity. From Palaces to Shops, Late Antique Archaeology* 3.2 (Leiden 2007) 239–81.

O. Paoletti, "Gorgones Romanae," *LIMC* 4.1 (Basel 1988) 345–62.

D. Parrish, "The urban plan and its constituent elements," in idem (ed.), *Urbanism in Western Asia Minor: New Studies on Aphrodisias, Ephesos, Hierapolis, Pergamon, Perge, and Xanthos, JRA* Suppl. 45 (Portsmouth, RI 2001) 8–42.

E. Patlagean, *Pauvreté économique et pauvreté sociale à Byzance, 4ᵉ–7ᵉ siècles* (Paris 1977).

W.R. Paton, *The Greek Anthology* 1, *Loeb Classical Library* (London and New York 1916).

J.G. Pedley, *Ancient Literary Sources, Sardis* M2 (Cambridge, MA 1972).

U. Peschlow, "Befestigungen lykischer Städte in spätantiker und frühbyzantinischer Zeit," in K. Dörtlük et al. (eds.), *The 3rd International Symposium on Lycia* 2 (Antalya 2006) 601–24.

U. Peschlow, "Das Südtor von Perge," in I. Delemen et al. (eds.), *Euergetes. Festschrift für Prof. Dr. Haluk Abbasoğlu zum 65.Geburtstag* (Antalya 2008) 971–88.

U. Peschlow, "Mauerbau in krisenloser Zeit? Zur spätantiken Stadtbefestigungen im südlichen Kleinasien. Der Fall Side," in D. Kreikenbom, K.-U. Mahler, and T.M. Weber (eds.), *Krise und Kult. Vorderer Orient und Nordafrika von Aurelian bis Iustinian, Millennium Studies* 28 (Wiesbaden 2010) 61–108.

G. Petzl, "Ländliche Religiosität in Lydien," in E. Schwertheim (ed.), *Forschungen in Lydien, Asia Minor Studien* 17 (Bonn 1995) 37–48.

G. Petzl, *Tituli Lydiae. Philadelpheia et ager Philadelphenus, TAM* 5.3 (Vienna 2007).

M. Pfanner et al., "Das Markttor von Milet. Die Sanierung der römischen Prachtfassade im Pergamonmuseum," *Jahrbuch der Stiftung Preußischer Kulturbesitz* 40 (2003) 183–96.

M. Pfanner et al., "Forschungen im Sumpf. Neue Untersuchungen zum Markttor und zur Agora in Milet," *Antike Welt* 36.2 (2005) 81–85.

C. Pharr, *The Theodosian Code and Novels and the Sirmondian Constitutions* (Princeton 1952).

G. Phillips (ed.), *The Doctrine of Addai, the Apostle* (London 1876).

P. Pinon, "Approche typologique des modes de réutilisationdes amphithéâtres de la fin de l'Antiquité au XIXe siècle," in C. Domergue, C. Landes, and J.-M. Pailler (eds.), *Spectacula I, Gladiateurs et amphithéâtres* (Paris 1990) 103–13.

G. Plattner and A. Schmidt-Colinet, "Beobachtungen zu drei kaiserzeitlichen Bauten in Ephesos," in B. Brandt, V. Gassner, and S. Ladstätter (eds.), *Synergia: Festschrift für Friedrich Krinzinger* (Vienna 2005) 244–45.

K. Polaschek, *Untersuchungen zu griechischen Mantelstatuen. Der Himationtypus mit Armschlinge* (Berlin 1969).

J.J. Pollitt, "The impact of Greek art on Rome," *TAPA* 108 (1978) 170–71.

G. Ponti, "Marmor Troadense: Granite quarries in the Troad. A preliminary survey," *Studia Troica* 5 (1995) 291–320.

R. Posamentir, "Innovation und Kulturtransfer in Anazarbos, der einstigen Metropole Kilikiens," in F. Pirson and U. Wulf-Rheidt (eds.), *Austausch und Inspiration. Kolloquium anlässlich des 65. Geburtstages von Adolf Hoffmann* (Berlin 2008) 89–106.

R. Posamentir, "Ohne Mass und Ziel? Anmerkungen zur Säulenstrasse von Anazarbos in Ebenen Kilikien," in I. Delemen et al. (eds.), *Euergetes. Festschrift für Prof. Dr. Haluk Abbasoğlu zum 65. Geburtstag* (Antalya 2008) 1013–33.

R. Posamentir and M.H. Sayar, "Anazarbos—ein Zwischenbericht aus der Metropole des Ebenen Kilikien," *IstMitt* 56 (2006) 317 –57.

D. Potter, "Recent inscriptions from Flat Cilicia," *JRA* 2 (1989) 305–12.

D. Potter, "Cultural archaism and community identity: The case of Xanthus and Paphos," *Διαλέξεις, Ομιλίες, Εκδηλώσεις Α* (Nicosia 1994) 427–41.

D. Potter, *The Roman Empire at Bay, AD 180–395, Routledge History of the Ancient World* (London 2004).

A.G. Poulter, *Nicopolis ad Istrum: A Roman, Late Roman, and Early Byzantine City. Excavations 1985–1992, JRS Monograph* 8 (London 1995).

A.G. Poulter, "The transition to late antiquity," in idem (ed.), *The Transition to Late Antiquity on the Danube and Beyond, ProcBritAc* 141 (Oxford 2007) 1–50.

A.G. Poulter (ed.), *The Transition to Late Antiquity on the Danube and Beyond, ProcBritAc* 141 (Oxford 2007).

A. Pralong, "Les remparts de Philadelphie," in H. Ahrweiler (ed.), *Philadelphie et autres études, Byzantina Sorbonensia* 4 (Paris 1984) 101–26.

T. Preger (ed.), *Scriptores originum Constantinopolitanarum* (Leipzig 1903–1907).

O. Puchstein, "Grundplan der Stadt Palmyra. Straßen und Plätze, Basilica und Wohnbauten," in T. Wiegand (ed.), *Palmyra. Ergebnisse der Expeditionen von 1902 und 1917* (Berlin 1932) 17–35.

A. Pülz, "Das Stadtbild von Ephesos in byzantinischer Zeit," in F. Daim and J. Drauschke (eds.), *Byzanz—Das Römerreich im Mittelalter.* Teil 2.2. *Schauplätze, Monographien des Römisch-Germanischen Zentralmuseums* 84.2.2 (Mainz 2010) 541–71.

H. Rabe (ed.), *Hermogenes opera edidit, Rhetores Graeci* 6 (Leipzig 1913).

J. Raeder, *Die statuarische Ausstattung der Villa Adriana bei Tivoli, Europäische Hochschulschriften* 38.4 (Frankfurt 1983) 81–82.

C. Rapp, "Bishops in late antiquity: A new social and urban elite?" in J. Haldon and L.I. Conrad (eds.), *The Byzantine and Early Islamic Near East* VI. *Elites Old and New, Studies in Late Antiquity and Early Islam* 1 (Princeton 2004) 149–78.

E. Rathmayr, "Die Skulpturenaustattung des C. Laecanius Bassus Nymphaeum in Ephesos," in F. D'Andria and L. Romeo (eds.), *Roman Sculpture in Asia Minor, JRA* Suppl. 80 (Portsmouth, RI 2011) 130–49.

C. Ratté, "New research on the urban development of Aphrodisias in late antiquity," in D. Parrish (ed.), *Urbanism in Western Asia Minor: New Studies on Aphrodisias, Ephesos, Hierapolis, Pergamon, Perge, and Xanthos, JRA* Suppl. 45 (Portsmouth, RI 2001) 116–47.

C. Ratté, "Aphrodisias," in W. Radt (ed.), *Stadtgrabungen und Stadtforschung im westlichen Kleinasien. Geplantes und Erreichtes, Byzas* 3 (Istanbul 2006) 37–48.
C. Ratté, "The founding of Aphrodisias," in C. Ratté and R.R.R. Smith (eds.), *Aphrodisias Papers* 4. *New Research on the City and its Monuments, JRA* Suppl. 70 (Portsmouth, RI 2008) 7–36.
C. Ratté, "Reflections on the urban development of Hellenistic Sardis," in N.D. Cahill (ed.), *Love for Lydia: A Sardis Anniversary Volume Presented to Crawford H. Greenewalt, Jr.*, *Sardis* R4 (Cambridge, MA 2008) 125–33.
C. Ratté, "The Carians and the Lydians," in F. Rumscheid (ed.), *Die Karer und die Anderen* (Bonn 2009) 135–47.
C. Ratté, "New research on the region around Aphrodisias," in R. Van Bremen and M. Carbon (eds.), *Hellenistic Karia, Ausonius Éditions, Études* 28 (Bordeaux 2010) 253–67.
C. Ratté and P.D. De Staebler (eds.), *Aphrodisias* V. *The Aphrodisias Regional Survey* (Mainz forthcoming).
C. Ratté, T.N. Howe, and C. Foss, "An early imperial pseudodipteral temple at Sardis," *AJA* 90 (1986) 45–68.
C. Ratté and R.R.R. Smith, "Archaeological research at Aphrodisias in Caria, 1997 and 1998," *AJA* 104 (2000) 221–53.
C. Ratté and R.R.R. Smith, "Archaeological research at Aphrodisias in Caria, 2002–2005," *AJA* 112 (2008) 713–51.
N.K. Rauh and K.W. Slane, "Possible amphora kiln sites in W Rough Cilicia," *JRA* 13 (2000) 319–30.
M. Rautman, "A late Roman townhouse at Sardis," in E. Schwertheim (ed.), *Forschungen in Lydien, Asia Minor Studien* 17 (Bonn 1995) 49–66.
M. Rautman, "Two late Roman wells at Sardis," *AASOR* 53 (1995) 37–84.
M. Rautman, "The aura of affluence: Domestic scenery in late Roman Sardis," in N.D. Cahill (ed.), *Love for Lydia: A Sardis Anniversary Volume Presented to Crawford H. Greenewalt, Jr.*, *Sardis* R4 (Cambridge, MA 2008) 147–58.
M. Rautman, "Daniel at Sardis," *BASOR* 358 (2010) 47–60.
M. Rautman, "Two menorahs from the synagogue at Sardis," *Qadmoniyot* 43 (2010) 44–48.
M. Rautman, "From mainstream to margin among the late Roman amphorae of Sardis," in P. Monsieur and J. Poblome (eds.), *From Amphorae to Modelling the Late Roman Economy* (forthcoming).
A. Rehm, H. Dessau, and P. Herrmann, *Milet* VI. *Inschriften von Milet.* Teil 1. A. *Inschriften n. 187–406.* B. *Nachträge und Übersetzungen zu den Inschriften n. 1–406* (Berlin 1997).
J.M. Reynolds and J. Ward-Perkins, *The Inscriptions of Roman Tripolitania* (Rome 1952).
K. Rheidt, "Aizanoi: Bericht über die Ausgrabungen und Untersuchungen 1992 und 1993," *AA* (1995) 693–718.
K. Rheidt, "Archäologie und Spätantike in Anatolien: Methoden, Ergebnisse und Probleme der Ausgrabungen in Aizanoi," in G. Brands and H.-G. Severin (eds.), *Die spätantike Stadt und ihre Christianisierung* (Wiesbaden 2003) 239–47.
A. Ricl, *The Inscriptions of Alexandria Troas* (Bonn 1997).
M. Ricl, "Society and economy of rural sanctuaries in Roman Lydia and Phrygia," *EpigAnat* 35 (2003) 7–101.
B.S. Ridgway, "The date of the so-called Lysippan Jason," *AJA* 68 (1964) 113–28.
B.S. Ridgway, *Roman Copies of Greek Originals* (Ann Arbor 1984).
A. Riegl, *Die Spätrömische Kunstindustrie* (Vienna 1901).
L. Robert, "Inscriptions de la synagogue," in idem, *Nouvelles inscriptions de Sardes* 1 (Paris 1964) 37–57.
L. Robert, *Hellenica* 13 (Paris 1965).
L. Robert, "Noms de métiers dans des documents byzantins," in idem (ed.), *Opera minora selecta, épigraphie et antiquités greques* (Amsterdam 1969) 915–21.
M. Roberts, *The Jeweled Style. Poetry and Poetics in Late Antiquity* (Ithaca 1989).
F. Rojas, *Empire of Memories: Anatolian Material Culture and the Imagined Past in Hellenistic and Roman Lydia* (Ph.D. dissertation, University of California–Berkeley 2010).
D. Roos, "Das Steinfachwerk-Gebäude," in A. Filges (ed.), *Blaundos. Berichte zur Erforschung einer Kleinstadt im lydisch-phrygischen Grenzgebiet, IstForsch* 48 (Tübingen 2006) 204–15.
D. Roos and A. Filges, "Die 'Dorische Portikus' und die Hauptstraße von Blaundos," in A. Filges (ed.), *Blaundos. Berichte zur Erforschung einer Kleinstadt im lydisch-phrygischen Grenzgebiet, IstForsch* 48 (Tübingen 2006) 199–203.
C.H. Roosevelt, "Central Lydia Archaeological Survey: 2005 results," *Araştırma Sonuçları Toplantısı* 24.2 (2007) 135–54.

C.H. Roosevelt, *The Archaeology of Lydia, from Gyges to Alexander* (Cambridge 2009).

C.H. Roosevelt and C. Luke, "Central Lydia Archaeological Survey: 2006 results," *Araştırma Sonuçları Toplantısı* 25.3 (2008) 305–26.

C.H. Roosevelt and C. Luke, "Central Lydia Archaeological Survey: 2007 results," *Araştırma Sonuçları Toplantısı* 26.2 (2009) 433–50.

C.B. Rose, "The 1991 post-Bronze Age excavations at Troy," *Studia Troica* 2 (1992) 43–60.

C.B. Rose, "The 1992 post-Bronze Age excavations at Troy," *Studia Troica* 3 (1993) 97–116.

C.B. Rose, "The 1993 post-Bronze Age excavations at Troy," *Studia Troica* 4 (1994) 75–104.

C.B. Rose, "The 1996 post-Bronze Age excavations at Troy," *Studia Troica* 7 (1997) 73–110.

C.B. Rose, *Dynastic Commemoration and Imperial Portraiture in the Julio-Claudian Period* (Cambridge 1997).

C.B. Rose, "The 1997 post-Bronze Age excavations at Troy," *Studia Troica* 8 (1998) 71–113.

C.B. Rose, "The 1998 post-Bronze Age excavations at Troy," *Studia Troica* 9 (1999) 35–71.

C.B. Rose, "Greek, Roman, and Byzantine research at Troy, 1999," *Studia Troica* 10 (2000) 53–72.

C.B. Rose, "Von Konstantin bis Mehmet II," in *Troia. Traum und Wirklichkeit* (Stuttgart 2001) 280–81.

C.B. Rose, "Ilion in the early empire," in C. Berns (ed.), *Patris und Imperium. Kulturelle und politische Identität in den Städten der römischen Provinzen Kleinasiens in der frühen Kaiserzeit* (Leuven 2002) 33–47.

C.B. Rose, "The temple of Athena at Ilion," *Studia Troica* 13 (2003) 27–88.

C.B. Rose, "The Granicus River Valley Archaeological Survey Project, 2004–2005," *Studia Troica* 17 (2007) 65–150.

C.B. Rose, "Separating fact from fiction in the Aeolian migration," *Hesperia* 77 (2008) 399–430.

C.B. Rose and R. Körpe, "The Granicus River Valley Survey Project, 2006," *Araştırma Sonuçları Toplantısı* 25.2 (2007) 103–16.

S.K. Ross, *Roman Edessa. Politics and Culture on the Eastern Fringes of the Roman Empire, 114–242 CE* (London and New York 2001).

S.K. Ross, "The last king of Edessa: New evidence from the Middle Euphrates," *ZPE* 97 (2003) 187–206.

S.I. Rotroff, *Hellenistic Pottery from Sardis, Sardis* M13 (Cambridge, MA 2003).

C. Roueché, *Aphrodisias in Late Antiquity: The Late Roman and Byzantine Inscriptions, JRS Monograph* 5 (London 1989).

C. Roueché, "Provincial governors and their titulature in the sixth century," *Antiquité tardive* 6 (1998) 83–89.

C. Roueché, *Aphrodisias in Late Antiquity: The Late Roman and Byzantine Inscriptions*, revised second online edition (2004) <www.insaph.kcl.ac.uk/ala2004>, ISBN 1 897747 17 9.

C. Roueché, "The Kuretenstraße: The imperial presence in late antiquity," in S. Ladstätter (ed.), *Neue Forschungen zur Kuretenstraße in Ephesos, DenkschrWien* 382 (2009) 155–70.

V. Rousseau, *Late Roman Wall Painting at Sardis* (Ph.D. dissertation, University of Wisconsin–Madison 2010).

V. Ruggieri, "Patara. Due casi di architettura bizantina e la continuità urbana," *Orientalia Christiana Periodica* 75 (2009) 319–41.

J. Rumscheid, *Kranz und Krone. Zu Insignien, Siegespreisen und Ehrenzeichen der römischen Kaiserzeit* (Tübingen 2000).

J. Rüpke, "Kaiserliche Religionspolitik und priesterliche Rekrutierungsmechanismen: Überlegungen zur Elitenformation am Beispiel der Sodalitäten des Herrscherkultes in Antoninischer Zeit," in H. Cancik and K. Hitzl (eds.), *Die Praxis der Herrscherverehrung in Rom und seinen Provinzen* (Tübingen 2003) 131–56.

D.A. Russell and N.G. Wilson (eds. and trans.), *Menander Rhetor* (Oxford 1981).

J. Russell, "The military garrison of Anemurium during the reign of Arcadius," in *Atti del XI Congresso Internazionale di Epigrafia Greca e Latina* 1 (Rome 1999) 721–28.

J. Russell, "The Persian invasions of Syria/Palestine and Asia Minor in the reign of Heraclius: Archaeological, numismatic and epigraphic evidence," in E. Kountoura-Galake (ed.), *The Dark Centuries of Byzantium (7th–9th c.)* (Athens 2001) 47–71.

E. Sachau, *Reise in Syrien und Mesopotamien* (Leipzig 1883).

M. Sage, "Roman visitors to Ilium in the Roman imperial and late antique period: The symbolic functions of a landscape," *Studia Troica* 10 (2000) 211–31.

S. Sande, "Zur Porträtplastik des sechsten nachchristlichen Jahrhunderts," *ActaAArtHist* 6 (1975) 65–106.

T. Saner, D. Roos, and P. Baumeister, "Keloşk Kale (Birecik) 2004," *Araştırma Sonuçları Toplantısı* 23.2 (2005) 217–24.

H.G. Saradi, "The *kallos* of the Byzantine city: The development of a rhetorical *topos* and historical reality," *Gesta* 34 (1995) 37–56.

H.G. Saradi, *The Byzantine City in the Sixth Century. Literary Images and Historical Reality* (Athens 2006).

W. Sauerlaender, "From stylus to style: Reflections on the fate of a notion," *Art History* 6.3 (1983) 253–70.

M.H. Sayar, "Mauererneuerungsinschriften aus Anazarbos," *Epigraphica Anatolica* 29 (1997) 111–15.

M.H. Sayar, *Die Inschriften von Anazarbos und Umgebung* I, *Inschriften griechischer Städte aus Kleinasien* 56 (Bonn 2000).

M.H. Sayar, "Aphrodite Kasalitis in Anazarbos," in M. Meyer and R. Ziegler (eds.), *Kulturbegegnung in einem Brückenland: Gottheiten und Kulte als Indikatoren von Akkulturationsprozessen im Ebenen Kilikien, Asia Minor Studien* 53 (Bonn 2004) 185–89.

M. Schapiro, "On style," in A. Kroeber (ed.), *Anthropology Today: An Encyclopaedic Inventory* (Chicago 1953) 287–312, reprinted in M. Schapiro, *Theory and Philosophy of Art: Style, Artist and Society* (New York 1994) 51–102.

V. Scheibelreiter, *Stifterinschriften auf Mosaiken Westkleinasiens, Tyche* Suppl. 5 (Vienna 2006).

V. Scheibelreiter, "Mosaik- und *opus-sectile*-Pavimente," in M. Steskal and M. La Torre, *Das Vediusgymnasium in Ephesos. Archäologie und Baubefund, Forschungen in Ephesos* XIV 1 (Vienna 2008) 259–75.

I. Scheibler, "Rezeptionsphasen des jüngeren Sokratesporträts in der Kaiserzeit," *JdI* 119 (2004) 179–258.

P. Scherrer (ed.), *Ephesus. The New Guide*, rev. ed. (Istanbul 2000).

P. Scherrer, "The historical topography of Ephesos," in D. Parrish (ed.), *Urbanism in Western Asia Minor: New Studies on Aphrodisias, Ephesos, Hierapolis, Pergamon, Perge, and Xanthos, JRA* Suppl. 45 (Portsmouth, RI 2001) 57–95.

P. Scherrer, "Die Fernwasserversorgung von Ephesos in der römischen Kaiserzeit. Synopse der epigraphischen Quellen," in G. Wiplinger (ed.), *Cura Aquarum in Ephesos, BABesch* Suppl. 12 (2006) 45–60.

P. Scherrer, "Hellenistische und römische Stadttore in Kleinasien unter besonderer Berücksichtigung von Ephesos," in T.G. Schattner and F. Valdés Fernándes (eds.), *Stadttore: Bautyp und Kunstform, Iberia Archaeologica* 8 (Mainz 2006) 63–78.

P. Scherrer, "Der *conventus civium Romanorum* und kaiserliche Freigelassene als Bauherrn in Ephesos in augusteischer Zeit," in M. Meyer (ed.), *Neue Zeiten—Neue Sitten. Zu Rezeption und Integration römischen und italischen Kulturguts in Kleinasien, WForsch* 12 (Vienna 2007) 63–76.

P. Scherrer and E. Trinkl, *Die Tetragonos Agora in Ephesos. Grabungsergebnisse von archaischer bis in byzantinische Zeit—ein Überblick. Befunde und Funde klassischer Zeit, Forschungen in Ephesos* XIII 2 (Vienna 2006).

A.M. Schneider, "Die Blachernen," *Oriens* 4 (1951) 82–120.

C. Schneider, *Die Musengruppe in Milet, Milesische Forschungen* 1 (Mainz 1999).

P. Schneider, "Die Faustinathermen," in O. Dally et al. (eds.), *ZeitRäume. Milet in Kaiserzeit und Spätantike* (Regensburg 2009) 121–41.

V. Schultze, *Altchristliche Städte und Landschaften 2. Kleinasien* (Gütersloh 1922–1926).

U. Schwertheim, "Die spätantik-byzantinische Bebauung," in A. Filges (ed.), *Blaundos. Berichte zur Erforschung einer Kleinstadt im lydisch-phrygischen Grenzgebiet, IstForsch* 48 (Tübingen 2006) 216–22.

R. Schwindt, *Das Weltbild des Epheserbriefes* (Tübingen 2002).

A.R. Seager, "The building history of the Sardis synagogue," *AJA* 76 (1972) 425–35.

A.R. Seager, "The building," in G.M.A. Hanfmann, *Sardis from Prehistoric to Roman Times. Results of the Archaeological Exploration of Sardis, 1958–1975* (Cambridge, MA 1983) 168–78.

J.B. Segal, *Edessa. The Blessed City* (Oxford 1970).

N. Sekunda, "Persian settlement in Hellespontine Phrygia," in A. Kuhrt and H. Sancisi-Weerdenburg (eds.), *Achaemenid History* III: *Method and Theory* (Leiden 1988) 175–96.

Ü. Serdaroğlu, *Surveys in the Lower Euphrates Basin* (Ankara 1977).

H.-G. Severin, *Zur Portraitplastik des 5. Jahrhunderts n. Chr.* (Munich 1972).

K. Shiuchi, "Bilingual inscriptions in Asia Minor. A preliminary survey," *Kodai* 13/14 (2003–2004) 103–9.

C. Şimşek, *Laodikeia* (Istanbul 2007).

T.A. Sinclair, *Eastern Turkey: An Architectural and Archaeological Survey*, 4 vols. (London 1987–1990).

F. Slavazzi, "Il ciclo di rilievi nella 'Kaisersaal' del Ginnasio di Vedio a Efeso," in I. Colpo, I. Favaretto, and F. Chedini (eds.), *Iconografia 2005. Immagini e immaginari dell'antichità classica al mondo moderno* (Rome 2006) 235–43.

F. Slavazzi, "Uso dei modelli e recupero del passato nei programmi scultorei ufficiali di età antonina in Asia Minore," in O.D. Cordovana and M. Galli (eds.), *Arte e memoria culturale nell'età della Seconda Sofistica* (Cantania 2007) 123–36.

R.R.R. Smith, "The public image of Licinius I: Portrait sculpture and imperial ideology in the early fourth century," *JRS* 87 (1997) 170–202.

R.R.R. Smith, "Statue life in the Hadrianic Baths at Aphrodisias, AD 100–600: Local context and historical meaning," in F.A. Bauer and C. Witschel (eds.), *Statuen in der Spätantike* (Wiesbaden 2007) 203–35.

J.-P. Sodini, "Archaeology and late antique social structures," in L. Lavan and W. Bowden (eds.), *Theory and Practice in Late Antique Archaeology, Late Antique Archaeology* 1 (Leiden 2003) 25–56.

J.-P. Sodini, "The transformation of cities in late antiquity within the provinces of Macedonia and Epirus," in A.G. Poulter (ed.), *The Transition to Late Antiquity on the Danube and Beyond, ProcBritAc* 141 (Oxford 2007) 311–36.

J.-M. Spieser, *Urban and Religious Spaces in Late Antiquity and Early Byzantium* (Aldershot 2001).

J. Spon, *Voyage d'Italie, de Dalmatie, de Grèce et du Levant, fait aux années 1675 and 1676* 3.1 (La Haye 1678).

T. Stefanidou-Tiveriou, "Τά αγάλματα τών Μούσων τής Θεσσαλονίκης," *Egnatia* 2 (1990) 73–122.

M. Steskal, "Zu den Stiftungen des M. Claudius P. Vedius Antoninus Phaedrus Sabinianus und ihrem Echo in Ephesos," *Tyche* 16 (2001) 177–88.

M. Steskal, "Bemerkungen zur Funktion der Palästren in den ephesischen Bad-Gymnasium-Komplexen," *ÖJh* 72 (2003) 227–39.

M. Steskal, "Rituelle Bestattungen im Prytaneion von Ephesos? Zu den Fundumständen der Artemis Ephesia—Statuen," *ÖJh* 77 (2008) 363–73.

M. Steskal, *Das Prytaneion in Ephesos, Forschungen in Ephesos* IX 4 (Vienna 2010).

M. Steskal and S. Ladstätter, "Vorbericht zur Baugeschichte des Vediusgymnasiums in Ephesos," *ÖJh* 73 (2004) 237–49.

M. Steskal and M. La Torre, "Das Vediusgymnasium in Ephesos. Die Geschichte der archäologischen Erforschung des Vediusgymnasiums und seines Umfeldes," *ÖJh* 70 (2001) 221–44.

M. Steskal and M. La Torre, *Das Vediusgymnasium in Ephesos. Archäologie und Baubefund, Forschungen in Ephesos* XIV 1 (Vienna 2008).

R.H.W. Stichel, *Die römische Kaiserstatue am Ausgang der Antike* (Rome 1982).

P. Stinson, "Imitation and adaption in architectural design: Two Roman basilical halls at Ephesus and Aphrodisias," in M. Meyer (ed.), *Neue Zeiten—Neue Sitten. Zu Rezeption und Integration römischen und italischen Kulturguts in Kleinasien, WForsch* 12 (Vienna 2007) 91–100.

S. Stiros, "The AD 365 Crete earthquake and possible seismic clustering during the fourth and sixth centuries A.D. in the eastern Mediterranean: A review of historical and archaeological data," *Journal of Structural Geology* 23 (2001) 545–602.

V.M. Strocka, "Neue archaische Löwen in Anatolien," *AA* (1977) 481–512.

V.M. Strocka, *Die Wandmalerei der Hanghäuser in Ephesos, Forschungen in Ephesos* VIII 1 (Vienna 1977).

V.M. Strocka, *Das Markttor von Milet, 128. Berliner Winckelmann-Programm* (Berlin 1981).

V.M. Strocka, "Zuviel Ehre für Scholastikia," in M. Kandler, S. Karwiese, and R. Pillinger (eds.), *Lebendige Altertumswissenschaft, Festgabe zur Vollendung des 70. Lebensjahres von Hermann Vetters* (Vienna 1985) 229–32.

V.M. Strocka, "Zeus, Marnas und Klaseas. Ephesische Brunnenfiguren von 93 n.Chr.," in N. Başgelen and M. Lugal (eds.), *Festschrift für J. İnan* (Istanbul 1989) 77–85.

C. Strube, *Baudekoration im nordsyrischen Kalksteinmassiv I: Kapitell-, Tür-, und Gesimsformen der Kirchen des 4. und 5. Jahrhunderts n. Chr., Damaszener Forschungen* 5 (Mainz 1993).

C. Strube, *Die "Toten Städte". Stadt und Land in Nordsyrien während der Spätantike* (Mainz 1996).

C. Strube, *Baudekoration im nordsyrischen Kalksteinmassiv II: Das 6. und frühe 7. Jahrhundert, Damaszener Forschungen* 11 (Mainz 2002).

H. Stümpel, "Geophysikalische Prospektion in Milet: Arbeiten in den Kampagnen 2000–2002," *AA* (2005) 183–94.

G. Tate, *Les campagnes de la Syrie du Nord du IIe au VIIe siècle: un exemple d'expansion démographique et économique dans les campagnes à la fin de l'antiquité, Bibliothèque archéologique et historique* 133 (Paris 1992).

G. Tate, "Un cas de croissance économique en zone marginale: la Syrie du Nord," *Histoire, économie et société* 3 (1997) 353–59.

G. Tchalenko, *Villages antiques de la Syrie du Nord: le massif du Bélus à l'époque romaine*, 3 vols., *Bibliothèque archéologique et historique* 50 (Paris 1953–1958).

B. Tekkök, S. Wallrodt, C. Günden, and C.B. Rose, "Two Roman wells in the Lower City of Ilion. Quadrats C29 and w28," *Studia Troica* 11 (2001) 343–82.

B. Tenger, "Troas zwischen Königsfrieden und Ankunft Alexanders," in E. Schwertheim and H. Wiegartz (eds.), *Die Troas. Neue Forschungen zu Neandria und Alexandria Troas* II, *Asia Minor Studien* 22 (Bonn 1996) 125–47.

B. Tenger, "Zur Geographie und Geschichte der Troas," in E. Schwertheim (ed.), *Die Troas. Neue Forschungen* III, *Asia Minor Studien* 33 (Bonn 1999) 103–80.

H.J. Thomson (ed.), *Prudentius* 1, *Loeb Classical Library* (London and Cambridge, MA 1969).

H. Thür, "Die spätantike Bauphase der Kuretenstraße," in R. Pillinger et al. (eds.), *Efeso paleocristiana e bizantina—Frühchristliches und Byzantinisches Ephesos, DenkschrWien* 282 (1999) 112–16.

H. Thür, "Die Bauphasen der Wohneinheit 4 (und 6)," in F. Krinzinger (ed.), *Das Hanghaus 2 von Ephesos. Studien zu Baugeschichte und Chronologie* (Vienna 2002) 41–66.

H. Thür, "Das spätantike Ephesos: Aspekte zur Frage der Christianisierung des Stadtbildes," in G. Brands and H.-G. Severin (eds.), *Die spätantike Stadt und ihre Christianisierung* (Wiesbaden 2003) 259–73.

H. Thür, "Das Gymnasion an der oberen Agora in Ephesos," in E. Christof, G. Koiner, M. Lehner, and E. Pochmarski (eds.), *ΠΟΤΝΙΑ ΘΗΡΩΝ. Festschrift für Gerda Schwarz zum 65. Geburtstag* (Vienna 2007) 406–14.

H. Thür, "Wie römisch ist der sog. Staatsmarkt in Ephesos?" in M. Meyer (ed.), *Neue Zeiten—Neue Sitten. Zu Rezeption und Integration römischen und italischen Kulturguts in Kleinasien, WForsch* 12 (Vienna 2007) 79–90.

H. Thür and W. Pietsch, "I.2 Prozessionsstraße (Via Sacra) in Bereich Kuretenstraße/Heroa/Hadrianstor," *ÖJh* 66 (1997) Grabungen 1996, 6–10.

H. Thür et al., "Die Wohneinheit 6 des C. Flavius Furius Aptus," *ÖJh* 75 (2006) Jahresbericht 2005, 326–27.

R. Tölle-Kastenbein, *Frühklassische Peplosfiguren. Typen und Repliken, Antike Plastik* 20 (Berlin 1986).

R. Tölle-Kastenbein, *Antike Wasserkultur* (Munich 1990).

J. Trilling, "The soul of the empire: Style and meaning in the mosaic pavement of the Byzantine imperial palace in Constantinople," *DOP* 43 (1989) 27–72.

F.R. Trombley, "The decline of the seventh-century town: The exception of Euchaita," in S. Vryonis (ed.), *Byzantine Studies in Honor of M.V. Anastos, Byzantina kai Metabyzantina* 4 (Malibu 1985) 65–90.

F.R. Trombley, "Korykos in Cilicia Trachis: The economy of a small coastal city in late antiquity (saec. V–VI)—a précis," *Ancient History Bulletin* 1.1 (1987) 16–23.

F.R. Trombley, "Town and *territorium* in late Roman Anatolia (late 5th to early 7th c.)," in L. Lavan (ed.), *Recent Research in Late-Antique Urbanism, JRA* Suppl. 42 (Portsmouth, RI 2001) 217–32.

H. Turnbow, "Roman sarcophagi," in C. Ratté and P.D. De Staebler (eds.), *Aphrodisias* V. *The Aphrodisias Regional Survey* (Mainz forthcoming).

T. Ulbert, "Stadttore in byzantinischer Zeit," in T.G. Schattner and F. Valdés Fernándes (eds.), *Stadttore: Bautyp und Kunstform, Iberia Archaeologica* 8 (Mainz 2006) 275–90.

R. Van Dam, *The Roman Revolution of Constantine* (Cambridge 2007).

L. Vandeput, "The re-use of Hadrianic architectural elements in basilica E1 at Sagalassos," in M. Waelkens (ed.), *Sagalassos* I: *First General Report on the Survey (1986–1989) and Excavations (1990–1991), ActaArchLov Monographiae* 5 (Leuven 1993) 93–109.

J.L. van Dieten (ed.), *Niketas Choniates Historia* (Berlin 1975).

C. van Eck, J. McAllister, and R. van de Vall (eds.), *The Question of Style in Philosophy and the Arts* (Cambridge 1995).

H. Vanhaverbeke, F. Martens, and M. Waelkens, "Another view on late antiquity: Sagalassos (SW Anatolia), its suburbium and its countryside in late antiquity," in A.G. Poulter (ed.), *The Transition to Late Antiquity on the Danube and Beyond, ProcBritAc* 141 (Oxford 2007) 611–48.

A. Van Millingen, *Byzantine Constantinople: The Walls of the City and Adjoining Historical Sites* (London 1899).

P. van Minnen, "The other cities in later Roman Egypt," in R.S. Bagnall (ed.), *Egypt in the Byzantine World, 300–700* (Cambridge 2007) 207–25.

R.L. Vann, *The Unexcavated Buildings of Sardis, BAR-IS* 538 (Oxford 1989).

D. Van Zanten, R.S. Thomas, and G.M.A. Hanfmann, "The city walls," in G.M.A. Hanfmann and J.C. Waldbaum, *A Survey of Sardis and the Major Monuments Outside the City Walls, Sardis* R1 (Cambridge, MA 1975) 35–52.

G. Varinlioğlu, "Living in a marginal environment: Rural habitat and landscape in southeastern Isauria," *DOP* 61 (2008) 287–317.

G. Varinlioğlu, *Rural Landscape and Built Environment at the End of Antiquity: Limestone Villages of Southeastern Isauria* (Ph.D. dissertation, University of Pennsylvania 2008).

C.C. Vermeule III, *Greek Sculpture and Roman Taste. The Purpose and Setting of Graeco-Roman Art in Italy and the Greek Imperial East* (Ann Arbor 1977).

F. Vermeulen, M. de Dapper, and T. Wiedemann, "Vers un approche géo-archéologique intégrée: le territoire antique de Pessinonte (Turquie)," in M. Clavel-Lévêque and A. Vignot (eds.), *Cité et territoire* 2 (Paris 1998) 123–39.

P. Verzone, "Città ellenistiche e romane dell'Asia Minore: Anazarbos," *Palladio* N.S. 7 (1957) 9–25.

P. Verzone, "Hierapolis," *Reallexikon zur byzantinischen Kunst* II (Stuttgart 1971) 1203–23.

H. Vetters, "Ephesos," *ÖJh* 49 (1968–1971) Grabungen 1969, 9.

H. Vetters, "Ephesos," *ÖJh* 50 (1972–1975) Grabungen 1971/72, 32–62.

P. Vladkova, "The late Roman agora and the state of civic organization," in A.G. Poulter (ed.), *The Transition to Late Antiquity on the Danube and Beyond, ProcBritAc* 141 (Oxford 2007) 203–17.

A. von Gerkan, *Milet* II 1. *Das Stadion* (Berlin 1921).

A. von Gerkan, *Milet* I 6. *Der Nordmarkt und der Hafen an der Löwenbucht* (Berlin 1922).

A. von Gerkan, *Milet* II 3. *Die Stadtmauern* (Berlin 1935).

A. von Gerkan and F. Krischen, *Milet* I 9. *Thermen und Palaestren* (Berlin 1928).

A. von Gutschmid, *Untersuchungen über die Geschichte des Königreichs Osroëne, Mémoires de l'Académie impériale des sciences de St.-Pétersbourg, VIIe Série* 35.1 (St. Petersburg 1887).

A. von Saldern, *Ancient and Byzantine Glass from Sardis, Sardis* M6 (Cambridge, MA 1980).

F. von Saldern, "Die Inschriften des Ceres-Tempels," in A. Filges (ed.), *Blaundos. Berichte zur Erforschung einer Kleinstadt im lydisch-phrygischen Grenzgebiet, IstForsch* 48 (Tübingen 2006) 189–98.

F. von Saldern, "Katalog der Inschriften," in A. Filges (ed.), *Blaundos. Berichte zur Erforschung einer Kleinstadt im lydisch-phrygischen Grenzgebiet, IstForsch* 48 (Tübingen 2006) 321–50.

M. Waelkens, "Sagalassos und sein Territorium. Eine interdisziplinäre Methodologie zur historischen Geographie einer kleinasiatischen Metropole," in K. Belke et al. (eds.), *Byzanz als Raum: Zu Methoden und Inhalten der historischen Geographie des östlichen Mittelmeerraumes, Tabula Imperii Byzantini* 7 (Vienna 2000) 261–88.

M. Waelkens, "The late antique to early Byzantine city in southwest Anatolia. Sagalassos and its territory: A case study," in J.-U. Krause and C. Witschel (eds.), *Die Stadt in der Spätantike—Niedergang oder Wandel?, Historia Einzelschriften* 190 (Stuttgart 2006) 199–256.

M. Waelkens, "Sagalassos," in W. Radt (ed.), *Stadtgrabungen und Stadtforschungen im westlichen Kleinasien. Geplantes und Erreichtes, Byzas* 3 (Istanbul 2006) 325–58.

M. Waelkens et al., "Two late antique residential complexes at Sagalassos," in L. Lavan, L. Özgenel, and A. Sarantis (eds.), *Housing in Late Antiquity. From Palaces to Shops, Late Antique Archaeology* 3.2 (Leiden 2007) 495–513.

J. Wagner, "Legio IIII Scythica in Zeugma am Euphrat," in D. Haupt and H.G. Horn (eds.), *Studien zu den Militärgrenzen Roms* II, *Beih. BJb.* 38 (Cologne 1977) 517–39.

J. Wagner, "Provincia Osrhoenae. New archaeological finds illustrating the military organization under the Severan Dynasty," in S. Mitchell (ed.), *Armies and Frontiers in Roman and Byzantine Anatolia*, *BAR-IS* 156 (Oxford 1983) 103–29.

J. Wagner, *Die Römer an Euphrat und Tigris*, *Sondernummer Antike Welt* (Feldmeilen 1985).

J.C. Waldbaum, *Metalwork from Sardis: The Finds through 1974*, *Sardis* M8 (Cambridge, MA 1983).

J.C. Waldbaum and G.M.A. Hanfmann, "The Roman Bath CG: Site, plan, and description," in G.M.A. Hanfmann and J.C. Waldbaum, *A Survey of Sardis and the Major Monuments outside the Walls*, *Sardis* R1 (Cambridge, MA 1975) 129–50.

A. Walmsley, *Early Islamic Syria: An Archaeological Assessment* (London 2007).

B. Walter, *Milet* II 4. *Topographische Karte von Milet* (Berlin 1968).

B. Ward-Perkins, "Urban continuity?" in N. Christie and S.T. Loseby (eds.), *Towns in Transition. Urban Evolution in Late Antiquity and the Early Middle Ages* (Aldershot 1996) 4–12.

B. Ward-Perkins, *The Fall of Rome and the End of Civilization* (Oxford 2005).

W. Warfield, "Report on the geology of Sardis," in H.C. Butler, *Sardis* I. *The Excavations*. Pt. 1, *1910–1914* (Leiden 1922) 175–80.

P.J. Watson, *Archaeological Ethnography in Western Iran* (Arizona 1979).

B.F. Weber, "Der Stadtplan des kaiserzeitlichen Milet," in L. Schwandner and K. Rheidt (eds.), *Macht der Architektur—Architektur der Macht*, *Diskussionen zur Archäologischen Bauforschung* 8 (Mainz 2004) 231–40.

E. Weber, "Zu den lateinischen Inschriften von Ephesos," in F. Krinzinger and H. Friesinger (eds.), *100 Jahre österreichische Forschungen in Ephesos* (Vienna 1999) 139–46.

K. Weitzmann (ed.), *Age of Spirituality. Late Antique and Early Christian Art, Third to Seventh Century* (New York 1979).

M. Whitby, "Procopius and the development of Roman defences in Upper Mesopotamia," in P.W.M. Freeman and D. Kennedy (eds.), *The Defence of the Roman and Byzantine East*, *BAR-IS* 297, *British Institute of Archaeology at Ankara Monograph* 8 (Oxford 1986) 717–35.

M. Whitby, "Procopius' description of Dara," in P.W.M. Freeman and D. Kennedy (eds.), *The Defence of the Roman and Byzantine East*, *BAR-IS* 297, *British Institute of Archaeology at Ankara Monograph* 8 (Oxford 1986) 737–83.

M. Whitby, "Recruitment in Roman armies from Justinian to Heraclius (ca. 565–615)," in A. Cameron (ed.), *The Byzantine and Early Islamic Near East* III. *States, Resources and Armies*, *Studies in Late Antiquity and Early Islam* 1 (Princeton 1995) 61–124.

M. Whittow, "Ruling the late Roman and early Byzantine city: A continuous history," *PastPres* 129 (1990) 3–29.

M. Whittow, "Recent research on the late-antique city in Asia Minor: The second half of the 6th c. revisited," in L. Lavan (ed.), *Recent Research in Late-Antique Urbanism*, *JRA* Suppl. 42 (Portsmouth, RI 2001) 137–53.

M. Whittow, "Nicopolis ad Istrum: Backward and Balkan?" in A.G. Poulter (ed.), *The Transition to Late Antiquity on the Danube and Beyond*, *ProcBritAc* 141 (Oxford 2007) 375–89.

C. Wickham, "Conclusion," in J. Haldon and L.I. Conrad (eds.), *The Byzantine and Early Islamic Near East* VI. *Elites Old and New*, *Studies in Late Antiquity and Early Islam* 1 (Princeton 2004) 285–98.

C. Wickham, *Framing the Early Middle Ages: Europe and the Mediterranean, 400–800* (Oxford 2005).

T. Wiegand, "Dritter vorläufiger Bericht über die von den Königlichen Museen begonnen Ausgrabungen in Milet," in *Sitzungsberichte der Königlich Preussischen Akademie der Wissenschaften: Philosophisch-historische Klasse* 1904 III (Berlin 1904) 72–91.

T. Wiegand, "Reisen in Mysien," *AM* 29 (1904) 254–339.

T. Wiegand, "Vierter vorläufiger Bericht über die Ausgrabungen der Königlichen Museen zu Milet," in *Sitzungsberichte der Königlich Preussischen Akademie der Wissenschaften: Philosophisch-historische Klasse* 1905 XXV (Berlin 1905) 533–48.

T. Wiegand, "Fünfter vorläufiger Bericht über die von den Königlichen Museen in Milet unternommenen Ausgrabungen," in *Sitzungsberichte der Königlich Preussischen Akademie der Wissenschaften: Philosophisch-historische Klasse* 1906 VIII (Berlin 1906) 249–65.

W. Wilberg, "Stierkopfkapitell aus Ephesos," *ÖJh* 12 (1909) 207–14.

T.J. Wilkinson, *Town and Country in Southeastern Anatolia* I, *Settlement and Land Use in the Lower Karababa Basin* (Chicago 1990).

C.J. Williams, *The Development of Monumental Street Architecture* (Ph.D. thesis, London 1979).

E. Winter, "On the regulations of the eastern frontier of the Roman empire in 298," in D.H. French and C.S. Lightfoot (eds.), *The Eastern Frontier of the Roman Empire, BAR-IS* 553 (Oxford 1989) 555–71.

E. Winter, *Staatliche Baupolitik und Baufürsorge in den römischen Provinzen des kaiserzeitlichen Kleinasien, Asia Minor Studien* 20 (Bonn 1996).

C. Witschel, "Statuen auf spätantiken Platzanlangen in Italien und Africa," in F.A. Bauer and C. Witschel (eds.), *Statuen in der Spätantike* (Wiesbaden 2007) 113–70.

C. Witschel, "Betrachtungen zum römischen Städtewesen in der Spätantike," in A. Lampen and A. Ozwar (eds.), *Schrumpfende Städte. Ein Phänomen zwischen Antike und Moderne* (Cologne–Weimar–Vienna 2008) 17–78.

R. Wittkower, "Eagle and serpent," *JWarb* 2 (1938/39) 293–325.

H. Wolfram, *Die Goten und ihre Geschichte* (Munich 2001).

C. Wolkersdorfer and J. Göbel, "Hydrogeologie der Troianischen Landschaft–eine Bestandsaufnahme," *Studia Troica* 14 (2004) 157–67.

J.T. Wood, *Discoveries at Ephesus* (London 1877).

C.W. Wooten, *Hermogenes on Types of Style* (Chapel Hill 1967).

H. Wrede, "Die spätantike Herme," *JAC* 30 (1987) 129–48.

R. Wuensch (ed.), *Liber de mensibus* (Stuttgart 1967).

U. Wulf, *Altertümer von Pergamon* XV. *Die Stadtgrabung*. Teil 3. *Die hellenistischen und römischen Wohnhäuser von Pergamon* (Berlin 1999).

U. Wulf, "Akören. Zur Stadtplanung und Wohnarchitektur zweier Siedlungen in Kilikien," in G. Brands and H.-G. Severin (eds.), *Die spätantike Stadt und ihre Christianisierung* (Wiesbaden 2003) 299–307.

W.W. Wurster, "Antike Siedlungen in Lykien," *AA* (1976) 23–49.

F.K. Yegül, *The Bath-Gymnasium Complex at Sardis, Sardis* R3 (Cambridge, MA 1986).

F.K. Yegül, *Baths and Bathing in Classical Antiquity* (New York 1992).

F.K. Yegül, "Memory, metaphor, and meaning in the cities of Asia Minor," in E. Fentress (ed.), *Romanization and the City. Creation, Transformations, and Failures, JRA* Suppl. 38 (Portsmouth, RI 2000) 133–53.

H. Yıldız, "La porta sud bizantina di Hierapolis (Pamukkale, Denizli)," in F. D'Andria and F. Silvestrelli (eds.), *Ricerche archeologiche turche nella valle del Lykos, Università di Lecce: Scuola di specializzazione in archeologia classica e medievale: Archeologia e storia* 6 (Galatina 2000) 193–207.

A. Zaccaria Ruggiu, "Regio VIII, insula 104. Le strutture abitative. Fasi e trasformazioni," in F. D'Andria and M. Piera Caggia (eds.), *Hierapolis di Frigia* I. *Le attività delle campagne di scavo e restauro 2000–2003* (Istanbul 2007) 211–56.

A. Zäh, "Eine spätantike Kirche in Nuhrud (heute Gürkuyu) im nördlichen Mesopotamien," *JÖB* 51 (2001) 365–71.

E. Zanini, "The urban ideal and urban planning in Byzantine new cities of the sixth century AD," in W. Bowden and L. Lavan (eds.), *Theory and Practice in Late Antique Archaeology, Late Antique Archaeology* 1 (Leiden 2003) 196–223.

E. Zanini, "Artisans and traders in the early Byzantine city: Exploring the limits of archaeological evidence," in W. Bowden, A. Gutteridge, and C. Machado (eds.), *Social and Political Life in Late Antiquity, Late Antique Archaeology* 3.1 (Leiden 2006) 373–411.

R. Ziegler, *Kaiser, Heer und städtisches Geld. Untersuchungen zur Münzprägung von Anazarbos und anderer ostkilikischer Städte, ETAM* 16 (Vienna 1993).

N. Zimmermann, "Ausstattungen von Haupt- und Nebenräumen. Zur Datierung der Wandmalereien des Hanghauses 2 in Ephesos," in F. Krinzinger (ed.), *Das Hanghaus 2 von Ephesos. Studien zu Baugeschichte und Chronologie* (Vienna 2002) 101–17.

Index

References to modern scholars are included only when those scholars are mentioned by name in the texts of individual contributions.

Abydus tariff, 163, 163n52, 179, 179n16
administration
    civic, 198
    ecclesiastical, 198
    imperial, 24, 120, 124, 248
    provincial, 83, 169, 247n2
Adramyttion, 167
Aegean sea, vii, 2, 258
Aesepus river, 151, 163, 164, 165, 167
Agathias, 13n49, 169n69
agora, 7, 112n31, 161, 247n3
    Aphrodisias, 124
    Ephesus, 23n89, 44–46, 49, 50, 55, 56, 58–66, 69, 70, 250
    Hierapolis, 120n67
    Miletus, 81n1, 86, 87, 88, 89, 93
    Sardis, 7
    Troy, 151, 155, 159, 162, 250, 254
agriculture, 124, 127, 131, 138, 173, 177n9, 179–187, 198, 200, 253, 256–257, 259
Aizanoi, 113nn32–34, 114n35, 119n60, 120, 121, 121n69
    streets, 112, 113
Akören I
    churches, 191
        West Church, 200
    houses, 199, 202
    public area, 200
    settlement pattern, 191, 198–200
    streets, 199
Akören II
    agriculture, 198, 200
    arch, 201
    churches, 191, 211, 214
        North Church, 191, 193, 200, 200 *fig. 12*, 201
        South Church, 191, 201, 202 *fig. 13*, 202 *fig. 14*
    houses, 193, 195, 198, 202
        House I, 192 *fig. 3*, 194 *fig. 6*, 195
        House II, 192 *fig. 3*, 195, 197 *fig. 8*
    public area, 196
    settlement pattern, 191, 195–196, 200
    streets, 191, 211
    tombs, 193
Alacaoluk, 167, 168 *fig. 17*, 169, 169 *fig. 18*, 253
Alaşehir. *See* Philadelphia
Alexander (the Great), 2n10, 151, 151n4, 152
Alexandria Troas, 152n8, 157, 157n25, 158 *fig. 8*, 159, 159n32, 163n54, 169
Algaze, Guillermo, 241, 242
Alzinger, Wilhelm, 43, 48, 49
Amida, 242
    walls, 221
Ammianus Marcellinus, 13n46, 179n15, 251
Amorium, 112n28
    walls, 111, 119, 119n57, 121n73, 251
amphitheater, 250
    Anazarbos, 207
Anastasius I, 112n28, 163, 169
Anazarbos
    amphitheater, 207
    arches, 206 *fig. 2*, 208, 221
        triumphal arch, 209–211, 209 *fig. 3*, 209 *fig. 4*, 215
    basilica (?), 207
    baths, 207
    cemeteries, 207
    churches, 208, 217, 221
        Church of the Apostles, 206 *fig. 2*, 210–212, 214, 222
        Rock-cut Church, 214
        tetra- or triconch, 214, 222

  - circus, 207
  - gates, 206 *fig. 2,* 207, 214, 217, 218, 222
  - grid plan, 207, 208, 212, 213 *fig. 10,* 214 *fig. 11,* 215 *fig. 12,* 216
  - inscriptions, 214, 217, 218, 222
  - sanctuaries, 207, 214, 215
    - Temple of Aphrodite Kasalitis, 208
  - shops, 214, 215
  - streets, 207, 208, 209, 210 *fig. 5,* 214, 214 *fig. 10,* 215, 215 *fig. 12a–b,* 216, 218, 223
  - theater, 206 *fig. 2,* 207, 218, 221
  - walls, 206 *fig. 2,* 208, 210, 212, 213 *fig. 10,* 214, 215–220, 222, 223, 224
- Anemurium, 111, 121n73, 251
- Antioch on the Orontes, 218, 221n64
- Antiochus, 4, 226
- Aphrodisias, vii, viii, 8n29, 48, 83, 103, 123–136, 152, 253, 260
  - agora, 45n9, 124
  - baths, 113, 123n2
  - bouleuterion, 136n13
  - cemeteries, 125, 127, 136
  - churches, 123, 127, 128 *fig. 2*
    - extra-urban, 125, 127
  - civil basilica, 45n9
  - fortifications, territorial, 134 *fig. 6*
  - gates, 115, 116, 117–118, 119, 119n57, 125
  - houses, 20n72, 113, 113n34, 127n9, 136n15
  - stadium, 124
  - streets, 112
  - temples, 127
    - Sebasteion, 160
    - Temple of Aphrodite, 123, 124, 125
  - theater, 123
  - walls, 10n36, 111, 114, 121n70, 123, 124, 125, 145, 251
- aqueduct, viii, 124, 156 (qanat)
  - Blaundos, 141, 142
  - (near) Constantinople, 116
  - Ephesus, 249 (water system)
  - Sardis, 5
  - Troy, 155
- Arabs, 109, 122, 171, 217, 226
- Arcadius, 13, 15, 29, 30, 30n11, 32, 33, 34, 111–112n28, 145, 249
- Archelaos, Flavios (vicar of Asia), 13, 13n50, 17
- arch, 141, 203, 233, 240
  - Akören II, 201, 202 *fig. 13*
  - Anazarbos, 206 *fig. 2,* 208, 209, 210–211, 215
  - Constantinople, 29
  - Rome, 36, 116, 117, 118
- Arles, 157, 250
- Armenians, 217, 219
- arms factory
  - Sardis, 8, 10, 11n38
  - Seleucia ad Calycadnum, 175, 187, 256
- Asartepe, 167, 169, 170 *fig. 9,* 253
- Asia, diocese/province of, 8, 65, 174n4
  - *asiarch*
    - Tatianos (= Antonios Tatianos?), 83, 91–92
  - proconsul of, 63–64n150
    - Asklepios, 56, 70
    - Lucius Caelius Montius, 62, 63, 65, 69
  - vicar of
    - Flavios Archelaos, 13, 17
    - Severos Simplikios, 13
    - Skylakios, 83
- Asklepios (proconsul of Asia), 56, 70
- Athens, 30, 250
- Augustus, 45, 46, 47, 48, 151, 158, 160, 260
- Auinger, Johanna, 44
- Aurenhammer, Maria, 249, 250
- Ausonius, 36, 36n40

- Babayaka, 165, 165 *fig. 15,* 166 *fig. 16*
- Balkans, 112, 247, 248, 257, 257n36, 258, 258n37, 258n38
- Banaji, Jairus, 252
- basilica, 7, 120n67, 173, 183, 221n60
  - Anazarbos (?), 207
  - Aphrodisias, 45n9
  - Blaundos, 137
  - Constantinople, 29, 34
  - Ephesus, 44, 45, 45n9, 46, 47, 48, 49, 50, 53, 55, 56, 57, 58, 59, 70
  - Lepcis Magna, 162
  - Miletus, 86, 87, 89, 107, 109
- Basiliskos (governor of Lydia), 13, 13n50
- baths, ix, 67n1, 69n6, 69n11, 93n40, 119
  - Anazarbos, 207
  - Aphrodisias, 113, 123n2
  - Constantinople, 29, 30, 30n8, 33, 34, 37, 40, 41, 248
  - Ephesus, 44, 45, 46, 50, 50n49, 53, 54, 54n76, 55, 55 *fig. 8,* 56, 57, 58, 58n111, 59, 61, 62, 63, 67–80, 66, 67, 67n1, 67n2, 69, 69n3, 69n4, 69n9, 69n10, 70, 70n15, 71, 72, 73, 76n51, 76n52, 77, 78, 79, 113, 249, 250
  - Hierapolis in Phrygia, 120
  - Miletus, 83, 84, 85, 88, 89, 90 *fig. 6,* 91, 92, 93, 94, 97, 97n53, 98, 99, 100, 101, 107, 108, 250

Sagalassos, 113
Sardis, 2, 5n15, 7, 8, 9, 9 *fig. 5*, 10n33, 11, 11n42, 11n43, 12, 12n44, 13, 13n47, 13n49, 14, 14n59, 15, 20, 21, 23, 23n89, 24, 26, 113, 254
Seleucia ad Calycadnum, 113
Troy, 113, 153 *fig. 3*, 155
Bell, Gertrude, 212
Beyburç, 238, 239, 240, 242, 242n50, 244, 245
Bier, Lionel, 45, 50, 51, 52
bishop, ix, 22, 83, 113n34, 125n7, 127n9, 140n12, 150, 227, 244n54, 248n6, 258
Blaundos, 112, 112–113n28, 137–150
aqueduct, 141, 142
basilica, 138
chora, 147
Christianity at, 150
gate, 115, 116n48, 119, 119n58, 140 *fig. 3*, 141, 142 *fig. 4a–b*, 149 *fig. 8*, 150
forum, 138, 148, 254
houses, 146–147, 148, 150
inscriptions, 140, 140n14
shops, 140
stadium, 142, 149 *fig. 8*
streets, 140, 148, 149 *fig. 8*, 150
temples, 138, 138n7, 138n8, 139 *fig. 2*, 148, 149 *fig. 8*, 150
Sanctuary of Apollo, 141, 146
theater, 139 *fig. 2*, 141
tombs, 140
walls, 111, 121n70, 141, 142, 142n19, 145, 146, 146 *fig. 7*, 147, 150, 221n61, 251, 254
Bol, Renate, 92
bouleuterion
Aphrodisias, 136n13
Ephesus, 45, 45n18, 47, 50 *fig. 5*, 50–51, 53, 58, 59, 61, 62n143, 63
Miletus, 86, 87, 87 *fig. 5*
Troy, 153 *fig. 3*, 162n48
Brad, 239
Butler, Howard Crosby, 1
Byzantium. *See* Constantinople

Cadario, Matteo, 58
Caelius Montius, Lucius (proconsul of Asia), 62, 63, 65, 69
Caesarea, 119n59, 251, 258
Cain, Hans-Ulrich, 85
Caligula (Gaius), 5, 48
Çaltılı, 8n24
Caracalla, 152, 152n11, 154, 155, 159, 226
Caria, 81, 124, 125n5
governor of
Flavius Marianus Michaelius Gabrielius Ioannes Eutropius, 83
Flavius Marianus Patricius, 83
Nonnos, 83
Vitianus, 83
Cassius Dio, 45, 226n7
cemetery (necropolis), 178, 179
Anazarbos, 207
Aphrodisias, 125, 125n7, 127
Görle, 136
Miletus, 109
Plarasa, 127
Sardis, 1, 14
Troy, 162, 250, 254
ceramics, 1, 5, 13n50, 17, 25, 46, 72, 98, 109, 112n28, 127, 129–131, 133, 135, 136n13, 138, 148, 155, 154, 162, 164, 165, 173, 175, 186, 193, 195n11, 207, 217, 221, 222, 224, 233, 241n46, 254
coarseware, 222n58
fineware, 24, 186
imported, 24, 25, 129, 140, 186
Chosroes II, 259
Christian destruction and mutilation, ix, 76, 76n51, 83, 93, 98, 100–101, 250, 250n13
Christianity, vii–viii, 98, 227
replacement of local cult, vii, 7n20, 14, 14n52, 60–61, 99, 123, 127, 171, 248
Christodoros of Thebes, 29n5, 30, 30n9, 33n28
Chronicles of Edessa, 226n11, 226–227
church, ix, 15n61, 66n164, 121, 171, 177, 189n2, 189n5, 222n67, 239n32, 239n36, 239n37, 241, 242n47, 242n48, 248n6, 251
Akören I, 189, 191, 200, 201, 203, 255
Akören II, 189, 191, 193, 200, 200 *fig. 12*, 201, 202 *fig. 13*, 202 *fig. 14*, 203, 212 *fig. 9*, 214, 255
Amorium, 119
Anazarbos, 206 *fig. 2*, 208, 210, 211, 211 *fig. 6*, 211 *fig. 7*, 212, 213 *fig. 8*, 214, 214 *fig. 11a–b*, 215 *fig. 12*, 217, 221, 222, 255
Aphrodisias, 123, 125, 125n7, 125n8, 127, 128 *fig. 2*, 135, 136
Attouda, 127
Babayaka, 165, 165 *fig. 15*, 166 *fig. 16*, 167
Beyburç, 238–239, 240
Constantinople, 116
Edessa, 227, 227n12, 244, 244n54, 255

Ephesus, 77, 120n61, 249
Gürkuyu, 239, 240, 244
Hierapolis in Phrygia, 120, 120n67
Hierapolis Kastabala, 255
Işıkkale, 183
Keloşk Kale (?), 233, 238 *fig. 15*, 244, 245
Limyra, 112n28, 120
Miletus, 83, 84, 97, 100, 109, 110 *fig. 8*, 110 *fig. 9*
Qalblozeh, 239
Sagalassos, 120, 120n67
Sardis, 14, 14n58, 254
Sitt er-Rum, 233, 234 *fig. 9*, 234 *fig. 10*, 238 *fig. 15*, 244
Tlos, 120, 120n67
Troy, 159, 161, 161 *fig. 12*, 162, 167, 171
church councils, 14, 249
Cibinören, 237, 238, 239
Cilicia, vii, 119n61, 120–121n68, 173, 175, 175n4, 175n7, 176 *table 1*, 176n8, 177, 179, 179nn15–16, 185–187, 189, 189nn2–3, 193, 201, 203, 254, 255–256, 256nn30–31, 257. *See also* Isauria
circus, 120n67, 248
Anazarbos, 207
Constantinople, 27, 34
Claudius, 5, 26n101, 48
coins, 2, 13n50, 16–17, 16n66, 22, 24, 25, 25n97, 46, 46n29, 118, 123, 138, 145, 154, 162, 162n48, 162n50, 207, 226, 226n6, 233
hoards, 17, 17n67
Comfort, Anthony, 240, 241
commercial businesses, 21, 178, 186, 252
Constans, 33n29, 57, 59, 62, 63, 69
Constans II, 24
Constantine, 8n30, 27, 29, 32, 33, 33n28, 33n29, 34, 83, 147, 159, 160n38, 164, 165n58, 247, 249, 254
Constantinople, vii, viii, 8, 23n88, 27–41, 29, 136, 169, 169n69, 169n71, 171, 179, 249–250, 252, 253, 254, 258
arches, 116
Milion, 29, 32, 32n27
basilica, 29, 34
Baths of Zeuxippos, 29, 30, 30n8, 33, 34, 37, 40, 41, 248
Capitol-Philadelphion complex, 29, 33, 33n28, 34
Church of St. John Studios, 116
circus, 27, 34
fora
Augusteion, 29, 32, 32n23, 32n27, 34, 36, 37, 41
Forum of Arcadius, 29, 33
Column of Arcadius, 30n11, 32, 34, 249
Forum of Constantine, 29, 30, 33, 33n28, 34, 37, 41, 248
Column of Constantine, 29, 30n6
Forum of Theodosius, 29, 33, 33n28, 41
Column of Theodosius, 30, 30n11, 32, 34, 249
Golden Gate, 115 *fig. 12*, 116, 116 *fig. 13*, 116n42, 117, 117n50, 118
Golden Horn, 29, 117n50
Great Palace, 32, 32n23
Chalke Gate, 32, 32n27
hippodrome, 29, 30, 30n8, 32, 32n23, 33, 34, 34n31, 37, 41, 248, 249
Built Obelisk, 34
Plataean Tripod, 29, 30n6, 248
Serpent Column. *See* Plataean Tripod
Theodosian Obelisk, 30n11, 34
library. *See* basilica
Strategeion, 29
streets
Mese, 29, 33
Regia, 29, 32, 32n27
temples
Capitolium. *See* Capitol-Philadelphion complex
See basilica
walls, 117n50, 118, 121n73
Theodosian, 116, 169, 169n69, 210n21, 219, 251
Constantius II, 57, 59, 249
construction techniques, 10, 15, 114, 137, 148, 169, 193, 201, 215, 216, 217, 218, 231, 233, 234 *fig. 10*, 235, 237, 240, 245
Corasium, 173, 175, 176 *table 1*, 178
Corycus, 173, 175, 176 *table 1*, 177, 178, 181, 186–187, 256
Council of Nicaea, 14
countryside, vii, viii, 109, 113n33, 120, 121n68, 124, 127, 137, 173, 175, 177n10, 178, 179, 181, 185, 185n33, 186, 187, 227, 240–244, 252, 253, 253n24, 255. *See also* rural settlement
Crete, 23n88, 155
Cyzicus, 164, 165, 167, 167n64, 167n66, 169n71

Dara, 242, 243n53
gates, 218
walls, 221, 221n66
Dardanelles, 151, 163
Daskyleion, 164

Deir Siman, 234
demographics (urban), 26, 65, 124, 147, 198
depopulation, viii, ix, 124, 136, 244, 253
De Staebler, Peter D., 252
deurbanization, 66n164, 207, 213 *fig. 10*, 217, 252, 253, 254, 258
Deyr Yakup, 242
Didyma, 43n1, 60n128, 61, 83
Didymateiche, 164
Diocletian, 8, 26, 120n65, 260, 165, 165n58, 165n59, 176n8, 240, 242, 243
Dorotheus of Gaza, 258, 258n42

earthquake(s) and aftermath, viii, 5, 7n22, 8, 9, 22, 23, 23n88, 46, 58, 58n116, 76, 81, 89, 120, 124, 138, 152, 154, 157, 162, 164, 164n56, 171, 209, 216, 221, 235, 249, 250, 253, 254
economy, vii, viii, 21n82, 22n85, 24, 26, 81, 109, 120n65, 124, 145, 155, 157n24, 159, 162, 171, 173, 175n4, 177, 179, 187, 226, 240, 243, 244, 247, 248, 251–260
Edessa, 35, 225n1, 225n3, 226, 226n4, 226n7, 226n10, 240, 241, 242n49, 244
    churches, 227, 244, 255
    kings of, 226, 226n5, 226n8
Egypt, 27, 27n2, 29, 155, 160n37, 163, 247n2, 248, 252, 252n22, 257, 256, 256n32, 257n33, 258, 259, 260
Elagabalus, 8
Elaiussa-Sebaste, 113, 113n34, 173, 175, 175n7, 181, 185
Empelus river, 167
Ephesus, vii, 8n29, 27, 27n2, 43, 43n1, 43n2, 69n3, 91, 111, 119, 119n61, 121, 122, 161n41, 161n42, 249, 249nn9–12, 250, 250n14, 250n15
    baths, 44, 67, 68 *fig. 1*, 69n6, 69–70, 70n15, 113, 249, 250
        baths in the Upper Agora, 45, 46, 50, 55 *fig. 8*, 55–56, 55n90, 58, 59, 61, 68 *fig. 1*, 69
        Baths of Scholasticia. *See* Varius Baths
        East Gymnasium, 68 *fig. 1*, 70, 76–79, 76n52, 77 *fig. 8*
            "Kaisersaal," 77, 77 *fig. 8*, 77n55, 78, 79
        Harbor Baths, 57, 68 *fig. 1*, 69, 69n9, 69n10
        Theater Bath-Gymnasium, 68 *fig. 1*, 69, 69n11, 79
        Varius Baths, 45, 53, 54, 54n76, 67n3, 68 *fig. 1*, 70, 70n19
        Vedius Gymnasium, 58n111, 67n1, 68 *fig. 1*, 69n4, 70, 70n23, 71 *fig. 2*, 71–76, 78, 79
            "Kaisersaal," 71, 71n28, 72, 72n34, 73, 74, 75, 75n44, 77, 79
    bouleuterion, 45, 45n18, 47, 50 *fig. 5*, 50–53, 51n51, 51n52, 53n71, 58, 59, 61
    churches, 77, 249, 254
        Church of St. Mary, 249
    Curetes Hall, 53, 54n76
    fountains, 44, 45, 56–58, 57 *fig. 9*, 59, 61, 62, 249
        Fountain of C. Laecanius Bassus, 45, 45n20, 45n21, 59, 61n141
        Fountain of Domitian, 45, 58
        Fountain of Trajan, 43n3
    four-columned monument, 249
    governor's palace, 69n3, 249
    Hercules Gate, 59
    houses, 69n8, 113
        "Hanghäuser"/Terrace Houses, 156–157, 156n22, 157n23, 160, 160n41, 249
        "Hanghaus"/Terrace House 1, 43, 43n3, 63n151, 161n42
        "Hanghaus"/Terrace House 2, 69n3, 156–157, 156n22, 157n23
    Magnesian Gate, 61, 62, 77
    Sebasteion, 48
    streets, 4, 65, 66, 112
        Arcadiane, 249
        Curetes Street, 44, 53, 59, 65n161, 66, 67n3, 70
        Embolos. *See* Curetes Street
    temples, 45, 48, 58
        Temple of Artemis, 82
    Tetragonos Agora/Lower Agora, 23n89, 49, 59, 59n121, 60, 63–65, 69n11, 250
    theater, 44
    Upper Agora, 44 *fig. 1*, 55, 58, 59, 60, 61, 62, 63–65, 66
        Basilica-Stoa, 44, 45, 45n9, 46–50, 47 *fig. 2*, 48 *fig. 3*, 49 *fig. 4*, 55, 58, 70
        prytaneion, 45, 45n12, 52 *fig. 6*, 53–55, 53 *fig. 7*, 53n73, 53n75, 58, 61, 62, 63
        Rhodian Peristyle, 45
        Temenos, 45, 53, 58
    water system, 59, 249
Eski Hisar, 237, 242, 243 *fig. 6*
Esmonde Cleary, Simon, 250
euergetism, viii, ix, 11, 13, 13n45, 13n49, 16, 17, 23, 44, 47, 50–51, 51n51, 52, 53, 57, 66, 69, 70, 71, 77, 78, 78n59, 81, 88, 154
Euphrates river, 225, 226, 227, 227n15, 228, 239, 240, 240n39, 241, 241n42, 241n43, 242, 243, 244
Eusebius, 30n7, 226

Faustina Minor, 91
Filges, Axel, 61, 254
Fittschen, Klaus, 51
forum, 69n11, 157n27
  Blaundos, 138, 148
  Constantinople, 29, 30, 33, 33n28, 34, 36, 37, 41, 248
  Lepcis Magna, 162
Foss, Clive, viii, 2, 103, 104, 106, 107, 108, 109, 111, 224, 247
fountain, 7, 7n23, 13, 16
  Ephesus, 43n1, 43n3, 45, 56, 57, 58, 58n107, 59, 61, 62, 63, 63n150, 65, 67n1, 76n51, 79n65, 249
  Miletus, 81n1, 87, 87 *fig.* 5, 97, 101
Frankel, Rafael, 185
Freshfield Album, 29n5

Gaius. *See* Caligula
gate, 106, 119n57, 121, 221n60, 231, 251
  Alacaoluk, 167, 169
  Anazarbos, 206 *fig.* 2, 210, 211, 212, 214, 217, 218, 220, 222, 223
  Antioch on the Orontes, 218
  Aphrodisias, 114, 114 *fig.* 11, 115, 116, 117, 118 *fig.* 15, 119, 119n57, 119n58
  Blaundos, 115, 115n38, 115n39, 116n48, 119n57, 119n58, 140 *fig.* 3, 141, 142 *fig.* 4a–b, 150
  Constantinople, 32, 115 *fig.* 12, 116, 116 *fig.* 13, 116n42, 117, 117n50, 118
  Dara, 218
  Ephesus, 49, 59, 62, 61, 77, 111n25, 119, 119n56, 120n61
  Hierapolis in Phrygia, 115, 115n38 118
  Laodicea on the Lycus, 119, 119n57
  Limyra, 112n28, 115, 115n38, 119, 119n57, 119n58
  Martyropolis, 218
  Miletus, 83, 84, 85, 85 *fig.* 2, 86, 87, 88, 89, 89n24, 91, 103, 104, 105 *fig.* 2, 105 *fig.* 3, 105 *fig.* 4, 106, 106 *fig.* 5, 107, 122
  Perge, 118, 118n55, 251
  Philadelphia, 10
  Sagalassos, 115, 115n38, 116, 119, 119n58
  Sardis, 10, 11, 12, 13, 17
  Side, 118, 251
  Tlos, 115, 115n38
  Troy, 153 *fig.* 3, 162
Germanicus, 5
Giese, Jürgen, 141
Gordian III, 82, 164, 169 *fig.* 14, 226
Görle, 136
Goths, 8, 69n8, 82, 84, 91, 112, 145, 169
Gough, Michael, 217
governors, ix, 8, 8n31, 13, 43, 65n161, 69n3, 83, 249
granary, 32n23, 256
  Tenedus, 163, 254
Granicus river, 151, 163, 164, 167, 171, 253
  Battle of, 164
Greenewalt, Jr., Crawford H., 2
guilds, 177, 178
Gümüşçay. *See* Didymateiche
Gündüz, Sema, 240
Gürkuyu, 239, 239n34, 240, 242, 244

Habur river, 225
Hadrian, 62n144, 88, 151, 151n7, 152, 152n8
Hanfmann, George M.A., 1, 2
harbor, 186, 187, 255
  Alexandria Troas, 157, 157n25
  Corasium, 173, 178
  Corycus, 173, 178
  Ephesus, 249
  Hermopolis, 260
  Miletus, 83, 85, 91n29, 107, 108 *fig.* 7
Heberdey, Rudolf, 47n35, 57n101, 69n8, 79n64
Hellenkemper, Hansgerd, 215, 217, 218
Hellespontine Phrygia, 163, 163n54
Heraclius, 25, 39n54, 117n50, 123, 162, 162n48, 169, 252n21, 259
hermits, 116, 222
Hermogenes of Tarsus, 27, 37, 37n43, 38, 41
Hermus river, 2, 4, 7, 8, 20
Herodotus, 4, 151n4
Herulians, attack of, 157
Hierapolis in Phrygia, 45n21, 103, 115n39, 115n40, 120n63, 121n70, 121n73, 140
  agora, 120n67
  bath, 120, 120n67
  churches, 120, 120n67
  gates, 115, 115n38, 118
  houses, 113, 113n34
  walls, 111, 112n28, 118, 145, 251
Hierapolis Kastabala, 212, 212 *fig.* 8, 212n29, 255
Hild, Friedrich, 215
hippodrome
  Constantinople, 29, 29n5, 30, 30n8, 30n11, 32, 33, 34, 36, 37, 41, 248, 249
Højte, Jakob Munk, 61
Howard-Johnston, James, 259
house/residence, 8, 8n31, 19n71, 20n75, 25n99, 100, 119, 119n60, 146, 177n10, 185, 189, 198, 231, 237, 248, 251
  Akören I, 191, 199, 200, 203, 255

  Akören II, 191, 194 *fig. 6*, 195, 196 *fig. 7*, 197 *fig. 8*, 198, 199, 200, 203, 255
  Aphrodisias, 113n34, 127, 136
  Blaundos, 146, 147, 148
  Dystos, 195, 195n10
  Ephesus, 43, 44n3, 62n143, 63n151, 69n3, 69n8, 156, 156n22, 157, 160, 160n41, 161n42, 249
  Hierapolis in Phrygia, 113, 113n34
  Pergamon, 113, 160
  Perge, 113
  Sagalassos, 113, 113n34
  Sardis, 2, 5, 11, 12, 14, 14n59, 17, 19, 19 *fig. 12*, 19n70, 20, 22, 23, 24, 25, 26, 113, 113n34, 161n42
  Troy, 156, 160, 161 *fig. 11*, 162
  Xanthus, 113, 113n34
Humann, Carl, 109
Huns, 169, 248, 258
Hyakinthos (bishop of Miletus), 83
Hypaepa, 10, 14
  embolos of. *See* Sardis, streets, *embolos* of Hypaepa

Ida mountains, 155, 160
Ilion. *See* Troy
imperial cult, 8, 45, 48, 56, 248
İnceler Köyü, 235, 236 *fig. 12*, 236 *fig. 13*, 237, 237 *fig. 14*, 237n26, 239, 244
inscriptions, 1, 7, 7n21, 7n23, 13, 13n45, 14n60, 23, 23n90, 26n101, 51, 51n51, 51n57, 51n59, 52n61, 52n64, 53, 56, 57n101, 60, 60n124, 61, 64, 69, 70, 81, 82, 84, 84n2, 88, 89, 91, 92, 92 *fig. 7*, 93, 94, 97, 103, 104, 105 *fig. 4*, 106, 109, 111n28, 116, 119n57, 123, 152n8, 157, 159, 159n32, 159n35, 160n37, 162n43, 162n44, 163–164, 189n6, 201, 208n13, 214, 217, 218, 222, 238, 256
  bilingual, 64, 64n156, 65n157, 138
  funerary, 8n24, 125n7, 140, 140n14, 173, 175, 178, 179, 189n6
  Greek, 1n1, 5, 13n49, 14n52, 16n64, 19, 19n72, 64, 154–155, 154 *fig. 5*, 159, 160, 160n38
  honorific, 5, 5n15, 5n16, 8n28, 13, 13n46, 15, 57, 62, 62n143, 62n144, 62n150, 63, 63n151, 63n153, 69, 71, 83, 91, 123, 159, 191, 193
  Latin, 1n1, 62, 63, 64–65, 65n158, 138, 160n38
Ionia, 4, 145, 157
Isauria, vii, 119n61, 120n61, 120n68, 173, 173n2, 174 *fig. 1*, 175, 176 *table 1*, 177, 179, 179n15, 179n16, 181n26, 183n28, 185, 186, 187, 189n2, 193, 201, 203, 215, 254, 255, 256, 257. *See also* Cilicia
Işıkkale, 181 *fig. 3*, 182 *fig. 4*, 183, 184 *fig. 7*, 186 *graph 2*

İstanbul Teknik Üniversitesi, 225n1, 228
Italy, 28n3, 39 *fig. 4*, 60n125, 66, 155, 155n19, 157n27, 211n27, 257

Jews/Judaism, vii, viii, 2, 7n20, 13n49, 15, 15n62, 15n63, 16, 16 *fig. 10*, 16nn64–66, 17, 21, 23, 254
Julian, 22, 33n29, 83, 159, 159n32, 160, 160n37, 160n38, 165n58, 226
Julius Caesar, 30, 160
Justinian, 83, 84, 89, 91, 104, 107, 108, 109, 119n59, 162, 163, 221, 240, 249, 251, 255, 257, 258

Kalinowski, Angela, 51
Kantırma, 240, 240n38, 245
Kasr el-Benat, 234
Kästner, Volker, 89
Keenan, James, 252
Keil, Josef, 71, 74, 77
Keloşk Kale, 225n1, 228–235, 228n17, 228n18, 229 *fig. 2*, 230 *fig. 3*, 231 *fig. 5*, 232 *fig. 6*, 233 *fig. 8*, 233–234n22, 234 *fig. 10*, 235 *fig. 11*, 235n25, 236, 237, 238, 238 *fig. 15*, 238n39, 239, 240, 241, 242, 244, 245
Kemerdere, 155
Kennedy, Hugh, 247, 248
Kirsten, Ernst, 1
Knackfuß, Hubert, 85, 88
Krischen, Fritz, 91, 92, 94, 97, 98, 100, 101

Ladstätter, Sabine, 72
Lampsacus, 171
Laodicea on the Lycus, 111, 111–112n28, 119, 119n57, 121n73, 251
Lausos, 36, 41n58
Lepcis Magna, 157, 162
Lesser Phrygia, 165
Liebeschuetz, J.H.W.G., 120
Limyra, 116n48
  church, 111–112n28, 120
  gates, 111–112n28, 115, 115n38, 119, 119n57, 119n58, 121n73
  streets, 112
  walls, 111, 121n70, 251
Lydia, 1, 1n1, 2n10, 4, 4n12, 7, 7n22, 8, 9n32, 14n55, 15n63, 17n67, 22, 22n85, 26n102, 113n34, 125n5, 253n25
  governor of, 8
    Basiliskos, 13, 13n50

Macestus river, 167
Macrinus, 84, 152, 154, 154 *fig. 5*, 155

Maeander valley, 140
Magnesia on the Maeander, 111, 111n24
manufacture/production
  agricultural, 178, 179–187
  animal products, 175, 176 *table 1*, 177, 179, 256
  arms. *See* arms factory
  ceramic, 175, 176 *table 1*, 179
  crafts, 177, 178, 179, 256
  food, 175, 176 *table 1*, 177–178, 178n11, 186, 198, 256
  metal, 22n84, 24, 24n92, 175, 176 *table 1*, 177, 187, 256
  olive oil, 136, 136n16, 178–179, 185–187, 198, 252, 252n21
    presses, 173, 175, 179–183, 179–180n17, 180n20, 180n22, 181 *fig. 5*, 185, 198, 198n13
  textiles, 24, 175 –177, 176n8, 180n18, 187, 256, 257
  wine, 178, 185–187
    presses, 173, 175, 179–183, 179n15, 183n28, 185, 185n33, 186, 198n13
Marianus Michaelius Gabrielius Ioannes Eutropius, Flavius (governor of Caria), 83
Marianus Patricius, Flavius (governor of Caria), 83
Marmara, sea of, 165, 167, 167n62, 171n73
Martyropolis, 218, 221, 223n69
Maurice, 257, 258, 259
Memnonios, 13
Menander of Laodicea, 38, 38n48
Mesopotamia, 227, 243n53, 259
metallurgy, 24, 24n92, 175, 257. *See also* manufacture/production, metal
Miletus, vii, 81
  agora, 82 *fig. 1*, 86, 87, 93
    altar in the, 82 *fig. 1*, 89
  baths
    Baths of Capito, 82 *fig. 1*, 85, 104 *fig. 1*, 108
    Baths of Faustina, 82 *fig. 1*, 83, 84, 88, 89, 90 *fig. 6*, 91–101, 97n53, 104 *fig. 1*, 107
    Hall of the Muses, 91, 92, 95, 95 *fig. 9*, 97n53
    baths south of the Ilyas Bey Mosque, 97, 108
  bishop of
    Hyakinthos, 83
  bouleuterion, 85, 86, 87, 87 *fig. 5*
  cemetery, 109
  Christian activity, 84, 93, 98, 99, 100
  churches, 83
    basilica, 82 *fig. 1*, 87, 89
    Church of St. Gabriel, 83
    Church of St. Michael, 82 *fig. 1*, 83, 84, 97, 104 *fig. 1*
    Great Church, 97
    Necropolis Church, 82 *fig. 1*, 104 *fig. 1*, 109, 110 *fig.* 8, 110 *fig* .9
    Round Church, 82 *fig. 1*, 104 *fig. 1*, 109
  harbors, 83
    Lion Harbor, 82 *fig. 1*, 85, 107, 108 *fig. 7*
    Theater Harbor, 91n29
  Heroon III, 82 *fig. 1*, 88
  Hometepe, 104 *fig. 1*, 108
  inscriptions, 81, 82, 83, 84, 89, 91, 92, 92 *fig. 7*, 93, 94, 97, 104, 105 *fig. 4*, 106, 106 *fig. 5*, 109
  North Market, 82 *fig. 1*, 85
  nymphaeum, 82, 86, 87, 87 *fig. 5*, 88, 89, 93, 104 *fig. 1*, 250
  Sacred Way, 83
  Selçuk *tekke*, 81
  South Market, 84, 87, 88, 89, 103
    "Antiochus Wall," 89
    Market Gate, 82 *fig. 1*, 83, 84, 85, 85 *fig. 2*, 86–91, 86 *fig. 3*, 86 *fig. 4*, 87 *fig. 5*, 103–107, 105 *fig. 2*, 105 *fig. 3*, 105 *fig. 4*, 106 *fig. 5*, 122
  stadium, 82 *fig.* 1, 88, 97, 97n52, 107
  temples
    extra-urban
      Sanctuary of Apollo Didymaios, 88
    Sanctuary of Apollo Delphinios (Delphinion), 88, 104 *fig.* 1
    Serapeion, 82 *fig. 1*, 88
    Temple of Dionysus, 82 *fig.* 1, 83
  theater, 82 *fig. 1*, 84, 88, 89, 105 *fig. 2*, 107
  Theater Hill, 103, 104 *fig. 1*
  walls, 250–251
    "Gothic Wall," 82 *fig. 1*, 83
    "Justinianic Wall," 84, 91, 107, 108
Miltner, Franz, 53, 77
Mithridatic Wars, 152, 159
monastery
  (near) Aphrodisias, 127, 135
  Keloşk Kale (?), 235, 241
  Syria
    Deir Siman, 234
    Kasr el-Benat, 234
Monastirli Köy. *See* Gürkuyu
Morsynus river, 125, 127, 136
mosaics, 15, 16, 17, 20, 25, 155, 157, 160, 161
Mysia, 160n37, 167
mythology. *See* sculpture, mythological
Mytilene, 29, 30, 30n6

Nazareth, 157
neokoros, 7, 7n20, 7n21, 8n28, 23–24n90
New Rome. *See* Constantinople
Nicaea, 169, 254
  Empire of, 171
Nicomedia, 112, 253
Niewöhner, Philipp, 91, 97
Nonnos (governor of Caria), 83
Notitiae Dignitarum/Register of Dignitaries, 8
Notitiae Episcopatuum/Register of Clerics, 140
Nuhrut. *See* Gürkuyu
nymphaeum. *See* fountain

oleoculture/olive oil production, 136, 136n16, 178, 179, 179–180n17, 180, 180n20, 181, 185–187, 185n33, 198
Osrhoene, vii, 225–246, 253, 255, 259

palace, 251
  Aphrodisias, 113n34, 127n9
  Constantinople, 32, 32n23, 116n47
  Ephesus, 68–69n3, 249
Palestine, 25n97, 173, 179, 179n17, 180, 183n28, 185n32, 198n50, 260
Palmyra, 157, 221n60
papyri, 260, 260n48
Parthians, 226, 242
Pax Romana, 145
Pegae. *See* Priapus
Pergamon, 4, 7n23, 11n40, 66n164, 121n70, 148, 157n24, 167
  houses, 113, 160
Perge, 118n54
  gates, 118, 118n55, 251
  houses, 113
Persians, 25n97, 81, 107n7, 109, 151, 163, 163n54, 164, 165, 225, 226, 247, 252, 254, 257, 259, 259n43, 260. *See also* Sassanians
Pfanner, Michael, 85
Philadelphia, 62–63, 62n150
  gates, 10, 119n57
  walls, 145
Philo of Byzantium, 118
Phocas, 257
Phrygia, 4, 22n85, 163n54, 165
plague, viii, 136, 162, 164, 253, 257
Plarasa, 135
  cemetery, 127
pottery. *See* ceramics
Priapus, 165, 171n73
Procopius, 37n41, 119n59, 163n52, 169n69, 177n9, 221, 221n60, 243, 243n53, 251, 255
Prudentius, 35, 36n38
prytaneion
  Ephesus, 45, 45n12, 52 *fig. 6*, 53, 53 *fig. 7*, 53n73, 53n74, 53n75, 54, 54n77, 54n83, 55n87, 58, 61, 62, 63, 63n151

Qalblozeh, 239, 239n32
quarry/quarrying, 14n56, 157n25, 242
  Estremoz, Portugal, 85
  (near) Herakleia under Latmos, 85
  Koç Ali, 157, 158 *fig. 8*, 162

Rathmayr, Elisabeth, 44
Ratté, Christopher, 252
Ravenna, 28n3, 37n43
  Mausoleum of Galla Placidia, 36
Register of Clerics/Notitiae Episcopatuum, 140
Register of Dignitaries/Notitiae Dignitarum, 8
rhetoric, 28, 37, 38, 38n48, 39–41, 40–41n56, 248n8, 249
road/street, viii, 24n91, 118, 119, 208n18
  Aizanoi, 112, 113 *fig. 10*
  Akören I, 190 *fig. 1*, 191, 199
  Akören II, 190 *fig. 1*, 201, 202 *fig. 14*
  Anazarbos, 207, 208, 209, 210 *fig. 5*, 214, 214 *fig.* 10, 215, 215 *fig. 12a–b*, 216, 218, 223
  Aphrodisias, 112, 123, 124, 125
  Blaundos, 140, 148, 150
  Constantinople, 29, 38
  Cyzicus, 164–165, 167
  Daskyleion, 164–165
  Didymateiche, 164
  Ephesus, 44, 53, 59, 61, 62, 65, 65n161, 66, 67n3, 70, 112, 250
  extra-urban, 4, 167, 167n64, 169, 243, 253
  Hypaepa, 10, 14
  Keloşk Kale, 231, 240, 241
  Limyra, 112
  Miletus, 91
  Nicomedia, 112
  Sagalassos, 112
  Sardis, 7, 8, 11–12, 12n44, 13, 15, 17, 19, 20, 21, 23, 24, 25n98, 26, 112, 254
  Side, 112
  (near) Taşoluk, 135
  Troy, 155, 160, 161
  Xanthus, 112

Roberts, Michael, 36
Rome, monuments of
Arch of Constantine, 117
Aurelianic wall, 251
Roueché, Charlotte, 44, 83, 123
rural settlement, viii, 25n99, 26, 109, 121, 125, 127, 135, 173, 203, 227. *See also* countryside

Sagalassos, 111, 113n33, 137n3, 253, 253n24, 260
baths, 113
churches, 12
gates, 115, 116n48, 118–119, 119n58
houses, 113, 113n34
streets, 112
walls, 111–112n28, 116, 119–120, 121n70, 121–122n73, 145, 145n24, 251
Samosata, 227, 241
Saradi, Helen, 248
Sardis, vii, viii, 111, 253
acropolis, 2, 4 *fig. 2*, 5, 7, 9, 11, 17, 22, 26
aqueduct, 5
arms factory, 8, 10, 11n38
baths, 113, 7
Bath CG, 7, 8n25, 11
Bath-Gymnasium Complex, 2, 5n15, 7, 9 *fig. 5*, 11, 10n33, 12, 12n44, 13, 13n47, 13n49, 15, 20, 23, 23n89, 24, 26
Marble Court, 8, 11, 13, 15, 23, 23n89
bishop of
Melito, 22
boule, 11n43, 23
Building C, 15n61
Building D, 14–15, 15 *fig. 9*, 15n61, 254
cemeteries, 1, 7–8, 11, 10n33, 14, 17, 20
churches, 14
Church EA, 14, 14n58
Church M, 14, 254
Field 55, 7, 7n21, 14, 20, 21
gates, 10, 11
Flying Towers, 11
Southwest Gate, 10, 12, 13
gerousia, 7n23, 11n43, 23
houses, 2, 5, 11, 12, 14, 17, 19 *fig. 12*, 19–20, 22, 23, 24, 25, 25n99, 26, 113, 161n42
House of Bronzes, 20
inscriptions, 1, 5, 5n15, 5n16, 7, 7n21, 7n23, 13, 13n45, 14n52, 14n60, 15, 23, 26n101
Sector ByzFort, 14n54, 20, 21
Sector CW6, 11n40
Sector HoB (House of Bronzes), 8n24, 12
Sector MD1/N, 21
Sector MD 2, 21
Sector MMS, 12, 19, 20, 25 *fig. 15*
Sector MMS/N, 5n15, 12n12
Sector MMS/S, 19, 19 *fig. 12*
Sector PN, 14, 14n59
shops, 2, 14
Byzantine Shops, 11–12, 12 *fig. 7*, 21, 21n82, 23, 24, 25
stadium, 5, 6 *fig. 4*, 7, 14, 22
streets, 7, 8, 11–13, 15, 20, 21 *fig. 13*, 23, 26, 112
embolos of Hypaepa, 13
Marble Road, 11–12, 12 *fig. 7*, 12n44, 17, 21, 24, 25n98, 254
MMS street, 12, 13 *fig. 8*, 17, 19, 25n98
synagogue, viii, 2, 13n49, 15, 16, 17, 21, 23, 25n98, 254
temples, 5, 6 *fig. 4*, 7–8
Sanctuary of Artemis, 5, 14
Artemis Temple, 1, 8, 14, 21
terraces, 4, 5, 7, 14, 14n54, 20, 22
theater, 4 *fig. 2*, 4–5, 6 *fig. 3*, 7, 9, 14, 14n56, 22, 23n89
tombs, 4, 22
Tomb 07.1, 11n39
Tomb 07.2, 22n87
Tomb 07.3, 22n87, 23 *fig. 14*
Tomb 76.1, 11n38, 12n87
Tomb 79.1, 11n29
Tomb 79.2, 22n87
Tomb 79.3, 22n87
Tomb of Flavios Chrysanthios. *See* Sardis, tombs, Tomb 76.1
Wadi B, 7, 7n22, 14, 20, 22, 24n92
walls, 3 *fig. 1*, 9–12, 14, 17, 21, 121n70, 122n73, 251, 253
Saros river, 201
Sassanians, 171, 225, 257n36, 259. *See also* Persians
Sayar, Mustafa, 191, 193
Scamander river, 160
Scherrer, Peter, 45, 48
Schneider, Carsten, 91, 92, 95, 97
Schultze, Victor, 1
Schwertheim, Ute, 147
sculpture, viii
antiquities, 29, 33, 34, 37
bronze, 13, 29–30, 31, 39, 60n128, 61, 63, 152, 159
honorific, ix, 27n1, 30–31, 32–33, 34, 44, 59, 66, 70,

87, 123
Lysippos, 27, 40n55
mythological, 27, 30, 35, 40, 43, 48–49, 52, 54, 56, 57–58, 71–72, 74, 75, 78, 92, 93, 94, 95, 97, 98, 100–101
portraits, 27, 30, 31, 32–33, 34, 37, 43, 46–47, 47–48, 51–52, 53, 54, 55, 56, 58, 59, 66, 78, 158
reworking of, ix, 61, 74, 76, 92, 93, 94, 95, 98, 99, 100–101
rhetorical theory and, 28, 37–41
sculptural programs, 33–35, 36–37, 51–52, 74–76, 78–79
spolia, 29–30, 34, 62n143, 71, 72, 74, 117–118
statue bases, 5, 29, 31–32, 46, 47, 50, 51, 52, 54, 55, 57, 58, 60–66, 72, 88, 92, 97
Sebasteion
Aphrodisias, 160
Ephesus, 48
Seleucia ad Calycadnum, 173, 174
arms factory, 175, 187, 256
baths, 113
Septimius Severus, 29, 165n58, 242
shop
Akören I (?), 200
Akören II (?), 195
Anazarbos, 214, 215
Blaundos, 140
Sardis, 2, 12, 12 *fig. 2*, 14, 21–22, 23, 24, 25, 254
Troy, 161, 162
Side, 112
gate, 106, 106 *fig. 6*, 118–119n55, 251
walls, 111, 111n25, 111n26, 121, 121n70, 122, 221, 222, 224
Simplikios, Severos (vicar of Asia), 13
Sitt er-Rum, 233, 234 *fig. 9*, 234 *fig. 10*, 237, 237 *fig. 14*, 238 *fig. 15*, 244, 245
Skylakios (vicar of Asia), 83
Smith, R.R.R., 123
Smyrna, 4, 5n14, 7n20, 111, 111–112n28, 251, 254
Sodoni, Jean-Pierre, 252
Sokolicek, Alexander, 250
spolia
architectural, ix, 12, 15, 34, 35n37, 50, 83, 94, 95, 97n51, 107, 121n70, 141, 147, 148, 161, 162, 167, 169, 185, 208, 210–212, 214, 217, 221, 223, 224
sculptural. *See* sculpture, spolia
stadium
Aphrodisias, 124
Blaundos, 142
Miletus, 88, 97, 107
Sardis, 5, 6 *fig. 4*, 7, 14, 22
Stephanos of Byzantium, 140
Steskal, Martin, 53
Strabo, 151n4, 171n74, 173
Strocka, Volker Michael, 88
synagogue, viii, 244n54
Sardis, 2, 13n49, 15–17, 21, 23, 25n98, 254
Syria, vii, 173, 177n10, 179, 180, 181n25, 183, 185n32, 185n33, 187, 198n13, 222n67, 223, 225, 233, 233n19, 234, 235, 237, 238, 239, 240, 243n52, 243n53, 244, 245, 247n2, 248n8, 252n21, 253, 258, 259, 260

Tabari, 259
Tacitus, 5
Taeuber, Hans, 51
Tarraco, 157
Tarsus, 1, 176, 176n8, 221n65
Tate, Georges, 252
Tatianos (= Antonios Tatianos?) (*asiarch*), 83, 91
Taurus mountains, 173, 189, 247, 248, 252, 254
taxation, 259, 260
Tchalenko, Georges, 252
temple, 83
Anazarbos, 208, 210
Aphrodisias, 123, 124, 125
Attouda, 127
Blaundos, 138, 150
Constantinople, 27, 29
Ephesus, 45, 48, 58, 82
Miletus, 83
Sardis, 1, 5, 6 *fig. 4*, 7, 8, 14, 14n54, 20, 21, 22, 24n92, 254
Troy, 153 *fig. 3*, 158 *fig. 9*, 159–160, 159 *fig. 10*
Tenedus
granary, 163, 254
theater
Anazarbos, 206 *fig. 2*, 207, 218, 221
Aphrodisias, 123
Blaundos, 141–142
Ephesus, 23n89, 44, 65n161, 69, 249
Miletus, 84, 87, 88, 89, 107
Sardis, 4 *fig. 2*, 4–5, 6 *fig. 3*, 7, 9, 14, 22
Theodosian Code, 14n51, 35, 162, 249
Theodosius I, 27, 29, 30, 32, 164, 165n58, 249
Theodosius II, 30, 30–31n12, 31, 32, 36, 169, 248n6
Tiberius, 5, 5n14, 5n15, 26
Tigris river, 242, 243
Tlos

churches, 120
gates, 115
walls, 111, 111–112n28, 116n48, 251
tomb, 125, 179, 207, 207n8
Akören II, 193
Blaundos, 140
Cibinören, 238
Görle, 136
İnceler Köyü, 237
Keloşk Kale, 231, 238
Miletus, 109
Plarasa, 127
Ravenna (Mausoleum of Galla Placidia), 36
Sardis, 4, 11n38, 11n39, 22, 22n87, 23 *fig. 14*
Troy, 152, 165, 171
trade, 124, 137, 140, 175, 179, 253
by sea, 186, 157, 162, 163
Trajan, 41n56, 88, 226
transport, 24, 179n16, 186, 186n37, 252n21
Trojan mythology, use of, 33, 34, 37, 151, 171
Troy, vii
acropolis, 151, 159, 162–163, 163 *fig. 13*, 254
agora, 151, 155, 159, 161, 162, 254
aqueduct, 155
Athenaion, 159, 160, 163
baths, 153n3, 155
bouleuterion, 153n3, 162n48
church, 159, 161–162, 161 *fig. 12*, 167
gate, 153 *fig. 3*, 162
Heroon of Hector, 159
houses, 113, 156–157, 160, 161 *fig. 11*, 162
inscriptions, 154–155, 157, 159, 160, 162n43, 164
Lower City, 152n9, 155–156, 156 *fig. 6*, 158, 159, 160, 161, 161 *fig. 11*, 162, 254
odeion, 153 *fig. 3*, 154–155
Quadrat D6, 162
Quadrat H17, 162n48
Quadrat t14, 163
shops, 161, 162
Spring Cave, 155, 157 *fig. 7*
streets, 155, 160, 161
temples, 153 *fig. 3*, 158 *fig. 9*, 159–160, 159 *fig. 10*
tombs, 171
Tomb of Achilles (alleged), 152
Tomb of Ajax, 152
Tomb of Festus, 152, 154
tumuli, 151, 163
Uveciktepe, 152, 154
Upper City, 250
walls, 151, 153 *fig.* 3, 155, 162
Turgutlu, 5n15

Umayyads, 258, 259
Uzunburç, 237, 242

Valens, 13, 83
Vanhaverbeke, Hannelore, 113n33, 253
Vedius Antoninus III, Publius, 51, 63n153, 77
village, viii, 14, 135, 136, 137, 140, 155, 157, 163, 173, 183, 185, 189, 191, 200, 214, 228, 235, 236, 237–239, 241, 242, 244, 248, 252, 253, 255, 256
Vitianus (governor of Caria), 83
viticulture/wine production, 179, 183n28, 185n33, 186, 187
Vitruvius, 7n23, 17, 180n22
von Gerkan, Armin, 97, 98 104, 107, 108, 109

Wagner, Jorg, 241
wall (city), ix
Alacaoluk, 167, 169
Amida, 221
Amorium, 111, 119, 119n57, 121n73, 251
Anazarbos, 206 *fig. 2*, 208, 210, 212, 213 *fig. 10*, 214, 215–220, 222, 223, 224
Anemurium, 111, 251
Aphrodisias, 114 *fig. 11*, 123, 124, 125
Asartepe, 167, 169
Blaundos, 111, 121n70, 141–142, 142n19, 145, 146, 146 *fig. 7*, 147, 150, 221
Constantinople, 116, 117n50, 118, 169, 169n69, 210n21, 219, 251
Dara, 218, 221
Ephesus, 119, 121, 122
Hierapolis in Phrygia, 111, 118, 120, 145, 251
Laodicea on the Lycus, 111, 145, 251
Limyra, 111, 120, 251
Magnesia on the Maeander, 111, 121, 122
Martyropolis, 218, 221, 223n69
Melitene, 221
Miletus, 81, 83, 84, 89–91, 97, 103, 104, 106, 107, 108, 109, 111–112, 114–115, 121, 122
Patara, 111, 121, 122
Philadelphia, 145
Rome, 251
Sagalassos, 111, 119–120, 145, 251
Sardis, 3 *fig. 1*, 9–12, 14, 17, 21, 121n70, 122n73, 251, 253
Side, 111, 111n25, 111n26, 121, 121n70, 122, 221, 222, 224
Smyrna, 111, 251

Tlos, 111, 111–112n28, 116n48, 251
Tripolis, 145
Troy, 151, 153 *fig.* 3, 155, 162
wall paintings, 11, 20, 22n87, 23n14, 157, 237
water systems and infrastructure, 249. *See also* aqueducts
Whittow, Michael, 147
Wiegand, Theodor, 84, 85, 91
Witschel, Christian, 66
Wood, John Turtle, 51, 52
Wulf-Rheidt, Ulrike, 255

Xanthus, 254n26
houses, 113
streets, 112
Xerxes, 151, 151n4

Yegül, Fikret, 93

Zeno, 17n67, 112n28
Zeugma, 227, 240n39, 241, 242n47